CONSTRUCTIONISM

Research Reports and Essays, 1985-1990
by the
Epistemology & Learning Research Group
Seymour Papert, Director

The Media Laboratory
Massachusetts Institute of Technology

edited by
Idit Harel and Seymour Papert

ABLEX PUBLISHING CORPORATION
NORWOOD, NEW JERSEY

Cover design by Betsy Chimento and the editors. Photography by Stephen Sherman.

Photographs within the book provided by Jacqueline Karaaslanian, LEGO Company, Stephen Ocko, and Stephen Sherman.

Figures and illustrations for Chapters 4, 5, and 6 by Idit Harel and Elizabeth Glenewinkel.

Printed in the United States of America.

Library of Congress Cataloging-in-Publication Data

Constructionism / edited by Idit Harel and Seymour Papert.
    p. cm.
   Includes bibliographical references and index.
   ISBN 0-89391-785-0 (cl).—ISBN 0-89391-786-9 (pp)
   1. Cognition. 2. Human information processing. I. Harel, Idit.
II. Papert, Seymour.
  BF311.C657 1991
  153—dc20   91-9389
                                             CIP

Ablex Publishing Corporation
355 Chestnut St.
Norwood, NJ 07648

Table of Contents

iii

PART III
THINKING ABOUT THINKING: EPISTEMOLOGICAL STYLES IN CONSTRUCTIONIST LEARNING

PART IV
CYBERNETICS AND CONSTRUCTIONISM

There is a line among the fragments of the Greek poet Archilochus which says: 'The fox knows many things, but the hedgehog knows one big thing.' Scholars have differed about the correct interpretation of these dark words, which may mean no more than that the fox, for all his cunning, is defeated by the hedgehog's one defence. But, taken figuratively, the words can be made to yield a sense in which they mark one of the deepest differences which divide writers and thinkers, and, it may be, human beings in general. For there exists a great chasm between those, on one side, who relate everything to a single central vision, one system less or more coherent or articulate, in terms of which they understand, think and feel—a single, universal, organising principle in terms of which alone all that they are and say has significance—and, on the other side, those who pursue many ends, often unrelated and even contradictory, connected, if at all, only in some *de facto* way, for some psychological or physiological cause, related by no moral or aesthetic principle; these last lead lives, perform acts, and entertain ideas that are centrifugal rather than centripetal, their thought is scattered or diffused, moving on many levels, seizing upon the essence of a vast variety of experiences and objects for what they are in themselves, without, consciously or unconsciously, seeking to fit them into, or exclude them from, any one unchanging, all-embracing, sometimes self-contradictory and incomplete, at times fanatical, unitary inner vision. The first kind of intellectual and artistic personality belongs to the hedgehogs, the second to the foxes; and without insisting on a rigid classification, we may, without too much fear of contradiction, say that, in this sense, Dante belongs to the first category, Shakespeare to the second; Plato, Lucretius, Pascal, Hegel, Dostoevsky, Nietzsche, Ibsen, Proust are, in varying degrees, hedgehogs; Herodotus, Aristotle, Montaigne, Erasmus, Molière, Goethe, Pushkin, Balzac, Joyce are foxes.

Of course, like all over-simple classifications of this type, the dichotomy becomes, if pressed, artificial, scholastic, and ultimately absurd. But if it is not an aid to serious criticism, neither should it be rejected as being merely superficial or frivolous; like all distinctions which embody any degree of truth, it offers a point of view from which to look and compare, a starting-point for genuine investigation.

Isaiah Berlin, 1978, *Russian Thinkers* (pp. 22–23)

PREFACE

This volume presents a representative set of chapters written by the first generation of graduate students in the Epistemology and Learning Research Group at the MIT Media Laboratory which began operations in 1985. Two chapters by Seymour Papert serve as an introduction to this collection, and chapters by Edith Ackermann and Sherry Turkle are included to represent their deep contribution to the intellectual life of the group.

The Media Lab's general mission is to advance the idea that computational technology would give rise to a new science of expressive media. Among its 12 research groups, some bring new approaches to areas traditionally regarded as media studies, such as movies, music, and graphics. The Epistemology and Learning Group extends the traditional definition of media by treating as expressive media the multiple materials with which children play and learn—from the sand on the beach through strings and plastic bricks to the silicon in the computer.

In this spirit, the first generation of graduate students from the group has been let loose on the creation of new media and new ways of using old media as playful materials in learning environments for children. In this volume they write about how they did this, how they researched this, and what they learned about learning and thinking in the process.

It is not simple to introduce the group or to identify the main features of its intellectual personality. It has multiple personalities: It can be seen as an interdisciplinary program of graduate study, and simultaneously, as a research laboratory concerned with cognition, learning, media, and technology, but also as a center of activism for the promotion of change in education.

In its aspect as an interdisciplinary program of academic study, the group tries to provide a supportive environment for graduate students to pursue personal research goals while working towards a PhD in what MIT now calls Media Arts and Sciences. The students, like the faculty and researchers who serve as their advisors, come to the group with a great diversity of backgrounds. Collectively we have degrees and experience in mathematics, physics, journalism, filmmaking, music, economics, fine arts, biology, mechanical engineering, and computer science, as well as in cognitive and experimental psychology, philosophy, education, and teaching at all levels from elementary school to college. What we have in common may be puzzling to an outsider. It is puzzling to us as well. And since we try to operate as a team in research and activism, the puzzlement sometimes blossoms into frustration. But being puzzled about what we are about is ultimately productive. The shaping of this group and its activities embodies an intuitive coherence whose import will become clear only through a slow process of active and reflective practice.

The group's work follows a program for learning research which Papert has named *constructionism*. Several of the chapters directly address the theoretical formulation of constructionism, and others describe experimental studies which enrich and confirm aspects of the idea. Taken with the introductory chapters by Papert, this volume of 23 chapters is by far the most extensive—even if still partial and tentative—exploration of a constructionist approach to media and education research and practice.

Among the authors included here, some completed their dissertation in the past three years (in order of completion): Idit Harel, Aaron Falbel, Judy Sachter, Ricki Goldman Segall, and Carol Strohecker. The authors Mitchel Resnick, Nira Granott, Greg Gargarian, Uri Wilensky, Fred Martin, and Aaron Brandes are planning to join the ranks of the group's doctoral alumni in a year or so. Yasmin Kafai is a doctoral student at Harvard who has been working closely with Idit Harel. Stephen Ocko was a Research Associate in the group during 1985-1989.

Work discussed in this volume was supported by a number of sponsors and funding agencies, which we hereby acknowledge with the usual statement that no one expects the supporting agencies to take responsibility for the opinions expressed here. The principal sources of funding for our work are: the National Science Foundation and the McArthur Foundation; as well as the following companies (in alphabetical order): the Apple Computer Inc., Fukutake Japan, the IBM Corporation, the LEGO Systems A/S, and Nintendo Inc. Japan.

Most of the chapters cut across goals supported by these various sponsors. The NSF mainly supported the conceptualization and validation of *constructionism*. This theory runs thematically through all the chapters in this volume, but especially in the development of materials most prominently mentioned in the chapters on children's software design projects and robotics research. The NSF has also supported our more recent work on teacher development (underrepresented in this volume).[1] The McArthur Foundation has provided general support

---

[1] Writing by and about teachers is a notable gap in this volume. The reason is *not* that we do not attach importance to teachers, rather, we attach so much that when we considered including a few papers on "teachers issues," we were overwhelmed by the sense of token representation. So we left them all out at this point. We are confident that current writing by the teachers we work with and by the members of the group, will soon redress the balance. Our group has developed increasing involvement in issues touching on the roles of teachers, the lives of teachers, the struggles of teachers, and, most importantly, the immense potential contributions of teachers as theoreticians, innovators, and researchers, as well as practitioners. For many reasons, some of which reflect intrinsic complexities, our inexperience, or simply the fact that research is still in progress and not ready for publication—this branch of the life of our group was late in budding and slower in maturing. But it is coming along.

for the enhancement of intellectual depth of the group and specifically for the work related to language, thinking, and literacy. LEGO and Fukutake have given very general support in the form of endowments, as well as in funding specific LEGO-related research and development projects. The grant from IBM made possible the original development of computational learning environments at the Hennigan School (''Project Headlight'') within which most of the work mentioned here was implemented and developed. Grants and donations of equipment by Apple facilitated an extension of the Headlight environment and our work with a larger network of teachers. With the most recent grant from Nintendo we continue to investigate learning through play, the psychology of game design in children, and the development of playful computational learning environments.

We structured the book in five parts: Part I, Introduction to constructionism; Part II, Learning through play, design, and programming; Part III, Epistemological styles in learning and thinking; Part IV, Children and cybernetics; and Part V, Video and multimedia tools for exploring and documenting constructionist environments. Grouping the chapters according to these themes was not an obvious task—most chapters can be placed under more than one theme. This division does announce some of the main branches of our work, but the reader must remember that it is quite artificial and was done mainly for clearness of presentation.

Finally, while we are fully aware of the risks involved in doing so, we think it is appropriate to predict the publication of further volumes that will present the work of other researchers and more aspects of the life of the Epistemology and Learning Group that are not well represented in this collection.

The Editors
MIT Media Laboratory
April, 1991

PART I

CONSTRUCTIONISM

Situating Constructionism

Seymour Papert

It is easy enough to formulate simple catchy versions of the idea of constructionism; for example, thinking of it as "learning-by-making." One purpose of this introductory chapter is to orient the reader toward using the diversity in the volume to elaborate—to *construct*—a sense of constructionism much richer and more multifaceted, and very much deeper in its implications, than could be conveyed by any such formula.

My little play on the words construct and constructionism already hints at two of these multiple facets—one seemingly "serious" and one seemingly "playful." The serious facet will be familiar to psychologists as a tenet of the kindred, but less specific, family of psychological theories that call themselves contructivist. Constructionism—the N word as opposed to the V word—shares constructivism's connotation of learning as "building knowledge structures" irrespective of the circumstances of the learning. It then adds the idea that this happens especially felicitously in a context where the learner is consciously engaged in constructing a public entity, whether it's a sand castle on the beach or a theory of the universe. And this in turn implies a ramified research program which is the real subject of this introduction and of the volume itself. But in saying all this I must be careful not to transgress the basic tenet shared by the V and the N forms: If one eschews pipeline models of transmitting knowledge in talking among ourselves as well as in theorizing about classrooms, then one must expect that I will not be able to *tell you* my idea of constructionism. Doing so is bound to trivialize it. Instead, I must confine myself to engage you in experiences (including verbal ones) liable to encourage your own personal construction of something in some sense like it. Only in this way will there be something rich enough in your mind to be worth talking about. But if I am being really serious about this, I have to ask (and this will quickly lead us into really deep psychological and epistemological waters) what reasons I have to suppose that you will be willing to do this and that if you did construct your own constructionism that it would have any resemblance to mine?

I find an interesting toe-hold for the problem in which I called the playful facet—the element of tease inherent in the idea that it would be particularly oxymoronic to convey the idea of constructionism through a definition since, after all, constructionism boils down to demanding that everything be understood by being constructed. The joke is relevant to the problem, for the more we share the less improbable it is that our self-constructed constructions should converge. And I have learned to take as a sign of relevantly common intellectual culture and preferences the penchant for playing with self-referentially recursive situations: the snake eating its tail, the man hoisting himself by his own bootstraps, and the liar contradicting himself by saying he's a liar. Experience shows that people who relate to that kind of thing often play in similar ways. And in some domains those who play alike think alike. Those who like to play with images of structures emerging from their own chaos, lifting themselves by their own bootstraps, are very likely predisposed to constructionism.

They are not the only ones who are so predisposed. In Chapter 9 of this volume, Sherry Turkel and I analyze the epistemological underpinnings of a number of contemporary cultural movements. We show how trends as different as feminist thought and the ethnography of science join with trends in the computer culture to favor forms of knowledge based on working with concrete materials rather than abstract propositions, and this too predisposes them to prefer learning in a constructionist rather than in an instructionist mode. In Chapter 2, I make a similar connection with political trends.

It does not follow from this that you and I would be precluded from constructing an understanding about constructionism in case you happened not to be in any of the "predisposed groups" I have mentioned. Of course not. I am not prepared to be "reductionist" quite to that extent about arguing my own theory, and in the following pages I shall probe several other routes to get into resonance on these issues: for example, stories about children are evocative for more people than recursions and can lead to similar intellectual positions.[1] But there is no guarantee; I have no argument like what is supposed to happen in formal logic where each step leads a depersonalized mind inexorably along a pre-set path. More like the tinkerer, the *bricoleur*, we can come to agreement about theories of learning (at least for the present and perhaps in principle) only by groping in our disorderly bags of tricks and tools for the wherewithal to build understandings. In some cases there may be no way to do it one-on-one but a mutual understanding could still be socially mediated: for example (to recall the context of discussing how to use this volume) we might both find ourselves in tune with Carol

---

[1] I understand Piaget better when he lets the concrete thinker in him emerge in his playing with extracts from children's dialogue than when he writes as a "formal" thinker. This does not mean that I do not agree with the essential core of Piaget's thinking though I am less sure that *he himself* always does.

Strohecker and her evocative descriptions of working with knots.[2] Through her we might come together. But what if we didn't find a route to any understanding at all? This would be tragic if we were locked into a classroom (or other power-ridden) situation where one of us has to grade the other; but in the best phases of life, including real science and mathematics, it turns out much more often than is admitted in schools to be right to say: *vivent les différences!*

I might appear in the previous paragraph to be talking about accepting or rejecting constructionism as a matter of "taste and preference" rather than a matter of "scientific truth." But a distinction needs to be made. When one looks at how people think and learn one sees clear differences. Although it is conceivable that science may one day show that there is a "best way," no such conclusion seems to be on the horizon. Moreover, even if there were, individuals might prefer to think in their own way rather than in the "best way." Now one can make two kinds of scientific claim for constructionism. The weak claim is that it suits some people better than other modes of learning currently being used. The strong claim is that it is better for everyone than the prevalent "instructionist" modes practiced in schools. A variant of the strong claim is that this is the only framework that has been proposed that allows the full range of intellectual styles and preferences to each find a point of equilibrium.

But these are not the questions to guide research in the next few years for they presuppose that the concept of constructionism has reached a certain level of maturity and stability. The slogan *vivent les différences* might become inappropriate at that stage. But when the concept itself is in evolution it is appropriate to keep intellectual doors open and this is where we are now. To give a sense of the methodology of this early "pre-paradigmatic" stage I shall tell some stories about incidents that fed the early evolution of the idea.

More than 20 years ago, I was working on a project at the Muzzey Junior High School in Lexington, MA, which had been persuaded by Wally Feuerzeig to allow a seventh grade to "do Logo" instead of math for that year. This was a brave decision for a principal who could not have known that the students would actually advance their math achievement score, even though they didn't do anything that resembled normal school math that year! But the story I really want to tell is not about test scores. It is not even about the math/Logo class.[3] It is about the art room I used to pass on the way. For a while, I dropped in periodically to watch students working on soap sculptures and mused about ways in which this was not like a math class. In the math class students are generally given little problems which they solve or don't solve pretty well on the fly. In this particular art class they were all carving soap, but *what* each students carved

---

[2] In Chapter 12 of this volume.

[3] This math/Logo class is the source of several anecdotes in my book *Mindstorms* (1980); it is also discussed in my paper *Teaching Children Thinking* (1971).

came from wherever fancy is bred and the project was not done and dropped but continued for many weeks. It allowed time to think, to dream, to gaze, to get a new idea and try it and drop it or persist, time to talk, to see other people's work and their reaction to yours—not unlike mathematics as it is for the mathematician, but quite unlike math as it is in junior high school. I remember craving some of the students' work and learning that their art teacher and their families had first choice. I was struck by an incongruous image of the teacher in a regular math class pining to own the products of his students' work! An ambition was born: I want junior high school math class to be like that. I didn't know exactly what "that" meant but I knew I wanted it. I didn't even know what to call the idea. For a long time it existed in my head as "soap-sculpture math."

Soap-sculpture math is an idea that buzzes in the air around my head wherever I go (and I assume it was present in the air the students who wrote the chapters in this volume breathed). Has it been achieved? Of course not. But little by little by little we are getting there. As you read the chapters you will find many examples of children's work that exhibits one or another of features of the soap-sculpting class. Here I mention two simple cases which happened to move me especially deeply.

Last year, at Project Headlight of the Hennigan School in Boston, MA, I watched a group of children trying to make a snake out of LEGO/Logo. They were using this high-tech and actively computational material as an expressive medium; the content came from their imaginations as freely as what the others expressed in soap. But where a knife was used to shape the soap, mathematics was used here to shape the behavior of the snake and physics to figure out its structure. Fantasy and science and math were coming together, uneasily still, but pointing a way. LEGO/Logo is limited as a build-an-animal-kit; versions under development in our lab will have little computers to put inside the snake and perhaps linear activators which will be more like muscles in their mode of action. Some members of our group have other ideas: Rather than using a tiny computer, using even tinier logic gates and motors with gears may be fine. Well, we have to explore these routes.[4] But what is important is the vision being pursued and the questions being asked. Which approach best melds science and fantasy? Which favors dreams and visions and sets off trains of good scientific and mathematical ideas?

Last week, I watched a tape of children from Project Mindstorm at the Gardner Academy in San Jose, CA. A fifth grader who was in his second year of working with LogoWriter was showing a spectacular sample of screen graphics he had programmed. When asked how he did it, he explained that he had to figure angles and curvatures to obtain the greatest "grace." His product was no less desirable than the soap sculptures, and its process much more mathematical

---

[4] For further descriptions of LEGO/Logo and LEGO Creatures learning environments, see Chapters 7, 8, 15, 18, and 19 in this volume.

than anything done in a usual math classroom. And he knew it, for he added with pride: *I want to be a person who puts math and art together.* Here again I hear answers to questions about taking down walls that too often separate imagination from mathematics. This boy was appropriating mathematics in a deeply personal way. What can we do to encourage this?

I'll tell another story to introduce a second idea. At the time of the Muzzey project in Lexington, "Logo" had not yet acquired the feature for which it is best known to most educators: It had no graphics, no Turtle. In fact, at Muzzey School there was no screen, only clanging teletype terminals connected to a distant "time-shared" computer. (In fact, the origination of the Logo Turtle was inspired by the soap-sculpture image and a few others like it.) About 10 years later, I was working with Sherry Turkle[5] and John Berlow at the Lamplighter School in Dallas, TX, the first elementary school where there were enough computers for children to have almost free access to them. The first space shuttle was about to go up, and in the tension of waiting it appeared in many representations on screens all over the school. "Even the girls are making space ships," one girl told us. But we noticed that although everyone had space ships they did not make them the same way. Some programmed their space ships as if they had read a book on "structured programming," in the top-down style of work that proceeds through careful planning to organize the work and by making sub-procedures for every part under the hierarchical control of a superprocedure. Others seemed to work more like a painter than like this classical model of an engineer's way of doing things. The painter-programmer would put a red blob on the screen and call over her friends (for it was more often, though not always, a girl) to admire the shuttle. After a while someone might say: "But its red, the shuttle is white." "Well, that's the fire!"—came the reply—"Now I'll make the white body." And so the shuttle would grow, taking shape through a kind of negotiation between the programmer and the work in progress.

This and many other such incidents initiated an intense interest in differences in ways of doing things, and during the next few years[6] (which means into the time when the work in this volume was starting), "style" was almost as much in the air than the "soap-sculpture." I was very much troubled by questions about whether styles were categorical or a continuum, whether they were correlated with gender or ethnic cultures or personality types. These two key ideas set the stage for the evolution of constructionism.

---

[5] Sherry Turkle has written a theoretical analysis of this experience which should be read by everyone interested in children and computers: *The Second Self: The Human Spirit in the Computer Culture.* See also Chapter 9 by Turkle and Papert in this volume.

[6] Observations on differences in styles of Logo programming were reported in Papert, Watt, diSessa, & Weir (1979). Sylvia Weir who participated very actively in the pre- and early periods of the Epistemology and Learning group developed an approach to style in her book *Cultivating Minds: A Logo Casebook* (1986).

Constructionism's line of direct descent from the soap-sculpture model is clearly visible. The simplest definition of constructionism evokes the idea of learning-by-making and this is what was taking place when the students worked on their soap sculptures. But there is also a line of descent from the style idea. The metaphor of a painter I used in describing one of the styles of programmer observed at the Lamplighter school is developed in Chapter 9 by Turkle and Papert in two perspectives. One ("bricolage") takes its starting point in strategies for the organization of work: The painter-programmer is guided by the work as it proceeds rather than staying with a pre-established plan. The other takes off from a more subtle idea which we call "closeness to objects"—that is, some people prefer ways of thinking that keep them close to physical things, while others use abstract and formal means to distance themselves form concrete material. Both of these aspects of style are very relevant to the idea of constructionism. The example of children building a snake suggests ways of working in which those who like bricolage and staying close to the object can do as well as those who prefer a more analytic formal way style.

Building and playing with castles of sand, families of dolls, houses of Lego, and collections of cards provide images of activities which are well rooted in contemporary cultures and which plausibly enter into learning processes that go beyond specific narrow skills. I do not believe that anyone fully understands what gives these activities their quality of "learning-richness." But this does not prevent one from taking them as models in benefiting from the presence of new technologies to expand the scope of activities with that quality.

The chapters in this book offer many constructions of new learning-rich activities with an attempt to reach that quality. A conceptually simple case is the addition of new elements to LEGO construction kits and to the Logo microworlds, so that children can build more "active" models. For example, sensors, miniaturized computers that can run Logo programs, and motor controllers allow a child (in principle) to build a LEGO house with a programmable temperature control system; or to construct forms of artificial life and mobile models capable of seeking environmental conditions such as light or heat or of following or avoiding one another. Experiments carried out so far still fall a little short of this idealized description, and, moreover, have been mounted systematically only in the artificial contexts of schools or science centers. But it is perfectly plausible that further refinement of the components (combined, be it noted for further discussion below, with suitable marketing) might result in such "cybernetic" activities (as we choose to call them), thus becoming as much part of the lives of young children as playing with toys and dolls, or other more passive construction kits. It is also plausible that *if* this were to happen, certain concepts and ways of thinking presently regarded as far beyond children's ken would enter into what they know "spontaneously" (in the sense in which Piaget talks about children's spontaneous geometry or logic or whatever), while other concepts—which children to learn at school but reluctantly and not very well—would be learned with the gusto one sees in Nintendo games.

This vision advances the definition of constructionism and serves as an ideal case against which results that have been actually achieved can be judged. In particular, it illustrates the sense of the opposition I like to formulate as *constructionism vs. instructionism* when discussing directions for innovation and enhancement in education.

I do not mean to imply that constructionists see instruction as bad. That would be silly. The question at issue is on a different level: I am asking what kinds of innovation are liable to produce radical change in how children learn. Take mathematics as an extreme example. It seems obvious that as a society we are mathematical underperformers. It is also obvious that instruction in mathematics is on the average very poor. But it does not follow that the route to better performance is necessarily the invention by researchers of more powerful and effective means of instruction (with or without computers).

The diffusion of cybernetic construction kits into the lives of children could in principle change the context of the learning of mathematics. Children might come to *want* to learn it because they would use it in building these models. And if they did want to learn it they would, even if teaching were poor or possibly nonexistent. Moreover, since one of the reasons for poor teaching is that teachers do not enjoy teaching reluctant children, it is not implausible that teaching would become better as well as becoming less necessary. So changes in the opportunities for construction could in principle lead to deeper changes in the learning of mathematics than changes in knowledge about instruction or any amount of "teacher-proof" computer-aided instruction.

This vision is presented as a thought experiment to break the sense of necessary connection between improving learning and improving teaching. But many of its elements can be related to real experiments described in the book. The potentially engaging qualities of the cybernetic construction kit is well established through work on the simpler version of it known as LEGO/Logo. The direct spill-over of LEGO/Logo onto mathematical learning is not discussed in this book, but a spill-over of something else in the same spirit was created and documented by Idit Harel for her doctoral dissertation.[7] Her experiments show that children's attention can be held for an hour a day over periods of several months by making (as opposed to *using*) educational software—even when the children consider the content of the software to be utterly boring in its usual classroom form. Moreover, here we do see statistically hard evidence that

---

[7] See Idit Harel's dissertation Software Design for Learning: Children's Construction of Meaning for Fractions and Logo Programming (1988) which was recently revised and published as *Children Designers: Interdisciplanary Constructions for Learning and Knowing Mathematics in a Computer-Rich School* (1991). See also Chapters 4, 5, 6, and 22 in this volume.

constructionist activity—which integrates math with art and design and where the children make the software—enhances the effectiveness of instruction given by a teacher in the same topic (in the case in point, fractions).

Although most of the examples in the book use computers, some do not. Most strikingly, a "knot lab" has children building such unorthodox entities as a family tree of knots. Why is it included in this volume? Its designer, Carol Strohecker, would say "why knot?"[8] Constructionism and this book are about learning; computers figure so prominently only because they provide an especially wide range of excellent contexts for constructionist learning. But common old garden string, though less versatile in its range, provides some as well. The point is that the Knot Lab, the Software Design Studio, LEGO/Logo workshops, and other learning environments described in this book all work in one way; while instructionist learning environments, whether they use CAI or the pencil-and-paper technology of traditional classrooms, work in a different way.

The assertion that the various constructionist learning situations described here "work in one way" does not mean they are not very different. Indeed, in form they are very different, and intellectual work is needed to see what they have in common. The construction of physical cybernetic creatures is made possible by novel hardware. In a closely related example, Mitchel Resnick opened a new range of activities by creating a new software system: an extension of Logo called *Logo which enables a child to create thousands of "screen creatures" which can be given behaviors to produce phenomena similar to those seen in social insects.[9] Judy Sachter created a software system for children to work in 3-D graphics.[10] Idit Harel used existing hardware and software; her invention (like Carol Strohecker's) was on a social level. She organized children into a Software Design Studio within which they learned by teaching, which gave cultural, pedagogical, as well as technical support for the children to become software designers.

There cannot be many research groups in education with the capability of innovating in so many ways. (Is this one result of constructionist environments?) Still, what makes the Epistemology and Learning Group unique is not this diversity as such, but the search for underlying unity. The creation of a multitude of learning situations (sometimes called learning environments or microworlds) is a great asset, but what gives constructionism the status of a theoretical project is its epistemological dimension.

Instructionism vs. constructionism looks like a split about strategies for education: two ways of thinking about the transmission of knowledge. But behind this there is a split that goes beyond the acquisition of knowledge to touch on the *nature of knowledge* and the *nature of knowing*. There is a huge difference

---

[8] See Carol Strohecker's dissertation (1991), and Chapter 12 in this volume.

[9] See Chapters 11 and 19 in this volume.

[10] See Chapter 17 in this volume.

in status between these two splits. The first is, in itself, a technical matter that belongs in an educational school course on "methods." The second is what ought properly to be called "epistemological." It is close to fundamental issues that philosophers think of as their own. It raises issues that are relevant to the nature of science and to the deepest debates in psychology. It is tangled with central issues of radical thinking in feminism, in Africanism, and in other areas where people fight for the right not only to think what they please, but to think it in their own ways.

Concern with ways of knowing and kinds of knowledge is pervasive in all the chapters in this volume[11] and this is what creates connection with a contemporary movement that goes far beyond education. Indeed, manifestations of the movement in question do not always label themselves as directly concerned with education. And even when they do, the educational concerns they express seem at first sight to be disconnected. This is demonstrated by the complexities of some common issues that appear in different guises in my own contributions to this collection. My chapter with Sherry Turkle ("Epistemological Pluralism and the Revaluation of the Concrete," Chapter 9) distills an epistemological essence from inquiry into the sociology of knowledge. My closing speech at the World Congress on Computers and Education ("Perestroika and Epistemological Politics," Chapter 2) looks at the same epistemological categories through political metaphors (which may well be more than metaphoric). And my chapter with Idit Harel ("Software Design as a Learning Environment," Chapter 4) looks at them through the lens of a particular educational experience. The understanding that my concerns with ways of knowing and kinds of knowledge are not disconnected form educational concerns grew out of my concerns with knowledge appropriation and styles of thinking (or one's style of making a piece of knowledge one's own); it is time to pick this thread up again.

In the chapter by Turkle and Papert the question of style takes on a new guise. The issue has shifted from the psychological question—Who thinks in one style or the other?—to the epistemological question of characterizing the differences. In that chapter we take a new look at the confluence of "noncanonical" epistemological thinking from sources as diverse as the ethnographic study of laboratories, intellectual movements inspired by feminist concerns, and trends within computer cultures. It is clear enough that each of these streams taken separately carries implications for education. But to capture a common implication one has to look beyond what one might call "a first impact," which in each case tends to be specific rather than common, focused on educational content rather than on underlying epistemologies. Thus, feminism's first and most obvious influence on education was tied to issues that very specifically affect women, for example, the elimination of gender stereotypes from school books,

---

[11] See especially Part III, "Thinking about Thinking: Epistemological Styles in Constructionist Learning" (Chapters 9 through 17) in this volume.

without in any way discounting its importance (and the likelihood that the waves it creates will go much further). I call this a "cleanup" because in itself it is compatible with similar books. While this can be, and usually is, implemented as a very local change, the implications of feminist challenges to received ideas about the nature of knowing run radically deeper. For example, traditional epistemology gives a privileged position to knowledge that is abstract, impersonal, and detached from the knower and treats other forms of knowledge as inferior. But feminist scholars have argued that many women prefer working with more personal, less-detached knowledge and do so very successfully. If this is true, they should prefer the more concrete forms of knowledge favored by constructionism to the propositional forms of knowledge favored by instructionism. The theoretical thrust of "Epistemological Pluralism" is to see this epistemological challenge as meshing with those made by the other two trends it analyzes.

The need to distinguish between a first impact on education and a deeper meaning is as real in the case of computation as in the case of feminism. For example, one is looking at a clear case of first impact when "computer literacy" is conceptualized as adding new content material to a traditional curriculum. Computer-aided instruction may seem to refer to method rather than content, but what counts as a change in method depends on what one sees as the essential features of the existing methods. From my perspective, CAI amplifies the rote and authoritarian character that many critics see as manifestations of what is most characteristic of—and most wrong with—traditional school. Computer literacy and CAI, or indeed the use of word-processors, could conceivably set up waves that will change school, but in themselves they constitute very local innovations—fairly described as placing computers in a possibly improved but essentially unchanged school. The presence of computers begins to go beyond first impact when it alters the nature of the learning process; for example, if it shifts the balance between transfer of knowledge to students (whether via book, teacher, or tutorial program is essentially irrelevant) and the production of knowledge by students. It will have really gone beyond it if computers play a part in mediating a change in the criteria that govern what *kinds of knowledge are valued* in education. The crucial thesis of "Epistemological Pluralism" is that while computers are often seen as supporting the abstract and impersonal detached kinds of knowing (which have drawn fire from feminists), computational thinking and practice has been shifting in the opposite direction towards a potential synergy with the feminist position.

Ethnographic studies of science provide a final example of a contrast between a superficial—though as in the other cases still valuable—first impact, and a potentially deep epistemological one. Work by Latour, Traweek, Keller, and many others has produced a picture of how scientist actually work that should be shared with children. But telling children how scientists do science does not necessarily lead to far-reaching change in how children do science; indeed, it cannot, as long as the school curriculum is based on verbally-expressed formal knowledge. And this, in the end, is what construction is about.

REFERENCES

Harel, I. (1991). *Children designers: Interdisciplinary constructions for learning and knowing mathematics in a computer-rich school.* Norwood, NJ: Ablex Publishing.

Papert, S. (1980). *Mindstorms.* New York: Basic Books.

Papert, S. (1970). *Teaching children thinking* (AI Memo No. 247 and Logo Memo No. 2). Cambridge, MA: MIT Artificial Intelligence Laboratory.

Papert, S., Watt, D., di Sessa, A., & Weir, S. (1979). *Final report of the Brookline Logo Project: Parts I and II* (Logo Memos Nos. 53 and 54). Cambridge, MA: MIT Artificial Intelligence Laboratory.

Strohecker, C. (1991). *Why Knot?* Unpublished doctoral dissertation. Cambridge, MA: MIT Media Lab.

Turkle, S. (1984). *The second self: The human spirit in the computer culture.* New York: Simon and Schuster.

Weir, S. (1986). *Cultivating minds: A logo casebook.* New York. Harper and Row.

Stephen Ocko Photography

Playing with LEGO/Logo at Project Headlight: Reaching some changes in how children do science and mathematics in schools.

In Gilda Keefe's 4th grade at Project Headlight, children design Native American Jewelry. Later they program these designs and other geometric patterns with Logo on the computer. These constructionist activities are part of their unit on Native American Culture & History.

2

Perestroika and Epistemological Politics

Seymour Papert*

During the week of the conference you have been immersed in exciting and focused discussions about actual uses of computers in real educational settings. So it should be. But it is equally appropriate at the beginning and at the end of the week to look at larger issues that are further removed from the reality of everyday work. I am delighted to be joined with Alan Kay for this aspect of the conference. His opening and my closing remarks will come together to define one side of the front in a battle for the future of education, a battle that goes far beyond the use of computers and indeed far beyond what is usually called "education."

My choice of political and militaristic metaphors was not made casually. I like to think of myself as a peaceful person, and come close to being a pacifist in international politics. I believe in consensus. But I have been driven to look at educational decisions with a confrontational eye. This does not mean giving up the ideal of consensual thinking, rather it means changing the community within which to seek the consensus. There is no chance that all educators will come together on the same side of the intellectual front I am trying to demarcate here. Many people in the education establishment are sincerely committed to positions with a firmness that is all the greater, because what is at stake is not simply a theory of education, but deeply rooted ways of thinking that touch on the relationship between individuals and society, cultures and subcultures, relativity and objectivity. What gives me confidence in the likelihood of significant educational change is the possibility of broad and unlikely seeming alliances between movements as diverse as progressive education, feminist "Aficonist" and other radical challenges to traditional epistemologies, and trends towards

---

* This chapter was edited from the transcript of my Closing Keynote Address given at the WCCE (World Conference on Computers and Education), Sydney, Australia, July 1990. The original was spoken, not read. In the editing the argument has been tightened but not so much as to lose the flavor of "orality" both in the rhythm and in the epistemology of the original presentation. Some points that seemed unclear have been elaborated. A more developed and "literate" form of the whole argument will be found in my 1992 book.

putting more emphasis on distributed, decentralized forms of computation. I believe that on a global scale, political winds of change are synergic with such alliances: Among these the political events from which I took my title.

I see the major theoretical challenge for thinking about the future of education as identifying the common element in these movements and the major issue for the World Community of Computer-literate Educators as deepening our understanding of the central role computers will play in translating them into educational reality. My goal today is to lead you to believe that there is such a common element and such a role for computers. I shall not do so by trying to give a precise definition of the Big Issue at stake. I don't know how to do that and doubt whether it is susceptible to precision. It is more in accordance with the epistemology I want to suggest here to stimulate the emergence of an idea in your minds by circling around my own version of it, touching it a little redundantly from different angles, pointing to a number of its multiple manifestations,[1] arguing that a real stand-off is developing, speculating about the role of computers and computer-educators.

It would be cozier to think that the large issues of educational policy could be settled consensually throughout the education world by the persuasive power of normal science—by the accumulation of incremental scientific knowledge about the "best" conditions for learning. But I am now convinced that, at the very least, something more akin to a Kuhnian revolution is needed. New paradigms are emerging and one cannot expect the established order of the old paradigms to give up their positions. Moreover, such a revolution would have to be of much broader scope than what is usually counted as "education." In particular, the emerging new paradigms require rethinking epistemological issues: while small changes in how to transmit knowledge do not call into question the nature of knowledge itself, the deep structure of our educational system is linked to our models of knowledge and cannot change unless they do. But perhaps even the concept of a Kuhnian revolution unduly limits the scope of what is necessary to bring about real change in education. For it is not only the established paradigms of knowledge that maintain the status quo in this field. In any science, the establishment holds its position in part through its control of institutions such as university departments, journals, and professional organizations. But in education there is a much vaster network of institutions—schools, universities, research labs, government departments, publishers—and the numerous people who work in them are more akin to a state bureaucracy than to the society of physicists. Exceptionally many people and institutions would be profoundly affected by any significant change and would defend their own interests by defending the status quo.

My title, "Perestroika and Epistemological Politics," is chosen to focus on

---

[1] See also Turkle and Papert (Ch. 9), and Resnick (Ch. 11), in this volume. Much of my thinking in this direction developed in collaborative work with Sherry Turkle.

these larger Issues, on the seriousness of the topic at hand, and on the high stakes of the revolutionary confrontation that awaits us. The analogy expressed by its use here has become significant for me in a number of ways.

The simplest is mostly inspirational. We have seen change happen with unexpected rapidity. No experts predicted the fall of the Berlin Wall or the newly found freedom of speech and religion in Soviet Union. Institutions that seemed firmly anchored have fallen, giving heart to those of us who have hoped for significant change in education. The backdrop of recent political events (in South Africa, Chile, and other places as much as in Eastern Europe) discourages one from even thinking "it can't change . . . it will never change!" And blocking this negative thought would remove one of the obstacles to change in school. But I also look at the events in these places as a source of insight into the nature of our own fight for change in education.

What is our fight really about? My reference to the Soviet Union comes from recognizing events there, not only as the most significant process of radical change in the world today, but also as one whose central issues are closely related to those that will dominate any deep change in education. What has happened in the Soviet Union is the collapse of a political and economic structure that invites descriptions like *hierarchical, centralized, depersonalized.* The confrontation I see in epistemology invites similar description as hierarchical–centralized–distanced vs. heterarchical–decentralized–personal conceptions of knowledge. The confrontation in education reflects both the political/social and the epistemological confrontations in the battle between curriculum-centered, teacher-driven forms of instruction, and student-centered developmental approaches to intellectual growth.

My reference to Alan Kay is a first shot at concretely drawing the lines of this confrontation in an educational context by pinpointing two positions situated on one side of the line. Placing us on the same side of this line is not meant to imply that we agree about everything. Far from it. For example, a difference of aesthetic taste showed itself in the movies Alan showed us about how children could create the behaviors of fish that live on a computer screen. This constructionist approach to biology is at the center of what we share. The study of biology is usually confined to observing natural creatures. We want to extend it by creating "make-an-animal" construction kits so you can learn by designing your own creatures and making them work. Given the depth of this agreement, it feels churlish even to mention such a trivial-sounding point of difference as my feeling that the look of the fish in his movie was a little too flashy and reminiscent of Hollywood. I'd like to see children construct fish that look like the children I used to know might have constructed them. But I think that if you could listen in to discussion between Alan and me on this point you would see that the difference really emphasizes the deeper commonality by the very fact of bringing issues of aesthetic taste into intimate relationship with the scientific study of biology. For children engaged in constructing "artificial fish," aesthetics and science merge more deeply than in the "gee, isn't nature pretty" invited by the usual superficial classroom form of nature study. And this merging energizes and enriches the children's work.

Besides our commitment to constructionism, another dimension on which I feel Alan to be closer than almost anyone else in the field of education is his deep understanding of real change—change that is more than incremental. One sees his openness to radical change in the content of what children would learn from the make-an-animal kit. This is not just a better way of transmitting the knowledge that is contained in a normal biology curriculum. Constructionism is not simply a better form of instructionism. Constructing the animals exercises a very different kind of knowledge and even leads to a very different placement of biology in the ensemble of intellectual disciplines. The model for biology projected by the traditional curriculum, and to some extent by the traditional practice of the science, is dominated by hierarchical notions of classification and description of structure. When you make your own animal your thinking is led naturally to focus on the emergence of functions and behaviors. Your role model is not Linnaeus the classifier but Tinbergen (1951) the ethologist or Wiener the cybernetician. One sees a biology affiliated as closely with what Herbert Simon (1989) has called "The Sciences of the Artificial" or "artificial science" as with "natural science." One sees that understanding biology requires a different logic: the logic of heterarchical (or self-organizing or decentralized) systems and the logic of design. The mindset of a designer or an engineer is better suited to understanding why animals are as they are than the mindset of a physicist.

I see this shift as representing a very significant change in education. But since people will have different ideas about what changes are big changes, I'd like to share with you a metaphor, a parable that I find useful for calibrating change and distinguishing "real" change—let's call it *megachange*—from incremental evolution.

I like to imagine a party of time-travelers from, it doesn't matter when, 1800 let's say, who had the opportunity to travel in the time machine to 1990 to see how people nowadays do things. Among them is a surgeon, who finds himself suddenly projected into an operating room 1990 style. Imagine his bewilderment with what's going on there. The flashing screens, beeping electronics. Even anesthesia is something totally new to him. So is the idea of antiseptics. Indeed, I think it's reasonable to say that nothing that's going on there makes any sense to him. Certainly, if the 1990 surgeon were to have to leave the room for a moment, the 1880 surgeon would not be in a position to take over.

Now imagine another member of the time-traveling party. A school teacher, who is projected into a classroom of 1990. Some things are puzzling, such as the funny little box with a window looking into another place, or maybe it's a magic mirror. But most of what's going on in that classroom is easily understood. And if the host teacher had to leave the room, the visitor wouldn't have the slightest trouble taking over and teaching the multiplication tables or spelling—unusual ideas about a few words would not make a big difference.

In some departments of human activity, such as surgery, telecommunications, and transportation, megachange has come in the wake of scientific and technological progress. The change has been so radical that the fields have become unrecognizable. Satellite television is not an incremental improvement over smoke signals, carrier pigeons, and couriers on horseback. It's a different ballgame. But in other departments, such as education, there may have been change, but it does not qualify as megachange in this sense.

Some people would argue that this is not surprising—it's simply not appropriate for megachange to happen in education. Not all activities are susceptible to megachange. Let's take eating, for example. The basic act of eating might be changed a little, it might be supported by technologies, but its essence is the same—you open your mouth, you put in the food, you chew it. Hopefully, you enjoy the food (and the company) and you swallow it down. Whether the food was cooked in a microwave oven, on an open fire, or not at all does not seem to be such a deep and radical change in the nature of the act. Eating is a natural act, it's not a technical act. It's a natural act that can be supported and modified by the technology around, but doesn't depend on it and doesn't change radically through its influence. We don't expect, and wouldn't welcome, megachange in the act of eating. Asking whether education is (in this respect) in the same category as eating or as medicine will help us clarify the educational lines of cleavage to a much greater extent than simply dividing people who, like Alan Kay and myself, hope for megachange from those who would look only for smaller "normal" change. The question also focuses on key epistemological issues underlying possible megachange. In particular it leads us to pay special attention to the *distinction between natural and technical acts.*

Isn't learning like eating? Isn't it also a natural act? And if so, should we expect megachange in learning? Well, I agree. Learning is a natural act, and it shouldn't be subject to megachange. Or rather, I agree that, if the kind of learning we're talking about is how a baby learns to talk, to walk, to love, to play—then learning is natural. And I don't look for any radical change in how it might happen. But school is not a natural act. School has become a technical entity permeated with "technical" ways of thinking even in situations where no "technology" is used.

What kinds of megachange might one anticipate in school? How should one think about the possibility of such change and the circumstances under which it might happen? Well, first I want to elaborate on the sense in which I think school is a technical act by focusing on how the teacher is cast in the role of a technician carrying out procedures set by a syllabus or curriculum designed hierarchically (from on top), and dictated to the teacher. Of course this is a simplification of what actually happens. In each classroom there is tension and compromise, a dialectical struggle between the role of technician in which the system tries to cast as the teacher, and the fact that the teacher is really a natural human being who loves and relates to people and who knows what it is to learn and to encourage development in a nontechnical spirit. Very few teachers fall completely, purely into the technician mold. The technician-teacher is an abstraction. But this is the mold into which the system tries to force the teacher. The abstraction helps us define the nature of the system. As we've heard recently in Britain, somewhat in America, and I believe here in Australia, whenever politicians get excited about the fact that something is wrong with the education, they start shouting "accountability," "tighten it up," "more hierarchical control," "let's have national tests." Why do they do it? You can say that this is what conservatives always do. But I think that it is helpful to have more theoretical, even if therefore more speculative, characterizations of an underlying process. I am suggesting that it is useful to think of what is happening as the system striving to define teaching as a technical act. This serves conservative purposes in many dimensions. It fits the conservatives' preferred mode of social organization. It fits the conservatives' preferred epistemological orientation. And, of course, in the most local sense, it suits the school bureaucracy to define the teachers' job as carrying out a technically specified syllabus following a technically specified teaching method.

So, the aspect of change that is moving to center stage in this discussion is *releasing education from its technical form and releasing the teacher from the role of technician.* But why am I talking about this here? This is a conference on computers in education. It is not a conference on "humanistic education"—computers *are* technology. Well, it might seem paradoxical—indeed is paradoxical—that technology should be the instrument for the achievement of a less technical form of education. But this is my goal, and I believe that such a trend has begun. I believe (and again I mention Kay as one who understands this in real depth) that the only plausible route to a "humanistic" education in the near future involves extensive use of computers. Technology can undermine technocentrism.[2] Specifically, having a strong technical infrastructure (e.g., in the form of computers as media of expression and exploration) allows the system to be less technical in its methodology (e.g., in laying down a centralized curriculum).

Let's go back to the time-travelling teacher to give ourselves a more concrete glimpse of what this might mean. There are a few classrooms where the teacher from 1800 would in fact fail to recognize most of the activities. Observing children designing fish in Alan Kay's "playground" is a case in point. And last weekend some of you might have seen children in this place working on building robots and other machines out of LEGO, connecting them to computers, and writing programs in Logo to control them. A teacher from 1800 who wandered

---

[2] Though maybe when it does, as Kay has noted, we shall stop calling it *technology*. No one calls pianos technology!

into those workshops would be slightly closer to the situation of the surgeon from 1800 wandering into a modern operating room—though still only slightly.

In the LEGO/Logo workshop we see glimmers of what a different kind of learning environment would be like. Here the children are engaged in constructing things rather than (as Freire would say) "banking knowledge". They are engaged in activity they experience as meaningful. And for this they don't need to be directed by a technician-policeman-teacher but rather to be advised by an empathic, helpful consultant-colleague-teacher. They are learning a great deal with a great deal of passion even though there is no technician to keep track of exactly what they are learning. Yes, it is true that this does not solve the technical problem of deciding the optimal sequence of their learning, but then Shakespeare and Picasso and Einstein did okay without anyone having to decide in advance the optimal sequence for them to do whatever brought them to their enviable state of creativity. I want to see children more like Shakespeare, Picasso, and Einstein, who did what was personally meaningful rather than what was laid down in someone else's program.

Does this threaten the jobs of teachers? In the sense of the bureaucracy's job description it does. But it opens new jobs: to guide students, to act as consultants, to help when a child may be in trouble, to spot a child who is in a cul-de-sac or on a plateau and could be encouraged to take a leap forward, or to spot a child who is on the track of something really wonderful and give encouragement. There's plenty of place for a teacher in this. In fact surely this image of the teacher, not as technician, not as policeman, not as an enforcer of curriculum, but as somebody who is part of a learning community, is an image of the teacher really being a teacher. The teacher would officially be given responsibility to exercise full individual judgment at each moment and to make individual decisions about where to go, what to do, and what action to take.

It is this freedom of the teacher to decide and, indeed, the freedom of the children to decide, that is most horrifying to the bureaucrats who stand at the head of current education systems. They are worried about how to verify that the teachers are really doing their job properly, how to enforce accountability and maintain quality control. They prefer the kind of curriculum that will lay down, from day to day, from hour to hour, what the teacher should be doing, so that they can keep tabs on it. Of course, every teacher knows this is an illusion. It's not an effective method of insuring quality. It is only a way to cover ass. Everybody can say, "I did my bit, I did my lesson plan today, I wrote it down in the book." Nobody can be accused of not doing the job. But this really doesn't work. What the bureaucrat can verify and measure for quality has nothing to do with getting educational results—those teachers who do good work, who get good results, do it by exercising judgment and doing things in a personal way, often undercover, sometimes even without acknowledging to themselves that they are violating the rules of the system. Of course one must grant that some people employed as teachers do not do a good job. But forcing everyone to teach by the rules does not improve the "bad teachers"—it only hobbles the good ones.

The change in education projected by the LEGO/Logo workshop can be seen from at least three different points of view. We're talking about a very different content material. The children are building robots, something that overlaps with doing math, doing physics, doing shop, doing writing, and doing spelling but is essentially different from any of them. We're talking about a different view of learning. And we're talking about a different form of control and organization of the school system.

But are these really three different dimensions of the system? I want to suggest that they are not. They are really manifestations of a common deeper structure. I would suggest that one reason education reform has not worked is that it almost always treats these dimensions as separate and tries to reform one or another—the choice depending on who is doing the reforming. Curriculum reformers try to put new curriculum in an otherwise unchanged system but ignore the fact that the old curriculum really suits the system and reverbs to type as soon as the reformers turn their backs. Similarly, when reformers introduce new forms of management of the old approach to knowledge and learning, the system quickly snaps back to its state of equilibrium. And, perhaps most dramatically from the point of view of people in this room, the same kind of process undermines any attempt to change education by putting a lot of computers into otherwise unchanged schools. But before talking about computers and schools, I shall take a closer look at how the study of Perestroika casts light on this kind of issue.

I have used the recent history of the Soviet Union and Eastern Europe in several ways as a powerful metaphor for thinking about change and resistance to change in education. First, there's the most elemental way: the events in Eastern Europe remind us that change is possible in systems that just 5 or 6 years ago seemed impregnable and unchangeable. Hardly any expert, maybe none, predicted that, in such a short time, the Berlin Wall would have crumbled, just as most people, all of us from time to time, feel that our education system is simply impregnable, and cannot change significantly, not in our lifetimes. But seeing how rapidly the Iron Curtain crumbled is sobering as well as heady in relation to our sense of the possibility of change in education.

But this incitement to believe that what seemed unchangeable isn't, is only one way to learn from the events in the Soviet world. These events can tell us a lot about the process, the pain, and the difficulty of changing a large, stable social structure.

When Gorbachev first began talking about Perestroika, he did not have any idea that there was going to be so much change so quickly. He didn't seem to predict it any better than the rest of us. It's more likely that he imagined a simple incremental restructuring. His intention seems to have been, not to induce megachange, but rather to jigger the bureaucratic organization in the hope of producing incremental improvements. But the system would not be jiggered.

Little by little in the Soviet Union and almost explosively elsewhere in Eastern Europe, it became clear that the problems of "Soviet" society could not be fixed by tinkering with details. By now it is painfully obvious that solving the urgent crisis of that society requires calling in question the fundamental ideas on which it is structured. Jiggering is not enough.

I believe that the same is true in our education system. Many reformers have tried to jigger the school system, to improve it by making small changes in the hope that it would eventually be transformed into a new modern, well-functioning system. But I think these reforms are victims of the same illusion that beset Gorbachev in the early days of Perestroika Reforming School requires more than jiggering. Here too we have to call into question the underlying, structuring ideas. But what are the structuring ideas of school?

A relatively easy step towards an answer is to note that what is wrong with our schools is not very different from what is wrong with the soviet economy—both suffer from rampant centralism. In fact, if we ask what aspect of American life is most like the Soviet economic system, it might well turn out that education is the closest parallel.

But it is easy to criticize bureaucracy superficially. It's harder to realize that, in both cases—our schools and the Soviet economy—the bureaucratic organization reflects underlying "structuring" ideas. I believe that a critique of bureaucracy can only be effective if it proceeds on this basis. Otherwise it cannot intelligently guide reform that will be more than jiggering. Gorbachev's Perestroika started as jiggering but was forced to move quickly toward calling in question the *fundamental* ideas of Soviet society, among them its deep commitment to a centrally planned economy.

Does the parallel between the central plan and our school's concept of curriculum need more explanation? In one case, a central authority decides what products will be manufactured in 5-year plans; in the other, it decides what children will learn in a 12-year plan: two-digit addition this year, three-digit addition next year, and so on. It is in the nature of this centralized planning that teachers be cast in the role of technicians whose job is to implement the plan. The very nature of a curriculum requires subordinating individual initiative to the Great Plan. Schools can see no way to make it work other than by exactly the methods and principles that have now been discredited in the Soviet system. All over the world, more and more people are recognizing that these principles do not work in economics. I think that more and more people are also beginning to see that they will not work in education either. These principles fail in the two cases ultimately for exactly the same reason: They hamper individual initiative, and deprive the system of the flexibility to adapt to local situations.

Thus when I talk about Perestroika in education, I refer to the conceptual organization of education as much as to restructuring its administrative organization. Indeed, ultimately conceptual organization and administration are so intertwined that one might as well say that they are the same thing.

In the Soviet Union, creating conditions for initiative and enterprise is emerging as the prerequisite for Perestroika. In education, initiative and enterprise (of students and of teachers) are blocked by the administrative bureaucracy and by the curriculum. The thrust of constructionism is to create a learning environment in which rich learning will come about in activities driven by enterprise and initiative. New technologies provide the opportunity for such learning by opening new possibilities for people of all ages to imagine and realize complex projects in which they implement a large range of important knowledge. "Learning by doing" is an old enough idea, but until recently the narrowness of range of the possible doings severely restricted the implementation of the idea. The educational vocation of the new technology is to remove these restrictions.

But even this does not go far enough toward a fullness of educational Perestroika. Real restructuring of the administration and of the curriculum can only come with an epistemological restructuring, an epistemological perestroika . . . *reshaping the structure of knowledge itself.*

One step in this direction is to break away from the traditional educator's role as someone who worries about transmitting knowledge but leaves the making of the knowledge to others. I illustrate this by recalling at least one of the lines of thinking that led to the development of the Logo Turtle. Instead of trying to "make children learn math" we tried to "make math that children will learn." Turtle Geometry offered a way to do math in the course of writing programs that would achieve purposes other than getting the right answer and getting a grade. Children write programs to make graphics on the screen, to make a game, to simulate something. They also write programs just to test out their own abilities, or just to have fun.

To do this, you need a somewhat different math. But it's mathematics nonetheless; it uses mathematical concepts, and above all it involves mathematical ways of thinking. It also leads children into thinking like mathematicians. Or rather, this is my opinion of it. But in order for this opinion to prevail, several layers of obstacles have to be overcome. These recapitulate the layers of Perestroika. First there is an administrative layer. The bureaucracy dislikes the change simply because it is change. A lot of money, effort and personal reputation has been invested in curriculum materials, definitions of job qualifications, textbooks, and so on. There is reluctance to change. On a second, more substantive level, a shift in content raises questions of authority. Who has the right to decide that this stuff really is math? Once posed in this way, the question effectively blocks anything remotely like a megachange. The only acceptable answer for the hierarchy would require an impossible consensus. But I really want to focus on a third level, where opposition to this kind of mathematics is firmly rooted in prevailing epistemological ideology. A shift here challenges more than particular knowledge: it challenges the very idea of knowledge. Inevitably the resistance will be fierce.

Scholars from different disciplines and with different purposes have criticized the role assigned by current epistemology to the hegemony of certain ways of thinking frequently described by terms like *formal, objective, abstract*.[3] Feminist scholars have argued that these categories express a male-centered approach. African scholars have associated these same ways of thinking with colonial domination. Such politically directed commentators on epistemology argue that the ways of thinking in question do not have an intrinsic superiority. Cases are cited of great intellectual works that proceed by other ways of thinking. And in this they are supported by recent work by ethnographers who go into laboratories to see what scientists actually do and how they actually think. A body of evidence is building up that puts in question, not only whether traditional scientific method is the *only* way to do good science, but even whether it is even practiced to any large extent. One can argue that it is nothing more than a shibboleth. But even if one takes a less extreme position, one has adequate grounds for several serious epistemological conflicts in the education system. An epistemological look at the turtle shows how these debates are close kin to issues in education.[4]

The most visible of Turtle Geometry's epistemological transgressions is bringing the body into mathematics. The turtle was chosen as a metaphor because it is so easy for a person to identify with it: You anthropomorphize the turtle: you solve a problem by putting yourself in its place and seeing what you would do. Of course, you can do Turtle Geometry in a formal way without any of this subjectivity. If this were not possible, I am not sure that I would accept it as "mathematics" (though this reluctance may be just residual conservatism that comes from being a white male of my generation who grew up in a series of elitist academic institutions—Cambridge University, Sorbonne, MIT, and so on). But if one were to refrain from doing "body math," most of the point of Turtle Geometry would be lost. Its intuitive attraction reflects epistemological preferences that would make Euclid wince—at least if we accept the image of him in the standard geometry curriculum.

The feminist and African critics of the traditional, canonical epistemology should understand the Turtle as a direct challenge to the ideology they wish to criticize. They have shown how the reduction of knowledge to precise formal rules in the name of "objectivity" is often male genderized and colored with colonialism. In the present context I can add another way in which it appears clearly as the ideological expression of an oppressive system. Control over teachers and students is simply easier when knowledge is reduced to rules stated so formally that the bureaucrat is always able to "know" unambiguously what is right and what is wrong. Technician-teachers and bureaucrats both like the true/false binary epistemology that insists on a right answer to every question, a right way to solve every problem. Constructionist mathematics has a different epistemology, whose criterion of success lies in the results rather than the method.

---

[3] See Turkle and Papert, this volume Chapter 9.

[4] See Papert, *Mindstorms* (1980); Abelson and diSessa, *Turtle Geometry* (1983).

Different methods can be used in a spirit of try, explore, test, debug, rethink. It becomes possible for the student to say, "Maybe the book says that, but this works. Just look and see."

Students working with LEGO/Logo show the beginnings of another area of new knowledge for children which is currently being actively developed by my colleagues and students at the MIT: an area we call *cybernetics for children*— using Norbert Wiener's name in a sense somewhat broader than its current American usage.[5] We are struggling to develop elementary forms of knowledge from control theory, theory of systems, and parts of AI that emphasize "emergence" and "society models." Doing so brings out in particularly sharp relief several aspects of my present theme. First, as I already noted, it is an area where the teacher from 1800 would be lost; thus it qualifies as an example for thinking about megachange. Second, it is highly constructionist. Children can exercise sophisticated ideas in pursuit of personal projects and fantasies (of which creating imaginary creatures is just the most obvious example,) Third, it shows us developing new knowledge rather than simply figuring out how to deliver existing knowledge. Each of these aspects has epistemological overtones, as I have already hinted. But cybernetics also brings out an epistemological issue I have not yet mentioned here.

Critics (such as the feminist and Africanist scholars already mentioned) of dominant epistemologies set up a line of demarcation that places formal, abstract kinds of thinking on one side, and intuitive, contextualized, concrete thinking on the other. In general, mathematics and computer science tend to be placed on the "dominant" rather than on the "alternative" side of this demarcation. I have already noted that Turtle geometry brings some of the personal into mathematics for children. Cybernetics, with an emphasis on self-organizing, decentralized, and distributed processes, provides more strong support for the alternative epistemologies. Through it children and teachers experience working in a precise way with heterarchical-decentralized forms of knowledge. This means they can "do science" without doing violence to their natural ways of thinking. Moreover, this kind of cybernetics represents a current of growing influence in the contemporary scientific world, including the culture of computer science. These two sides of cybernetics make it a powerful ally for an antihierarchical epistemological perestroika.

This is as far as I can go here in the direction of developing the idea of an epistemological perestroika. I move towards closure by recapitulating. I have used Perestroika in the Russian political sense as a metaphor to talk about change and resistance to change in education. I use it to situate educators in a continuum: are you open to megachange, or is your approach one of seeking Band-Aids to fix the minor ills of the education system? The dominant paradigm is the Band-Aid—most reform tries to jigger the curriculum, the management of schools, the

---

[5] See Section 3 of this volume about Children and Cybernetics.

psychological context of learning. Looking at the Soviet experience gives us a metaphor to talk about why this doesn't work. For stable change a deeper restructuring is needed—or else the large parts of the system you didn't change will just bring the little parts you did change back into line. We have to seek out the deeper structures on which the system is based. On this level, too, the Soviet case provides an analogy: for the same categorization—hierarchical–centralized–depersonalized vs. heterarchial–decentralized–personal—applies to the organization of education, to the structure of the curriculum, and to a deeper underlying epistemology. It offers a handle to grasp the conditions for change. Moreover, it suggests a close tie between educational change and the winds of change that seem to be blowing in many other domains in many parts of the globe. In short here is my conjecture and my call to arms: There is a powerful force in the world which could in principle—perhaps will inevitably—carry education in a certain direction. Moreover this is a direction which I and Alan Kay and all the people I love and admire most consider to be a good one. Let's go with it! It's our responsibility.

But why us? First, because we are, I hope, good and right-thinking people, who want to see education change for the better. And second, more specifically, because we have an instrument for such a change. But in recognizing this I must state a qualification. I do not see the computer as a "cause" of change—certainly not of this change: much thinking about the computer goes in the opposite direction, strengthening the idea of teaching as technical act, supporting centralization in organization of institutions and of ideas. I've seen models of a school of the future in which there's a computer on every desk wired up to the teacher's computer, so that the teacher can see what every child is doing. And then the teacher's computers are wired up to the principals computer, so the principal can see what every teacher is doing. And all the principals are wired up to well, you know where. Nothing could be more hierarchical.

The computer is not an agent that will determine the direction of change. It is a medium through which different forces for change can express themselves with special clarify. One might describe its role as sharpening the choices. In traditional school there is a mixture of centralized and decentralized. If you contrast the LEGO/Logo workshop with the image of the wired-up school, you see a purer form of each than can easily be found in traditional schools. It is for us to choose.

The response of schools to computers brings other issues as well into sharp relief—for example, the issue of megachange vs. Band-Aid. The first microcomputers I saw in classrooms were brought there by visionary teachers who saw the computer as a way to improve the general learning environment of the classroom. This was a small step . . . but a step in the direction of megachange. In the last 10 years there has gradually been a process of "normalization"—like a living creature, the education system has known how to make the foreign body part of itself. As the school administration took control from the individual teacher conservatism set in. "Computer Rooms" were set up that isolated the computer from the learning environment of the classroom. In many places a curriculum was to set up replete with tests on precisely defined fragments of knowledge about computers. In other places the computer was used to deliver the most technical and rote parts of the traditional curriculum. The computer accentuates the choice. It is for us to make it. Which image will guide the long-run growth of educational computing?

But what about the short run? I said that schools recuperate the computer from being an instrument of revolutionary change and make it a Band-Aid. But that doesn't always happen. There's room for insertion of individual acts to subvert the normalization. I have found useful the metaphor of the Trojan horse. LEGO/Logo is a very good Trojan horse. It looks acceptable to people who just want to do "technology studies," so these kids will be "computer literate" and "technology literate." This way the bureaucracy will accept it, because it seems to be innocuous. But, in fact, within it is a seed you can nurture, a seed of real deep restructuring of relationships and ways thinking about education. The system has an inherent tendency to use you for its ends. But you don't have to be used.

There's another way in which the computer lab normalization is breaking down. We're beginning to see in the United States that there are now too many computers to put into a computer lab. And so they're overflowing back again, so that the question arises of what to do with the computers. Will they go back in the mainstream of learning? Or will you make another computer lab with another specialized computer teacher? You can be influential in the decision whether to let them spill them over into the main stream of learning.

My last words are about what this implies for the status of computer teachers, of whom there are many here present at WCCE. Some of things I've said might be felt uncomfortable for a computer teacher cast in the role of agent of the reaction. I don't mean to do that. Although it's true that the system might be using the teacher in that role, the teacher doesn't have to follow the script. As the computers spill out of those labs back into the mainstream, the person who knows about the computer will have the opportunity to take on a new role and a much more exciting exalted role within that school. Now there is an opportunity to become the person whose job is to facilitate rethinking the whole learning environment of the school, the whole structure of ecucation. We are entering a period in which the person who was "the computer teacher" has the chance to become the educational philosopher and the intellectual leader of the school, of the education world.

It was said at one of the reflection sessions this morning that, compared with the previous World Conference on Computers and Education, this one was much less about computers and much more about education. I'd like to push this trend by asking: Well, how many more WCCEs should we have? Isn't it time for us to grow up? And as we grow up, we should stop seeing ourselves as specialists of computers in education, because that casts us in the role of a kind of service profession. Accepting the role allows that other people are the ones to decide the big goals of education, what the curriculum is, how learning happens, what's a school. And at our conferences we talk about how their decisions can be served by the computers. Well, fine, up to a point. This certainly allows revolutionary actions as long as we are at the stage of crafting Trojan horses to throw into the system. But at some point we have a responsibility to break out of that marginal role and take on our true vocation, which is not one of service but one of leadership. At some point it will be as ridiculous to have a world conference in computers and education as to have a world conference on pencils and education.

And with that I'll stop. And thank you for listening to me.

REFERENCES

Abelson, H., & di Sessa, A. (1983). *Turtle geometry*. Cambridge, MA: MIT Press.
Papert, S. (1980). *Mindstorms*. New York: Basic Books
Simon, H. (1989). *The science of the artificial*. Cambridge, MA: MIT Press.
Tinbergen, N. (1951). *The study of instinct*. Oxford: Oxford University Press.
Wiener, N. (n.d.) *Cybernetics: Communications & control in animal and machines*. Cambridge, MA: MIT Press.

Stephen Sherman Photography

Project Headlight teacher Gwen Gibson and Armone School teacher Denise O'Malley with Seymour Papert, at a Science and Whole Learning (SWL) Project Meeting: "What's the curriculum? How does learning happen? What's science? What's a school?"

28

3

The Computer as a Convivial Tool

Aaron Falbel

What is the effect of the computer on the mind of the child? Does the computer enhance thinking skills? Or does the computer promote heartless, mechanical, instrumental reason? In short, is the computer good for kids, or bad for them?

It is understandable that these questions should be of great concern to parents and teachers who are confronted with the growing presence of computers in the workplace, in schools, as well as in the home. A critical outlook is indeed a healthy one. But I would like to point out that these are nonetheless *badly formed* questions. Trying to answer them in this form will only lead to confusion and reactionary logic.

TECHNOCENTRISM

The problem with asking questions regarding "the effect" of "the computer" is that such questions presume that the computer itself can somehow directly affect thinking and learning, that the computer, solely by virtue of its being a computer, can change the way people think and learn. It is all too easy for the technical object, because it is new and not well understood, to loom too large and eclipse our finer critical sensibilities. Seymour Papert has called this type of reasoning, where one gives undue centrality to a technical object, "technocentric thinking." In an essay that appeared in *Educational Researcher*, Papert asks us to consider other "obviously absurd" technocentric questions:

> Does wood produce good houses? If I built a house out of wood and it fell down, would this show that wood does not produce good houses? Do hammers and saws produce good furniture? These betray themselves as technocentric questions by ignoring people and elements that only people can introduce: skill, design, aesthetics . . . Everyone realizes that it is carpenters who use wood, hammers and saws to produce houses and furniture, and the quality of the product depends on the quality of their work. (Papert, 1987, p. 24)

It ought to be equally obvious that *people* are the agents when it comes to thinking and learning, not computers. People use computers to do things. If we are to say anything meaningful about the thinking and learning involved, then we should look at what people are doing with computers and not at what "the computer" is allegedly doing to them. For in reality, there is no such thing as "the computer" in general—only specific uses of computers in specific contexts.

EDUCATION: ACTIVE OR PASSIVE?

The fact that this is not obvious, that technocentric questions abound in discussions concerning children and computers, is due to a certain basic fallacy in people's thinking about education generally. The fallacy equates education with schooling or instruction: a designed process or technical act that is *performed on* the learner. With such a definition of education, it is not hard to see how questions regarding the effect of the computer enter into the picture.

But education—real education—is not something performed on someone, nor is it something one *gets;* it is something one *does* for oneself. I generally prefer to use the word *learning* instead of *education. Learning* has a more active feel to it, whereas *education* carries with it a sense of passivity.

With such a passive view of education, we open the door to technocentrism when we speak of the computer as an "educational tool." It should not be an *educational* tool, but just a tool. Like other tools, it allows us to do some things that we couldn't do before, or, more usually, to do some things better that we could do before.

It is somewhat vacuous to distinguish the computer by calling it "a tool for learning." In a sense, *all* tools are learning tools: we learn when we do things, and tools can help us do things better. Unfortunately, most of the time, when people describe the computer as a learning tool, what they really mean is that they see it as a teaching tool, that is, something you learn *from* (as opposed to something you learn *with*), or—even worse—something that they think can *make* children learn.

I really do want to discourage people from using the type of educational software or "courseware" in which the computer fires questions at the learner or in some way directs the learner's behavior. My argument has little to do with computers; I would argue just as strongly against teachers or parents firing questions at children. The point here concerns courses of action rather than tools: What shouldn't be done, shouldn't be done *at all*. A computerized workbook is just as bad as a paper one. The real problem with workbooks, whether on the computer or off, is that they are based on, and hence convey to children, a bad model of learning. When children are responding to questions and exercises in workbooks, one of the things they are learning—regardless of the content of the workbook—is the very idea that learning itself consists of answering other people's questions rather than your own. This model of learning is ultimately harmful and is one of the many elements that leads people to view learning as a passive process, as something that is done to them.

This whole active/passive distinction is not as straightforward as it seems. One must be wary of falling into the trap of saying that people are "active" when using computers, because they are pushing buttons or in some way responding to events on the screen, whereas they are "passive," when, say, watching television, because they are just looking at it. Such a use of the word *active* or *activity* is a rather shallow one; it takes the defining characteristic of activity to be mere movement rather than volitional, purposeful, intentional action. The social psychologist Erich Fromm noted this very distinction between the shallow and deeper senses of "activity" in his book *Man For Himself:*

> Activity is usually defined as behavior which brings about a change in an existing situation by an expenditure of energy. In contrast, a person is described as passive if he is unable to change or overtly influence an existing situation and is influenced or moved by forces outside himself. This current concept of activity takes into account only the actual expenditure of energy and the change brought about by it. It does not distinguish between the underlying psychic conditions governing the activities.
>
> . . . The person in a deep hypnotic trance may have his eyes open, may walk, talk, and do things; he "acts." The general definition of activity would apply to him, since energy is spent and change is brought about. But if we consider the particular character and quality of this activity, we find that it is not really the hypnotized person who is the actor, but the hypnotist who, by means of suggestions, acts through him. While the hypnotic trance is an artificial state, it is an extreme but characteristic example of a situation in which a person can be active and yet not be the true actor, his activity resulting from compelling forces over which he has no control. (Fromm, 1947, pp. 92–93)

Computer-assisted instruction (CAI) essentially places the computer in the role of the hypnotist: "Answer *this* question, solve *this* problem," it demands. The user of such a program can only react to whatever appears on the computer's screen. The learner is not *in* control, but *under* control.

If this is a bad model of learning, then what is a good one? How might a child learn by using a computer? The answer is, the same way he or she learns by using a pencil. Pencils don't make you a better writer, but they can be used to write with. Computers, too, can be used to write with, or to draw with, or to calculate with, or to store and retrieve information with, or to solve certain types of problems. One learns by doing these things and by thinking and reflecting about what one does. There is nothing magical about the computer in all of this. Like a pencil, it can be a "convivial tool."

A CONVIVIAL TOOL

The philosopher and social critic Ivan Illich has coined the phrase "convivial tool" to refer to tools or social arrangements that can enhance a person's freedom and autonomy. The issues he raises here mirror the concerns I have raised thus far with regard to computers. Illich writes:

> Tools are intrinsic to social relationships. An individual relates himself in action to his society through the use of tools that he actively masters, or by which he is passively acted upon. To the extent that he masters his tools, he can invest the world with meaning; to the degree that he is mastered by his tools, the shape of the tool determines his own self-image. Convivial tools are those which give each person who uses them the greatest opportunity to enrich the environment with the fruits of his or her vision.
>
> . . . Tools foster conviviality to the extent to which they can be used, by anybody, as often or as seldom as desired, for the accomplishment of a purpose chosen by the user. The use of such tools by one person does not restrain another from using them equally. They do not require previous certification of the user. Their existence does not impose any obligation to use them. They allow the user to express his meaning in action. (Illich, 1973, pp. 22–23)

There is nothing inherent in a tool that makes it convivial or not. While it can be argued that the certain tools (such as telephone networks) lend themselves more easily, due to their design, to convivial uses than do others (such as commercial television), the key to a tool's potential for conviviality lies also and especially in the social arrangements people create around its use. With a different social arrangement, telephone networks could become less convivial (through limiting access, surveillance, or restricting the content of conversations), or, alternatively, television and video technology more convivial (by making available cheap, compact video recording and playback equipment plus a supply of tapes on which people could record whatever they wish and then send these tapes, either physically or electronically, to others).

However, it can be argued that, in some ways, the design of computers is becoming less convivial. One aspect of a tool's capacity for conviviality is its simplicity or transparency, or, conversely, its complexity or opacity. When home computers started to appear in the mid-1970s, they were largely bought by people who considered themselves to be "computer hobbyists." Frequently, these early computers were bought in kit form to be assembled at home. The early Apple computers had a large lid on top which could be easily removed, revealing many "expansion slots" or places to plug in additional hardware. These early computers were designed to be tinkered with. Not so any more. On the back of today's Macintosh computer one finds a label conveying a very different sort of message:

CAUTION

▲WARNING:▲

To prevent electric shock, do not remove cover. No user serviceable parts inside. Refer servicing to qualified service personnel.

This constitutes a reduction in conviviality, the hallmark of which is self-reliance. The computer is becoming more and more opaque—a veritable black box. The message here is clear: You cannot understand it; you must rely on the experts. Illich underscores this point in *Deschooling Society:*

> The nonspecialist is discouraged from figuring out what makes a watch tick, or a telephone ring, or an electric typewriter work, by being warned that it will break if he tries. He can be told how a transistor radio works but he cannot find out for himself. This type of design tends to reinforce a noninventive society in which the experts find it progressively easier to hide behind their expertise and beyond evaluation. (Illich, 1971, p. 115)

Commercial software, too, suffers from opacity and nonconviviality. More convivial software could be written in a programming language that is easy to understand. MacWrite may be a first-class word processor, but as a user, you're stuck with whatever features have been designed into it. You can't customize it. You can't "look under the hood" and see how it works. And while it is possible to drive a car without knowing how it works or how to repair it, this places one at the mercy of specialists. Similarly, it is possible to use a computer without knowing how it works, how to program it, or how to repair it, but this, too, limits one's freedom. We must settle for whatever the experts send our way.

I have already mentioned certain *uses* of computers that I believe are bad; namely, using computers for the purposes of instruction, using programs that do things to people. I want to mention other uses of computers that can liberate people to do things better or more easily, uses that increase a person's range of choices.

Many professional writers today use a word processor as their main writing instrument. Why shouldn't children have access to the same quality writing tools as professional writers? The computer can turn a piece of text into a fluid, plastic substance that can be edited and manipulated at the touch of a few buttons. Revision is no longer the arduous task it once was, and ease of editing can liberate people to be more expressive and free with their writing. The effort one needed to put into rewriting, in precomputer days, often meant that one's first draft was identical to the final draft. The pen may be mightier than the sword, but the eraser is mightier still. And the computer's delete key is one of the most powerful erasers ever invented.

Electronic mail, or "E-mail," takes advantage of computer networks (often making use of existing telephone lines) to enhance the speed and power of regular mail. A message sent via E-mail is delivered nearly instantaneously, and sending copies to other persons (or, through the use of mailing lists, to a large group of people) is made vastly easier via this technology. So is replying to a message or forwarding a piece of mail to another reader. Many children enjoy writing to pen pals, and I believe that many more would enjoy writing to an even wider range of people via E-mail, especially if they received the prompt replies to their messages that the technology enables.

Learning to program a computer can in some sense make it a more convivial tool and can counteract the current trend toward nonconvivial hardware. Knowledge of a programming language allows one to shape the computer to one's needs and tastes. This allows for more freedom and flexibility as far as what the computer can be made to do and what it can be used for.

I have listed only a few convivial uses of the computer here. My short list is far from exhaustive. Many other productive ways of using computers are discussed in greater detail in the other chapters in this collection: The computer is explored as a tool for music making, for art, for controlling robots, for exploring or presenting ideas in physics or mathematics, and as a tool to aid research. None of these chapters attempts to measure the "effect" of the computer. Collectively, they signal that the age of computer euphoria is over, and that we can direct our attention away from the machine itself and towards what the machine can empower us to do. We must ask ourselves: What are these things? Are they worth doing?

VALUE NEUTRALITY

At the start of this chapter, I dismissed as technocentric the question of whether computers were good or bad for kids. In doing so I leave myself open to attack by certain critics who will accuse me of saying that technology is "value neutral." They would argue that technology is "value laden," that tools and machines themselves "embody" certain values which are in turn imposed on their users. But to ascribe values to tools is also a form of technocentrism, for it is not the tools themselves but the use of tools that we should be evaluating, and such uses are certainly *not* value free.

Sherry Turkle, who has written a highly detailed and sensitive account of people's interactions with computers, has commented on the question of value neutrality in the following way:

> I have often been asked, "Are computers good or bad?" The question was usually
> asked in regard to children, but as home computers moved aggressively into the
> workplace, I was increasingly asked to answer this question in regard to adults. The

question deserves some comment. No one asks whether relationships with people are good or bad in general. Rather, we seek out information to build our own model of a *particular* relationship. Only then do we make judgments about the possible effects of the relationship . . . Computers are not good or bad; they are powerful. (Turkle, 1984, pp. 2–3; emphasis added)

The crucial point is: It does not make sense to talk of good or bad machines outside of any reference to the particular ways they are being used.

If find myself asking, Why do the critics get so hot under the collar when it comes to this issue of value neutrality? Why do they devote endless pages to argue this point, pages thick with quotes from Hegel, Weber, Marx, and Cassirer? I understand their fear well enough: a fear that science is an arena sanitized of ethical values, that science deals with truth and falsity, not good and bad. This is indeed a dangerous misperception. Science is a human activity and as such deals with right and wrong, good and bad. But unfortunately the critics further confuse the issue by saying that ethical values are inherent in tools. I can use a pencil to write a beautiful sonnet, or I can use it to stab someone. Similarly, I can use a computer to write a novel, or I can use it to embezzle funds from someone's bank account. The blame-the-tools argument actually hurts their cause, because it directs our attention toward machines and away from the real concern of ethics: human actions and their consequences.

COMPUTER LITERACY VS. COMPUTER CULTURE

A number of computer companies, overzealous innovators, and aggressive advertising agencies have convinced many educators and legislators of the importance of something they call "computer literacy." While it is almost never clear just what is meant by this phrase, one can assume that computer literacy entails some sort of general knowledge about computers, how they work, and how to use them. The importance of such knowledge is vastly overrated: It is assumed to be necessary when in fact it is, under certain circumstances, convenient or useful. We must not let ourselves become intimidated by people who claim that children will be left behind, or ill prepared for the "computer age," unless they are "exposed" to the computer early on. This is nonsense. It must be remembered that people who say such things are almost always trying to sell you something.

The only reason to become "computer literate" right now is that you need or want to use a computer right now. Talk of the future has very little to do with it. Besides, today's computer literacy will be woefully out-of-date when applied to tomorrow's computers. If computers will indeed be "everywhere" (as the prophets of the computer age claim), then it should be very easy to find out about them, how to use them, and so on. Children learn to talk because talk is everywhere and it is useful. Learning about computers in the computer age need not be any different.

I believe that children of all ages should have *access* to the tools that we adults use in our culture, and the computer is one such tool. Access means that something is *within reach*. It is up to the individual whether he or she actually wants to reach out and take advantage of this accessibility. I get the feeling, though, that when people talk about computer literacy, they are not talking about access but *exposure*. This is something very different. Again, the active/passive distinction comes into play here. Exposure to, say, a compulsory course in computer literacy puts the learner in a passive role; he or she is acted upon. The alternative would be to provide someone with access to computers and to people who have knowledge about computers. This gives that person an opportunity to enter a computer culture. The learner *acts,* first by choosing to become involved, and then by actually becoming involved.

My remarks here about "computer literacy" are equally applicable to achieving alphabetic literacy, that is, learning to read and write. Becoming literate chiefly involves access to books and writing materials, and to people who can read and write. Likewise, becoming computer literate involves access to computers and to people who can use them. Both entail entering a culture, or, as the educator Frank Smith has put it, "joining a club" (Smith, 1988). Contrary to all this, however, the computer-literacy campaign, through exposure and through institutionalization, ends up turning the computer from a convivial tool into a compulsory one.

The assumption behind the exposure tack is that only adults know what is good for children. The children are not to be trusted. They must be taught what is important. They do not know what they want or need. I flatly disagree with this. If given free access—not exposure—to computers with as much help and assistance as is asked for, children will make their way into the computer culture in the right way and at the right time, something no computer-literacy program can hope to do. Most of the common pedagogical arguments (regarding "the appropriate computer curriculum") fall by the wayside: No child will work on something that really is too hard or too abstract or too boring, provided that he or she is *free to leave* the computer. But this is almost never the situation in schools, where exposure is the rule. Children are *told* to work on the computer or are brought into the computer lab for 45 minutes—they are not free to leave. Such a situation goes against the grain of Illich's definition of conviviality.

Computers can be used to enslave people, to program them, to dehumanize them; or they can be used in a liberatory manner, to extend our creative and expressive reach, to foster conviviality. The choice is ours and depends on our values. Do we want a society that manipulates and controls, or do we want a society that fosters choice, freedom, and autonomy? The way we use *tools*—in Illich's broad sense of the word—reveals our true intentions.

ACKNOWLEDGMENTS

This chapter is based on a chapter written for the book, *Schooling at Home: Parents, Kids, and Learning,* published by *Mothering* magazine in conjunction with John Muir Publications. Subscriptions: $18.00 per year (4 issues), P.O. Box 1690, Sante Fe, NM 87504. Excerpted with permission.

REFERENCES

Fromm, E. (1947). *Man for himself.* New York: Ballantine Books.

Illich, I. (1971). *Deschooling society.* New York: Harper & Row.

Illich, I. (1973). *Tools for conviviality.* New York: Harper & Row.

Papert, S. (1987). Computer criticism vs. technocentric thinking. *Educational Researcher, 16* (1).

Smith, F. (1988). *Joining the literacy club.* Portsmouth, NH: Heinemann Educational Books.

Turkle, S. (1984). *The second self: Computers and the human spirit.* New York: Simon and Schuster.

Stephen Ocko Photography

Technology can be used to enslave people, to program them, to dehumanize them; or in a liberatory manner, to extend creativity and expressivity, to foster conviviality.

PART II

LEARNING THROUGH DESIGN, PLAY, AND PROGRAMMING

4

Software Design as a Learning Environment

Idit Harel and Seymour Papert*

CHILDREN AS SOFTWARE DESIGNERS

This chapter has a double intention: It adds to the description and discussion of an experiment that formed the centerpiece of Harel's doctoral dissertation (Harel, 1988), and it uses the discussion of this particular experiment to situate a general theoretical framework (developed over the years by Papert and his colleagues) within which the experiment was conceived. The experiment will be referred to here as the "Instructional Software Design Project" (ISDP), and the theoretical framework as "Constructionism" (e.g., Papert; 1990).

The ISDP experiment involved studying a class of fourth-grade students. Each student worked for approximately four hours per week over a period of 15 weeks on designing and implementing instructional software dealing with fractions. A narrow description of our intention in doing this is that we wished to turn the usual tables by giving the learner the *active* position of the teacher/explainer rather than *passive* recipient of knowledge; and in the position of designer/producer rather than consumer of software. This idea is in line with Constructionism's use of "building," "constructing," or "knowledge-representing" as central metaphors for a new elaboration of the old idea of learning by doing rather than by being told ("Constructionism" rather than "Instructionism").

The usual passive view of integrating computers into education supports *Instructionism and Technocentrism* (Papert, 1987). ISDP, like all projects at Papert's Epistemology and Learning Group, attempted to change this approach by giving children the control over their learning with computers. Children were the agents of thinking and learning—not the computer. Our view is: Computers cannot produce "good" learning, but children can do "good" learning with computers.

---

* This chapter was previously published in *Interactive Learning Environments, 1*(1), 1–32.

> Does wood produce good houses? If I built a house out of wood and it fell down, would this show that wood doesn't produce good houses? . . . These . . . questions ignore people and elements that only people can introduce: skill, design, aesthetics . . . (Papert, 1987, p. 24)

> It ought to be equally obvious that *people* are the agents when it comes to thinking and learning, not computers. People use computers to do things. If we were to say anything meaningful about the thinking and learning involved, then we should look at what people are doing with computers, and not at what "the computer" is allegedly doing to them. For in reality, there is no such thing as "the computer" in general—only specific uses of computers in specific contexts . . . With a passive view of education, we open the door to technocentrism when we speak about the computer as an "educational tool" . . . It should not be an *"educational"* tool, but just a tool. Like other tools, it allows us to do things we couldn't do before, or more usually, to do some things that we could do before better. (Falbel, this volume, Chapter 3)

Building on the computer (or with the computer) a piece of instructional software about fractions is discussed here as a privileged way for children to engage with fractions by constructing something personal. In this, it may overlap educational techniques that employ materials such as cuisenaire rods, fraction bars, or pattern blocks. But constructing software goes far beyond the physical manipulations involved in using such materials. To the adage "you learn better by doing," Constructionism adds the rider, "and best of all by thinking and talking about what you do." Without denying the importance of teaching, it locates the important *directions of educational innovation* less in developing better methods of teaching than in developing "better things to do and more powerful ways to think about what you are doing" (e.g., Papert, 1971a, 1971b).

The key research question is to determine what kinds of things are "better." In this paper we focus on attributes such as *appropriability* (some things lend themselves better than others to being made one's own); *evocativeness* (some materials are more apt than others to precipitate personal thought); and *integration* (some materials are better carriers of multiple meanings and multiple concepts).

We see several trends in contemporary educational discussion such as "situated learning," and "apprenticeship learning" (e.g., Brown, Collins, & Diguid, 1989; Collins & Brown, 1987; Suchman, 1987) as being convergent with our approach, but different in other respects. Two features will be discussed here as giving specificity to Constructionism in relation to this essentially synergistic body of literature. The first is our emphasis on developing new kinds of activities in which children can exercise their doing/learning/thinking. (Turtle Geometry is one example. ISDP is another.) The second is our special emphasis on project activity which is self-directed by the student within a cultural/social context that offers support and help in particularly unobtrusive ways. ISDP provides us with insights into the unique ways in which constructing instructional software generates and supports personal reflection and social interaction favorable to learning.

In elaborating the Constructionist vision we take the time to dissipate misunderstandings by contrasting it with derivatives of Papert's early work that radically miss its epistemological essence. In particular, we emphasize the fact that ISDP has little to do with the idea that learning Logo is in itself either easy or beneficial.

WHAT WAS ISDP?

Context

ISDP was conducted as part of a larger project to study the uses of computers in elementary schools. Project Headlight, as it is called, is based in an inner city public school, the Hennigan School, in Boston. Only *one third* of Hennigan students, with children from first through fifth grade, participate in Headlight. (The experimental ISDP class and control class C1, which did daily programming in Logo, were both part of Project Headlight. Control class C2 was not.) As at many Boston public schools, the majority of the student population at Hennigan is Black and Hispanic, and in most ways the school is quite conventionally structured. A major purpose of Headlight was to gain understanding of how a computer culture could grow in such a setting. One feature that is not typical in Hennigan is its building, which dates from the early seventies when there was a fad for "open architecture." When we first saw the school its architectural features were virtually unused, but we viewed them as an opportunity to reinforce our open-ended educational philosophy through the design of the space. We saw the *physical environment* as a very important factor in shaping a learning culture. These open spaces allowed us to bring the technology closer (physically and conceptually) to students and teachers; to integrate the computer activities with the regular classroom activities; and to facilitate movement and action around the computers; to reinforce communication and information-sharing regarding computer-based activities across grade levels and among teachers.

In Headlight there is no long hallway leading into one classroom called the "Computer Lab" where children take their weekly "Computer Literacy Class." Rather, there are two large open areas (the "Pods") housing four large circles with 100 computers, and each pod is surrounded by 6 classrooms. At Headlight, children use computers at least one hour a day, for working on their different computer projects, as an integral part of their homeroom learning activities.

In Headlight there is virtually no use of "ready to use software" and little emphasis on learning *about* computers and learning programming as ends in themselves. The students learn programming but programming is a means to different ends, which we conceptualize as entering a new learning culture—developing new ways of learning and thinking.

Our vision focuses on using technology to support excellence in teaching, in learning, and in thinking *with* computers—technology as a medium for expression. We particularly eschew naive views of the computer as replacing (in the guise of improving) some of the functions of the teacher. Headlight students are encouraged to tackle exceptionally complex problems and work on exceptionally large-scale projects in a culture where they have a great responsibility for their own learning. They are able to work individually and collaboratively in a variety of styles where the differences are reflected in gender, ethnicity, cognitive development, and in the individual personality of the teachers as well as in the personality of the learners (see also, Goldman Segall, 1989a-b; Harel, 1986, 1988, 1989a-e; Motherwell, 1988; Resnick, Ocko, & Papert, 1988; Resnick, 1989; Sachter, 1989; Turkle & Papert, 1990).

ISDP Procedures

During the period of the ISDP project, one of the "pods" in Headlight was turned into a software-design studio, where 17 fourth-grade students worked on constructing personally designed pieces of instructional software; the only requirement was that they should "explain something about fractions" to some intended audience. Before they started their software design work, the students were interviewed individually and were tested on fractions and Logo programming. Presenting herself as a researcher and a "helper," Harel explained to the students that they were not being graded, but were involved in a new kind of activity which she wanted to observe, evaluate, and report on for the benefit of others. Students were encouraged to think of themselves as collaborators in the project and its data collection.

ISDP was open-ended, but somewhat more structured than the other Headlight projects. It included a series of activities that all the experimental students performed. Each working day, before going to the computer, the students spent 5 to 7 minutes writing their plans and drawing their designs in their personal Designer's Notebooks. Then, they worked at their individual computers for approximately 45 to 55 minutes. They implemented their plans and designs, created new ones, and revised old ones. When they wished, students were allowed to work with friends, help each other, or walk around to see what other students were doing. At the end of the ISDP daily period, students saved their daily Logo files on a diskette. In their Designer's Notebooks, they then wrote about the problems and changes of the day (related to Logo, fractions, instructional design, teaching, etc.) and sometimes added designs for the next day. The students had full freedom to choose which concepts they wanted to teach (within the domain of fractions), how to design their screens, what the sequence of their lesson should be, and what instructional games, quizzes, and tests to include, if any. In short, the project was open-ended in terms of what the students chose to design, teach, and program. The only two requirements were: (1) that they write in their Designer's Notebooks before and after each working session; and (2) that they spend a specific amount of time at the computer each day. The purpose of this second requirement, regarding time limitations, was to allow the project to fit into the schedule of the class and of the school. This requirement also made it possible to estimate and draw generalizations about what students could accomplish in a project of this kind, within time periods that could fit into the regular schedule of any class or school in the future.

Several "Focus Sessions" about software design, Logo programming, and fraction represention were conducted in the classroom during the project. In the first session, Harel briefly introduced and discussed with the students, the concept of instructional design and educational software. Together—the children, teacher, and Harel—we defined the meaning and purpose of instructional software, and briefly discussed a few pieces of software with which the students were familiar. Harel showed the students her own designs, plans, flowcharts, and screens from various projects she had worked on in the past. She also passed among the students the book *Programmers At Work* (Lammers, 1987) and asked them to look at notes, pieces of programs, and designs by "real" hardware or software designers and programmers—such as the people who had designed the Macintosh, PacMan, Lotus 1-2-3, and others. In this first session the students also received their personal diskettes and their Designer's Notebooks (see Appendix), and we discussed the ways in which they should and could be used during the project.

Other Focus Sessions encouraged the students to express themselves on issues such as the difficulties of specific concepts and on how they might be explained, represented, or taught. For example, in two of these discussions, we hung two posters, one on each side of the blackboard. On one poster we wrote, "What is difficult about fractions?" and on the other, "What screens and representations could be designed for explaining these difficult concepts?" We asked the students to generate ideas for both posters simultaneously.

Other discussions focused on specific Logo programming skills. For example, in some of these short sessions about programming, the teacher, the researcher, or one of the students, could stand next to one of the computers that were in the classroom or in the "computer pod", in front of the whole class or a group of students, and explain how to use REPEAT, IFELSE, variables, and so on. The students could take notes on such concepts and programming techniques in their notebooks, or go directly to their computers and write a procedure which included that new programming technique or concept.

In addition, the fourth-grade students/designers worked with third graders from another Headlight class, who visited the ISDP class once a month, for the purpose of trying out ("evaluating") the students' pieces of software as they were developed. The fourth graders gave the third graders "demos," and then, different pairs of children were engaged in discussing different aspects of the software projects: some were teaching/learning fractions; some were teaching/ learning Logo programming; some discussed design issues; and so forth. A great deal of teaching/learning through socializing went on during these sessions. However, the actual teaching was not as important as the fourth graders' feeling that they were working on a real product that could be used and enjoyed by real people. It reinforced the "thinking about explaining things to others" during their product development, and it placed them in the role of epistemologists.

The teacher and the researcher (Harel) collaborated and actively participated in all the children's software design and programming sessions during the project: walked around among the students, sat next to them, looked at their programs, helped them when asked for, and discussed with them their designs, programming, and problems in a friendly and informal way. In general, there were no specific plans for the Project's sequence, or for our presentations and focus discussions; rather, they were initiated by the teacher or by the researcher "as needed," at times when they were relevant to the children's work or problems, or according to the children's requests.

To summarize, the children's daily activities resulted in 17 different pieces of instructional software about fractions—one product for each child in the experiment—and 17 personal portfolios consisting of the plans and designs they wrote down for each day's work, and the pieces of Logo code they had programmed, as well as their written reflections at the end of each session on the problems and changes they had dealt with that day.

To our pleasure, we observed that students worked with great intensity and involvement, over a period of four months, on a subject that more often elicits groans or yawns than excitement—namely fractions. What seemed to make fractions interesting to these students was that they could work with them in a context that mobilized creativity, personal knowledge, and a sense of doing something more important than just getting a correct answer.

ISDP Atmosphere

Procedures answering to the descriptions in the above section could be carried out in very different atmospheres but would then, from our point of view, constitute radically different projects. It is therefore appropriate to devote some space here to capture the particular ambience of this project.

The ISDP environment was marked by the deep involvement of all participants. There were interactions and reciprocal relations among the students, teacher, researcher, members of the MIT staff, and sometimes visitors—all of whom walked around the computer-area, talked together, helped each other, expressed their feelings on various subjects and issues, brainstormed together, or worked on different programming projects individually and collaboratively. Knowledge of Logo programming, design, and mathematics was communicated by those involved. Children, much like the adults in this area, could walk around and observe the various computer screens created by their peers, or look and compare the different plans and designs in their notebooks.

Young students were developing knowledge and ideas without workbooks or worksheets, working within a different kind of a structure. They became software designers, and were representing knowledge, building models, and teaching concepts on their computer screens. They were thinking about their own thinking and other people's thinking—simultaneously—to facilitate their own learning. The following "snapshot" briefly illustrates the atmosphere of this noisy, flexible, and productive learning environment.

Debbie is swinging her legs while sitting at her computer and programming in an apparently joyful way. To her right, Naomi is busy programming letters in different colors and sizes. To her left, Michaela is engaged in programming and debugging a screen that shows a mathematical word-problem involving fractions, comparing thirds and halves by using a representation of measuring cups that are filled with different amounts of orange juice and water. She is very involved with her design, typing with one hand on the keyboard while her other hand is moving and touching the figures on her computer screen. A few computers away, the teacher is trying out Tommy's program, giving him feedback on one of his explanations about "what mixed fractions are." In the background, Charlie is walking around the other computer circle, holding his Designer's Notebook in one hand, and chewing on the pencil that is in his mouth. He suddenly stops next to Sharifa's computer. He chats with her for a moment, presses a key or two on her keyboard, and observes Sharifa's designs as they appear on her computer screen. After looking at her Logo code, moving the cursor up and down on the screen, he calls out, "Hey Paul, come see Sharifa's fractions clock!" The noise and movement around Michaela and Debbie do not seem to bother them at all at this moment. Now Naomi, who sits next to Debbie, has just completed the "title screen" for her software, which reads: "Welcome To My Fractions Project! by Naomi." She is stretching her arms while moving her head to the left and to the right, looking around to see "what is new" in her friends' programs. She then stretches towards Debbie's computer, and asks her to show her what she is doing.

Debbie shows Naomi her programming code. "It's a long one," she says, running the cursor down the screen, very proud of the 47 lines of code she has programmed for her "HOUSE" procedure. She then gets out of the programming editor to run her program, which impresses Naomi, who moves her chair even closer to Debbie's computer. In a quiet and slow voice, pointing to the pictures on her screen, Debbie explains to Naomi: "This is my House Scene. All these shapes [on the screen] are one-half. In the house, the roof has halves, the door has two halves, and I will add to this scene two wooden wagons and a sun. I'll divide them into halves too . . . The halves [the shaded parts] are on different sides [of the objects]. You can use fractions on anything. No matter what you use . . . Do you like the colors?" Their conversation goes on and on.

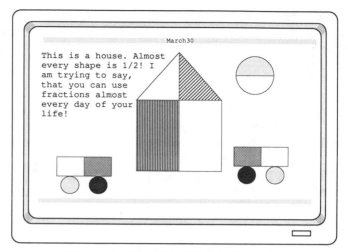

Figure 1. Debbie's "House Scene"

The idea of representing halves on the different sides of the objects, the objects being "regular human things" in a real-life situation, is Debbie's. In her final version of the teaching screen, there will be an explanatory text accompanying the pictures on the screen which says: "This is a house. Almost every shape is ½! I am trying to say that you can use fractions almost every day of your life!" Debbie is the only child in her class who has designed such a screen. She is very clear about why she designed it: to teach other children that fractions are more than strange numbers on school worksheets. As she discovered, fractions can be all around us; they describe objects, experiences, and concepts in everyday life.

Debbie has painted half of each object a different color, and left the other half blank. The house half is painted in light blue, the roof half in orange, the sun half in yellow, the door half in red, the wagon half is red, etc. While Debbie is working on this, the only advice she asks of her friend Naomi is about the colors: "Do you like the colors?" Naomi, who has adopted a different design strategy for her software, tells her: "It's nicer if all the halves are in the same color." They negotiate it for a minute or two. But Debbie doesn't agree: "No. It will be boring." Naomi and Debbie continue to work on their projects with the computer keyboards on their laps . . .

EVALUATION OF ISDP

The evaluation of ISDP was designed to examine how students who learned fractions and Logo through the ISDP differed from students who learned fractions and Logo through other pedagogical methods. Three fourth-grade classes from the same inner-city public school in Boston were selected for this evaluation. One class, from Project Headlight ($n = 17$), was involved in the ISD

Project (Experimental Class). Control Class 1, or C1 ($n = 18$), studied fractions only in their regular math curriculum and programmed in Logo as part of Project Headlight. Control Class 2, or C2 ($n = 16$), studied fractions in their regular math curriculum, was not part of Headlight, and programmed only once a week in the school's "computer laboratory."

Experimental Design

In January 1987, all three classes were pre-tested on specific skills and concepts in fractions and Logo. Thereafter, one of the classes participated in the four-months ISDP experiment. All 51 pupils were then tested again in June on their knowledge of fractions and of Logo (see Figure 2).

Using the set of pre-tests, it was established that no significant differences existed between the experimental and the control children's knowledge of fractions and Logo before the experiment began (Harel, 1988, 1989e). Four months after the pre-tests, by using a similar set of post-tests, the ways in which these students differed in their knowledge and understanding of fractions and Logo were investigated in detail. In addition, during the project the researcher and the teacher conducted careful observations and interviews with the experimental students, and assessed (by the use of case study methods and videotaping) the development of the students in the ISD Project.

Many research questions could have been raised concerning the ISDP experiment, since it involved many variables within a complex pedagogical situation. However, for the purpose of this study, the objectives and questions were narrowed down to two main sets of assessments:

1.   An assessment of the experimental children's knowledge of basic fraction concepts; and

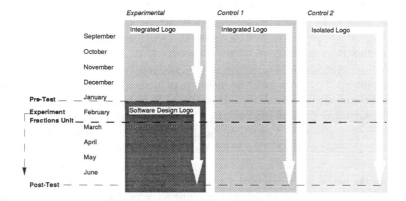

Figure 2.   Experimental Design and Procedure

2.   An assessment of the experimental children's knowledge of Logo programming concepts and skills.

The "experimental treatment" integrated the experimental children's learning
of fractions and Logo with the designing and programming of instructional
software. Since the experimental students and the C1 class had equivalent,
though differently styled, exposure to Logo (i.e., both classes were part of
Project Headlight), it was an open question whether participation in ISDP would
result in greater Logo knowledge, but one naturally expected both of these
groups to exceed class C2 in this area. With respect to fractions learning, the
experimental group had additional (but not formal) exposure to fractions concepts through ISDP, so that improved performance of the experimental class was
expected in this area as well, but the assessment sought to determine whether this
was in fact true and, if so, what the nature of the improvement was. As will be
seen in the next sections, the assessment uncovered some surprising results,
more finely-textured than these general surmises.

Within the fractions domain, emphasis was placed on children's ability to
translate between various modes of fractional representations. This aspect has
been shown to be a crucial part of rational-number knowledge, and particularly
difficult for young children (e.g., Lesh & Landau, 1983; Behr, Lesh, Post, &
Silver, 1983; and others). But standard school tests were also used, which
concentrated on students' use of algorithms. In Logo, the evaluation investigated
the children's knowledge, use, and understanding of programming commands,
instructions, and operations. More specifically, it assessed whether the students
from the experimental class knew and understood more programming commands
and operations such as REPEAT, IFELSE, SETPOS, variables, and inputs in
their projects, and became better at these skills, than the students in the two
control classes. The evaluation also investigated whether the experimental students could understand, implement, debug, transform, optimize, and modify
someone else's programming code better than the students from the control
classes. Finally, the evaluation assessed whether the experimental students were
able to construct Logo routines for someone else's design or picture and were
better at this than the students in the two control classes.

Given the breadth of the learning experience and the mixed methodology of
the assessments—including the extensive case studies of several students (i.e.,
examination of the children's progress, Designer's Notebooks, finished products, interviews with participants during and following completion of the project), as well as the more formal pre- and posttests—it was possible to trace in
detail the microgenesis of Logo and fractions skills and concepts, exploring
different approaches taken by the experimental students with different personal
and learning styles (e.g., Debbie's Case in Harel, 1988, pp. 76–245; and the
Appendix in Harel's paper in *Journal of Mathematical Behavior*, 1990a), as well
as to draw inferences concerning their acquisition of metacognitive skills.

The experimental design of ISDP and the analysis of its results we present here raise methodological issues for education research. Most acutely, these concern the question of what *kinds of rigor* are appropriate.

A simplistic position would maintain that the highest standard of rigor is always required. But we argued elsewhere (e.g., Papert, 1987) that this can sometimes result in an analog of the complementarity principle in physics, stronger formal rigor sometimes being obtained only at the cost of thinner results. Thus Harel (1988) adopted different kinds of rigor for different aspects of her work, and we will do likewise in this article.

The first results section demonstrates with statistical rigor *that learning* took place: the ISDP subjects learned *quantitatively measurable skills* in the programming and in standard school domains. The section that follows illustrates some aspects of the in-depth investigations into *what and how* they learned, going beyond test scores to obtain qualitative insights into the changes that occurred in students' thinking about fractions, and the dynamic of the process that lead to those changes. Finally, a discussion section follows, where we discuss *why* the students learned what they learned.

RESULTS

Quantitative Results from ISDP

The "thinnest" and most formally rigorous part of the analysis shows that the subjects in the experiment did improve in their ability to perform on standardized quantitative tests of performance in their work with fractions (as presented in the following subsection). Here the solidity of the results derives from the existence of a large established body of data on how students perform in such mathematics tests (e.g., Behr et al., 1983; or Lesh et al., 1983). We also present some quantitative data to show that the ISDP subjects did learn much more about Logo programming than the subjects in the two control groups (as presented in the subsection about Logo results).

Results from the Fractions Posttests of the Three Classes

All the teaching of fractions, for all the three classes, was conducted for two months, during regular math lessons only and following the city-wide curriculum and traditional teaching methods (see Figure 2). The experimental class was not provided with any additional formal instruction on fractions, although we note that the representations of fractions in the context of instructional design was discussed in a few informal Focus Sessions. (More information about the characteristics of the pupils, teachers, and their math curriculum is available in the dissertation and the Appendix of Harel, 1988.)

**Table 1.   Average Percentage Correct of Pre-
and Posttests on Fractions Knowledge**

	Fraction Knowledge	
Treatment	Pretest (%)	Posttest (%)
Experimental Class	52	74
Control Class 1	54	66
Control Class 2	47	56

The posttest included 65 multiple-choice questions. Out of these, 60 were taken from the Rational-Number Project (RN Project, Lesh et al., 1983, pp. 309–336). The remaining five were designed by the researcher and included word problems and construction of representations. Of the 60 RN Project questions, 43 were given to the students in the pretest, then again in the post-test. As examples, Table 1 shows the children's average percentages of correct answers on the fractions pre- and posttests; Table 2 shows the table of results for the Two-Way Factor Analysis of Variance with repeated measurement for the fractions pre- and posttest scores; and Figure 3 shows the interaction diagram of the two main factors. In general, the difference in pre- and posttest scores of the students from the experimental class was almost twice as great as that achieved by the students from class C1, and two-and-a-half times as great as that of class C2.

Results from the More Difficult Questions on the Fractions Test

We gave specific attention to the analyses of the most difficult translation modes between rational-number representations that the students had to carry out in the test. Some of these translations were the most difficult for students of all ages in previous studies, and were equally so for all students in the present study's pre-tests. In the posttests however, these translation modes were still relatively

Table 2.   Two-Way Repeated Measurement Analysis of Variance
(The results account for the unequal sample sizes of Factor A).

Source	d.f.	F-Statistics
A (Groups)	2	15.31**
Subjects between Samples	48	
Within Subjects	50	
B (Pre-Post)	1	110.99**
A × B	2	8.29**
B × Subjects	48	
Between Subjects	51	
Total	101	

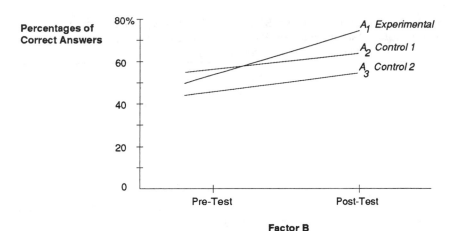

Factor B

Figure 3. Interaction Diagram of the Two Main Factors in the Analysis of the Pre- and Posttests Scores

difficult for the control students, but dramatically less so for the experimental students. Let us consider an example. Lesh et al. considered question 50 to be so complex that it was not given at all to the fourth graders in the RN Project, only to sixth-, seventh-, and eighth-grade students (Lesh et al., p. 326). To answer this question, the students had to translate a pictorial representation into a written (verbal) representation of a fraction.

Question 50 presented students with a polygonal region representation, with a numerator that was higher than 1, a denominator, a representation of a rational number lower than 1, in a discrete object that included a perceptual distraction (i.e., one part was "outside" the triangle area). In order to choose one of the options, the students had to (1) translate the given picture into symbols or words (two fifths are shaded in), (2) read the question again and realize that the question referred to the denominator of the shaded fraction, and (3) find the correct answer, which was b. Option a is confusing because it is written like a spoken symbol and includes "relevant" numbers—five and thirds. Option b is confusing because it does not mention "fifths," but rather "five" (the denominator is "five"). Table 3 shows the scores in their percentage of correct answers for question 50.

The ISDP students scored twice as high on question 50 as did the control students, and twice as high as the sixth to eight graders from the RN Project. The Chi Square analysis shows that the differences of frequencies are highly significant.

Perhaps there is some "transfer" from Logo programming experience at work here. Decomposing a given picture into its geometrical components is a common process in Logo programming, and a skill students usually acquire in their ongoing programming experiences. What Lesh et al. (1983) and Behr et al.

Table 3.   Contingency Table Statistics, Comparing Performance of the Study Sample with the Performance of the Background Sample (Lesh et al., 1983, Average of Grades 6–8)

	(%) Correct in Study Sample	(%) Correct in Background Sample
Experimental Class	66	33
Control Class 1 & Control Class 2 (Average)	29	33

$\chi^2 = 33.49$

(1983) consider as a ''perceptual distraction'' (i.e., the one little triangle that was ''outside'' the big triangle area) was probably not at all a distraction for the students who looked at the picture with ''Logo eyes'' and decomposed it into its five geometrical components.

Another example is Question 42. It involved a translation of pictorial into symbolic representation (see Figure 5). This question, number 42, was the 13th most difficult of the 18 asked in this subset. It was the 44th most difficult in the whole set of 60 questions given in the RN Project to students from fourth through eighth grades (Lesh et al., 1983, p. 323). It included a discrete object representation in which the represented rational number was less than one; moreover, parts of this object were not congruent and were visually distracting. Table 4 shows the scores (given as percentage of correct answers) on this question according to the children's division into math groups (see Harel, 1988, for the detailed description of the math groups).

As seen in Table 4, none of the high-math experimental students made any mistakes. The medium-math experimental students scored like the high-math

50) What is the denominator of the fraction that tells us what part of the picture below is shaded?

a. five-thirds   b. five   c. three   d. two   e. not given

Figure 4.   Question #50

42) What fraction of the balls are tennis balls?

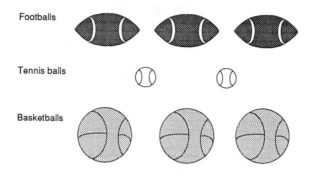

a. 2/8   b. 3/2   c. 2/6   d. 6/2   e. not given

Figure 5.   Question #42

students in the two control classes. The experimental class as a whole scored 100% better on this subset as the students in the RN Project, and 14 percentage points better and 27 percentage points better than class C1 and class C2, respectively. Table 5 shows that the Chi Square analysis of differences of frequencies is highly significant.

Table 4.   Percentage of Subjects Responding Correctly to Question #42, by Treatment and Mathematical Ability

	Mathematical Ability		
Treatment	**Low (%)**	**Medium (%)**	**High (%)**
Experimental Class	50	72	100
Control Class 1	40	68	72
Control Class 2	20	50	72

Table 5.   Contingency Table Statistics, Comparing Performance of the Study Sample with the Performance of the Background Sample (Lesh et al., 1983, Grade 4)

	(%) Correct of Study Sample	(%) Correct of Background Sample
Experimental Class	74	36
Control Class 1, Control Class 2 (Average)	53.5	36

$\chi^2 = 42.62$

Results from Standard Boston Public Schools Math Tests

In addition, all the pupils were tested in math, as part of their end-of-year public school series of "referenced tests." This mathematics test included 40 multiple-choice questions. The average number of incorrect answers was 5.06 incorrect answers per child in the experimental class, 6.27 per child in class C1, and 9.45 per child in class C2.

Of the 40 questions, six were specifically on fractions ordering and equivalence, four on decimals, four on measurements of distance and time that required the use of fractions, and one on understanding geometrical shapes (i.e., this was the subset of 15 questions directly related to rational-number concepts, their representations and computation). The average number of incorrect answers to this subset of 15 rational-number questions was 1.60 per child in the experimental class, 3.16 per child in class C1, and 4.62 per child in class C2.

Several conclusions can be drawn from analyzing these results. The first is that the experimental students, in general, did much better on the entire conventional school test than the two control classes. The second conclusion is related to the children's incorrect answers in the rational-number concepts subset of this test. In the experimental class, only 29% of the incorrect answers in the whole test (40 questions) were incorrect answers about rational-number concepts. But in both class C1 and class C2, approximately 50% of the incorrect answers were on rational-number concepts. This shows the superiority of the experimental class on rational-number knowledge in particular—as measured by this standard test. Table 6 shows the proportion of incorrect answers in this rational-number subset to the whole test.

The third conclusion is related to "transfer." By subtracting the average of incorrect answers on the fractions subset from the average of incorrect answers on the whole test, we can examine the children's average of incorrect answers to all the non-fractions questions: for the experimental class, $5.06 - 1.60 =$ an average of 3.46 incorrect answers per child on non-fractions questions; for class C1, $6.27 - 3.16 = 3.11$; and for class C2, $9.45 - 4.62 = 4.83$. The differences between the experimental class and class C1 are not significant here, but the differences between these two classes and class C2 are. This finding is interesting because it might be that the experience of Project Headlight students

Table 6.   Contingency Table Analysis, Comparing the Proportion of Rational-Number Subset to Whole Test in the Boston School Math Test between the Experimental and Control Classes (of incorrect answers)

Experimental Class (%)	Control 1 Class (%)	Control 2 Class (%)
29	51	48

$\chi^2 = 6.631$

(experimental class and class C1) with Logo programming contributed to their general mathematical ability.

SAMPLE RESULTS FROM THE LOGO POSTTESTS

In the pencil-&-paper Logo Test the students were asked: "*Please list all the Logo instructions and commands that you know and use—in column A; then, write an explanation and give an example for each one—in column B.*" The results for this question were divided into two major groups of findings. The first are simple findings that relate to how many instructions and commands each child actually listed. The second relate to the children's understanding of the meaning and functions of these commands and instructions in the Logo language. Table 7 represents the differences between the students in terms of how many Logo commands, operations, function keys, control keys, and so on, they listed in the posttest. The number in each slot shows the average number of commands and instructions the children from all three classes listed and explained. The advantages of the experimental students over the students from the two control classes become clear from examining this table.

The students were also evaluated on the quality of their definitions and examples for each of the items they had listed. In class C1 no one was evaluated as "Very Good," whereas in the experimental class, three students who wrote over 40 commands and instructions, and four who wrote over 30, and gave very good examples and definitions of each, were evaluated as "Very Good." No one was evaluated "Low" or "Very Low" in the experimental class. However, four students in class C2 were evaluated as "Low" since they listed fewer than five commands and instructions and did not provide examples or definitions for all or most of those.

We also tested the children's ability to analyze given programming code and "execute" it on paper. A long, linear Logo code composed of short strips of Logo primitives was given to the students, and the students were asked to draw the graphics. This task required that students read the given linear code, comprehend it, understand its flow of control, build a mental model of what the computer would do when each of the lines in this program was executed, and draw the picture accordingly, step by step.

Table 7. Contingency Table Analysis, Comparing the Average Number of Listed Logo Commands between the Experimental and Control Classes

Experimental Class	Control 1 Class	Control 2 Class
25.6	12.0	8.3

$\chi^2 = 10.8426$

Many researchers in the field of programming distinguish between writing a linear program and a modular program. These researchers consider a linear program as one which emphasizes the generating of effects without any consideration and understanding of the inner structure of the code (e.g., Papert, 1980; Papert, Watt, diSessa, & Weir, 1979; Carver, 1987; Soloway, 1984; several researchers in Pea & Sheingold, 1987; and others). On the other hand, a modular program emphasizes elegant and efficient programming, and is accompanied, they claim, by a higher level of understanding of programming in general, and of the programming language characteristics in particular.

Our results show that students who had written linear as well as modular programs during their process of learning to program were better able to understand and correctly execute this confusing linear program. The students in C2, who only knew how to write linear programs, were not able to solve this problem accurately unlike many of the ISDP students. We should note that ISDP students often introduced structure (i.e., subprocedures and functional naming) into their programs only after a long period of purely linear programming, and only when they themselves decided it was necessary; it was not imposed on them from the outside. They learned to introduce structure, modularity, and elegant coding when they themselves realized the need for it in maintaining their *long* programs, in adding new parts to them, or in re-using (instead of re-writing) certain subprocedures in several places in their programs.

Another interesting aspect of these results came to view in the "number of trials" category. Many of the ISDP students tried more than once to draw the picture on paper, and finally found the right solution; but the students in the control classes who had gotten it wrong in their first trial were apparently not motivated or determined to try again or to find the right solution. Many of them simply wrote "I don't know how to do it," and went on to the next task on the test.

Finally, we mention that on a "Debugging Task" given to the students on the computer, the ISDP students were faster at identifying the bugs, locating them, and then re-evaluating the program in order to create an output that corresponded perfectly with the original goal given to them. The data in Table 8 shows the results for "Tasks 1 and 2" on the computer, which required that the students run a given bugged program, analyze the features of the resultant graphics, identify the discrepancies between them and the desired graphics, enter the Logo code on the computer, locate the different bugs causing the discrepancies, fix the program on the computer, and add the corrections on the program that were written on the paper.

Table 8 speaks for itself. The superiority of the ISDP students over the other pupils is clear, as is that of class C1 over class C2. Table 9 shows a Chi Square Analysis of these results.

In addition to the above quantitative results we made a number of qualitative observations about the children's debugging strategies. For example, the first

Table 8.   Results from the Debugging Task

	No. of Bugs Found and Fixed	Identify & Fix Bugs in *Computer* Prog.	Identify & Fix Bugs in *Paper* Program	Average Time for Solving 1 & 2
Experimen. class $n = 17$	16—all bugs 1—one bug	17 children—yes 100% succeeded	17 children—yes 100% succeeded	15 min per child
Control 1 $n = 18$	9—all bugs 4—one bug 5—none	13 children—yes 5 children—no 70% succeeded	8 children—yes 10 children—no 44% succeeded	35 min per child
Control 2 $n = 16$	2—all bugs 4—one bug 10—none	6 children—yes 10 children—no 37% succeeded	2 children—yes 14 children—no 12% succeeded	55 min per child

thing all the ISDP students did was to change the HT (Hide Turtle) command at the very beginning of the procedure, to ST (Show Turtle), so that they could follow the turtle as it executed the code. On the other hand, the first strategy that most of the students in class C2 and many in class C1 used was to copy the program given to them on paper (in subtask 2) into the Logo Command Center and execute it line by line. This strategy worked well until they reached the REPEAT statements, which were written on more than one line. Then, the students got confused because the program still did not work, though they were sure that they had located a bug. Instead of trying a new strategy, these students then erased everything and started to copy the procedure into the computer in "direct mode" again, which resulted in the same thing happening again, and so on.

In "Tasks 3 and 4 on the computer," the students were asked to optimize the code given to them in Tasks 1 and 2, and make it clearer and shorter. In order to solve these sub-tasks, the students had to cease operating on the individual command level, and start thinking in a procedural mode, using REPEATs, procedures, and inputs. To summarize these results, the experimental students

Table 9.   Contingency Table Analysis, Comparing the Number of Bugs Found in the Debugging Task between the Experimental and Control Classes

	Experimental Class (%)	Control 1 Class (%)	Control 2 Class (%)
Bugs found:			
2	94	50	13
1	6	22	25
0	0	28	62

$\chi^2 = 138.92$

were more flexible and attempted to explore a greater variety of ways for producing the same Logo drawings. They understood and reached a more modular level of code, and many of them tried to use repeats, subprocedures, and variables. The experimental students also performed significantly better than the control students on the three other items of this test, covering use of inputs, modification of procedures according to specific requests, and prediction of results of short but confusing graphics programs (see Harel, 1988, 1989b, d,e).

Interestingly, all the ISDP students, who had already performed much better than the control students in the similar pencil-&-paper tasks, performed even better when using the computer. But the students from class C2 got more confused at the computer, and performed less well than they had on the pencil-&-paper task. Class C1 was somewhere in between: the high-math students, like those from the ISDP class, performed much better at the computer, and the medium- and low-math students performed similarly to those from class C2—far less successfully than they had in the pencil-&-paper task.

Similar trends were found in the results of the Logo post-tests and in the Fractions posttest: the ISDP students consistently scored higher than the other two classes; but class C1 usually scored higher than class C2. Also, the high-math students from class C1 made up a special group. They were never as good as the high-math ISDP students, but most of the time they were as good as the medium-math ISDP students. Their scores in the fractions test were often higher than those of the students from the RN Project, and stood out from those of the other control students. What does this mean? It seems as though only the high-math students in class C1 strongly benefited from Project Headlight experience with respect to the pictorial-to-symbolic translation of fractions. This was probably due to their programming expertise, which contributed to their ability to translate picture representations into written ones, and vice versa. This phenomenon requires further investigation. It is an interesting one, since it suggests a correlation between the children's level of understanding and involvement in Logo programming, and their ability to understand different representational systems.

QUALITATIVE RESULTS ABOUT *WHAT AND HOW* THE STUDENTS LEARNED

Thicker descriptions than "getting better at" fractions or Logo in the school's terms were derived from an analysis of a large body of qualitative data derived in three ways: formal interviews, preservation of students' work, and observations of process. The 51 students in the experimental and control groups were interviewed before and after the ISDP experience. The ISDP students' work was preserved in Designer Notebooks and in computer files showing the state of their software projects at the end of each day. In addition to direct daily observations

by the researcher and teacher, videotape made in two modes gave many opportunities for micro-analysis of behaviors: in one mode the videocamera was
carried by an observer and directed at interesting events, in the other it was
placed in one position on a tripod for an entire session and simply allowed to run.
These sources of data allowed us to see subjects discovering new ways of talking
about fractions and relating to fractions spatially and kinesthetically as well as
linguistically and conceptually (e.g., Harel, this volume, Chapter 22).

The interpretative nature of such conclusions required rigor that is different in
kind from statistical analysis that checks whether or not the probability of
differences in scores could be due to chance. But it is the richness of observation
obtained from so many different sources that yielded a coherent sense of the
development of individual subjects as well as of shared developmental trends,
and this gave us confidence in our conclusions that we could not have obtained
by any other means. To appreciate this coherence in full it is necessary to refer to
finer textured case studies published elsewhere (Harel, 1988, 1990a). Here we
focus on four issues which we label as *development of concept*, *appropriation of
project*, *rhythm of work*, and *cognitive awareness and control*.

Development of Concept. Under the rubric development of concept we
analyze the movement from rigidity, particularity and isolatedness toward flexibility, generality, and connectedness. In the initial interviews questions such as
"What is a fraction?" or "When you close your eyes and think about fractions
what images do you have?" or "Can you give me an example of a fraction"
revealed several aspects of particularity. There was particularity in the use of
particular rational numbers (usually one half or one fourth) as prototypes. Most
strikingly there was particularity of restriction to the spatial: A fraction is a part
of something, and "something" means something physical or geometrical. Of
course children from an early age use fraction words linguistically to refer to
parts of other kinds of entities, such as time ("half an hour" or "I am eight-and-
three-quarters") and money ("a quarter"). But in the interviews they very
seldom seemed to connect such usages to a general notion of a fraction. When
specifically prompted to look for fractions in a real calendar or clock, subjects
gave answers referring to the squares on the calendar or shapes on the clock face.
One student even referred to the pattern strap-watch-strap as analogous to the
numerator, the slash, and the denominator in the school representation of fractions! And even within the spatial there was a high degree of particularity in
choosing examples that happened to coincide with those one expects to meet in
school books: "a fraction is a half a pie" or "a fraction is like an apple or an
orange divided in the middle." When asked to draw a fraction most commonly
they would draw a circle or a square, divide it vertically (not necessarily
equally), and shade some parts. In some cases the degree and rigidity of the
particularity bordered on the bizarre. For example, Debbie was committed to the
idea that a fraction is the right shaded part of a circle divided by a vertical
diameter. When asked whether the unshaded part of the circle is a fraction, she

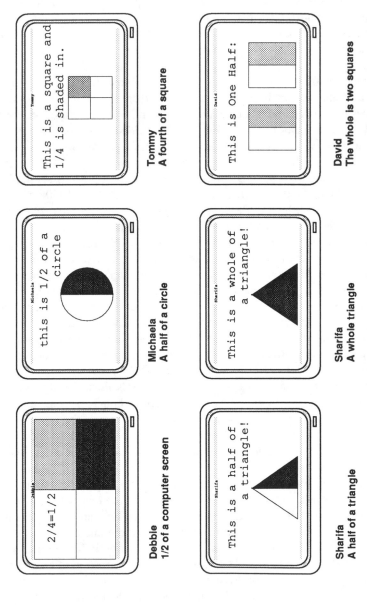

Debbie
1/2 of a computer screen

Michaela
A half of a circle

Tommy
A fourth of a square

Sharifa
A half of a triangle

Sharifa
A whole triangle

David
The whole is two squares

Figure 6.   Some Children's Initial Representations on the Computer

62

said, "No. It's not a fraction. It's nothing." Such tendencies were also seen in the choice and modes of representation of fractions in the very first examples of computer screens made in the experimental students' software projects.

All this changed dramatically in the course of the project. The content of the software as well as the post-interviews revealed a widening diversity of kinds of examples and representations among the ISDP students. Even more significantly, there was often a conscious—indeed, one might well say philosophical, recognition of the achievement of greater generality. In Figures 7a–f we show a few examples of some children's further representations. Although it is difficult to capture the colorfulness and playfulness of those animations in this static black and white medium, the children's general ideas, their diversity, and complexity is captured here.

Consider Debbie again. After a whole month of explaining about fractions—by creating a representation showing a half of her computer screen, and different geometrical shapes divided into halves and fourths—Debbie discovered something. Her discovery was expressed in her choosing to teach an idea of a different, more "philosophical" nature than how to cut a shape into thirds or how to add a third and a half.

She chose to explain that, "there are fractions everywhere . . . you can put fractions on anything." To teach this idea, Debbie designed a representation of a "house, a sun, and two wooden wagons" (see Figure 1). She worked very hard on implementing this representation using some quite complex Logo program-

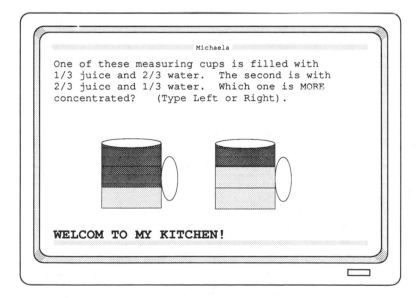

Figure 7a.   Michaela's Kitchen Scene

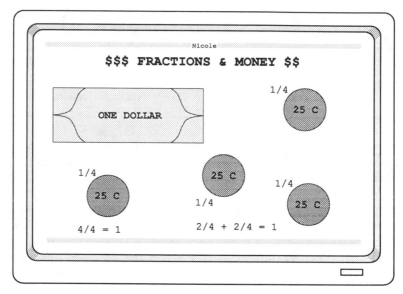

Figure 7b. Nicole's Money Scene

ming code (see Harel, 1988, pp. 118–140, for a detailed description of her lengthy and complex programming process and her work on this particular screen).

Debbie was not alone. A few weeks later, Tommy's House appeared, and then Paul's. The idea that it is important to teach others that "fractions are everywhere," and that one could "find fractions in regular human things" was spreading around the Design Studio.

Michaela and Sharifa, who used Debbie's software and received her full set of explanations about it, also chose to teach the same principle, but in another way. Sharifa selected to represent fractions by using a clock, teaching her users that "Half an hour is a half of ONE hour!" Her enthusiasm in announcing to the world that, "half of an hour is a fraction too!" (and her use of exclamation points) is evidence for the philosophical importance of the breakthrough as she experienced it. Michaela chose to teach this principle through using a representation of "two measuring cups filled with different quantities of orange juice, water, or flour—depends on the fraction . . ." Later she confessed, "I found so many fractions in my kitchen . . . I told my mom about it too . . ."

These observations are consistent with the ways in which ethnographers such as Scribner and Lave (1984) have demonstrated the separation of school knowledge of mathematics from practical, everyday knowledge. But we note something further that has a disquieting as well as an educationally hopeful aspect. The disconnection seems to be well entrenched within both the *practical* and *everyday* side and on the school side, as shown for example by the fact that

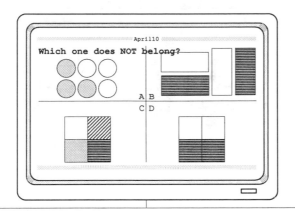

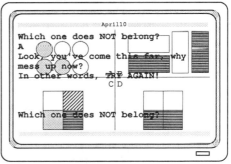

If the user typed C, the computer answered...

If the user typed A, B, or D, the computer answered...

And the program continued to the next screen...

The question was printed again and again, until the user found the right answer. Then, the program continued to the next screen...

Figure 7c.

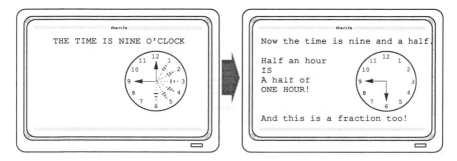

Figure 7d.

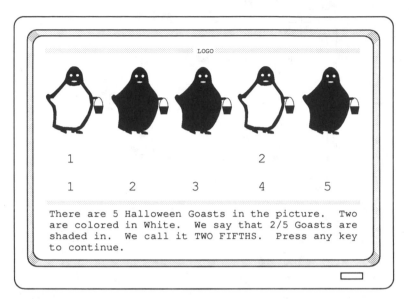

```
1                      2

1        2        3        4        5
```

There are 5 Halloween Goasts in the picture.   Two
are colored in White.   We say that 2/5 Goasts are
shaded in.   We call it TWO FIFTHS.   Press any key
to continue.

Figure 7e.

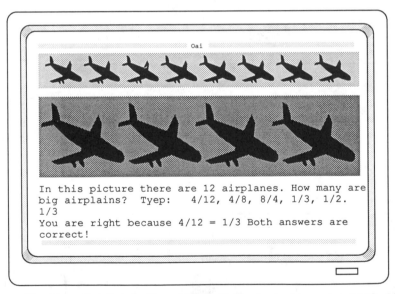

In this picture there are 12 airplanes. How many are
big airplains?   Tyep: 4/12, 4/8, 8/4, 1/3, 1/2.
1/3
You are right because 4/12 = 1/3 Both answers are
correct!

Figure 7f.   Pay attention to the options Oai gave to his users (4/12, 4/8, 8/4, 1/3, 1/2). He probably had an idea of what could be their problems with understanding this representation. He programmed it so both the answers 4/12 and 1/3 would receive the same feedback ("you are right . . ."). He also had an explanation for the users for *why* their answers were incorrect.

Shariffa had to discover a connection between "half an hour" and "half an apple." On the other hand, she did make the discovery, and did so without explicit or directive prompting by adults. Similarly, we see clear evidence that many students do not see "a quarter" as related to either the ¼ in their school worksheets or the "25% off" in a store's sale pricing.

Our conjecture is that "disconnection of knowledge" must not be seen primarily as a limitation of "schoolish" knowledge but rather as a universal characteristic of how knowledge develops, first as "knowledge in parts" (to use Andrea diSessa's phrase) and then by the unifying effect of control mechanisms such as those described by Lawler in *Computer Experience and Cognitive Development* (1985), by Minsky in *Society of Mind* (1986), and by Papert in *Mindstorms* (1980).

Appropriation of the Project. Our second rubric, appropriation of the project, refers to observations about a shift from a reluctant, impersonal, and mechanical mode of working to a growing personal engagement, assertive individuality, and creativity. Debbie's case once more illustrates this process. Her initial response to the project was globally very negative. She simply did not want to develop software about fractions. In the culture we tried to maintain, she was allowed to hold back but gradually began to succumb to generalized social pressures. So by the end of the second week, she was beginning to put fractions on her computer screen. But what she put up was still a direct reflection of the stereotyped model of fractions she had derived from math class. However, a new process was also beginning. We would say that she was "working through" her ideas (and no doubt her feelings too) about fractions. It took her approximately a month to achieve her breakthrough. Now she had an individual philosophical position which she pursued with something of a missionary zeal. She had given herself the task of leading the rest of the world to her discovery.

Time Frame and Rhythm of Work. This category appears to be an essential element of the process of appropriation. Switching in and out of projects in the fragmented time of the regular school, simply does not provide the conditions for personal appropriation and expression of personal intellectual style. Observations in the ISDP also show the importance of pace in the student's rhythm of daily work and in the radical differences in individual style of work, action, and thought. Analysis of videotapes set up to run continuously at fixed places show a pattern of work in striking contrast with the regular school notion of "efficient time on task." In the videos, we do see periods of intense concentration. But we also see periods in which students' attention is elsewhere: sometimes looking at a neighbour's work, sometimes engaged in play, chatting, and interactions that have no discernible connection with the project. Is this an "inefficient" use of time? While we did not measure this with any rigor, it appears to us that the rhythms of work adopted by the individual students have an integrity that contributes to getting the job done and especially to getting it done creatively. And in making this assertion we feel supported by such ethnographic studies as

Bruno Latour's (1987) description of the ways in which engineers and scientists at work mix "serious" talk about the problems in hand with intrusions from everyday life and personal concerns.

Metacognitive Awareness. In this rubric we describe in what ways ISDP encouraged children's metacognitive awareness (i.e., children's thinking about their own thinking), their cognitive control (i.e., planning, self-management, and thinking about these processes), and their meta-conceptual thinking (i.e., children's thinking about their own knowledge and understanding of concepts).

Through the project the students developed *problem-finding skills.* For four months, students involved themselves in discovering problems they wished to solve. No one specified the problems for them; rather, they were the ones in charge of deciding, for example, what was difficult about fractions, what screens to design to explain fractions, what Logo procedures to create and how, and so on. Students also developed an awareness of the skills and processes needed to solve the various problems they posed. The Designer's Notebooks, as another example, required that children design and think about their screens on paper. Their initial drawings and plans demonstrated that they were not very aware of either the programming or the fractions knowledge and skills needed to accomplish their designs; however, as the project progressed they rarely came up with a design they could not manage in Logo. They also had to be aware of their target users' knowledge of fractions so that they could make the representations they had created on the computer comprehensible to them. Not only did children become *aware of strategies* to solve a problem at hand, they also learned to *activate* them. The Logo posttests, for example, showed that the experimental children were able to optimize, modularize, and debug Logo procedures better and faster within given time constraints.

Over the course of the project, children developed the ability to discard inefficient designs, plans, and solutions and to search for better alternatives. In other words, they developed *cognitive flexibility.* During the project they learned to adjust their cognitive efforts to match the difficulty of the problem. They would often begin to implement their designs in Logo, but when they realized that too much effort was needed to accomplish a simple or "unimportant" design, they stopped working on it and moved on to a screen that was more crucial for their software or decided to redesign the screen that was giving them problems. As a result the ISDP students were not rigid in their solution processes in the Logo posttests, and did not stop working on difficult problems (unlike many of the control children who simply answered "I don't know"), but kept trying until they found the solution.

Another thing they learned was how to *control distractions and anxiety.* In this project (and in Project Headlight in general), children worked in an open area next to their classroom. Different children worked on different problems, with other children, teachers, and visitors often walking around. Children learned to keep their attention focused on the problems they were working on, and to resist being distracted by external stimulation. They also learned to control their anxiety when a problem was difficult. Posttests showed that Project Headlight children (both ISDP and C1) did better in avoiding anxiety, focusing efficiently on the problems given to them and not letting external interference distract them from their thinking and writing.

The community supported a *practice of continual evaluation*: Children evaluated their own and each other's performance every day when they ran their software and made entries in their Designer's Notebooks, and when they looked at other children's software—sometimes making suggestions or borrowing ideas. They were constantly relating their current performance and implementation phases to the general goals of the task and making appropriate changes if the result was too slow or unclear.

The students learned to *monitor their solution processes*. Since they were in charge of their own learning and production, they knew that when they had a problem or difficulty they could look first to themselves for a solution. They developed self-reliance and faith in their thinking.

Finally, the students *became articulate* not only about general planning and specific design tasks, but about the subject domain as well. They talked, thought about, and actually related to fractions, both during their involvement in the project and in the interviews and tests that took place afterwards. From their point of view, it was having to teach and explain fractions to someone else that caused them to embrace it so thoroughly because, as they said, "how can you teach it if you don't know it yourself?" Much like professional educational-software producers, who gain deeper understanding of the topics involved in their software by thinking of ways to build explanations and graphical representations for their future software users—the experimental children, through teaching and explaining, also gained an awareness of what fractions were or of what they knew and did not know about fractions. To give some examples of students' metacognitive expressions, here are four related quotes from the post-interviews.

Andy: "It's supposed to be for littler kids, right? But to program it so they can understand it, you have to be sure that you know what you are talking about. 'Cause the teacher has to know more . . . You don't know how the other kid will react to it and all of that . . . It was really hard to get it so they will like it . . . Always to think about and imagine that you are small, right, and how would *you* like it?!"

Naomi: "It is hard to teach. You have to have a pretty good understanding of something, so you'll be able to explain it well to others . . . and a lot of times it's really hard to understand what's happening with these fractions . . ."

Debbie: "You have to show them fractions and explain, little by little. To program the scenes, so they will learn how to do fractions, and what they did wrong . . . then, someone can listen to you, to the computer, I mean, and understand."

Paul: "It's hard to tell someone else that doesn't know about fractions how to do these things. So I program this software for them, to help them understand it . . . But I have to think a *lot* about what I really know and how to show it on the computer, and how to explain it. And at the end, how to test them about it."

DISCUSSION: *WHY* DID THEY LEARN?

The simplest description of the ISD experiment reads like a "treatment" type of experiment: These subjects did something particular (made instructional software) for so many hours (close to 70 hours of work). In fact, the situation is vastly more complex than anything that could be sensibly described as "changing one variable while keeping everything else constant" because there were too many particulars involved. To make their pieces of software, the students used particular computers (IBM PCjrs) and a particular programming language (LogoWriter). The project included focus sessions where the specific content of fractions was discussed in a particular way—informally and compared with school classes, briefly. The project took place in a particular part of the school with a particular "computer culture." And during the ISDP the culture developed further in a particular way, with particular customs of interaction, attention, mutual help, secrecy, humor, and so on. The students and their teacher were aware of having a unique relationship with the research staff. They reacted in particular ways to the presence of video cameras, question-askers, and note-takers.

One can raise innumerable conjectures about the "real" source of their learning about fractions, for example. Did the simple fact of spending some 70 hours programming representations in Logo contribute to the results? Was the "moral climate" in the project largely responsible? Or the fact that the teacher felt she was part of something important or simply different? Some such conjectures, or aspects of such conjectures, we can, and do, try to check by studying control groups. But there are far too many of them to treat in a rigorous way.

What can be said with some certainty is that we created a *total learning environment* in which some impressive learning took place. Teasing out the contributions of particular aspects of the environment is not a reasonable goal for any single well-defined experiment. Understanding will come through a process of gradual accumulation of many projects and of a great deal of theory building (e.g., Kafai & Harel, 1990; Jackson, 1990; Resnick, 1989). What we can do here is to share our own intuitions and, as part of the larger scientific enterprise, to formulate and discuss some conjectures concerning these intuitions.

In the following sections we speculate that improvement in performance might be affected by factors related to the *affective side* of cognition and learning; to the children's process of *personal appropriation* of knowledge; to the children's use of *LogoWriter*; to the children's constructive involvement with the deep structure of fractions knowledge (namely, *construction of multiple representations*) to the "*integrated-learning*" principle; to the "*learning by teaching*" principle; to the *power of design* as a learning activity.

However, the main point we would like to make here is that each one of these conjectures, when considered alone, would only give very partial information about why ISDP took the form and yielded the results that it did. Only by considering them together, and by speculating about their interrelations, can we take a step towards understanding the holistic character of Constructionism in general and of ISDP in particular.

The Affects of Affect

From certain Instructionist points of view (e.g., Papert, 1990) one could see a paradox in the results obtained here. Here are a few examples from the ISDP students' test scores: Debbie scored 51% correct on the fractions pretest and 84% on the post- (33% difference); Casey scored 55% on pre- and 83% on post- (28% difference); Rachel, 55% on pre- and 87% on post- (32% difference); or Oai, 55% on pre- and 97% on post- (42% difference). Debbie's, Oai's, Casey's and other children's ability to work with fractions, improved considerably from working on a project that was entirely self-directed, gave them no "feedback" in the form of marking responses right or wrong, gave them very little guidance or information about fractions. How could worrying about whether "fractions are everywhere," to take Debbie's concern as an example, lead to greater ability to do school problems in manipulating fractions?

The "obvious" explanation, which nevertheless surely has more than a little truth, is that the students developed a better attitude towards fractions, perhaps even came to *like* fractions. We recall that Debbie was initially reluctant to have anything to do with such stuff but ended up with enthusiastic missionary zeal. One does not need any complex theory of affectivity to conjecture that she might therefore be more likely to engage her mind with fractions both in the regular math class, so that she would learn more of what she wanted to teach, and in test situations, so that she would score more.

Pursuing the idea that Debbie changed her "relationship with fractions" leads into an area where the line between the affective and the cognitive becomes hard to maintain (e.g., Turkle, 1984; Turkle & Papert, 1990). We see something happening that is analogous to the development of a greater intimacy in relationships with people. Debbie becomes willing to take more risks, to allow herself to be more vulnerable, in her dealings with fractions. As long as fractions-knowledge was teacher's knowledge regurgitated, she was emotionally safe; the risk of poor grades is less threatening than the risk of exposing one's own ideas.

Our view of people like Debbie is strongly colored by the sense that when they allow themselves to tap into personal knowledge, they allow knowledge about fractions to become connected with the personal sides of themselves. We conjecture that improvement in performance is related to the extent to which the students respond to a problem about fractions by "digging around" in their own stocks of knowledge as opposed to trying to follow set procedures. We note that this point could be formulated in Scribner's (1984) language by saying that their thinking about fractions shifts from scholastic intelligence, characterized by rigid, inflexible, externally imposed methods, to practical intelligence characterized by the use of multiple, flexible, and personal methods.

The Importance of Situatedness

The idea, though not the word, is an important theme in the development of Logo-based Constructionism (Ackermann, this volume, Chapter 14; Papert 1980, 1984a–b, 1987). In this spirit we attribute the fluency with which our students work with fractions to the fact that this knowledge is situated in computational microworlds, much as Jean Lave's weight watchers benefit from the supportive consequences of the fact that fractions are situated in the microworld of the kitchen. A similar example is how Michaela was able to grasp fractions' significance in the context of using cooking tools for representing fractions. An even more striking example is provided by Sherifa, who got a grasp on the fractional nature of time through support from an overlap between the way the clock face represents fractions as angles, and the way in which the Logo turtle (which by then was familiar to her) does something very similar.

In that sense, our observations are consistent with those of Lucy Suchman, Jean Lave, and John Seeley Brown about "situated knowledge." Like these researchers, we are strongly committed to the idea that no piece of knowledge stands and grows by itself. Its meaning and its efficacy depend on its being situated in a relation to supporting structures. However, we attach more weight than we think those writers do to the Society of Mind metaphor (e.g., Lawler, 1985; Minsky, 1986; Papert, 1980) which would allow the situating of knowledge in internalized, mental environments to act in much the same way as situated in external, physical environments. Looking at the performance of Sherifa from this point of view we would say that her work with the computer enabled her to bring together *in her thinking* mutually supportive internal microworlds, in this particular case, microworlds of clock-time and of simple fractions.

The Contribution of Logo

There is a body of literature that addresses the question whether "programming" in general or "Logo" in particular can induce cognitive effects, and if so to what extent. In this sense, Logo would be seen as a causal factor in the improvement of fractions-knowledge or cognitive skills seen in our study.

But Papert (1987) has used the term "Technocentrism" to warn against simplistic forms of this question. In different contexts the import of the phrase "learning Logo" can differ so greatly that the question borders on meaninglessness. Nevertheless, in the particular context of the ISD project, where Logo was not isolated from a total context, and where students programmed intensively and extensively, one can meaningfully *begin* to ask how various features of Logo contributed to the success of the children's work.

At least one important contribution of Logo in this study was *indirect*— having less to do with acquiring cognitive skills than with mastering a subject domain—learning how to program and using Logo enabled these students to become more involved in thinking about fractions knowledge.

But we do think that Logo, because of its structure (or ISDP, because of the unique way it used the structure of Logo), had direct affects. Sharifa's ability to see the analogy between the clock and the turtle is one example of these affects. Our conjecture here, stated in its most general form, is that the structure of Logo brings students into direct and concrete contact with issues of *representation*—in the case of ISDP, representation of the specific object of study, fractions; and more generally, with the representation of objects, projects, structures, and processes in terms of subprocedures, LogoWriter pages, and other computational structures.

It is relevant to note that much of what the ISDP students did, could in principle be done by other methods, such as using pencil and paper to draw representations, or using physical manipulatives of various kinds (for representation construction). This might seem to make the contribution of Logo quite incidental. But in practice, we find it implausible that traditional media could equal the ease with which Logo allows students to save and connect concepts and their different representations, and especially how it allows them to develop and modify such representations over long periods of time. Even more important, working in Logo on one's own machine, in a culture where that's what everybody else is doing, reinforces the learner's contact with his or her personal knowledge that is expressed in a real product—a piece of software—that can be used and re-used by oneself or others, changed, modified, and grow with the knowledge of the learner and of the culture. Logo facilitated this ongoing personal engagement and gradual change of knowledge; and at the same time, it also facilitates the sharing of the knowledge with other members of the design studio, and it allowed learners to continue and build upon their and others' ideas and comments very easily. Logo facilitated communications about the processes and acts of cognition and learning.

Of course we do not maintain that only Logo could do this. Surely, many new media will develop that can do it better. But looking carefully at the features of Logo that contribute here, and the ways it was used in the ISDP context, will be of use in guiding such developments (e.g., Harel & Papert, 1990). Pursuing such issues requires much further research. However the research that will elucidate them is not well guided by the kind of questions that have often been posed in the literature, such as "Does Logo have such and such a cognitive effect?" but rather "Can Logo be used to amplify and support such and such a direction of children's intellectual development, or such and such a change in a learning culture?"

The Deep Structure of Rational-Number Knowledge

Whereas most school work touches only on the surface structure of rational-number knowledge, we believe ISDP puts students in touch with the deep structure.

Elementary-school children's processes as well as difficulties in learning fractions and understanding their representations have been well documented. Unlike whole numbers, the meaning of which students largely come to grasp informally and intuitively out of school, learning the rational-number system is confined almost exclusively to school. Because rational-number concepts and algorithms are so difficult for so many pupils, they figure prominently in school curricula from the second grade on, mainly in the form of algorithmic tasks and the working out of specific well-defined mathematical problems. Even so, several national assessments have found that children's performance on fraction-ordering and computation was low and accompanied by little understanding (see the discussion of this topic in Harel, 1988, 1989b, d, 1990a). This is particularly unfortunate because fractions are ideal tools for learning about number systems and representational systems in mathematics.

We see the understanding of the rational-number representational system as a privileged piece of knowledge among the other pieces of rational-number knowledge. Representations form part of the deep structure of rational-number knowledge, whereas algorithms put students in touch with only the surface structure (e.g., Janvier, 1987; Lesh & Landau, 1983).

Logo can be a direct route to this encounter with the deep structure, enabling students to explore the concept of fractions through various on-screen representations of their own devising. In ISDP, this process was catalyzed by setting students the task of creating good pedagogical aids for other students, in the course of which they thought to create fractions representations in such forms as money, food, or clocks, as well as geometric shapes, and to accompany them with symbolic or verbal explanations, they thought would be helpful to their target audience.

By becoming designers of instructional software, the students gained distance and perspective in two senses. In the first place, they were dealing not with the representations themselves, but with a Logo representation of the representations. Moving between representations was subordinated to programming good examples of representations. Secondly, the students programmed, not for themselves, but for others. They had to step outside and think about other children's reactions. The depth and creativity of such an experience contrasts with the rote, superficial quality of what typically occurs when a student is put through the paces of an externally conceived sequence of learning.

In summary, ISDP recasts fractions learning in essentially three ways:

1. It emphasized more involvement with the deep structure (representations) over the surface structure (algorithms) of rational-number knowledge;

2. It made fractions learning simultaneously incidental and instrumental to a larger intellectual and social goal, that is, having students think about and explain what they think and learn, in an interactive lesson for younger children; and
3. It encouraged both personal expression and social communication of rational-number knowledge and ideas.

The "Integrated Learning" Principle: Learning More Can Be Easier Than Learning Less

It must be admitted that there are certain problems with integrating instructional software design activity into a school's curriculum. Software design is a time-consuming and complex enterprise for a teacher to handle, and it is not yet clear how it can fit into the average class schedule. Also, at the present time, it is not very clear which school subjects would lend themselves best to this process of learning (e.g., Jackson, 1990; Kafai & Harel, 1990).

But knowledge about computation (such as programming) and the sciences of information (involving control over one's own processing, metacognition, and information construction) has a special character in this respect because it has a reflexive synergistic quality—it facilitates other knowledge. In ISDP, the learning of fractions and the learning of the complex skills (programming, design, etc.) encompassed in the phrase "software design" did not compete for time; rather we maintain that each took place more effectively than would have been the case had they been taught separately.

The reflexive quality of information science offers a solution to the apparent impossibility of adding another component to an already full school day. If some knowledge facilitates other knowledge, then, in a beautifully paradoxical way, more can mean less!

The idea that learning more science and math necessarily means learning less of something else shows a wrong conception. If these domains are properly integrated into individuals' knowledge and into learning cultures, they will be supportive, not competitive with other learning. We believe in the possibility of integrating science, mathematical concepts, art, writing, and other subjects and making them mutually supportive. We also believe that in ISDP this principle of integration—which meant that young students learned fractions, Logo programming, instructional designing, planning, story-boarding, reflection, self-management, and so on, all at the same time and in a synergistic fashion—greatly contributed to the results.

Special Merits to Learning By Teaching and Explaining

As educators or teachers, producers, computer programmers, software developers, or professional people in general, we are rarely encouraged to draw on our own learning experiences in order to better understand the reasons, purposes, and processes of learning and teaching our subject matter. Too often we tend to forget what was really difficult for us to understand, or why one learning experience was more or less valuable for us than others in the course of our own intellectual and professional development.

It has been observed by students and educators in our group as well as by many "experts" that the best way to learn a subject is to teach it. Let us consider for a moment, experiences that are common to professional people in all fields in the course of their everyday work or professional training. Teachers, for example, often remark that they "finally understood something today for the first time" when a student asked for an explanation of something he did not understand. Some of our friends (professional computer programmers) at MIT have told us that they "really" learned how to program when they had to teach it to someone else—or when they were involved in a real, complex, long, and meaningful programming job. Many university professors choose to teach a course on the theory of topic of their research while they are actually working on it; so that the process of teaching and discussing their work with students, will enable them to clarify and refine their own ideas and theories. And it certainly seems to be the case in the educational software field, that the people who are having the most fun, and are learning the most, are the software designers and programmers. With most educational software today, especially the drill-and-practice kind, the users rarely gain *deep* understanding of the concepts taught, unless the software is supplemented by instruction and explanations from a good teacher. But the designer, who spent a long and intensive period of time designing, learning, and thinking of ways to build explanations and graphical representations for given concepts (even for the simplest form of educational software), has probably mastered these concepts and gained a much deeper understanding of them than they were able to convey in the software product itself.

The intellectual benefit of generating one's own explanations have been stressed by a number of theorists. Piaget, for example, has argued that higher-level reasoning occurs in a children's group in the form of arguments. These arguments, according to Piaget, help children construct and internalize ideas in the form of thought. Such observations prompted Piaget to conclude that the very act of communication produces the need for checking and confirming one's own thoughts (e.g., Piaget, 1953). Furthermore, in the Child's Conception of Space (1967), Piaget emphasizes how difficult it is for young children to decenter—that is, to move freely from their own point of view to that of another, in either literal or metaphorical senses. Increasing communication develops the child's ability to decenter, and to come closer to an objective view of the whole. The process of decentering, says Piaget, is fundamental to knowledge in all its forms.

Among contemporary researchers, Brown, for example, has done many studies to elucidate the ways in which explanatory processes, as part of reciprocal teaching activities, motivate learners and encourage the search for deeper levels of understanding and subject mastery. Brown characterizes these explanatory-based interactive learning environments as ones that push the learners to explain and represent knowledge in multiple ways and therefore, in the process, to comprehend it more fully themselves. The interactions could be supported by computers, teachers, or other learners (e.g., Brown, 1988).

Hatano and Inagaki (1987) also argue that comprehension and interest is enhanced where students have to explain their views and clarify their positions to others. In the process of trying to convince or teach other students, they explain, "one has to verbalize or make explicit that which is known only implicitly. One must examine one's own comprehension in detail and thus become aware of any inadequacies, thus far unnoticed, in the coordination among those pieces of knowledge." Their studies demonstrate how persuasion or teaching requires the orderly presentation of ideas, and better intra-individual organization of what one knows. It also invites students to "commit" themselves to some ideas, thereby placing the issue in question in their personal domains of interest (Hatano & Inagaki, 1987, p. 40).

Fourth-grade children seldom have such opportunities. Peer teaching or reciprocal teaching can be used to take a small step in that direction. We feel that ISDP took a much larger step.

Designing For Learning

In *Knowledge as Design*, Perkins (1986) discusses in detail the instructional philosophy that supports the creation of a design environment for learning, arguing that the act of designing promotes the active and creative use of knowledge by the learner—the designer. In the designing process, Perkins says, the problem's meaning is not given by the problem itself; rather, the designer imposes his own meanings and defines his own goals before and during the process. The goals and the subgoals may change over that period of time, and keeping track of these changes is a central interest when the design task is not for the purpose of "getting it right," but is instead aimed at producing something useful through the use of creative and critical thinking.

Schön's work (1987) is also relevant to this theme. He is interested in how different designers (e.g., architects) impose their own meaning on a given open-ended problem, and how they overcome constraints (created by themselves, or given as part of the problem they solve) and take advantage of unexpected outcomes. This interactive process requires high levels of reflection and develops the ability to "negotiate" with situations in "as needed," and creative ways.

What is the difference between programming as such and designing a piece of instructional software? How does it relate to the "knowledge as design" framework?

A "computer program" is an independent entity consisting of a logically arranged set of programming statements, commands or instructions, that defines the operations to be performed by a computer so that it will achieve specific and desired results. We use the term "instructional software design" to refer to the building of a computer program that has a specific instructional purpose and format—much more is involved than mere programming. In this context, the lessons constructed by children were composed of many computer procedures or routines (i.e., isolated units) that were connected to each other for the purpose of teaching or explaining fractions to younger children. A unit of instructional software is a collection of programs that evolve through consideration of the interface between product and user. The instructional software must facilitate the learning of something by someone.

Designing and creating instructional software on the computer requires more than merely programming it, more than merely presenting content in static pictures or written words, more than managing technical matters. When composing lessons on the computer, the designer combines knowledge of the computer, knowledge of programming, knowledge of computer programs and routines, knowledge of the content, knowledge of communication, human interface, and instructional design. The communication between the software producers and their medium is *dynamic*. It requires constant goal-defining and redefining, planning and replanning, representing, building and rebuilding, blending, reorganizing, evaluating, modifying, and reflecting in similar senses to that described by Perkins and Schon in their work.

In terms of the programming end of it, software designers must constantly move back and forth between the whole lesson and each of its parts, between the overall piece and its subsections and individual screens (e.g., Adelson & Soloway, 1984; Atwood, Jefferies, & Polson, 1980; Jeffries, Turner, Polson, & Atwood, 1981). Because of the computer's branching capabilities, the designer has to consider the multiple routes a user might take, with the result that the nonlinear relationship between the lesson's parts can grow very complex. Moreover, the producer needs to design interactions between learner and computer: designing questions, anticipating users' responses, and providing explanations and feedback—which require sophisticated programming techniques. Finally, the child-producer who wants to design a lesson on the computer must learn about the content, become a tutor, a lesson designer, a pedagogical decision-maker, an evaluator, a graphic artist, and so on. The environment we created in ISDP encouraged and facilitated these various processes, and therefore we believe, contributed to the results.

SUMMARY AND CONCLUSIONS

This chapter had a double intention: to describe ISDP, and to situate this particular project in a general theoretical framework called Constructionism. ISDP offered a realistic and comprehensive model for our constructionist vision of education in general, and for the use of computers in education in particular. It also offered a model for the kinds of research that we find insightful and beneficial to our understanding of learning and development, thinking, teaching, education, and the use of computers to facilitate these processes.

We described how the participant ISDP class, comprised of 17 fourth-grade students, integratively learned mathematics, design, and programming, and so on, in the course of using LogoWriter to develop pieces of instructional software for teaching third graders. We illustrated various aspects of our evaluation— quantitative and comparative results, as well as qualitative ones. Our evaluation showed that the ISDP students achieved greater mastery of both Logo and fractions as well as improved metacognitive skills than did either control class. The ISDP approach of using Logo programming as a tool for reformulating fractions knowledge was compared with other approaches to using Logo, in particular the traditional learning of programming per se in isolation from a content domain, and was also compared with other approaches of learning fractions. The ISDP experiment showed that simultaneously learning programming and fractions was more effective than learning them in isolation from each other.

The ISD Project recast fractions learning in essentially three ways:

1. It emphasized more involvement with the deep structure (*representations*) over the surface structure of rational-number knowledge (*algorithms*);
2. It made fractions learning instrumental to a larger intellectual and social goal, that is, having students think about and explain what they think and learn, in an interactive lesson designed for younger children; and
3. It encouraged both personal expression and social communication of rational-number knowledge and ideas.

We emphasized the fact that ISDP had little to do with the idea that learning Logo is in itself either easy or beneficial. We asserted that in different contexts the import of the phrase "learning Logo" can differ so greatly, that the question borders on meaninglessness. Nevertheless, in the particular context of the ISD Project, where Logo was integrated into a total context, and where students programmed intensively and extensively, one can meaningfully *begin* to investigate the question of how various features of Logo contributed to the success of the children's work.

We found that Logo facilitated the ongoing *personal engagement* and gradual evolution of different kinds of knowledge; and at the same time, it also facilitated the *sharing* of that knowledge with other members of the community, which in turn encouraged the learners to continue and build upon their own and other people's ideas. In short, Logo facilitated communications about the processes and acts of cognition and learning. We do not maintain that only Logo could do this. But looking carefully at what specific features of Logo enhanced individual cognition and social learning can help guide us in future technological developments. And indeed, ISDP provided us with many insights—cognitive/developmental as well as technological—into what kinds of learning tools we want to develop for constructionist learning.

We mentioned that the ISDP should not be viewed as a "very controlled treatment" type of experiment. The pedagogical situation was quite complex, and one could formulate innumerable conjectures about the "real" source of the experimental children's learning. We concluded that ISDP allowed us to create a total learning environment in which some impressive integrated learning took place.

It was beyond the scope of this study to single out the contribution of the individual aspects of that environment. In our view, a more complete understanding of this learning process can come through an integrative and accumulative process of experimentation and theory-building (and there are several projects of this kind within our group at the Media Laboratory, e.g., Harel, 1990b). This chapter is also intended as a contribution to that process, in which we shared our conjectures and the bases on which we formulated them. We hypothesized, for example, that improvements in performance among ISDP students could have been affected by factors related to: the affective side of cognition and learning; the children's process of personal appropriation of knowledge; the children's use of LogoWriter; the children's constructivist involvement with the deep structure of fractions knowledge; the integrated-learning principle; the learning-by-teaching principle; and the power of design as a learning activity.

However, the main point we wanted to make here was that each one of those conjectures, when considered alone, would give only very partial information about the meaning of the results. By considering them together, and by speculating about their interrelations, we are endeavoring to make use of the very kind of holistic approach—to knowledge and cognition, and to the development of learning technologies—that we believe informs and characterizes Constructionism in general, and ISDP in particular.

ACKNOWLEDGMENTS

The research reported here was conducted at Project Headlight's Model School of the Future during 1987–88 as part of Idit Harel's Ph.D Thesis at the MIT's Media Laboratory; and was supported by the IBM Corporation (Grant # OSP95952), the National Science Foundation (Grant # 851031-0195), the McArthur Foundation (Grant # 874304), the LEGO Systems A/S, and the Apple Computer Inc. The preparation of this chapter was supported by the National Science Foundation (Grant # MDR 8751190) and Nintendo Inc. Japan. The ideas expressed here do not necessarily reflect the positions of the supporting agencies.

We are deeply grateful to Linda Moriarty, who made an essential contribution to the Project and to the research ideas reported here. Over the years, many other teachers in Project Headlight at the Hennigan School contributed indirectly, but very importantly, to the work. We thank all the students and teachers of Headlight—without whom this project would not have been possible.

We thank Aaron Falbel and Beth Rashbaum for their editorial assistance, and other members of our Epistemology and Learning Group for their contribution in their inspiring discussions of the ideas presented in this chapter. We thank Yasmin Kafai for her help in the preparation of the statistical tables.

REFERENCES

Adelson, B., & Soloway, E. (1984a). *A cognitive model of software design* (Cognition and Programming Project, Res. Rep. No. 342). New Haven, CT: Yale University.

Adelson, B. & Soloway, E. (1984b). *The role of domain experience in software design* (Cognition and Programming Project, Res. Rep. No. 25). New Haven, CT: Yale University.

Atwood, M.E., Jefferies, R., & Polson, P.G. (1980, March). *Studies in plan construction I and II* (Tech. Rep. No SAI-80-028-DEN). Englewood, CO: Science Applications Inc.

Behr, M.J., Lesh, R., Post, T.R., & Silver, E.A. (1983). Rational number concepts. In R. Lesh & M. Landau (Eds.), *Acquisition of mathematics concepts and processes*. New York: Academic Press.

Behr, M.J., Wachsmuth, I., Post, T.R., & Lesh, R. (1984). Order and equivalence: A clinical teaching experiment. *Journal of Research in Mathematics Education, 15* (5), 323–341.

Brown, A.L., Bransford, J.D., Ferrara, R.A., & Campione, J.C. (1983). Learning, remembering, and understanding. *Handbook of child psychology: Cognitive development* (Vol. 3). New York: Wiley.

Brown, A.L. (1984). Reciprocal teaching: Comprehension-fostering and comprehension-monitoring activities. *Cognition and Instruction, 1*(2), 117–175.

Brown, A.L. (1988). Motivation to learn and understand: On taking charge of one's own learning. *Cognition and Instruction, 5*(4), 311–322.

Brown, J.S., Collins, A., & Duguid, P. (1989). Situated cognition and the culture of learning. *Educational Researcher, 18*(1), 32–42.

Carver, S.M. (1987). *Transfer of LOGO debugging skill: Analysis, instruction, and assessment*. Unpublished doctoral dissertation, Carnegie-Mellon University, Pittsburgh, PA.

Chipman, S.F., Segal, J.W., & Glaser, R. (1985). *Thinking and learning skills* (Vol. 1 & 2), Hillsdale, NJ: Erlbaum.

Collins, A., & Brown, J.S. (1987, April). *The new apprenticeship*. Paper presented at the American Educational Research Association, Washington, DC.

Goldman Segall, R. (1989a, February). *Videodisc technology as a conceptual research tool for the study of human theory making*. Unpublished manuscript. Media Laboratory, MIT, Cambridge, MA.

Goldman Segall, R. (1989b, November). *Learning constellations: A multimedia ethnographic description of children's theories in a logo culture.* Unpublished PhD Thesis Proposal, Media Laboratory, MIT, Cambridge, MA.

Harel, I. (1986, July). *Children as software designers: An exploratory study in project headlight.* Paper presented at the LOGO '86 International Conference, MIT, Cambridge, MA.

Harel, I. (1988, June). *Software design for learning: Children's construction of meaning for fractions and logo programming.* Unpublished doctoral dissertation. Media Laboratory, MIT, Cambridge, MA.

Harel, I. (1989a, April). Tools for young software designers. *Proceedings of the Third Workshop of Empirical Studies of Programmers (ESP Society).* Austin, TX.

Harel, I. (1989b, June). Software design for learning. In W.C. Ryan (Ed.), *Proceedings book of the National Educational Computer Conference (NECC).* Boston, MA: The International Council of Computers in Education.

Harel, I. (1989c, September). Software designing in a learning environment for young learners: Cognitive processes and cognitive tools. *Proceedings of the FRIEND21 international symposium on next generation human interface technologies.* Tokyo, Japan.

Harel, I. (1989d, September). Software design for learning mathematics. In C. Maher, G. Goldin, & R. Davis (Eds.), *Proceedings book of the eleventh annual meeting of psychology of mathematics education.* New Brunswick, NJ: Rutgers University, Center for Mathematics, Science, and Computer Education.

Harel, I. (1990a). Children as software designers: A constructionist approach to learning mathematics. *Journal of Mathematical Behavior,* 9(1), 3–00.

Harel, I. (Ed.). (1990b). *Constructionist learning: A 5th anniversary collection of papers.* Cambridge, MA: MIT Media Laboratory.

Harel, I., & Papert, S. (1990). *Instructionalist products vs. constructionist tools: The role of technology-based multimedia in children's learning.* Cambridge, MA: MIT Media Laboratory.

Hatano & Inagaki (1987). A theory of motivation for comprehension and its applications to mathematics instruction. In T.A. Romberg & D.M. Steward (Eds.), *The monitoring of school mathematics: Background papers. (Vol 2.): Implications from psychology, outcomes from instruction.* Madison, WI: Center for Educational Research.

Jackson, I. (1990). Children's software design as a collaborative process: An experiment with fifth graders at project headlight. In I. Harel (Ed.). *Constructionist learning: A 5th anniversary collection of papers.* Cambridge, MA: MIT Media Laboratory.

Janvier, C. (Ed.). (1987). *Problems in representation in the teaching and learning of mathematics.* Hillsdale, NJ: Erlbaum.

Jefferies, R., Turner, A.A., Polson, P.G., & Atwood, M.E. (1981). The processes involved in designing software. In J.R. Anderson (Ed.), *Cognitive skills and their acquisition.* Hillsdale, NJ: Erlbaum.

Kafai, Y., & Harel, I. (1990). The instructional software design project: Phase II. In I. Harel (Ed.), *Constructionist learning: A 5th anniversary collection of papers.* Cambridge, MA: MIT Media Laboratory.

Lammer, S. (1987). *Programmers at work.* Redmond, WA: Microsoft Corp Press.

Latour, B. (1987). *Science in action: How to follow scientists and engineers through society.* Cambridge, MA: Harvard University Press.

Lawler, R. W. (1985). *Computer experience and cognitive development: A child learning in a computer culture.* West Sussex, England: Ellis Horwood Limited.

Lesh, R., & Landau, M. (1983). *Acquisition of mathematics concepts and processes.* New York: Academic.

Minsky, M. (1986). *Society of mind.* New York: Simon and Schuster.

Motherwell, L. (1988). *Gender and style differences in a logo-based environment.* Unpublished doctoral dissertation, Media Laboratory, MIT, Cambridge, MA.

Papert, S. (1971a). *Teaching children thinking* (AI Memo No. 247, and Logo Memo No. 2). Cambridge, MA: MIT.

Papert, S. (1971b). *Teaching children to be mathematicians vs. teaching about mathematics* (AI Memo No. 249 and Logo Memo No. 4). Cambridge, MA: MIT.

Papert, S., Watt, D., diSessa, A., & Weir, S. (1979). *Final report of the brookline logo projects. Part I and II* (Logo Memo No. 53). Cambridge, MA: MIT.

Papert, S. (1980). *Mindstorms: Children, computers, and powerful ideas.* New York: Basic Books.

Papert, S. (1984a). *Microworlds transforming education.* Paper presented at the ITT Key Issues Conference, Annenberg School of Communications, University of Southern California, Los Angeles.

Papert, S. (1984b). *New theories for new learnings.* Paper presented at the National Association for School Psychologists' Conference.

Papert, S. (1987). Computer criticism vs. technocentric thinking. *Educational Researcher, 16*(1), 22–30.

Papert, S. (1990). An introduction to the 5th anniversary collection. In I. Harel (Ed.), *Constructionist learning: A 5th anniversary collection of papers.* Cambridge, MA: MIT Media Laboratory.

Pea, R.D., & Sheingold, K. (Eds.). (1987). *Mirrors of mind: Patterns of experience in educational computing.* Norwood, NJ: Ablex.

Perkins, D.N. (1986). *Knowledge as design.* Hillsdale, NJ: Erlbaum.

Piaget, J. (1955). *The language and thought of the child.* New York: New American Library.

Piaget, J., & Inhelder, B. (1967). *The child's conception of space.* New York: W.W. Norton.

Resnick, M., Ocko, S., & Papert, S. (1988). Lego, LOGO, and design. *Children's Environments Quarterly, 5*(4).

Resnick, M. (1989, April). *Lego Logo: Learning through and about design.* Paper presented at the American Educational Research Association, San Francisco, CA. (Appeared in Harel, I. (1990). (Ed.). *Constructionist learning: A 5th anniversary collection of papers.* Cambridge, MA: MIT Media Laboratory.)

Sachter, J.E. (1989). *Kids in space: Exploration into children's cognitive styles and understanding of space in 3-D computer graphics.* Unpublished PhD Thesis Proposal. Media Laboratory, MIT, Cambridge, MA. A short version of this proposal appeared in Harel, I. (1990). (Ed.). *Constructionalist learning: A 5th anniversary collection of papers.* Cambridge, MA: MIT Media Laboratory.)

Schön, D.A. (1987). *Educating the reflective practitioner.* San Francisco: Jossey-Bass.

Scribner, S. (1984). Practical intelligence. In B. Rogoff & J. Lave (Eds.), *Everyday cognition: Its development in social context*. Cambridge, MA: Harvard University Press.

Soloway, E. (1984). *Why kids should learn to program?* (Cognition and Programming Knowledge Res. Rep. No. 29). New Haven, CT: Yale University.

Suchman, L. (1987). *Plans and situated actions: The problem of human machine communication*. Cambridge, MA: Cambridge University Press.

Turkle, S. (1989). *The second self: Computer power and the human spirit*. New York: Simon & Schuster.

Turkle, S., & Papert, S. (1990, in press). *Epistemological pluralism: styles and voices within the computer culture. Signs Journal*. Chicago, IL: The University of Chicago Press. (Also appeared in Harel, I. (1990). (Ed.). *Constructionist learning: A 5th anniversary collection of papers*. Cambridge, MA: MIT Media Laboratory and this volume Chapter 9.)

1/2 of Project Headlight area at the Hennigan School in Boston. The Hennigan School's "open architecture" allows us to bring the technology closer (physically and conceptually) to students and teachers; to integrate computer activities with ongoing classroom activities; to facilitate movement and action around the computers; and to reinforce communication across grade levels and among teachers.

5

Learning Through Design and Teaching:
Exploring Social and Collaborative Aspects of Constructionism

Yasmin Kafai and Idit Harel

EXPLORING ISDP'S SOCIAL NATURE

Students in our instructional software design projects (ISDP; see Harel & Papert, this volume) learn about fractions by designing a piece of software that will teach fractions to younger students. They are involved in issues of representation, communication, instructional design, programming, and teaching of fractions. Later, when these same students become consultants to other younger software designers, they refine their knowledge of fractions, programming, design, and teaching. They consider their own reasoning once again, and, in this playful mode, they actively construct a broader and deeper understanding of fractions—while strengthening other concepts and skills.

Our aim is to explore various aspects of the design/teaching/consulting method of learning, while emphasizing the *social nature* of the ISDP environment. By exploring social and collaborative aspects in ISDP, we attempt to define in more detail the interactionist and affective characteristics of constructionist learning environments (e.g., Harel & Papert, this volume) and to relate our models to the ongoing research on collaborative learning and social construction of knowledge.

The thesis that cognitive change is as much a social as an individual process prompted the educational and psychological research communities to focus on the role of social contexts in learning and development (e.g., Newman, Griffith, & Cole, 1989). Researchers are now looking at individual and social worlds as intertwined, and while they continue to consider ways to capture an individual's constructivist development (e.g., in the spirit of Piaget), they simultaneously pay careful attention to social processes within which the individual participates (e.g., in the spirit of Vygotsky). The contribution of social interaction to the individual's learning has been conceptualized in several ways: as "cognitive-apprenticeship learning" (Collins, Brown, & Newman, 1990; Palincsar & Brown, 1984), or as "peer-collaboration learning" (e.g., Daiute & Dalton, 1989; Johnson, Johnson, & Jolubec, 1986; Slavin, 1983)—to name but a few. One general assumption of these approaches is that working and learning in close interactions with adults, peers, or people in general is sometimes a richer experience than learning by oneself. Another assumption is that during social interactions, participants communicate their ideas and make their thoughts explicit—to examine their own as well as someone else's views and problems and react accordingly. Finally, complex shared activity with another is often viewed as a context for building arguments substantially different from those one would build without group interaction. We agree with the above assumptions but intend to add a twist. The purpose of this chapter is to reveal our "twist," express some of its aspects explicitly, and relate it to the approaches mentioned above.

During the 1989–1990 school year, three different teachers and their classes participated in our ISDP reimplementation studies—our second look at ISDP (which also occured in Project Headlight at the Hennigan School, an inner-city elementary school in the Boston area). The *learning by teaching* aspect of the original ISDP provided the students with a new kind of audience—the younger students, rather than the audience they usually have—their teacher. This aspect contributed greatly to the original ISDP students' understanding and learning (e.g., Harel, 1988). We chose to expand it in the following way: fifth graders designed software for fourth graders, established relationships with them, and then became consultants for the fourth graders, as they designed software for third graders (see Figure 1).

In the following sections we will explore various aspects of ISDP's social nature. We will describe our conceptualization of collaboration in ISDP and, for demonstration purposes, focus on three case studies of young software designers as they navigate through a particularly sensitive phase—what we will call the

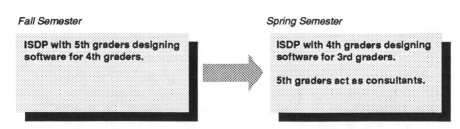

Figure 1. Research procedure in ISDP-II.

Incubation Phase. Our other chapter which follows (see Kafai & Harel, this volume) deals with the extension of the learning-by-teaching principle and explores how young software designers make sense of their "consulting activity." In the discussion, we summarize the findings from our case studies and define the particular social features of the ISDP constructionist learning culture and how they contribute to the individual's learning.

REDEFINING COLLABORATION WITHIN ISDP

The ISDP learning environment leads to better understanding of fractions and programming, through enhancing opportunities for social contacts and mutual exchange. Multiple and flexible interactions are a primary feature of ISDP. Students in ISDP interact with each other in requesting help and in giving advice, both as teachers to younger students and as software designers and content presenters.

In educational research, an interactional style of learning is usually described as "collaboration" or "cooperation." These words are being used to describe two or more students collaborating, cooperating, expressing themselves, and working together—towards *one* product. In other words, the collaborators have one common goal—finishing their project; and another common goal—working on it together and finding ways of incorporating each collaborator's ideas in a process of mutual work and negotiation towards one product. Many studies show the advantage of working collaboratively in this style (e.g., Slavin, 1983; Johnson et al., 1986; Daiute & Dalton, 1989); we refer to it here as the conventional conceptualization of collaboration.

The collaborative style of ISDP shares the spirit of this conventional conceptualization of collaboration but implements it in a different way and with some additional features. For example, ISDP includes a collaborative process among two or more students where each of the students is working towards his or her *own* project. In ISDP, all the students have a common "umbrella" goal—to use LogoWriter to design a piece of software that teaches about fractions—but each of them also expresses his or her own ideas and produces his or her own project. Everyone faces similar "problems" and finds occasions for sharing ideas, asking for help, or discussing technical problems. They may choose to discuss problems with a partner, or even to jointly design and implement certain aspects of their software.

In summary, we found ourselves conceptualizing collaboration in a different way within the framework of ISDP. The main features of the ISDP collaborative style are: (a) *Optional Collaboration:* students can work alone on their own piece of software, but they can also work with others on the same piece if they wish; and (b) *Flexible Partnerships:* students can decide with whom they want to work, when, for what purposes, and so on. In other words, in the ISDP framework, students can move between both collaborative styles according to their own needs and desires.

The spatial arrangement of the working areas at Headlight allows students to be flexible in their seating arrangements. This facilitates their movement, communication, and ongoing interactions. As a result, a particular kind of interactional process caught our attention. We would like to characterize it as *collaboration through the air*. This refers to a process described by two sociologists, Berger and Luckman (1966), in their book *The Social Construction of Reality*. They state that constructing reality involves, not only "face-to-face" interaction, but also interaction with the world of the "knowledge surrounding us." This last aspect is very similar to the learning situation in ISDP.

In our projects, the students are sitting at their computers, in two large circles. They are "surrounded by" other students' computer screens, ideas, knowledge, Logo code, and fractions designs. A number of different ideas are floating around in this "software design studio," waiting to be "picked up"—as Harel (1988) described in Debbie's Case in her dissertation on the original ISD Project, and as Gerald's Case (see below) illustrates in our analysis of ISDP-II.

These floating ideas are programmed (represented) in various ways on different computer screens. Eventually, most children honestly believe that they originated the ideas on their own, although in most cases the ideas probably originated with one person and then spread throughout the group. The daily interaction among students—the ability to walk around and see other students' projects, to try them out, and so on—facilitates this collaboration through the air.

Berger and Luckmann (1966) also stress the idea that there are "different timings" for the appearance of knowledge within specific individuals. Transferred to ISDP, this means that the concept of fractions equality (when realized in the context of fractions of areas) can be very important to one person at a certain time, but not important to others at that same time. Only if and when the other students are "ready" for it will they appropriate it. We believe that the basis for appropriation has to do not only with social aspects of learning, but also with a child's readiness. The following fieldnote by Kafai explains what we mean by "readiness" for knowledge appropriation.

> On Day 13, we introduced the QUIZ procedure to the students, which allows the student to ask a question on the screen, to read in the user's answer, and to give a reply corresponding to that answer. This procedure introduced many new and different programming concepts to the students, such as conditionals, variables, and branching. Many students adopted the procedure for their program immediately; they copied it and then tried it out.
>
> In the following days I observed that some students integrated this procedure in most of their screens, while other students deleted it completely—as did one student, Alicia.
>
> After some days we had a Focus Session in the classroom, where I asked the students if they had problems. Alicia told me she really wanted to know about

READLIST (which is a component of QUIZ) because she didn't understand it. But she also told me that she didn't want to know it right then. Rather, she would tell me when.

After 3 weeks, Alicia suddenly told me: "Now I am ready to learn about READLIST. Can you come and explain it to me?" I went to see her and discovered she had prepared everything in her program. She had put all the questions already in the Logo code, but did not include the part where you read in the answer and give the reply. After I explained this to her, and we worked together on integrating it into one of her procedures, she then proceeded to integrate it into the rest of program—on her own.

This simple example tells us that appropriating an idea is easy when you are ready for it. The same is true for understanding new ideas or concepts. Harel (1988) gave several examples of this readiness in Debbie's Case in relation to her learning new Logo techniques (e.g., Random, GetPage) and new ideas about fractions (e.g., "All these shapes show one half," or "Fractions are everywhere!").

To summarize, we see "collaboration through the air" as working in two ways: it provides individuals (or society) with many examples of what one person can do and how he or she can do it; and it allows space and time for individuals (or society) to pick up (or rediscover) such ideas when they are ready.

CASE STUDIES

As the project begins, the only assignment given to the students is to "design a piece of software to teach younger students about fractions." No further well-defined specifications are given about the task. It is up to the participants to make their own decisions as they slowly slip into the role of educational software designers. In this beginning phase of the project—which we call the *incubation phase*—the new designers are at once confronted with many hard questions: What should be the main theme of their project? What are fractions? How do you represent fractions? How do you teach fractions? Or on a more practical level: What should be programmed on the computer screen? Which colors should be used? What text might be included? Where should it be placed on the screen? and so forth. At first, the selection of themes and representations, as well as the design problems involved in handling this project, seem to be endless and quite overwhelming. Our experience shows that one of the challenges for the young software designers is to decide where and how to begin.[1]

---

[1] In the literature on problem solving and programming, the incubation phase is usually called *planning*. The importance of this planning phase, for experts as well as novices, has been stressed repeatedly (e.g., Soloway, 1988). In the planning phase, the problem solver is engaged in building up the "problem space" while decomposing the problem into smaller, more manageable parts, as

The following case studies exemplify what we call *flexible and optional partnerships* and *collaboration through the air*. We focus here on the incubation phase—the first 3 weeks of ISDP-II in the fifth grade. These cases demonstrate that some students actually look for and strongly need interactions with peers, while other do not. Some children, who work collaboratively at first in a "face-to-face" style, eventually do make a decision to continue their work independently. Other children prefer to work individually throughout the project. However, it would be wrong to perceive their processes as individualistic per se, because of collaboration through the air.

We found that the initial phase has a rather "messy" character: students are trying out different designs; some get started, then stop, only to start all over again; others seem to do nothing at all for 5–10 days. From the outside, it often looks like a period of nonproductive activity. There appears to be no visible progress. However, because this is the phase when learners "mess around" (Duckworth, 1987) with their ideas, intuitions, and "dirty thoughts" (Harel & Papert, this volume) about fractions and software design, we consider this initial starting phase to be particularly important for learning. Eventually, this messing about—both cognitively and socially—might become finalized into a good design or an idea that is followed through for a whole week, an entire month, or until the end of the project. In fact, ISDP is advancing in individual cycles and rhythms. Individual and collaborative planning and evaluation of achievements occur quite often during the project: as students complete a representation, an entire instructional screen, a procedure, a super procedure, a Logo Page, a topic, and so on.

Following is a description of the incubation phase as seen through the work of several software designers. In the case of Gerald, for example, we shall see that he is not ready for collaboration at the beginning of the project and needs some time on his own to identify the goals he wishes to pursue. On the other hand,

---

well as laying out initial "subplans" for further steps to follow. This approach seems to be particularly appropriate when dealing with well-defined problems of which the end state is known.

In addition, many studies show that planning is not common in novice behavior (e.g., Dalbey, Tourniaire, & Linn, 1986) and more prototypical of experts (e.g., Kurland et al., 1984). Observations of expert programmers, for example, reveal that a major portion of their time is devoted to planning. In these studies, however, novices are rarely given the chance to work on problems large enough to engage them in substantial planning activities. We argue that the provision of time, complexity, and the open-ended structure of the problem in ISDP give the student designers a chance to explore further activities and therefore to engage in collaborative planning activities of various kinds.

In an ill-defined, design-based problem-solving process, the student designers have to define the problem before they can identify potential obstacles and desired end-states. In short, the particularities of ISDP are never defined entirely in advance. As the project moves along and becomes more complex, further issues and problems are identified by the participants (students, teachers, researchers) with great sensitivity to time and context involving social interactions and collaborative efforts.

Stacey and Amy worked together at the beginning but later decided to work alone. Jeannine's case is an example of a girl who preferred to work on her own most of the time. Still, there were students who met for short periods of time on a day-to-day basis to discuss each other's projects, and then returned to their own projects.

Case study 1: Gerald. Consider Gerald, a 10-year-old boy. He is one of only four boys in the class. Most of the other students do not like to work with him. In the preinterviews they described him as "bossy" and "not doing his work,"—remarks which were similar to what his teacher said about him. Gerald, however, does not see himself this way. He thinks that when he "is right," things should be always done his way ("YK" stands for the researcher):

YK: And can you tell me on what project you were working with Eugene?
G: I was working with Eugene on the Science Project.
YK: What were you doing?
G: . . . making the street lights. I was working on making them go on and off.
YK: Did you have discussions, arguments?
G: A little.
YK: What did you argue about?
G: Well, if you want to make a stop you had to put the tape on it and I was telling him "We have to put on the tape" and he was telling me "Don't put the tape there." But then I got it to be my way and I put it there, and so it worked.

Several days after the interview, when we introduced ISDP, the idea of a Nintendo-styled fraction-game was in everybody's mind. Gerald's first screen design in his Designer's Notebook showed a man holding something in his hand facing two towers (in "Mario Brothers" terminology these would be the Warp Zones, see Figure 2).

All four boys went to the computers to start working on their Nintendo-like projects, and all four sat next to each other. They started by taking animation programs (from their other projects) and transferring them into their fraction project. This idea remained the dominant one during the first few days, until Matt decided to start working on his own project and Eugene began designing geometrical shapes in the Logo Shapes Page representing 1/2, 1/3, 1/4, and so on. Eugene's program was designed so he could assign the Logo Turtle a fraction shape (by using SETSH and a number) and have it move across the screen. In this way, the user could control the movement of several fractions on the computer screen, resulting in an animated sequence of fractions moving on the screen. Antonio immediately used Eugene's idea for his project, and they both started working on the idea together.

For a while, at least, the idea of a very sophisticated Nintendo-like game had died. Gerald remained the only one pursuing this idea. For the next 3 days we saw complicated mazes and various race tracks in his Designer's Notebook. His

MY PLANS FOR TODAY

Figure 2.   Gerald's first Designer's Notebook entry of a Nintendo-like design.

reflection entries were always the same: *"I had no problems. I didn't make any changes. I don't know."*

Gerald's insistence on working on this particular Nintendo design isolated him from the other three boys. He kept trying day after day to change one of the already existing programs called "car racing." At one point, as Kafai tried to help him with something, she accidently deleted his whole procedure, and he stopped working on his project completely. He wrote in his notebook: *"I lost everything."*

For the next 3 days, whenever Kafai asked Gerald what he wanted to do, he would say: "I am not working on the project." After 10 days, Kafai found a design in his notebook with wild scribbles on it: *"I am not doing this project anymore."*

On Day 11 we had a 'show and tell' session in the class. Mira, Stacey, and Robin volunteered to present their problems to the other students. Not all of the children came to look, but Gerald did. Later that same day, he started programming some fraction representations on his computer screen for the first time. He began by working on displaying a circle divided into fourths. When Kafai asked him why he gave up on his car program, Gerald answered: "It's too difficult for now."

After the 'show and tell' session, we had a meeting with all the children in the class to discuss project ideas and any problems they were having. This was the first time a competitive atmosphere clearly emerged. Most of the students expressed their feelings about how they "did not want to have other students look over their shoulders" and "take away their ideas." Through this discussion

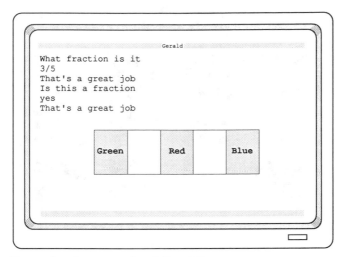

```
                                Gerald
What fraction is it
3/5
That's a great job
Is this a fraction
yes
That's a great job



              Green        Red        Blue
```

Figure 3.   An example of Gerald's screen on fractions.

they reached an agreement that "Logo ideas could be shared, but not fraction representations ideas." Strangely enough, Gerald was one of the students who strongly advocated this agreement![2]

Nevertheless, it seemed that Gerald grasped something during the 'show and tell' session which allowed him to redirect his approach to his own project. Did seeing the other students' projects stimulate his thoughts about what to do? Every day, he would start by working on a new screen, a new representation of a fraction. He even invited Kafai to see what he was working on—something he had refused to do before (see Figure 3). One day, we had a guest student from another class. Gerald eagerly took him to his computer for his own 'show and tell' session, during which he explained to the guest what he was doing.

A week later, Matt and Gerald decided to put both their programs together. Matt had designed a maze with fractions displayed all over it. A PacMan-like shape was running across the screen, in a maze, and passing over fractions (see Figure 4). Interestingly, he had incorporated the concept of equal fractions in the design of the maze: opposing each other were equal fractions, such as 3/6 to 4/8, 2/4 to 5/10, and 1/2 to 6/12.

Matt's initial ideas displayed in his Designer Notebook and software were the Mario Brothers warp zones, a little man standing on them with fractions. When I asked him what his game was all about, Matt presented an elaborated perspective of what his software project would be once it was finished:

---

[2] This session is further discussed in the following chapter (Chapter 6) by Kafai and Harel, Episode 8.

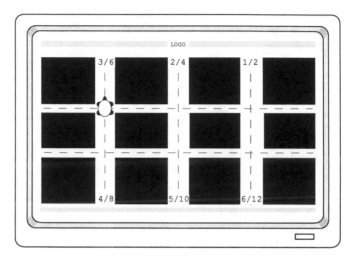

Figure 4. Matt's PacMan fractions maze.

I will make a man on the Shapes page. The man is going to have a fraction on his shirt saying 1/2 or 2/4. And then he goes to the dimension where there is a lot of mumbles [he pointed on the screen to the warp zones]. And they are going through the pipes . . . and when they come out of the pipes, they go over there. And the person who has 1/2, he has to jump up and down. They will come up real fast and on another warp, when he got one false, the guy grows as tall as this, he grows and he runs. That's what happens. Creatures come out, birds come down dropping things on him, when you make it to the King Tut, he throws fractions at you. You have to dodge the fractions so you don't die . . If you get this, you go to another dimension.

For several days, Matt elaborated his software, called "videogame," trying out different placements of the figure shapes and warp zones. Much in contrast to the detailed designs, he wrote in his Notebook most of the time: *"I have no plans and ideas for tomorrow. None."*

Gerald, on the other hand, had so far designed five screens displaying different fractions. For 3 days, they both sat together and worked on copying all the procedures and shapes from both of their programs into one. At one point, Matt indicated to Gerald the incorrect phrasing of one of his fraction questions:

M: You have to write 'What fraction is *this?'* and not 'What fraction is it?'
G: Why 'this'?
M: Because that's what you are asking your users, about this one (points to the representation Gerald created on the computer screen).

At the end of this collaborative period between Matt and Gerald, Matt had a fractions project combining both his and Gerald's program segments. Gerald also

incorporated Matt's segments. However, after a week, Gerald decided to continue working only on the fractions representations he had created, and to leave
Matt's part out. From then on, both students continued working individually on
their fractions project, although every once in a while they did interact on various
matters.

Case study 2: Amy and Stacey. Amy and Stacey decided to work together at
the beginning of the project. Amy is a short, rather shy, girl. Stacey, in contrast,
is much taller and has a more outgoing personality. She smiles quite often and
enthusiastically jumps up and down when she gets excited. She is always ready
to laugh and joke around with a visitor or a friend. Frequently she would hug her
teacher or her classmates.

The entries in their Designer's Notebooks reflect this difference: Stacey wrote
on the first day, in a determined voice: *"I am going to give the students 20
questions, and if they get them all right they will win a TV, and if they get half of
them right they will win a radio."* Her notebook's screen design (see Figure 5)
included many ideas at once: examples for different fractions, how to represent
fractions with either shaded or circled parts, a question she remembered from the
Fractions Interview about how to cut a cake.

The next day she had a new idea and wrote, *"I will make a maze and the
pacman will get you. If you do not get to home first you must get all the fractions
right in 20 minutes and I will put 20 fractions for you to do."*

Amy, in contrast, was less sure of her plans and she wrote: *"I am going to just
make some fractions."* Her screen design in the notebook included two fractions,
a circle cut into quarters and a rectangle cut into eighths.

MY PLANS FOR TODAY

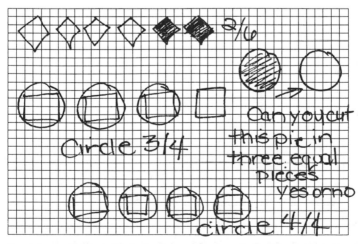

**Figure 5.   Stacey's first design of quarters and eighths in her Designer's
Notebook.**

Once they decided to work together, the two girls had a discussion with Kafai about how they could do that. She said that it was "perfectly o.k. to share ideas, give help to each other, and to work on the same program if they wanted to." Amy then asked if they could work together on one computer. Again, the researcher said this was fine if that was what they wanted.

Their writings in their Designers Notebooks were nearly the same for the first 2 weeks. Stacey wrote, *"Amy and I had problems today we couldn't figure out what we were trying to do,"* or on the following day, *"My problem was that my procedure didn't work and my partner and I were getting very angry. I added a whole procedure."* Amy put it this way: *"Stacey and I couldn't get it to work when the kids type the answer. I didn't make any changes."* They both decided to continue working, and Amy added in her notebook: *"[we need] to work on the game and fix our problems."*

For 2 weeks, we could also see Amy and Stacey finishing their designs (one of which is shown in Figure 6) at the same time, walking together to the computer area, and always choosing to sit next to each other. However, at one point, they decided to continue working on the same thing, but implementing it using two adjoining computers, one for each girl. While Amy and Stacey sat next to each other, they checked each other's screens continuously and waited for each other before continuing work. The following discussion at the computer shows Stacey and Amy discussing their screen design.

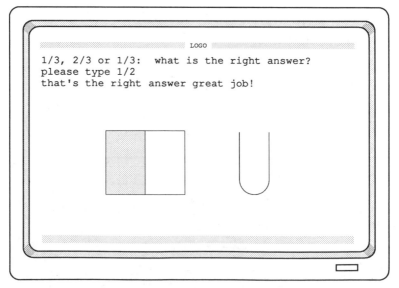

Figure 6. Amy's and Stacey's fractions screen representing a 1/2 and the pit.

Stacey: "We should it put up there [she gestures with her head over Amy's screen, Figure 6]." A few minutes later, Stacey asks: "Ok, what do we do?" Amy answers: "Now how we are going to type this in [she talks loud while she is typing in code in the command center] if . . . [unclear]?" Stacey: "What are you doing?" and she discusses different examples of how to provide feedback to the user. A few minutes later, in the same session, both talk about screen design again. Stacey [while she is talking she is pointing with her hand to the corresponding parts on the screen]: "Maybe we could do this stuff here. Make some things smaller, have a lot of them here."

We observed that Stacey, the more outgoing of the two girls, had the more active part in the team as far as deciding what to do next, and how. One day, we introduced the QUIZ procedure to the students. Most of the students tried to integrate this procedure into their programs. Amy tried, and when she didn't know how to continue, she asked the researcher to help her. In the meantime, Stacey sat and waited. Afterwards, she asked Amy to leave the Flip Side on the screen (the Logo Editor) so that she could correct the procedure she had copied onto her own Logo Page. Because Amy wanted to work on her Shapes Page, she leaned over to Stacey's computer and said: "Let me do this for you fast." During this time, it was very important to the girls that they proceed at the same pace and create identical programs but on two different computers.

Suddenly, on Day 10 of the project, Stacey began designing a new representation: It had a rectangle divided into unequal pieces, some of which were shaded in. She also printed a question at the top of the computer screen, above the representation: "Are these fractions equal? Type yes or no" (see Figure 7).

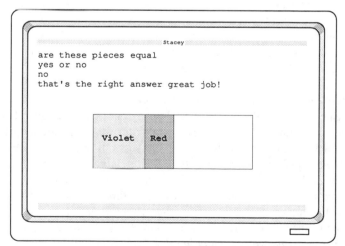

Figure 7.   Stacey's screen representing and quizzing about fractions equality.

The researcher asked Stacey why she thought the equality of fractions was an important thing to teach. She answered that one must know how to cut areas into equal pieces. Later, the researcher asked why she was "designing this screen alone, and why Amy doesn't have it, too." Stacey answered: "Because it was my idea." The girls did not fight, and it seemed that their agreement to take a break from working together was mutual. In their Notebooks, both write on the same day, *"I will continue to work on my game. It is getting easier for me. I changed something in my procedure"* (Stacey), and *"I had no problems today. I didn't make any changes. I will continue to work on my game. It is getting easier"* (Amy).

After that, Amy and Stacey did not work together again in this fashion. In fact, both started new partnerships with others: Stacey working most of the time with Karen, and Amy worked with Sara and Jeannine.

Case study 3: Jeannine. Jeannine's teacher, Mrs. Mar, regards Jeannine as a very successful student and thinks very highly of her school work and her accomplishments with LogoWriter. In an interview we conducted at the end of ISDP-II, Mrs. Mar talked about Jeannine's software design project:

> Jeannine always puts a lot of time in anything she does. Her software program includes [an animation of] the bus picking up the people showing them [fractions]. That something, a little extra, I am not sure if anyone else has that. That's nice. Jeannine always goes above and beyond for anything she does!

We will follow Jeannine through her incubation phase. For one-third of the project, Jeannine explored, on her own, different ideas of what to do in her project. She first designed a candy bar, then a baseball game, until she settled down on her final idea. Even though Jeannine worked mostly on her own, she rarely sat alone. Every day she changed partners. One could frequently see her looking at other students' projects, trying them out, or making a comment. On several occasions Jeannine was hanging around and playing with her classmates.

On her first day of the project, Jeannine wrote in her Designer's Notebook: *"I want to make a candy bar and make it into half and as I go on I want to make it harder.'* She then drew the picture of a Hershey bar in her Designer's Notebook and wrote the symbol 1/2 over it. In LogoWriter that day, she programmed a picture of a Hershey bar. At the end of the session, she wrote again: *"I had absolutely no problem. And it's fun! I made not changes but I might change my mind on what I am going to do on the game"* (see Figure 8).

For some reason, Jeannine chose not to save this program. The next day she started with another idea and erased the whole Hershey bar procedure she programmed. She wrote in her Designer's Notebook: *"I am going to try to think of a new project, and while I am doing that I am going to finish what I did. My problem I had was to think of what I am going to do but I found out. I erased my*

MY PLANS FOR TODAY

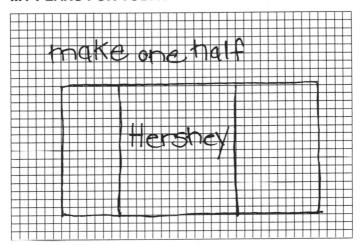

Figure 8.   Jeannine's design of a Hershey chocolate bar.

Hershey Bar because I thought it was stupid. So I made a baseball game'' (see Figure 9). Figure 10 is the directions screen she designed for her students.

For the next 3 days, Jeannine elaborated upon the idea of the baseball diamond, adding other features such as bases. She included a procedure which takes the name of the user as an input and says "Hello [name]." At the computer, where other students tried out her software, she kept saying: "It is not finished yet!" and then explained to Leslie that she was trying to fix something. However, she was still not sure whether this was what she wanted to do. In her Designer's Notebook entry from the third day of the project, she wrote: *"I am going to finish what I had on Friday and if I get frustrated I am going to erase it."* After this session she decided to stick further with this plan: *"I had no problems and I didn't need to erase my procedure but I almost erased it."* She also corrected the spelling mistakes in the instructions screen, and changed the shape of the turtle from a diamond into a bus stop sign. Furthermore, she added a little procedure:

```
to  r
game
end
```

On the next day, there were no changes in her code. During the day, some students, among them Jeannine, Stacey, and Amy asked Kafai how to quiz people ("How to ask a question and to give an answer back."). Kafai started explaining it to them but had the vague feeling they did not understand. How-

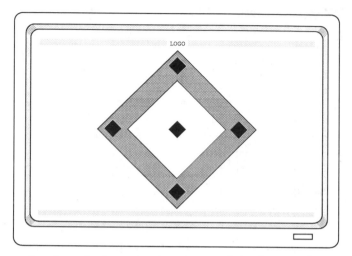

Figure 9. Jeannine's computer screen of the baseball diamond.

ever, a day later, Jeannine changed her directions screen (Figure 10), indicating that she had a new idea for her project. Even though the programming part of quizzing seemed unclear, Jeannine grasped the idea of what it would do and integrated it accordingly into her project (Figure 11).

After we introduced the students to the idea of a quizzing procedure (as was requested by the students), Jeannine changed her strategy once again. On Day 6 of the project, she started working on representation of a square cut into five

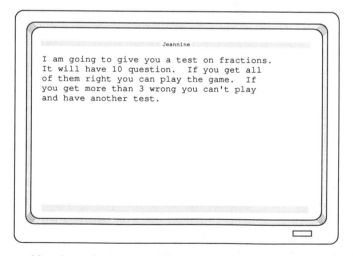

Figure 10. Jeannine's instructions for how to use her software.

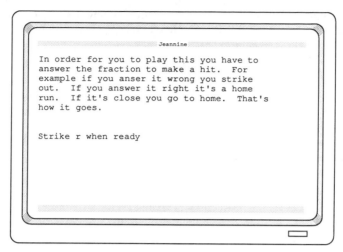

Figure 11.   Jeannine's new instructional screen.

pieces, two of which were colored in different shades of blue. In her quiz, she asked the student to choose an answer from the given fractions: 1/2, 2/3 or 2/5 (see Figure 12).

At this point, the diamond procedure had been disconnected from the program, and on the following days Jeannine continued to work on different fraction representations without the baseball diamond idea. She also added new fraction

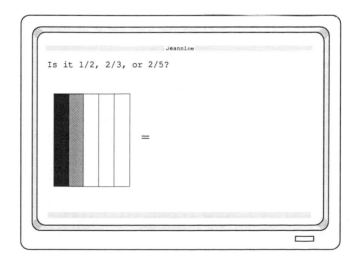

Figure 12.   Jeannine's representation of 2/5.

representations to her software. Her program was now more modularized: she had separated the parts of the program that quizzed the user. A further feature of her program's flow of control was that each procedure called the next.

Then, for the first time a new design idea emerged: she created a shape in the form of a man that was stamped at the bottom of the computer screen below the fraction. For the following days, she disconnected part of the program from the control flow and worked separately on each fractions screen procedure to include the little man. When Kafai asked her what she was planning to do, she replied: ''With every correct answer, the student will see an additional little man at the bottom of the screen.'' At the end of her game, ''a bus will come and pick them all up'' (see Figure 13).

In the following weeks, Jeannine expanded her idea, and by the end of ISDP, her software included 10 instructional screens asking questions about fractions. In the course of ISDP, she changed the shape of the little man twice and worked on completing her quizzing procedures. She managed to implement the feedback animation with the little men. After each time a correct answer was given by the software user, a little man is placed on the bottom of the screen. After 10 correct answers, 10 little men are waiting in line. Then, at the end, after all the fraction quizzes are completed by the user, there is an animation of a bus which comes to pick the men up—motivating feedback (or reward) for Jeannine's software users.

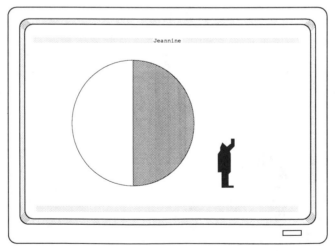

Figure 13. Jeannine's screen of a fraction representation with the "little man," which appears when the user's answer to the fraction problem is correct.

SUMMARY: COLLABORATIVE FEATURES IN ISDP

In this chapter, we examined the interplay between social and individual processes in ISDP. In describing the dynamics in ISDP, we identified some prominent collaborative features that are partly different from those found in existing literature. We also specified two particular kinds of interactions that influenced this learning process: one of collaborative nature, where students actually worked together on specific designs and problems, the other, a *collaboration through the air*, in which students interacted with free-flowing ideas and concepts. We strongly believe that the success of ISDP is drawn upon the *integration* of these interaction processes. The case studies provided examples of the flexibility of ISDP, and the different ways students can use the building of software to explore their individual ideas and meet their individual learning styles, needs, and desires—by working alone or with a partner.

The "Incubation Phase" of the project was chosen to explore these issues of collaboration. It is a challenging stage within which students tease out their intuitions and preliminary design ideas and is a useful period for illustrating the optional and flexible collaborative features of the project. In the process of constructing an understanding of this complex enterprise, students chose what seemed best-suited to their styles and personal knowledge of programming and fractions. Gerald, for example, was not able to immediately build the cornerstone for his project. Initially, he lost interest and was somewhat frustrated. However, his interest in the project was sparked again through his walking around, chatting with friends, and watching other students' software projects. He eventually decided to collaborate with one of them. This collaboration turned out to be a fruitful act which resulted in Gerald's creating very interesting designs. In contrast, Stacey and Amy needed the collaboration in order to get started. Jeannine, on the other hand, preferred to work on her own, although other students used her procedures and were inspired by her designs. We illustrated the ways in which students took advantage of the ideas and knowledge floating around the computer circles and how they shared their impressions with each other. However, they chose different ways of building their own ideas of what *their* project would be.

In many ways, this is comparable with the environment of professional software designers, or scientists in general, as described by Latour (1987) or Schoenfeld (1988). Schoenfeld, for example, describes the influence of "ideas in the air" on his own research agenda within the culture of his scientific community:

> I have claimed that our work is, in large part, the product of our environment, and that in other locales the work could not have evolved the way it did here . . . It

shows how two of the most important features of our analysis [of data from videotapes, for example] have their roots in ideas current in our local intellectual community—how we are conditioned to see new or different things in our data, as a result of living in a community whose 'common sense' supported our seeing things that way. (Schoenfeld, 1988, p. 6)

Two features of Schoenfeld's work are of a similar nature to the atmosphere and activities of ISDP: His casual conversations with other researchers in his community, which were seemingly unrelated to the ongoing work; and the culture that he worked in, which supported the growth of these conversations.

In addition, the culture created during the Incubation Phase can be described as providing a "home base" for the young software designers. It supported conversations and interactions that allowed students to explore various ideas, to experiment with different approaches, to continue working on some ideas, and to dismiss notions that were not working. Our vision of the "home base" is that of a place where students can return to start new ideas while retaining the original task of designing a piece of software. In the same sense, it is also a "comfortable zone" where students can explore more familiar ideas—individually and collaboratively—until they are able to "break away" with their new concepts and make discoveries. The home base is established in different places: in the Designer's Notebook, where the students can invent, describe, and scribble their designs without actually having to implement them, and/or share them; in their programs, where the students can write segments of code and disconnect them later from the flow of the program; and in trying out different screens before settling on one design idea to implement throught their software. Harel also described in Debbie's case (e.g., Harel, 1988) how Debbie was frustrated at first, and did not know how to get started. She also generated many ideas in her Designer's Notebook, but did not implement all of them in her software project. She used the Designer's Notebook as well as her software project as a home base for exploration. In one particular example, Debbie first expressed her personal feelings by writing poems before she could actively begin work on her software project. In this case, writing poems was a comfortable zone for Debbie to start thinking about the fractions project.

In short, this time spent wrestling with different perspectives and ideas—individually and collaboratively—during the Incubation Phase proved to be very important in Harel's as well as in the present study. It resulted in students' conversing and starting to build their conceptual models of what their instructional piece of software would be, and it helped them conceptualize what they wanted to communicate about fractions. Later, we were able to expand this by implementing "consulting activities" (see Kafai & Harel, Chapter 6, this volume) which allowed students to revisit their knowledge of fractions and Logo programming through play and social interaction, without feeling at risk.

ACKNOWLEDGMENTS

We wish to thank the fifth-grade teacher Marquita Minot and her students, the fourth-grade teacher Gwen Gibson and her students, as well as the third-grade teacher Fran Streeter and her students for their collaboration with us and their great contribution to this work. Without them, this research would not have been possible. The research reported here was conducted at Project Headlight's Model School of the Future and was supported by the IBM Corporation (Grant # OSP95952), the National Science Foundation (Grant # 851031-0195), the McArthur Foundation (Grant # 874304), the LEGO Company, Fukatake, and the Apple Computer Inc. The preparation of this chapter was supported by the National Science Foundation (Grant # MDR 8751190), and Nintendo Inc., Japan. The ideas expressed here do not necessarily reflect the positions of the supporting agencies. We thank Seymour Papert, Ricki Goldman Segall, Uri Wilensky, Mitchel Resnick, Aaron Falbel, and Colette Daiute for their insightful comments on our work and on previous drafts of this chapter.

REFERENCES

Berger, P., & Luckmann, T. (1966). *The social construction of reality*. New York: Irvington.

Collins, A. S., Brown, J. S., & Newman, S. (1990). Cognitive apprenticeship: Teaching the craft of reading, writing, and mathematics. In L. B. Resnick (Ed.), *Cognition and instruction: Issues and agendas*. Hillsdale, NJ: Erlbaum.

Dalbey, J., Tourniaire, F., & Linn, M.C. (1986). Making programming instruction cognitively demanding: An intervention study. *Journal of Research in Science Teaching, 23.*

Daiute, C., & Dalton, B. (1989, April). *Collaboration between children learning to write: Can novices be masters?* Paper presented at the American Educational Research Association, San Francisco, CA.

Duckworth, E. (1987). *The having of wonderful ideas and other essays on teaching and learning*. New York: Teachers College Press.

Harel, I. (1988). *Software design for learning: Children's construction of meaning for fractions and Logo programming*. Unpublished PhD. Thesis, Media Laboratory, MIT, Cambridge, MA. (Available through Ablex, Spring 1991)

Johnson, D., Johnson, R., & Jolubec, E. (1986). *Circles of learning: Cooperation in the classroom*. Englewood Cliffs, NJ: Prentice-Hall.

Kafai, Y. & Harel, I. (1990). Replicating the instructional software design project: A preliminary research report. In I. Harel (Ed.), *Constructionist learning: A 5th anniversary collection,* (pp. 150–170). Cambridge, MA: MIT Media Lab.

Kurland, D. M., Pea, R. D., Clement, C., & Mawby, R. (1989). Development of programming ability. In E. Soloway & J. C. Spohrer (Eds.), *Studying the novice programmer* (pp. 83–112). Hillsdale, NJ: Erlbaum.

Latour, B. (1987). *Science in action: How to follow scientists and engineers through society*. Cambridge, MA: Harvard University Press.

Newman, D., Griffith, P., & Cole, M. (1989). *The construction zone: Working for cognitive change in school.* Cambridge: Cambridge University Press.

Palincsar, A. S., & Brown, A. L. (1984). Reciprocal teaching. *Cognition & Instruction, 1,* 117–175.

Schoenfeld, A. H. (1988). *Ideas in the air. Speculations on small-group learning, environmental and cultural influences on cognition and epistemology* (Rep. No. 1RL88–0011). Palo Alto, CA: Institute for Research on Learning.

Slavin, R. (1983). *Cooperative learning.* New York: Longman.

Soloway, E. (1988). It's 2020: Do you know what your children are learning in programming class? In R. S. Nickerson & P. P. Zodhiates (Eds.), *Technology in education: Looking toward 2020.* Hillsdale, NJ: Erlbaum.

Yasmin Kafai

Stephen Sherman Photography

Idit Harel

Jacqueline Karaaslanian Photography

Scenes from the Software Design Studio
Project Headlight, Joanne Ronkin's 4th graders

Optional Collaboration and Flexible Partnerships

Jacqueline Karaaslanian Photography

Our case studies show that students often look for interactions with peers, occasions for sharing ideas, asking for help, or solving technical problems. However, after they jointly design and implement parts of their software together, they often choose to continue their work independently.

Stephen Sherman Photography

Stephen Sherman Photography

Stephen Sherman Photography

109

Idit Harel helping fourth-grade Logo programmers at Project Headlight.

Stephen Sherman Photography

6

Children Learning Through Consulting:
When Mathematical Ideas,
Knowledge of Programming and Design,
and Playful Discourse
are Intertwined

Yasmin Kafai and Idit Harel

CHILDREN AS SOFTWARE CONSULTANTS

The "learning-by-teaching" aspect of the original ISDP (Harel & Papert, this volume) provided the students with a new kind of audience—the younger students, rather than the audience they usually have, their teacher. We chose to expand this feature in the following way: fifth graders designed software for fourth graders, established relationships with them, and then became consultants for the fourth graders as they designed software for third graders. In the process of consulting, mathematical ideas, programming knowledge, instructional design, and playful and social discourse became intertwined. In the following chapter we present an analysis of two consulting sessions and discuss this in relation to other relevant models of interaction.

In *cognitive apprenticeship* (e.g., Collins, Brown, & Newman, 1990), for example, the expert/adult models the important processes and makes them more transparent to the novice/apprentice. In addition to providing the apprentice with a clear conceptual model (or mental model) of the processes involved (and the desired product), the expert also helps to focus the apprentice/learner's attention, provides coaching for the important steps, and assists in certain problematic moments. This is done until the expert eventually fades away from the learner's activity completely. This interplay between observing an expert, being scaffolded, and becoming increasingly independent assists the learner/apprentice in developing self-monitoring and self-correction skills and supports the integration of the skills and conceptual knowledge needed to advance toward expertise. One concrete example of cognitive apprenticeship is the "reciprocal teaching" method (Palincsar & Brown, 1984), in which teachers/experts are explicitly modeling comprehension-monitoring and other sophisticated reading skills to their students/apprentices. The students' role is to internalize the teacher's questioning strategies and comprehension processes. Eventually students accomplish on their own what they previously could only achieve with their teachers. The cognitive change is taking place as part of the instructional interaction between teacher/expert and learner/apprentice.

In contrast to cognitive apprenticeship, *peer collaboration* (e.g., Daiute & Dalton, 1989) relies on student-to-student interaction (i.e., apprentice-to-apprentice), in which students engage in learning as they work and play together, reviewing, synthesizing, and elaborating what they have gathered from the world around them. One important feature in peer collaboration is the role of "cognitive conflict"—disagreeing, arguing, contesting—for the enhancement of knowledge and processes. In these collaborative situations, the roles among the collaborating students may switch between those of "experts" and "apprentices."

Here we explore a cocktail of the two approaches described above. In a nutshell, consulting is characterized here as a learning environment, in which older students are asked to become advisors for younger students. This context includes at least two learning agendas: the agenda of the younger students (consultees), and the agenda of the older students (consultants). The younger students (fourth graders) were working on programming a piece of instructional software to teach third graders about fractions; and the older (fifth grade) students' role was to help. It so happened that several months before these consulting sessions, the fifth graders themselves were involved in a similar software design project (e.g., see Kafai & Harel, 1990). Thus becoming advisors or helpers to the new group of software designers made a lot of sense to these children.

Learning-through-consulting shares several features with cognitive-apprenticeship and peer-collaboration approaches. At the same time, however, it is also distinguished from these approaches in the following ways.

1. *The nonexpert consultants activate and modify their knowledge through the process of modeling and teaching.* In the consulting situation the older students are placed in the role of an expert. However, they are only experts in a relative sense. To a certain degree, we see this context as facilitating a deeper learning experience for the older students than for the younger ones. Through the effort of searching for, and modeling, solutions to the consultees, the consultants reactivate and apply "old" knowledge as well as gain "new" understandings about concepts they could not fully explore and acquire previously.

2. *The student is the epistemologist who generates the "conceptual models."* Through their own software design process, the older student-consultants

encountered design and programming problems, learned how to devise their own strategies, and explored ways to handle a variety of situations related to fractions-knowledge specifics, representing fractions ideas on computer screens, programming aspects, teaching and explaining, or reading and writing skills. We believe that these personal conceptual models serve as organizers, interpretative structures, and guides for the students-consultants in the interaction with their younger consultees during the sessions.

3.   *The instructional interaction is an ill-defined and complex task.* Consulting confronts the older students with many complex problems. The consultees may present the older students with a wide range of problems—from Logo programming questions and design questions to teaching strategies or spelling and writing problems. Because the consultants may be confronted with several kinds of problems at once, it is their choice to determine what will be the most adequate or desirable aspect to deal with at any given moment.

4.   *It is easier to solve a problem when it is "someone else's problem."* Since the consultants work on someone else's product, the problems they encounter are not their own. However, quite often, they may be similar to those problems they themselves have encountered in their own projects. Working on another student's project gives the consultants a second chance to deal with these problems. We believe it is easier for them to delve into another student's problems than into their own. We also believe that they can relate to the other student's problem because it is one they have previously encountered themselves.

5.   *Learning-through-consulting is similar to "playing doctor."* For various psychological reasons this microworld is similar to "playing doctor." First, it allows learners to explore the role of consultants/teachers in the much-disliked terrain of fractions (as much as going to the doctor is also disliked and feared by children). Second, learning-through-consulting places learners in a playful mode in which they can explore their intellectual confusions, overcome doubts, and release fears related to social roles and mathematical understandings (they can "undress" their thoughts about fractions). The student-consultants can create their own terms and rules with their consultees. Drawing from a large spectrum of possible issues, they can elect to investigate topics that are important to them. Above all, within this framework, they can assume a position of control.

One of our main purposes in ISDP-II was to explore the processes involved in the consulting context, *from the point of view of the consultants,* and to study how these relate to the claims and ideas presented above. At this point, we initiated and examined only two consulting sessions, which we carefully observed and videotaped. Our research aimed to explore different aspects of these sessions and to gain insight on issues such as the children's modes of interaction, the contents of their discourse, the topics of their learning and thinking, and the

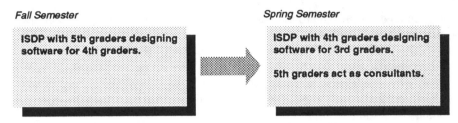

Figure 1.   Research procedure in ISDP-II.

kinds of problems they chose to work on. Several questions guided our analysis of the data from our observations and from the videotapes:

- What *kind of knowledge* do fifth graders activate and communicate when talking with the fourth graders about their software projects? Do they choose to discuss the programming aspects? Do they focus on the fractions representations? Or, do they discuss the fourth graders approaches to teaching and explaining?
- What *modes of interaction* do the consultants use with the fourth graders? In what ways do they identify and understand the consultee's ideas, notions, or problems? Which interactive strategy do the fifth graders use: do they give "clues" about what to do, or "do it for" the younger students?
- What do the fifth grade students *learn* through engaging in the activity of software-design consulting? (It should be noted that it was not in the aim of this study to focus on the learning experiences of the student-consultees, although we see it as an interesting aspect in itself.)

The investigation of learning-by-consulting is situated in our year-long study called ISDP-II (see Kafai & Harel, 1990, and in this volume. See Figure 1 for the year-long research procedure). In addition to the data we collected during the consulting sessions, we have observed these students over a period of 1 year and collected many in-depth interviews with the students and their teacher; we also recorded several classroom discussions and saved the students' daily work (designs, writing, programming). Many of our interpretations of the consulting sessions are based on this larger body of data.

PROCEDURE OF CONSULTING SESSIONS

The first consulting session took place 3 months after the fifth-grade students had completed their software projects, and after the fourth-grade students had spent 3 weeks on their projects. The second session took place 3 weeks later. As we describe the procedure of each of the consulting sessions in the following paragraphs, we shall also explain: (a) how the idea of consulting was introduced to the student-consultants, (b) how the activity itself took place during the two consulting sessions, and (c) what the students reported about their consulting experiences in the follow-up classroom discussions.

Description of the First Consulting Session

The idea of consulting was introduced to the student-consultants by one of the researchers (Kafai) and their teacher (Mrs. Mar) in their classroom. The intention was to have the students define what consulting could mean. For that purpose, we installed a poster asking "What is Consulting?" on the blackboard. One girl, Robin, volunteered to write the other students' suggestions on the poster. As she transcribed the students' ideas and wrote them on the poster, there was some confusion in the room: the students seemed to have an idea what consulting is, but were having difficulty expressing it in words. At about this time, Alicia asked to look in the dictionary for the word "consulting." She later read to everybody the definition she found. The teacher then suggested to think about concrete examples of "who a consultant can be." The students came up with the examples of "a lawyer," "a doctor," "a priest," and "a psychiatrist." The content of the poster at the end of the introduction session is shown in Figure 2.

Then we asked the students to think about what it could mean for them to become 'software design consultants' for the fourth graders. The students' ideas about the content of consulting were, for example: "You ask questions about software" and "Tell them what's wrong with it." The teacher modeled one kind of feedback the students could give to their consultees.

Mrs. Mar: One of the things to keep in mind . . . when you give somebody your opinion about it [about their software], you don't go 'That stinks.' [Laughter] It's called *constructive criticism.* Do you understand what I mean by constructive criticism?

Karen: You could say like 'Maybe you could change this to that?' or something like it.

Mrs. Mar: If you don't like it, if there is something in particular, you don't understand, you could give your idea about something in a nice way. Say, they have a screen that doesn't make sense to you, don't say 'That's garbage.' You could say 'This is really confusing, what are you trying to say?' And then, you can try and help that person to work it out. Okay. You should always try to be nice.

The rest of the introductory discussion was spent on the problem of how to say "critical things in an acceptable way." The students kept expressing one particular dilemma they encountered in their thinking about consulting: "If we really don't like it [the fourth graders' pieces of software] and they ask us "What do you think?"—what do we say?"

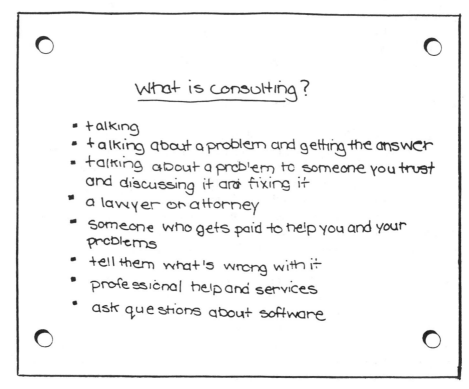

Figure 2.   Students' poster after the consulting introduction.

In general, we had the feeling that all fifth-grade students were willing and eager to do the consulting with the fourth-grade students. After this 20-minute introductory discussion, we asked the children ''Are you ready to go?'' Fourteen voices answered: ''Yeah!'' and we all left the classroom to go to the computer pods.

At the computer pods, the teacher assigned the consultant–consultee pairs.[1] Since there were more consultees than consultants, some students did not have a consultant. Kafai walked around with the videocamera on her shoulder and recorded the activities. Many times she stopped next to one of the pairs and asked them to tell her about what their ideas were, and what they were working on. When asked, she also gave advice about issues the pairs could discuss, etc. The

---

[1] The teacher was concerned about the combination of certain consultant–consultee pairs. For example, she did not want to have particular students in her class work with the special needs students because she considered their interaction style not adequate for them (''too bully''). We, in fact, questioned this, and felt the students could have profited from these interactions in particular. However, we respected the teacher's decision.

two teachers were also walking around the computer pods and helping the students.

The general impression of this session is that all the pairs were engaged in their "job" but in different ways. Some of the fifth-grade students were watching the fourth graders' programs; some of them ran it by themselves; some were helping with programming problems; some focused on the fourth graders' explanation of fractions or the quality of their fraction games. The modes of interactions varied as well: some pairs sat next to each other with almost no talking, while others were actively involved in discussing things and changing things in the Logo programming code.

In the follow-up discussion, the teacher asked each student about his or her experience with consulting. The students briefly described what they had observed and what they had suggested to the fourth graders. In the beginning, most of the discussion focused on issues related to programming. One of the fifth graders said that her fourth-grade student used "no procedures." Another child reported that her consultee "did not know SETPOS," and another child added that his consultee did not know "how to use STARTUP."

Then Alicia brought up that she didn't understand one of the student's screens, and that she had simply "found one of the fraction representations wrong." An interesting discussion with the teacher and other students emerged (a more detailed discussion of this can be found in the next section). Another student continued with a further example of how "fractions can be wrong" (as described below in Episode 1). The students referred to the problem that some questions can have more than one right answer (as described below in Episode 2). One student introduced another problematic aspect: the phrasing of questions and spelling of words on the screen (as described in Episodes 5 and 6).

Towards the end of the discussion, the teacher asked the students if they would volunteer to continue helping the fourth graders on a regular basis. All the children agreed to do that and even requested to work with the same partners again.

Description of the Second Consulting Session

Three weeks later, we had the second session. The fourth graders' projects grew since the first consulting session, and they were ready for another round of consulting and feedback from the fifth graders. We did not have an introductory discussion, nor did we assign the consultant–consultee pairs for this second consulting session. After the student-consultants were told that the fourth graders were waiting for them at the computers, they walked out to the computer pods to find their partners.

All students were engaged in their consulting activity. The observations from the first consulting session are also applicable to the second consulting session. A particular 'consulting session' took place during this time between the teacher and one of her students discussing the teaching strategies used in his software. The students worked together for approximately 20 minutes before returning to their classroom. We used the remaining time for a general class discussion similar to the one we had had at the end of the first session.

Again, we asked the students to talk about what they had observed and what they had done as consultants to the fourth graders. Children's accounts of their consulting experiences in this second session were related to Logo programming problems, design issues, and teaching strategies. Unfortunately, we did not have enough time to get a report from all the consultants.

OBSERVATIONS AND DISCUSSION OF CONSULTING SITUATIONS

The following episodes indicate the potential role of consulting in the process of learning—at least for the consultants. Students applied different kinds of knowledge in this context: they were involved in several content areas such as fraction representations, programming issues, the correct spelling and phrasing of questions, teaching strategies, design issues, and so on. They were engaged in problem solving when helping the consultees debug the programming code, fix and clarify instructions, and fraction representations.

This gave students an opportunity to revisit and confront their own knowledge about fractions, programming, and software design 3 months after the completion of their own projects. The fifth graders could reevaluate their knowledge. They found that many of their own "misconceptions" were reflected in the fourth graders' pieces of software. They were also confronted with situations that made them observe problems that, in fact, they themselves had with fractions and Logo programming. For example, when referring to one fourth grader's particular screen showing a representation of 2/4, Karen said: "I know it could be 1/2, but that's not what is on [her] screen." This problem, in fact, existed already when the fifth graders were working on their own software. Students "knew" that 2/4 could also be 1/2. However, "knowing it" is not the same as "understanding it." This brings the reflective function of consulting into play. Through digging into the consultees' concepts, the student consultants could challenge their own understandings without a threat to their personal intellectual ability.

In the introductory discussion (before the consulting session) they used words such as "not liking the game"; however, in the follow-up discussion (after the consulting session) there was a shift from the criterion of "liking–not liking" to deeper and more specific dimensions. Students referred, for example, to the quality of their consultees' programming knowledge, their fraction representations, the quality of explanations in the instructional screens, and issues related to spelling and writing. The follow-up discussion also allowed the fifth-grade students to share and compare their past experiences in ISDP.

In addition, the follow-up discussions required complex teacher-intervention strategies. Though the time-frame in this study did not allow for an extended interaction among students and teachers on deep-structure knowledge, we see these follow-up sessions as providing a potentially rich opportunity for exploring the complexity of the *teacher's role* in constructionist learning environments. (We will discuss this aspect of our observations in greater detail in the conclusions.)

In the following subsections, we shall briefly present several model cases or episodes to show how the consulting process created a context that confronted the students with a multitude of problems. This context encouraged a large spectrum of 'cognitive conflicts' (e.g., Posner, Strike, Hewson, & Gertzog, 1982) among learners, forcing them to rethink and reconsider their own knowledge across the board.

Activating Knowledge of Fractions and their Representations

Episode 1. What Alicia discovered in her consulting session with Tracy: "How can 6/6, 7/7 and 8/8 be the same as 5/5?" Moreover, "How can one whole be made out of five discrete objects?" During the first session's follow-up discussion, Alicia (fifth grader) raised this important issue related to rational-number concepts and their representations: It took only one of Tracy's (fourth grader) screens to create a cognitive conflict in Alicia's mind. Her not-so-simple puzzle was related both to understanding part–whole relations and to understanding the concept of discrete and continuous fractions.

In general, this episode revealed several things. First, the fourth grader's (Tracy) screen was an excellent vehicle for eliciting the fifth grader's (Alicia) thinking about her own understandings. It created a situation where Alicia had a strong need to announce to her classmates and teacher what she could not understand—a rare situation in school practice. By doing so, Alicia also encouraged other students to report on similar cases.

Alicia:	. . . And Claudia didn't have hers ready. So I looked at Tracy's. And Tracy, I couldn't understand hers [one of the screens].
Mrs. Mar:	What couldn't you understand about Tracy's?
Alicia:	She showed me one part of her screen, it had 5 diamonds with different colors and she said [printed on the top of her screen] 'What's this fraction?' And it had [as options for the user to choose as the correct answer] 6/6, 7/7 and 8/8. And there was no 5/5! And I said "I don't understand that." And she said "Oh, what didn't you [understand]?" And then I said "I still don't understand it.' And then they said "Time to logout."

Mrs. Mar: So you didn't have a chance to explain [to her], how she needed to make this [screen] more clear?

Alicia: But I [also] don't understand [in the first place] how can 5 pieces be a whole?

Mrs. Mar: Well, it can.

Alicia: It cannot.

Mrs. Mar: Yes, it could be if it is individual pieces. Because sometimes you can take fractions as [she pauses]. See, we haven't talked about fractions, and their class has done fractions. See, Mrs. Kin's class, are, is now doing fractions.

Some students: We did.

Mrs. Mar: [A bit uncomfortable] Maybe when we do fractions [in a few months, within the school's curriculum], we'll come back to this.

[Other children report on similar cases. There is noise in the class. The teacher says:]

Mrs. Mar: Advice. If you have a denominator and numerator of the same number, it equals to one whole.

Mira: Oh so it divides.

Stacey: You can divide it by the same number like 5/5 is divided by 5 and you get 1/1, you get a whole.

Mira: I told her too [Frida] about the one whole and she changed all 5/5 and 4/4 [to say '1 whole'].

Mrs. Mar: Well, technically, it's still correct [to say 5/5 and 1 whole] and usually, what you do is you reduce it to the lowest terms, but 5/5 has to be reduced to a whole.

Consulting is a very rich problem-finding environment. This discussion could have been the springboard for the teacher and students to create *conversational cycles* of finding ways to help children solve their puzzles. As we see in the transcript, the time constraints did not allow the group to engage in meaningful explorations of mathematical knowledge. We want to use this example to explain what we think Alicia is referring to—Tracy's computer screen (Figure 3).

We believe that Alicia's concern was twofold. First, she was simply confused because there were five diamonds on the screen, but no reference to the number 5 in any of the options Tracy gave to her users as the possible answers. So Alicia's first reaction was: *"And it had 6/6, 7/7, and 8/8. And there was no 5/5!"* Moreover—even if 5/5 was given as an option by Tracy—Alicia was not at all sure that 5/5 was the right answer: *"But I don't understand how can 5 pieces be a whole?"*

Alicia thinks that, since there are five objects on the screen, the corresponding symbolic representation has to have the number 5 in it in some way. However, at the same time, Alicia's frame of reference is a single diamond. And since there were five diamonds on the screen, they must be five wholes. But how can one whole be composed of five wholes? In her mind she cannot yet shift her frame of reference and consider a set of five objects as one whole. Recall her strong opinion:

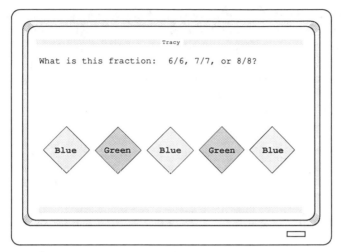

Figure 3. Tracy's screen of a representation with diamonds from April 27.

Alicia: But I don't understand how can 5 pieces be a whole?
Mrs. Mar: Well, it can.
Alicia: It cannot.

Pronouncing her different opinion so clearly for herself and to the teacher provided an entry for intervention. Although the teacher did not deepen the discussion around this issue, other students reported cases where they believed that the fourth graders had "similar problems" about fractions (e.g., Mira and Stacey in the above transcript). In the second consulting session, for example, Antonio (fifth grader) reported on a similar problem he had had with Annie's (fourth grader) software. He, however, was able to switch perspectives quite well:

Antonio: The girl's name is Annie. And then she had a big circle, right, and then she split it into halves. And two of them, two sides were painted in different colors. And then I put [answered] 'one whole.' That wasn't it. I put 'one-half.' That wasn't it. It was 2/2!
Yasmin: So how did you come to think that she thinks 2/2 is the right answer?
Antonio: I don't know. But it should have been one whole.
Gerald: Couldn't it be 2/2? It could. [Discussion in classroom, difficult to understand the tape.]
Alicia: You feel so stupid in front of a fourth grader [she then says with a funny voice:] 'I know it, but.'
Antonio: I was trying to figure it out [by myself, until I found what she meant:] 'Oh, I got it 2/2' and then she goes: 'Great job!' Then, the second one [another screen Annie programmed] had a split line and it messed up [the program crashed].

Episode 2. What Karen discovered in her Consulting Session with Alice: "How can a representation of 2/4 be equal to 1/2?" After the first consulting session the students also discussed two kinds of "frustrating situations" in their consultees' pieces of software. These were: (a) when there is more than one correct answer, and the designer chose (as the right one) something different than they did; and (b) when the 'right answer' does not correspond with the representation that is on the designer's screen. This led to the following discourse:

Karen: So, if I have 2/4 on the screen [stopped by the teacher].

Mrs. Mar: Or it could be 1/2.

Karen: No. But if you are doing the fractions game and it's like . . . four pieces on the screen and two are colored in, and two aren't. How, can I know that it could be 1/2? But that's not really what is on the screen?!

Mrs. Mar: Well . . . they give you a choice of answers, such as, 2/4, 1/2, or 5/8 or something. If they give you a choice of answers, then it makes it easier, for 2/4 is equal to 1/2. [It is not clear to us what the teacher meant to say here. But Stacey raised her hand and interrupted her talking. She looked at her and said:] Stacey?

Stacey: I had the same thing in my program. But I had, I had 2/4 and 1/2 and chose one answer of it. And when they [the users] got the answer, I explained to them *why* I did that [i.e., why their answer is right or wrong].

Mrs. Mar: But back to Karen's. It doesn't come into Karen's. It's the same thing [2/4 and 1/2]. Basically it's the same thing. Let's say they give you a choice of answers, but if they don't give you a choice of answers, sometimes you might *not* get the right answer.

Alicia: Then you feel stupid.

Mrs. Mar: Well, oh no. [i.e., you shouldn't feel stupid]. It's also part of programming. If we had learned about lists [in Logo] when you were doing your projects . . . see, you had the same problem coming up the way. Do you see what I am saying?

This discussion demonstrates how fraction representations and programming problems can become intertwined. In Logo, there are several ways to write a procedure which accepts more than one answer as the correct one (e.g., by using lists). The students did not know about lists, which would have allowed them to accept different "right" answers at the same time for their instructional quizzes. After this issue was raised, we realized that the students lacked an important programming skill that could facilitate their design and teaching strategies as well as their fractions knowledge (e.g., of fractions equality). Here we find an ideal context in which Logo programming knowledge could have supported particular aspects in the fractions knowledge, and vice versa. It reemphasizes the idea that learning in integration can be easier than learning things in separation (Harel & Papert, 1990).

Activating Knowledge of Logo Programming

Episode 3. How Jeannine finds out what Caroline needs to know in Logo. While working as consultants and in follow-up discussions, much of the students' work referred to Logo programming problems. Their accounts covered a range of problems—from simple syntax errors to Logo Page arrangements and program control. Furthermore, the consultants often introduced the younger students to "new Logo programming tricks" and discussed in the classroom how to go about teaching Logo. For example, in the follow-up discussion of the first session, Jeannine (fifth grader) remarked that Caroline (fourth grader) "did not know about procedures."

During the first consulting session, Jeannine was sitting next to Caroline and simply watching her. Since Jeannine did not know Caroline very well, it did not occur to her that knowing about procedures was far out of reach for Caroline, who was still using Logo in the direct mode (i.e., writing the code at the Logo Command Center only). Although Jeannine was quite astonished to find out that one can program "such long programs without using procedures," she was not sure whether Caroline was ready for learning about procedures. During the second consulting session, Jeannine copied Caroline's code from the Command Center to the Flip Side, wrote a procedure, and then searched for something to teach Caroline at her level. Jeannine chose to teach Caroline how to use SETPOS (the Logo command for placing the Turtle on the screen by specifying two numbers, the Cartesian coordinate positions).

Idit [to Caroline]:	Was she helpful, was Jeannine helpful?
Caroline:	Ahem.
Idit:	What did she help you with?
Caroline:	SETPOS.
Idit:	With SETPOS. Did you ever use SETPOS before?
Caroline:	[nods 'yes' with her head].
Idit:	But she explained it to you. I see . . . she put it in certain places . . .
Idit [to Jeannine]:	What was her problem with SETPOS, Jeannine?
Jeannine:	She really didn't use it.
Idit:	Oh, she really didn't use it. So you put it . . . where did you put it in the program?
Jeannine:	On the Flip Side.
Idit:	On the Flip Side. Where do you think she needed it?
Jeannine:	Whenever she "function-9!"
Idit:	Function-9. Great!

Shortly after Jeannine taught SETPOS to Caroline, and they went through Caroline's code and implemented it at various places, we asked Caroline, "Did you ever use SETPOS before?" She nodded and smiled. Jeannine smiled too,

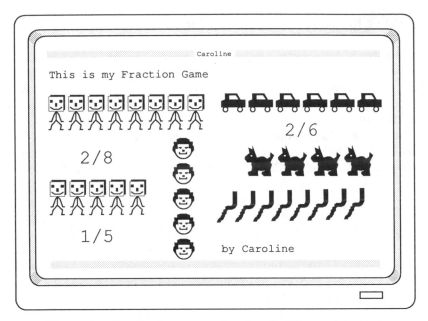

Figure 4. Caroline's screen showing 6 different fractions.

and said that was not true. We interpret this as Caroline's appropriation of the new skill (see Figure 4).

Episode 4. Alicia and Tracy working on debugging Tracy's Logo code together. We have already described one episode from the first consulting session when Alicia (fifth grader) was working with Tracy (fourth grader) and had problems understanding one of her representations. In the second consulting session, Alicia worked with Tracy again, this time on a debugging problem related to variables and conditionals. Alicia's description of this situation in the follow-up discussion demonstrates that she understands the Logo syntax for conditionals and variables very well (i.e., at what places the quotes and colons have to appear when dealing with variables in a program).

Interestingly, Alicia herself had many difficulties with this aspect of programming when she was previously working on her own software. (Recall that the fifth graders were involved in ISDP during the fall semester.) Here is an example from Alicia's Logo code from the fall. The procedure "half.circle" draws on the computer screen a fraction representation of a circle divided vertically into halves. At the top of the screen a question appears, asking, "What is this fraction?" The question is printed, but Alicia did not write the appropriate code for accepting the user's input (answer). The following is a code fragment from Alicia's fractions project from November 28, 1989:

```
. . . .
to half.circle
rg ct
pu setpos [ − 45 0]
rt 90 setc 5
fd 45 fd 45 fd 23 fd i
pu setpos [14 10]
setc 5 pd fill
pr [What is this fraction?]
pr [4/5 or 3/4 or 1/2]
end
. . . .
```

The procedure "half.circle" is one of three such examples in Alicia's program. In fact, Alicia was one of the very few students who did not immediately implement the appropriate code for a "quiz procedure" after it was discussed in the classroom. She waited a few weeks before implementing it in her program (see Kafai & Harel, 1990). One day she came to Kafai and asked for her help (with the implementation of the quiz procedure within the pre-prepared program segments). More than 3 months later, in the consulting session, Alicia approached this problem very professionally:

> Alicia in the Spring (in classroom followup discussion): Tracy has, had problems with her . . . her, ahm, you know, the stuff you use with answers [taking user's input], the two dots, she kepts on putting the dots in the wrong places. She didn't know what was the matter. And she also doesn't know how to use SHOW-POS and SETPOS. But she wanted her, ahm, letters to go all over the screen and come back to their places, and then to leave them alone. That's it. I helped her.

We captured on videotape the beginning of this particular consulting session when Alicia and Tracy were working at debugging Tracy's quizzes. The video segment starts with the two girls running Tracy's program and realizing that something is wrong. They move back and forth between running the program and debugging the code on the Flip Side. What is remarkable in this consulting situation is the way these two girls share the access to the computer keyboard. The video gives a nice example for how both girls closely interact as they work on quite a complex debugging problem.

Consulting on Spelling and Writing

Episode 5. What did Gerald discover in his consulting session with Brian: spelling and writing problems. In the following excerpt from the discussion, Gerald (fifth grader) raises the problem of Brian's (fourth grader) misspellings. The teacher puts it in the context of what she had seen in her own students'

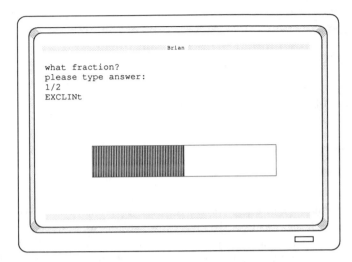

Figure 5.   Brian's screen representing 1/2 (note his spelling mistake).

programs while they were working on their projects in the Fall. This is the screen
to which Gerald, Eugene, and Matt are referring in this episode (see Figure 5):

Gerald:	I was working with Howard. He, Howard, he was good, but then Brian's, he was good too, but he prints [the word] excellent and he didn't spell it right like 'e' then 'x' . . .
Mrs. Mar:	Did you tell him that his 'excellent' was spelled wrong?
Gerald:	Yes, and he said 'Oh' and then he just went along.
Mrs. Mar:	Did he fix it?
Gerald:	No [looks a bit upset].
Mrs. Mar:	Maybe, well, it will be very interesting to see if he fixes it later on. Maybe, he just wanted you to look at his program. [Looking at Eugene who raises his hand, saying] Eugene?
Eugene:	I did this too with him, and I saw this 'excellent' thing too.
Mrs. Mar:	Ah, so you noticed what I have noticed in a lot of your projects. Because one of the first things which catches my eyes is when [you print] 'what fractions' and that 'w' was not capitalized. Or, I was looking to see where was your question mark?
Gerald:	Yeah, he didn't have that either, [a question mark].
Mrs. Mar:	But those are the kind of things that you can tell them. [Looking at Matt who raises his hand, saying] Matt?
Matt:	I went over to look at Brian's software. And when I looked at it, he spelled excellent all in huge letters and then he had this small ''t'' and I said, 'What is this: excellennnnn t?'
Mrs. Mar:	Maybe with that one, he wanted that. I don't know.
Alicia:	Tracy, she put the two little dots at the end of her question. Like, 'What fraction is this:' [shows the two dots with her fingers in the air] What does that mean, the two dots? You know, the two dots?

Mrs. Mar: Colons. She did go on, may be. Was there a question mark?
Alicia: But it is a question. Why does she have to put dots in there?

Interestingly, the student, Gerald, who brought up this question in the first place, had a similar language problem while designing his own piece of software. Here is an excerpt of a discussion from October 1989 that Gerald had with Matt, while they were working together on their software projects. At one point, Matt indicated to Gerald:

Matt: You have to write "What fraction is *this?*" and not "What fraction is *it?*"
Gerald: Why *this?*
Matt: Because *that's* what you are asking your users, about this one (points to the representation Gerald created on the computer screen).

It was interesting for us to observe that the consulting did not only deal with the core issues such as the correctness of fraction representations, but also with little details such as correct spelling and grammar. This seemingly little detail caught our attention, since the fifth-grade teacher repeatedly indicated her concerns about writing and spelling to her students during the previous term. However, most students ignored this type of comments. As consultants, the students shifted perspectives, and became more concerned with this aspect of the software.

Episode 6. Instructional and pedagogical concerns. An example of the children's awareness of the instructional or pedagogical quality of the software can be found in the second consulting session, particularly when Gerald (fifth grader) was working with Howard (fourth grader) on the feedback he gives his users about their answers. The following is the code of Howard's program before the consulting session 1:

```
to fract
. . .
{first screen shows a rectangle divided into halves, both colored in}
. . .
print [what is this fraction?] print [please type your answer!]
name readlist "answer
ifelse: answer = [1/1]
[print[ good answer]] [print[ go ahead]]
wait 15 ct rg cc
. . .
end
```

Howard included all his screens in one procedure. The only distinction between the feedback he gave to correct vs. incorrect answers is the printed message on the screen: either "good answer" or "go ahead"—but in both cases the program continues ahead. After that first session, Gerald told his classmates:

Gerald: I was working with Howard and . . . everything was good, except one thing he put 'Go ahead and correct.' He did this everytime. Instead of printing 'try again,' he put 'go ahead' and he goes to the next problem! And I had to fix all of that.

Gerald's sensitivity to this issue surprised us. He proposed a solution to Howard: to include "try again" as a reply for a wrong answer, and to have users go back to the beginning of the project. Howard implemented Gerald's suggestions.

Consulting on Design

Episode 7. Eugene, Matt, and Marion: Fixing the look of shapes and symbols. In the second session, for example, Eugene and Matt (fifth graders) and Marion (fourth grader) worked together. This episode provided us with an example of consulting on a nearly finished piece of software. Since there seemed to be no fraction or programming problems, the three students focused on correcting minor design problems related to the symbolic representation of 3/4 which Marion had designed using the Logo Shapes-Page.

In the following scene, Marion had the keyboard on his lap. Matt discussed in detail with Eugene how to improve the look of the 3/4, in particular the look of the number 4 in the 3/4 representation:

Matt [to Eugene]:   I showed you that shape here . . . look. [They are looking at the Shapes Page. Matt moves his hands on the screen and points to the Shape showing a symbolic representation of 3/4.]

Marion: Yeah. I am gonna change that.

Matt: [His finger touches the computer screen, pointing on the fraction denominator '4.' He doesn't like the way the number 4 looks on the screen; he looks at Marion, and says:] Make this one over one, and move this block, too.

Marion: [flips back to the Shapes page, points to Shape number 4, and says:] That's what it's got to look like. [He then moves back to the Shapes building area. One can see the cursor moving on the screen, for adding blocks to the number 4 to make it look more like a 4. The three boys say:] There.

Episode 8. Leslie and Sara: "How many fractions do you need for your software to be really good?" A recurring discussion theme in all the ISDP projects is related to how many fraction representations would qualify a project to be finished and good. In the beginning, students were asking us frequently "How many fractions [representations or screens] do I need to make for this project?" It was difficult to convince them that the number of screens was not a decisive point.

While Leslie (fifth grader) was looking at Sara's (fourth grader) software, she was a bit disturbed by the fact that Sara had included only four representations and was already working on her software's title page:

Leslie: I was working with Sara. She didn't have any problems [she means screens showing a representation of a fraction and a related problem to solve]. She didn't have any problems. She had about *only* four problems, she was working on another one. She asked me to help her on the front page and I didn't know . . .

Yasmin: Why do you think she didn't have enough problems?

Leslie: Because she was [already] working on her front page!

Idit: Is it good or bad, or, it doesn't matter?

Leslie: I don't know. I guess it's good . . .

Leslie's insecurity pointed to a particular concern of the designers regarding the size of the fractions software (or the number of screens), which we had discussed during the fall with the designers and their teacher. In the midst of the fifth graders' project in the fall, the students started talking about *"how many screens are actually needed in order to say I am done."* Very frequently one could hear students asking each other when talking about their own projects "How many screens do you have?" On the other hand, when giving presentations in our fall "show and tell" session, you could hear one student say to the presenter (Antonio): "And this is all?" referring to the four fractions screens of Antonio's project.

Leslie's insecurity about taking a clear position on this case reflected her ambivalence and that of the other class members on this issue. However, an interesting discussion emerged about whether one way to evaluate whether a piece of software is good or not is related to how many problems/representations are presented in the software. The question of whether this is a criteria, or a category, for judging a piece of software is related to both design and pedagogy.

Social and Moral Issues Involved in Consulting

Episode 9. Using other students' ideas. A special situation occurred when Nora (fifth grader) and Wanda (fourth grader) were working together. Quite often, Wanda had problems in 'adjusting' her design ideas to her Logo-programming skills. One of her very first ideas was to design a fractions game in the spirit of Nintendo's Mario Brothers. She spent an enormous amount of time designing screens for the different "worlds" (i.e., a Nintendo metaphor) both in her Designer's Notebook and in Logo. However, making her ideas work as an interactive fractions game (like Mario Brothers) required sophisticated Logo-programming skills she did not have. After a while, Wanda became frustrated and decided to do something else more closely related to what other students were doing. Therefore, she was one of the few students who did not have much to show in terms of an implemented project, yet she had a great deal to share in terms of her imagination and ideas.

When Nora came to consult Wanda, they talked for a while about Wanda's ideas. When Nora realized that Wanda did not have much of a program to show, she decided to show her the software she had designed 3 months before. Wanda liked Nora's project very much and asked Nora if she could copy her programming code as is, and add some of her ideas to it. Here is what Nora told her classmates after this session:

Nora: I was working with Wanda. From her whole game, she had only her front page! She didn't save anything. And then I decided to show her my game, and then she said she wants to do exactly like my game. I said, she couldn't have it just like that. And I showed her my front page with the music on it. And she wanted it like that, and I said: 'You can't.' And then she started acting like she was crying and she was mad. She wanted it like Mario Brothers at first, and then she saw my game, and she wanted it different. Like mine. So she kept on changing her ideas back and forth.

Idit: How did you solve it?

Nora: I just asked her which one she is going to do. And she said, I want to do my game just like yours.

Idit: And your cover page too? [Nora loved her opening page with the music.]

Nora: Yeah.

Idit: Why didn't you want her to have it just like yours?

Nora: Because.

Alicia: [answers for Nora] It's mine!

Nora: Yeah. It's mine, not hers.

This was an issue which was of particular importance for the consultants: "Who owns an idea?" Or, "Can one copy someone else's program? Why or why not?" In the Fall, we had a long animated discussion on this topic (e.g., Kafai & Harel, 1990), and the fifth-grade students came to the conclusion that it was "o.k. to share Logo programming tricks but not to pick up screen ideas from other students." The following short excerpt from the *classroom discussion on "software rights and confidentiality" of November 3, 1989* illustrates the students' concerns about ownership and the sharing of ideas:

Amy: If we have an idea and we share it with a couple of people, is this fair?

Mrs. Mar: Do you think it is fair? To learn something new? If it is *their* idea and you want to share it with one or two people . . . An idea or procedure or something new. Well. Do I have to share everything I know with you all?

Students: No.

Mrs. Mar:	Do you get mad if you think I don't? [Idit laughs] It's a personal thing. You share something with whom you want to share it. It's a personal thing. [Talking to Nora] Nora?
Nora:	I don't think that's fair because, say, like Antonio said, right, if he got something new, he will only tell a boy and he will leave us [the girls] without knowing it.
Mrs. Mar:	Do you think if you have something new you're gonna walk over to Antonio, Eugene, Gerald and Matt and tell them?
Students:	No you won't.
Nora:	No. I tell girls first.
Mrs. Mar:	What makes you think . . . what's the difference between that? [telling boys or telling girls]
Nora:	Because, see, they always tell boys first and I just tell girls first.
Idit:	Let me tell you something, in a software company, there is a policy. Do you know the word confidential? [Several students at the same time: No, no, yes, yes no . . .] Could you explain it?
Mrs. Mar:	Confidential. It means like if I have this folder on my desk and the word confidential was written on it, that means that *no one* has the right to open up that folder. Just like nobody has the right to go into my copy book. Like nobody has the right to go into your personal journal. It's confidential. It's for certain people who have certain permissions to do it.
Idit:	O.K. So what usually happens in software companies, and if we agree we are like a software company here, we can say: the information we are producing here, the products we are producing here are confidential to the outside world. And it will be sort of o.k. to say: Ok we do not want other people to see what we are doing. But, it is pretty common in a company to work together and share information within the company. Because, on one day you might not want to share your invention. That's fine. But always remember that other people have great ideas and inventions too, and that we can a learn a lot from those. See, you always have to remember the other side of the coin. You can decide to make your project confidential if you want too, that's fine. But then it will not be fair for you to walk around and see what's going on [on other people's computers]. So always remember that. The minute you say 'my project is confidential,' or 'I am only sharing information with my teacher, with Yasmin and with two other children,' then, remember it is not fair to walk around and look at other people' ideas.
Antonio:	You mean, if we mind only our own business, and if we do have a secret, we don't have to tell anybody?
Mrs. Mar:	You don't have to tell anybody; but don't expect that somebody else who learns something new is going tell you about it.
Antonio:	But they won't know if it is, if I already ahm . . .
Mrs. Mar:	They might find something different that could be beneficial to you. But if you are going to act like Mr. Snootie or Mr. Stinky and not share your ideas, why should they share it with you?! That's basically what we are saying here. So you learn something, and you will feel good enough about sharing

> it then somebody will share something new with you. [Looking at Leslie, saying:] You'll be the last one [to talk] and we have to go to the library.

Nora's initial reaction has to be understood in this context. Furthermore, it put her in a difficult social situation because Wanda was having a hard time accepting that she could not copy Nora's game: *"And then she started acting like she was crying and she was mad."*

In Wanda's fourth-grade class, students did copy Logo tricks and design ideas from each other. In fact, 1 week before this consulting session, Kafai helped Wanda to copy several shapes from Caroline's (fifth grader) computer, because she liked them so much. She only wanted to have them, not use them. Caroline did not mind. Through this consulting session Nora worked through this issue as well, and managed to solve it:

Idit: But I saw you working on something. So what did you work on?
Nora: It's the same, but it sounds different and it looks different.
Idit: So you decided to do almost the same but a slightly different music and slightly different colors. Right?
Nora: Yes.
Idit: But the same concept and the same idea. Did she agree to this at the end?
Nora: Yes.
Idit: So, now she is happy?
Nora: Yes. [smiling].
Idit: O.K. Now, how did you deal with it at that moment, when she was acting out. What did you do?
Nora: I just was looking to her, and then, she stopped and looked at me. I said to her 'What's wrong with you?' and she said: 'I want my game like yours.' And I said: 'So?' and she said: 'Hey, let's forget it then.' And I said: 'No. Then do it. That's okay, you can do it.'

DISCUSSION: WHY CONSULTING FOR LEARNING?

In this chapter, we continued to examine the interplay between social and individual processes in ISDP. We followed and observed a class of students over a period of one school year. This allowed us to situate their thinking and activities in a larger context. During our research, we chose to investigate and describe two features of social interaction that are quite contrary in terms of their openness: one feature we described was the flexible nature of collaborative processes in ISDP (Kafai & Harel, Chapter 5 in this volume), whereas this chapter focused on the function of the consulting process. From the outside, learning through consulting might project a more contrived picture. However, we found that interactions and themes chosen by the consultant-consultee pairs were rich and diverse. In that sense, even learning through consulting left the definition of goals up to the students. Special importance was given to the fact that conceptual models were generated by the students in their processes of interaction. In several instances, we were even able to trace how the consultants' questions and observations were related to their own past work and interviews.

Originally, we generated and implemented the idea of "consulting" with some reluctance. Our reluctance stemmed from the fact that we did not know what to expect from the students-consultants, who three months before the consulting sessions were quite happy to finish their projects and move on to a new project. Taking into consideration students' typical attitudes in relation to schoolwork and its routines, we were not sure whether they would be enthusiastic about revisiting an "old" finished project three months after its completion. And as much as we strongly believed in the intrinsic importance of the "consulting pedagogy" and thought of it as an important constructionist activity to experiment with in the context of ISDP, we were also ready to cancel the consulting sessions in the case of students' rejections or negative attitudes.

However, the students' attitudes surprised us. There was not one objection about becoming software-design consultants to the fourth graders. Observing and interacting with the students during the consulting sessions and the follow-up discussions did not lead to any misunderstanding: The students were engaged and enthusiastic about the consulting activities. Moreover, it seemed that the students were excited about helping the fourth graders, showing their own finished pieces of software, and revisiting and discussing (once again!) their own knowledge of fractions and Logo.

Our hypothesis is that, above all, students liked discussing their mathematical and design ideas within this playful context. On one hand, helping the younger children was familiar to most of the students who are used to help their young siblings at home. On the other hand, consulting was like a game to these students with roles and rules they usually don't play in school. It provided students with a different audience from the one they usually have. In regular school-like situations—by facing a teacher, who by definition seems to know everything—students might feel intimidated to announce their ideas or problems, discuss their theories and raise hypotheses. We found this not to be the case in this study.

The collection of nine episodes from the two consulting sessions shows an extensive range of questions the consultants were engaged in: about fractions, Logo programming, design, pedagogy, writing, and so on. They were free to choose what they wanted to work on. The observations and analyses of these two sessions provided multiple examples supporting the hypotheses that consulting can be a rich context for learning. We saw Alicia and Karen expressing their confusions about equality of fractions and the different frames of references used to understand fraction representations. We also saw Gerald, Matt, and Alicia learning about spelling, punctuation mistakes, and question phrasing.[2] In fact,

---

[2] The topics under discussion ranged from concerns regarding deep issues (e.g., representation of fractions or fractions equality) to concerns regarding surface issues (e.g., spelling and punctuations).

there were many more episodes during the two consulting sessions, as well as in the follow-up discussions, where students had a chance to make explicit their knowledge and understanding about Logo programming, software design, fractions knowledge, or teaching strategies. It is beyond the scope of this chapter to describe all of them here. Our point is that many questions and reflections were raised during this context *by the children,* in forms which made them learn a great deal, without perhaps, them noticing they were actually doing so.

Our questions of whether learning through consulting actually works and why have been touched upon at several points in this chapter. We will use these two consulting sessions as a springboard to tie our reflections to the social aspects of the ISDP environment.

Learning with Multiple Perspectives

The idea of learning through consulting has been created to provide learners with multiple ways of building knowledge in several contexts simultaneously. Our assumption is that, some times, learning takes place in a deeper and richer way when a child has the opportunity to approach a problem or explore a domain of knowledge from different angles (e.g., Perkins, 1986). ISDP builds on this very point of how the process of designing a piece of software about fractions can become an "object" with which to think about fractions—the "object" is conceived and seen from various perspectives: the perspective of the designer, the programmer, the child as a teacher, and the further target user (e.g., Harel, 1988, 1990).

Later, when students become software-design consultants, they gain an additional perspective. As consultants, they advise students on software design and fraction representations and deepen their own understanding. This is done by trying to understand the other designers' problems, debugging their programs, and improving their software's functionality. In particular, consulting fosters a different epistemological style of interaction with software in that the students can have a much greater *cognitive distance* to the piece of software than when they are engaged directly in their own production process. Like Collins, Brown, and Newman (1990), we think that an important part of building understanding is to have that distance. It gives another opportunity to reflect upon what one has done and what one knows. This "cognitive distance" first takes place during the software design process, when students think about teaching others or play with each other's pieces of software. But the social context of learning, as expressed in the consulting sessions, provided a motivational rationale for the students to make their thinking even more transparent to the consultees in order to be helpful, communicative, and productive—together. The process of making their implicit knowledge "explicit" for the consultees allows them to compare their own ideas/knowledge with that of the consultees.

To summarize, in the consulting situation the student consultants have a cognitive distance to the product which they are evaluating. This cognitive distance has a reflexive character, because it allows the consultant to see the fraction representations of others—which they could have constructed on their own. The consulting situation has a mirror-like character which can reflect both solutions and misunderstandings.

Often, this process generates "cognitive conflicts." The student-consultants are engaged in the process of comparing their own understandings (and conceptual framework) to what they see in the consultees' products of learning. Possible differences become clearer and allow the consultants to express their conflicts clearly (as, for example, Alicia and Karen did in the followup discussions). Therefore, through the effort of searching for and modeling solutions to the consultees, the consultants confront many cognitive conflicts. Thus, as much as they reactivate and apply "old" knowledge, they also gain "new" understandings about concepts they could not fully explore and acquire previously.

We propose the following model (Figure 6) as one that illustrates this context for learning that provides students with multiple perspectives on the same problems or domains of knowledge.

At the center of the model (the area of the overlap of the three small circles) we can see the product of ISDP—a piece of software. The piece of software itself is a product of an interdisciplinary, multifaceted process of learning (i.e., the integration of Logo programming with the developing of fraction representa-

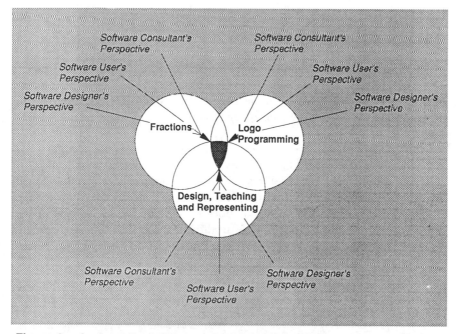

Figure 6. An interdisciplinary and multifaceted process of learning and knowing in ISDP in general, and in consulting activities in particular.

tions, designing, teaching, explaining, etc.). Whether it is the learner's own piece of software or another pupil's piece of software, the learner has multiple routes for evaluating the piece of software, which reflects his or her process and product of learning and knowing.[3]

The consulting situation in particular, and the social interactions in general, in the ISDP learning environment provide ground for this model. As the student software designers look to their neighbors' screens, and as they walk around in the computer pods and try out each others projects, they encounter multiple models of what other designers want to incorporate in their projects. In that sense we argue that both sides—allowing students to find their own perspective and giving them multiple opportunities and routes for learning and knowing—are essential.[4]

Wrestling with Ideas Through Play and Without Feeling at Risk

We believe that the time spent wrestling with different perspectives and ideas in the Incubation Phase is the place when students start to build their conceptual models of what their instructional piece of software will be and what they want to communicate about fractions. We described these different processes in three case studies (of Gerald, Amy and Stacy, and Jeannine). The consulting activity provided a similar place in which these students were allowed to revisit their knowledge of fractions and programming through play, without feeling at risk.

One characteristic of children's play is the ability to experiment with and transform reality. Through this process, children can assume control over given situations and select the important issues they want to deal with (e.g., Bruner, Jolly, & Sylva, 1976). We were interested in using this aspect of play in the context of consulting. By inviting learners to play the role of expert software designers and consultants, we encouraged deep thinking about fractions, programming, and design.

However, we draw a fine line between play situations and the playfulness of consulting: On one hand, the students were able to grasp the situation of "playing consultants" because it resembled other familiar play situations, such as playing doctor, lawyer, or secretary. On the other hand, in contrast to the imaginary aspects involved in playing doctor, consulting in the context of the present study required the principle of truthfulness: the students were actually asked to become consultants because of their real expertise gained by participat-

---

[3] We must take into account in this model that learning takes place over *a long period of time* and that students use *different styles* to accomplish this integration and to apply their multiple perspectives meaningfully (i.e., Harel, 1988, 1990).

[4] Some aspects of learning through multiple perspectives have also been applied to other learning activities, such as writing (e.g., Daiute & Dalton, 1989). Students can learn how to write by acting as readers, writers, editors, book designers, and publishers of their own or other students' writing.

ing in a similar project in the fall. This is in contrast to typical play situations, where students use the imaginary and not realistic quality of the situation to create adventure in their plots.

Learning While Playing Experts

Certain episodes in our current study lead us to believe that novices can successfully establish themselves in the role of an expert and greatly benefit from that role. Our observations closely follow the results of a recent study conducted by Daiute (1989), where she explores the interactions among fourth graders as they collaboratively work on writing text. Daiute found evidence that novices can also demonstrate or acquire expertise in summarizing, questioning, rephrasing, and so on, during their interactions with each other.

We used a nontraditional lens in our study: We did not ask what the novice learned from the interaction with the expert, but rather what the educational benefits were for the expert. We found that students in the role of experts can gain insights not previously available to them. Our claim is based on the idea that our nonexpert experts themselves developed their expert conceptual models; whereas in the "cognitive apprenticeship" approach (Collins, Brown, & Newman, 1990) this model is provided to the apprentice/learner by someone else—the expert/teacher. Our episodes showed us how students interact with their consultees on the basis of their own notions of what was appropriate and correct. Gerald (fifth grader), in his interaction with Howard (fourth grader), for example, had a clear model in his mind for what was an acceptable way of phrasing the feedback the software should provide its target users. In Alicia (fifth grader) reaction to Tracy's (fourth grader) screen we saw that Alicia definitely had a set of expectations for how a particular fraction representation had to look and how to phrase the instructional questions and explanations of the representations. When Alicia was confronted with a screen she found difficult to understand, there was a conflict in her mind. But since she was playing expert, she had to find ways to understand what was going on in her consultee's project. She had a responsibility. Her conceptual model (which was developed in her own software design process) needed to be expanded or transformed. Her role as a consultant or teacher required her to reflect upon the problem, express it in the classroom, and find ways to accomodate the situation.

One can ask, however, in what way these personal models constitute expert models in the traditional sense? We would agree that the student-consultants' models themselves are not like the real domain expert models in the formal sense; nevertheless, the students' *processes of searching for and constructing* these models are very similar to those of real experts. Also, these models are quite sophisticated in relation to the fourth graders' models. Our argument is that the students' benefit lies first and foremost in their own process of constructing these models. This process is the one that later allows them to speak with confidence about difficult matters. One example we saw was Alicia, who herself had problems dealing with the variables in her fractions software programming code, and who could, in the context of consulting, apply this knowledge and refer to the case as *"She* [the consultee] didn't know what the matter was!''

A Rich Role for the Teacher

In the follow-up discussions (after the consulting sessions), the student-consultants could replay their consulting experiences while trying to explicitly explain to others how they had made sense of the consulting situation.

In a further step, these follow-up discussions could provide a springboard for mathematical discourse not traditionally known in the school context. A student-consultant could raise many fascinating questions about what he or she did not understand. Then, as others joined in, they could describe similar experiences and raise new questions. We observed that students used the classroom as a place to brainstorm about mathematics and software design as experts would do in their domain. We can see these follow-up discussions in our consulting context as an example of how these discipline-like discussions can be initiated in the classroom by the students as well as by the teacher.

In our two consulting sessions, the students came back confused about what they had seen in the consultee's programs. By voicing that they do not understand the fraction representations, they offered ''gates'' for the teacher to discuss these problems in class. In consulting, the teacher's role is to provide room/space for discussion and to think about thinking with her students. As we have already described, the context of consulting confronts the student-consultant with an ill-defined mix of problems. Therefore, as a teacher and researcher, we could only speculate about the possible outcomes of the students' interaction in consulting. In the constructionist tradition, we believe that this is an appropriate model, with *students* bringing up the issues to discuss. The problems we raise here are, what can a teacher do with these issues? How can she or he facilitate the epistemological concerns that his or her students bring with them from their constructionist experiences? We are in the process of exploring these important questions.

CONCLUSIONS

We presented our explorations of the social and collaborative aspects of learning in ISDP to provide an example of how collaboration can be conceived in alternative ways. Our point is that ISDP can be seen as an exemplar environment for the social aspects of constructionist vision. ISDP facilitates the social pro-cesses supporting the individual construction of understanding in various domains. In this environment, which invites students in a multifaceted way to explore their own and other students' ideas, social interaction becomes a natural mode of being. Social skills involving giving and requesting help, about giving and receiving explanations and asking and answering questions, are tapped continuously.

This is in contrast to recent approaches in the collaborative literature (e.g., Johnson & Johnson, 1989; Sharon & Sharon, 1989) that request explicit training in collaborative skills. We do not train for collaboration. We do not teach consulting skills. We assume that the environment itself can create a context of a learning culture in which collaboration-though-the-air allows ideas to circulate and enter students' minds; an environment in which optional collaboration and flexible partnerships facilitate the students' construction of knowledge and of conceptual models; a culture in which brainstorming and consulting provide a context to travel through multiple perspectives while learning.

ACKNOWLEDGMENTS

We wish to thank the fifth-grade teacher Marquita Minot and her students, the fourth-grade teacher Gwen Gibson and her students, as well as the third-grade teacher Fran Streeter and her students for their collaboration with us and their great contribution to this work. Without them, this research would not have been possible. The research reported here was conducted at Project Headlight's Model School of the Future and was supported by the IBM Corporation (Grant # OSP95952), the National Science Foundation (Grant # 851031-0195), the McArthur Foundation (Grant # 874304), the LEGO Company, Fukatake, and the Apple Computer Inc. The preparation of this chapter was supported by the National Science Foundation (Grant # MDR 8751190) and Nintendo Inc., Japan. The ideas expressed here do not necessarily reflect the positions of the supporting agencies. We thank Seymour Papert, Ricki Goldman Segall, Uri Wilensky, Aaron Falbel, Mitchel Resnick, and Colette Daiute for their insightful comments on our work and on previous drafts of this chapter.

REFERENCES

Bruner, J., Jolly, A., & Sylva, K. (Eds.). (1976). *Play—Its role in development and evolution.* New York: Penguin Books.

Collins, A. S., Brown, J. S., & Newman, S. (1990). Cognitive apprenticeship: Teaching the craft of reading, writing, and mathematics. In L. B. Resnick (Ed.), *Cognition and instruction: Issues and agendas.* Hillsdale, NJ: Erlbaum.

Daiute, C., & Dalton, B. (1989, April). *Collaboration between children learning to write: Can novices be masters?* Paper presented at the American Educational Research Association, San Francisco, CA.

Harel, I. (1988). *Software design for learning: Children's construction of meaning for fractions and Logo programming.* Unpublished PhD Thesis, Media Laboratory, MIT, Cambridge, MA. (Available through Ablex, Spring 1991)

Harel, I. (1990). Children as software designers: A constructionist approach for learning mathematics. *The Journal of Mathematical Behavior, 9*(1), 3–93.

Johnson, D. W., & Johnson, R. (1989). Social skills for successful group work. *Educational Leadership, 47,* 29–31.

Kafai, Y., & Harel, I. (1990). Replicating the instructional software design project: A preliminary research project. In I. Harel (Ed.), *Constructionist learning: A 5th anniversary collection* (pp. 150–170). Cambridge, MA: MIT Media Lab.

Newman, D., Griffith, P., & Cole, M. (1989). *The construction zone: Working for cognitive change in school.* Cambridge: Cambridge University Press.

Palinscar, A. S., & Brown, A. L. (1984). Reciprocal teaching. *Cognition & Instruction, 1,* 117–175.

Perkins, D. N. (1986). *Knowledge as design.* Hillsdale, NJ: Erlbaum.

Posner, G. J., Strike, K. A., Hewson, P. W., & Gertzog, W. A. (1982). Accommodation of a scientific conception: Toward a theory of conceptual change. *Science Education, 66* (2), 211–227.

Sharan, Y., & Sharan, S. (1989). Group investigation expands cooperative learning. *Educational Leadership, 47,* 17–21.

Stephen Ocko Photography

LEGO/Logo: Learning Through and About Design.
Design projects can give mathematical and scientific concepts a new relevance in the minds of children.

7

LEGO/Logo:
Learning Through and About Design

Mitchel Resnick and Stephen Ocko*

INTRODUCTION

Problem solving can be divided, very roughly, into two categories: analysis and design. Analysis involves decomposing problems into simpler subproblems, typically with the help of formalized rules. Design is different in several ways. In design, the problem goals are typically ill structured; defining the problem is part of the designer's job. Moreover, there is a somewhat fuzzy sense of what it means to "solve" a design task. Rather than seeking *optimal* solutions, designers typically seek *satisficing* solutions (Simon, 1969)—that is, solutions that roughly satisfy a given set of constraints.

Design is important in almost all fields of human activity. Of course, an architect uses design skills when preparing a blueprint. But so does a writer when writing a report, and a manager when restructuring an organization. Given the central role of design in human activity, one would expect design to play an important role in school classrooms. But it doesn't. In the minds of many educators, the ill-structured nature of design activities makes them ill suited for the classroom. Design activities, they complain, are difficult to "manage" and to evaluate. As a result, students rarely get the opportunity to design, to build, to create, to invent.

This chapter explores the role of design in the classroom. In particular, it focuses on the use of LEGO/Logo, a computer-based robotics system that supports a variety of design activities. The chapter examines how students using

---

* Portions of this chapter previously appeared (under the title "LEGO, Logo, and Design") in *Children's Learning Environments* (vol. 5, no. 4), Winter 1988.

141

LEGO/Logo can learn important mathematical and scientific ideas *through* their design activities, while also learning *about* the design process itself.

LEGO/LOGO

LEGO/Logo links the world of LEGO construction with the world of the Logo programming. In using LEGO/Logo, children start by building machines out of LEGO pieces, using not only the traditional LEGO building bricks but newer pieces like gears, motors, and sensors. Then they connect their machines to a computer and write computer programs (using a modified version of the programming language Logo) to control the machines. For example, a child might build a LEGO merry-go-round, then write a Logo program that makes the merry-go-round turn three revolutions whenever a particular touch sensor is pressed.

LEGO/Lego builds on several decades of research on computers and children. In the late 1960s, Seymour Papert and colleagues at MIT developed Logo as a programming language for children (Papert, 1980). The most popular application of Logo involved the "floor turtle," a simple mechanical robot connected to the computer by a long "umbilical cord." Logo included special commands like FORWARD, BACK, LEFT, and RIGHT to control the floor turtle. For example, children would type FORWARD 50 to make the turtle move forward by 50 "turtle steps," or RIGHT 90 to make the turtle turn right through 90 degrees.

With the advent of personal computers, the Logo community shifted its focus to "screen turtles." With personal computers, children still use commands like FORWARD and RIGHT, but these commands control small graphic images on the computer screen, not actual mechanical robots. Screen turtles are much faster and more accurate than floor turtles, and thus allow children to create more complex graphic effects.

LEGO/Logo brings the turtle back off the screen, but with several important differences from the early days of the floor turtle. First of all, LEGO/Logo users are not given ready-made mechanical objects; they build their own machines before programming them. Second, children are not restricted to turtles. Children have used LEGO/Logo to build a wide assortment of creative machines. A few examples: a programmable pop-up toaster, a "chocolate-carob factory" (inspired by the Willy Wonka children's stories), a machine that sorts LEGO bricks according to their lengths, and an "ejection bed" that automatically tosses its occupant onto the floor when the sun shines through the window in the morning. Working on projects like these, children experiment with many different types of design: structural design, mechanical design, software design. LEGO/Logo might be viewed as a "multimedia construction kit," allowing students to build and create in several different (though interconnected) media.

The LEGO/Logo system includes new types of LEGO blocks for building machines, and new types of "Logo blocks" for building programs. On the LEGO side, there is an assortment of gears, pulleys, wheels, motors, lights, and sensors. For example, there are optosensors that report when they detect changes in the level of light, and touch sensors that report when they are pressed. The computer communicates with LEGO devices through a custom-designed interface box, which connects to a slot card in the computer. Information flows through the interface box in both directions: children can send commands to LEGO motors and lights, and receive status information from LEGO sensors.

As its programming language, LEGO/Logo uses an expanded version of Logo. Students can use any of the traditional Logo commands and control structures (such as FORWARD, RIGHT, IF, and REPEAT), plus any of 20 new commands added specially for the LEGO environment. The new commands include words like ON and OFF for controlling LEGO motors and lights, and words like SENSOR? for getting information from LEGO sensors.

Just as students can build increasingly complex machines by snapping together LEGO bricks, they can build increasingly complex computer programs by "snapping together" Logo commands. Imagine, for example, a LEGO car with a touch sensor on the front. A student can write a program called CAR that turns the car on, waits until the car bumps into something, then turns it off. The program would look like this:

```
to car
on
waituntil [sensor?]
off
end
```

When we work with students, we attempt to create an Inventor's Workshop environment. We show students copies of actual patent drawings by famous (and some not-so-famous) inventors, and we encourage them to keep Inventor's Notebooks to document their own designs. In some classes, we have established a system of "LEGO/Logo patents," awarded to students who document their "inventions" with drawings and descriptions.

Students use their Inventor's Notebooks in many different ways (see Figure 1). Some students make preliminary sketches of their machines. Others make careful mechanical drawings of their constructions and write elaborate instructions on how to use the machines. Still other students use their notebooks to write stories about their machines. Indeed, we find that LEGO/Logo is a rich environment, not only for math, science, and design, but also for language arts, since students are often interested in writing about the machines that they have built.

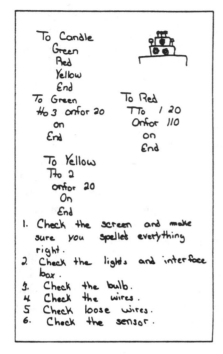

Figure 1. Pages from Inventor's Notebooks.

LEARNING THROUGH DESIGN

LEGO/Logo activities can be organized in many different ways. For example, a teacher could tell each student in the class to build a LEGO car, according to particular "building instructions." Then the teacher could tell the students to perform a prescribed set of experiments on the car. Certainly, the students would learn something. But such a "recipe-based" approach runs counter to the ideas that informed the development of LEGO/Logo.

In our experience, design activities have the greatest educational value when students are given the freedom to create things that are meaningful to themselves (or others around them). In such situations, students approach their work with a sense of caring and interest that is missing in most school activities. As a result, students are more likely to explore, and to make deep "connections" with, the mathematical and scientific concepts that underlie the activities. This idea is at the core of Papert's theory of *constructionism* (Papert, 1986).

Our work with LEGO/Logo supports this idea. LEGO/Logo projects typically involve a variety of mathematical or scientific concepts—such as fractions, friction, and mechanical advantage. In many cases, the students have previously "learned" these concepts in the classroom. But students seem to gain a deeper understanding when the concepts are embedded in meaningful design activities.

Particularly striking are the experiences of students who have been unsuccessful in traditional math and science activities. Quite a few of these students thrive in the LEGO/Logo environment. These students often have strong design and mechanical skills, but many have been frustrated by the analysis-centered approach of traditional math and science classes. As a result, their teachers typically view them (and they typically view themselves) as poor learners. In some cases, LEGO/Logo experiences have had a profound effect on how these students view themselves as learners (and on their subsequent performance in other classroom activities).

Example 1: Mathematics through design. George, a third-grade student, began his LEGO/Logo work by building a simple LEGO car. First, he connected the car's motor to a battery box and watched the car roll forward. Next, he connected the motor to the computer and began experimenting with some of the new Logo commands. We explained the commands ON, OFF, ONFOR (which takes an input and turns on the motor for a designated amount of time), and RD (for reverse direction). After a while, George put several commands together in the following expression: REPEAT 4 [ONFOR 20 RD]

When George executed this expression, the computer turned on the motor for two seconds (ONFOR 20), reversed the direction of the motor (RD), then repeated those commands three more times. The result: the car moved forward and back, then again forward and back, completing two forward-back cycles.

Next, George changed the numerical input to REPEAT. He tried REPEAT 3 and REPEAT 6 and REPEAT 7. After this experimentation, George noticed a pattern:

When I use an even number, the car ends up where it began. When I use an odd number, it ends up away [from where it started].

George paused for a moment and then added:

So that's why there are even and odd numbers!

Clearly, George had previously learned about even and odd numbers in the classroom. But George's experimentation with the LEGO car provided him with a new (and more personally relevant) representation of the concept. Moreover, the LEGO activity allowed George to *relate* to numbers in a new way: he *played* with the ideas of even and odd. This new relationship with even and odd numbers helped George develop a new level of understanding.

Example 2: Science through design.

In some classes, we suggest that students begin their LEGO/Logo work by building motorless "soap box derby" cars. We set up a ramp in the classroom, and students race their cars down the ramp. Some students see a challenge: they want to make their cars go as fast and as far as possible. They measure how far their cars go beyond the bottom of the ramp, then design their cars to try to make them go farther.

As students discuss why some cars go further than others, we encourage students to look for places where "pieces are rubbing together" (for example, gears rubbing against other gears, or axles rubbing against the girders that support them). Before long, discussions about *friction* become part of the standard discourse between us and the students—and, more importantly, among the students themselves. In one class, a student removed some pieces from his car, explaining (correctly) that "more weight makes things tighter, you know, more friction." Other students give similar explanations. Even after students finish working on their cars and start designing other LEGO/Logo projects, many of them continue to talk about friction in describing and analyzing the motions of their new machines.

As with even and odd numbers, friction is not a new concept for these students. But the LEGO/Logo activities provide a more meaningful context for students to talk about and think about friction. Students *want* to make their cars go farther, so friction assumes a new relevance. In short, students *care* about friction. At first, students' models of friction are rather fragile, and their explanations are often misleading. But as they work on their LEGO/Logo projects (and participate in a "culture" where friction is a standard part of the discourse), students gradually construct richer models of how friction influences the motions of their machines.

diSessa (1986) describes science learning as a *re-experiencing* process. Children do not learn a new concept when they are taught the definition. Rather, they must experience and re-experience the concept in different contexts. Through these experiences, children gradually reorganize their intuitions into more complete models. In this case, students, by exploring the motions of LEGO/Logo machines, seem to develop richer and more robust models of friction.

LEARNING ABOUT DESIGN

While working on LEGO/Logo design projects, students can learn not only about mathematical and scientific ideas, but about the process of design itself. In particular, students can learn important *heuristics,* or rules-of-thumb, for dealing with design tasks. Such heuristics are particularly important when working in complex design environments like LEGO/Logo, in which the designer needs to consider several different interrelated design tasks.

As an example, consider the "vibrating walker" developed by Nicky, a fourth-grade student at a Boston public elementary school. Nicky started by building a car out of LEGO. After racing the car down a ramp several times, Nicky added a motor to the car and connected it to the computer. When he turned on the motor, the car moved forward a bit—but the motor fell off the body of the car and began vibrating across the table.

Rather than trying to fix this bug (or giving up, since his car had "failed"), Nicky became intrigued with the vibration of the motor. He began to wonder whether he might be able to use the vibrations to power a vehicle. In effect, he decided to turn the vibrations from a bug into a feature.

Nicky mounted the motor on a platform atop four "legs" (LEGO axles) (see Figure 2). After some experimentation, Nicky realized that he needed some way to amplify the motor vibrations. To do that, he drew upon some personal experiences. Nicky enjoyed riding a skateboard, and he remembered that swinging his arms gave him an extra "push" on the skateboard. He figured that a swinging arm might accentuate the vibrations of the motor as well. So Nicky connected two LEGO axles with a hinged joint to create an "arm." Then, he placed a gear on the motor and inserted the arm slightly off-center in the gear. As the gear turned, the arm whipped around—and amplified the motor vibrations, just as Nicky had hoped.

In fact, the system vibrated so strongly that it frequently tipped over. A classmate suggested that Nicky create a more stable base by placing a LEGO tire horizontally at the bottom of each of the legs. Nicky made the revision, and his "vibrating walker" worked perfectly. In fact, Nicky was even able to steer the walker. When the motor turned in one direction, the walker vibrated forward and

Figure 2.   Nicky's Walker.

to the right. When the motor turned in the other direction, the walker vibrated forward and to the left.

Next, Nicky set out to make the walker follow a black line on the table top. He attached a LEGO light sensor (pointing down) at the front of the walker. When the walker passed over a black line, the sensor reported TRUE. With a bit of assistance from us, Nicky wrote the following program to make the walker follow the line. (We have ''cleaned up'' Nicky's code to make the program more readable.)

```
to follow
look-for-line
go-past-line
reverse-direction
follow
end

to look-for-line
waituntil [floor-color = "black]
end

to go-past-line
waituntil [floor-color = "white]
end

to floor-color
if sensor? [output "black]
if not sensor? [output "white]
end
```

When the FOLLOW procedure is executed, the walker veers in one direction until it ''finds'' the line, continues in that direction until it passes over the line, then reverses the direction of its motor and repeats the process. As a result, the walker weaves back and forth over the line, making a bit of forward progress with each cycle.

What did Nicky learn through this project? For one thing, he gained an introductory understanding of some specific engineering concepts. In building the walker, Nicky ended up with an appreciation for both the constructive uses and the destructive potential of vibration in mechanical systems. And in programming the walker to follow the line, Nicky explored basic ideas of feedback and control. Nicky used these same ideas in a later project, when he programmed a LEGO ''turtle'' to find its way out of a large cardboard box.

Equally important, Nicky gained a sense of the *process* of design. In building the walker, Nicky used an impressive array of *design heuristics*. Among Nicky's heuristics:

- *Take advantage of the unexpected.* When the motor fell off of his car, Nicky did not see it as a sign of failure. He saw it as an opportunity. He was on the lookout for unexpected events, and took advantage of them when they happened.
- *Use personal experience as a guide.* When Nicky needed to amplify the vibrations of the motor, he relied on knowledge of his own experiences and body movements.
- *Try using materials in new ways.* The designers of LEGO bricks probably did not envision LEGO axles used as arms or legs. Nor did they imagine that LEGO wheels would be turned 90 degrees and used as feet. But Nicky did not feel constrained by standard usage.
- *Collaborate with others.* When the vibrations kept tipping the walker over, Nicky was uncertain how to solve the problem. So he consulted with a classmate who had a reputation for mechanical-design skills. The collaboration was a success. Such collaborative efforts are particularly important in multidisciplinary activities like LEGO/Logo.

In discussing LEGO/Logo projects, we encourage students to think and talk explicitly about such design heuristics. In many cases, we believe that LEGO/ Logo activities have helped students develop a more principled approach to design and invention.

BEYOND HANDS-ON

What makes LEGO/Logo successful as a design environment (and as a learning environment)? Certainly, the materials (LEGO bricks and Logo software) are part of the answer. But only part of the answer. Good tools and materials are necessary but not sufficient for effective design (and effective learning). Our experiences with LEGO/Logo have highlighted several other key ingredients for creating rich design environments for children:

- *Put children in control.* In many hands-on activities in the classroom, students recreate someone else's experiment. Our LEGO/Logo classes have been most successful when children formulate their own designs and experiments, and work on projects that they care about personally.
- *Offer multiple paths to learning.* Not everyone wants to start by building a car. It is important to allow students to approach design projects from different directions and different perspectives. With LEGO/Logo, some students start with mechanical design, others with programming, still others with architectural aesthetics. Some build moving vehicles, others build moving sculptures. But providing multiple paths does not mean that each student gets

"stuck" in his or her own niche. In fact, we have found that many students use their initial "regions of comfort" as a foundation from which to explore other areas—areas that might have seemed intimidating in isolation.

* *Encourage a sense of community.* In LEGO/Logo workshops, we encourage groups to share ideas, designs, and actual constructions—and to critique one another's designs. In this way, students combine "hands-on" activities with what Seymour Papert has termed "heads-in" activities. Moreover, students get a deeper sense of the way in which real designers go about their work, as part of a community of designers.

Implementing these strategies is not easy. There are many unanswered questions—such as how to help students "break away" from their initial "regions of comfort." And coordinating open-ended design activities is a challenge for any teacher. Indeed, organizing an inventor's workshop is far more difficult than delivering a lecture on mechanical advantage or developing a step-by-step hands-on lesson. As Dewey (1938) noted more than a half-century ago (in words that still ring true today): "The road of the new education is not an easier one to follow than the old road but a more strenuous and difficult one." But it is a road well worth taking.

ACKNOWLEDGMENTS

Many of the ideas in this chapter are based on collaboration with Seymour Papert. We are grateful to David Cavallo for sharing transcripts of his LEGO/Logo work with children. Edith Ackermann, Idit Harel, Fred Martin, and Andee Rubin provided helpful comments on earlier drafts of this chapter.

Our research on LEGO/Logo is supported by grants from the LEGO Group and from the National Science Foundation (Grants 851031-0195, MDR-8751190, and TPE-8850449). LEGO Systems, Inc. markets a version of LEGO/Logo under the product name *LEGO TC logo*.

REFERENCES

Dewey, J. (1938). *Experience and education*. New York: Macmillan.

diSessa, A. (1986). Artificial worlds and real experience. *Instructional Science, 14*, 207–227.

Papert, S. (1980). *Mindstorms: Children, computers, and powerful ideas*. New York: Basic Books.

Papert, S. (1986). *Constructionism: A new opportunity for elementary science education*. Proposal to the National Science Foundation.

Resnick, M., Ocko, S., & Papert, S. (1988). LEGO, Logo, and design. *Children's Environments Quarterly, 5*(4), 14–18.

Simon, H. (1969). *The sciences of the artificial*. Cambridge, MA: MIT Press.

8

Xylophones, Hamsters, and Fireworks:
The Role of Diversity in Constructionist Activities

Mitchel Resnick*

INTRODUCTION

There is growing enthusiasm for "hands-on" approaches to education. Increasingly, educators agree that learning should be an active process, with students participating in hands-on experiments and explorations, not just sitting back and listening to the teacher.

Unfortunately, "hands-on" alone is not enough. Too many hands-on activities involve little more than following a recipe. In many hands-on activities, students are asked to re-create someone else's experiment. Such activities might be hands-on, but they are heads-out. Students are unlikely to become engaged in or inspired by activities where the goals and results are defined by someone else.

The Constructionist approach to education (Papert, 1986) goes beyond typical hands-on activities in that it aims to give children more control over finding and defining the problems they work on. Constructionism places a high priority on *making projects personal*. It asserts that students (and teachers) who make *personal connections* with their projects invariably do the most creative work—and learn the most from their experiences.

But the goal of "making projects personal" is not necessarily easy to achieve. It raises difficult questions: In what types of environments are students and teachers most likely to make personal connections with their projects? How can classroom activities be organized to insure that students and teachers care about their projects in a deep and personal way?

This paper examines these questions in one particular context: a workshop introducing teachers to LEGO/Logo (Resnick, Ocko, & Papert, 1988). Using

* An earlier version of this article appeared (under the title "Making Projects Personal: Reflections on a LEGO/Logo Workshop") in *Logo Exchange* (vol. 8, no. 5), Jan. 1990.

sample projects from the workshop, it explores the factors that led to a flourishing of personally meaningful projects.

SAMPLES FROM A WORKSHOP

The Science and Whole Learning (SWL) workshop was organized in the summer of 1989 by Seymour Papert's Epistemology and Learning Group at the MIT Media Lab. The goal of the 3-week workshop was to help teachers explore new ways of thinking about and learning about science. Roughly 60 teachers, mostly from Boston-area schools, attended the workshop.

The first 3 days of the workshop served as an introductory period. During this time, the teachers were introduced to LogoWriter and LEGO/Logo—two "basic tools" that they would be using throughout the workshop (and throughout the following school year). Each teacher spent 2 days working with LogoWriter and 1 day with LEGO/Logo.

For the remaining 12 days of the workshop, teachers attended special-interest sessions and worked on "personal projects" of their own choosing. An entire room was set aside for teachers working on LEGO/Logo projects. Three of us from MIT (Steve Ocko, Natalie Rusk, and myself) supported the teachers as they worked on their projects. In addition, Eadie Adamson (a New York City teacher) and Cathy Helgoe (of LEGO Systems, Inc.) offered a miniworkshop on "Kinetic Art" using LEGO/Logo. The main goal of this activity was to make teachers consider the creative and aesthetic aspects of machines and structures. Eadie and Cathy brought a variety of art materials (colored papers, pipe cleaners, etc.) to the workshop, and they showed how these materials could be combined with LEGO mechanisms to create moving sculptures.

Roughly a dozen teachers decided to make LEGO/Logo the focus of their personal projects. Following are examples of the teachers' projects.

Xyloman. Carole Carter works as a music teacher at the Brimmer and May School, so it is not that surprising that she adopted a musical theme for her LEGO/Logo project. On the first day of the workshop, she decided that she would like to build a LEGO robot that plays the xylophone. The next day, she brought in a toy xylophone from home, and she began to build her robot, Eventually, Carole built a robot with two motors: one motor controlled the robot's arm, making it hit the keys on the xylophone; the other motor made the robot rotate so that it could hit different keys. She named the robot "Xyloman."

Next, Carole began writing computer programs to make Xyloman play sequences of notes. The programs used input from an optosensor to control the rotation of the robot. The sensing mechanism wasn't very accurate, so the robot had difficulties when successive notes were far apart. So Carole carefully chose songs in which the notes were close together. By the end of the workshop, the machine could play several different songs. Carole was clearly pleased by her machine's performance, but she added: "I haven't taught it how to bow yet."

Carousel. Before the workshop, Natalie Isbitsky had never built anything out of LEGO bricks. But early in the workshop, she became obsessed with an idea: She wanted to build a LEGO carousel like the one she had ridden as a little girl at Revere Beach near Boston. Building a simple carousel proved relatively easy. But Natalie, a teacher at the Donald McKay School, wasn't satisfied. She wanted the horses to go up and down as the carousel rotated—just as they had on the carousel at Revere Beach. Natalie struggled with this idea, but she finally developed a mechanism that worked. She found a way to put a gear on the vertical axle so that the gear would remain stationary as the carousel turned. Then she connected the horses to a set of gears positioned around (and at right angles to) the stationary central gear. As the carousel turned, these gears rotated around the stationary central gear—and made the horses go up and down.

Once the mechanism was working, Natalie wrote a computer program that played the song *And the Band Played On* while the carousel rotated. She also decorated the carousel with some non LEGO art materials—an idea she got from attending the Kinetic Art miniworkshop. At the end, Natalie reflected on her experiences: "Learning has always been a struggle for me. I'm amazed at how much I've learned during the past 3 weeks. At the start of the workshop, I didn't know how I would fill the time from 9 to 4. Now, there is never enough time in the day." She added: "My students are really reluctant to try new things. I can relate to that. I didn't know anything about Logo or music, and I felt uncomfortable about science. Now when I go back to school, I'll work differently with the students and give them more opportunities to try things. Letting the students do things hands-on will make them feel more engaged and make learning more personal."

Pole-balancing machine. In the orientation session for the workshop, Seymour Papert led the teachers in an experiment. He asked the teachers to try to balance a yardstick vertically on their hands. Then he asked them to try to balance a pencil the same way. This experiment led to a discussion: Why is a yardstick easier to balance than a pencil? At one point, Seymour wondered aloud whether it would be possible to build a LEGO machine that could balance a pole on its "hand."

Kip Perkins of the Atrium School took up the challenge. He built a LEGO cart that moved along racks, and he placed a 1.5-meter wooden pole on top of the cart. He used just a single sensor for feedback: the sensor indicated which direction the pole was leaning. Kip "cheated" a bit to make the problem easier—he constrained the pole so that it could move in only one dimension, and he put a wing at the top of the pole to slow its motion. Still, many of us felt that Kip would not be able to make the machine work. We were wrong. By the end of the workshop, Kip's machine was reliably balancing the pole. His program was remarkably simple: It simply made the cart move (with a slight time delay) in the direction that the pole was leaning.

Fireworks machine. The Sunday before the workshop began, Irene Hall went to watch the annual July 4 fireworks along the Charles River in Boston. So, when she sat down to work on a LogoWriter program on the first day of the workshop, she decided to draw fireworks on the screen. The next day, at the introductory LEGO/Logo workshop, Irene (who teaches at the Leonard School) decided to continue with the same theme and build a fireworks machine.

Irene wasn't sure how to build a mechanism for throwing the fireworks, so she consulted the book *The Way Things Work* by David Macauley. She tried several different mechanisms: a spring, a cam, and finally a catapult. Irene used the catapult mechanism to throw glitter into the air—and ultimately onto a paper that had been covered with glue. The result was an interesting pattern of glitter glued to the paper. By the end of the workshop, Irene had developed a complete multimedia presentation. While the Logo turtle drew fireworks on the screen, the computer played the *William Tell Overture* and the LEGO machine threw glitter into the air. Said Irene: "I followed a path that just developed. That's why I learned so much. This exploration feels like everything learning should be about."

International drawbridge. Ida Fallows, one of three Costa Rican teachers attending the workshop, had never seen a drawbridge before coming to Boston for the workshop. So Ida had no doubt what she wanted to do for her LEGO/Logo project. She looked through various LEGO building instructions until she found a mechanism that reminded her of the drawbridge. She built the mechanism according to the LEGO plans, then added some extra features to make it look more like the drawbridge she had seen.

When Ida was about to start programming her drawbridge, she discovered that another teacher, Steve Wachman of the Brimmer and May School, had been building a LEGO boat with motorized paddle wheels. So Ida and Steve decided to work together. Steve found a rolling cart in another lab and filled it with water. (As he put it: "I borrowed an ocean.") They put the boat and bridge into the water, added a light and optosensor, then wrote a program to coordinate the whole system. Whenever the boat passed in front of the optosensor, the drawbridge opened and gave the boat a chance to pass through. Finally, Ida added a song to the computer program: As the drawbridge opened, the computer played a Costa Rican children's song about a boat that couldn't navigate.

Mardi Gras. The Kinetic Art workshop captured the imaginations of several teachers, including Sharon Beck of the Ellis School. Sharon wanted to build something that would evoke the carnival-like atmosphere of the annual Mardi Gras celebration in New Orleans. She combined LEGO motors and gears with a variety of non-LEGO materials, including pipe cleaners and flashy colored paper with optical patterns. One LEGO motor catapulted confetti into the air while also controlling the dance of a pipe-cleaner turtle. A second motor spun a dazzling array of optical patterns. With both motors on, the LEGO machine turned into a lively and colorful work of art. Another teacher told Sharon: "We'll be thinking of you at Mardi Gras time."

LEGO/Logo zoo. For a long time, Steve Ocko and I have talked about building a LEGO/Logo zoo, using LEGO sensors to monitor animal activity. During the workshop, we decided to give it a try. We bought a hamster and brought it into the lab. By coincidence, one of the teachers, Julie Fine of the Agassiz School, had also brought her hamster to the workshop. Julie planned to do a video analysis of her hamster running. After talking with us, she decided to work on the LEGO/Logo zoo as well. We attached optosensors to the exercise wheels in each of the hamster cages, and we wrote a program to keep track of how far (how many revolutions) each hamster ran every 10 minutes.

The first day, the hamsters slept all day. The program reported a long list of zeros. We were pretty frustrated. But when we came back to the lab the next morning, the computer showed that there had been lots of activity overnight. One hamster ran several hundred revolutions between 8:00 and 10:00 pm. The other hamster ran more than 1,000 revolutions between 9:00 pm and midnight. We did a quick calculation and found that the hamster had run nearly a quarter mile! After midnight, both hamsters apparently went back to sleep. We continued to monitor the hamsters' activity for the next week. The hamsters ran exclusively at night, usually in 2-hour bursts of activity. But our results weren't entirely reliable: Several nights, one of the hamsters gnawed through the LEGO wires.

Cybernetic house. At one of the tutorials during the workshop, I showed how analog sensors could be used in connection with LEGO/Logo. We borrowed some analog light and temperature sensors from the Technical Education Research Centers (TERC) in Cambridge. These sensors, which plug into the game port of the computer, can be read with the *paddle* command in the LEGO/Logo software. I suggested that someone might be interested in building a "cybernetic house"—that is, a house that regulates its own internal conditions.

Dave Mellen, who teaches at the Kingwood Oxford School, decided to work on the cybernetic house as his project. He and his son built a house out of LEGO bricks, and then Dave started adding sensors. He installed the TERC temperature sensor in the wall of the house and built a fan to cool the house when necessary. The TERC light sensor wasn't responsive over the relevant range, so Dave bought a different light sensor at Radio Shack and added it to the house. Dave's program continually checked the two sensors and then took the necessary actions. If the light intensity dropped below a certain threshold, it would turn on LEGO lights inside the house. If the temperature rose, it would turn on the LEGO fan. Dave saw this as just the beginning: with more sensors and a more complex program, the house could behave almost like a living organism.

REFLECTIONS: THE ROLE OF DIVERSITY

It is clear that these projects were rich in *personal meaning* for the teachers. For Costa Rican teacher Ida Fallows, who had recently seen her first drawbridge, the LEGO drawbridge symbolized her visit to the United States. For Natalie Isbitsky, the LEGO carousel symbolized her childhood. The carousel at Revere Beach, where Natalie had ridden as a child, is no longer there. Building a LEGO/Logo carousel was, in Natalie's words, "a way of regaining my youth."

What led to such a flourishing of personally meaningful projects? The answer, I believe, revolves around the idea of *diversity*. The environment in our LEGO/Logo workshop encouraged and promoted diversity in several ways. The environment encouraged a diversity of project themes, a diversity of working styles, and a diversity of entry paths.

Diversity of project themes. Question: What do a xylophone-playing robot, a sensor-monitored hamster cage, a multimedia fireworks display, and a self-regulating house have in common? Answer: Not much. But that is exactly the point. None of the projects in the workshop was "typical." Each was special in its own way.

To a certain extent, this diversity of project themes was a result of the tools we used. Both LEGO and Logo are open-ended construction sets: Each can be used in many different ways. But tools alone do not lead to diversity. In organizing the workshop, we made diversity of projects an explicit goal. We didn't want the teachers to have preconceived notions of what LEGO/Logo projects *should* look like. We encouraged them to explore the boundaries of LEGO and Logo, to try to use the materials in new ways. Of course, we provided models and examples to give teachers a sense of what might be possible. We even suggested that, in the beginning, they might want to try some of the LEGO building instructions to get a "feel" for the LEGO materials. But we encouraged the teachers not to feel constrained in choosing themes for their longer term projects. We wanted the teachers to be free to develop projects that were personally meaningful to them.

Diversity of working styles. Different people work in different ways. Some people like to develop a plan then execute it; others like to tinker with the materials, letting a plan emerge as they work. Some people like to work in groups; others like to work alone. If a workshop (or a classroom) encourages and supports only some of these styles, some people will be left out. Only if a workshop respects and supports a diversity of working styles will participants feel comfortable enough to work on personally meaningful projects.

Consider, for example, the question of collaborative vs. individual work. LEGO/Logo can serve as an ideal environment for people to work together as a team. Consider a group of people collaborating on a LEGO/Logo factory. One approach is for each person to build an individual machine, then to link all of the machines together. Another approach is for one person to work on building the machines while another works on the programming. The value of collaboration was clear in the drawbridge project that Ida Fallows and Steve Wachman worked on together. The LEGO/Logo zoo can also be viewed as a collaboration— between the "teachers" (Steve and me) and the "student" (Julie Fine). Such teacher–student collaborations (regrettably rare in most school classrooms) can be rich learning experiences for both sides.

But for all the benefits of collaboration, people sometimes need to work alone. Consider the case of Natalie Isbitsky. For the first several days of the SWL workshop, Natalie collaborated with another teacher in building a conveyor belt. That was a good learning experience, but Natalie didn't really get involved in the LEGO/Logo activity until she began working on the carousel. She felt much more of a personal stake in the carousel. She had a clear and compelling vision of what she wanted to do. It was *her* project.

Carole Carter went through a similar progression. From the very start of the workshop, she knew that she wanted to build a robot to play the xylophone. For the first few days, two other teachers worked with Carole on the project. The other teachers suggested that they put a rack on the xylophone, so that the xylophone could move back and forth. Carole preferred to make the robot, not the xylophone, move. (After all, that's the way it is in the real world.) Being a good team member, Carole agreed to put the xylophone on a rack, but inside she was feeling frustrated. After a few days, the other teachers lost interest in the project. Carole was relieved. She took the rack off of the xylophone and continued with the project as she had originally envisioned it.

Diversity of entry paths. The books accompanying the LEGO/Logo kit present a sequence of introductory activities involving LEGO cars and traffic lights. For some students and some teachers, these activities provide a good introduction to LEGO building and Logo programming. But these activities represent only one of many possible entry paths for LEGO/Logo. Cars and traffic lights do not appeal to all teachers or all students. Alternate entry paths are needed to capture the imaginations of other teachers and students.

Kinetic Art represents one alternative. During the SWL workshop, about a dozen teachers worked on some sort of Kinetic Art project. For several of these teachers, Kinetic Art fundamentally changed the way they viewed LEGO/Logo. These teachers had started out by building LEGO cars or other "standard" LEGO machines. But it wasn't until they worked on Kinetic art projects that they became excited about LEGO/Logo. Kinetic Art resonated with these teachers. Finally, they had something that they really *wanted* to make.

The Kinetic Art activity could help address what some people see as a gender bias in the introductory LEGO/Logo activities involving cars and traffic lights. Although both boys and girls have participated enthusiastically in these activities, some people worry that the boys feel a stronger personal involvement in the car-related activities. They worry that the girls, while participating, aren't as emotionally involved in the projects and thus do not have as rich a learning experience.

Alternative entry paths for LEGO/Logo can help ease this problem. The teachers who built Kinetic Art sculptures at the SWL workshop were just as sophisticated in their use of LEGO materials as anyone else. In short, Kinetic Art seems like a excellent alternative approach for introducing LEGO/Logo. That is not to say the Kinetic Art is *the* right approach for everyone. There is no one "right approach." For the future, we need to develop more alternative paths, so that more teachers (and children) can make deep personal connections with LEGO/Logo.

ACKNOWLEDGMENTS

Most of all, I would like to thank all of the teachers who participated in the Science and Learning Workshop. I would also like to thank the Epistemology and Learning Group members (particularly Steve Ocko and Natalie Rusk) who supported LEGO/Logo activities during the workshop. Funding for our work with LEGO/Logo has been provided by the LEGO Group and the National Science Foundation (Grants 851031-0195, MDR-8751190, and TPE-8850449).

REFERENCES

Papert, S. (1986). *Constructionism: A new opportunity for Elementary Science education.* A proposal to the National Science Foundation.

Resnick, M. (1990). Making projects personal: Reflections on a LEGO/Logo workshop. *Logo Exchange, 8*(5), 15–19.

Resnick, M., Ocko, S. & Papert, S. (1988). LEGO, Logo, and design. *Children's Environments Quarterly, 5*(4), 14–18.

Stephen Ocko Photography

In some cases, students' or teachers' experiences with LEGO/Logo seemed to have a profound effect on their images of themselves as learners.

PART III

THINKING ABOUT THINKING:
EPISTEMOLOGICAL STYLES IN CONSTRUCTIONIST LEARNING

_____**9**

Epistemological Pluralism
and the Revaluation of the Concrete

Sherry Turkle and Seymour Papert*

EPISTEMOLOGICAL PLURALISM

The concerns that fuel the discussion of women and computers are best served by talking about more than women and more than computers. Women's access to science and engineering has historically been blocked by prejudice and discrimination. Here we address sources of exclusion determined, not by rules that keep women out, but by ways of thinking that make them reluctant to join in. Our central thesis is that equal access to even the most basic elements of computation requires an epistemological pluralism, accepting the validity of multiple ways of knowing and thinking.

With this assertion we find ourselves at the meeting point of three epistemological challenges to the hegemony of the abstract, formal, and logical as the privileged canon in scientific thought. The first of these challenges comes from within feminist scholarship. Here, the canonical style, abstract and rule driven, is associated with power and elitism, and with the social construction of science and objectivity as male.[1]

_____

*A similar version of this chapter appeared in *SIGNS: Journal of Women in Culture and Society,* Autumn 1990, Vol. 16 (1).

[1] Edited collections include Bleir (1986) and Harding and Hintikka (1983). An overview that highlights many of the issues we deal with in this essay is provided by Elizabeth Fee (in Bleir, 1986).

In this chapter we situate our position by focusing on two writers, Carol Gilligan and Evelyn Fox Keller. Gilligan, with her emphasis on moral discourse, might seem out of place in a discussion of noncanonical approaches to science and technology. But here we argue that key issues in the critique of science are not about *scientific* reasoning but about *reasoning*. Juxtaposing moral and computational reasoning helps us make this point. In addition, Gilligan's critical relationship to the theories of Lawrence Kohlberg is analogous to our own critical relationship to Piaget's work. We emphasize Keller because her work underscores, as does ours, the importance of relationships with objects in the development of noncanonical styles. Using Gilligan and Keller as a contrasting pair allows us to highlight two different dimensions of what we shall call the "soft" approach to science. See Gilligan (1982), Keller (1983, 1985).

A second challenge comes from social scientists who have undermined the privileged status of canonical ways of knowing through their studies of scientific and mathematical practice. They show us how within laboratories there is a great deal of thinking that does not respect the canon and how "ordinary" people in their kitchens and workplaces make very effective use of a down-to-earth mathematical thinking very different from the abstract and formal math they were taught at school.[2]

Although few members of this community make a direct connection with feminism, there is a convergence of intellectual values—a "revaluation of the concrete." These challenges to the dominant epistemology are intellectually assertive and politically self-conscious. A third challenge most often presents itself as neutral and technical. It is a challenge from within computation, as when the maverick Macintosh with its iconic interface made its bid against the established IBM personal computer. That the computer should be an ally in the revaluation of the concrete has a certain irony; in both the popular and technical cultures there has been a systematic construction of the computer as the ultimate embodiment of the abstract and formal. But the computer's intellectual personality has another side: Computers provide a context for the development of concrete thinking. When we look at particular cases of individuals programming computers, we see a concrete and personal approach to materials that runs into conflict with established ways of doing things within the computer culture. The *practice* of computing provides support for a pluralism that is denied by its social construction.[3]

Since the prevailing image of the computer is that of a logical machine, and since programming is seen as a technical and mathematical activity, the existence of anything but an analytic approach in this area makes a dramatic argument for pluralism. But the computer's most specific contribution to the critique of canonical styles depends on something more fundamental. The computer stands betwixt and between the world of formal systems and physical things; it has the ability to make the abstract concrete. In the simplest case, an object moving on a computer screen might be defined by the most formal of rules and so be like a construct in pure mathematics; but at the same time it is visible, almost tangible, and allows a sense of direct manipulation that only the encultured mathematician can feel in traditional formal systems. (see Davis & Hersh, 1981; Papert, 1980a)

---

[2] A sample of relevant studies in scientific ethnography is provided by Knorr-Cetina and Mulkay (1983). See also Knorr-Cetina (1981), Latour and Woolgar (1979), Traweek (1989). A sample of studies on everyday thinking is contained in Rogoff and Lave (1984). Also see Lave (1988).

[3] The Macintosh's replacement of proposition-like commands by the use of concrete icons has theoretical roots in a style of programming usually called "object oriented." For a nontechnical discussion, see Kay (1977), pp. 230–44; 1985, pp. 122ff.). The reaction within artificial intelligence against abstract, propositional, rule-driven methods was given literary expression in the writings of Douglas Hofstadter. See, for example, Hofstadter (1985, pp. 631–65). Two other manifestations of this reaction are Minsky (1987) and Rumelhart, McClelland, and the PDP Research Group (1986).

The computer has a theoretical vocation: to bring the philosophical down to earth.[4]

While many can emphathize when Carol Gilligan describes people making "contextual" moral decisions (you can cast yourself and acquaintances in the different roles) there is a more of a problem when people try to get close to what it feels like to do science in a style that rejects standard notions of "objectivity."[5] Evelyn Fox Keller, describing such a style in the work of geneticist Barbara Mclintock, notes that this is the "less accessible aspect" of a scientist's relationship to nature (Keller, 1985). We believe she is right. A personal appropriation of epistemological pluralism in science requires, at the limit, that we get close to the experiences of an Einstein or a McClintock or a Salk. But you can imagine yourself in the place of a programmer more easily than in the place of an Einstein. And when you yourself program (an activity within the reach of everyone), you can experience the degree to which your style of solving logical problems is very much your own.

In this chapter, we use the computer as an instrument for observing different styles of scientific thought and developing categories for analyzing them.[6] We find that, besides being a lens through which personal styles can be seen, it is also a privileged medium for the growth of alternative voices in dealing with the world of formal systems. After presenting cases in which the computer serves as an expressive medium for personal styles, we turn to this more speculative them: As a carrier for pluralistic ideas, the computer holds the promise of catalyzing change, not only within computation but in our culture at large.

PERSONAL APPROPRIATION

Consider Lisa, 18, a first-year Harvard student in an introductory programming course. Lisa had feared that she would find the course difficult because she is a poet, "good with words, not numbers." But after years of scorning teachers who had insisted that mathematics is a language, the computer has made Lisa ready to reconsider the proposition, and with it her characterization of herself as someone "bad at math." Lisa started well, surprised to find herself easily in command of

---

[4] For a fuller discussion of the computer as an evocative and concretizing object see Turkle (1984).

[5] Gilligan (1982). For a critical discussion of Gilligan's proposals and her reply, see Kerba, et al. (1986, pp. 304–33). Its methodological criticisms of Gilligan's treatment of the relationship between "voice" and gender do not detract from how her subjects illustrate the way of thinking we shall call "bricolage."

[6] Research reports that emphasize approach to programming or programming style in the sense we are using it here include Papert, di Sessa, Weir, and Watt (1979), Turkle (1980, 1984, esp. chap. 3), Weir (1987), Turkle, Schön, Nielsen, Orsini, and Overmeer (1988), Motherwell (1988), and Harel (1988).

the course material. But as the term progressed she reluctantly decided that she "had to be a different kind of person with the machine." She could no longer resist a pressure to think in ways that were not her own. She was in trouble, but her difficulty expressed a strength not a weakness. Her growing sense of alienation did not stem from an inability to cope with programming but from her ability to handle it in a way that came into conflict with the computer culture she had entered.

Lisa wants to manipulate computer language the way she works with words as she writes a poem. There, she says, she "feels her way from one word to another," sculpting the whole. When she writes poetry, Lisa experiences language as transparent, she knows where all the elements are at every point in the development of her ideas. She wants her relationship to computer language to be similarly transparent. When she builds large programs she prefers to write her own smaller "building block" procedures even though she could use pre-packaged ones from a program library; she resents the latter's opacity. Her teachers chide her, insisting that her demand for transparency is making her work more difficult; Lisa perseveres, insisting that this is what it takes for her to feel comfortable with computers.

Two months into the programming course, Lisa's efforts to succeed were no longer directed towards trying to feel comfortable. She had been told that the "right way" to do things was to control a program through planning and black-boxing, the technique that lets you exploit opacity to plan something large without knowing in advance how the details will be managed. Lisa recognized the value of these techniques—for someone else. She struggled against using them as the starting points for her learning. Lisa ended up abandoning the fight, doing things "their way," and accepting the inevitable alienation from her work. It was at this point that she called her efforts to become "another kind of person with the machine" her "not-me strategy," and began to insist that the computer is "just a tool." "It's nothing much," she said, "just a tool."

A classmate, Robin, is a pianist. Robin explains that she masters her music by perfecting the smallest "little bits of pieces" and then building up. She cannot progress until she understands the details of each small part. Robin is happiest when she uses this tried and true method with the computer, playing with small computational elements as though they were notes or musical phrases. Like Lisa, she is frustrated with black-boxing or using prepackaged programs. She too was told her way was wrong: "I told my teaching fellow I wanted to take it all apart, and he laughed at me. He said it was a waste of time, that you should just black box, that your shouldn't confuse yourself with what was going on at that low level."

Lisa and Robin came to the programming course with anxieties about not "belonging" (fearing that the computer belonged to male hackers who took the machines and made "a world apart"), and their experiences in it only served to make matters worse.[7] Although imaginative and carefully designed, the Harvard course taught that there is only one right way to approach the computer, a way that emphasizes control through structure and planning. There are many virtues to this computational approach (it certainly makes sense when dividing the labor on a large programming project), but Lisa and Robin have intellectual styles at war with it. Lisa says she has "turned herself into a different kind of person" in order to perform, and Robin says she has learned to "fake it." Although both women are able to get good grades in their programming course, they represent casualties of this war. Both deny who they are in order to succeed.

In their response and their defense, Lisa and Robin are not alone. In a survey, 37 women members of a local computer society included 17 who "changed their style to suit the fashion" when they began to interact with the "official" computer world. "I got my wrists slapped enough times and I changed my ways," says a college student for whom programming on her Macintosh was a private passion until she entered MIT. The cost of such "wrist slapping" is high: On an individual level, talent is wasted, self image eroded. On the social level, the computer culture is narrowed.

Such casualties are unnecessary. The computer can be a partner in a great diversity of relationships. *The computer is an expressive medium that different people can make their own in their own way.* But people who want to approach the computer in a "noncanonical" style are rarely given the opportunity to do so. They are discouraged by the dominant computer culture, eloquently expressed in the ideology of the Harvard course. Like Lisa and Robin, they can pass a course or pass a test. They are not computer phobic, they don't *need* to stay away because of fear or panic. But they are computer reticent. They *want* to stay away, because the computer has come to symbolize an alien way of thinking. They learn to get by. And they learn to keep a certain distance. One of its symptoms is the language with which they neutralize the computer as they deny the possibility of using it creatively. Recall how Lisa dismissed it as "*just* a tool."

These responses begin to show how discrimination in the computer culture takes the form of discrimination against epistemological orientations, most strikingly, against the approach preferred by Lisa and Robin.

STYLE AS SUBSTANCE

Lisa and Robin share a preferred strategy for organizing work and a particular manner of identifying with computational objects. To capture the difference

---

[7] Lisa and Robin were part of a larger study of Harvard and MIT students taking introductory programming courses. The study found anxiety about an identity as a "computer person" to be an important aspect of reticence towards computers, especially among women. See Turkle (1988). See also Kiesler, Sproull, and Eccles (1985).

between them and their instructors, we describe a complex of attributes, an "approach" to knowledge, that encompasses several dimensions of difference. We isolate two approaches which serve as ideal types, theoretical prisms through which to see simplified projections of more complex realities. Lisa and Robin use a "soft" approach, and the instructors in their course are encouraging them to use a "hard" one.

Our culture tends to equate soft with feminine and feminine with unscientific and undisciplined. Why use a term, *soft*, that may begin the discussion of difference with a devaluation? Because to refuse the word would be to accept the devaluation. Soft is a good word for a flexible and nonhierarchical style, open to the experience of a close connection with the object of study. Using it goes along with insisting on negotiation, relationship, and attachment as cognitive virtues. Our goal is the revaluation of traditionally denigrated categories. We do not argue that valuable thinking is not soft; we explore ways in which soft is a valid approach for men as well as women, in science as well as the arts.

Hard and soft are more than different approaches to computation. The phrase *epistemological pluralism* (rather than, for example, *computational pluralism*) underscores the generality of the issues. The computer forces general questions about intellectual style to reveal an everyday face. Even schoolroom differences in how children program computers raise issues that come up in a more abstract form in scholarly debates about scientific objectivity. The computer makes ideas about alternative scientific voices more concrete and therefore more appropriate because we can relate them, not only to the science of the scientists, but to our own thinking.

Observation of the soft approach to programming calls into question deeply entrenched assumptions about the classification and value of different ways of knowing. It provides examples of the validity and power of concrete thinking in situations that are traditionally assumed to demand the abstract. It supports a perspective which encourages looking for psychological and intellectual development within rather than beyond the concrete and suggests the need for closer investigation of the diversity of ways in which the mind can use objects rather than the rules of logic to think with.

The ideal typical hard and soft approaches are each characterized by a cluster of attributes. Some involve organization of work (the hards prefer abstract thinking and systematic planning; the softs prefer a negotiational approach and concrete forms of reasoning); other attributes concern the kind of relationship that the subject forms with computational objects. Hard mastery is characterized by a distanced stance, soft mastery by a closeness to objects.

Hard mastery is resonant with the logical and hierarchical elements of the traditional construction of "scientific method." Soft mastery has always had its place in the discourse of the arts and has always been glimpsed in the autobiographical writings of scientists. Only recently has it gained academic recognition as an integral element of scientific practice.[8]

When we say that hard and soft approaches are ideal types, we signal that individuals will seldom conform to either exactly, and that some will be so far from both that it is impossible to assign a type. In other words our contention is not that the attributes in a cluster are exactly correlated, but that each approach has internal coherency in the way that a stable culture is coherent. So for example, closeness to objects tends to support a concrete style of reasoning, a preference for using objects to think with, and a bias against the abstract formulae that maintain reason at a distance from its objects. Conversely, a distanced relationship with objects supports an analytic, rule- and plan-oriented style. Our theoretical conjecture is that degree of closeness to objects has developmental primacy; it comes first. The child forms a proximal or distant relationship to the world of things. The tendency to use the abstract and analytic or concrete and negotiational style of thinking follows.

But although closeness to objects favors contextual and associational styles of work, it does not exclude the possibility of using a hierarchical one. Planning is not always an expression of personal style. It can be acquired as a skill, sometimes because it is needed to get a job done, sometimes as a facade to hide rather than express individuality.

Thus, the elements of each cluster are not invariably associated with each other; still less are they invariably associated with gender.[9] But in our observations of people learning to program we have found an association between gender and approach to programming. When people are free to explore programming without preconceptions about the "right" way to do it, more women use soft approaches and more men hard approaches, although many men are alienated from the dominant engineering style and many women work creatively within it.[10]

Using clinical methods inspired by the Piagetian and psychoanalytic traditions, we built up case studies of children using computers in grade-school settings where they were encouraged to explore programming without precon-

---

[8] See, for example, the ethnographic studies referenced in Note 3 and the writings on scientific epistemology from the tradition of feminist scholarship referred to in Note 1.

[9] Empirically, we sometimes find each aspect of soft mastery—bricolage as a style of organization and closeness to the object—without the presence of the other. In particular, one finds people who are planners but who enjoy a close relationship with concrete objects (and who experience computational objects this way). On the pairing of planning and what they call an interactive style with the computer, see Sutherland and Hoyles (1988).

[10] In our research, the male/hard and female/soft dichotomy was most dramatic in a predominantly white, wealthy private school in the South, where traditional patterns of socialization would favor boys learning the ways of control, hierarchy, and distance, and girls learning the ways of negotiation and closeness.

ceptions about the "right way" to go about it. We took 40 cases for which we had material both on individual personality and programming style. Of 20 girls, 14 favored the soft approach; of 20 boys, there were 4 who followed this route. In case material on college students taking a first programming course, of the 15 women, 9 were soft style programmers; of 15 men, 4. What we say in this chapter about gender, programming, and intellectual style is based on the analysis of these cases. But we believe that what is most important is not any statistical association between gender and programming styles, but what lies behind the styles and behind the resistance of our intellectual culture to recognize and facilitate them both. In our culture, those who use hard approaches don't simply share a style, they constitute an epistemological elite.

Here, we focus on the soft approach; the canonical style is well known and well defended. But implicity, our discussion of soft approaches is a discussion of hard ones; it contributes to the deconstruction of the latter as *the* way to do things. It also situates it: the supervaluation of the hard approach owes much of its strength within computation to the support it gets in other intellectual domains. To state simplistically a position we shall elaborate in the following pages: "Hard thinking" has been used to define logical thinking. And logical thinking has been given a privileged status that can be challenged only by developing a respectful understanding of other styles where logic is seen as a powerful instrument of thought but not as the "law of thought." In this view, "logic is on tap not on top."

It is beyond the scope of this essay to spell out the multiple relationships between our definition of "soft" and the large body of feminist writings on intellectual approaches. But we use the work of Gilligan and Keller to bring out the two most striking constituent elements of the soft approach. The negotiational and contextual element, which we call *bricolage,* recalls Gilligan's material on moral reasoning. Then we look "beyond bricolage" to a second element of the soft approach, underscored by Keller in her work on Barbara McClintock. This is a style of relating to objects, be they physical objects such as gears or chromosomes, or conceptual objects such as the elements of programming. Whereas bricolage is negotiational, this aspect of the soft approach is proximal, a closeness to objects.

BRICOLAGE

Levi-Strauss used the idea of bricolage to contrast the analytic methodology of Western science with what he called a "science of the concrete" in primitive societies.[11] The bricoleur scientist does not move abstractly and hierarchically

---

[11] Levi-Strauss (1968). Levi-Strauss contrasted bricolage with Western science, ignoring the significant aspects of bricolage present in the latter. Several recent writers have written in a way that begins to redress this imbalance. See, for example, Feyerabend (1975), Hanson (1958), and Wittgenstein (1953). In a less formal vein, see Feynman (1985).

from axiom to theorem to corollary. Bricoleurs construct theories by arranging and rearranging, by negotiating and renegotiating with a set of well-known materials.

If we take Levi-Strauss's description of the two scientific approaches as ideal types and divest them of his efforts to localize them culturally, we can see both in how people program computers. For some people, what is exciting about computers is working within a rule-driven system that can be mastered in a top-down, divide-and-conquer way. Their structured "planner's" approach, the approach being taught in the Harvard programming course, is validated by industry and the academy. It decrees that the "right way" to solve a programming problem is to dissect it into separate parts and design a set of modular solutions that will fit the parts into an intended whole. Some programmers work this way because their teachers or employers insist that they do. But for others, it is a preferred approach; to them, it seems natural to make a plan, divide the task, use modules and subprocedures.

Lisa and Robin offer examples of a very different style. They are not drawn to structured programming; their work at the computer is marked by a desire to play with the elements of the program, to move them around almost as though they were material elements—the words in a sentence, the notes on a keyboard, the elements of a collage.

While hierarchy and abstraction are valued by the structured programmers' "planner's" aesthetic, bricoleur programmers, like Levi-Strauss's bricoleur scientists, prefer negotiation and rearrangement of their materials. The bricoleur resembles the painter who stands back between brushstrokes, looks at the canvas, and only after this contemplation, decides what to do next. Bricoleurs use a mastery of associations and interactions. For planners, mistakes are missteps; bricoleurs use a navigation of midcourse corrections. For planners, a program is an instrument for premeditated control; bricoleurs have goals but set out to realize them in the spirit of a collaborative venture with the machine. For planners, getting a program to work is like "saying one's piece"; for bricoleurs, it is more like a conversation than a monologue.

We introduced bricolage through the programming styles of college students Lisa and Robin. To consider it in finer detail, we look at the work of two 9-year-olds. In the spirit of Jean Piaget, we find that children's thinking often allows particularly transparent access to processes that extend far beyond childhood.

Alex, 9 years old, a classic bricoleur, attends the Hennigan Elementary School in Boston, the scene of an experiment in using computers across the curriculum. There, students work with Logo programming and computer controlled Lego construction materials. The work is both frequent enough (at least an hour a day) and open-ended enough for differences in styles to emerge.

When working with Lego materials and motors, most children make a robot walk by attaching wheels to a motor that makes them turn. They are seeing the wheels and the motor through abstract concepts of the way they work: the wheels roll, the motor turns. Alex goes a different route. He looks at the objects more concretely, that is, without the filter of abstractions. He turns the Lego wheels on their sides to make flat "shoes" for his robot and harnesses one of the motor's most concrete features: the fact that it vibrates. As anyone who has worked with machinery knows, when a machine vibrates it tends to "travel," something normally to be avoided. When Alex ran into this phenomenon, his response was ingenious. He doesn't use the motor to make anything "turn," but to make his robot (greatly stabilized by its flat "wheel shoes") vibrate and thus "travel." When Alex programs, he likes to keep things similarly concrete.

Learners are usually introduced to Logo programming through the "turtle," an icon on a computer screen which can be commanded to move around the screen and leave a trace as it goes. So, for example, the turtle can be told to move forward a hundred steps and turn ninety degrees with the commands FORWARD 100 RIGHT 90. Four such commands would have the turtle drawing a square. Programming occurs when a set of commands, such as REPEAT 4 [FORWARD 100 RIGHT 90], are defined as a procedure: TO SQUARE. Alternatively, a subprocedure TO SIDE might be defined and repeated four times.

Alex wanted to draw a skeleton. Structured programming views a computer program as a hierarchical sequence. Thus, a structured program TO DRAW SKELETON might be made up of four subprocedures: TO HEAD, TO BODY, TO ARMS, TO LEGS, just as TO SQUARE could be built up from repetitions of a subprocedure TO SIDE. But Alex rebels against dividing his skeleton program into subprocedures; his program inserts bones one by one, marking the place for insertion with repetitions of instructions. One of the reasons often given for using subprocedures is economy in the number of instructions. Alex explains that doing it his way was "worth the extra typing" because the phrase repetition gave him a "better sense of where I am in the pattern" of the program. He had considered the structured approach but prefers his own style for aesthetic reasons: "It has rhythm," he says. In his opinion, using subprocedures for parts of the skeleton is too arbitrary and preemptive, one might say abstract. "It makes you decide how to divide up the body, and perhaps you would change your mind about what goes together with what. Like, I would rather think about the two hands together instead of each hand with the arms."[12]

In his own way, Alex has resisted the pressure to believe the general superior to the specific or the abstract superior to the concrete. For Alex, thinking about

---

[12] In its ideal, the structured method would have the programmer go beyond subprocedures to make one procedure that could be given different parameters to produce arms and legs, right and left sides, even differently shaped people. This aesthetic, known as *procedural abstraction,* wants to see a right arm and a left leg disappear into a generalized abstract idea of "limb." But for someone like Alex, the top priority is staying in touch with the concrete. He is aware of the importance of organizing his program in order to find his way around it, but he does so by giving it what he calls "rhythm" rather than a hierarchical structure of procedures and subprocedures.

hands as a subset of arms is too far away from the reality of real hands, just as taking a motor that was most striking as a vibrating machine, and using it to turn wheels in the standard fashion was too far away from the real motor he had before him. While the structured programmer starts with a clear plan defined in abstract terms, Alex lets the product emerge through a negotiation between himself and his material. In cooking, this would be the style of chefs who don't follow recipes but a series of decisions made as a function of how things taste. Or we might think of sculptors who let themselves be guided by the qualities of the stone that reveal themselves as the work progresses.

The turtle that Alex used to draw a skeleton is the best known Logo object, but there are others. For example, *sprites* are turtles that can be set in motion. Once you give a sprite a speed and a heading, it moves with that state of uniform motion until something is done to change it, just like an object obeying Newton's first law.

Anne, whose favorite hobby is painting, has become expert at using sprites in programs that produce striking visual effects.[13] In one, a flock of birds (each of them built from a sprite) flies through the sky, disappears over the horizon, and reappears some other place and time. If all the birds were red, then it would be easy to make them disappear and reappear. The command SETCOLOR :INVISIBLE would get rid of them and SETCOLOR :RED would make them reappear. But Anne wants the birds to have different colors, and so making the birds reappear with their original color is more complicated.

A classical method for achieving this end calls for an algebraic style of thinking: You make the program store each bird's original color as the value of a variable, then you change all colors to invisible and recall the appropriate variable when the bird is to reappear. Anne knows how to use this algorithmic method, but prefers one that allows her to turn programming into the manipulation of familiar objects. As Anne programs, she uses analogies with traditional art materials. When you want to hide something on a canvas, you paint it out, you cover it over with something that looks like the background. Anne uses this technique to solve her programming problem. She lets each bird keep its color, but she makes her program "hide" it by placing a screen over it. Anne designs a sprite that will screen the bird when she doesn't want it seen, a sky-colored screen that makes the bird disappear. *Anne is programming a computer, but she is thinking like a painter.*

"Thinking like a painter" does not prevent Anne from making a significant technical innovation in the context of her fourth-grade computer culture. She is familiar with the idea of using two sprites to form a compound object. Her

---

[13] Although we have described Anne's program elsewhere, we redescribe it here in enough detail for the reader to appreciate how the concrete and the formal can come to the same place by alternative routes. Anne's program has the merit of showing in compact form a set of qualities characteristic of the bricoleur that are usually more diffusely represented. See Turkle (1984, pp. 110–115).

classmates and teachers have always done this by putting the sprites side by side. Anne's program is like theirs in using two sprites, one for the screen, one for the bird. But she places them on top of each other so that they occupy the same space. Instead of thinking of compound objects as a way of getting a picture to be bigger, she thinks of compound objects as a way of getting sprites to exhibit a greater complexity of behavior, an altogether more subtle concept.

Thus, Anne's level of technical expertise is as dazzling in its manipulation of ideas as in its visual effects. She has become familiar with the idea of data structures by inventing a new one—her "screened bird." She has learned her way around a set of mathematical ideas through manipulating angles, shapes, rates, and coordinates in her program. As a bricoleur, her path into this technical knowledge is not through structural design, but through the pleasures of letting effects emerge.

In describing bricoleur programmers, we have made analogies to sculptors, cooks, and painters. Bricoleurs are also like writers who don't use an outline but start with one idea, associate to another, and find a connection with a third. In the end, an essay "grown" through negotiation and association is not necessarily any less elegant or easy to read than one filled in from an outline, just as the final program produced by a bricoleur can be as elegant and organized as one written with the top-down approach.

Anne's case makes it clear that the difference between planners and bricoleurs is not in quality of product, it is in the *process* of creating it. As in the case of Alex, Anne does not write her program in "sections" that are assembled into a product. She makes a simple working program and shapes it gradually by successive modifications. She starts with a single black bird. She makes it fly. She gives it color. Each step is a small modification to a working program that she has in hand. If a change does not work, she undoes it with another small change. She "sculpts." At each stage of the process, she has a fully working program, not a part but a version of the final product.

Anne is perfectly capable of producing a program with well-delineated sub-procedures, although her way of creating them has little in common with the planner.[14] Devotees of structured programming would frown on Anne's style. From their point of view, she should design a computational object (for example, her bird) with all the required qualities built into it. She should specify, in advance, what signals will cause it to change color, disappear, reappear, and fly.

---

[14] Bricolage does not exclude the use of subprocedures; it simply does not give their a priori delineation the status of a privileged method. Some ways that bricoleurs use subprocedures in a way that feels natural to them are captured in the following examples. First, a part of a program first conceived holistically can be demarcated as a subprocedure at any stage of programming. Second, subprocedures need not be "black boxes"; they too can grow by sculpting as the program grows as a whole. Finally, the bricoleur may use as subprocedures programs that happen to be "lying around," possibly even programs that were originally made for very different purposes.

One could then forget about "how the bird works." In engineer's jargon, it could be treated as a black box. Anne's work dramatizes the features of bricolage that was so salient for Lisa and Robin: the desire for transparency.

With a structured programming style, one usually does not feel comfortable with a construct until it is thoroughly black-boxed, with both its inner workings and all traces of the perhaps messy process of its construction hidden from view. Many programmers feel a sense of power when they use black-boxed programs, perhaps because of the thought that others might take them up exactly as frozen.

But black-boxing makes other programmers nervous rather than exultant. Anne did not want to package her constructs into opaque containers. Like Lisa and Robin, she enjoys keeping open the possibility of renegotiating their exact form. And this means staying in touch with that form at all times. When programming, bricoleurs tend to prefer the transparent style, planners the opaque, but *the program's authorship is a critical variable in this preference.* Planners want to bring their own programs to a point where they can be black-boxed and made opaque, while bricoleurs prefer to keep them transparent. *But when dealing with programs made by others, the situation is reversed.* Now, the bricoleurs are happy to get to know a new object by interacting with it, learning about it through its behavior the way you would learn about a person, while the planners usually find this intolerable. Their more analytic approach demands knowing how the program works with a kind of assurance that can only come from transparent understanding, from dissection and demonstration.

Do programmers "graduate" from bricolage when they develop greater expertise? Will Anne become a structure programmer in junior high? Our observations suggest that, with experience, bricoleurs reap the benefits of their long explorations, so that they may appear more "decisive" and like planners when they program on familiar terrain. And of course, they get better at "faking it." But the negotiating style resurfaces when they confront something challenging or are asked to try something new. *Bricolage is a way to organize work. It is not a stage in a progression to a superior form.* Indeed, there is a culture of adult programming virtuosos, the hacker culture, that would recognize many elements of the bricolage style as their own. And interviews with graduate students in computer science turned up highly skilled bricoleurs, most of them aware that their style was "countercultural."

In the case of computation, the existence of the countercultural style challenges the idea of one privileged, "mature" approach to problems. This challenge is supported by countercultural styles in other domains, for example, those observed by Gilligan in the domain of moral reasoning.

Gilligan's work presents us with two moral voices. We can hear both in children's responses to classical examples of moral dilemmas. When confronted by the story of Heinz, who must decide whether to steal a drug to save a life, 11-year-old Jake sees the dilemmas as "sort of like a math problem with humans" (Gilligan, 1982, p. 26). He sets it up as an equation and arrives at what he believes is the universal response: Heinz should steal the drug because a human life is worth much more than money. Eleven-year-old Amy takes an approach in which we see elements of bricolage. While Jake accepted the abstractly given problem as a quantitative comparison of two evils, Amy looks at the problem setting in concrete terms, breaks the restrictive formal frame of the given problem, and introduces a set of new elements. These elements include the druggist as a concrete human being who probably has a wife of his own and feelings about her. Amy proposes that Heinz talk things over with the druggist, who surely will not want anyone to die.

In Gilligan's description of Jake, justice was like a mathematical principle. It resembled the structured programmer's black box. To solve a problem, you set up the right algorithm, the right box, you crank the handle, and the answer comes out. Amy's style of reasoning required her to stay in touch with the inner workings of her arguments, with the relationships and possibly shifting alliances of a group of actors. Amy's resemblance to the programmers Alex and Anne is striking. They are all negotiators, stay close to their materials, and require transparency as they arrange and rearrange them. Despite Anne's high level of achievement, theorists of structured programming would criticize her style for the same kinds of reasons that Lawrence Kohlberg would classify the impressively articular Amy at a lower intellectual level than Jake. In both cases, criticism would center on the fact that neither of the two young women is prepared to take the final step to abstraction.

Kohlberg saw moral development as a sequence of stages which move from judging rightness by one's immediate feelings to judging rightness by the application of absolute principles. Between egocentrism and the Kantian imperative lie intermediate stages of reasoning based on balancing and assessing the consequences of actions for individuals. Gilligan finds many adult women speaking as did Amy. In Kohlberg's terms, they are "blocked" at this intermediate level: Instead of looking to universal principles in making their decisions, they consider concrete situations. Gilligan uses her observations to reject Kohlberg's theory, particularly its positing of a determinate end-point to development.[15] If one branch of the development of moral reasoning moves towards the primacy of "justice," of the formal and analytic, Gilligan insists on equal respect for a different branch of development which leads toward increasingly sophisticated ways of thinking about morality in concrete terms of care through relationship and connection.

---

[15] Gilligan (1982). Kohlberg had already been challenged on other grounds. See, for example, Gibbs (1977). Similar issues have been raised in critiques of Jean Piaget. See, for example, Toulmin (1972). Toulmin argues that Piaget's experimental investigations reflect an a priori commitment to a Kantian position. We single out Toulmin because, unlike most of Piaget's critics, he does not quarrel with the detail of how the stages are described but with the epistemological assertion of the final end point.

In making the analogy between Amy and Anne, we shift the emphasis of Gilligan's analysis of the "different voice." Is her work about morality or epistemology? Gilligan is certainly concerned with both morality and epistemology when she says: "[for women] the moral problem arises from conflicting responsibilities rather than from competing rights and requires for its resolution a mode of thinking that is contextual and narrative rather than formal and abstract" (Gilligan, 1982, p. 19). But her language expresses a priority, a primary concern with the character of the morality which, as she says, requires a certain mode of thinking. *Our concern is with the mode of thinking.*

Gilligan's priority shows itself in recent writing where she redescribes Kohlberg's theory as being about only one side of moral reasoning. In this view, Kohlberg is talking about justice, thus leaving the other side of morality, namely care, to her (Gilligan, 1988).

This compromise, which splits off the *content* of moral judgment, blunts the force of Gilligan's observations as a challenge to something more general than moral reasoning. Kohlberg's theory of the development of moral judgment mirrors Piaget's theory of the development of intelligence per se. Both express the value-laden perspective on intellectual growth that has dominated Western philosophy. Piaget sees a progression from egocentric beginnings to a final, "formal stage" when propositional logic and the hypothetico-deductive method "liberate" intelligence from the need for concrete situations to mediate thinking (Piaget & Inhelder, 1958). In this vision, mature thinking is abstract thinking. We disagree: for us, *formal reasoning is not a stage, but a style.*

Although Piaget would place the "concrete" Anne squarely in the preformal stage, her level of achievement undermines standard assumptions about the privileged status of the analytic and formal. And it undermines standard assumptions about the "objective." There is little distance between Anne and her objects. This aspect of Anne's work—her close, almost tactile involvement with the sprites—enables us to make a bridge between styles of programming and styles: this time, not of moral discourse, but of doing science. The fact of diverse styles of *expert* programming supports the idea that there can be different but equal voices even where the formal has traditionally appeared as almost definitionally supreme: logic, mathematics, and the "hard" sciences. And this aspect of Anne's work bring us to the second constituent element of the soft approach. We go "beyond bricolage" to the question of closeness to the object.

BEYOND BRICOLAGE: CLOSENESS TO THE OBJECT

There is a tradition of scientific epistemology which sees the essence of science in objectivity and the essence of objectivity in a distanced relationship with the object of study. Feminist scholars have related this notion of objectivity to the construction of gender: objectivity in the sense of distancing the self from the object of study is culturally constructed as male, just as male is culturally constructed as distanced and objective. In a moving case study of a scientist at work, Keller demonstrates that this is not the only possible stance. She sees another in the work of geneticist Barbara McClintock, who talked about her relationship to objects of scientific study as one of proximity rather than distance. For McClintock, the practice of science was essentially a conversation with her materials. "Over and over again," says Keller, McClintock "tells us one must have the time to look, the patience to 'hear what the material has to say to you,' the openness to 'let it come to you.' Above all, one must have a 'feeling for the organism.' "[16]

McClintock said that the more she worked with neurospora chromosomes (so small that others had been unable to identify them), "the bigger [they] got, and when I was really working with them I wasn't outside, I was down there. I was part of the system. I actually felt as if I were right down there and these were my friends . . . As you look at these things, they become part of you and you forget yourself" (Keller, 1983, p. 117). McClintock came into increasing conflict with the formal, "hard" methods of molecular biology. McClintock was recognized by the scientific establishment, indeed she was awarded the Nobel Prize, only when the formal approach came independently and much later to conclusions that she had derived from her "softer" investigations.

When we study programmers at work we see differences reminiscent of the two approaches to genetics. Alex and Anne relate to computational objects much as McClintock related to chromosomes, while many of their peers, like the mainstream molecular biologists, take a more distant approach.

Anne psychologically places herself in the space of her objects. She experiences her screens and birds as tangible, sensuous, and tactile. She is down there, in with the sprites, playing with them like objects in a collage. Or consider the computer science graduate student Lorraine, who explains how she uses "thinking about how the program feels like inside" to break through difficult problems. "For appearances sake," she wants to "look like I'm doing what everyone else is doing, but I'm doing that with only a small part of my mind. The rest of me is imagining what the components feel like. It's like doing my pottery." This is in sharp contrast to structured programmers who use their favorite device of black-boxing as a way to maintain distance. The idea of the black box, designed not to be touched, mediates between the structured (planning) style of organizing work and their relationship to computational objects. Structured programmers are not *among* the sprites, they act *on* the sprites.

An example from outside of computation clarifies the role of identification with objects as a way of appropriating formal systems. Children using gears illustrate how closeness to objects allows alternatives to abstract thinking.

---

[16] Keller (1983, p. 198). Keller describes McClintock's approach as dependent on a capacity to "forget herself," immerse herself in observation, and "hear what the material has to say."

At the Hennigan School where we met Alex, many students work as he does with a Lego construction kit with which they can build mechanisms and write computer programs to make them function. Sooner or later in building their objects, the children run into the need for gears.[17]

The motors in the construction set turn at a high speed with low torque. A car built by attaching these motors directly to the wheels will go very fast but will be so underpowered that the slightest slope or obstruction will cause it to stall. The solution to the problem with Lego cars is the same as that adopted by designers of real cars: use gears. But in order to use them effectively, children need to understand something about gear ratios. Contrary to their teachers' expectations, the girls in this project did extremely well, both in the quality of their work with the gears and in their performance on a test of underlying principles.[18]

If a small gear drives a larger gear, the larger gear will turn more slowly and with greater torque. It is the relative and not the absolute size of the two gears that counts. But when we interview children, we find that some of them reason as if the size of only one gear matters, as if they were following a set of rules such as "large gears are slow and strong" and "small gears are fast and weak." Without the notion of relative size, such rules fail. Other children, among them the girls who excelled, are less articulate and more physical in their explanations. They squirm and twist their bodies as they try to explain how they figure things out. And they get the right answer.

Theorists who look at intellectual development as the acquisition of increasingly sophisticated rules would say that children run into problems if the rules they have built are not yet good enough.[19] But armed with the idea of "closeness to objects," we can consider a different kind of theory. Perhaps the girls who did so well did not have better rules, but a tendency to see things in terms of relationships rather than properties. Perhaps the girls had easy access to a style of reasoning which allowed them to imagine themselves "inside the system." They used a relationship to the gears to help them think through a problem.

This kind of "reasoning from within" may not be adequate for all problems about gears, but for the kind of problem encountered by the children in our project, it was not only adequate, but much less prone to the errors produced by a too-simple set of rules. Relational thinking puts you at an advantage: You don't suffer disaster if the rule isn't exactly right.

---

[17] These experiments with Lego and programming are undertaken in a Piagetian spirit. See Piaget (1951) for experiments that deal with how mechanisms work. For a personal statement about the power of gears as an introduction to formal systems, see Papert (1980).

[18] Our sample does not allow us to say that girls did systematically better than boys. Research is in progress on this point. Our present discussion is about styles of explanation (rule driven vs. body syntonic), not distribution of abilities.

[19] For example, most of those inspired by the Carnegie-Mellon schools of artificial intelligence. See Michalski et al. (1983).

This way of thinking about girls and gears is supported by the hypothesis, familiar in recent writing about women, that boys are more comfortable with boundaries and girls with attachments.[20] This notion, drawn from accounts of development in the psychoanalytic tradition of object relations, stresses that for girls, identity formation takes place in a context of greater continuity than for boys.[21] The girl's sexual identification is with the mother, with whom she is encouraged to maintain a close relationship. Girls don't need to define themselves through a denial of the early, closely bonded relationship with the mother to the same extent as boys. They grow up with a stronger basis for experiencing the needs and desires of another as their own. Since girls do not have to renounce the pleasures of attachment to the mother as sharply as do boys, it is easier for them to play with the pleasures of closeness to other objects as well.

For boys, the separation from the mother is sharper, because in a certain sense, it happens twice, first in the rupture of the earliest bonded relationship, then in the course of the Oedipal struggle. The double separation translates into a lifelong tendency to be most comfortable with clear boundaries between self and nonself. It makes distanced, "objective" relationships feel like safe, approved ground.

The contemptuous comment of one fourth-grade boy who overheard a classmate talking about "being a sprite" when he programs can be interpreted from this point of view. "That's baby talk," he said. "I am not in the computer. I'm just making things happen there." The remark reflects an insistence on boundaries and the development of a world view that will fall easily into line with the canonical, objective science whose male meanings Keller has delineated.

The object relations school of psychoanalysis focuses on the way development progresses by a process of internalization of the things and people of the world. They come to live within us; they become our objects to think with. When psychoanalysts talk about "objects," they usually mean people.[22] Keller, in her work on McClintock, has explicitly extended the idea of closeness to the object to elaborate a theory of relationships to nature. Here we further extend this idea to relationships with specific artifacts. In doing so, we find ourselves addressing questions more familiar in discussions about relationships between people than between people and things. *What kinds of individuals choose to manipulate or make what kinds of objects, and what kinds of relationships follow?* From this perspective, it is not enough to ask whether individuals "like" or "don't like" to

---

[20] Among the most influential writings that integrate this hypothesis are Keller (1985) and Chodorow (1978).

[21] For an excellent overview of the object relations perspective perspective, see Greenberg and Mitchell (1983).

[22] In contrast, D. W. Winnicott has some suggestive ideas about the power of the "transitional object"—the baby's blanket, the teddy bear—that, in developmental terms, mediates between experience of self and nonself. In the current context, it suggests the power of the inanimate in inner life.

program, because that puts the question on too high a level of generalization. *"Liking" to program depends on forging an appropriate relationship with a computational object that "fits."*

The choice of a computational object that fits has several elements. First is the choice among objects offered by the system. Even people who like to be close to objects don't all like to be close to the same ones. For example, in the version of Logo used by Anne there was a choice between sprites and turtles. Some prefer the turtle, its static nature, the fineness in the way it draws. For others, these same qualities are reasons to reject the turtle as constraining, even unpleasant. They prefer the sprites, which move with flash and speed.

Second, when an object has been chosen, it can be thought of in different ways. As computational objects, turtles and sprites stand on the boundary between the physical and the abstract. In some ways both are like physical objects. You can see them, move them, put one on top of another. But at the same time, they are abstract and mathematical. Ambivalent in their nature, computational objects can be approached in different ways. Hard-approach programmers treat a sprite more like an abstract entity—a Newtonian particle— while soft-approach programmers treat it more like a physical object—a dab of paint or a cardboard cutout.

Because of this ambivalence, computational objects offer a great deal to those whose approach requires a close relationship to an object experienced as tactile and concrete. Computational objects offer a physical path of access to the world of formal systems. Some people are comfortable with mathematical experiences that manipulate symbols on quadrille-ruled paper. But for many *the ambivalent nature of computational objects means quite simply a first access to mathematics.*[23]

A third dimension of difference in people's choice of computational object has to do with differences in the degree to which these objects are anthropomorphized. The anthropomorphization extends from the computational objects ("That sprite doesn't want to do what I tell it now") to the computer itself. Anne, like many soft-approach programmers, has an easier time working with the computer if she anthropormorphizes it. She has no doubt that computers have psychologies: They "think" but can't really have "emotions." She believes, however, that the computer has preferences. "He would like it if you did a pretty program." And when it comes to technical things, Anne assumes the computer

---

[23] The Logo turtle was designed to be "body syntonic," i.e., to allow users to put themselves in its place. When children learn to program in Logo, they are encouraged to work out their programs by "playing turtle." The classic example of this is developing the Logo program for drawing a circle. This is difficult if you search for it by analytic means (you will need to find a differential equation), but easy if you put yourself in the turtle's place and pace it out. (The turtle makes a circle by going forward a little and turning a little, going forward and little and turning a little, etc.) Turtles are a path into mathematics for people whose surest route is through the body. See Papert (1980c).

has an aesthetic: "I don't know if he would rather have the program be very complicated or very simple."

We know and she knows that the computer is "just a machine." But those who want to treat it in certain ways "as if" it were a person are able to see the machine as sufficiently alive for it to serve as a companion, if only a limited one. When the computer "moves the queen" in a game of chess, it tempts us to think of it as having intentions. And programs within a computer system interact with each other in a way that supports models of the computer as composed of "agents" in communication. Anthropomorphization, both of a computer system and its parts, does not follow from lack of technical expertise. Computer scientists talk about a concept such as recursion with anthropomorphic metaphors: one agent "calls up" another, "wakes up" another, and "passes on a job." They sometimes even refer to the agents within a computer system as citizens of a "society of mind" (Minsky, 1987; Papert, 1980c).

Very young children are in fact uncertain whether computers should be counted as alive or not alive, and argue the question hotly, debating the computer's aliveness on the basis of its psychology, intentions, consciousness, and feelings (Turkle, 1984, esp. chap. 1). By age 10, most are sure that the computer is not actually alive. But at this point, some children, like Anne, continue to behave with and talk about the computer as if it were sentient. They brag that it is helping them or complain that it doesn't. In this, they are not showing confusion about biology. They do not think that the computer is alive the way an animal is. But it has a "kind of life," the kind of life appropriate to a computer. This is a psychological life.

Other children have a very different reaction. Once they are no longer perplexed by whether the machine might actually be biologically alive, they shy away from anthropomorphization. When they complain about the computer they do so in objective terms: It is too slow, it doesn't have enough memory. Talking about the computer usually means "talking shop" about technical details.

Lise Motherwell, a researcher at the Hennigan School, did an intensive study of eight fifth-grade students in a computer-rich classroom (Motherwell, 1988). She found she could capture children's stances towards the anthropomorphization of the computer by distinguishing two styles: relational and environmental. *Relational* children treat the computer as much like a person as they can get away with, while *environmental* children treat it like a thing. Three out of the four girls in her study were relational; three out of the four boys environmental. Motherwell's research supports our observation that children who anthropomorphize the computer are no less technically sophisticated than those who do not. The degree of anthropomorphization does not reflect expertise but psychological approach. Motherwell's research also supports our association of programming style and gender.

Looking at Motherwell's data through our theoretical prism, it is as though, once they have placed the computer in the not-alive category, the boys tend to settle with relief into treating it as a thing. This helps them to appropriate it through a relationship that involves distance, objectivity, and control. And it is as though the girls, once having settled the question of biological aliveness, get more comfortable with the machine by making it an interactive partner. In the computer they have found something in the domain of formal systems to which they can relate with informality.

The conventional route into formal systems, through the manipulation of abstract symbols, closes doors that the computer can open. The computer, with its graphics, its sounds, its text and animation, can provide a port of entry for people whose chief ways of relating to the world are through movement, intuition, visual impression, the power of words and associations. And it can provide a privileged point of entry for people whose mode of approach is through a close, bodily identification with the world of ideas or those who appropriate through anthropomorphization. The computational object, on the border between the idea and a physical object, offers new possibilities.

CLOSENESS AND CONFLICTS

Different intellectual perspectives provide suggestive hypotheses about why women tend to adopt the approaches that we have clustered under the rubric *soft*. Some perspectives, such as the psychoanalytic account, place the roots of difference at an early stage of human development. If the earliest and most compelling experiences of merging are with the mother, the process of differentiation takes on gender meanings. Experiences where boundaries are not clear are associated with something female. Differentiation and delineation are male.

The psychoanalytic focus on early experience does not necessarily undermine a more sociological perspective, where the emphasis is on our culture's sharp gender division of parenting roles and on the very different socializations of men and women. As a birthday gift, a boy receives toy tanks and soldiers; a girl receives dolls, presented to her, not as objects to command, but as children to nurture. In our culture, girls are taught negotiation, compromise, and the capacity for intimacy as social virtues, while models of male behavior stress decisiveness, cool impartiality, and the imposition of will. It would not be surprising if women felt more comfortable, more "themselves," with negotiation and compromise among elements of thought, and men preferred to make decisive plans and impose principles on a separate reality.

From its very foundations, objectivity in science was metaphorically engaged with the language of male domination and female submission. Francis Bacon used the image of the male scientist putting the female nature "on the rack" (Keller, 1985, pp. 33 ff.; Merchant, 1980; Haraway, 1979, pp. 206–237). Objectivity has been constructed, not only in terms of the distance of the knower from nature, but in terms of an aggressive relationship towards it (or rather towards her). And from its very foundations, objectivity in science has been engaged with the language of power, not only over nature, but over people and organizations. Such associations have spread beyond professional scientific communities; aggression has become part of a widespread cultural understanding of what it means to behave in a scientific way. Its hard methods are expected to involve "demolishing" an argument and "knocking it down" to size. Here the object of the blows is not a female nature but a male scientific opponent. If science is first a rape, it is then a duel.

In either case, it is not surprising that many women feel uncomfortable both with science and with ways of thinking that have been associated with it. The traditional discourse of computation has not been exempt from these connotations. Programs and operating systems are "crashed" and "killed." We write this chapter on a computer whose operating system asks if it should "abort" an instruction it cannot "execute." This is a style of discourse that few women fail to note.

Such observations about language, power, and the genderization of scientific discourse suggest pressures that push women to look for alternative approaches to knowing, and this means pressure to adopt soft approaches. A psychoanalytic perspective might suggest that women have a predisposition towards a soft approach. And then, the social construction of science reinforces this preference. Science waves its flag as "hard" in a way that repels women. This means that, in our culture, women are too often faced with the not necessarily conscious choice of putting themselves at odds either with the cultural meanings of being a scientist or with the cultural constructions of being a woman.

Such choices do not have to be made in an all-or-nothing way. The "not-me" strategy we mentioned earlier anticipated a phenomenon of costly partial surrender. Women who enter centers of power give eloquent testimony, not only to the pressure, but to the seduction of having achieved the right to use the male discourse that predominates there. And they also speak to the conflict that this engenders, a kind of conflict that considerably complicates our story of how women appropriate technology.

We have suggested that many women have a preference for attachment and relationship with technological objects as a means of appropriating them—but we have also pointed to the association of these objects with a construction of the male that stresses aggression, domination, and competition. This construction of technology may lead to a conflict between a close encounter with technology and women's image of themselves as women. Such a conflict is apparent when we look at women and computers.

When women neutralize the computer as "just a tool," it is more than a way of withdrawing because of a lack of authenticity in style of approach. Insisting that the computer is just a tool is one way to declare that what is most important about being a person (and a woman) is incompatible with close relationships to technology.

When Lisa first found herself doing well in her programming course, she found it "scary," because she felt she needed to protect herself from the idea of "being a computer science type." In high school, Lisa saw young men around her turning to computers as a way to avoid people: "They took the computers and made a world apart." Lisa describes herself as "turning off" her natural abilities in mathematics that would have led her to the computer. "I didn't care if I was good at it. I wanted to work in worlds where languages had moods and connected you with people." And although Robin had gone through most of her life as a musician practicing piano 8 hours a day, she too had fears about "guys who established relationships" with the computer. "To me, it sounds gross to talk about establishing a relationship with the computer. I don't like establishing relationships with machines. Relationships are for people."

In the vehemence with which many women insist on the computer's neutrality, on its being nothing more than a mere tool, there is something more than alienation of culture and style. Many women are fighting *against* an experience of the computer as psychologically gripping. They are fighting against an element of their soft approach. For some, it can be because they want to "belong" to the dominant computer culture. Lorraine, who programs by imagining what "the components feel like," ends her description of her programming style by adding, "Keep this anonymous. I know it sounds stupid." But for others, their experience of closeness to the object is a source of conflict.

When Lisa began programming, she saw herself as communicating with the computer, but the metaphor soon distressed her. "The computer isn't a living being, and when I think about communicating with it, well, that's wrong. There's a certain amount of feeling involved in the idea of communication, and I was looking for that from the computer." She looked at it, and she frightened herself. "It was horrible. I was becoming involved with a thing. I identified with how the computer was going through things."

Lisa, like the soft-approach programmer Anne, placed herself in the space of the computational objects she worked with and was prone to anthropomorphization, responding to the computer as though it had (at least) an intellectual personality. In Lisa's case, her own style came to offend her. As a programmer with a soft approach to the discipline, she rebelled against where her style had led her, because it had led her to what she experienced as a too-close relationship with a machine.

Carol Gilligan talks about the "hierarchy and the web" as metaphors to describe the different ways in which men and women see their worlds (Gilligan, 1982, p. 62). Men see a hierarchy of autonomous positions. Women see a web of interconnections among people. Men can be with the computer, content that it leaves them alone, even isolated, within a larger organization. When women see computers demanding separation from others, they perceive the machines as dangerous. They use metaphors from their programming classes to frame a view of people as what computers are not. So, for example, Robin says that people have "great flashes of abstract thought without any logical sequence before it. If you tried to do that with a computer, it would tell you it's a system error or illegal!" Lisa boils down what computers can't do to a starker form: They cannot love.

> I suppose if you look at the physical machinery of the computer mind, it is analogous to the human mind. But the saving grace, the difference, is emotion. That's the line you can draw. That's where you say, "This thing may be able to do something like thinking, but it can't love anybody."

The computer presence has provoked a "romantic reaction" in our culture.[24] As people take computers seriously as simulated mind, many are in conflict with the mechanistic image that is reflected back to them in the mirror of the machine. They define the specificity of people in terms of what computers cannot do. Simulated thinking may be thinking, but simulated love is never love. Women express this sentiment with particular urgency. We believe this is because a conflict fuels their conviction. A comfortable style of thinking would have them get close to the objects of thought. The computer offers them objects of thought. But the closer they get to this machine, the more anxious they feel. The more they become involved with the computer, the more they insist that it is only a neutral tool. A way out of the impasse would require profound change in the culture that surrounds the computer tool. If the computer is a tool, and of course it is, is it more like a hammer or more like a harpsicord?

The musician Robin is not distressed by her close relationship with her piano. A woman who finds attachment to the computer "unnatural" is not upset by her passion for the beautiful, heavy antique ink pens she uses to write. We infer that, if Lisa had been in music school, she would not experience as threatening her sense of communicating with her instrument or her emotional involvement with it. Music students live in a culture that, over time, has slowly grown a language and models for close relationships with music machines. The harpsicord, like the visual artists' pencils, brushes, and paints, is "just a tool." And yet we understand that artists' encounters with these can (and indeed, will most probably) be close, sensuous, and relational. And that artists will develop highly personal styles of working with them.

The development of a new computer culture would require more than technological progress and more than environments where there is permission to work with highly personal approaches. It would require a new and softer construction of the technological, with a new set of intellectual and emotional values more like those we apply to harpsicords than hammers.[25] If computers are really the tools we use to write, to design, to play with ideas and shapes and images, they

---

[24] See Turkle (in press). For more on women and the romantic reaction, see Turkle (1988a).
[25] On values for a new computer culture, see Papert (1987).

should not be addressed with the language of desktop calculators. Moving out of the impasse also would require the reconstruction of our cultural assumptions about hard logic as the "law" of thought. Addressing this question brings us full circle to where we began, with the assertion that epistemological pluralism is a necessary condition for a more inclusive computer culture.

ROADBLOCKS AND OPENINGS FOR CHANGE

Achieving epistemological pluralism is no small thing. It requires calling into question, not simply computational practices, but dominant models of intellectual development and the rarely challenged assumption that rules and logic are the highest form of reason. Anne was able to escape the damaging effects of these models because, at her age, she was not expected even by the most committed Piagetian to have achieved the "formal stage"—and at the stage of "concrete operations," bricolage can seem acceptable. But in many educational settings, even this would not have saved her; her work with the computer would have been taken by teachers as the opportunity to encourage the development of "more advanced" cognitive skills. She would have been given the message that her style of programming (and so, also, her style of thinking) was inadequate, that she was capable of something better, such as, "the real thing."

The message that she could do better would not necessarily lead someone like Anne to reject computers or "do badly" with them on a technical level. We see many Annes following in the path of a Lisa or Robin. They respond to the dominant ethos of the computer culture by entering into an inauthentic relationship with the computer. This response can lead to a paradoxical reaction: frustrated bricoleurs appear at first sight to be extremely rigid "planners." Some turn to a "cookbook" approach—as when, in third grade, we were told to divide fractions by turning "the second fraction" upside down. When denied a chance to do their "real thinking," they turn to rules that do not require them to think at all. People like Lisa and Robin "escape to conformity," a reaction that muffles the manifestation of a significantly "different voice" in computing. But that voice is there. Recall the graduate student Lorraine, who says she tries "to look like I'm doing what everyone else is doing" in order to preserve "appearances." Her style is hidden beneath her efforts to fit in.

We have said that, in our culture, the structured, plan-oriented, abstract thinkers don't only share a style but constitute an epistemological elite. Language such as "pure science" and "pure mathematics" implies that their superiority is achieved by filtering out the concrete, and this means a continual put-down of people like Lisa and Robin. But although this way of thinking is deeply entrenched, there is cause for measured optimism. We conclude by describing how one opening for change is coming from within the technological culture itself. It takes the form of a new emphasis on computational objects which is making itself felt in domains as diverse as debates about which personal computers are the best and how to build artificial brains.

Its simplest manifestation is the fashion for using icons in controlling personal computers. Consider two ways of getting a computer to copy information—for example, the text of a section of this chapter—from one diskette to another. In a traditional computer operating system, this requires typing an instruction. In an iconic system, the same effect may be achieved by moving a screen symbol for the text on top of a screen symbol for the diskette. The current technology for the act of moving something on a screen falls short of what the computer industry expects to provide quite soon, but existing systems, such as the "mouse" or touch-sensitive screen, already give a tactile sense that recalls Anne's experience of programming as collage.

Even superficial use of icons is enough to transform the perception of the computer by people who are using it in computationally simple ways. For example, many writers who began to use computers reluctantly, as a necessary evil, are finding that warmer relationships are mediated by the icons, the mouse, and the cozier appearance of a Macintosh. And although these particular warmer relationships do not involve programming, their cultural influence means that the next generation people like Lisa and Robin will come to programming courses with a different sense of who "owns" the computer.

But a multiplicity of technical methods doesn't by itself lead to pluralism. It can simply lead to competition. This point has been recently dramatized by the terms of the competition between the IBM PC and the Apple Macintosh computers. Many have been party to heated conversations between those who argue the superiority of each. (In the IBM the typical interaction with the computer is typing an instruction; in the Macintosh it is manipulating a screen object.) But when we understand the computer as a projective screen for different approaches to knowledge, we can listen to these conversations in a new way. Different people are comfortable with each system. When people fight about the IBM versus the Macintosh, what they are really trying to do is defend their cognitive style. And yet, the debate has both industry and consumers arguing in terms of whether IBM or Apple got it "right."

The Logo language allowed Anne and Alex to program in their own styles. But in many educational settings where Logo is defined as the computer language for children who have not reached the top stage in Piaget's hierarchy, allowing even as sophisticated a thinker as Anne or as creative a thinker as Alex to use their styles would be bought at the cost of defining their intellects as immature. Similarly, the very success of the Macintosh has often been cast in terms that reflect the elitism of the dominant computer culture. The Macintosh iconic interface has been brilliantly marketed as "the computer for the rest of us," with the implication that "the rest of us" need things made simple and don't want to "be bothered with technical things." And from the beginning, the implication has been that it is a good system for women and children. If it is, it is not, in any simple sense, because it is "easy." When the Macintosh is experienced as good, it is experienced as good because, for some people, it feels like a thinking environment that "fits," while for others, and for very different reasons, the IBM feels like a thinking environment that "fits."

As it happens, the Macintosh's iconic style may be winning this argument. The designers of computer interfaces might interpret this as final proof of the technical superiority of icons. A psychologist might read it as putting in question the hard/soft split. Perhaps everyone is really "soft" after all, and "hard" is a construct that is dropped when it is not needed for acceptability or prestige or functionality. Others might simply say that icons are "easier." All of the above may be in part true. But from our perspective what is important is that the iconic victories are part of a larger cultural shift towards an acceptance of concrete, relational ways of thinking.

The icons in the Macintosh reflect something deeper, a philosophy of "object-oriented programming." In the traditional concept of a program the unit of thought is an instruction to the computer to do something. In object-oriented programming the unit of thought is creating and modifying interactive agents within a program for which the natural metaphors are biological and social rather than algebraic. The elements of the program interact as would actors on a stage. This style of programming is not only more congenial to those who favor soft approaches, but puts an intellectual value on a way of thinking that is resonant with their own. It undermines the elitist position of the "hards" in two ways. First, within the world of programming, it legitimates alternative methods. Second, in the larger intellectual culture, it supports trends in cognitive theory that challenge the traditional canon.

Until recently, prevailing models of cognitive theory have bolstered the commitment of psychologists and educators to the superiority of algorithmic and formal thinking. They were given support by the cognitive theorists most influential in the computer world, the leaders of the artificial intelligence community. In the late 1970s and early 1980s, the model of AI with the greatest visibility was the rule-based "expert system" with its model of mind as a structured information processor. Critics of how computers influence the way we think cited the information-processing model as demonstrating the instrumental reason and the lack of ambiguity allegedly inherent in all computational thinking about intelligence (see, e.g., Dreyfus, 1979; Weizenbaum, 1976). But artificial intelligence is not a unitary enterprise. And recently, another model has become increasingly prominent: "emergent AI."[26]

Emergent AI does not suggest that the computer be given rules to follow but tries to set up a system of independent elements within a computer from whose interactions intelligence is expected to emerge. Its sustaining images are drawn,

---

[26] For more extended comments on the "two AIs," see Papert (1988b).

not from the logical, but from the biological. Families of neuronlike entities, societies of anthropomorphized subminds and sub-subminds, are in a simultaneous interaction whose goal is the generation of a fragment of mind. We noted that these models are sometimes theorized in notions of "mind as society," where negotiational processes are placed at the heart of all thinking. Those who espouse and support such models are more inclined to find bricolage acceptable than are classical Piagetians. What concerns us here is not which of these trends in AI is "correct," just as we aren't advocating a choice between the use of icons and the use of textual instructions in computer operating systems. What does concern us is that the new trends—icons, object-oriented programming, actor languages, society of mind, emergent AI—all create an intellectual climate in the computational world that undermines the idea that formal methods are the only methods.

Thus, recent technological developments in interfaces, programming philosophy, and artificial intelligence have created an opening for epistemological pluralism. There is the possibility for new alliances between computation and the theorists as well as the practitioners of a science of the concrete. We began by presenting the notion of epistemological pluralism by reference to three streams of thought which, although different in many ways, converge in reasserting the importance of things in thinking. We close by noting the opportunity for their theoretical unification.

Louis Althusser wrote about psychoanalysis that the important breakthrough was not any particular statement about the mind, but the step of recognizing the unconscious as an object of study that defines a new theoretical enterprise (Althusser, 1964–1965). Psychology had considered the rational and the conscious as the quintessential mental activity; Sigmund Freud shifted the ground to the irrational and the unconscious. The unconscious was not only given recognition as an important "factor," but became an object of science in its own right. Similarly, we believe there is an opening for a break with ways of thinking that take the abstract as the quintessential activity of intelligence. We believe that the three intellectual movements we have noted—feminism, ethnography of science, and computation—are elements of a sea change that would not only recognize concrete thinking as important, but promote it to an object of science in its own right.

On a more down-to-earth level, there is every reason to think that revaluing the concrete will contribute to a computer culture that treats the computer as an expressive medium and encourages differentiated styles of use and relationship with. There is every reason to think that this computer culture will be more welcoming and nurturing to women—and to men. Gilligan has said that "women's place in man's life cycle" is to protect the recognition "of the continuing importance of attachment in human life (Gilligan, 1982, p. 23). We conclude with an analogous point. The role of feminist studies in the nascent computer culture is to promote the recognition of diversity in how we think about and appropriate formal systems and encourage the acceptance of our profound human connection with our tools.

REFERENCES

Althusser, L. (1964–1965, December–January). Freud et Lacan. *La Nouvelle Critique,* Nos. 161–162.

Bleir, R. (Ed.). (1986). *Feminist approaches to science.* New York: Pergamon.

Chodorow, N. (1978). *The reproduction of mothering: Psychoanalysis and the sociology of gender.* Berkeley, CA: University of California Press.

Davis, P. J., & Hersh, R. (1981). *The mathematical experience.* Boston: Houghton Mifflin.

Dreyfus, H. (1979). *What computers can't do: The limits of artificial intelligence* (2nd ed.). New York: Harper and Row.

Feyerabend, P. (1975). *Against method: The outline of an anarchistic theory of knowledge.* London: NLB.

Feynman, R. (1985). *Surely you must be joking Mr. Feynman.* New York: Norton

Gibbs, J. (1977). Kohlberg's stages of moral judgement: A constructive critique. *Harvard Education Review, 47*(4), 43–61.

Gilligan, C. (1982). *In a different voice: Psychological theory and women's development.* Cambridge, MA: Harvard University Press.

Gilligan, C. (1988). Two moral orientations. In C. Gilligan, J. V. Ward, & J. M. Taylor (Eds.), *Mapping the moral domain.* Cambridge, MA: Harvard University Press.

Greenberg, J. R., & Mitchell, S. A. (1983). *Object relations in psychoanalytic theory.* Cambridge, MA: Harvard University Press.

Hanson, N. R. (1958). *Patterns of discovery.* Cambridge, UK: Cambridge University Press.

Haraway, D. (1979). The biological enterprise: Sex, mind, and profit from human engineering to sociobiology. *Radical History Review, 20,* 206–237.

Harding, S., & Hintikka, M. B. (Eds.). (1983). *Discovering reality: Feminist perspectives on epistemology, metaphysics, methodology, and philosophy of science.* London: Reidel.

Harel, I. (1988). *Software design for learning: Children's construction of meaning for fractions and Logo programming.* Unpublished doctoral dissertation, MIT, Cambridge, MA.

Hofstadter, D. (1985). Waking up from the Boolean dream, or subcognition as computation. In D. Hofstadter (Ed.), *Metamagical themas: Questing for the essence of mind and pattern* (pp. 631–665). New York: Basic Books.

Kay, A. (1977). Microelectronics and the personal computer. *Scientific American, 237,* 230–244.

Kay, A. (1985). Software's second act. *Science, 85,* 122.

Keller, E. F. (1983). *A feeling for the organism: The life and work of Barbara McClintock.* San Francisco: W. H. Freeman.

Keller, E. F. (1985). *Reflections on gender and science.* New Haven, CT: Yale University Press.

Kerba, L. K. (1986). On *In A Different Voice:* An interdisciplinary forum. *Signs, 11*(2), 304–333.

Kiesler, S., Sproull, L., & Eccles, J. S. (1985). Poolhalls, chips, and war games: Women in the culture of computing. *Psychology of Women Quarterly, 9.*

Knorr-Cetina, K. (1981). *The manufacture of knowledge: An essay on the constructivist and contextual nature of science.* Oxford: Pergamon.

Knorr-Cetina, K., & Mulkay, M. (Eds.). (1983). *Science observed: Perspectives on the social studies of science.* London: Sage Publications.

Latour, B., & Woolgar, S. (1979). *Laboratory life: The social construction of scientific facts.* Beverly Hills, CA: Sage Publications.

Lave, J. (1988). *Cognition in practice: Mind, mathematics and culture in everyday life.* Cambridge, UK: Cambridge University Press.

Levi-Strauss, C. (1968). *The savage mind.* Chicago: University of Chicago Press.

Merchant, C. (1980). *The death of nature.* New York: Harper and Row.

Michalski, R. S., Michalsky, J. G., & Mitchell, T. M. (Eds.). (1983). *Machine learning: An artificial intelligence approach.* Los Altos, CA: Morgan Kaufmann.

Minsky, M. (1987). *Society of mind.* New York: Simon and Schuster.

Motherwell, L. (1988). *Gender and style differences in a Logo-based environment.* Unpublished doctoral dissertation, MIT.

Papert, S. (1980a). The mathematical unconscious. In J. Wechsler (Ed.), *Aesthetics and science.* Cambridge, MA: MIT Press.

Papert, S. (1980b). The gears of my childhood. In S. Papert (Ed.), *Mindstorms: Children, computers, and powerful ideas.* New York: Basic Books.

Papert, S. (1980c). *Mind storms: Children, computers, and powerful ideas.* New York: Basic Books.

Papert, S. (1987). Technological thinking versus computer criticism. *Educational Researcher, 16*(1), 22–30.

Papert, S. (1988). One AI or many. *Daedulus, 117*(1), 1–13.

Papert, S., de Sessa, A., Weir, S., & Watt, D. (1979). *Final Report of the Brookline Logo Project* (Logo Memos 53 and 54). Cambridge, MA: MIT.

Piaget, J. (1951). *La prise de conscience.* Paris: Universitaires de France.

Piaget, J., & Inhelder, B. (1958). *The growth of logical thinking from childhood to adolescence.* New York: Basic Books.

Rogoff, B., & Lave, J. (Eds.). (1984). *Everyday cognition: Its development in social context.* Cambridge, MA: Harvard University Press.

Rumelhart, E. D., McClelland, J. J., & the PDP Research Group. (1986). *Parallel distributed processing: Explorations in the microstructure of cognition.* Cambridge, MA: MIT Press.

Sutherland, R., & Hoyles, C. (1988). Gender perspectives on Logo programming in the mathematics curriculum. In C. Hoyles (Eds.), *Girls and computers* (Bedford Way Papers, No. 34), London: Institute of Education, University of London.

Toulmin, S. (1972). *Human understanding.* Princeton, NJ: Princeton University Press.

Traweek, S. (1989). *Beantimes and lifetimes: The world of high energy physicists.* Cambridge, MA: Harvard University Press.

Turkle, S. (1980). Computer as Roschach. *Society, 17,* 15–22.

Turkle, S. (1984). *The second self: Computers and the human spirit.* New York: Simon and Schuster.

Turkle, S. (1988a). Computational reticence: Why women fear the intimate machine. In C. Kramarae (Ed.), *Technology and women's voices: Keeping in touch.* New York: Pergamon.

Turkle, S. (1988b). Artificial intelligence and psychoanalysis. *Daedalus, 117*(1), 241–268.

Turkle, S. (in press). Romantic reactions: Paradoxical responses to the computer presence. In M. Sosna & J. J. Sheehan (Eds.), *Boundaries of humanity: Humans, animals, machines.* Berkeley, CA: University of California Press.

Turkle, S., Schön, D., Nielsen, B., Orsini, M. S., & Overmeer, W. (1988). *Project Athena at MIT.* Unpublished manuscript.

Weir, S. (1987). *Cultivating minds: A Logo casebook.* New York: Harper and Row.

Weizenbaum. (1976). *Computer power and human reason.* San Francisco: W. H. Freeman.

Wittgenstein, L. (1953). *Philosophical investigations.* New York: Macmillan.

Stephen Ocko Photography

Revaluing the concrete will contribute to a computer culture that treats computers as expressive media and encourages differentiated styles of use; thus, being more welcoming and nurturing to women, and to men.

Seymour Papert with some Logo programs at Project Headlight.

10

Abstract Meditations on the Concrete
and Concrete Implications for Mathematics Education

Uri Wilensky

"No ideas but in things"—William Carlos Williams

INTRODUCTION

Seymour Papert has recently called for a "revaluation of the concrete": a revolution in education and cognitive science that will overthrow logic from "on top and put it on tap." Turkle and Papert (Chapter 9, this volume) situate the concrete thinking paradigm in a new "epistemological pluralism"—an acceptance and valuation of multiple thinking styles, as opposed to their stratification into hierarchically valued stages. As evidence of an emerging trend towards the concrete, they cite feminist critics such as Gilligan's (1982) work on the contextual or relational mode of moral reasoning favored by most women, and Fox Keller's (1983) analysis of the Nobel-prize-winning biologist Barbara McClintock's proximal relationship with her maize plants, her "feeling for the organism." They cite hermeneutic critics such as Lave (1988), whose studies of situated cognition suggest that all learning is highly specific and should be studied in real world contexts.

For generations now we have viewed children's intellectual growth as proceeding from the concrete to the abstract, from Piaget's concrete operations stage to the more advanced stage of formal operations (e.g., Piaget, 1952). What is meant then by this call for revaluation of the concrete?

And what are the implications of this revaluation for education? Are we being asked to restrict children's intellectual horizons, to limit the domain of inquiry in which we encourage the child to engage? Are we to give up on teaching general strategies and limit ourselves to very context specific practices? And what about mathematics education? Even if we were prepared to answer in the affirmative to all the above questions for education in general, surely in mathematics education we would want to make an exception? If there is any area of human knowledge that is abstract and formal, surely mathematics is. Are we to banish objects in the head from the study of mathematics? Should we confine ourselves to manipulatives such as Lego blocks and Cuisinaire Rods? Still more provocatively, shall we all go back to counting on our fingers?

We often use phrases, such as "concrete thinking," "concrete-example," "make it concrete," when thinking about our own thinking as well as in our educational practice. In this chapter I will show that such phrases, although often used, are not well understood—indeed the standard definitions we have of "concrete" are flawed and inadequate. I present a new characterization of the concrete that addresses these inadequacies, expands our notion of the concrete, draws implications for our educational practice and, in the sense I will develop, concretizes it.

To begin our investigation we will need to take a philosophical detour and examine the meaning of the word *concrete*. What do we mean when we say that something—a concept, idea, piece of knowledge (henceforward an *object*)—is concrete?

STANDARD DEFINITIONS OF CONCRETE

Our first associations with the word concrete often suggest something tangible, solid; you can touch it, smell it, kick it[1]; it is real. A closer look reveals some confusion in this intuitive notion. Among those objects we refer to as concrete there are words, ideas, feelings, stories, descriptions. None of those can actually be "kicked." So what are these putative tangible objects we are referring to?

One reply to the above objection is to say: No no, you misunderstand us, what we mean is that the object referred to by a concrete description has these tangible properties, not the description itself. The more the description allows us to visualize (or, if you will, *sensorize*) an object, to pick out, say, a particular scene or situation, the more concrete it is. The more specific the more concrete, the more general the less concrete. In line with this, Random House says *concrete* is "particular, relating to an instance of an object" not its class.

Thus, my pillowcase is concrete; it is a unique instance with its particular color (faded milky white), texture (abraded cotton, but soft, like a well-worn jean), and elasticity (less than it was). But a mathematical triangle is not; it is

---

[1] As in Samuel Johnson's famous refutation of idealism by kicking a stone.

described purely by its formal properties and has no color, thickness, nor any richness of detail apart from its defining properties.

A common opposition or dichotomy is to oppose abstract to concrete. Webster's says "a poem is concrete, poetry is abstract." We thus have an implied continuum that, as it moves from pillowcases to triangles, gets less concrete and more abstract. This particular pen that I am currently using, which is made by Papermate, is black, and has a cap roughly one-sixth as long as the stem, which has some chew marks on it, is much more concrete than just plain "pen" or even "Papermate pen." These descriptions of my pen ascend[2] in levels of abstraction and can be further abstracted by making the move to "writing implement" or "communication tool." Note that, in the last case, objects which are not at all similar to pens,[3] objects such as language itself, are subsumed together with plain Papermates under the heading of "communication tool." Under this view, an attempt to operationalize a criterion for deciding if a concept or description is concrete might look like: "determine how many objects in the world could fit this description; the lower the number the more concrete."[4]

Let us call the notion of concrete specified by the above the *standard view*. If we adopt the standard view, then it is natural for us to want our children to move away from the confining world of the concrete, where they can only learn things about relatively few objects, to the more expansive world of the abstract, where what they learn will apply widely and generally.

Yet somehow our attempts at teaching abstractly leave our expectations unfulfilled. The more abstract our teaching in the school, the more alienated and bored are our students, and far from being able to apply their knowledge generally across domains, their knowledge displays a "brittle" character, usable only in the exact contexts in which it was learned.[5] Numerous studies have

---

[2] Our language uses height as a metaphoric scale to measure concreteness. Thus, the very concrete is down and the abstract up (where presumably it is hard to reach and to "grasp" and to "hold on to").

[3] That is, if we use a sensory metric as a measure of similarity.

[4] Provided that there is at least one such object. If there are no objects satisfying the description, the concreteness of the object is not specified. An amusing probably apocryphal anecdote concerns a mathematician giving a guest lecture at a research university. He defines a Rotman-Herstein group and then proceeds to spend the next hour proving all kinds of marvelous theorems about groups of this kind. Towards the end of the lecture a graduate student gets up and asks: "Esteemed professor, I am very impressed by all these amazing theorems that you have proved about Rotman-Herstein groups, but I have been trying to come up with specific (concrete) examples of such groups, and I can't find any except the trivial cases of which your theorems are manifestly true." It took the professor and the student only a little more time to show that no other examples of Rotman-Herstein groups exist.

[5] A fruitful analogy can be made here between this kind of brittleness and the brittle representation of knowledge that so called expert systems in AI exhibit. In effect this kind of abstract teaching is akin to programming our children to be rule-driven computer programs. A similar kind of brittleness can be found in simple animals, such as the sphex wasp. For a discussion of "sphexish" behavior and how it differs from human behavior, see Hofstadter (1982) and Dennett (1984).

shown that students are unable to solve standard math and physics problems when these problems are given without the textbook chapter context. Yet they are easily able to solve them when they are assigned as homework for a particular chapter of the textbook (e.g., diSessa, 1983; Schoenfeld, 1985).

CRITIQUES OF THE STANDARD VIEW

Upon closer examination there are serious problems with the standard view. What does it mean for something to be specific as opposed to general? Surely, we know what we mean by that. Well, let's see: Specific descriptions can be satisfied by only a few objects, while general ones can be satisfied by many. Let's take an example, say the word "snow."[6] Is snow concrete? Your first reaction would probably be: Of course, snow, that fluffy stuff that falls from the sky each winter, t at stuff that covers the ground and for a moment makes the land a virgin untouched by human imprint, that stuff that fell on Robert Frost's horse while they were stopped one evening. Surely, if anything is specific and concrete, snow is!? Unless, of course, you are an Eskimo (and my apologies for presuming otherwise). For Eskimos, as we all know, have many words for snow (22 according to my Funk and Wagnalls), and each of them describes a particular kind of snow with its particular sensory qualities. Snow, for an Eskimo, is a vast generalization, combining together 22 different substances, some of which may be as different to an Eskimo as "pens" and "languages" are to us.

So we see here one faulty assumption that underlies the standard view: the assumption that there are a fixed number of objects in the world, such as, that people's ontologies are identical,[7] or that there is one universal ontology in an objective world.[8] But as was first noted by Quine (1960), this is not the case: There are a multitude of ways to slice up our world. Depending on what kind and how many distinctions you make, your ontology can be entirely different. Objects like snow which are particulars in one ontology can be generalizations in another. Indeed for any concrete particular that we choose, there is a world view from which this particular looks like a generalization.

An even more radical critique of the notion of a specific object or individual comes out of recent research in artificial intelligence (AI). In a branch of AI called emergent AI, objects that are typically perceived as wholes are explained as emergent effects of large numbers of interacting smaller elements. Even the

---

[6] Famous for its inclusion in the defining sentence of the logicist's account of the correspondence theory of truth: " 'Snow is white' is true if and only if snow is white" (see Tarski, 1956).

[7] For if this were not the case, then each person who applied the definition would get a different result, and moreover, the same person would get a different result at different periods of his or her development.

[8] A tenet of the empiricist world view. For an illuminating comparison of the empiricist, rationalist, and hermeneutic stances, see Packer and Addison (1989).

human mind, our once archetypal example of an individual, is now said to be made up of a society of agents (Minsky, 1987). Research in brain physiology as well as in machine vision indicate that the translation of light patterns on the retina into a "parsing" of the world into objects in a scene is an extremely complex task. It is also underdetermined; by no means is there just one unique parsing of the inputs. Objects that seem like single entities to us could just as easily be multiple and perceived as complex scenes, while apparently complex scenes could be grouped into single entities. In effect the brain constructs a theory of the world from the hints it receives from the information in the retina. Thus it is entirely possible to imagine a visiting alien "seeing" what you call this concrete chair as a random collection of variegated particles designated by some strange abstract label. The alien might not even perceive the area of space you call.chair to be filled at all, or to be filled partially by one object and partially by another. To make this alien more concrete, just imagine for instance a virus's "eye"-view of say a wicker chair. It is because children share a common set of sensing apparatus (or a common way of obtaining feedback from the world, see Brandes & Wilensky, Chapter 20, this volume) and a common set of experiences such as touching, grasping, banging, ingesting,[9] that children come as close as they do to "concretizing" the same objects in the world.[10]

This critique of the standard view is also beholden to Piaget. But instead of focusing on the progression of the child through stages, this view takes as its focus Piaget's emphasis on construction—that the child actively constructs his or her world. Each object constructed is added to the personal ontology of the child. The phenomenon of conservation indicates the creation of a new stable entity that is added to the ontology. Before the conservation of number, there is no number object in the child's world.[11] One consequence of this view is that we can no longer maintain a simple sensory criterion for concreteness, since virtually all objects, all concepts which we understand, are constructed, by an individual, assembled in that particular individual's way, from more primitive elements.[12] Objects are not simply given to the senses; they are actively constructed.[13]

We have seen that when we talk about objects we can't leave out the person who constructs the object. (To paraphrase Papert: You can't think about *some-*

---

[9] I ignore here the social experiences which play a large role in determining which objects are useful in construct.

[10] Alternatively, we can say that children construct a *model* of the world through feedback they receive from their active engagement with the world (again, see Wilensky, 1991a).

[11] Or alternatively, there is a number concept, but it is incommensurable with the adult concept (see Carey, 1985).

[12] In other words, whether something is an object or not is not an observer-independent fact, there is no universal objective (sic) way to define a given composition as an object. It thus follows that when we call an object concrete, we are not referring to an object "out there" but rather to an object "in here," to our personal constructions of the object.

[13] Even the recognition of the most "concrete" particular object as an object requires the construction of the notion of object permanence.

thing without thinking about *someone* thinking about *something*.) It thus follows that it is futile to search for concreteness in the object—we must look at a person's construction of the object, at the relationship between the person and the object.

As an example, let us return to play in the "snow" one more time. As we have seen, "snow," which for a New Englander is concrete, is an abstract generalization for an Eskimo. The particular varieties of snow which for an Eskimo are concrete are not even objects in the New Englander ontology. The distinctions, unimportant to most New Englanders, have not been made, leaving the specific snow objects unconstructed. We search in vain if we seek a property of snow that will determine its concreteness. We must look at our construction of a snow description, our relationship with snow, in order to find out if it is concrete for us or not.

TOWARDS A NEW DEFINITION OF CONCRETE

> *"Only Connect"*—E. M. Forster

The above discussion leads us to see that concreteness is not a property of an object but rather a *property of a person's relationship to an object*.[14] Concepts that were hopelessly abstract at one time can become concrete for us if we get into the "right relationship" with them.

I now offer a new perspective from which to expand our understanding of the concrete. The more connections we make between an object and other objects, the more concrete it becomes for us. The richer the set of representations of the object, the more ways we have of interacting with it, the more concrete it is for us. Concreteness, then, is that property which measures the degree of our relatedness to the object, (the richness of our representations, interactions, connections with the object), how close we are to it, or, if you will, the *quality of our relationship* with the object.

Once we see this, it is not difficult to go further and see that any object/ concept can become concrete for someone. The pivotal point on which the determination of concreteness turns is not some intensive examination of the object, but rather an examination of the modes of interaction and the models which the person uses to understand the object. This view will lead us to allow objects not mediated by the senses, objects which are usually considered abstract—such as mathematical objects—to be concrete; provided that we have

---

[14] Or as we shall say later, *"concretion"* is the process by which "stuff" (i.e., sense data, more primitive objects) become objects for an individual—in other words the process of an individual coming into relationship with an object.

multiple modes of engagement with them and a sufficiently rich collection of models to represent them.

When our relationship with an object is poor, our representations of it limited in number, and our modes of interacting with it few, the object becomes inaccessible to us. So, metaphorically, the abstract object is high above, as opposed to concrete objects, which are down and hence reachable, "graspable." We can dimly see it, touch it only with removed instruments; we have remote access, as opposed to the object in our hands that we can operate on in so many different modalities. Objects of thought which are given solely by definition, and operations given only by simple rules, are abstract in this sense. Like the word learned only by dictionary definition, it is accessible through the narrowest of channels and tenuously apprehended. It is only through use and acquaintance in multiple contexts, through coming into relationship with other words/concepts/experiences, that the word has meaning for the learner and in our sense becomes concrete for him or her. As Minsky says in his *Society of Mind:*

> The secret of what anything means to us depends on how we've connected it to all the other things we know. That's why it's almost always wrong to seek the "real meaning" of anything. A thing with just one meaning has scarcely any meaning at all. (Minsky, 1987, p. 64)

This new definition of concrete as a relational property turns the old definition on its head. Now, thinking concretely is seen not to be a narrowing of the domain of intellectual discourse, but rather as opening it up to the whole world of relationship. What we strive for is a new kind of knowledge, not brittle and susceptible to breakage like the old, but in the words of Mary Belenky, "connected knowing" (Belenky, Clinchy, Goldberger, & Tarule, 1986).

Keeping in mind that the adjective concrete applies not to things, not to concepts or ideas or physical objects, but rather to relationships between people and these things, it follows that what we would like to achieve in the schools by revaluing the concrete is not a restriction of children's knowledge to a smaller but more "concrete" domain, but rather an enrichment of the child's relationship to the whole panorama of human intellectual endeavor. The lesson we take from Piaget is not that the child develops by leaving behind the primitive world of concrete operations and leaping into the enlightened world of adult formal operations. Rather what we desire is that the child concretize his or her world by engaging in multiple and complex relationships with it.

CONSEQUENCES OF THE NEW VIEW

Let us return to the classroom and try to gain insight by seeing how these ideas work out in a school setting. We will take as our example the teaching of fractions, a subject thought to be difficult for most children to apprehend because the material is "so abstract."[15] Indeed fractions are an appropriate example for study, since one of the primary difficulties in understanding fractions is in grasping that the fraction expresses a *relationship* between a part and a whole (e.g., Harel, 1988). The difficulty lies in the child's confusion about what the whole is, the very same difficulty we encountered when trying to define *concrete*.

The traditional approach to teaching the manipulation of fractions is to give rules for each operation, rules such as "to add fractions, make a common denominator," "to divide fractions, invert and multiply."[16] These rules are given as if they were definitions: They are supposed to serve as the meaning of their corresponding operations. They are not connected to each other, nor to previous knowledge about fractions. Indeed, studies have shown that, in the case of dividing fractions, no connection is made between the notion of division in fractions and familiar division of whole numbers (e.g., Ball, 1990; Wilensky, 1991b). These practices lead to a disconnected knowing, a knowledge of fractions that can only bear up if one is given problems that just call for application of these rules.[17]

The solution to this problem, is not to avoid abstract objects like fractions, or even to replace rules for manipulating them with situated practices such as those suggested by Lave (1988). These solutions use the old mistaken notion of concrete, a notion of concrete as a property of certain objects but not others, in order to restrict the domain of learning. Rather, we must present multiple representations of fractions, both sensory (pies, blocks, clocks) and nonsensory (ratios, equivalence classes, binary relations), and give opportunities for the child to interact with all of these and establish connections between them. This kind of enrichment of the relationship between the child and the fraction will make the fraction concrete for the child and provide a robust and meaningful knowledge of fractions.

By establishing this kind of complex and multifaceted relationship with the fraction, the child may still not fall in love with fractions as Papert did with the

---

[15] For those of us who think that fractions are not abstract, substitute imaginary numbers for fractions. I recall that, in grade school, when I first encountered imaginary numbers, they were very mysterious. What, I wondered, made some numbers imaginary and others real? Reflection on this question helped me see that despite the suggestive language real numbers weren't so real and imaginary numbers weren't so imaginary. Later, a high school student told me: "a mathematician is someone for whom imaginary numbers are just as real as real numbers." Not a bad definition.

[16] A rhyme gathered from one classroom goes, "Ours is not to reason why, just invert and multiply."

[17] Though one can go remarkably far with such limited knowledge. When a class of MIT graduate students was asked, "What does it mean to divide two fractions?" almost no one could muster any kind of answer. Of course, all of them knew how to perform the calculation, yet each student, when made aware of the question, expressed a lack of understanding of what's going on. Though they could all state the flip and multiply rule, no one felt that this was a sufficient explanation of what division of fractions meant.

gears of his childhood (Papert, 1980), but at least fractions will be brought into the "family" thus enabling a lifelong relationship with them.

Most of us who have participated in mathematics classes have had the experience of myriad definitions and theorems swirling about you, in the air, out of reach, any attempt to grab hold of one sends the others speeding away. Okay, so you can do the homework, but what is really going on here?

If you were one of the fortunate ones, at some point in the class something clicked and it all came together.[18] But the fact that it all came together for you, though doubtless due in part to your own native talent, is largely a matter of happy accident. Almost nothing is done in our math classrooms to facilitate this clicking into understanding.

Those of us who click are rewarded, and often pursue the study of mathematics. Those of us who do not, learn that they "aren't good at math" and rarely continue on in it. I argue here that this sudden click of understanding, this dawn of early light, is nothing other than our old friend the concretizing process (henceforward *concretion*) at work. Concretion is the process of the new knowledge coming into relationship with itself and with prior knowledge, and thus becoming concrete.

It would thus appear again that the standard Piagetian view of stage is turned on its head. In the school setting, rather than moving from the concrete to the formal, we often begin our understanding of new concepts (just as we often do with new people) by having a formal introduction. Gradually, as the relationship develops it becomes more intimate and concrete. Outside of school, in the world, our nascent understanding of a new concept, while not usually formal, is often abstract because we haven't yet constructed the connections that will concretize it. The reason we mistakenly believed we were moving from the concrete to the abstract is that the more advanced objects of knowledge (e.g., permutations, probabilities) which children gain in the formal operations stage are not concretized by most adults. Since these concepts/operations are not concretized by most of us, they remain abstract and thus it seems as if the most advanced knowledge we have is abstract. It follows that the actual process of knowledge development moves from the abstract to the concrete. Only those pieces of knowledge that we have not yet concretized remain abstract.

HOW SHOULD EDUCATORS RESPOND?

Translated into practical advice for educators, this perspective gives a few answers and raises many questions. How do we foster the concretion process? What kind of learning environment nurtures it and promotes its growth? Clearly,

---

[18] Like a self-organizing system reaching a stable state?

much more research is needed to explore the many facets of this question. Here we point to only one: the *constructionist paradigm* for learning (see Harel & Papert, 1990). When we construct objects in the world, we come into engaged relationship with them and the knowledge needed for their construction. It is especially likely then that we will make this knowledge concrete. When Harel's fourth and fifth graders (Harel, 1988) construct a computer program for representing and teaching fractions, they have the opportunity to meet and connect multiple representations of fractions and to construct their own idiosyncratic relationships with and between them.

When people construct objects in the world external to them, they are forced to make explicit decisions about how to connect different pieces of their knowledge. How does one representation fit with another? Which pieces of knowledge are the most basic? Which are important enough to incorporate into the construction, and which can be safely left out? Which really matter to them and which don't engage them at all? The constructionist paradigm, by encouraging the externalization of knowledge, promotes seeing it as a distinct other with which we can come into meaningful relationship.

I leave you with a thought experiment: What kinds of relationships between people would be fostered by a society which stipulated that people be introduced to each other formally and thereafter relate only in prescribed, rule-driven ways? If you shudder at this prospect, consider the analogy between this scenario and the *instructionist paradigm* for learning (see Harel & Papert, 1990). It is through people's own idiosyncratically personal ways of connecting to other people that meaningful relationships are established. In a similar way, when learners are in an environment in which they construct their own relationships with the objects of knowledge, these relationships can become deeply meaningful and profound.

ACKNOWLEDGMENTS

I wish to thank Seymour Papert and Ellie Baker for stimulating discussions which gave birth to this chapter. Donna Woods, David Rosenthal, Mitchel Resnick, Idit Harel, David Frydman, and Aaron Brandes provided helpful and insightful comments on earlier drafts.

REFERENCES

Ball, D. (1990). Prospective elementary and secondary teachers' understanding of division. *Journal of Research in Mathematics Education, 21*(2), 132–144.

Belenky, M., Clinchy, B., Goldberger, N., & Tarule, J. (1986). *Women's ways of knowing.* New York: Basic Books.

Carey, S. (1985). *Conceptual change in childhood.* Cambridge, MA: MIT Press.

Dennett, D. (1984). *Elbow room: The varieties of free will worth wanting*. Cambridge, MA: MIT Press.

diSessa, A. (1983). Phenomenology and the evolution of intuition. In D. Gentner & A. Stevens (Eds.), *Mental models*. Hillsdale, NJ: Erlbaum.

Fox Keller, E. (1983). *A feeling for the organism: The life and work of Barbara McClintock*. San Francisco, CA: W. H. Freeman.

Gilligan, C. (1986). *In a different voice: Psychological theory and women's development*. Cambridge, MA: Harvard University Press.

Harel, I. (1988). *Software design for learning: Children's learning fractions and Logo programming through instructional software design*. Unpublished PhD Dissertation, Media Laboratory, MIT, Cambridge, MA.

Harel, I., & Papert, S. (1990). Software design as a learning environment. *Interactive Learning Environments Journal, 1*(1), 1–32.

Hofstadter, D. R. (1982). Can Creativity be mechanized? *Scientific American, 247.*

Lave, J. (1988). *Cognition in practice: Mind, mathematics and culture in everyday life*. Cambridge, England: Cambridge University Press.

Minsky, M. (1987). *The society of mind*. New York: Simon & Schuster.

Packer, M., & Addison, R. (Eds.). (1989). *Entering the circle: Hermeneutic investigation in psychology*. Albany, NY: State University of New York Press.

Papert, S. (1980). *Mindstorms: Children, computers, and powerful ideas*. New York: Basic Books.

Piaget, J. (1952). *The origins of intelligence in children*. New York: International University Press.

Quine, W. (1960). *Word and object*. Cambridge, MA: MIT Press.

Schoenfeld, A. (1985). *Mathematical problem solving*. Orlando, FL: Academic Press.

Tarski, A. (1956). *Logic, semantics, metamathematics*. Oxford, England: Clarendon Press.

Wilensky, U. (1991a). *Feedback, information, and domain construction*. Unpublished paper, MIT Media Laboratory, Cambridge, MA.

Wilensky, U. (1991b). *Fractional division*. Unpublished paper, MIT Media Laboratory, Cambridge, MA.

A simulation of "self-organizing" behavior, developed in *Logo, a new version of Logo with thousands of Turtles. By developing *Logo simulations, students can explore how patterns arise from decentralized interactions.

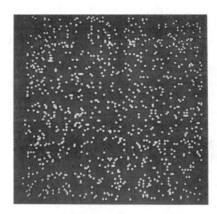

1000 creatures

As the creatures move, they drop a green pheromone.

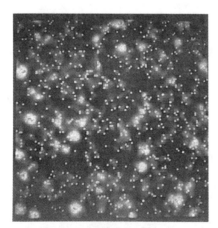

The creatures also "sniff" for the pheromone. If they sense the pheromone, they try to follow the gradient, to higher pheromone concentrations.

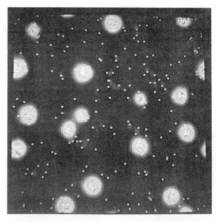

Each cluster is self-reinforcing: the more creatures, the more pheromone—making it more likely for the creatures to stay in the cluster.

11
Overcoming the Centralized Mindset:
Towards an Understanding of Emergent Phenomena

Mitchel Resnick

INTRODUCTION

Almost everywhere you look, in almost every domain of life, the forces of decentralization are on the rise. In Eastern Europe, centrally planned economies are crumbling. In American school systems, the effort known as "school-based management" is shifting power from centralized bureaucracies to individual schools. At the same time, scientists are gaining a deeper appreciation of the decentralized nature of many natural-world phenomena. In cognitive science, for example, the traditional centralized-planning model of the mind is being challenged by the decentralized models of Connectionism (e.g. Rumelhart, McClelland, & the PDP Research Group, 1986) and Society of Mind (Minsky, 1988).

There is little doubt that we have entered an Era of Decentralization. But how well prepared are we to understand the workings of decentralized systems? Researchers are finding that decentralized approaches are often more robust and parsimonious than their centralized counterparts (see, for example, Langton, 1989)—but decentralized systems also seem more difficult to understand. Decentralized systems typically consist of thousands (or more) components. The behavior of the overall system "emerges" from the interactions among these components. Trying to make sense of these emergent behaviors is a challenging task. Often, the behavior of the overall system bears little resemblance to the behaviors of the individual components. In an ant colony, for example, individual ants follow very simple rules, but the colony as a whole acts in rather sophisticated ways. Similarly, brains act very differently from individual neurons, and economic markets act very differently from individual buyers and

205

sellers. Indeed, in the upside-down world of decentralized systems, complexity can emerge from simplicity; order can emerge from randomness; global patterns can emerge from local rules; and sequential behaviors can emerge from parallel interactions.

This chapter presents a preliminary inquiry into how people think about decentralized systems. In particular: What heuristics and metaphors do people use when trying to make sense of decentralized systems? What new heuristics and metaphors could help them better understand the workings of such systems? What new tools could help people explore ideas about emergent phenomena?

To explore these questions, I developed a new computer-based environment called *Logo (pronounced *star-logo*). With *Logo, people can write rules for thousands of interacting "creatures," then observe the group behaviors that emerge. For example, people can simulate the emergence of foraging trails as ants search for food, or the emergence of traffic jams as cars interact with one another on a freeway. Initially, I am working with a small group of high-school students. By working with these students, I have begun to gain preliminary insights into how people think about certain simple decentralized systems.

THE CENTRALIZED MINDSET

Before students began using *Logo, I asked them to consider a hypothetical situation (inspired by Steels, 1990):

> Suppose that we discovered large deposits of gold on some distant planet. It is too dangerous and costly to send human astronauts to this planet, so we decide to send a spaceship with several thousand small robots. Each robot has a sensor to detect when it gets near gold, and a scoop to dig for (and carry) the gold. Once the spaceship lands on the planet, we want the robots to explore for gold and bring the gold back to the spaceship. How should we program each of the robots? In other words, what type of rules and strategies should the robots follow?

I chose this problem since it has strong similarities to a problem in the natural world: How do ants find and collect food? Ants generally solve the problem in a very decentralized way. They begin by searching randomly. When an ant finds food, it carries the food back to the nest, emitting a chemical pheromone as it walks. If another ant happens to detect this pheromone trail, it follows the trail to the food source, then reinforces the trail on its way back to the nest.

In presenting the robots-searching-for-gold problem, I asked the students to suggest general rules and strategies for the robots. (In particular, I told them *not* to write actual computer programs for the robots.) The students developed a variety of interesting and creative strategies. But there were certain consistencies in the student responses. Certain ideas came up again and again:

- *Centralized decision making.* In most of the strategies, one robot (or a small group of robots) was put in charge of the exploration process. For example: The "leader" tells the "explorer robots" where to explore. If an explorer finds gold, it reports back to the leader at the spaceship. The leader then assigns other robots to help the successful explorer.
- *Global communications.* The strategies generally assumed that each robot could communicate with every other robot, no matter where the robots were located, no matter how many robots were trying to communicate at the same time.
- *Absolute coordinates.* Many of the strategies assumed that the robots always had perfect knowledge of their locations. In one case, the "leader" assigned each robot a specific Cartesian coordinate to explore. Once a robot found gold, it communicated its exact location to the other robots (so that they could come and help).

In short, the student strategies conflicted with the ant strategies in almost every way. Ant strategies are decentralized rather than centralized, local rather than global, relative rather than absolute. That is not to say that the student strategies were *wrong;* in fact, many of the student strategies seemed like they would work. But it is intriguing that the students were so committed to centralized approaches, even in a situation specifically tailored to decentralized strategies.

Why did the students opt for more centralized strategies? Part of the answer, I think, is that people are familiar with many systems that are, in fact, organized by a central designer. When people see neat rows of corn in a field, they assume (correctly) that the corn was planted by a farmer. When people watch a ballet, they assume (correctly) that the movements of the dancers were planned by a choreographer. And from an early age, many children participate in systems (such as school classrooms) where power and authority are centralized.

But *familiarity* with centralized systems is not a totally satisfying explanation. People are also familiar with many decentralized systems. Indeed, the world is full of decentralized systems. The animals in the woods form a decentralized system; the cars in a traffic jam form a decentralized system. So why didn't the students use these familiar systems as metaphors in thinking about the robots and gold?

The reason, I think, is that people's experience with decentralized systems is largely *passive.* To be sure, people observe many decentralized systems, and they even participate in decentralized systems. But they rarely if every have the opportunity *to actively design* decentralized systems. When a person designs something, that person typically plays the role of the "central actor" in the system. Every time a person organizes a birthday party or arranges a softball game, it reinforces the idea that orderly activities must be centrally controlled.

As a result, people tend to develop what might be called a *centralized mindset.* When people see phenomena in the world, they tend to assume centralized control where none exists. When people see a flock of birds or a school of fish, many of them assume (incorrectly) that there must be a leader of the group. And when people see the diversity of complex creatures in the world, many of them assume (incorrectly) that there must be a single Designer of Life.

This centralized mindset is quite resistant to change. People need better models and metaphors for thinking about decentralized systems. And they need a way to design their own decentralized systems and to "play around" with emergent phenomena. That is what *Logo aims to provide.

*LOGO: A PROGRAMMING LANGUAGE FOR DECENTRALIZED SYSTEMS

There is an old saying that goes something like this: If a person has only a hammer, the whole world looks like a nail. Indeed, a person's perceptions and models of the world are strongly shaped by the objects that exist in the world. The same is true for computational systems. The way people interact with (and think about) a computational system depends strongly on the *objects* that compose the system. If the objects are well chosen for the intended task, even novices will use the system productively. If the objects are not well chosen, even experts will struggle.

*Logo is designed around two primary types of objects, chosen specifically to facilitate the modeling of decentralized systems and emergent phenomena. One type of object is a *creature*. Traditional versions of the Logo programming language include a graphic "turtle" on the screen. Students can command the turtle to move and draw lines on the screen (Papert, 1980). *Logo creatures go beyond the standard Logo turtle in several ways. Most important, *Logo programmers can control *hundreds* or *thousands* of creatures, and all of the creatures can act in parallel. In addition, *Logo provides programmers with built-in primitives to control local interactions between the creatures, and to create new creatures dynamically.

Programmers can use *Logo creatures to represent birds or ants or molecules or automobiles—or any other type of object that moves in the world. By creating different "breeds" of creatures, programmers can simulate situations with multiple object types—for example, foxes and rabbits in an ecology model, or antibodies and antigens in an immunology model.

The second type of *Logo object, called a *patch,* is a more striking departure from traditional Logo (and other programming languages). A patch is a small section of the "environment" in which the creatures live. (The term *patch* is borrowed from Hogeweg, 1989.) If, for example, the creatures are programmed to release a "chemical" as they move, each patch can keep track of the amount of chemical that has been released within its borders. Like creatures, patches are "active" objects, capable of computation. So, as the creatures move, each patch could diffuse some of its chemical into neighboring patches, or it could grow "food" based on the level of chemical within its borders. *Logo includes several special-purpose primitives (such as FOLLOW-GRADIENT) to facilitate interactions between creatures and patches, and others (such as DIFFUSE) to facilitate interactions between neighboring patches.

Thus, the environment is given equal status to the animals that inhabit it. Animals (in the form of creatures) and the environment (in the form of patches) are both computationally active objects. They can mutually influence one another, somewhat in the spirit of James Lovelock's (1979) Gaia. Of course, other "creature-oriented" programming languages (e.g., Steels, 1989; Taylor, Jefferson, Turner, & Goldman, 1989; Travers, 1989) allow programmers to control both creatures and the environment. But none treats the environment as an equal-status object. They tend to treat the environment as a passive entity, manipulated by the creatures that move within it. This view, not surprisingly, matches the way many people view the Earth itself. By reifying the environment, *Logo aims to change the way people think about creature–environment interactions—perhaps leading to new and richer ways of thinking about how phenomena emerge in the world.

The current version of *Logo is implemented on the Connection Machine, a massively parallel computer with at least 16,000 processors (Hillis, 1985). In this implementation, each Connection Machine processor controls one creature and several patches. But massively parallel hardware is not theoretically important to the *Logo approach. *Logo aims to provide the programmer with a clear *conceptual model* for massive parallelism. The programmer writes programs *as if* the creatures and patches are all acting in parallel, regardless of the underlying implementation.

EXAMPLES

This section describes several *Logo projects. Two were initiated by me, one by a pair of high-school students. These examples are intended to give a flavor of the types of issues and questions that arise while experimenting with decentralized systems.

Example 1: Aggregation. Under certain conditions, the larvae of some creatures (including bark beetles) aggregate into clusters (Prigogine & Stengers, 1984). The mechanism for this self-organizing behavior involves a chemical pheromone that the larvae emit. With each step, the larvae drop a bit of pheromone, but they also "sniff ahead" for the pheromone. If they can sense some pheromone, they follow the gradient of the pheromone (that is, they move in the direction of greatest concentration). The behavior of each creature can be simulated with a simple *Logo program:

```
to creature-rule
if ask-my-patch [pheromone] > smell-threshold
  [follow-gradient pheromone]
ask-my-patch [make "pheromone pheromone + 1]
right random 40 left random 40
forward 1
end
```

Meanwhile, each patch follows this rule: Let a little of your pheromone evaporate, then let the pheromone diffuse into neighboring patches.

```
to patch-rule
make "pheromone pheromone * (1 - evaporation-rate)
diffuse pheromone
end
```

If you start the simulation with a small number of creatures, not much happens. The creatures wander around randomly, trying to detect the pheromone. But the pheromone diffuses and evaporates too quickly. The creatures look somewhat like the particles in an ideal gas.

But if you add enough creatures to the simulation, the behavior changes drastically. With lots of creatures, there's a better chance that a few creatures will wander near one another. When that happens, the creatures will collectively drop a fair amount of pheromone, creating a sort of pheromone "puddle." The pheromone in the puddle will be above the "smell-threshold," so the creatures in the puddle will follow the pheromone gradient. Thus, they stay within the puddle and drop even more pheromone—a type of "positive feedback." If other creatures wander into the puddle, they are likely to join the group. Before long, there are clusters of creatures all over the screen.

Next, nearby clusters start to merge. Why? Randomness plays an important role. If one creature happens to wander out of one cluster and into another, the first cluster becomes "weaker" (less pheromone) and the second cluster becomes "stronger" (more pheromone). So even more creatures are likely to escape the first cluster and join the second—another example of positive feedback.

This aggregation simulation highlights several "core concepts" that are important to understanding the workings of decentralized systems. One core concept is *feedback*. Another is *critical density*—only when the density of creatures surpasses a particular threshold do clusters begin to form. A third core concept is *randomness*. Without any randomness, the clusters will "freeze" into static entities; with randomness, creatures will move in and out of clusters, and clusters will eventually merge together into superclusters.

This simulation suggests many "what-if" questions. For example: What would happen if the creatures had a better sense of smell (that is, a lower smell threshold)? It is rather straightforward to deduce that the creatures will form more and smaller clusters, and that they will form the clusters more quickly. (And indeed, this happens.) Interestingly, this result seems to run counter to many people's intuitions. I conducted an informal study with a small sample of people (including high-school students and adults). Most people predicted (correctly) that clusters would form more quickly, but most predicted (incorrectly) that the clusters would be larger than before. Why do people have this false intuition? Some people seem to reason like this: The creatures are trying to form clusters, so if the creatures have a better sense of smell, they will do a "better job" and form larger clusters. What's the flaw? Creatures are not really trying to form clusters; they are simply trying to follow a pheromone gradient. The clusters are an emergent phenomenon, on a different "level" from the creatures. By confusing the levels, people develop false intuitions.

Example 2: Traffic Flow. Two high-school students (one of whom recently received his driver's license) decided to design a simulation of traffic flow. They started with the simplest of rules. When a car sensed another car ahead of it, it slowed down. If it didn't sense another car, it sped up. With this simple rule, the students didn't expect much to happen. But when they started the simulation, the cars bunched into a realistic-looking traffic jam.

The students were surprised. Why should a jam form at all? The ensuing discussion highlighted the importance of small fluctuations. If all cars were evenly spaced, travelling with the same velocity, there would be no traffic jam. But certain small fluctuations (such as two cars spaced close together, or one car with a higher velocity) can ripple through the cars like a shock wave, causing a traffic jam.

When the students started watching the traffic jam, they were in for another surprise: the traffic jam moved backwards. They found this behavior counterintuitive. How could a traffic jam move backwards when all of the cars within it are moving forward? This behavior highlighted an important idea: emergent structures (like traffic jams) often behave very differently from the elements that compose them.

Next, the students added a "radar trap" on the highway and equipped the cars with radar detectors. When the cars detected the radar, they slowed down. Not surprisingly, a traffic jam formed at the radar trap. Somewhat more surprising was what happened when the students equipped only a quarter of the cars with radar detectors. The cars with detectors slowed down, causing other cars to slow down as well. So the emergent effect was exactly the same as before. Finally, the students removed the radar trap (after the traffic jam had already formed). They were surprised at how long the jam lingered, even though the direct cause of the jam was not longer present.

As a next step, the students plan to add new rules so that faster cars can pass slower cars. By doing so, the students hope to observe a phenomenon that (according to them) is known as "snaking." Evidently traffic jams (on real highways) often shift from one lane to another, in a snaking pattern. The reason is fairly clear: If one lane of traffic is jammed up, cars in that lane tend to shift to a faster-moving lane. But if too many cars adopt that strategy, a jam will form in what used to be the fast-moving lane. A key research question: As students construct emergent behaviors like snaking, will their understanding of those phenomena improve? If so, in what ways?

Example 3: Decentralized graphing. The first two examples involved simulations of real-world behavior. This example is different. It shows how decentralized thinking can provide a new way of looking at mathematical structures.

Imagine the screen is filled with thousands of creatures at random positions. Then, you give each creature the following rule: SETY XPOS. In other words, each creature should calculate its x-position, then sets its y-position to have the same value. Visually, the result is striking: the random mess of creatures transforms itself into a diagonal line, from the bottom-left corner of the screen to the upper-right. It is the line $y = x$.

You can use this same approach to graph any function. If you give the creatures the rule SETY XPOS * XPOS, the creatures align themselves into the parabola $y = x.^2$ If you give them the rule SETY SIN XPOS, they align themselves into a sin wave.

This type of graphing amounts to a new form of "turtle geometry." In traditional Logo programming, students can program the turtle to draw various geometric shapes and patterns (Abelson & diSessa, 1980). But in the *Logo form of turtle geometry, the turtles themselves form the geometric shapes and patterns.

*Logo-style graphing feels very different from the way students traditionally learn about graphing. Typically, students plot one point at a time, then fit a line through the points. In the *Logo approach, students imagine the whole plane filled with creatures, then think about where each creature should move. As in traditional Logo, students can "play turtle," imagining that they themselves are one of the creatures, then thinking about where they should move.

What if you wanted to graph a circle of radius 10, centered on the point (-3, 8)? Again, fill the screen with creatures in random positions, with random headings. Then, give each creature the following commands:

```
setpos [-3 8]
fd 10
```

Since the creatures have random headings, they will move out from the center of the circle in all different directions, forming a complete circle (as long as there are *lots* of creatures). To get a different radius, just change the input to FD.

*Logo provides yet another approach for thinking about graphing. For this approach, you need to focus on the *patches* rather than the creatures. Imagine that each patch follows the rule:

```
if ypos = xpos [setcolor green]
```

Each patch asks itself: "Does my x-position equal my y-position? If so, I should turn green." So every patch on the line $y = x$ turns green. Again, you could use this approach to graph any function.

Are these new approaches to graphing necessarily superior in all cases? Certainly not. But educators have long argued that students need *multiple representations* for mathematical problems. *Logo provides precisely that, offering students alternative ways to think about functions and graphs.

THINKING ABOUT DECENTRALIZATION

These examples are just a sampling. *Logo has also been used to simulate the foraging patterns formed by ants in a colony, the spread of a fire through a forest, the immune-system battle between antibodies and antigens, the chain-reaction of uranium-atom fission, and the oscillating populations of predators and prey. And, of course, there are many more simulations that could be written.

Even from our preliminary work with high-school students, we have begun to gain a sense of some "core concepts" that are useful for thinking about decentralized systems. Among them: feedback, critical density, randomness, diffusion, gradients, levels, trapped state, and local maxima and minima. And we have begun to develop some *heuristics* that might be helpful in understanding the workings of a decentralized systems. A few examples:

- *Complex patterns can emerge from simple rules.*
- *Large-scale patterns can emerge from local rules.*
- *Randomness can promote stability and order.*
- *Systems don't necessarily act like their parts.*
- *Small fluctuations can lead to big changes.*
- *Everything depends on everything else.*

These heuristics are not very helpful in making definitive predictions about what will happen with a particular decentralized system. But they can provide an initial framework for "making sense" of decentralized systems. As we continue our work with *Logo, we hope to develop better ways to help people develop heuristics like these.

Of course, a "decentralized mindset" is not appropriate for all situations. Some natural-world phenomena involve centralized decision making. And for certain design tasks, centralized approaches are most appropriate. But nature provides a rich inventory of robust and effective decentralized systems. A better understanding of these systems could lead not only to a better understanding of nature, but better methods for designing man-made systems, organizations, and societies.

ACKNOWLEDGMENTS

Hal Abelson, Seymour Papert, Brian Silverman, and Ryan Evans have provided encouragement, inspiration, and ideas for the *Logo project. Idit Harel and Natalie Rusk provided helpful comments on an earlier draft of this chapter. The LEGO Group and the National Science Foundation (Grants 851031-0195, MDR-8751190, and TPE-8850449) and Nintendo Inc., Japan have provided financial support.

REFERENCES

Abelson, H., & diSessa, A. (1980). *Turtle geometry: The computer as a medium for exploring mathematics*. Cambridge, MA: MIT Press.

Hillis, W. D. (1985). *The connection machine*. Cambridge, MA: MIT Press.

Hogeweg, P. (1989). MIRROR beyond MIRROR, Puddles of LIFE. In C. Langton (Ed.), *Artificial life*. Redwood City, CA: Addison-Wesley.

Langton, C. (Ed.). (1989). *Artificial life*. Redwood City, CA: Addison-Wesley.

Lovelock, J. (1979). *Gaia: A new look at life on Earth*. New York: Oxford University Press.

Minsky, M. (1988). *The society of mind*. New York: Simon & Schuster.

Papert, S. (1980). *Mindstorms: Children, computers, and powerful ideas*. New York: Basic Books.

Prigogine, I., & Stengers, I. (1984). *Order out of chaos*. New York: Bantam Books.

Rumelhart, E. D., McClelland, J. L., & the PDP Research Group. (1986). *Parallel distributed processing*. Cambridge, MA: MIT Press.

Steels, L. (1989). *The RDL manual* (AI Memo 89-11). Brussels: University of Brussels.

Steels, L. (1990). Cooperation between distributed agents through self-organization. In Y. Demazeau & J. P. Muller (Eds.), *Decentralized A.I.* Amsterdam: North-Holland.

Taylor, C., Jefferson, D., Turner, S., & Goldman, S. (1989). RAM: Artificial life for the exploration of complex biological systems. In C. Langton (Ed.), *Artificial life*. Redwood City, CA: Addison-Wesley.

Travers, M. (1989). Animal construction kits. In C. Langton (Ed.), *Artificial life*. Redwood City, CA: Addison-Wesley.

12

Elucidating Styles of Thinking about Topology through Thinking about Knots

Carol Strohecker

INTRODUCTION

This chapter describes a research project concerned with the development of understandings of *topology*, a branch of geometry concerned with properties of objects that are invariant when the object is distorted or deformed. Arriving at an understanding of such properties can involve a process of constructing ways of identifying relationships among parts of the object. Children's styles of making such identifications were elicited through activities done in the experimental setting described here. Knots, with their complex processes of formation and changing appearances as they are loosened and tightened, proved to be ideal objects for such a study. While the research does not relate directly to the branch of mathematics known as "knot theory," certain aspects of the exploration recall questions that the algebraists seek to answer. I make this analogy in the spirit of an approach shared by Piaget and Papert:

> [A] belief in the heuristic value of trying as hard as one can to understand as much as one can of children's mathematics and mathematicians' mathematics in the same categories. Doing so can illuminate both sides. (Papert, 1986, p. 1)

Knots are also well suited to such a study in their double offering as "microworlds" (Papert, 1980). Each knot is, in a sense, its own universe, which invites contemplation of its topology both as it is being formed and as a completed object. Additionally, different knots are often quite similar, so that understanding something fundamental about one can lead to an understanding of another. In this sense, knots as a category of objects can be a microworld for learning about topology. The research involved close examination of both levels. Different thinking styles became evident as participants worked with knots in a unique setting that encouraged immersion in the activity and communication of ideas about it.

Making others' thoughts available for study requires a well designed environment and a relationship between researcher and participant that is characterized by trust and mutual respect. The research described here was greatly enhanced by the noteworthy features of a relatively long duration for the project, and a flexibility of approach that allowed participants to contribute by determining directions for their work and enquiry.

EXPERIMENTAL DESIGN AND DATA

Two pilot studies were conducted, one involving children and one with adults. In each, participants gave instructions to someone else for how to tie a knot. The approach of the actual study extended the pilot studies in terms of constraints and setting. Longer duration and a wider variety of activities enabled greater access to the participants' thinking.

For a period of 3 months, I worked with 20 10- and 11-year-old, multicultural children as they learned to tie various knots. My aim was to encourage, observe, and document the childrens' thinking. I collected data through note-taking, audiotaping, videotaping, and tangible projects that the children produced. At the end of the study, I had an individual meeting with each child. We conversed while the child tied various knots, compared two similar knots, and arranged a set of knots into groups, according to perceived similarities. These comparative techniques were useful in eliciting understandings of relationships among parts of the configurations. A large part of the data analysis involved developing illustrated protocols from transcripts of the videos and from my research notes, coordinating this information with the children's writing and project work. The result was a basis for describing different styles of thinking about the topological relationships embodied by certain knots.

The design of the learning environment cannot be underestimated in its importance to collecting this data. I was concerned with developing appropriate conditions for both learning and research at two levels: that of the overall environment in which the research was conducted, and that of particular problems or enquiries in which the participants were engaged. The definition of the environment at each level relied on both the researcher's instigation of ideas and ongoing adjustments based on the participants' responses and suggestions. Thus the research design is best characterized in terms of malleability rather than imposition of a predetermined structure. The setting was designed to be flexible enough for the project to evolve in response to ideas and events that occurred during its course. An initial context for learning about knots was presented and gradually modified as the children became immersed in the project.

The project began with an introduction to a video "pen pal" who showed the participants how to tie various knots and responded to questions as the project progressed. The pen pal was an older child who was a Boy Scout, himself in the process of learning to tie certain knots. As the researcher, I assumed the roles of facilitator and "courier," the person common to each end of the communication, who videotaped the sessions and arranged for the children and the Boy Scout to see each others' video mail. Videotaping the exchanges between the children provided a means of recording visual and aural data, and also stimulated the children's excitement about the project.

This "video correspondence" served a kick-off purpose but did not define the scope of the project, which quickly took on a life of its own. Most dramatic in its evolution were gradual shifts from an emphasis on video as an instruction and communication medium, to the children's initiation of their own activities and greater use of paper correspondence. The children worked individually or in teams, initially within four separate working groups. As the end of the school year approached, distinct boundaries between these groups relaxed, and increasingly frequent, but casual, merging of the groups occurred. With this change came increases in the incidence of borrowing of ideas and of collaboration between members of initially different working groups. The children were building not only understandings of certain knots, but a culture dedicated to the learning.

Evidence of the children's appropriation of the project and the knots accumulated visibly over the 3 months. The room in which the groups met came to be known as the "Knot Lab," which was adorned by a wealth of printed and video information about knots, as well as bulletin board displays that the children constructed, showing knots in different stages of being tied, stories about the knots, a "family tree" of knots, and special words and graphic devices for describing knots.

SURFACING TOPOLOGICAL THINKING

Similarities and differences. Comparing knots became an important way of distinguishing the relationships characteristic of their configurations. In noticing the similarity between the Square knot and the Sheet Bend, for example, one of the children came to talk about them as being "related." From his initiation of this idea grew a project on which he and two of his friends worked, that of making a "family tree" of knots (Strohecker, 1991). They bound together twigs so that they resembled a tree, and carefully arranged knots on the different branches according to ways in which they deemed the knots to be related. Their intense involvement with the work is illustrated by the following dialog, in which Tony and Jill have a disagreement that becomes philosophical as well as topological. Their discussion involves the configurations in Figure 1.

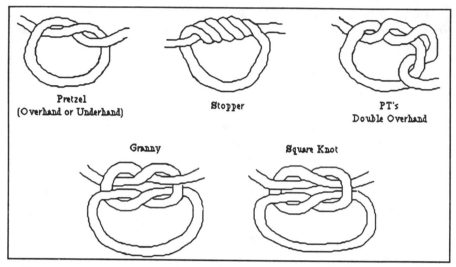

Figure 1. Configurations in Tony's and Jill's discussion of the "Family Tree of Knots."

Above the Pretzel knot they put a Stopper, and then moved to the Granny knot, about which Tony said, "Some people call it the Double Pretzel." This name is to be contrasted with his earlier designation of the Double Overhand, which was Stopper-like in its repetition of the wrapping motion that produces the Overhand knot. (A simplified instruction might be: "cross, wrap, wrap.") The Double Pretzel involves a more complete repetition: not just the wrapping motion is repeated, but also the crossing motion that precedes it ("cross, wrap, cross, wrap"). Thus Tony used the terms *pretzel* and *overhand* interchangeably when referring to the basic knot, but used the same terms differently when referring to specific derivatives of the knot. (Given the passage of time between his adoption of these designations, it is doubtful that he realized the discrepancy—or, for that matter, even remembered that he had named the Double Overhand.)

They put the Granny knot on a node between two branches. Tony explained:

Tony: The granny is a kind of bridge between the Pretzel and the Square . . . It's like a Pretzel, double, but it's not quite a Square, 'cause it's a Square if you keep on going instead of if you do it right. Some people say that a Square is you do it one way and then you do it the other way, but since the string—strings change places, it's really doing it twice.

Instead of using the "left over right, right over left" adage for the Square knot, Tony came to think in terms of a single active end: again the pattern is "cross, wrap, cross, wrap," but with the same end each time, crossing it consistently over or consistently under the other end (or ''cross x over y, wrap, cross x over y, wrap'').

Tony: And the Granny's when you do it once one way and the other time the other way . . . But it looks like you're doing it the same way.

In other words, the pattern for the Granny was ''cross x over y, wrap, cross y over x, wrap.'' But disregarding the path of the initial end, a local view of the tying yielded the appearance of more consistent action: ''left over right, left over right.'' He continued:

Tony: And, um, Square knot family—this whole branch. This is the Square knot, which is the knot—which is a really good knot. It's good for—well, it's good for, when you tie it, it's like a Pretzel, like I said, it's—it's an exact Double Pretzel, is a Square.

Jill pointed out the contradiction of his earlier designation of the Granny as the Double Pretzel. To do so, she used Tony's own earlier reasoning in considering the Square knot as, basically, two loops:

Jill: No, not exactly. It's more like two loops with sides coming out, which is not exactly a Pretzel.
Tony: Yeah, it's a Double Pretzel, exactly.
Researcher: Which is the Double Pretzel?
Tony: The Square. (*points to it*)
Researcher: Oh, the Square.
Jill: But I thought you said *that* was a Double Pretzel (*points to the Granny at the node*). That's what you said. (Tony *shakes his head ''no.''*) Yes, you did. You said that—
Tony: I said *it can be called* a Double Pretzel, but—in the way you tie it, it's a Double Pretzel—but in this (*he points to the Square knot*), the way it *is* is a Double Pretzel. I mean, it looks like you're tying it one way, and then the other way.
Jill: No—
Tony: But since the stings change, it's a Double Pretzel.

What Tony meant is that the *appearance* of symmetrical movement in tying the Granny may lead to calling it a Double Pretzel, but that appearance is distracting. The sense of repeating what you have done before (''left over right, left over right'') dulls the awareness that the knot can be understood in terms of the movement of a single end. For Tony, the second step of the Granny was properly understood as an interruption rather than a continuation, since the motion of the first end is eclipsed by the movement of the second one. The second step of the Square, though, truly *is* a continuation, as the same end travels smoothly along the path that produces the knot. It is the change of position

Figure 2.   Localized views of the Square Knot and the "Mystery" Knot.

resulting from the first crossing that produces the apparent alternation of ends ("left over right, right over left"). Yet the result of the second step of the Square knot is an exact repetition of the topology of the initial step, and therefore, for Tony, it was the Square knot that could rightfully be called the Double Pretzel.

Tony illustrated his point by tying the Square knot, and it became clear that he and Jill had in mind different criteria for the meaning of "double":

Jill: Well, I don't think that's double—Tony, once you tie it, and once it's tightened, it doesn't look like a double—it doesn't look like a Double Pretzel.

Tony: I didn't say it looked—I said it is. There's a difference, you know. There's such a thing as, "I look, therefore I am." It's—I mean—(*does back-and-forth motion as the check for the Square knot*)—see? It *is* a Square.

Jill based her concept of "double" on appearance and therefore referred to the finished Granny, in which the two crossings sit in nearly perpendicular planes. Their "doubleness" is obvious in that a glance reveals the two components, which look identical except for the shift in orientation. Tony based his concept of "double" on the essence of how the knot was produced, and therefore chose the Square. Never mind that a vertical view of the finished knot seems to reveal the second crossing as a mirrored image rather than a duplication of the first. Duplication may be more subtle in the finished Square knot, but the end appearance was not to be trusted as a sole indicator of what the object embodies and therefore what it *is*.

Such an exchange illuminates how differences in the way of thinking about a knot, while they may seem minor at first, can lead to fundamentally different

Square Knot   **"Mystery" or "Thief" Knot**

Figure 3.   Looking at the entire configurations makes it clear that the Square Knot and the "Mystery" Knot are different.

understandings. As in this exchange, much of what is special about an individual's learning or thinking style can best be appreciated in comparison to someone else's approaches to a given problem. One child's use of serializations of knots seems all the more significant when seen with the work of a child whose conception of knots as resulting from a single motion leads her to show only the final step; a child's trial-and-error method of discovering and validating new knots contrasts more "by-the-book" approaches of other participants; and a child's deep exploration of one configuration and closely related topologies contrasts other children's preference for trying many significantly different knots.

The distinctive Family Tree display drew attention from other Knot Lab participants, many of whom began working on their own family trees. The idea tended to precipitate and express the children's understandings of the knots so well that I incorporated a version of it into the final interviews: each child arranged the knots into groups according to his or her interpretation of which ones "go together," and we talked about why. The result was a rich set of information about their thinking about such relationships.

Also in the final interviews were specific comparisons of two knots, which tended to elicit a more detailed discussion of the configurations and relationships among components. The Square knot and a variant of it, the Thief or Bread knot (known as the "Mystery" knot and the "Reef" knot in the Knot Lab), provided a compelling problem. In a very localized view, the knots seem identical (Figure 2). Yet, looking at the entire configurations (Figure 3), it becomes clear that they are different.

Articulating the nature of this difference posed a challenge for many of the children. Some of them, like Patrick in the situation described below, found it easier to keep track of the intertwining by imagining themselves to be so small that they could walk along the string. The anatomical diagram in Figure 4 explains some of the terminology used in the protocol.

Patrick had some trouble following the imaginary ant's path at first. He complained about the "blockades" obstructing his way and lost track of the path

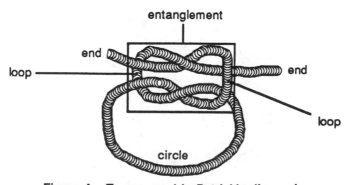

Figure 4.   Terms used in Patrick's discussion.

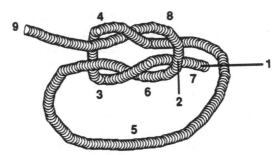

Figure 5. Patrick's initial pathway through the "Mystery" Knot.

as he got confused at the crossings. He then modified his descriptions at subsequent crossings, including more detail in order to keep track of where he was:

Patrick: Okay. I would start here (1) and then, I'd go um—hmm. Let's see. It's hard. It's a blockade (2). I'd probably go there (3), and then I'd switch to here (4), come around (5), go across over this (6), go—oh no! (7). (*He realized that he would leave the knot too early.*) Then come back here (8), and go around there (9). Okay, 'cause of those things in it, it's hard (see Figure 5).

Interviewer: Uh huh. What about this one?

Patrick: This one. I start here (1), walk all the way to the end where this one (2) starts, and then I'd walk over this (3), and come back to where it would come in (4), walk onto the one that it was connected to (5) ('cause I couldn't go under it), and then I'd walk on this (6) and come over here (7), and then I'd walk on this (8), and come here (9), and walk over this (10)—like that (11).

His "U-curve" concept breaks down the Square knot into two interlocking loops (Figure 6). He tried applying this view to tying the Thief knot, but without success.

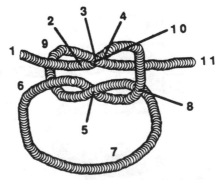

Figure 6. Patrick's pathway through the Square Knot.

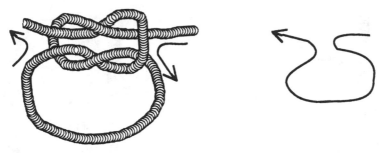

Figure 7. Patrick's "U-curve" formulation of the two interlocking loops of the Square Knot.

Patrick: So, I'd just actually make a U curve and make a U (*he traces out a curve with his fingers*) (see Figure 7).

Interviewer: So, that's like one continuous pathway?

Patrick: Sort of.

Interviewer: Sort of. A U and another U. And are these two pathways the same (*on the Square and on the Thief*)?

Patrick: Um—not really. I don't know why. I just thought of a better idea for this one.

Interviewer: *And how are they different?*

Patrick: This one (*the Thief*), I just—I had this one all over the place (*moves his finger along the knot in a dancing motion*)—I just came from this to this one—I just switched. (*He moves the knot around a bit, ultimately flipping it.*)

Patrick inadvertently flipped the Thief knot during the conversation, which may have helped to get him "unstuck" in his way of looking at the knot. The novel approach of turning the knots sideways enabled him to distinguish the Square and Thief knots. In this view, the question is not whether Patrick chose the entanglement or the circle as a referent—by changing the orientation in the way that he did, the two components no longer seemed separate. He made his distinction based on properties they share, which were made more obvious by taking a different view of the knot. In the Square knot, the lower part of the entanglement (or the right part, in Patrick's orientation) *is* part of the circle, and in the Thief knot, the *upper* part (his left part) is part of the circle. In the original orientation, the circle can become a distractant; Patrick found a way to use it, instead, to his advantage. He considered it as a fundamental aspect of the knot.

Interviewer: . . . you think they're the same—they're both a Square knot?

Patrick: They look the same—Oh! Wait a minute. (*He turns the knots sideways.*) I found it! Right here (*on the Square*), this Square—the one on the right is a loop, and the one on the right here (*the Thief*) is not. The one on the *left* is the loop. (See Figure 8.)

Interviewer: What made you suddenly see it?

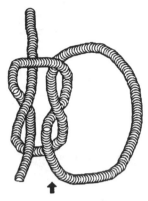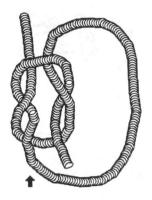

Figure 8. Patrick's reorientation of the Square and "Mystery" Knots.

Patrick: I was comparing (*he turns the knots upright again*)—to find out which one—and I was looking at this one, and this one (*he points to loops of knots*), and I thought, "Wait a minute! Something's wrong here!" (See Figure 9.)

Later, in tying the Thief, Patrick produced a knot that is a flipped version of the one he had come to understand (though this flipped version matched the knot he started with). He was confused at first, but it didn't take him long to realize that the knot is the same either way.

(He tries tying the Thief, manipulating the string while holding it in his two hands. He makes two loops, puts the left over the right (so the right is surrounded by the left), and tries tucking the left end in various ways over, through, etc., then stops.) (See Figure 10.)

Patrick: Humm—don't know. Well—I can't do this. How about if—well, I'll show what I do. I try to look at—like, make that loop, and then go around, and then make that one.

Interviewer: Oh, okay.

Patrick: (*He tries it: he makes a right loop, then left*)—this would go (*tries putting left in the right, reversing his previous try*)—I was trying that.

Interviewer: Yeah, I saw you were trying that. How about if you put it flat on the table,

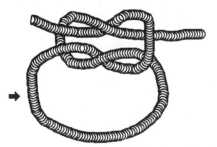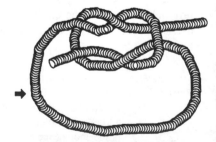

Figure 9. After reorienting the knots, Patrick transfers the realization to the original view of the knots.

and try to match what you see there? (*He begins.*) If you want, I can put
my finger to hold it somewhere. (See Figure 11).

Patrick: Let's see. I'm following it—

Interviewer: Very good! (*He maneuvers more off the table than on, twisting hands and
string awkwardly.*) (See Figure 12.)

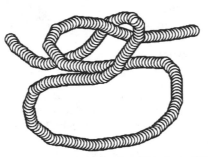

**Figure 10. Patrick's attempt to tie the Thief, or "Mystery" Knot, by
surrounding one loop with another.**

**Figure 11. The finished Thief Knot becomes a model for Patrick as he
ties.**

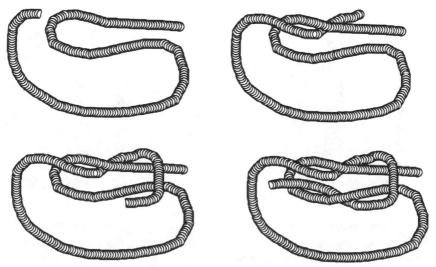

Figure 12. Patrick manages a pathway that reconstructs the Thief Knot.

Figure 13. Patrick's result is the reverse of his model.

> *(Though he has started and proceeded in a way that would produce the Thief on the table, he was managed to turn it around in tightening it, so he gets the confusing variation in Figure 13).*

Interviewer: Is that it? That's certainly close, if it's not it—*(he rotates it one way)*—that is *extremely* close! (*He rotates the other way.*) (See Figure 14.)

Patrick: Close, but not it. (*He plays with it, tightening, straightening.*)

Interviewer: That might be it—let's see if we can—

Patrick: Yeah. (*He flattens the knot, and puts it next to the Thief.*)

Interviewer: Very good—you tied it! You didn't think you could, but you did!

Strategies. Patrick's "turn it sideways" idea is just one example of many strategies that emerged as the children worked at tying and describing different knots. Such techniques became part of a Polya-like repertoire for problem solvers in the Knot Lab (Polya, 1973). Other strategies included considering more detail in examining a knot, varying the context in which the knot was viewed, reversing a process, and finding metaphors for the tying process, such as

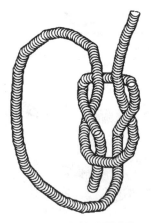

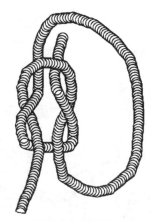

the original Thief   Patrick's Thief

Figure 14. By again using the strategy of turning the knots sideways, Patrick sees that they are the same.

riding on a highway or imagining a snake moving along. Such characterizations of the children's thinking contrast traditional problem-solving paradigms that favor strictly procedural approaches. Many knot-tyers attempted to develop step-by-step instructions, but embedded within their attempts were a variety of highly individualized and diverse heuristic techniques.

Language. Another way in which the children's thinking about knots was facilitated was the development of a language that enabled them to describe the peculiar twists, turns, and overlaps encountered in knot-tying. As cultures in computer science centered around a particular "language" have demonstrated, a well-honed, restricted set of expressions for particular kinds of operations or approaches to problem solving is crucial. With the children's knot-tying culture grew particular ways of expressing thoughts about configurations, relationships within and among them, and ways of producing them. The terminology included words, gestures, and pictorial symbols.

That the individual children's expressions gradually expanded into a small-scale, shared "language" is significant for its reflection of the culture that gradually developed, a culture devoted to learning about knots. The children worked individually, in pairs, and in teams, transforming the schoolroom into a "lab" that was an outward expression of the many approaches to the subject that their minds were generating. One of the purposes of the research was to consider what elements of their thinking were reflected through this activity.

APPROACHES TO THE STUDY OF TOPOLOGICAL THOUGHT

The Piagetian tradition proposes looking beyond a concept as we know it, such as "number" or "movement," to find precursor and constituent concepts. My research was conducted in this vein, but strove to extend Piaget's spirit (if not his words) in its particular focus on "concrete" thought. Papert's (1990a, 1990b) discussion of "constructionism" is relevant, as it pertains to the processes of tying knots and developing mental models of the spatial relationships they embody. An aspect of the constructionist philosophy is its illumination of a shift of emphasis on "abstract, formal, and logical" thought to an acknowledgement of the importance of concrete thinking, a trend that Papert and Turkle call a "revaluation of the concrete" (Turkle & Papert, 1990, p. 345). They characterize concrete thinking as a *style of thought* that is present throughout life, and which many adults prefer, rather than a step in a developmental progression in which concrete thought is ultimately replaced by a more mature, abstract kind of thought.

Papert's concept of "body syntonicity" is a kind of concrete thinking, used in discussions of the Logo turtle and relevant to the work with string described here. In *Mindstorms,* Papert develops the idea of a mathematics that is not separate from the body, a mathematics that depends on concrete experience as well as on abstractions such as the formalisms of mathematical language:

Jean Piaget's work on genetic epistemology teaches us that from the first days of life a child is engaged in an enterprise of extracting mathematical knowledge from the intersection of body with environment. The point is that, whether we intend it or not, the teaching of mathematics, as it is traditionally done in our schools, is a process by which we ask the child to forget the natural experience of mathematics in order to learn a new set of rules. (Papert, 1980, pp. 206–207)

Logo's array of computer microworlds includes "Turtle geometry," in which children write programs to guide the movement of a graphic turtle on the computer screen. To do so, the children make use of the knowledge of their own movement through space. As they develop more precise and sophisticated specifications for the turtle, they are encouraged to think more deeply about their own movement, and this deeper understanding is, in turn, translated to the computer programs. Papert develops the term *body syntonicity* to describe the nature of the correspondence between the child's experience and the turtle's behavior. He explains how this phenomenon can help to understand another object as well—a gear:

The gear can be used to illustrate many powerful "advanced" mathematical ideas, such as groups or relative motion. But it does more than this. As well as connecting with the formal knowledge of mathematics, it also connects with the "body knowledge," the sensorimotor schemata of a child. You can *be* the gear, you can understand how it turns by projecting yourself into its place and turning with it. It is this double relationship—both abstract and sensory—that gives the gear the power to carry powerful mathematics into the mind. (p. viii)

The microworlds of knots make a similar offer. By twisting and turning with a piece of string, and by seeing and feeling the relationships of different parts of a knot, a child can construct vivid understandings of what is crucial about those relationships. Several of the children demonstrated this sort of "body syntonic" approach in their learning. One boy, for example, likened the configuration of the Sheet Bend to a wrestling hold, and other children habitually tied string around parts of their bodies as they were working with knots.

Related to the concept of body syntonicity is Papert's discussion of "objects to think with" (Papert, 1980). Gears can be objects to think with, as can string and knots. As physical objects, such things assist in the construction of ideas and the development of modes of thought that rely on producing and thinking with objects—of thinking concretely.

An aspect of the "revaluation of the concrete" in doing science is the "society of mind" theory developed by Minsky and Papert (Minsky, 1986), in which thinking processes are described in terms of societies of "agencies" that grow, organize, and reorganize in certain ways. In this model, thinking emerges from the interactions of many small parts that comprise the societies, "agents." Each part is skilled at performing some particular function, but unaware of the skills—or even existence—of the others. Agents become associated with other agents based on useful functions that result from their combined efforts. In time, entire "societies" of agents develop, with their member agencies assuming various roles—of finding a match to some scene or event, performing a calculation, sending a message to another agency, deciding what information to ignore, and so on.

Minsky's explication of "Papert's Principle" forms a model that is useful in describing the changing nature of children's thinking as they learn more about properties of knots. This is:

> The hypothesis that many steps in mental growth are based less on the acquisition of new skills than on building new administrative systems for managing already established abilities. (Minsky, 1986, p. 330)

One child's transfer of knowledge about the Square knot to learning about a very similar knot, the Sheet Bend, is an example of how adjusting a few familiar topological properties can lead to outward results that seem new and different. Recognizing when existing abilities are being channeled to new contexts requires personal knowledge of the child and an in-depth analysis of her work and thinking. Case studies provide a form for such analysis (Strohecker, 1991).

In elucidating the children's thinking, I considered other psychological aspects as well. My observations are supported by literature in cognitive psychology and in psychoanalytic theory, which for purposes of comparison might be called "affective psychology." This double focus supports an effort to consider both cognition and affect in interpreting the data. These realms often have been kept separate in psychological research, but, recently, some authors have attempted a more complete way of reporting on subjects' thinking, by including acknowledgments of both aspects (e.g., Papert, 1980, 1986; Keller, 1983, 1985; Turkle, 1984). Like these authors, I both acknowledge and question the usefulness of a distinction between cognition and affect, and strive to incorporate both aspects in my data analysis. Together, they comprise what I call *thinking*.

Several studies in the realm of cognitive psychology have made use of knots, strings, or strings figures. Piaget and Inhelder (1967) worked with young children (ages 2–7) in studying their abilities to recognize and tie some simple knots. Olson is a researcher whose work on spatial understandings has raised comparisons to Piaget's work. Although Olson did not work specifically with knots, Forman uses knots as an example is describing a difference between Olson's approach and Piaget's (Eliot & Salkind, 1975). Olson's tendency would be to keep his observations localized to a particular area of thought in which a research inquiry is being made, whereas Piaget used specific research scenarios as a launching point for generalizations about thought processes and their development. Another researcher, Caron-Pargue (1983), elicited and analyzed adult subjects' graphic and verbal instructions for making knots. Of particular interest were the subjects' construction and use of notations, which Caron-Pargue catalogued and systematized. Van Sommers (1984) developed a comparative measure of adult subjects' abilities to reproduce from memory graphic representations of "difficult" graphic designs, including representations of Overhand and Figure 8 knots. In a completely different vein, the child psychiatrist Winnicott (1971a, 1971b) noted a preoccupation with string in the play of a young boy who had experienced traumatic separations from his mother.

Among these psychologists, the work of Piaget and Inhelder, and of Winnicott, become most useful in reporting on my study.

Piaget and Inhelder. In Piaget's (1965) theory, classification and sequence are considered as "mother structures" with which children construct the concept of "number." Classifications are a cardinal concern, involved with ways of arranging things that are similar. Sequence, or seriation, is an ordinal concern, involved with giving order to things that are dissimilar.

The concern with "order" appears again in the later work of Piaget and Inhelder (1967) as they discuss childrens' constructions of the concept of "space." This complex understanding consists of concepts of topological space and of geometric space, which includes projective and euclidean components. The understanding of topological space, characterized by properties intrinsic to a certain object, precedes the understanding of geometric space, with which different objects can be related in terms of measures or coordinates. The mother structures of topology include "proximity," "separation," "order," "enclosure," and "continuity." Piaget and Inhelder come to their study of children and knots through an elaboration of the structure of "order." They begin with the idea that an element of a series is arranged "between" other elements. This relationship—"between"—is an instance of the relationships of "surrounding," a property that is easily studied with the use of string and knots. In this domain, "surrounding" can be expressed as "intertwining." My study delved deeply into conceptions within this category of relationships.

The case studies present the work and thinking of three children through the source of the project, with particular focus on the precipitation and nature of changes in their conceptions (Strohecker, 1991). The children are characterized with regard to stylistic differences, partly in terms of a Piagetian "mother structure" that tended to prevail in their approach:

Child	Case Title	Structure	Conceptual Area
Jill	"Step by Step"	seriation (order)	topology and number
Alice	"All at Once"	continuity	topology
Tony	"Relatives & Mutations"	classifications (groupings)	number

Winnicott. Where appropriate, the children are also characterized with regard to the role of their personal lives in influencing their thinking about knots.

Winnicott's work supports these interpretations. His contributions are part of the object-relations school of psychoanalysis, in which the concept of introjection plays a key role (Freud, 1965; Fairbairn, 1963). An important process is thought to occur early in each person's life, and variations of it to be repeated throughout life: It is painful and difficult for an infant to spend time alone, without its mother—yet the mother cannot be with the infant all the time. Enabling the child to separate is a way of internalizing the mother, of developing a concept that represents her and which the infant can keep with it all of the time. This representative concept is called an "object," and with some others that also develop, it influences later ways of being and thinking about the world. (Papert's 1980 discussion of the Logo turtle as a kind of "transitional object" considers introjection as a process that can occur throughout life. The "object to think with" idea extends the concept in its supposition that not only people, but any physical object, can be introjected.)

Winnicott (1971a, pp. 15–20) describes a case in which he interprets a boy's play with string to be expressive of certain feelings. In particular, the boy experienced anxiety when apart from his mother, and obsessively tied together objects in the house. Winnicott surmised that the boy was "dealing with a fear of separation, attempting to deny separation by his use of string" (p.17). I make use of a similar way of interpreting the peculiar absorptions of two participants in the Knot Lab project. Jill was interested in knots that move, and came to focus on the True Lovers' knot, in which two component knots can be moved repeatedly together and apart. Her fascination is partially discussed in terms of her back-and-forth visits to her divorced parents. Tony, the lab's "Square Knot expert," spent a lot of time working with variations of this configuration. His manipulations sometimes led him to discover another version of the knot, but sometimes he produced indecipherable variants, embarrassments, which he called "mutations." The derogatory term seemed to reflect his low self-esteem from his sense of being overweight and, often, intellectually separate from the other knot tyers. However, an interesting validation of these "mutations" occurred as he made a place for them on a display, next to their recognizable counterparts.

SUMMARY

This work joins the growing body of literature on the nature of thinking and thinking styles, which emphasizes the characterization of thought in terms of multiplicity and diversity. I supplement this discussion with ideas and models for describing varying processes of thought. My concerns are with problem-solving strategies, descriptions of topological relationships, and affective components of the childrens' thinking.

With its examination of the structure and growth of topological thinking, the analysis also contributes to the literature on microgenetic development. The

Piagetian "mother structures" of topological thought become a basis for characterizing a certain prevalence in an individual's thinking.

Although perspectives from the disparate fields of artificial intelligence and psychoanalysis have been compared or combined previously (e.g., Turkle, 1990), my work concretizes the relationship between ideas from computation and affective psychology by rooting the discussion at the level of case studies.

ACKNOWLEDGMENTS

This research was conducted through Project Headlight. I would like to thank the students, teachers, and administrators who participated in the research project, as well as Troop 224 of the Boy Scouts of America for their cooperation.

Funding and administrative support were provided by the MIT Epistemology and Learning Group, whose work is supported by grants from Apple Computer, Inc., Fukutake Japan, IBM Corporation (Grant #OSP95952), the LEGO Group, MacArthur Foundation (Grant #874304), National Science Foundation (Grants #851031-0195, #MDR-8751190, #TPE-8850449), and Nintendo, Inc., Japan. The ideas expressed here do not necessarily reflect those of the supporting agencies.

REFERENCES

Caron-Pargue, J. (1983). Codage verbal et codage graphique de noeuds. In *Proceedings of La pensée naturelle: Actes du colloque de Rouen*. Paris: Presse Universitaire de France (Publications de l'Université de Rouen).

Eliot, J., & Salkind, N.J., (Eds.). (1975). *Children's spatial development*. Springfield, IL: Charles C. Thomas.

Fairbairn, W. R. D. (1952). *Psycho-analytic studies of the personality*. London: Tavistock Press.

Fairbairn, W. R. D. (1963). Synopsis of an object-relations theory of the personality. *International Journal of Psycho-Analysis, 44*, 224-225.

Freud, S. (1965). Lecture XXXI: The dissection of the psychical personality. *New introductory lectures on psychoanalysis* (Trans. and ed. by James Strachey). New York: W. W. Norton.

Gruber, H. E., & Vonèche J. J., (Eds.). (1977). *The essential Piaget*. New York: Basic Books.

Keller, E. F. (1983). *A feeling for the organism: The life and work of Barbara McClintock*. San Francisco: W. H. Freeman.

Keller, E. F. (1985). *Reflections on gender and science*. New Haven, CT: Yale University Press.

Minsky, M. (1986). *The society of mind*. New York: Simon and Schuster.

Papert, S. (1980). *Mindstorms: Children, computers, and powerful ideas*. New York: Basic Books.

Papert, S. (1986). *Beyond the cognitive: The other face of mathematics*. Cambridge, MA: MIT Epistemology and Learning Group.

Papert, S. (1987). *About project headlight*. Cambridge, MA: MIT Epistemology and Learning Group.

Papert, S. (1990a). *A unified computer environment for schools: A cultural/ constructionist approach* (Proposal to National Science Foundation). Cambridge, MA: MIT Epistemology and Learning Group.

Piaget, J. (1965). *The child's conception of number*. New York: W. W. Norton.

Piaget, J., & Inhelder, B., (1967). *The child's conception of space* (Trans. by F. J. Langdon & J. L. Lunzer). New York: W. W. Norton.

Polya, G. (1973). *How to solve it: A new aspect of mathematical method*. Princeton, NJ: Princeton University Press.

Strohecker, C. (1991). *Why knot?* Unpublished doctoral dissertation, MIT Epistemology and Learning Group, Cambridge, MA.

Turkle, S. (1984). *The second self*. New York: Simon and Schuster.

Turkle, S. (1990). Romantic reactions: Paradoxical responses to the computer presence. In M. Sousua & J. Sheean (Eds.), *Boundaries of humanity: Humans, animals, machines*. Berkeley: University of California Press.

van Sommers, P. (1984). *Drawing and cognition: Descriptive and experimental studies of graphic production processes*. Cambridge, UK: Cambridge University Press.

Winnicott, D. W. (1971a). *Playing and reality*. London: Tavistock Publ.

Winnicott, D. W. (1971b). *Therapeutic consultations in child psychiatry*. London: Hogarth Press.

Carol Strohecker introducing the Knot Lab to some students at Project Headlight.

Documentary videography and videodisc technology were used by Ricki Goldman-Segall in her ethnographic investigations of the Project Headlight computer culture, and its students' development and thinking styles.

Stephen Sherman Photography

13

Three Children, Three Styles:
A Call for Opening the Curriculum

Ricki Goldman Segall

THINKING STYLES AND THE CURRICULUM

In many schools today the way of thinking about subjects is fixed. Often educators believe that children should think about a given subject in the way the subject "should be" thought about. For example, one should think about literature in a narrative way, about chemistry in a causal manner, and about psychology using a relational approach. As a result, teachers are often educated to teach each subject in "its own language." They are not taught to encourage the child to think about a subject according to his or her own preferred style, or, even to acknowledge that diverse thinking styles exist and are fundamental in understanding how children make what they learn their own. Indeed, it would seem strange to most educators to encourage the child whose thinking is social and interpersonal to approach history in that style, to invite narrative thinkers to build narratives about Curric, Euclid, and Newton, or to promote empirical thinkers to think about understanding human behavior. Yet, this is precisely what is happening and what has been happening in scholarship in many academic settings around the world. People are beginning to question the traditional approaches to scholarship. Studies *are* being developed around intellectual issues rather than disciplines. Barbara Tuchman wrote scholarly works in her personal style, one of which gave us rich insights into the lives and conditions of people in 14th-century Europe (Tuchman, 1978). Scholarly books and films about the lives of Norbert Weiner, Victor Weisskopf, and Neils Bohr, provide more complete pictures of the discovery process. However, students have to be enrolled at universities to consider approaching a subject from their preferred style. Our schools have tried to incorporate interdisciplinary studies, but success has been small. The position of this chapter is that it is the child who comes to the subject from a variety of perspectives and thinking styles. It is the responsibility of the educator to provide experiences within the subject matter which open the curriculum to the child.

"Is opening the curriculum" possible in our schools? Could children benefit from a more open approach to the school curriculum? Are there children in schools who are "kept back" or expelled from schools who could have their chance to succeed if educators simply encouraged diverse styles? How can children with diverse thinking styles contribute to the understanding of any given subject?

In a time of national concern over educational issues, it seems timely to propose that a child's preferred style will not block him or her from full participation within the educational system. We can no longer expect all our children to think the same way about any given school subject. Although I am not devaluing the effect of a multitude of factors such as size of classrooms, salaries of teachers, introduction of higher technology, and so on. I suspect that addressing those factors will not make fundamental changes in solving the crisis in our schools today *unless* more attention is paid to the diverse thinking styles of children, so that all children have the opportunity to participate fully in their learning.

Learning environments such as the particular Logo Constructionist culture at the Hennigan School in Boston have begun to open the curriculum to a diverse style of thinkers. Seymour Papert, Sherry Turkle, and others have often claimed that diverse thinking styles exist. My ethnographic research provides new evidence. It also suggests that many children who are presently rejected from the educational system could participate more fully if educators changed their way of thinking about how what needs to be learned is made available to learners.

This chapter provides a theoretical discussion of pluralism in thinking styles, the results of my research—excerpts from the case studies of three children studied during my 2½-year fieldwork at the Hennigan School, and the implications of my results for thinking about changes within the school curriculum. The complete case studies, theoretical background, and methodology using video and videodiscs as research tools are available in other articles and my dissertation.[1]

ALTERNATIVES TO STAGE THEORY

The Narrative Mind

Over the last 20 years, a new breed of epistemologists has been examining the range of thinking styles which affect the way people approach any given domain

---

[1] Collections of relevant work include the following papers and video/videodisc projects: Goldman Segall (1986, 1987, 1988, 1989a, b, c, d, e, 1990a, b); Goldman Segall, Mester, & Greschler (1989).

of knowledge and, by their doing this, they have challenged existing theories of how people learn.

Stage theorists used science-like models to show how maturation takes place in logical causal sequences according to observable stages in growth patterns. Always the final stage is the highest and best. Developmental theories, such as Freud's oral, anal, and genital (Freud, 1952), Erikson's eight stages of psychological growth from basic trust to generativity (Erikson, 1950), or Piaget's stages from sensori-motor to formal operational thinking (Grubner & Voneche, 1977), are based on the belief that the human organism must pass through these stages at critical periods in its development in order to reach full healthy integrated maturation—be it psychological or intellectual.

Carol Gilligan (1982), among many others, suggests that there is a "different voice" as powerful in its origins throughout the last few thousand years as the stage-theory voice. To describe the narrative part of this voice, one may need to think about human thinking before what Ivan Illich and Barry Sanders (1989), refer to as "the book," to a period of preliterate thinking.

This relativistic narrative mode is in sharp contrast to the stage theory of thinking. To think about the "unfolding" of the narrative, Illich and Sanders take their readers back to the thinking of Plato to reflect upon thinking in preliterate, prehistoric times:

> Prior to history, Plato says, there is a narrative that unfolds, not in accordance with the rules of art and knowledge, but out of divine enthusiasm and deep emotion. Corresponding to this prior time is a different truth—namely, myth. In this truly oral culture, before phonetic writing, there can be no words and therefore no text, no original, to which tradition can refer, no subject matter that can be passed on. *A new rendering is never just a new version, but always a new song. Thinking itself takes wing; inseparable from speech, it is never there but always gone, like a bird in flight. The storyteller spins his threads, on and on, never repeating himself word for word.* No variants can ever be established. This is often overlooked by those who engage in the 'reading' of the prehistorical mind, whether their reading is literary, structuralist, or psychological. (1989, p. 4; emphasis added here and in later citations)

Our knowledge of this preliterate period is limited by the obvious: We can only know how dead people thought through the records they left behind. However, our only records of the prehistoric period are the few remaining hieroglyphics. Inasmuch as words are artifacts of thinking and incomplete pictures of how people really think, we have to accept that the written word of dead people is the most reliable means for making hypotheses about how they thought. According to Illich and Sanders, understanding the thinking of our pre-alphabetic ancestors in terms of how we understand thinking today is impossible. The prehistoric mode of thinking was a relativistic experience; what was expressed at any given moment in time changed from the previous time it was expressed. In this way, there could be no fixed recall, no truth as we define it today. ''A new rendering is never just a new version, but always a new song'' (Illich & Sanders, 1989, p. 4).

The concept of knowledge as a continually changing ''truth,'' dependent on the cultural rules established by both the will of the community as well as the ability of the storytellers, dramatically changed with the introduction of a system of written rules. The moment a statement could be written down, it could be referred to. Memory changed from being an image of a former indivisible time to being a method of retrieving a fixed, repeatable piece or section of an experience.

One might say that, before alphabetic script, facts could not exist. If we think of the mind as a bucket, then the preliterate mind could be compared to a bucket of water being both filled and emptied by experience, whereas the alphabetic mind is more comparable to a crate of carefully marked boxes containing the groups of experiences or facts most aligned to the box type. The ''facts'' travel from box to box given the nature of the operation. Although the perception of the box changes, the facts remain constant. According to the literate mind, we can change our minds by changing the point of view, but facts are fixed.

The Relational or Social Mind

Evelyn Fox Keller addresses the relational model as a style of doing science. Science is a ''deeply personal as well as a social activity. (Fox Keller, 1985, p. 7). She reaches a conclusion that scientific thinking is currently gender-biased— preferential to the male and ''objective'' way of thinking. Fox Keller combines Thomas Kuhn's ideas about the nature of scientific thinking with Freud's analysis of the different relationship between young boys and their mothers and between girls and their mothers. The fact that boys are encouraged to separate from their mothers, and girls to maintain attachments, may influence the manner in which children relate to physical objects. The young boy, in competition with his father for his mother's attentions, learns to compete in order to succeed. Girls may realize that becoming personally involved with the things in her world— getting *a feeling for the organism*[2]—is their preferred mode of making sense of their relationship with physical objects.

Fox Keller's insights about the impersonal and the personal approach to doing science could open the door for thinking about science in personal and social, rather than in an objective and often ''antisocial'' way:

> Just as science is not the purely cognitive endeavor we once thought it, neither is it as impersonal as we thought: science is a deeply personal as well as a social activity. (1985, p.7)

---

[2] See *A Feeling for the Organism* (Fox Keller, 1983), about the life of geneticist, Barbara McLintock.

Turkle and Papert (Chapter 9, this volume), in a direction similar to Fox Keller's, introduce the terms *hard thinking* and *soft thinking* to name equally significant styles of thinking. Papert, a mathematician working with Jean Piaget, departed from the genetic epistemology of developmental stages to an examination of how different kinds of thinking—sensori-motor, concrete, formal—interact throughout life. Papert's learning theory recognizes all learners as constructionists learning in accordance with their thinking styles.

Turkle and Papert's theory is that, traditionally, hard thinking has been the basis of defining logical thinking. "And logical thinking has been given a privileged status which can be challenged only by developing a respectful understanding of other styles where logic is seen as a powerful instrument of thought but not as the 'law of thought' " (Turkle & Papert, Chapter 9, this volume). According to Turkle and Papert, among others (Linn, 1978; Ackermann, this volume, Chapter 14; Globerson, 1987) soft thinking is more negotiational and contextual, or what Lévi-Strauss terms *bricolage*. This orientation focuses on the closeness to objects aspect of the soft style of thinkers.

When Turkle and Papert (Chapter 9, this volume) compare the programming approaches of hard-thinking *planners* and soft-thinking *bricoleurs,* this is what they say:

> While hierarchy and abstraction are valued by the structured programmers' "planner's" aesthetic, bricoleur programmers, like Lévi-Strauss' bricoleur scientists, prefer negotiation and rearrangement of their materials. The bricoleur resembles the painter who stands between brushstrokes, looks at the canvas and only after this contemplation, decides what to do next. Bricoleurs use a mastery of associations and interactions. For planners, a program is an instrument for premediated control; bricoleurs have goals, but set out to realize them in the spirit of collaborative venture with the machine. For planners, getting a program to work is like "saying one's piece;" for bricoleur's it is more like a conversation than a monologue.

Although Turkle and Papert use the terms *hard* and *soft* to explain different and equally significant approaches to computation, their contribution reaches out to broader domains. Their aim is to contribute to the acceptance of *epistemological pluralism*. They cite "feminism, ethnography of science and computation" as three of several movements which promote concrete thinking "to an object of science in its own right." They also believe that, by accepting diverse styles of appropriating knowledge and understanding formal systems as being equally significant to the world of scientific thought, the personal relational perspective of concrete human thinking will gain respectability within the scientific community.[3]

To explore his theories, Papert encourages the creation of learning environments wherein individuals with diverse styles of thinking can have equal oppor-

---

[3] To understand Papert and Turkle more fully, see Shapiro (1965), Gilligan (1982), and Fox Keller (1985).

tunity to the tools they need to build their own (micro) worlds. It was this belief in the importance of exploring the growth of learning cultures in the context of new technologies which led to the implementation of Project Headlight, a computer-rich constructionist learning environment at the Hennigan School, a Boston inner-city elementary school.

Papert also addresses the interpersonal through the concept of *objects to think with*. He has a genuine love of objects as intellectually challenging models to understand. While engaged in a conversation, he often holds an object (that he can move) in his hands, even if he is not discussing the object. The tactile relationship with objects seems to stimulate his thinking. When he describes understanding an idea, he often uses the expression "getting a handle on it," as if the idea is a three-dimensional object. His relationship with functionality and concreteness underlies much of the philosophical premises embedded in Logo. Children in the Logo culture are encouraged to play with ideas by manipulating real or virtual objects, turning them around and then putting them together to construct powerful ideas.

Objects to Think With **and** *Relationships to Think With*

The theoretical premise that guided my research is my belief that the starting point for thinking about science is embedded in our human relationships. My view is that, if we are going to make this world into a more convivial place, as Illich proposed in 1972, then we need to promote negotiation, as Gilligan says, and commensurability, as Clifford Geertz (1973, 1988⁶) says. Tools can help us build contextually supportive learning environments for conviviality and commensurability. The *known, knowing,* and *knowable* are intimately connected by the interaction between being known to oneself and others, and knowing others. In the relational model, knowledge is a *tool* for human relationships and not a goal in and of itself.

Underlying this premise is the willingness to search for the wholeness of what is known and what is knowable, the objective and the subjective as an indivisible unity. Thinking about thinking *without* thinking about the narrative or the soft, bricolage, relational aspects is to be less scientific and less representative in reporting the whole of human inquiry.

To illustrate what I have been discussing, let me introduce three children— Josh, a predominantly empirical thinker; Andrew, a narrative thinker; and Mindy, a social thinker.

CASE STUDIES

The Empirical Mind of Josh

In the Classroom. I first met Josh at the Hennigan School on a day when the fourth-grade teacher, Joanne Ronkin, used carrots as a prop to help the children learn how to describe objects. Josh's classroom was typical of the Hennigan School: the clock hanging on the wall, the posters of children's work placed around the room, the overhead fluorescent lighting, and the typical formica tables and chairs. The overall impression was one of brightness, color, and order.

Ronkin sat at the head of a circle of tables. The children were comfortably scattered around the table, some sitting on chairs, others on tables. An assortment of carrots was strewn on the table. Some were in a plastic bag. Small index cards were held in Ronkin's hands; she read the description of the carrots written on each card to the class. The children were very engaged, trying to match the carrot to the description. She read the text from one of these pages describing a carrot.

The following excerpt is taken from my video data:

Ronkin: This person was very specific, telling us his carrot was exactly five inches long. Very specific in his description. And that's what you need. And it has black marks at the top. So, how many people think it's this one?

Ronkin held up one carrot, and the children hummed, "No" or "Maybe." Ronkin held up another, and the children again hummed, "No" or "Maybe." When she held up the third one, the children in unison answered, "Yes!"

Ronkin: Whose carrot is this?
Josh: It's mine.
Ronkin: Is this your carrot?
Joseh: That's my carrot!"
Ronkin: Excellent! Excellent description! Great carrot!

Josh had been sitting on a desk towards the back of the room. His body was thin and lanky; his hair light brown; his eyes twinkly alert. He squeezed his knees with both arms extended while Ronkin praised him for his excellent description. He then glanced furtively at the camera, unconsciously pushing the sleeve of his shirt up.

He called out to his classmates, "Did you see the little engravement?" (He meant "engraving," I believe.) Ronkin asked if he wanted to point it out to everyone, so Josh jumped from his place and excitedly walked toward his teacher who was holding the carrot lengthwise between her two hands.

Josh: Wait a minute, hold on! This *isn't* my carrot!
Ronkin: That's not his carrot!

With the realization that the carrot he had thought was his wasn't his at all, Josh became very flustered. When the other children began to tease him for not knowing his carrot, he became embarrassed.

Josh:	It's not? Hold on.
Ronkin:	Wait a minute . . .
A child:	(off camera, in a teasing voice) I thought you knew your carrot, Josh!
Ronkin:	Josh insisted he knew his carrot. (*The children laugh while Josh looks at the carrot and the other carrots on the table.*)
Josh:	My carrot's not here!
Ronkin:	We have to call the FBI. I tell you what, check in this bag and see if someone else claimed your carrot.

Following the carrot incident, Josh often approached me during my visits to the school, asking, "Can I see the carrot video?" I would respond by trying to set up a time to do this, finally realizing that the banter was a way for Josh to begin our friendship and to put his embarrassment to rest. Josh did not often make mistakes.

Building Objects With Move and Change. Over the following 2 years, I spent one or two afternoons a week with Josh at the Hennigan School. We had time to share many experiences and stories. I observed Josh in hundreds of situations in the classroom and in the computer area *pods*. What I discuss in the following description is my understanding of Josh's empirical mind as reflected in both his building objects and programs and his thinking about the nature of moving things.

Building objects with Lego bricks, and using Logo as the interface for sending commands to these objects, was a common experience for Josh and his classmates. Josh 'learned' about the transfer of energy from one object to another by making this transference happen. He could connect an object—such as a Lego car—to a wire, which was connected into an interface box, and then write a range of commands in Logo for that car object to move, to wait for a few seconds, and then to turn and move again. He experienced the meaning of sending messages and causing actions to be carried out. More than experiencing simple cause/effect, or input/output relationships, he made things move according to his own design.

Josh was exposed to playing with Lego bricks in a choice-driven manner; with Lego, there was no curriculum to follow, no rules, no grades and no expectations. From the beginning of his Lego experiences, Josh would approach these Lego workshops with wonder and excitement. At first, he built (what most children start off building in Lego)—his cars, which, I presume because of his love of expensive sports cars, were Lamborghinis and Porsches in his mind's eye. Within weeks, he was building other personal creations of moving things. For example, he built a room with a person who was propelled out of bed. He called it his *Alarm Clock Bed*. Josh's theory was that getting out of bed in the morning is usually a problematic event. Therefore, as a precaution against falling back to sleep, the little Lego person would be ejected from bed and propelled onto a conveyor belt taking him into the next room.

Another invention of his was equally imaginative. He was playing around with a Lego motor, pretending it was an electric shaver and rubbing his 10-year-old face—not finding any whiskers to remove. While shaving, he kept scrounging through a large bucket of Lego bricks, not seeming to be particularly inspired. With characteristic puttering, Josh put a wheel on the bottom of the motor and held the Lego motor from its wire, allowing the motor to touch the table. The thing contorted in strange and unpredictable ways. When I asked Josh what it was, he told me it was an *Electronic Breakdancer*. He then proceeded to build a Lego discotheque with strobe lights for his dancer. He explained the disco with its lights to me in this way:

Josh: See, I just made a light here. Like, there are these little blocks and he goes down [and] there is a wheel spinning on the motor, and all he does is, when he goes down, he goes wild.

Curiously, the *Breakdancer* remained a motor and a wheel. He never felt the compunction, as other children might have, to make the *Breakdancer* look like a person. The object stood for or represented a breakdancer; Josh was not interested in making the object look real, he was interested in what the object did.

Josh's work with Logo had the same imaginative flair. He redesigned the car game he and his friend Joe had started a school term earlier, building a rather sophisticated interface for users called *Obstacle Mania*. In *Obstacle Mania*, the computer screen was divided into two sections by a lime-green line with a small opening. The user had to control the direction of the car cursor by hitting the L or the R key. L turned the car 15 degrees and moved it 5 steps forward to the left, and R turned it 15 degrees and moved it 5 steps forward to the right. This is how he explained it to me:

Josh: The only way you die is if your very middle hits. The only way you die is if, watch the screen, watch the screen: L, R, see, my bumper can hit; anything can hit except the very middle. See, only the very middle can make it die. 'Cause, see, the very middle is the very middle of the turtle [cursor] and everything.

Josh makes it sound as if it is very hard "to die" in his game. Speaking from experience, I found it very easy "to die" in his game—the car exploding in vivid colors on the monitor. In fact, in many of Josh's creations in Logo there were dramatic events: explosion, fires, take-offs, or ejections from one place to another. His concern was with things that moved and changed. Ultimately, he used these actions as objects to think about the nature of moving things—why and how energy is transformed from one thing to another to produce more powerful effects.

Josh's Thinking about Moving Things. The inventiveness embedded in Josh's constructions seemed to be without limits when his imagination was allowed full reign. More powerful, though, was when his thinking was given the same freedom.

On a sunny day Josh and I sat outside the school on a hill, talking for more than half an hour. He philosophized, not only about gears and cars, but about the nature of energy. Needless to say, the conversation was never very far away from his favorite subject, moving things.

Josh examined the steps in a process of energy transferring from one object to another. While explaining how procedures in Logo work, or how information is stored on a disc, his body movement accentuated his amazement about this physical phenomenon of energy transfer. He sat squatted with his left arm relaxing on his left knee. With his right hand, he squeezed the watch band on his left wrist and unconsciously flicked his fingers against the skin by his watch. He looked directly into my eyes, with his eyebrows raised. As he spoke, he moved his eyes away from me, towards the open field, and said:

Josh: How can a disc hold information? How can it hold little words? Like, in the eighteen hundreds, things weren't as easy as they are now—cars; we have so many advanced new things—cars, video cameras, VCR's. It's amazing how people . . . Even computers. If you think about the Logo we do, FD has to be a procedure somewhere, right? And the things you put in a procedure has to be a procedure, right? And it just goes back to electronic pulses and micro-chips!

Josh did not stop at this level of explanation. He took the idea deeper. In other words, he tried to understand just what was happening at each step, "pushing the beginning back further and further," as my colleague Mitch Resnick says about Josh's thinking. These few words, "pushing the beginning back," seem to touch at the core of Josh's soliloquy, because Josh was searching for the origin of energy. At one point he took his own theory to the ridiculous in order to make it clear to me why this process is so amazing, by saying, "How does an electronic pulse hold information? I mean, do you just stuff a word in it?" To quote him more fully, our conversation went like this:

Josh: You'd have to meet a genius who knew how little electronic pulses traveled through computers, hit the microchip and it changed something around, and a word pops up. You press something and a letter comes. Now, how could they do that? I mean, you press a key and a letter comes.
Ricki: Are there any books which might help you find the answers?
Josh: Well, it would be impossible to explain. An electronic pulse comes and it holds the information. How does an electronic pulse hold information? I mean, do you just stuff a word in it? How can an electronic pulse hold it, go into a microchip and travel around a lot and pop up on a screen? Amazing!!

In the above citation, Josh introduced another element in his theory about energy here: information is converted to pulses of energy, which are somehow held or stored in microchips, or, as he explains later, in CDs, or in computer discs. In Josh's thinking, energy and information (similar to motion and particle) are almost interchangeable. Consider the way he connects movement and information in the following citation:

Ricki: What other kinds of things do you think about, Josh?

Josh: Mostly things that move. Like, how does a muscle move? Even if it is a muscle and it has strength and everything, how does it move? How does a disc contain information? How can it hold little words? Whoever came out with a disc is amazing! What about CDs—a laser reads these things. You can put it on the ground, step on it, and it won't do anything. The only way you can break it is if you split it in half or something. And it's amazing—a laser goes down onto a piece of metal and it makes sounds, makes music. A tape, a slit of paper, cellophane—it makes music. Isn't that amazing? If you look at cellophane, it's amazing that it can hold music. Even records, it's not like, I used to think that it was carved into it and when the needle went over it, it scratched out the sound. But how does it scratch out: Ahhhh? You can't. Like, how does a laser read off a CD? It's so amazing!

Transfer of energy is not limited to mechanical objects in Josh's scheme of things. In the same conversation Josh showed an equal fascination about the speed of a fast ball thrown by Boston Red Sox pitcher Roger Clemens:

Ricki: What else do you think about Josh?

Josh: Roger Clemens. Like, Roger Clemens can throw a fast ball, like, 95 miles an hour. Now the fastest person that ever ran, ran about 15 miles an hour. And you can throw something 95 miles an hour. In just 60 minutes it would go 95 miles if it didn't, like, run out of power. That's how fast some people can throw.

This comparison shows two significant things about Josh's thinking. First, it shows how Josh is trying to understand how an object thrown by a person can go faster than the person herself or himself; something happens to the ball which gives it the power to do that, but what? How? Second, and most important, this comparison shows that Josh's thinking is pervasive throughout domains and is independent of the level of sophistication of the technology. His sense of wonder about the transfer of energy is shown whether speaking about baseballs, computers, CDs, records or tape decks. The point is that Josh used what he was exposed to in order to think about how things move and how energy is changed.

Josh the Empiricist, on Ideas and Inventions. The empiricist in Josh says that there is an objective external reality from which we derive our thoughts. We couldn't imagine something new if we first didn't see "the facts."

Josh: Well, people, like, get ideas but they have to get it from something. You see a rock, you might think of something carved out of it, or something. But you could never know if there were no rocks. You never think of rock, unless you were trying to think of something new. Like, [if] you were trying to think of a new substance or something. Most imagination; you see a car and an airplane, you put them together in a picture.

Josh's empiricism begins to mix with some rationalist thinking by mentioning that "you might never think of rock, unless you were trying to think of something new." Although seeing the rock might give you the idea to carve something on the rock, Josh acknowledges that the new thing you do to the rock is determined to some degree by internal human factors which may have nothing to do with the rock. This may be why Josh begins to play with the notion that if a person is trying to think of something new, or to invent something, then something other than objective reality may be of concern.

When he concluded this round of thinking, however, he returned to his basic premise that most imagination is putting things that we see or experience together. In other words, when Josh had the opportunity to reflect on his own imagination processes, he understood them to be the putting of known things together in his own way.

When Josh thinks about imagination, he thinks that imagination gives us the power to create new things, such as, cars, video cameras, VCR's, computers, and compact disks. His mind revels in the technological advances made in the last hundred years.

On Neon Lights and Video Cameras. Connecting imagination and invention in a very concrete manner Josh explains how inventors came up with the idea to turn lights into the neon lights used in signs. First, inventors had to think really hard; then they had to use things that existed in the world around them; then they manipulated it in such a way that something new was invented. In a sense, this explanation differs to some extent from what he said earlier. Josh begins to emphasize the role of the person who is creating, rather than the existence of "facts that you see." This is his explanation of how neon signs and video cameras were invented:

Josh: But, like, if you're really, if you're really, like, thinking real hard of something new, maybe, like inventions; they think real hard, and they use things that people have already come up with. Like the light bulb. People thought of it real hard and they came up with neon. Not neon, but, y'know, those lights that light up and are in different shape, to light up signs and everything . . . They just thought about the light bulb and they just put it in things.
Ricki: How do you think they thought up a light bulb?
Josh: (ignoring my question) And like when they made video cameras, like you're shooting me now. When they made them, they probably thought about cameras. You take a picture, each second, if you put them together, you made a video, a scene happening. That's how somebody discovered it!

What Josh was talking about in the above quotation was not the making of video cameras, but the creation of the moving image—how many individual pictures with a small difference in movement placed one after the other and viewed quickly enough, one after the other, give the impression of movement.

Obviously, Josh was influenced by the fact that, while he was telling me his theory about inventions, I was using one of these new inventions to record his thoughts. Given his exposure to the process, Josh's thinking about the moving image is not very surprising, yet it is interesting to see how he incorporated the videomaking into thinking about the things he wanted to think about.

His rationale for the invention of the moving image is that the people who thought about it had to first think about camera, or the individual shots when shot "1 second" apart would yield this impression. (One second apart would not yield this result, but the general idea is expressed rather well for a 10-year-old.)

Closing Remarks about Josh. The constructionist Logo culture provided many opportunities for Josh to deepen and expand his empirical style of thinking by providing him with tools to build multiple representations or ways of looking at a problem. It gave him a larger repertoire of mental models to build with and to think about. Moreover, it gave him the experience of experimenting with the process of moving things with which he was so fascinated.

Josh was able to speak about many moving things, including procedures in his Logo programming, in ways most children do not. Using Logo, Josh built programs which gave him an opportunity to direct and control moving things. He also had many opportunities to explain his programming, which gave him a chance to begin conceptualizing how they worked. Most important, Josh had the encouragement of reflecting upon the origin of energy, imagining the stream and flow of movements upon other movements. As he put it: "FD has to be a procedure somewhere, right? And the things you put in a procedure has to be a procedure, right? And it just goes back to electronic pulses and microchips!" Josh traced the route of electronic pulses through microchips in order to find the source of the energy flow which enables words to pop up on the screen by pushing a key. This gave Josh a glimpse at the power of creation.

The Narrative Mind of Andrew

Introducing Andrew. When I met Andrew, he was a fourth-grade pupil who could make up complicated stories by linking diverse segments of other stories he had heard or read in a unique, if not integrated, manner. The story I am about to tell is of a child whose strengths in the narrative mode of thinking[4] did not fit into the traditional classroom environment. My hypothesis is that, had Andrew had a longer and earlier exposure to the Logo constructionist culture and a greater opportunity to integrate his imaginative creations into constructions that were his own,[5] he may have had a chance at not being suspended from school and succeeding within the school environment.

---

[4] See Bruner (1986) for a somewhat different use of the term *narrative*. Bruner's narrative has more to do with a story genre than a thinking style. Also see Cole (1989).

[5] See Harel (1988) for description of her Instructional Software Design Project (ISDP) at the Hennigan School.

Andrew was an active child who moved fast—especially in class, where he would squirm on his chair as if it were slippery. When he spoke, he used grammatically correct sentences. His diction was dramatic and clear. He knew how to emphasize a phrase and to pace his speech with just the right amount of pauses so the listener could follow his ideas. Conversations with Andrew were always experiences of hearing his thinking. Often he would tell his stories in intricate detail—using the exact time of the event. This use of dates and times struck me as curious. Why did a young child feel he had to be that precise? Was he used to being cross-examined?

Andrew had an average build and an excellent posture. His curly black hair was cut short and neat, and often his clothes were a bit too grown-up compared with other children's. On regular school days, he wore his shirts tucked in his pants, with a belt. If he wore a sweatshirt to school, the collar of his shirt would be neatly sticking out. He also wore shirts with collars under his assortment of well-designed sweaters, and clean white running shoes. On special occasions, Andrew would be especially decked out—wearing his pink cotton shirt with a black bow tie and black pants. However, Andrew's commanding presence was not determined by his clothing.

Andrew had a special aura about him which others found either very attractive or very unattractive. His persistence with adults when he wanted things done his way tended to distance him from those very persons with whom he most wanted contact. Children tended to respond quite similarly: some, like Mark and José, thought Andrew "dangerous" and wanted to be his friend so that they could experience the forbidden fruits of getting into trouble; others avoided him, thinking him too straightforward for their gentler sensibilities. Few, if any, of these 'friendships' with other children or adults seemed to give Andrew a positive feeling about himself during grade four.

Andrew's most special ability was to tell stories. He could make them up in an instant, "without missing a beat," as his home room teacher, Linda Moriarty, would say. My favorite story about Andrew's making up stories is one I did not have the opportunity to observe. However, it seems to represent the essence of his personal struggle to gain recognition as a person. Moriarty told me that a storyteller had come to the class one day. The storyteller told the children how some famous people had gotten their names. Then she asked the children how they got their names. This is how she described it to me:

Moriarty: So, Andrew, hand waving madly, said, 'Oh, I was named after a famous basketball player.' And [then] he named the basketball player, and [said], 'because I'm good at basketball.'

So, one of the kids said, 'Well how did you mother know that you were so good at basketball when you were just born?'

(*Moriarty clicks her fingers in the air.*) Without missing a beat, he said, 'Oh, well, I wasn't named Andrew until I was 5.'

So they said, 'Well, what was your name [those first 5 years]?

And he said, 'They just called me Baby A.'
For 5 years of his life! And he just shot this out—no smile on his face,
complete, you know, God's Truth stuff. That was the most hysterical thing.
But that is Andrew!

This small anecdote about a child begging for recognition is tenderly tragic. At
first one laughs at his getting caught in a lie and then at having the imagination to
follow through with a possible explanation. Then the question hits: Why did
Andrew feel he had to impress his classmates by being named after someone
famous? And why, for example, did Andrew name his dog Scott Lincoln, after
Abraham Lincoln? One of Andrew's stories called *The Sheep and the Goat and
the Duck* may address this question more clearly.

    A Story by Andrew. Andrew and I sat in a barren room by a big table
catching up on the few weeks which had passed since our last serious talk. I
asked him if he had been writing any stories, and he told me about the goat, the
sheep, the duck, the owl, the shark, and the hunter. (Although Andrew told me
the story in one sequence, it seems to divide quite well into four acts or scenes
with a preface.) The following is the verbatim transcript:

The Sheep and the Goat (. . . and the Duck!)

PREFACE

Andrew: Now I'm trying to make up a new story. This time it might be a whole, might
           be three pages, yeah, three pages worth of it. It's going to be a book.''
Ricki: About what?''
Andrew: The goat and the sheep.''
Ricki: You want to tell me about it?''
Andrew: Not too much, because I wrote it like the beginning of April before school
           vacation, and it's about a duck; his name was Alfred and his friend the goat;
           his name was Freddy.

ACT 1

Andrew: So I have a goat. So the goat goes one day to the supermarket, gets some hay,
           and he meets the duck there getting a swimsuit. And so they talk on the way
           home. Then the duck didn't know that she was pregnant. Her stomach—she
           began to hurt and hurt. She thought she was eating a lot and that's what made
           her fat; so he said: "We'd better see the doctor about this."

ACT II

Andrew: So he takes her to the doctor, Doctor Owl. Her doctor tells her that she's
           pregnant. She has a fit! And finally, while she's having a fit, the baby comes
           out—wide awake, three little babies, three little ducklings. Both of them were

pretty, you could say. One of them was the ugliest duckling you ever saw in your life.

ACT III

Andrew: So one day, the girls and their mother were going out to take a swim. A shark came. The ugly duckling was on the beach putting sand on him. The shark came after the mother and ducklings. The ugly duckling grabs a rock, runs out in the water, hits the shark [and] gets his family back in safety. They're still calling him ugly. They still think he's not very brave. They just keep saying, 'he's lucky, he's lucky.'

ACT IV

Andrew: So another time when they were about to get shot by a hunter, flying in the air; the hunter was shooting bullets; the ugly duckling didn't [fly], he always wanted to play; he didn't want to learn how to fly, so he didn't. So he had to stay on the ground. He sees the hunter; he goes over and bites the hunter and his family gets away safely. And now they're starting to be convinced that the ugly duckling is brave, and it doesn't matter if he's ugly or not. It just matters how he acts, how he acts, what's his personality. And THE END (May 1987).

At least three aspects of this story are worth a close examination in getting to understand the thinking of Andrew through his storytelling: the structure of the overall story, the attention to detail, and the content itself.

The Structure of the Story. Structurally, the story has an introduction (Act 1), a problem to resolve (Act II), a first attempt to resolve the problem through an active event (Act III), and a resolution—a happy fairy tale ending (Act IV). Each section unintentionally begins with the word *so,* because Andrew punctuates his pauses with that word. It is Andrew's clue to the listener that she or he should expect a change. (Maybe the *so* also gives Andrew a chance to think of the next scene.)

In the introductory Act I, the main characters are introduced. The goat, who was previously the sheep, meets the duck (who was previously a male named Freddy) at the supermarket. The goat is the male, and the duck is now female. The female duck is buying a swimsuit. On the way home, she realizes that she is pregnant. The male goat suggests she comes to his doctor.

In the next scene, or Act II, the problem emerges or, rather, is born. The duck has three little ducklings, and two, the female ducklings, are pretty; but one, the male, is "the ugliest duckling you ever saw in your life." Here, Andrew states the problem of the story: How will the ugly duckling gain acceptance from the others?

In Act III, the ugly duckling has his first opportunity to find a solution to his not being appreciated by his family. He saves his mother and the girl ducklings from a shark. This act or scene has action but not resolution—after being saved, his mother and sisters think he was just lucky. The resolution comes in Act IV, when he saves his family from being shot by the hunter. This time his family realizes that it was no accident; the ugly duckling is worthy of their respect. They are "starting to be convinced" that he is brave, and that what really matters is not how someone looks but rather how they act, "what's his personality."

Attention to Details Which Keeps Changing. What is remarkable about this story is that it is structurally so strong and complete in every part. Moreover, Andrew is making it up as he goes along. Notice how at first Andrew tells me, "I'm trying to make up a new story," and then, when I ask him to tell me about this new story, he tells me he already wrote it, in April to be exact.

Andrew is very specific about the time as well as about the size: the story "might be a whole, might be three pages—yeah, three pages worth of it. It's going to be a book."

The story itself is a tribute to details within an organized whole. Andrew has introduced many characters who all have active roles in keeping the plot moving. He also assigns a gender to many of the characters. In fact, the story partially revolves around a gender issue—the mother duck gets pregnant and "has a fit." Although we don't know the gender of the hunter, the shark, and the owl, it is not hard to speculate that they are all male, as those needing to be saved are all female—the mother and the girl ducks! And the ugly duckling is male. He, the ugly duckling, of course, saves the females from the predators and gains their approval at the same time.

Another example of Andrew's attention to detail is his inclusion of details that don't enhance the plot but enrich the context. The ugly duckling who didn't go off with his mother and sisters is lolling about on the beach, throwing sand on himself! Consciously or not, Andrew has built drama into the plot with these details; it is just at the moment of seeming peacefulness that the shark comes along.

Linking Different Stories Together. If we agree that our stories reflect what we experience, then several significant features emerge while looking closely at *The Sheep and the Goat (and the Duck)*. The first feature is the most obvious: this story is extremely similar to *The Ugly Duckling*. In fact, when I asked Andrew how he got the idea for this story, he told me he put two stories together, *Two Friends* and *The Ugly Duckling*. As he explained to me that same day in Turtle Cove,

Andrew: Well, I started to think that I should make a book. And I had no ideas at first. So, I thought of something; I looked at a story, *The Ugly Duckling*. I got part of it from there, and I got part of it from *Two Friends*, a book that just came out. And I saw the duckling and the goat. And the name, it was *Two Friends*, and not *Duckling and Goat; Two Friends* and like that. So I decided I'd make my own title, and I used each. I used half from *The Ugly Duckling* and it was half from *The Two Friends*. So I did, and that's how my story turned out.

Notice how once again Andrew pays attention to exact amounts—"I used half from *The Ugly Duckling* and it was half from *The Two Friends.*" One also has to remember that, based both on what Moriarty later told me and on how Andrew keeps changing the details about the story, this story is probably being made up by Andrew on the spot! So, when I ask Andrew why his story is more than a combination of the two stories, his response is very interesting. He returns to his position that he had had a plan for the story and had made decisions along the way, meaning that he was not making this up on the spot but that it was a product he had already produced. This is what he said to me:

Andrew: Oh, because I made a little change in it . . . In *Two Friends,* the lady does not get pregnant and she has the Doctor Owl. She's not pregnant; she's just fat. So I decided I should change it and, 'cause I couldn't think of any way to put the ugly duckling in it. So I started thinking that maybe she was pregnant and she had another ugly duckling. And that's what I think's unique about it.

This example of Andrew's ability to find a way to explain how, despite the fact that his story is so similar to other stories, it is still unique to him is comparable to the Baby A story told at the beginning of this chapter. Andrew has the ability to make his stories come out "realistic" even when he is "caught" in the act of making up a story at that moment.

Autobiographical Theme of Andrew's Stories. The second outstanding feature of the story is its autobiographical theme—the hero's saving others will win him the approval he is so anxiously awaiting. Andrew's main character is put in the position where he must fight the shark and the hunter. Fighting off the bad guys provides a way for Andrew's duckling to overcome his rejection. His family no longer sees him as being ugly; they begin to understand his brave personality through the way he acts.

One is reminded of what Josh said: Ideas come from things that you experience. If you see people fighting, that's what you put in your picture. One can only speculate about Andrew experiences as an inner-city child which make him feel that he has to win the admiration of others by fighting. As his teacher, Linda Moriarty, said when she had just finished watching this video chunk,

Moriarty: That is so autobiographical to me, Ricki.
Ricki: How is it autobiographical?
Moriarty: I just feel a little bit now; you know, this could be very carried away or something, but I just feel that he is, trying to be important and, special. I don't know if it's brave or whatever; and he has such a reputation with his mother and with people of not being credible—you know, making up stories, doing all this stuff and he is bit by bit changing. But it's being accepted by his family; like, doing something special for the family and saving them or helping them and I think that's important. But getting recognized for that. He doesn't feel he's recognized for anything. He is talented, he is special but his

environment is not, it's not . . . He's not getting re-enforced at all. He's not fitting into the standard school environment because his writing skills and his behavior kinds of stuff are not the norm.

While watching Andrew on video, Moriarty's perspective was that he is moving "into the real world but he's still so needy and needs to be paid attention [to] for his strengths." She also noticed that what Andrew chooses to tell and what he chooses not to tell reflect some deeper aspect about Andrew's perspective, although she isn't able to articulate what that is.

Bits and Pieces of Computer Programs. Moriarty's observation about Andrew's overall classroom and computer work was that Andrew took "big chunks of stuff" from other children, which he couldn't work with himself because they were just bits and pieces—this was especially true while programming in Logo. Since many of the children shared their programs, it was not uncommon for children not to be the creator of each part of their project. But with Andrew, who liked to roam around the pod looking for ideas, it seemed that the parts that he had taken from others were not functioning together as an integrated whole. As a teacher who spent much of her time working with individual children, Moriarty would walk around the pods, helping children with their programming difficulties. Often I observed her trying to work with Andrew and getting frustrated. When other children would call for help, she seemed relieved to have to leave. Andrew's bits and pieces often remained bits and pieces, because, as she said, "he confuses himself." This is her description of what working with Andrew was like:

Moriarty: His program so confused me Ricki. I didn't know where to start with him. I mean, when I worked with him, some pieces he would grab from other kids, some he would do himself. I didn't have a length of time. I couldn't sort out where he was at, so I found it very hard to work with him at the computers. I didn't know what to grab onto with him, so I think that's part of it. Well, I found that sometimes with the computer he would be engaged and a lot of times just not. But he'd have so much there. But he confuses himself. And that's where it's hard because he has a whole block of stuff that he got from someone and doesn't really understand that much, so it's hard to fill in at that point with him (Summer 1987).

On one occasion, Moriarty was sitting on the chair beside Andrew, trying to help him get his program to work. He was working on the Instructional Software Design Project (ISDP), which Idit Harel, another member of the MIT research team, had initiated with Moriarty and her pupils. The children were to design and carry out a program which would help younger children learn fractions. Because the project's duration was approximately 4 months, Andrew had no choice but to continue developing his program. In an interview with Andrew near the beginning of the project, he told me he found the fractions project very boring because he "already learned fractions" in his previous school. However, when he discovered he could use the program as a vehicle to say nasty things to potential users who answer his quizzes incorrectly, he found the project more to his liking. For example, he wrote a program which first asked the user a question, then evaluated the answer, and then, if the answer was incorrect, delivered a nasty message.

On one occasion, Moriarty had come to help him because Andrew had decided to modify commands in Logo! He had wanted get the computer to send a specific nasty message to the user if the user typed in anything other than *one-third*, the correct answer to the question in his program. Instead of using the command called *"IFELSE,"* which would instruct the computer to recognize the input by the user which was incorrect, Andrew deduced that there could be a command called, *"IFWRONG"*, a logical assumption—if the answer is wrong, then tell the user the following statement. Moriarty, a proficient Logo facilitator, noticed the problem immediately.

Moriarty: Oh, I see what you did. You can't [say that]. Logo doesn't know, IF-WRONG. What it knows instead is a command called IFELSE, alright? And then, what IFELSE does is—it takes three inputs, O.K.? The first one is the condition, the thing that you want to be true, O.K.? Now, that fraction was ⅔, so that you want to be true is for the person to write in two-thirds.

Andrew: No. One-third.

Moriarty: I thought you shaded in two-thirds (in his graphic representation of an object divided into parts)?

Andrew: No, it was three things and I shaded in one (Spring 1987).

Throughout this instruction Andrew was very silent. He sat quietly and stiffly, listening to his teacher while she deleted and, uncharacteristically, typed her corrections onto his program. Andrew's voice was very meek when he told Moriarty that the shaded part of his graphic representation was one-third and not two-thirds. Nevertheless, he did have the courage to point this out to Moriarty, a person whom he obviously perceived as the authority.

Trying to Put the Pieces Together. The type of questions the participant observer tends not to ask of the members of the culture is the prescription global one, such as: "Do you think that there's a way in which the computer can bridge the gap between reality and fantasy? And if so, how? And if not, why?" Nevertheless, sitting with Moriarty watching hours of tapes of Andrew provided a context wherein that question seemed appropriate. Having reached an understanding of each other's concerns about and actions toward Andrew, Moriarty and I found ourselves reflecting on what could make Andrew's life in his classroom more successful during the following school year.

Moriarty: Well, I think one thing with the computer that he's learned [is that] all the dribs and drabs and messing around was not really getting him any place in building a program. And it wasn't until really the last couple of months when a couple of the things he did, almost on his own, started to work for him that he realized—

As Moriarty started to speak of Andrew, she spoke without moving. Her eyes seemed to be looking for a way to address the issue. Her shoulder lifted ever so slightly and she nodded her head softly and blinked her eyes as in deep thought as she listened to my response to her thoughts.

Ricki: [Do] you remember how you told me about his fractions project—how he gets pieces from here and pieces from there, it's similar to how he builds his stories!
Moriarty: That's right.
Ricki: It just occurred to me now.
Moriarty: And how he knew almost everything even in classroom discussions. You can see he takes some of what's happening, but he hasn't . . . It's a different . . . He takes it and builds it into something different. He's not following the thread of things.

What is different? Is it the way he understands what he hears in the classroom discussions? And why is building something different problematic? Because he's not following the thread of things? This image of the thread describes more than his relationship to things; it also seems to hint at the delicate balance for Andrew between maintaining his unique way of following his own thoughts while he follows the conversation of others.

Andrew obviously had a great ability to join bits and pieces of stories (and programs) together. The question is, did he integrate them and make them his own? His stories at first seem well pieced together; however, an element of separate chunks placed side by side seems to describe them more than the feeling of an integrated story—a story where Andrew shows how he has appropriated the chunks and made them his own creation.

Moriarty once thought about Andrew as a troublesome pupil in her class. Getting to the point of thinking about him as a fascinating and interesting child rather than a liar and storyteller was a major change for her. As she thought more deeply about Andrew and watched more and more video, she became extremely animated and excited about finding ways to work with Andrew the following year. She spoke about how Andrew's putting his personality into his programs seemed to build his self-esteem. She spoke about how to help him integrate the pieces so that they could form a whole that was his own creation.

Moriarty: We did some list processing and that's when [working on the computer] really grabbed him. While he did some word processing and he could then have the computer respond to the user; and it was Andrew! You know, the name-calling and stuff like that. He loved doing that, and he did some modifications. He was so amused when I sat down next to him and I said: 'Andrew!' (*in a humorously reprimanding voice*) I would say, 'How could you!' and you know, he got a little silly. And [then] he made some change, keeping [the name-calling] there and [he] put something that wasn't quite so name calling in it.

Ricki: But in a way that [name-calling] was making it his own!

Moriarty: That's right—that was his; and he, then, got much more involved with the computer and worked [for] longer periods of time; so he was really sitting through some problem solving stuff with it. Now that was very good. That, to me, was a major growth for him. He stayed with something and followed the same strand long enough to come to sort of a conclusion. He didn't leap into something else immediately, and so he that he was working on solving a bug in a specific program that he wanted to work and that he had planned the way he wanted it to work.

Postscript on Andrew. Like many children in the classrooms of inner-city schools, Andrew was struggling to distinguish between fantasy and lies. Oddly, we encourage children to make up stories and yet we punish them for making up stories, expecting children to be able to distinguish between when it is O.K. to tell make-up things and when it is not. Our message to children—that to gain our approval, they have to tell us only the kind of make-believe we want to hear—may need to be reexamined. Many children at risk are children who are still flexible enough to discover their own reality, a reality that could contribute to our civilization instead of undermining it. For Andrew, unfortunately, certain less flexible patterns had already taken hold. Moriarty transferred schools the following year; Andrew's new teacher was not able to prevent his being expelled from school; and to make matters even worse, he was moved from his home to one foster home, then to another, and then to an institutional residence.

The Social Mind of Mindy

Introducing Mindy. Mindy had a way of engaging me in conversation. Maybe it was how her big round eyes would grab my glance and then diagonally look up to the right or left. Maybe her exaggerated gestures—her winks, her shrugging shoulders with her upturned face, or her hand resting on her hip—signalled her wondrous range of emotional responses, which included intrigue, joy, desire, anger, frustration, sadness, and embarrassment. Or maybe it was simply her warm, responsive nature which made it so easy to spend time with her. Whatever the combination of interpersonal skills, Mindy was a joy to listen to. More than Josh or Andrew, Mindy could and would share intimacies with me about how she understood herself and those around her. Mindy was the only child in my study who did not need stories or objects to reflect upon the nature of life. Her own life and fantasies were the stuff of her inventions.

Mindy often had her nails painted red or wore frilly clothes to school. On regular school days it was not unusual to see Mindy wearing an off-white satin dress, white lace stockings, and white shoes. I often asked myself whether or not Mindy chose to wear this dress to school. Maybe the dress was hers or an older cousin's old "going-out" clothes which needed to be worn before she grew out of them, or maybe she was expected to look like a pretty little girl to please her family.

When I asked Mindy what she liked doing on the computer, she first mentioned how she liked "discoverin' stuff and playing." However, as she caught herself saying the word "playing," she nodded her head from side to side wistfully. Watching this gesture and hearing her say the word "playing" gave me the clue to pursue her notion of play a bit further. For Mindy, playing on the computer meant making, or programming, girls:

Ricki: What do you like doing on the computer?
Mindy: I like discoverin' stuff. And I like playing.
Ricki: You like playing?
Mindy: Yeah! That should be the first thing I should say.
Ricki: What kind of things do you play on the computer?
Mindy: I play games, and *I make, like, girls. I love making girls—on paper, on computer, on cardboard, on chalk, on anything, chalkboard!*

Indeed, one of Mindy's favorite Logo projects was a graphic illustration of a girl in a dress with a bright yellow triangle as the skirt.

On Girls and Boys. Scoring well on aptitude tests, Mindy was in the grade-four Advanced Work Class. In class, she watched everyone very closely. She would focus intensely on each movement in the classroom, her eyes moving from child to child. She seemed to be watching and gathering information with each quick turn of her body. Her eyes rarely rested for a moment (although she was not hyperactive in any sense). Her theatrical movements could create the perfect effect at a moment's notice.

In one of our conversations in the classroom, during an independent work period, she maintained a conversation with me while simultaneously responding to a number of contextual events within the classroom: her teacher's comments in another part of the room, what was happening within different groups of children, and what was happening in her immediate vicinity. She had what is called "peripheral vision" and used it without losing her train of thought.

While we spoke, my camera was placed on a table beside me, quite close to her. In the foreground of the frame is Mindy, in her off-white satin dress, the white line of a bra strap on her shoulder showing; in the background are Tammy and Moses, on each at their own desk.

We were discussing may things that day—boys, stories, and computers. Our first discussion was about Josh and Joe and her reactions to how they worked together. Mindy was a good informant about Josh and Joe, because she spent a lot of her time interacting with them in the computer pods. For more than half a year, Mindy sat to Josh's left and often engaged Joe, who sat on Josh's right, in conversations to tease Josh. This day in the classroom she was telling me about Josh and Joe's style of working together. She told me how she thought Josh was weird because he asked so many questions: "Josh, I think he's very weird." Her voice was a bit whiny, as if she were imitating Josh, and, as she spoke to me, her eyes caught the look from a classmate and she waved her fingers across the room. She switched her attention back to me and told me how when her teacher, Ronkin, talks to them about their work, Josh asks questions "which are very stupid."

What is remarkable about her reflections on Josh and Joe is not only what she says about them, but also what it shows about the relationship between boys and girls. Josh and Joe were not stupid, as Mindy suggests, but just not interested in the things that Mindy was interested in. In spite of all the hours the three children spent sitting next to each other at their computers, Josh and Joe rarely acknowledged Mindy's presence while they worked on their exploding cars and airplanes. Usually, the boys ignored her, which provoked Mindy into teasing them; sometimes, they would decide to pay attention to her teasing and seemed to enjoyed it. (This struggle to engage boys in talking instead of playing with their cars and blowing up things seemed to strike familiar chords in my memory.)

Keeping Her Focus Throughout Distractions. Tammy did not agree with Mindy's interpretation about Josh's asking stupid questions, and she was not shy about telling Mindy so. She interrupted the conversation between Mindy and myself to say, "Uh, uh! They're good questions, but they're hard to answer." Mindy turned dramatically and yet good-heartedly, lifting her eyes in a wide-open stare as if to tell Tammy to stop interfering with her conversation with me.

Meanwhile, Moses jumped into the scene and looked right into the lens of the camera to tell me, "She lives in a Housing Project!" Mindy remained calm and did not respond at all. In fact, I have examined this segment of video many times, trying to understand how Mindy remained so calm while a classmate of the same ethnic background used her living in a housing project as a weapon. My interpretation is that Mindy, being a good observer of human nature, did not take Moses too seriously. Moses was a child whom Mindy would have named a "troublemaker." She had probably heard him say this kind of class-related put-down many times before—as I had.[6] Another interpretation is that Mindy was enjoying being the center of the camera's and my attention and was probably more interested in being appreciated by me than put down by Moses. A third

---

[6] Although Moses' comment does not seem to be racist, it's roots are most likely racist. Within a racially stratified culture, class stratification within the races begins to grow as a way of maintaining the status quo that one person is always better than another. During this same conversation, I remember thinking that I heard Moses saying, "Jews, Jews, Jews!" also with a derogatory intonation. I still think that is what he is saying on tape. To this day, I am confused about what was happening with Moses, and sense that he provides us with interesting clues to problems of self-esteem and self-worth.

interpretation is that Mindy was too proud to admit that she was the subject of discrimination. Denial?

Mindy just continued our conversation as if nothing at all had happened. She told me about Josh and Joe, how they always talk in class and want to do the opposite of what their teacher, Ronkin, wants them to do. She stayed right with me—her eyes metaphorically *holding* the camera.

Mindy: Him, him and Joe, yeah! They always TALK!! They sort of, like, they always make a struggle. Like, Mrs. Ronkin says something and they say something the opposite way. They say: 'But No!' And then when Mrs. Ronkin says: 'Let's go' . . . They say: 'No, I wanna finish it!' (*She whines, pretending to be them.*)

When comparing herself to how Josh and Joe do things, she pointed out that they can do things she can't do, like making the computer make sounds and doing animation, "making things move." But as impressed with what Josh and Joe do, she was very confident about what she could do well on the computer—make pictures of girls!

Continuing to be interrupted by Tammy and Moses, Mindy began to show greater disapproval by her even more exaggerated manner of turning her whole body around and giving her nasty stare to both of them. Then Mindy's composure returned, and she quite matter-of-factly explained to me:

Mindy: [Josh and Joe] like make things . . . They make things move . . . In the computer they make sounds. But I just like making, like, pictures and writing procedures. Yeah, I love writing procedures. Yup, 'cause it's like I'm inventing something.

Mindy told me this with confidence and a sense of enjoyment about her own ways of looking at the world.

Mindy's Teasing Josh. As mentioned earlier, Mindy had very strong feelings towards Josh. For most of the school year, she sat within two or three chairs of Josh and Joe in the computer pods. Mindy would tease Josh to get his attention, making fun of his Logo grasshopper-shaped figure, provoking him by telling him that "Joe is magnificent" and encouraging the kinds of fights that often occur between 9-year-old girls and boys. During one particular occasion, she sat in the chair beside Josh in the computer pods, with her hair held up in a big red plastic clip and her right arm leaning over the side of her chair. Her fingers were moving emphatically with every word, and her dark brown eyes were rolling up to the ceiling for emphasis.

Ricki to Mindy:	I want to hear why you think that Joe is so magnificent.
Mindy to Ricki:	'Cause he's . . .
Josh to Ricki:	Who? Who? Who's so magnificent?
Mindy to Josh:	Notchu! (*she means, not you!*) (*All four of us giggle at the way she says this, including herself.*) Joe!

Ricki to Mindy:	Josh is too.
Josh to Mindy:	Joe is magnificent?
Mindy to Josh:	I don't like you! You just want me to like you, but you're too ugly, and you have a hard head, with your Pinnochio nose.
Ricki to Mindy:	O.K. So, tell me about Joe's program.
Mindy to Ricki:	He's the one who taught Josh everything he know.
Josh to Joe:	C'mom, I taught Joe everything. C'mom, Joe, admit it, Joe, just say it. Who taught you how to do the airport? Who did most of the airport? (*Joe continues working, not paying much attention to this whole interaction.*)
Mindy to Ricki:	Josh wanted Joe to help him do the grasshopper.
Josh to Mindy and Ricki:	Oooo, ooo, it was the best file he ever did. And I did most of it!

Whether Josh was the better programmer of Joe was is not as significant as the fact that Josh took her so seriously. Mindy, unlike anyone else that I observed in contact with Josh, knew how to get his feathers ruffled.

Nevertheless, Mindy was a keen observer of others and she knew what was happening between people. Joe often had very good ideas that seemed to be Josh's. As in the above incident, Joe often helped Josh figure out what to do, and Josh probably did not realize the extent to which Joe contributed to their mutual projects. Josh's focus was so goal directed that he just did not see that others were part of the process. Mindy did.

Making "New Inventions."

Mindy: I just like making, like, pictures and writing procedures. Yeah, I love writing procedures. Yup, 'cause it's like inventing something.

Women from the age of young childhood, knowing they will probably become mothers, never question their ability to make girls (and boys). Our dolls are our first babies, and we are guided by our mothers and sometimes our fathers how to hold the doll, how to put it to bed, how to change its clothes, and how to talk to it. The culture of the female child and her dolls is as powerful and enculturated as are the toys soldiers and guns boys are expected to become engaged with. Not surprisingly, boys become stimulated by their toys, which have the power of detachment, and girls becomes domesticated by theirs which offer the comfort of attachment (Gilligan, 1982; Fox Keller, 1985). Many things have changed over the years, and the biggest change is that girls play with cars, trucks, and airplanes, and liberated boys cuddle dolls. (Or, rather, some parents encourage their children to explore a range of activities.) What has not been adequately addressed is the way in which girls (and boys) bring these relationships with their dolls (and "girls" as Mindy would say) into a larger context of their interpersonal skills.

I mention these issues because Mindy was very attached to her make-believe girls, her dreams of having a sister and of becoming a teenager.

Dolls and Girls as People to Think With. Mindy told me she loved writing procedures. Her procedures were pieces of graphic representations which when assembled became girls. For Mindy, this was inventing.

Mindy: Like, when you make a picture, you're not sure how it's gonna come out; you're not sure it's gonna come out like you want it to come out, and if it doesn't, you kinda like it. Yeah, and you sort of say—it's a new invention!

A new invention is a new way of looking at what you did. For Mindy, the end product does not have to be a perfect match with what she has in her mind while she is programming. Instead, she is open to the possibility of a new creation. It may not "come out as you want it to come out" but you like it, she says.[7]

One of the times we sat together at the computer, I remember Mindy becoming very animated about showing me one of the girls she had "invented." She looked at me and asked, "Wanna see?" I told her I did, and then she turned the event into a surprise. She put her hands over the computer monitor as if to hide the surprise. I was told to close my eyes and she would make magic on the computer monitor. "Her it goes," she told me with a song in her voice:

Mindy: Wanna see it? Close your eyes first. O.K. I'll turn it on. Here it goes. This is what I have so far . . . (*A graphic drawing of a girl appears on the monitor*). See. I'm making the hair on the shapes page and the other foot on shapes page. I made this on shapes page (*pointing to part of the girl*); this on shapes page (*pointing to another part*); and I'm going to make the lips on shapes page and the hair and the hands and feet.

When she started showing me her girl, she sat by the computer, munching on a wad of gum and holding the computer with both arms. It was an affectionate and proud gesture. Even when she pointed at the monitor to the places that had been built on the shapes page, she still kept one hand touching the side of the computer.

Mindy on Marriage. A conversation we had about marriage provided me with an even deeper or thicker understanding of how Mindy tries to work out how to be who she is, do what she needs to do, and to come to terms with how others view her priorities. One cold February morning, Mindy and I were sitting on the floor near a muraled wall outside her classroom. She sat leaning to one side, her head tilted toward me and resting on her shoulder. The substitute teacher was not particularly concerned about what Mindy was doing, so we had

---

[7] People often tell me that they wish all children could see things as Josh sees them. On many instances I agree with them. I wish more people who heard Mindy speak about liking the unknown, the unexpected, and the different would say the same thing.

the rare opportunity of just letting the conversation move to where it moved. The mood between us was very casual and the pace very slow, despite the fact that, all around us, the room was filled with the movement and excitement of twenty or more children at the computers.

The moment that stands out as being most characteristic of Mindy's approach to life was when she said the following:

Mindy: Well, when I grow up, if I get married, this is what I want my husband to be: I want him to be helpful, loving, and I want him to be understanding. Like, if I date someone else, he won't get all huffy and puffy. And, if he dates someone else, it's O.K. by me.

For Mindy, it was important that her husband be "cute, loving, have a nice personality, and have a job." He should like her mother, go to church with her every Sunday, and give her all the money so she could go shopping. When I asked her what she would shop for, she told me that first she would go food shopping and then go clothes shopping.

Mindy's father had recently married a young woman from Haiti. At the time of this interview, Mindy had just returned from a 3-week trip to Haiti, where she attended the wedding and celebrations. Her father's bride and a brother remained in Haiti; Mindy, her other brothers, and her father returned. The bride and brother would be joining her family soon.

Mindy lived with her mom. She visited her father "once in a while." At first, when she told me about this arrangement, she said, "I go over to my father's house *every* weekend. Well, every other, every next weekend" and then under her breath, added, "once in a while."

The parts of our conversation I find the most provocative are those that illustrate how she integrates personal challenges in the realm of social interaction. Mindy thinks of herself as an expert on human relations and has very definite ideas about what constitutes a good marriage. I once asked her to tell me more about how she will decide who to marry. This is what she told me:

Ricki: How will you know who to marry?
Mindy: I'll try a couple of dates. Until I see how he really; until I really know him. Yeah, like, if I ask him to baby-sit, see how he reacts on the children; say if he's going to be coming back. See, if he's O.K. when he comes back.
Ricki: If he keeps his word?
Mindy: Yeah. Honesty.
Ricki: So, that is the most important thing [for you]?
Mindy: (*She nods*)
Ricki: How do you deal with it when people you love are not always honest all the time?
Mindy: Well, I try to make them understand that, like, if you're not honest, you go to stealing and if you go to stealing you'll go to drugs, and if you go to drugs,

> you'll die. If you lie, you'll steal, if you steal, you'll go to jail and if you go into
> drugs, or commit suicide, then you die.

Ricki: So, how could you help someone who is a thief, or who . . .

Mindy: Lies?

Ricki: Or who lies! Everybody lies a little bit, right?

Mindy: Yeah! Not big lies! Like a whole pack of lies, just one little bit.

Ricki: Sometimes one lie leads to another . . .

Mindy: And then the other leads to another and then it becomes a pack of lies! (*She nods.*)

Ricki: It's hard to be honest.

Mindy: I know, like if you get into trouble, you're thinking of a way to get out of this; and then the next time you get in trouble, like, another day and then you have to come up with another lies.

In this conversation Mindy examines the realm of marital issues in relation to honesty; lying and deception are intrinsically tied to a culture of drugs and death. Issues are dealt with in exaggerated terms but nonetheless relevant in light of the fact that Mindy often felt she was forced into lying because her teacher or her mother wouldn't understand her choices. Once she told me how she was willing to be punished and felt it fair to be punished if she decided to go to a party instead of doing her homework. She felt that going to the party was more important than doing her homework. What she did not like was having to lie about going to a party. Sometimes she felt she had to lie because no one understood her choices.

Thinking about what Mindy said about not minding if her husband went out with other women and that she too should be free to date others, one can see that what Mindy is struggling with is how to be herself, be accepted and loved as herself, and how to treat others. In her cultural milieu, these are indeed the issues to be addressed.

"Sustaining the Settings in Which Individuals Can Grow." I would like to conclude the section on Mindy with the hope that we caregivers and educators of young children "can sustain settings in which individuals can grow," the words of Mary Catherine Bateson (1984, p. 56) Mindy's story holds many of the keys to the problem of understanding what childhood thinking is about for many children whose style of thinking is not invited into the culture of schools. Perhaps a short explanation of why it took me 4 years to "acknowledge" Mindy's thinking style is called for.

The problem I was struggling with was how to "get a handle" on the development of a girl with excellent social skills like Mindy who was mostly interested in thinking about boys (and drawing girls) and who, as a result, was not doing very well in school. In fact, I believe that I did not focus my attention and the attention of the camera on Mindy as much as I did on Josh and Andrew because I was still evaluating success in the traditionally male way. Only after spending 2 years in data selection and analysis, while working with the video-discs, did I begin to realize that what was happening to Mindy and what has been happening for generations to many young girls who approach puberty is that they "drop out" of being smart—they lose in sports to make the boys look better, and they feign behavior that will help them achieve male and older female approval, at the expense of their own intellectual needs.

Certainly one might say that I did not need to study Mindy to learn these things. I could have thought deeply about Melanie, my childhood buddy from Winnipeg, Canada. Melanie was considered among the smartest pupils in the school until grade five. Suddenly, she was demoted into the "dumb" all-girls class. Ironically, the girls who thought most about boys were separated from the boys, who were busy studying advanced mathematics and introductory physics. Only after Melanie's divorce in her early thirties did she remember that she had once loved learning new things. A socially skilled observer, Melanie became a successful school psychologist and continued to pursue advanced degrees.

Working with the videodisc data of Mindy flooded my memory of Melanie and the girls of my childhood who, like me, had to come to terms with not having our interpersonal skills recognized as being very interesting, even by our women teachers. Working with the data has taught me compassion instead of anger, which was my earlier, more activist, response to female subjugation through gender stereotyping. Instead of trying to remake Mindy into a male scientist or to prove that Mindy and other girls can be as good as boys in the sciences, I have begun to see the value of the female voice in working out very complicated human dramas. Some may contend that these dramas are not the stuff of scientific investigation. It will be my contention that, until we begin to accept the interpersonal skills of persons whose main focus is the lives of human beings, we will never begin to reach below the tip of the iceberg at solving the fundamental balance between humankind and science. As Mary Catherine Bateson so elegantly states:

> The need to sustain human growth should be a matter of concern for the entire society, even more fundamental than the problem of sustaining productivity. This, surely, is the deepest sense of homemaking, whether in a factory or a college or a household. For all of us, continuing development depends upon nurture and guidance long after the years of formal education, just as it depends on seeing others ahead on the road with whom it is possible to identify. A special effort is needed when doubts have been deeply implanted during the years of growing up or when some fact of difference raises barriers or undermines those identifications, but all of us are at risk, not only through childhood but through all the unfolding experiences of life that present new problems and require new learning. Education, whether for success or failure, is never finished. *Building and sustaining the settings in which individuals can grow and unfold, not "kept in their place" but empowered to become all they can be, is not only the task of parents and teachers, but the basis of management and political leadership—and simple friendship.*
> (1984, pp. 55-56)

In thinking about Mindy's dreams, her aspirations, and her fantasies, I ask the reader to question the nature of our biases about home and family and to consider the notion of honest human relationships as being an essential ingredient of the growth of an intellectual scientific and humanistic community.

I now ask myself, What could have happened to Mindy had she been able to develop her interest in "making girls" to the extent where her girl/boy skills became the guiding force in a class project? What would happen to many young girls who are physically experiencing strong hormonal changes in grades four, five and six if they could use their skills of understanding people to follow their interests within a curriculum? It seems quite obvious that the existing grade-four learning modules on insects, explorers, and the planets may not hold as much excitement for the budding young women more interested in the social dimension of human discovery and learning as might a module in psychology and human development.

IMPLICATIONS OF THINKING STYLES ON CURRICULUM DEVELOPMENT

Two assumptions are made about learning that I believe the resulting case studies of my research put into question. The first one is that people are probably more empirical in some situations or domains and more social or narrative in others. Another assumption is that certain subject areas lend themselves best to being thought about in a certain thinking style. Style is usually linked with the style of the discipline. What is hard for educators to deal with is that children may have diverse thinking styles that do not match the accepted style of learning a given subject. When this happens, learners either adjust their personal style to fit the accepted one, suppress their own style and adopt the external accepted style, or, more often, lose interest in the subject. My concern is that, when children compromise their individual style, they forfeit the opportunity to develop a strong sense of who they are as unique individuals. They are told that who they are and how they think about things is not valuable. Unfortunately, succeeding in the traditional school system usually means abdicating one's unique style.

Building written and video portraits from the extensive video data of these three children resulted in the emergence of three dominant and pervasive thinking styles—the empirical, narrative, and social/interpersonal. I am not suggesting that the styles I uncovered represent the full gamut of thinking styles. I *do* propose that, within the situations I encountered these children (in situ and on video), their preferred and dominant style was pervasive. What I elucidate is that their success and/or failure are linked to how their styles enabled them to appropriate their experiences. Josh's empirical thinking style matched the accepted approach within most of the existing curriculum; he did not have problems in appropriating. Andrew's narrative style was not a match; he did not appropriate as well. Mindy appropriated her experiences, but her appropriation was not thought to be a contribution to the way subjects are discussed in schools.

I propose that children would better appropriate their experiences if, first, they could do so within their styles, and, second, if their style were welcomed.

In am certainly *not* claiming that all children with narrative and social/ interpersonal styles will encounter problems, or that curriculum developers believe that the empirical style of thinking is the superior style for doing *all* subjects in the school curriculum. Instead, I show, in the full and complete case studies of my dissertation, that two of the three children did not have an opportunity to think about a given school subject in their style in order to succeed within the traditional school curriculum. They did not have the chance to become engaged in what they were doing, because their individual styles were not welcomed. The Logo constructionist culture provided them with some opportunities to express their preferred style, but many more changes will need to be made to keep the Mindys and the Andrews from failing and being expelled from school.

At this time we can only speculate about what could have happened to Andrew and Mindy had the curriculum been open to their way of thinking. Moreover, we can ask ourselves: How many other children are not being given their opportunity to succeed because no one is listening?

ACKNOWLEDGMENTS

I would like to thank Josh, Andrew, Mindy, who reminded me how to build unconditional relationships. They gave so much of themselves and asked only for respect in return. For the countless hours of joy, while either being with them in person or working with the video data, I thank them and all the children of Project Headlight. May they each find many people who will welcome who they are and how they think. To the children's parents and teachers, I send my gratitude for giving me the permission to enter through doors which are usually locked. Many of them welcomed me (and my camera) into spaces without setting rules. This took courage and confidence. I hope even more doors will open for them in the future.

I would also like to acknowledge individual persons and agencies: Silvia McFadyen-Jones, for her unconditional friendship and her intellectual and spiritual guidance; Seymour Papert, for sharing his thinking with me for 5 years; Glorianna Davenport, for her encouragement and support, Idit Harel, for initiating this book and pursuing it with her usual vigor; Howard Gardner of Harvard University; Andrew Molnar of the National Science Foundation; The MIT Council of the Arts; and the National Science Foundation: grant #851031-0195, #MDR-8751190, #TPE-8850449; The McArthur Foundation; grant #874304; IBM Corporation: grant #SP95952; LEGO Systems A/S, Apple Computer, Inc., and Fukatake. Although the ideas expressed in this work do not necessarily reflect the positions of the supporting agencies or individuals, I am very grateful for their support.

And, to my friends, family, and husband, I thank you for helping me continue to learn the value of rich and meaningful social relationships.

REFERENCES

Bateson, M. C. (1984). *With a daughter's eye.* New York: Pocket Books.

Bruner, J. (1986). *Actual minds, possible worlds.* Cambridge, MA, and London: Harvard University Press.

Cole, R. (1989). *The call of stories, teaching and the moral imagination.* Boston: Houghton Mifflin.

Erikson, E. H. (1950). *Childhood and society.* New York: Norton.

Fox Keller, E. F. (1983). *A feeling for the organism. The life and work of Barbara McLintock.* San Francisco: W. H. Freeman.

Fox Keller, E. F. (1985). *Reflections on gender and science.* New Haven, CT, and London: Yale University Press.

Freud, S. (1952). *On dreams.* New York: Norton.

Geertz, C. (1973). *The interpretation of cultures.* New York: Basic Books.

Geertz, C. (1988). *Works and lives, the anthropologist as author.* Palo Alto, CA: Stanford University Press.

Gilligan, C. (1982). *In a different voice: Psychological theory and women's development.* Cambridge, MA: Harvard University Press.

Globerson, T. (1987). What is the relationship between cognitive style and cognitive development? In T. Globerson & T. Zelniker (Eds.), *Cognitive style and cognitive development* (pp. 71-85). Norwood, NJ: Ablex Publishing Corp.

Goldman Segall, R. G. (1986). *Epistemological styles.* Unpublished manuscript, MIT Media Laboratory, Cambridge, MA.

Goldman Segall, R. G. (1987). *The growth of a culture* [Video of Project Headlight at the Henningan School]. Cambridge, MA: MIT Media Laboratory.

Goldman Segall, R. G. (1988). *Thick descriptions: A language for articulating ethnographic media technology.* Unpublished manuscript, MIT Media Laboratory, Cambridge, MA.

Goldman Segall, R. G. (1989a). *Children and programming: Gracefulness* [Video portraits of children speaking about the Logo mathematics culture]. Cambridge, MA: MIT Media Laboratory.

Goldman Segall, R. G. (1989b). *Children are the future* [Video of Project Mindstorms in San Jose, CA]. Cambridge, MA: MIT Media Laboratory.

Goldman Segall, R. G. (1989c, July). Videodisc technology as a conceptual research tool for human theory making. *Proceedings of the Fourth International Conference for Logo and Mathematics Education.* Haifa, Israel: Technion, Israel Institute for Technology.

Goldman Segall, R. G. (1989d, November). Thick descriptions: A tool for designing ethnographic interactive videodiscs. *SIGCHI Bulletin, 21,* 2.

Goldman Segall, R. G. (1989e). *Thinking about the future* [1-hour documentary about the future of global issues in education]. Cambridge, MA: Cambridge Center for Adult Education.

Goldman Segall, R. G. (1990a). Learning constellations: A multimedia research environment for exploring children's theory-making. In I. Harel (Ed.), *Constructionist learning.* Cambridge, MA: MIT Media Laboratory.

Goldman Segall, R. G. (1990b). *Learning constellations: A multimedia ethnographic research environment using video technology to explore children's thinking.* Unpublished doctoral dissertation. Cambridge, MA: MIT Media Laboratory.

Goldman Segall, R. G., Orni Mester, V., & Greschler, D. (1989). *Learning constellations* [Six videodiscs and interface]. Cambridge, MA: MIA Media Laboratory.

Grubner, H. E., & Voneche, J. J. (1977). *The essential Piaget.* New York: Basic Books.

Harel, I. (1988). *Software Design for Learning: Children Constructions of Meanings for Fractions and Logo Programming.* Unpublished doctoral dissertation, MIT Media Laboratory, Cambridge, MA.

Illich, I. (1970). Education without school; how it can be done. *New York Review of Books,* p. 25.

Illich, I. (1971). Why we must abolish schooling. *New York Review of Books,* p. 15.

Illich, I. (1972). *Deschooling society.* New York: Harrow and Row.

Illich, I. (1973). *Tools for conviviality.* London and New York: Marian Boyars.

Illich, I., & Sanders, B. (1989). *ABC, the alphabetization of the popular mind.* New York: Vintage Books.

Linn, M. C. (1978). Influence of cognitive style and training on tasks requiring the separation of variables scheme. *Child Development, 49,* 874-877.

Shapiro, D. (1965). *Neurotic styles.* New York: Basic Books.

Tuchman, B. (1978). *A distant mirror: The calamitous 14th century.* New York: Ballantine Books.

Stephen Sherman Photography

Edith Ackermann discusses her work at the Epistemology & Learning Group Research Seminar. To her left, Isaac Jackson; to her right, Robert Rusmussen and Lars Bo Jensen from the LEGO Company.

14

From Decontextualized to Situated Knowledge:
Revisiting Piaget's Water-Level Experiment

Edith Ackermann

INTRODUCTION

Piaget's stage theory provides a model for describing children's ways of thinking at different levels of their cognitive development. Its main contribution is to show that children have their own views of the world (which differ from those of adults), that these views are extremely coherent and robust, and that they are so for good reasons. Children are not incomplete adults. Their thinking has a consistency of its own, mostly well suited to their current needs and possibilities. This is not to say that children's views of the world, as well as of themselves, do not evolve through contact with others and with things. The views are continually evolving. Yet knowledge, Piaget suggests, grows almost at its own pace, and according to very complex principles of self-organization. For a child—or an adult—to abandon a current working theory requires more than just being exposed to a better theory. Conceptual changes in children, like theory changes in scientists, are constructed internally and require deep and global restructuring (Carey, 1987).

What stage theory provides is a fixed sequence of progressive differentiations and reintegrations that, in Piaget's view, are needed in order to overcome current limitations and reach deeper levels of understanding. The limitation of stage theory is, however, that it almost completely overlooks the constructive role of specific contexts and media, as well as the importance of individual preferences or styles in knowledge acquisition. While capturing what is common in children's thinking at a given developmental stage and describing how this commonality evolves over time, stage theory tends to ignore singularities.

Situated knowledge—or knowledge in situ—is best captured by what I call the *differential* approach.[1] Because of its focus on differences rather than commonalities, the differential approach provides a framework for studying how ideas get formed and transformed when expressed through different media, when actualized in particular contexts, when worked out by individual minds. In recent years, an increasing number of psychologists and cognitive scientists have come to the view that knowledge is essentially "situated" and thus should not be detached from the situations in which it is constructed and actualized (e.g., Brown & Collins, 1989; Rogoff & Lave; 1984; Schön, 1983). To use Schön's words, learners are "reflective practitioners" who think and act in situ, no matter how sophisticated their thinking. This growing interest in the idea of situated knowledge, or knowledge as it lives and grows in context, is leading many researchers to look at singularities in people's ways of thinking, to analyze individual and group interactions with, and descriptions of, specific situations, and to study how these interactions and descriptions evolve over long periods of time.

Consistent with this approach, Papert and others have shifted our attention from the study of general stages of development to the study of individual or culturally related learning styles. In accordance with many women scholars (e.g., Gilligan, 1987; Fox Keller, 1985; Turkle, 1984), they question the prevalent view among developmentalists (e.g., Piaget, Kohlberg) that formal thinking is necessarily the most mature form of intellectual development. They show that formal thinking is by no means the most powerful tool for everyone, and not necessarily the most appropriate in all situations. Different individuals may develop different ways of thinking in given situations and nonetheless remain excellent at what they do. Such an emphasis on the richness and diversity of learning paths challenges the normative view of cognitive growth as a universal increment toward some specific form of hypothetico-deductive thinking! In her book on Barbara McClintock, *A Feeling for the Organism*, Evelyn Fox Keller shows that even "hard" science can be practiced the "soft" way, and that a rigorous scientific approach should not be equated with removal from specific contexts through purely abstract and analytical thinking (Fox Keller, 1985). In a similar way, Carol Gilligan's study of girls' attitudes toward moral dilemmas offers a strong alternative to Kohlberg's normative model of moral development (Gilligan, 1987). For all of these authors, formal thinking is far less crucial for reaching deep understanding than is normally assumed by scientists and educa-

---

[1] By *situated knowledge* I mean knowledge as it gets actualized by a person in a given context. The *differential approach* refers to the method by which a researcher captures knowledge in situ. By *decontextualized knowledge* I mean cognitive invariants, or that which is transferable across situations. Stage theory refers to the method used to access the progressive construction of cognitive invariants.

tors. Such a claim has important implications in the fields of cognitive research and education.

My purpose in this chapter is to incorporate such views in guiding the reader through a specific experiment, the water-level task, initially designed by Piaget and Inhelder to study children's construction of the horizontal/vertical coordinate system (Piaget & Inhelder, 1967). This system is, in the authors' view, the most stable and external reference frame used to describe objects and movements in space. Many years ago, I replicated this experiment from a differentialist's perspective, which I contrasted with Piaget's stage analysis (Ackermann, 1981, 1987). My current aim is to make explicit the epistemological assumptions underlying Piaget's stage theory, and to show that a situated approach can enrich the developmentalist's perspective. I describe how different children manage to organize and make sense of various situations presented to them, and I pay attention to the contexts that trigger, or hinder, their understanding. I also hope to illustrate the importance of variations, or as Piagetians say, of *décalages* (discrepancies) in the construction of cognitive coherence. Thus, my approach represents a synthesis of what I view as most valuable in the stage and differential perspectives.

PIAGET AND PAPERT: SIMILAR GOALS, DIFFERENT APPROACHES

My description of the microworld of the water-level experiment will be enriched by a further characterization of the developmental and situated approaches to knowledge acquisition. Piaget and Papert each represent a strong view in the debate between decontextualized and situated theories of knowledge acquisition. At the same time, they share enough common background for a comparison to be meaningful.[2]

Piaget and Papert are both *constructivists* in that they view children as the builders of their own cognitive tools as well as of their external realities. For them, knowledge and the world are both constructed and constantly reconstructed through personal experience. Each gains existence and form through the construction of the other. Knowledge is not merely a commodity to be transmitted, encoded, and retained, but a personal experience to be actively constructed. Similarly, the world is not just sitting out there waiting to be uncovered but gets progressively shaped and transformed through the child's, or the scientist's, personal experience.

---

[2] Describing the difference between Piaget and Papert has been useful for me, and might be of general interest for the reasons mentioned in the text. It was through working directly with both thinkers (first, at the Piaget Institute, and currently at MIT) that I became progressively convinced of the need for integrating structural and differential approaches in describing human development.

Piaget and Papert are both *developmentalists* in that they share an incremental view of children's cognitive development. The common objective is to describe the processes by which children come to outgrow their current views of the world and to construct deeper understandings about themselves and their environment. In their empirical investigations, both Piaget and Papert try to analyze the conditions under which learners are likely to maintain or change their theories of a given phenomenon through interacting with it during a significant period of time. Despite these important convergences, the approaches of the two researchers nonetheless differ. Understanding these differences requires a clarification of what each thinker means by intelligence and of how he chooses to study it.

Both Piaget and Papert define intelligence as *adaptation,* or the ability to maintain a balance between stability and change, closure and openness, continuity and diversity, or, in Piaget's words, between assimilation and accommodation. And both see psychological theories as attempts to model how people handles such difficult balances. The main difference is that Piaget's interest was mainly in the construction of internal stability (*la conservation et la réorganisation des acquis*), whereas Papert is more interested in the dynamics of change (*la découverte de nouveauté*). Allow me to elaborate:

Piaget's stage theory relates how children become progressively detached from the world of concrete objects and local contingencies, gradually becoming able to mentally manipulate symbolic objects within a realm of hypothetical worlds. He studied children's increasing ability to extract rules from empirical regularities and to build cognitive invariants from variations in the environment. He emphasized the importance of rules and invariants as means of interpreting and organizing the world, and he presented abstract and formal thinking as the most powerful ways to handle complex situations. One could say that Piaget's interest was in the assimilation pole, as his theory emphasizes all those things needed to maintain the internal structure and organization of the cognitive system. And what Piaget describes particularly well is precisely this internal structure and organization of knowledge at different levels of development.

Papert's emphasis lies almost at the opposite pole. His main contribution is to remind us that intelligence should be defined and studied in situ; alas, that being intelligent means being situated, connected, and sensitive to variations in the environment (Papert, 1980). In contrast to Piaget, Papert draws our attention to the fact that "diving into" situations rather than looking at them from a distance, that connectedness rather than separation, are powerful means of gaining understanding. *Becoming one with the phenomenon under study* is, in his view, a key to learning.

Papert's research focuses on how knowledge is formed and transformed within specific contexts, shaped and expressed through different media, and processed in different people's minds. While Piaget liked to describe the genesis of internal mental stability in terms of successive plateaus of equilibrium, Papert is interested in the dynamics of change. He stresses the fragility of thought during transitional periods. He is concerned with how different people think once their convictions break down, once alternative views sink in, once adjusting, stretching, and expanding their current view of the world becomes necessary. Papert always points toward this fragility, contextuality, and flexibility of knowledge under construction.

The type of "children" that Piaget and Papert depict in their theories are very different and much in tune with the researchers' personal styles and scientific interests. Piaget's "child," often referred to as the epistemic subject, is a representative of the most common way of thinking at a given level of development. And the "common way of thinking" that Piaget captures in his descriptions is that of a young scientist whose purpose is to impose stability and order over an ever-changing physical world. I like to think of Piaget's child as a young Robinson Crusoe in the conquest of an unpopulated yet naturally rich island. Robinson's conquest is solitary yet extremely exciting, since the explorer himself is an inner-driven, very curious, and independent character. The ultimate goal of his adventure is not the exploration as such, but the joy of stepping back and being able to build maps and other useful tools in order to better master and control the territory under exploration.

Papert's "child," on the other hand, is more relational and likes to get in tune with others and with situations. He or she resembles what Sherry Turkle describes as a "soft" master (Turkle, 1984). Like Piaget's Robinson, he or she enjoys discovering novelties, yet, unlike him, likes to remain in touch with situations (people and things) for the very sake of feeling at one with them.[3] Like Robinson, he or she learns from personal experience rather than from being told. Unlike him, he or she enjoys gaining understanding from singular cases, rather than extracting and applying general rules. He or she likes to be engaged in situations and not step back from them. He or she might be better at pointing at what he or she understands while still in context, than at telling what he or she experienced in retrospect. He or she is what Schön (1983) calls a "reflective practitioner."

My own perspective is an integration of the above views. Along with Piaget I view separateness through progressive decentration as a necessary step toward reaching deeper understanding. I see constructing invariants as the flipside of generating variation. Distancing oneself from a situation does not necessarily entail disengaging but may constitute a necessary step toward relating even more intimately and sensitively to people and things. In any situation, it would seem, there are moments when we need to project part of our experience outwards, to detach from it, to encapsulate it, and then reengage with it. This view of

---

[3] The switch from the pronoun "he" to "he or she" is here intentional. It points to the fact that, unlike Piaget, many researchers on individual learning styles have tried to correlate soft/hard distinctions with gender. I take the stance that either gender may demonstrate both.

separateness can be seen as a provisory means of gaining closer relatedness and understanding. It does not preclude the value of being embedded in one's own experience. I share Papert's idea that diving into unknown situations, at the cost of experiencing a momentary sense of loss, is a crucial part of learning. Only when a learner has actually traveled through a world, by adopting different perspectives, or putting on different "glasses," can a dialogue begin between local and initially incompatible experiences.

My claim is that both "diving in" and "stepping back" are equally important in getting such a cognitive dance going. How could people learn from their experience as long as they are totally immersed in it? There comes a time when one needs to translate the experience into a description or model. Once built, the model gains a life of its own and can be addressed as if it were "not me." From then on, a new cycle can begin, because as soon as the dialog gets started (between me and my artifact), the stage is set for new and deeper connectedness and understanding.

In his book, *The Evolving Self,* Kegan beautifully develops the view that becoming embedded and emerging from embeddedness are both essential to reaching deeper understandings of oneself and others. To Kegan, human development is a lifelong attempt on the part of the subject to resolve the ongoing tension between getting embedded and emerging from embeddedness (Kegan, 1982). In a similar way, I think of cognitive growth as a lifelong attempt on the part of the subject to form and constantly reform some kind of balance between closeness and separation, openness and closure, mobility and stability, change and invariance.

The water-level experiment, which is described below, offers a rich setting for describing how different children, at different ages and in different situations, handle this subtle balance. The questions I attempt to illuminate include: How do children come to progressively impose order upon the extremely labile world(s) that we present to them? What kinds of reference frames do they select in order to give meaning to each situation? Are these reference frames local and changing, or global and invariant? Under which conditions are children likely to hold on to some current idea, or rather, to let go of it? How do they come to understand that the orientation of the surface of liquid at rest remains the same, or invariant, regardless of the orientation of its container?

THE WATER-LEVEL EXPERIMENT: A MICROWORLD FOR STUDYING THE CONSTRUCTION OF SPATIAL INVARIANTS

My discussion is based on studies involving Piaget's well-known water-level experiment, which I conducted several years ago from two different perspectives.

The experimental setting was the following: Forty-one children from age 4 to 10 were shown a cylindrical bottle partially filled with liquid. The bottle was quickly turned around, and covered with a cloth to hide the water level. We asked the children to anticipate the orientation of the water-level when the container was presented in different static orientations. In the classical experiment, children were asked to express what they anticipated by means of drawings. They drew the position of the surface for all positions (as shown in Figure 1). Only if the drawings did not provide enough information were they also asked to *show* the level on the bottle (covered) with their finger, or to *verbally describe* the orientation of the surface.

This experimental setting is obviously restricted. It is a contrived task, presented to children under very controlled conditions and over short periods of time (three sessions of half an hour each). Despite these limitations, the water-level experiment nonetheless offers a rich environment in which to study the role of context and style in the construction of cognitive invariants, and (conversely) the role of invariants in the handling of variations. These qualities will become more obvious as I further describe the experiment.

The original experiment was designed by Piaget and Inhelder (1967) to study how children progressively build a stable and external reference frame—the coordinate system—necessary in order to describe orientations and movements in space. The water level task was initially coupled with an experiment on children's understanding of verticality. Children were asked to anticipate the position of a plumb-line once the context was tilted, and to draw smoke stacks on slanted roofs, or straight poles on slopes. Both experiments require the construction of an invariant: horizontality in the case of the water-level task, and verticality in the case of the other experiment. In Piaget's view, the cartesian coordinate system as modelled by mathematicians is nothing but an elaborate version of the most stable and reliable reference frame spontaneously constructed by adults to situate objects and movements in space.

The water-level task can be described as a conservation experiment in which the constructed invariance is the permanent position of the water level independent of the position of the container. An interesting feature of the water-level task is that, for each position of the jar, children need to define the orientation of the water level in relation to other objects. Without the use of external and stationary

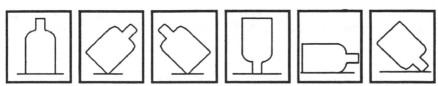

Figure 1.   Children are asked to draw the water-level for all the positions of the bottle.

objects of reference, the horizontality of the water level—which might well remain invariant for all positions of the container—can simply not be identified. The children need to fix some objects in order to give meaning to others. They need to select, among all potential landmarks within a given situation, the ones that will serve as referent objects.

Note that the questions addressed to children involve static rather than dynamic properties of liquids: What they need to evaluate is the orientation of the surface of liquid at rest in immobile containers. This does not imply that the dynamic properties of liquids can be ignored. Would it ever be possible to anticipate the placement of water at rest without knowing anything about the displacement of liquids in motion? Piaget has shown, and my experiment largely confirmed, that children as young as 4 actually know quite a bit about static and dynamic properties of water. In a conversation prior to the experiment, I asked the 41 children (from 5;4 to 10;8) to tell me how they think water "behaves" in familiar contexts such as lakes, rivers, bath tubs, water dropping into sinks, and so forth. It was generally obvious to them that water is "uncatchy" (or slippery), while moving water "always goes down" ("falls"); once at rest, it tends to "put itself flat" ("on its belly" or "lying down"). Children agreed that water "can't stick on a ceiling" or "stay on a slope," that "rivers can't possibly stop flowing" because their course is necessarily downwards. Water "has to go down." It "always goes as far down as it can."

To conclude, all the children knew perfectly well that water flows downward, and that it necessarily remains flat once at rest. This necessity is itself an invariant, expressed by words such as "always." "it has to go down," "it cannot stay on the slope."

If all children do so well, the question then becomes: Why is it that the same children have such difficulties in identifying the orientation of the water level in the context of the water-level experiment? What is it that makes the experimental setting different and harder?

Piaget suggests that in order to make use of their physical knowledge in the context of the experiment, children need to possess another kind of knowledge that he called "geometrical." The function of geometrical knowledge is to specify a given orientation in relation to a larger context. In our preliminary interviews we saw that within the frame of reference of their everyday experience, children can easily relate "down" to "the floor," "up" to "the sky," and "flat" as being "parallel to the floor." Yet the water-level experiment introduces an additional difficulty, similar to that found in Witkin's rod-and-frame experiment (Witkin & Goodenough, 1981): Tilting the bottle is almost like tilting the world, and as a result, all familiar referents disappear and need to be reconstructed.

For each position of the bottle, the child needs to describe water levels in relation to its container (the bottle), and the container in relation to an even larger context (the table, the walls, etc.). Under such circumstances, it becomes hard to just "apply" the otherwise known properties of water at rest. One no longer knows in relation to what referent these properties should be described.

TWO APPROACHES TO THE SAME EXPERIMENT: STAGE THEORY AND A DIFFERENTIAL APPROACH

The water-level task is a good setting in which to study the construction of a reference frame as a means of orienting objects in space. From a stage-theorist's perspective, the main assumption of such a study is that the choice of referent-objects will homogeneously enlarge throughout ontogeny. As Piaget states, the referent-objects will first be limited in character, and then they will gradually become more extensive and abstract. Children will progressively purge and clarify space, emptying it from its objects in order to organize the container itself [the horizontal–vertical coordinate system] (Piaget & Inhelder, 1967).

My own assumption was different. I thought that, unlike mathematicians, children might never totally purge the space into the XYZ coordinate system. Or they might do so in certain areas of their activities but not necessarily in others. I thought that the choice of reference-objects would surely change with age, but also according to each context (the shape and orientation of the bottle) and to the particular medium used to describe the orientation (drawing, showing, or telling). I knew from other water-level studies and studies of similar tasks that different people—children as well as adults—tend to consistently choose different kinds of reference-objects, depending on their style (Olson, 1970). Like Witkin's rod-and-frame task, the water-level task seems to be extremely style-sensitive: "Field-dependent" people, whose tendency is to favor contextual rather than body-centered referents, seem to have a harder time perceiving the horizontality throughout contexts than their "field-independent" counterparts.

Like Piaget, I used the clinical investigation as a way to access children's thinking. Yet I did so for different reasons. Piaget's main objective in varying contexts and in proposing counter-suggestions to children was to access the hidden coherence behind apparent contradictions. He saw different media, such as drawing, telling, and showing as vehicles through which the same representation of the phenomenon could be expressed. To him, working in different media was not supposed to alter children's representations, at least not deeply enough to require particular attention.

I felt, though, that different media and contexts would trigger different representations, which led me systematically to ask children to first draw, then show, and ultimately tell the orientation of the water level for all positions of the bottle. I also asked the children to choose between drawings done by others (see Figure 2) to see whether they could recognize correct representations before being able to actually generate them.

In other words, I considered each modality as a context in and by itself, and

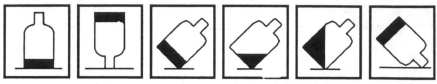

Figure 2.   Children are asked to choose between different drawings done by others.

my objective was to better understand: (a) what children wanted to show through their drawings, pointing, and telling; (b) what children thought their drawing, gestures, and words, once achieved, actually showed; (c) which situations helped children to generate, and/or to recognize the horizontality of the water level; and (d) what was needed to discover the permanence of the water level across contexts.

PRESENTATION OF RESULTS: PIAGET'S CLASSICAL EXPERIMENT

In the original experiment, Piaget and Inhelder grouped children's responses into three main stages, including various substages. The description of these stages reflects Piaget's strongly held orientation towards coherence. I hope to show that these descriptions of children's intermediary stages (all except 1 and 3b) desperately seek hidden coherence where coherence refuses to reveal itself, and for developmental levels where levels seem to blur.

Piaget and Inhelder's Description of Stages

*   At stage 1, up to 4–5 years, children do not identify the water level as a plane surface. The drawings show systematic scribbles, or at best a small ball-like shape put inside the jar independently of its orientation (Figure 3). Stage 1 children respect only topological relations such as proximities and separations.

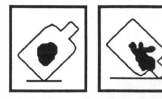

Figure 3.   Stage I children draw a small ball-like shape inside the jar.

Figure 4.   Stage II children draw the water-level parallel to the bottom of the jar.

- At stage 2, from 4 to 6 years, children represent the water level as a straight line, and its direction is related to the boundaries of the bottle itself (Figure 4). Children make no use of a stable and external frame of reference, and thus cannot conserve the horizontality throughout contexts. Stage 2 is subdivided into 2 substages.
- At substage 2a, children mostly draw the water level parallel to the base of the jar, which means that children actually conserve its orientation, but in relation to a frame of reference that is itself not stationary. When the bottle is tilted, or placed upside down, the children sometimes place the parallelism near the neck.

  In a few cases, they totally fill the bottle (see Figure 5).

  Piaget interprets these filled drawings by saying that children think the water is actually expanding, increasing in volume while moving toward the neck. We shall see that such an interpretation takes drawings as too direct an expression of children's ideas.
- At substage 2b, called "intermediary types of responses," children indicate the water level correctly by placing a finger on the bottle (showing). Most of them describe the water level verbally as "moving toward the neck" or, in the case of tilted bottles "slanted in the same direction as the bottle." Yet the drawings still show the water level parallel to the base. In some cases, children draw the level parallel to the lower side of the tilted bottle (see Figure 6).

Piaget's overall comment on "these seemingly contradictory results" is that:

Each of these children can reproduce the horizontal in certain situations and not

Figure 5.   Two variations of the filling procedure.

Figure 6.   Children draw the level parallel to the lower side of the tilted bottle.

in others, and this is because in each situation he bases his judgment on a different reference frame without realizing it.

It is obvious to him that the child's idea of the horizontal is not an operational concept, but a merely intuitive one, governed by the perceptual contexts. Piaget concludes:

Despite such superficial appearances of incoherence, the children of stage 2b have nevertheless in common the fact that they no longer imagine the water level as parallel to the base. They rather regard it as moving relative to the jar. But since they cannot relate the surface to a stable external frame of reference, they draw it in relation to the boundaries of the jar. (Piaget & Inhelder, 1967, pp. 399–400)

- Stage 3, which ranges from ages 6 to 12, is descried as the stage in which the progressive discovery of horizontality occurs. Three main types of intermediary reactions may be distinguished.
- At substage 2b–3a, children discover the horizontal when the jar is lying on its side or stands straight upside down. In other words, a stable external reference frame can be found for all orthogonal positions of the jar (as seen in Figure 7).
- At substage 3a, "One is faced with an astonishing fact. Children ranging between the ages 6,4 and 11 years only succeed after repeated attempts, after reproducing the same errors as were seen seen in stage 2" (p. 408). Yet after a long process of trial-and-error, they finally construct the horizontality for all positions of the bottle.
- At substage 3b horizontality is logically, immediately and consistently applied to all situations right from the start of the interview (see Figure 8).

Figure 7.   Children use a stable and external reference frame.

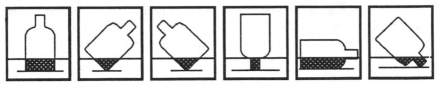

Figure 8.   The water level is horizontal for all positions of the jar.

As Piaget states: "About the age of nine, substage 3b begins with the immediate prediction of horizontal and vertical as part of an overall system of coordinates" (Piaget & Inhelder, 1967, p. 384). At stage 3b, the idea of horizontality is no longer context dependent but is effectively and immediately applied to all positions and inclinations.

BEYOND DEVELOPMENTAL STAGES

Piaget's stages are useful in that they describe children's activities as a sequence of increasingly sophisticated solutions to the problem. They show that the use of an external and stable reference frame, needed to identify the horizontality of the water level, is indeed progressively constructed, and that it cannot be present at all ages or in all situations. From Piaget's stages, we learn that children progress from using local to global referents and that orthogonal positions of the container facilitate the choice of external referents.

On the other hand, Piaget's stage theory has limited explanatory power in this particular experiment because, unlike other conservation experiments, the water-level task is a poor indicator of general levels of operativity. We find children of all ages in almost all stages. Many of them travel through various substages until they reach their final "plateau." The reason for these strong discrepancies can be attributed to the style-sensitivity of the task: different children approach the problem in very different ways.

Another particularity in the experiment is that different stages stand for different aspects in the construction of horizontality: If stages 1 and 3b actually describe periods of relative equilibrium, all intermediary substages (2a, 2b, 2b–3a, and 3a) mark the extreme heterogeneity, contextuality, and fragility of though that are characteristic of all periods of cognitive change. One could argue that stages are, in a way, nothing but "markers in an ongoing process. Yet, they usually indicate periods of relative balance in the process of evolution" (Kegan, 1982, p. 114). In this experiment, the myriad of substages seems to defeat the very essence of what developmental stages are supposed to capture, namely, coherence, closure, organization. Piaget could have used this explosion of substages to stress the constructive role of disparities,. or *décalages*, in the discovery of the permanence of horizontality. Yet he did not. Rather, he treated *décalages* as a hierarchy of steps within an ideal construct. And by doing so, he lost sight of the actual path by which intermediary children eventually find their way through the multiplicity of conflicting descriptions that they themselves generate.

THE DIFFERENTIAL APPROACH

By using a differential approach, one can pay particular attention to singular paths or learning curves. It involves looking closely at how individual children deal with particular contexts, how they use different media, and how they try to bridge initially incompatible situations in order to make sense of them.

Paying attention to individual learning paths seems the only way, at least in this experiment, to tackle some of the questions left open by Piaget's stage theory, namely: Why can a child "see" the horizontality in all orthogonal positions of the jar, and not in the tilted ones? Why can a child conserve horizontality by means of gesture and words, but not in drawings? Why is it that we find children of all ages in all of Piaget's stages?

In my study, I sought to analyze the pattern of *décalages* characteristic of "intermediary" children. Specifically, I hoped to stress the role of *décalages* in the construction of horizontality.

From a child's point of view, *décalage* means conflicting descriptions. In my study, I wanted to capture a few privileged moments in which children were able to build new bridges between initially incompatible descriptions.

Within this overall framework, I became particularly interested in the role of media—drawing, showing, and telling—in shaping children's representation of the phenomenon. I analyzed how the construction of an external model, used to describe a situation, can in turn modify (in a sort of feedback loop) the understanding of the phenomenon. I asked children to describe the orientation of the water level by means of drawings, gestures, and words. Then I studied how their ideas were translated within the constraints of each medium, and how different productions, once achieved, reshaped their initial ideas. Finally, I looked at differences between children's ability to evaluate other people's drawings and to generate their own.

METHOD: STUDY OF CASES

Examining particular cases is a useful method for grasping individual learning processes. Yet it entails a loss of the overall picture, as provided by Piaget's stage theory. Richness of singular cases, versus the power of general laws, encompasses the ensuing debate. Those of us who have tried to integrate both stage and case studies know the impossibility of the endeavor: It would take a lifetime to combine accurately detailed analysis of singular cases with systematic comparison of a significant number of cases. In this respect, Piaget's overall framework has provided generality without prohibiting my inspection of specific contexts whenever they seemed to reveal a microprocess relevant to a child's construction of horizontality. Piaget's stages provide an ideal construct. Detailed case studies provide a microscopic description of significant moments within this ideal construct.

SOME RESULTS

My purpose in presenting some results here is to give the reader a taste of how the differential approach might enrich stage theory. I will limit the discussion to describing how intermediary children anticipate the position of the water level using different media in different contexts. And I will present some detailed vignettes of particularly rich moments of confusion or transition.[4]

Group One

Even the youngest among our "intermediary stage" children (eight children from 4;4 to 5;7) know very well how to *show* the water level with their finger (horizontal gesture). And they usually do so for all positions of the jar. Yet, when asked to *tell* the orientation of the surface, these same children say, for tilted positions: "the water goes to the side where you tilt the bottle," or "it goes toward the neck," and for orthogonal positions of the jar: "the water goes down" or "to the neck." In their *drawings* these same children almost invariably mark the water level parallel to the bottom of the jar, and when asked to explain, in retrospect, what they wanted to show through their drawings, they say that "the water is flat," that "it goes down" (or both), that it "goes to the neck." A more detailed analysis of children's drawings, especially for the cases of the tilted and upside-down positions, is necessary in order to better understand what the children actually tried to represent.

Vignette 1. When the jar is tilted (up or downwards), children sometimes draw the water level by filling up the whole bottle. Either they draw an array of lines parallel to the bottom, or else, a continuous zig-zag from the bottom to the top of the jar (see Figure 9).

When asked what they wanted to show, the children say "that the water is flat and goes toward the neck." To the counter-suggestion: "Doesn't your drawing show that the bottle gets all filled up with water?" children clearly say, "No." This dialogue between experimenter and children indicates that filling pro-

---

[4] For an extensive report on the 41 subjects, see Ackermann (1987).

Figure 9. Filling procedures.

cedures should not be interpreted literally: drawings of filled bottles do not express the idea, as Piaget had actually suggested, that water expands in tilted jars, or that its volume increases. Rather, filling procedures are cartoon-like attempts to show that the water remains flat *while* going toward the neck. Children represent these static and dynamic properties of the liquid separately: "flat" is represented by the parallel line, and "going toward neck" is represented by an animation repeating the parallelism. The filling itself is nothing but a side effect. It results from the fact that the trace does not go away and thus fails to indicate in what order it has been produced.

Vignette 2. For the upside-down position of the jar, young children never *draw* the water level parallel to the bottom without, at the same time, *showing* a movement in the opposite direction (downward) with their finger. Sometimes, they *draw* lines or arrows going downwards outside of the bottle itself (see Figure 10).

When asked what they wanted to show in their drawings, these children say: "The water goes down" or "to the neck" (with gesture indicating a movement toward the floor) *and* "it is flat." Here again, drawings are descriptions of both static and dynamic properties of the water: *flat* is translated into a line parallel to the bottom, and *down* or *toward the floor* is translated into a gesture or an arrow downwards.

I use *mixed schematizations* to refer to cases in which children describe the phenomenon using different media. Most frequently, the red rectangle drawn at the bottom of the bottle stands for the position of water at rest in the bottle: flat and down. The gesture toward the table stands for dynamic properties of liquids: water goes down. Note that the two locations of *down* are not defined according to the same reference frame.

Figure 10. An example of mixed schematization.

In most cases, young children shift between different media such as drawing, gesture, and spoken description without ever noticing that their description of the phenomenon keeps moving as well. In a few cases, though, two conflicting descriptions are suddenly identified, which leads to momentary states of confusion, usually followed by a new cycle of exploration and reflection.

Zooming into such moments of sudden awareness and describing how children negotiate between conflicting views is very useful in understanding how children come to build locally coherent concepts out of initially scattered worlds. Vignettes 3 and 4 tell the story of a particularly interesting moment of confusion/transition, as seen in Figure 11.

Vignette 3. Monica, 4;11, is presented with a jar in a tilted downwards position. She first *draws* the water parallel to the base, trying to show that "it is down and flat" (Figure 11).

When she has completed her drawing, I ask her: "Is the water well drawn?" Monica then looks back at her drawing and comments: "Oh no, it's wrong! because like this the water can't come, the baby can't drink." Experimenter: "What do you mean?" Monica : "It's stuck. It can't go down." Experimenter: "Can you show me where down is?" Monica goes back to her drawing with the intention of pointing "down." Yet, as she does so, she ends up pointing to the bottom of the bottle again, and says: "Oh no! I was right!"

Monica is caught in a loop: Each time she emerges from her drawing and looks at it from a distance, she realizes that "a baby could not drink because the water does not come down." Yet, as she wants to actually point out the location "down" in her drawing, she dives back into the restricted universe of the bottle, and loses the external reference frame (the baby). As a result, she finds her initial drawing (showing the level as parallel to the bottom) to be correct. But then again, she comes out of her drawing, and tries to read it, which makes her realize that "the baby cannot drink."

In order to get the child out of the loop, the experimenter restates her question as follows: "Can you draw the water so that the baby could drink?" This particular formulation helps the child tie together the two alternating and incompatible schemes ("baby drink" and "down with reference to the bottle").

Vignette 4. A variation of the same behavior is found in Ada (5;5). Like Monica, she begins to draw the water parallel to the bottom.

Figure 11. **"A baby couldn't drink because the water does not come down."**

Yet as soon as she is done, she spontaneously comments: "It's wrong. I put the water down. I should have put it up." Notice Ada's use of the words *up* and *down*": after a first trial, she immediately realizes that the water should be near the neck (or *down* in reference to the sheet of paper), yet she still uses the bottle as a reference frame to name directions. *Up* means "up with reference to the bottle," and *down* means "down with reference to the bottle." As a result, she decides to call *up* the place where she thinks the water should be (namely, *down* in relation to the sheet of paper).

Early distinctions between up and down (in "orthogonal" positions of the container) can lead to interesting compromise solutions when the bottle is presented lying on its side. The most striking example is that of Rodolph.

Vignette 5. Rodolph (7;6) draws the water like a vertical ribbon cutting the reclining jar through its middle (see Figure 12). Before he begins to draw, he spontaneously says: "Aie, Aie, I'd say that the water is right in the middle, because it's neither at the bottom nor at the top."

Rodolph found an elegant solution to the problem that he had set for himself: he thought of the (lying) position of the bottle as *neither pointing upwards nor pointing downwards*. Once stated, this description determines how he will think about the position of the water level. He already knew that, *if the bottle stands upwards, the water is going to be down*, and that, *if the bottle is upside-down, the water is going to be down*. He had actually drawn these two positions previously. From these premises, he then drew the natural conclusion: *If neither up nor down, then in the middle*, and he gave life to his idea by sliding the ribbon or rectangle that represents the water from the bottom to the middle of the bottle.

Note that Rodolph's previous drawings determine his actual solution to the problem. At no moment does Rodolph really think about water and its properties (which he does very well elsewhere in the experiment). Rather, he works on his own previous figural representation of water. If the ribbon stands for the water, why shouldn't he operate directly on ribbons rather than on water? In this case, it is precisely Rodolph's reliability on his own model of water that dictates the solution.

All of the vignettes presented so far suggest that children's drawings should not be taken too literally. Drawings are not analogues of the ideas that they express. They are usually quite abstract schematizations of the most salient

Figure 12.   Rodolph (7;6): "The water is right in the middle because it's neither at the bottom nor the top."

properties to be represented. But this is not to say that, once achieved, the drawings might not be misinterpreted by the children themselves, as well as by the researchers who try to read them.

Vignette 6. A last set of examples comes from the verticality situation that I examined in a pilot study. Most intermediary children know very well how to actually stick a pole onto a 3-D cone (toy-mountain) so that it is "straight" (Figure 13a). Yet when asked to draw the pole vertically on a 2-D representation of the mountain, they trace a line perpendicular to the slope (Figure 13b).

When further invited to compare their results and to explain the different outcomes, all children mention that they actually wanted the pole to be "straight" in both cases. Young children give no further explanation for the different outcomes, whereas all of a sudden, they begin to give reasons for the discrepancy. According to a six-year-old "It's normal (that they are not the same in both tasks). This (points * in B) is straight in the drawing. And this (gesture downwards) is straight when I stick the pole in the heep. This (shows * in drawing) would be wrong here (3-D maquette)."

The beauty of this explanation is that the child makes explicit the contextuality of the result in relation to each medium used. To him, the results do not have to be identical for each task. Only older children become bothered by the discrepancy and try to come up with a common solution to both tasks.

Group Two

Group two intermediary children seem to share an altogether different view of the world. To them, the water level should not, as for Group One, be flat and down, but rather *tilted for all tilted positions* of the bottle. These children treat orthogonal positions differently from tilted positions: The former (orthogonal) dictate that the water level be "flat and down," while the latter (tilted) imply that the water level be tilted relatively to the orientation of the jar. Group two children consistently represent "down," in orthogonal positions, relative to a stable and external reference frame, even in their drawings. I shall limit my comments to

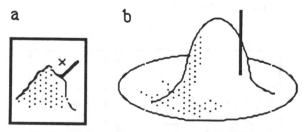

Figure 13. **"Straight" in the drawing is not like "straight" in the maquette.**

the tilted positions of the jar, trying to show how the new idea of *relative orientation* is actually expressed through different media.

The most striking result is that, in *showing* the water level with their finger, all children actually maintain the horizontality of the water level for all positions. Yet when asked to *verbally specify* the orientation that they just showed, they say, "The water is tilted in the same direction as the bottle." In their *drawings*, children come up with a large variety of solutions (see Figure 14). In all cases, they argue that they have drawn the level the way they did to show that the water is *tilted*.

A large subgroup of children actually draws the water perfectly straight (horizontal) for all positions of the bottle (except sometimes for the titled downwards position, which is particularly difficult). The arguments used to justify these drawings include: "My drawing shows that the water always goes exactly in the same direction as the bottle," and "you can put the water in any different shape; by moving the bottle, it will always follow the bottle. It will shape itself like the bottle." To the question: "Is the water level actually the same for different positions of the bottles?" these children initially say, "No," indicating that they reconstruct the level for each context, and that they do not see the invariance that they actually demonstrated through the actions that produced their drawings. Even when they look at their drawings in retrospect, they do not recognize that something has actually stayed the same for each position. The drawings, in these cases, are like gestures that leave a trace. Yet, the similarity of the trace for each position is not perceived.

In some cases, we captured shifts, or moments of confusion/transition, between nonconservation and conservation.

Vignette 7. When asked to *tell* the orientation of the water level, some of the children exhibit an interesting behavior: Instead of naming the direction of the water level by means of words like *straight* or *tilted*, they insist upon showing it with their finger (horizontal gesture for all positions). At best, they say things like "It's like this" (gesture horizontal), or "It's just always like the bottle," or "I can't really tell." It almost feels as if the words *straight* or *tilted* were suddenly recognized as misleading descriptors of the beginning of a sense of invariance. The children do not trust these words any more and thus avoid using them, which puts them in a momentary state of confusion. They are reluctant to

Figure 14.   The water level is tilted for all tilted positions of the jar.

describe the water level as being straight, since it remains, in their minds, oriented relative to each position of the bottle, and is thus tilted in a variety of ways. On the other hand, their drawings and gestures exhibit a regularity from which they no longer depart.

The way permanency is usually discovered by these children is very sudden, and based on three main arguments:

Vignette 8. "Oh, am I stupid, of course it [the water level] remains the same. The more the bottle goes down [or is tilted downwards], the more the water goes up [or is tilted upwards]. So it's the same. It's always the same." I call this discovery *conservation by compensation.* Children understand that any movement downward of the container is compensated by an equal movement upward of the water level (and vice versa). As a result they produce the invariant horizontal position of the water level.

Vignette 9. Another kind of insight is: "Oh, no! . . . I thought the water moved in the bottle, but it's the bottle that moves around the water." In this case, the liquid does not move at all, while the bottle turns around it. This discovery resembles a Necker effect: What was previously seen as moving is actually fixed, and what was previously seen as fixed is actually moving. Depending on how you decide to look at them you see things differently.

Vignette 10. A last type of insight is the recognition that the water level always stays parallel to the top of the table. In this case, the children do not describe the water level relative to the container, but to a steady and external reference frame. Their thinking goes as follows: I see that the water level stays parallel to the top of the table; I know that the top of the table is flat; thus, the water level has to be flat, too.

EXPERIMENTAL CONCLUSIONS

The study of the water-level task shows that even young children (4–5 years) know quite a bit about water in motion and at rest. At given moments in the experiment, all of them express ideas such as "the water level is always flat," "water always goes down," "water goes toward the neck," "water goes in the direction where you tilt the bottle." Note that they explicitly mention the invariant character of these properties by using words like *always,* or *necessarily.*

The study also shows that most children's knowledge remains fragile in that it appears in particular situations and vanishes in others. And it does so with unexpected consistency across our population.

Just as a reminder, the permanence of horizontality of the water-level is generally first discovered for orthogonal positions of the bottle, and only later for tilted positions. In both cases (orthogonal and tilted bottles), upside-down positions appear as harder than upright positions. In all cases, the horizontality of the water level can be indicated by gesture, before it is signified by words or represented in drawings. Within the particular medium of drawing, children are able to recognize correct drawings achieved by others, before they can generate their own. For each intermediary child, we observe a pattern of *décalages* that shows the "consistency in their inconsistencies" across contexts and usages!

As a result, we end up with a contradictory picture: On one hand, young children come to the experiment with a series of quite general "pieces of knowledge" (diSessa, 1988), or cognitive invariants, that they use to make sense of different specific situations (e.g., water *always* goes down; water levels are *always* flat). On the other hand, these "pieces of knowledge" remain local, in that they do not always help to make useful distinctions within and across contexts: They are general, yet they are only locally valid.

Two main questions I wish to discuss in the experimental conclusions are: (a) How can we explain the *décalages,* or disparities between contexts and media? (b) If it is true that each context, and medium, leads to a different understanding of the phenomenon, how can children ever build coherence? In other words, how do children learn to bridge initially incompatible descriptions, and build trans-contextual invariants?

A first explanation of *décalages,* suggested by Piaget and Inhelder, is that some contexts trigger the use of an external reference frame, whereas others hinder it (Piaget & Inhelder, 1967, p. 405). For example, in the orthogonal positions, the contours of the bottles are isomorphic to the axes of a "natural" horizontal–vertical reference frame which children already know how to use (in their everyday experience.) When bottles are tilted, this isomorphism breaks down, and two conflicting reference frames appear. In this case, children need to define the water level either relative to the contour of the bottle, or relative to a larger context, such as the room or, in the case of drawing, to the sheet of paper. Our results show that younger children tend to use closer neighbors as reference.

For each orientation of the jar, the choice of a reference frame is in addition influenced by the medium used to describe the water level. The main ideas that children express through each medium are:

1.   The water goes "down";
2.   The water goes toward the neck;
3.   The water goes to the side where you tilt the bottle (for tilted positions);
4.   The water level is flat and down;
5.   The water level is flat and goes to the neck;
6.   The water level is tilted for tilted bottles (group two children adopt view 6).

The ways in which these ideas are implemented through each medium are extremely different, and once the representations are embodied, are likely to modify children's initial understanding.

In drawing, the code adopted to translate the basic ideas is:

DOWN => bottom of bottle (for group one),
FLAT => straight line
TOWARD NECK => trace located near neck (or) arrow toward neck
FLAT AND DOWN => straight line parallel to bottom of jar (for group one)
FLAT AND TOWARD NECK => straight line to bottom of jar, plus arrow
toward neck (or) straight line parallel to bottom of jar repeated till neck
(animation).
TILTED => straight line joining diagonal corners of bottle

— Note that figural representations are not an ideal medium for capturing
dynamic properties of moving water, except if we think of drawing as a
process, a gesture that leaves a trace (which some of our children do). In
the majority of cases, drawings are used to capture the static properties of
water at rest: when children want to describe movement, they usually
complete their drawings by means of gestures and arrows.

Through *gesture,* directions tend to be described in reference to the position of
the child's own body within a larger natural coordinate system (the room). A
gesture is particularly well suited to describing dynamic properties of liquids
(such as going down, going toward the neck). This explains why children
gesturally enact horizontality across contexts, before they even notice that they
are doing so.

Verbal descriptions of spatial orientations require an explicit mention of the
objects chosen as referents: if I describe an object as being "slanted,"
"straight," "above," or "below," I usually say in reference to "what" I see it
as "slanted," "straight," "above," or "below." Our results also show that
younger children tend to choose the neck of the bottle as a privileged descriptor
of dynamic properties. The idea that "the water goes to the neck" usually stands
for "if you tilt the bottle, the water will flow out" (and the neck is the place
through which it will flow out). Note that verbal descriptions are equally well
suited to capture static and dynamic properties of water.

How do children come to build invariants? As mentioned earlier, none of the
children in the study proceed exclusively from local to global (or bottom-up)
when constructing new knowledge. They certainly induce general laws (or
invariants) from the empirical regularities that they discover in specific contexts.
And in this sense, the coordination of local knowledge remains a crucial mechanism in building cognitive invariants. We were able to capture a few of such
transitions-by-coordination in our case studies. All the children proceed from the
general to the particular (or top-down) by applying prior pieces of knowledge
that they had made into a general rule in order to interpret local contexts. For
example, the idea that water *always* goes down is by no means a situated piece of
knowledge: It is itself an "invariant" used by children to impose order upon the
ever changing local worlds that we present to them. Readjusting general working
ideas to fit a new local context is no easy tradeoff. Yet once achieved, it allows
for new distinctions, which can themselves grow into new general rules.

To conclude, both *differentiation* of global knowledge and *coordination* of local knowledge are equally important at each level of cognitive development. And between levels, children can be said to move from concrete to abstract—or from situated to decontextualized—only because the materials that their minds differentiate and coordinate are broader and can be removed from here-and-now contingencies. The horizontal–vertical coordinate system is, in this sense, the most stable and external reference frame, used by most adults to describe objects and movements in space. Generally speaking, the achievement of ontogenetic development is less the victory of the abstract and general over the concrete and particular, than the triumph of the stable and mobile over the unstable and rigid. Such an achievement is made possible through an increasingly far-reaching equilibrium between *coordination of local knowledge* and *differentiation from general rules.*

TOWARDS NEW VIEWS OF COGNITIVE DEVELOPMENT

In her book on Conceptual Change in Childhood, Susan Carey points at a major risk of abandoning Piaget's stage theory:

> A new view of cognitive development is emerging, one that challenges Piaget's description of child development (Carey, 1983; Fischer, 1980; Gelman and Baillargeon, 1983). Many students of cognitive development now feel that there are no across-the-board changes in the nature of children's thinking. The new view denies that preoperational or operational thinking exist . . . I do wish to emphasize one extremely undesirable consequence of this new view: Piaget's theory brought order to otherwise bewilderingly diverse developments. In giving up stage theory, we seem to be left with tracing large numbers of piecemeal developments through the childhood years . . . This is a high price to pay for a new view, and no doubt explains, in part, why many developmental psychologists have resisted abandoning Piaget's stage theory. (Carey, 1987, pp. 13–14)

On the other hand, I have argued in this chapter that stage theory is an extremely idealized construct, and, as such, it cannot account for how individual learners, using different lenses, evolve in different contexts. Stage theory is moreover very normative, making us believe that formal, or hypothetico-logical reasoning, is necessarily the most mature form of thinking in and across domains.

I see Kegan's work as a major contribution to all psychologists interested in contrasting stage-theory and differentialists' approaches. In *The Evolving Self,* he proposes a developmental model that is integrative enough to avoid the explosion mentioned by Carey, flexible enough to allow the multiplicity of developmental paths, and specific enough to account for individual differences.

Kegan's principles of functioning are universal, not because they ignore individual difference, but because they offer a unifying tool to account for differences, both individual and contextual.

Kegan defines *human development* as: "a history of successive emergence from embeddedness (differentiation) in order to relate better (integration)" (Kegan, 1982, p. 31). People grow by traveling through a succession of cycles during which they attempt to resolve the endless tension between embeddedness and emergence from embeddedness. Of course, individuals develop preferences for connectedness or separation, depending on how comfortable or threatened they feel at given times and in given situations. And preferences turn into "styles" when they rigidify over time. This is not to say that individuals cannot, through external help or by themselves, learn to displace a current set of dominances, modify the ways they set their boundaries, and thus optimize their interactions with the world.

Kegan's model is useful in rethinking cognitive development. In the beginning, one could say, worlds were scattered, and our relation to these worlds— people and things—was fusional: we were [embedded in] them. Then came a time when we wanted to remove ourselves from our experience, and to encapsulate it in some kind of description. We stepped back, and we told ourselves and others what we had done (through words, scribbles, or rituals). Once the model was built, or the description achieved, it gained a life of its own, and could be addressed as if it were "not me." From then on, a new cycle could begin, because as soon as the dialogue got started (between me and my artifact), the stage was set for new and deeper [connectedness and] understanding.

This cycling back and forth punctuates our interactions with the world, and simultaneously determines our way of thinking: Situated knowledge is knowledge that helps us become more intelligently connected by being sensitive to variations in the environment. Decontextualized knowledge helps us master complex situations from a distance, giving them form. And cognitive growth is achieved through a progressive widening of the field of experience in the practice of both.

ACKNOWLEDGMENTS

I wish to thank those who helped me write this article. Their inspiring comments, suggestions, criticisms, and encouragements were precious to me. I also wish to thank those whose minds were present while I was writing. I am deeply grateful to Greg Gargarian, Idit Harel, Bärbel Inhelder, Robert Kegan, Lise Motherwell, Seymour Papert, Jean Piaget, Mitchel Resnick, and Carol Strohecker. I also wish to thank all the children who participated in the research: Their creative and generous minds are a main motivator in all my work. The preparation of this chapter was supported by the National Science Foundation (Grant #MDR 8751190 and #TPE 8850449) Fukatake, and Nintendo Japan. The ideas expressed here do not necessarily reflect those of the supporting agencies.

REFERENCES

Ackermann, E. (1981). *Statut fonctionnel de la représentation dans les conduites finalisées chez l'enfant.* Unpublished doctoral dissertation, University of Geneva, Switzerland.

Ackermann, E. (1987). Que deviennent les idées a propos d'un phénomène une fois retraduites á travers différent media? *Archives de Psychologie, 55,* 195–218.

Brown, J. S., Collins, A., & Duguid, P. (1989). Situated knowledge and the culture of learning. *Educational Researcher, 18*(1), 32–42.

Carey, S. (1983). Cognitive development: The descriptive problem. In M. Gazzaniga (Ed.), *Handbook for cognitive neurology.* Hillsdale, NJ: Lawrence Erlbaum.

Carey, S. (1987). *Conceptual change in childhood.* Cambridge, MA: MIT Press.

diSessa, A. (1988). Knowledge in pieces. In Forman & Pufall (Eds.), *Construction in the computer age.* Hillsdale, NJ: Erlbaum.

Fischer, K. W. (1980). A theory of cognitive development: the control and construction of hierarchies of skills. *Psychological Review, 87,* 477–531.

Fox-Keller, E. (1985). *Reflections on gender and science.* New Haven, CT: Yale University Press.

Gelman, R., & Baillargeon, R. (1983). A review of some Piagetian concepts. In J. H. Flavell & E. M. Markman (Eds.), *Carmichael's manual of child psychology* (Vol. 3). New York: Wiley.

Gilligan, C. (1987). *In a different voice: psychological theory and women's development.* Cambridge, MA: Harvard University Press.

Kegan, R. (1982). *The evolving self.* Cambridge, MA: Harvard University Press.

Olson, D. (1970). *Cognitive development: The child's acquisition of diagonality.* New York: Academic Press.

Papert, S. (1980). *Mindstorms. Children, computers and powerful ideas.* New York: Basic books.

Piaget, J., & Inhelder, B. (1967). *The child's conception of space.* (See especially: Systems of reference and horizontal–vertical coordinates pp. 375–418). New York: W. W. Norton and Co.

Rogoff, B., & Lave, J. (Ed.). (1984). *Everyday cognition: Its development in social context.* Cambridge, MA: Harvard University Press.

Schön, D. (1983). *The reflective practitioner: How professionals think in action.* New York: Basic Books.

Turkle, S. (1984). *The second self: Computers and the human spirit.* New York: Simon and Schuster.

Witkin, H., & Goodenough, D. (1981). *Cognitive styles: Essence and origins.* New York: International University Press.

15

Puzzled Minds and Weird Creatures:
Phases in the Spontaneous Process
of Knowledge Construction

Nira Granott*

INTRODUCTION

Problem solving, viewed as the culmination of intelligent human activity (Polya, 1962), often serves as a context for the exploration of thinking processes. Different paradigms direct researchers to investigate different aspects of problem solving. Gestalt theory stresses the reorganization of the problem's elements, which yields a solution to the problem in a swift moment of insight (Wertheimer, 1945; Duncker, 1945; Adamson, 1952; Metcalfe, 1986). The information-processing approach focuses on problems of encoding, decoding, pattern recognition, and selection in the problem-solving process; the influences of the way the problem is presented; the underlying structure of the problem, and the subjects' strategies. It highlights the issue of "bottlenecks" created by the limitations of short-term memory (for example, Simon, 1978; Atwood & Polson, 1976). Researchers influenced by artificial intelligence use computer simulations to model mental processes (Newell, Shaw, & Simon, 1958; Newell & Simon, 1972; Sacerdoti, 1974; Simon & Reed, 1976; Carbonell, 1983, 1986; Anderson, Farrell, & Sauers, 1984).

---

* An earlier version of this chapter appeared in I. Harel (Ed.). (1990). *Constructionist learning.* Cambridge, MA: MIT Media Laboratory.

This study is based on another paradigm for exploring the problem-solving process—the epistemological one. In line with Piaget, the epistemological paradigm portrays the construction of knowledge as a developing process that evolves through qualitatively different stages of thought (Piaget, 1954, 1970; Ginsburg & Opper, 1979). This knowledge-construction process can only be explored within a particular context. Sufficient time must be allowed for the appropriation of the task at hand by the individual, which can only happen when the activity in question emanates from the person's own interest and is not imposed from the outside (Papert, 1973, 1980). When these processes are investigated extensively, microgenetic traits (Werner, 1957) can be discerned, showing that thought undergoes microdevelopment during brief periods of time (Flavell & Draguns, 1957). Studies adopting this approach try to analyze the underlying representations and processes that give rise to knowledge and can help identify factors that lead to understanding (Siegler & Jenkins, 1989). The evolution of knowledge can be explored through such microdevelopmental processes, looking at small-scale changes that occur spontaneously throughout experimental sessions (Karmiloff-Smith, 1979).

Microdevelopmental studies involve intensive data analysis and are not easy to conduct, which probably explains their relative scarcity. They usually show that the microgenetic process proceeds through discontinuous discernible phases (Draguns, 1984), though the transition does not take place at a single identifiable moment (Wertsch, 1979).

Werner (1957) formulates an orthogenetic principle, suggesting that development proceeds from a state of relative globality and lack of differentiation to increasing differentiation, articulation, and hierarchic integration. According to Werner, this applies to microprocesses as well. In problem solving, as in other domains, microgenesis follows from a global state to an analytic one, and then in the final stage to a synthesis where the parts are integrated into a whole.

One of the examples Werner refers to is Duncker's work. In an early study, first published in 1935, Duncker analyzes the problem-solving process and its phases. When the problem is presented, the problem solver starts with a general conception. He or she then analyses alternative outlines of a solution. The next phase consists of analysis of these outlines into means of solutions. Later, a solution is constructed out of these means (Duncker, 1945).

Fischer (1980) suggests that microdevelopmental changes occur in a systematic order, forming a sequence of qualitatively different behavioral organizations. Fischer finds four phases in this sequence. Starting with no recognition of the problem, the first phase shows a vague diffuse definition of the problem. During the second phase, a general outline of the solution develops. The third phase shows an unintegrated control of the solution's components, but only in the fourth phase does a real integration occur, so that all the components are synethsized into a single unit. Fischer (1980) shows that this pattern of behavior exists in the problem solving behavior of animals, as well as in human subjects

(Fisher, 1972, 1975) and corresponds to recurrent levels within developmental stages (Fisher, 1980a).

Another sequence of phases in the microdevelopmental process is suggested by Karmiloff-Smith. Karmiloff-Smith (1984) analyzes the micro- and macro-developmental changes that occur in the spontaneous behavior of children while solving problems, or in the process of language acquisition. She suggests a three-phase model for these spontaneous changes (Karmiloff-Smith, 1986a, 1986b). According to this model, implicit knowledge undergoes some "explicitation" that is unconscious in the first phase. In the second phase, knowledge is redescribed and becomes available to conscious access. In the third and most developed phase, the explicit redescription allows translation into different representational codes, thus generating multi representational links.

In a way similar to the studies mentioned above, this chapter explores microprocesses of knowledge construction and analyzes the phases through which these processes evolve. However, this study explores also the function of these phases. While research of problem solving is usually geared toward the solution of problems, which is the culmination of the process, this study shows the important function of the phases preceding the solution. It also identifies conditions for natural and spontaneous processes of problem solving and discusses their implications.

METHOD

The present study uses an ethnographic approach. Adult subjects faced ill-defined problems in an environment with materials unknown to them. Thus, they had to define the problem as well as the procedures they could use. The social dimension of the exploration was not structured in advance. Teams formed, changed, and reformed spontaneously. The resulting process of knowledge construction was thus fueled by the existing social reality, where collaboration and social interaction formed a part of the knowledge-construction process (i.e., Vygotsky, 1978; Wertsch, 1979; Wertsch, Minick, & Arns, 1984; Resnick, 1988), where human behavior was situated in the particular context (Suchman, 1987; Brown, Collins, & Duguid, 1989), and where context influenced the definition of the problem and its solution (Lave, Murtaugh, & de la Rocha, 1984; Rogoff, 1984; Lave, 1988). The subjects negotiated the meaning of the ill-defined situation and the phenomena they encountered; they reasoned with causal models, and their understanding was socially constructed—attributes that characterize real-life and professional problem solving (Brown et al., 1989).

The social context helped to cope with the problem of delayed verbal reports and their distracting effect (Draguns, 1984). During the collaborative exploration, the subjects immediately and spontaneously expressed their reactions, thoughts, and discoveries while calling their partners' attention to them.

Procedure

Thirty-five adults participated in the study. They were divided into three groups. Each group met twice, in consecutive days. The duration of each meeting was about 1½ hours (3 hours for the two sessions). Three participants came for additional sessions or joined other groups (having 4½ to 6 hours each).

The first part of each session consisted of free exploration. The second part, which took approximately half an hour at the end of each session, was a whole group discussion. During the discussion the participants talked about their experiences, compared approaches, and discussed their findings.

The participants were asked to write notes during their explorations, and to describe their experiences and findings. The sessions were also videotaped (both the exploration and the discussion periods). The videotapes and the notes served as data for the study.

Materials

The study used a specialized set of Lego Bricks (called Braitenberg Bricks, after Valentino Braitenberg, 1984) that were developed in the Lego-Logo Laboratory of the Epistemology and Learning group (Martin, 1988). These Lego bricks incorporated sensors (detecting light, sound, and touch), included logic bricks (and, or, inverter, etc.), and motor bricks. Small vehicles or "creatures" were built out of these bricks. Different wiring connections between bricks generated varied and sometimes complex "behaviors." The *Weird Creatures,* as they came to be called, moved, changed directions, made noise, stopped from time to time, and started moving again—in fact, they "behaved" very much like living organisms. However, the causes of these patterns of "behavior" were not obvious.

Six different Weird Creatures were used for this study (see Appendix). Each Weird Creature was put in an environment that generated varied stimuli. Some of the stimuli activated the specific "creature" in that environment. Other stimuli could activate other Weird Creatures, but not necessarily the one in their proximity. When the Weird Creatures were turned on, they started to "behave" in complex ways, responding to stimuli they encountered. Some of the patterns they showed were avoiding light and retreating for a while when bumping into something; following the direction of light; oscillating quickly along a line of a shadow cast on the floor; stopping at a sound, and stopping according to an internal timer and restarting by sound.

Varied objects were scattered around the environment to provide additional stimuli. These included different light-generating objects (flashlights, lamps, etc.), shadow-generating objects, items to generate sound with, and items that were touched or bumped into. The participants could use these objects (as well as their hands or sounds they made) to generate different stimuli in order to investigate the Weird Creatures' responses.

In a corner of the room, there were extra parts, divided into small drawers with labeled categories. Ready-made bases that included batteries set on wheels could be used for building additional Creatures, or for testing the function of specific bricks.

RESULTS

There were distinct phases in the way the participants explored the Weird Creatures and in the kinds of explanations they gave. The different phases of exploration were expressed in the way the participants interacted with the Weird Creatures. Another distinguishing attribute was the physical distance between the subjects and the Weird Creatures. These phases corresponded to different modes of discourse, in which different kinds of explanations were generated to account for the observed phenomena. The phases of exploration and modes of discourse are described in the following section.[1]

A. Different Phases of Exploration

The participants' way of interaction with the creatures evolved throughout the sessions. They usually started by watching the "behaviors" of the Weird Creatures. Later, they held them in their hands and explored closely the effects of different stimuli. At the same time, their observations changed with respect to level of detail, as will be specified below.

The Behavioral Phase. The phases of exploration started with a *behavioral* phase, in which the participants focused on the weird creature's "behavior". While the Weird Creatures were moving and responding to stimuli, the subjects watched them, generated varied stimuli, and tried out the Weird Creatures' responses to these stimuli. For example, they tried to find out a weird creature's response to different lights—flashlight, lamp, sunlight coming in through the window. They tried to make different kinds of shadows—with a box, a finger, a hand, a shoe, a notebook, and so on. They also tried the effects of different densities and different lengths of shadows. In a similar way, they tried different touch and sound stimuli.

---

[1] The analysis of results includes excerpts from the video transcripts. In these excerpts, the first roman numeral indicates the number of the group, the second number indicates the number of the session of that group, and the following numbers correspond to the page numbers in the transcripts—that is II.1.2-3 indicates that the excerpt is taken from the second group, first session, pages 2-3 of the written transcript.

In these explorations the participants were trying to find out patterns in the Weird Creatures' behaviors. These varied and repeated experimentations aimed at making sense of the Weird Creatures' "behaviors", establishing regularities, and understanding causal patterns. The participants tried to understand the way different patterns of movement related to different external conditions. The following examples show this search for patterns.

- "Let's try turning on the little light . . . Why does it go to the box? Put it in the box!" (II.1.2.-3).
- "Our theory is that it circles until it finds the light . . ."(II.1.5)
- "Look—look—look!! See—it's much easier with the light on top!"(II.1.5)
- "Trying to decide whether it's speed or distance or time that—[cause the change]"(II.1.6)
- "Change with sound will cause it to change direction . . . same with the change of light."(II.1.7)
- "We don't know what happens—you put your hand and it stops forever."(II.1.7)
- "We noticed a pattern of going forward more and back less."(II.1.7)

To specify these conditions, the participants varied, not only the sources of the stimuli, but also the other qualities of these stimuli. For example, when they moved their hands to create a shadow, they did it at varying speed. They also tried to vary the distance and the relative position between their hands and the Weird Creature (for example, they put their hands above the Weird Creature, then around it from different sides, closer and further away). When they tried to vary one variable (such as shade or touch), they also tried to eliminate it altogether. While experimenting with shade, they also tested the behavior of the Weird Creature without any shade. When they tested a Weird Creature carrying a touch sensor and bumping into a wall, they also tried it further away from the wall.

When the Weird Creature's "behavior" was complex, the participants tried more elaborate techniques in order to find out the patterns, sometimes using external devices. While experimenting with a Weird Creature which has a complex forward and backward motion, for example, some of them looked at a watch to measure the duration of each movement. Others used counting in order to compare the durations of the forward and the backward movements.

The Close-up Investigation Phase. In the second phase of the exploration, participants held the Weird Creatures in their hands and examined them closely. The subjects generated different stimuli and looked at the corresponding responses, as they did before. However, at this phase they did not focus on varying the stimuli as much as they were closely checking the different variations of the responses. For example, while they were watching the direction in which the wheels were turning, the subjects made a variety of sounds, like clicking, whistling, snapping fingers, and so on. Then they watched the effect of these sounds upon the direction of the wheels' movement. In this phase they also made more subtle distinctions about the phenomena they observed. For example, they noticed the blinking lights on the bricks:

- "Now why is *this* constant and *this* blinking?" (II.2.6)
- "Oh, you see, it goes either on or off. But the green one stays" (II.2.4)

They were paying attention to details to which they did not pay attention before, such as the position of a brick on the Weird Creature:

- "Do you know on the sound sensor whether *that* has to be sticking out or *that*?" (II.2.1).
- "Maybe the motor has to be plugged [in] a certain way?" (II.2.2)

During this phase of exploration subjects used working hypotheses that were also related to the wiring connections between the bricks:

- "Maybe we have to connect it to both! Let's connect it to both! . . . Oh, there's only one place to put it in" (II.2.6-7)

They focused on the function that they were looking for and tried to find a way to achieve it using the different components. For example, a team that was working with the touch sensor said:

- "We need something to make it completely back . . . We need to add something else here. Maybe a timer." (II.2.7)

They also started to build up Weird Creatures from parts. Sometimes they "cloned" a Weird Creature according to another one; sometimes they changed the order of the components on a Weird Creature and experimented with the results:

- "We decided rather than do a dissection to clone it . . . That was after we watched it for quite a while . . . So we spent most of our time physically working with the parts, explaining what connections worked and didn't work." (I.2.7)

Yet this exploration was linked to the previous kind of exploration: From time to time the participants went back to "behavioral" examinations. While trying to expand their understanding, they frequently alternated between the two modes of exploration. It seemed as if they wanted to establish the connection between the new phenomena they watched and those they had investigated before, in order to anchor the new understanding to that previously formed. In other words, they wanted to make sure the Weird Creature they were investigating was still functioning in the same way as they saw before. The following example demonstrates the alternation of the two modes of exploration:

*   The participants let the Weird Creature move, watched it, and stated: "It goes forward to the light . . ." [referring to the behavorial level].
    After this remark, they started a close-up investigation: they held the Weird Creature and looked at it closely. They talked about the inverter, took it apart, then connected it again. They checked the light sensor, checked its dial, and then connected it again [close-up investigation]. Then they turned the Weird Creature on, held a box above it, and tried out the way it reacted to the box's shadow [behavioral level]. Later, they took the Weird Creature again, held it and watched it closely. Afterwards, they turned it on again and continued to check its "behavior" when the box was held above it. This pattern repeated itself a few more times. (III.2.1-4)

In a similar vein, when they built a new Weird Creature, they wanted to check its behavior. A group who was building a clone with some variations, having finished building the Weird Creature, turned it on and tried out its "behavior" while clapping, whistling, and counting for the estimation of time duration.

Thus, when they had a theory about how a certain way of wiring generated a specific "behavior", they wanted to check back the wiring and to check the "behavior" of the Weird Creature again, in order to assess their theory on the behavioral level as well:

*   "It changed, instead of plugging it into direction we plugged it into the speed! . . . So I guess it doesn't back up any more—let's change it again and see if it works." (III.2.5)

The Piecemeal, In-Depth Investigation Phase. This third phase usually appeared after two sessions. Participants who came for additional sessions either joined another group or came to work with the Weird Creatures in their spare time. In this phase, participants focused on specific bricks, differentiated between kinds of bricks, and explored their corresponding functions. In other words, they were not exploring a Weird Creature as a whole, but rather specific bricks.

At the end of a second session, one of the participants already stated her intentions and wish to pursue this direction, if time permitted. (It didn't.)

*   "We didn't get to the point of analyzing the effects of each of the pieces and how you'd have to, maybe remove a piece and (connect) it later to see how it would change it . . . To see: oh, it's a flip flop, oh, it's connected to direction, so no wonder it's going back and forth." (I.2.8)

One of the participants, coming for additional time, chose—from the collection of spare parts—one brick of each kind. She set the bricks on a paper, wrote down next to each brick its name (as was marked on the corresponding drawer), then systematically connected a brick at a time to the battery and the motor and explored what each brick "did:"

- "So you've written the names of all the pieces, and now you're trying one by one?"
- "To see what if anything they do." (I.3.1)

B. Corresponding Levels of Explanation

The way in which participants explored the Weird Creatures evolved throughout the sessions. At the same time, the way they explained the phenomena they observed evolved in a similar fashion.

The Descriptive Level. In the first phase, which corresponded to the behavioral exploration, the participants' discourse was related to the global behavior of the Weird Creatures and was of a descriptive quality. In this phase the participants were mainly describing the "behavior" of the Weird Creature:

- "It's following the light on the wall." "The reflection?" (I.1.4)
- "At first it seemed pretty random, and then it became clear it wasn't random at all. It would go forward, hit a wall, and go backward, somebody would make a sound, it would change direction. One pattern we found was that first it seemed to go back a certain distance . . ." (I.1.5)
- "It circles until it finds the light." (II.1.5)

Sometimes the discourse was not only descriptive but also explanatory, relating cause and effect. However, during this phase the explanations were based on a behaviorist level:

- "It wasn't as sensitive to light . . . Light controls direction but not movement" . . . "It seems to escape the light." (III.1.7-8)
- "Something relating to light is controlling that machine, that's very clear. It has some mood, or mode, or . . . that is happy feeling or blue feeling that after some 5 or 4 or 5 seconds that hits the wall it goes backwards, and another rule, in that time the machine behaves another way, after it hits the wall. So he's afraid of something so he'll go out (away) of the wall . . ." (III.1.7)
- "He liked P.—you were blocking all the light sources from behind you—so he kept going toward you . . ." (III.1.8)
- "What did you find out?"—"It didn't like total darkness." (III.2.2)

Transition: Linking the Descriptive Level to the Functional Level. During the close-up investigation, the participants' discourse was pointing to more specific functions in the Weird Creatures' responses. They noted the changing direction in which the wheels were turning; they noted the different kinds of bricks; they guessed what their functions could be. Focusing their attention to these specifics, they related them to the overall "behaviors" which they had observed before, such as the change of movement direction—forward or backward, and the stopped movement in reaction to sound:

- "So that's how it reverses direction! (Looking at the wheels). That's some sort of sensor. This one here looks like a light sensor, and this like a sound sensor . . ." "I wonder if the sensor works until it changes direction . . . It only changes direction when it's moving forward." (I.2.1)
- "Oh, this is the sound sensor, it has a little microphone in it. That's what you (pop?) to stop." (II.2.2)

With their expanding experience of focusing on the parts' functions, of building and cloning, and of changing the position of the parts and the wirings, they also made more subtle explanations about the relationship between the wiring connections and the Weird Creatures' "behaviors:"

- "When the sensor is plugged to direction, it goes forward. When the sensor is plugged to an inverter, which is plugged to direction, it goes backward." (II.4, in III.2.2)

The Functional Piecemeal Description Level. At this phase, which appeared during the third and forth sessions, participants focused on the function of the different parts, seeing the Weird Creature as a system combined of these parts. Their discourse was a kind of "technotalk," of a much more technical quality:

- "At the signal, it [the inverter] makes the engine do the opposite of what it did before. When it's one signal it goes one way, when it's the other signal it goes the other way." (I.3.3)
- "The inverter only changes the message while the sensor is . . . The flip-flop doesn't do that—it keeps it flipped." (I.3.5)
- "I originally thought that the engine was programmed to always move forward, I realized from changing plugs that the directionality is controlled by one of the plug outlets . . ." (II.3, in III.1.9-10)

They focused on the relationships among the different parts, the connections among them, and the way they are composed together into one system:

- "It seems like words in a sentence, they only make sense together . . . It seems like there's a couple of things I have to think about. One is what is each brick and what it's supposed to do, and two is the sequence they're hooked in . . ." (I.3.1)

- "The next brick I want to work on is the flip-flop, to see what it does. And I'm worried that it might have to be in connection to something else, but we'll see." (I.3.4)
- "I know it has to be a complete circuit." (I.3.2)

DISCUSSION

The evolution of subjects' responses was similar to those suggested in the literature, as discussed above. In the first phase, subjects' understanding was global and implicit. They considered the Weird Creature as a whole and explored its "behavior". Their explanations were fuzzy and had a psychologistic character. In the second phase, subjects' knowledge evolved through progressive differentiation and more explicit understanding. They noticed more subtle details and were able to distinguish phenomena unnoticed before. They also started focusing on specific components (bricks) and their respective functions. In the third phase, subjects started to integrate the components and to synthesize them into a single unit. They started to see relations and connections among the bricks and to understand the Weird Creature as a composed system.

Their knowledge about the Weird Creatures seemed to evolve from fuzzy, diffuse, and implicit, to differentiated, analytic, and more explicit. On the face of it, it seemed that subjects made continuous progress from less scientific to more scientific thinking. Nonetheless, I claim that the whole process is equally scientific. Even though the first phase was global, less differentiated, fuzzy and descriptive, it can by no means be considered less scientific. Subjects' exploration at that phase aimed at establishing regularities, understanding patterns, and structuring the phenomena they observed, which is an important scientific process.

Not only were the phases equally important, but it seems they were also equally necessary. Each of the phases served as a prerequisite for the following one. Each was a necessary step in the sequence of scientific inquiry. Understanding patterns and regularities was a prerequisite for later inference of causal relations. The regularities (which the subjects conceived of while watching the "behavior" of the Weird Creatures) guided their further explorations and directed what they tested, what they were looking for, and what they were looking at in the next phase. For example, only after having a well-formed familiarity with, and an intuitive feeling for, a forward and backward movement and the relevance of sound could subjects focus on the direction in which the wheels rotated and test it in response to sound inputs. In a similar way, the exploration of specific bricks and their functions during the second phase was a prerequisite for understanding relations between bricks and their integration into one system in the following phase.

The function of previous understanding for establishing further knowledge and for directing further exploration is also seen in the subjects' temporary regressions from the second phase to the first. It seemed that, when the correspondence between the two phases—global and close-up investigation—was not clear, subjects needed to alternate between them frequently. Apparently, they tried to use this alteration as a means for fostering their understanding of the link between the two. This frequent alternation helped them keep in mind the behavioral pattern while focusing on the way specific parts functioned.

The study also sheds light on the conditions for spontaneous inquiry and a natural way of knowledge construction. It shows the importance of hands-on experience, of first-hand exploration, and of experimentation. It shows the importance of *redundancy*—having abundant opportunity to try and try again, interact, change conditions and change them back again, vary the situation, and alter factors in a search for the relevant variables influencing the phenomena they observed.

The study shows the importance of the subjects' autonomy in their explorations. It seems that the way they interact with the Weird Creatures feeds their understanding at the corresponding phase. Choosing whether to hold the Weird Creature in their hands or to let it move on the floor is therefore an important function, which could be obstructed if constraints were imposed on their activity. Given autonomy, subjects can choose the mode of exploration they need at a certain time and move forward when they are ready. Also, they can form their understanding of regularities through different kinds of explorations in a way that corresponds to their particular style of thought and the availability of related experience in the past.

SUMMARY

The study shows that, when subjects are given time and autonomy, their process of knowledge construction evolves through qualitatively different phases. Analysis of their spontaneous inquiry reveals distinct phases that are related both to the mode of action and to the kinds of explanations they gave to the observed phenomena.

The study suggests that, in the process of natural inquiry, exploration evolves from general and global to specific, from exploratory to investigatory, and from random to systematic. The study also indicates that, during each phase, subjects can perceive certain phenomena, while other phenomena are not accessible to them at that time.

The study illuminates the connection between different phases of exploration and the corresponding evolution of understanding. During these phases of exploration, the explanations which the participants generate—in order to account for the different behaviors they observe—also change. These evolve from psychologistic explanations, through explanations that tie the structure and components of the Weird Creatures to their "behaviors", and ultimately to explanations that are functional and technically orientated. The relationship between the subjects' activities and explanations might indicate that different kinds of exploration feed corresponding kinds of knowledge.

Adults' exploration of unknown material and unfamiliar technological devices that operate in a way that is a complete mystery to them, can help us gain insight into children's understanding. It can help us look afresh at children's struggle to explore and understand phenomena that are new to them. When we, as adults, are faced with a phenomenon for which we have no intuition, and feel the fragility of our understanding, we are forced to reconsider a few questions. How thorough could such an understanding be without sufficient direct experimentation? How understandable are abstract explanations given by another knowledgeable person in that case? And if such explanations are repeated and memorized, how much transfer can one expect in understanding a slightly altered situation? Keeping the educational context in mind, the relevance of these questions becomes apparent. While not every learning should start from the beginning, it is important to verify whether children have had direct experimentation with relevant experiences. When this is not the case, this study might indicate that this is where learning should start.

ACKNOWLEDGMENTS

I am very thankful to Summer Whole Learning workshop teachers, who took part in the Weird Creatures activity and shared with me their experiences.

Many thanks to Fred Martin, the inventor and developer of the Braitenberg Bricks, for introducing me to their mysteries. Many thanks to Seymour Papert, Edith Ackermann, and Aaron Falbel for their fruitful suggestions and the stimulating discusssions of the topic, and to Aaron and Edith especially for their help in the workshop. Special thanks to Kurt Fischer for enlightening discussions and encouragement. To Idit Harel, for the help and support in discussing ideas and giving a hand when needed, and to all my friends in the Epistemology and Learning group and outside of it—thank you all for the support.

The research reported here was supported by the National Science Foundation (Grant #851031-0195), The McArthur Foundation (Grant #874304), The LEGO Systems A/S, and Apple Computer, Inc. The preparation of this chapter was sponsored by Nintendo, Inc., Japan.

REFERENCES

Adamson, R.E. (1952). Functional fixedness as related to problem solving: A repetition of three experiments. *Journal of Experimental Psychology, 44,* 288–291.
Anderson, J.R., Farrel, R.G., & Sauers, R. (1984). Learning to program in LISP. *Cognitive Science, 8,* 87–129.

Atwood, M.E., & Polson, P.G. (1976). A process model for water jar problems. *Cognitive Psychology, 8,* 191–216.

Braitenberg, V. (1984). *Vehicles: Experiments in synthetic psychology.* Cambridge, MA: MIT Press.

Brown, J.S., Collins, A., & Duguid, P. (1989). Situated cognition and the culture of learning. *Educational Researcher, 18*(1), 32–42.

Carbonell, J.G. (1983). Learning by analogy: Formulating and generalizing plans from past experience. In R.S. Michalski, J.G. Carbonell, & T.M. Mitchell (Eds.), *Machine learning: An artificial intelligence approach.* Los Altos, CA: Morgan Kaufmann.

Carbonell, J.G. (1986). Derivational analogy: A theory of reconstructive problem solving and expertise organization. In R.S. Michalski, J.G. Carbonell, & T.M. Mitchell (Eds.), *Machine learning: An artificial intelligence approach* (Vol. 2). Los Altos, CA: Moran Kaufmann.

Draguns, J.G. (1984). Microgenesis by any other name. In W.D. Froehlich, G. Smith, J.G. Draguns, & U. Hentschel (Eds.), *Psychological processes in cognition and personality.* Washington, DC: Hemisphere Publishing.

Duncker, K. (1945). On problem solving. *Psychological monographs, 58* (Whole no. 270).

Fischer, K.W. (1972). *Learning as skill acquisition.* Unpublished manuscript, University of Denver, Denver, CO.

Fischer, K.W. (1975). Thinking and problem solving: The cognitive approach. In K.W. Fischer, P. Shaver, & A. Lazerson (Eds), *Psychology today: An introduction* (3rd ed.). Del Mar, CA: CRM.

Fischer, K.W. (1980a). Learning as the development of organized behavior. *Journal of Structural Learning, 6,* 253–267.

Fischer, K.W. (1980b). A theory of cognitive development: The control and construction of hierarchies of skills. *Psychological Review, 87*(6), 477–531.

Flavell, J.H., & Draguns, J. (1957). A microgenetic approach to perception and thought. *Psychological Bulletin, 54*(3), 197–217.

Ginsburg, H., & Opper, S. (1979). *Piaget's theory of intellectual development* (2nd ed.). Englewood Cliffs, NJ: Prentice-Hall.

Karmiloff-Smith, A. (1979). Micro and macrodevelopmental changes in language acquisition and other representational systems. *Cognitive Science, 3,* 91–118.

Karmiloff-Smith, A. (1984). Children's problem solving. In M.E. Lamb, A.L. Brown, & B. Rogoff (Eds.), *Advances in developmental psychology* (Vol. 3, pp. 39–90). Hillsdale, NJ: Erlbaum

Karmiloff-Smith, A. (1986a). From meta-processes to conscious access; Evidence from children's metalinguistics and repair data. *Cognition, 23* (2) 95–147.

Karmiloff-Smith A.(1986b). Stage/structure versus phase/process in modelling linguistic and cognitive development. In I. Levin (Ed.), *Stage and structure: Reopening the debate.* Norwood, NJ: Publishing Corp. Ablex (pp. 164–190).

Lave, J. (1988). *Cognition In practice.* Boston, MA: Cambridge University Press.

Lave, J., Murtaugh, M., & de la Rocha, O. (1984). Dialectic of arithmetic in grocery shopping. In B. Rogoff & J. Lave (Eds.), *Everyday cognition: Its development in social context.* Cambridge, MA: Harvard University Press.

Martin, F. (1988). *Children, cybernetics, and programmable turtles.* Unpublished masters dissertation, MIT Media Laboratory, Cambridge, MA.

Metcalfe, J. (1986). Premonitions of insight predict impending error. *Journal of Experimental Psychology: Learning, Memory, and Cognition, 12*, 623–634.

Newell, A., Shaw, J. C., & Simon, H. A. (1958). Elements of a theory of human problem solving. *Psychological Review, 65*, 151–166.

Newell, A., & Simon, H. A. (1972). *Human problem solving.* Englewood Cliffs, NJ: Prentice-Hall.

Papert, S. (1973). *Uses of technology to enhance education* (AI Lab Logo Memo No. 8, AI Memo No. 298). Cambridge, MA: MIT.

Papert, S. (1980). *Mindstorms: Children, computers and powerful ideas.* New York: Basic Books.

Piaget, J. (1954). *The construction of reality in the child.* New York: Basic Books.

Piaget, J. (1970). Piaget's theory. In P.H. Mussen (Ed.), *Carmichael's manual of child psychology* (Vol. 1). New York: Wiley.

Polya, G. (1962). *Mathematical discovery* (Vol. 1). New York: Wiley

Resnick, L. (1988). Learning in and out of school. *Educational Researcher, 16* (9) 13–20.

Rogoff, B. (1984). Introduction: Thinking and learning in social context. In B. Rogoff & J. Lave (Eds.), *Everyday cognition: Its development in social context* (pp. 151–171). Cambridge, MA: Harvard University Press.

Sacerdoti, E. D. (1974). Planning in a hierarchy of abstraction spaces. *Artificial Intelligence, 5*, 115–135.

Siegler, R. S., & Jenkins, E. (1989). *How children discover new strategies.* Hillsdale, NJ: Erlbaum.

Simon, H. A. (1978). Information processing theories of human problem solving. In W. K. Estes (Ed.), *Handbook of learning and cognitive processes.* Hillsdale, NJ: Erlbaum.

Simon, H. A., & Reed, S. K. (1976). Modeling strategy shifts in a problem-solving task. *Cognitive Psychology, 8*, 86–97.

Suchman, L. A. (1987). *Plans and situated actions: The problem of human–machine interaction.* Cambridge, UK: Cambridge University Press.

Vygotsky, L. S. (1978). *Mind in society: The development of higher psychological processes.* Cambridge, MA: Harvard University Press.

Werner, H. (1957). The concept of development from a comparative and organismic point of view. In D. B. Harris (Ed.), *The concept of development: An issue in the study of human behavior* (pp. 125–148). Minneapolis: University of Minnesota Press.

Wertheimer, M. (1945). *Productive thinking.* New York: Harper & Brothers.

Wertsch, J. V. (1979). From social interaction to higher psychological processes: A clarification and application of Vygotsky's theory. *Human Development, 22*, 1–22.

Wertsch, J. V., Minick, M., & Arns, F. J. (1984). The creation of context in joint problem solving. In B. Rogoff & J. Lave (Eds.), *Everyday cognition: Its development in social context* (pp. 151–171). Cambridge, MA: Harvard University Press.

APPENDIX: EXAMPLES OF TWO WEIRD CREATURES

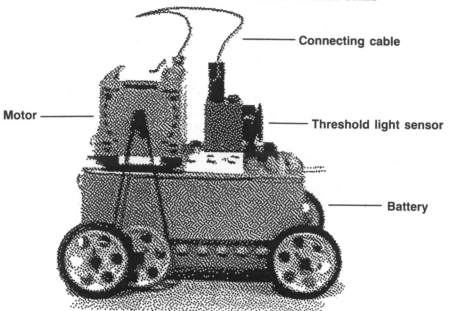

Connecting cable

Motor ——————

Threshold light sensor

Battery

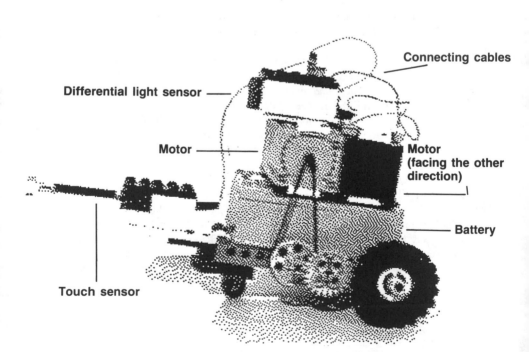

Connecting cables

Differential light sensor ——————

Motor ——————

Motor (facing the other direction)

Battery

Touch sensor

16

Towards a Constructionist Musicology

Gregory Gargarian

INTRODUCTION

This chapter introduces a way of looking at musical understanding which blends ideas from music, psychology, and computing in order to develop a framework for a constructionist musicology. Section 3 demonstrates compositional strategies using the Logo programming language. Section 4 demonstrates compositional strategies in a more traditional compositional context. Section 4 also presents three related research themes: In the first theme I use ideas about design to discuss compositional process, in the second theme I use ideas from the psychology of expectations to discuss the interpretive process, and in the third I discuss how the social context aids in the negotiation of musical meaning.

DESIGN PROBLEMS

Mathematics presented in the Euclidean way appears as a systematic, deductive science; but mathematics in the making appears as an experimental, inductive science. (Polya, 1973, p. 18)

Well-defined problems are all alike, but every ill-defined problem is ill-defined in its own way. (Holland, Holyoak, Nisbett, & Thagard, 1986, p. 11)

Music is one of the most ancient of the sciences of the artificial, and was so recognized by the Greeks . . . When we view composition as a problem in design, we encounter just the same tasks of evaluation, of search for alternatives, and of representation that we do in any other design problem. (Simon, 1985, pp. 157–158)

Polya was one of the first people to show the inductive nature of mathematical discovery. According to him, mathematicians often need strategies for varying the *form* of a problem in order to solve it. Some of the strategies Polya suggests in his *How to Solve It* are redefinition, analogy, generalization, specialization, decomposition, and recombination (Polya, 1973). He also suggests problem-solving heuristics, questions like: What is the unknown? What is given? Do you know a related problem? Can you restate the problem? Can you decompose the problem into simpler distinct parts? Such strategies and heuristics are components of what is generally called the *inductive process*.

Composers also have strategies and heuristics for making the problem-solving process easier to manage. It is remarkable how many of Polya's suggestions can be transposed from mathematics to music composition. However, there is a catch: I am not able to take Polya's advice in the domain of mathematics, nor would I expect him to apply his own advice in music composition. Inductive thought is different within each problem context, because it gets its shape from the problem-solving context. General strategies can't capture this particularity of thought, especially in ill-defined problems where they are desperately needed.

> The rules that people induce for events are always local ones to some degree. They are learned in the context of people's attempts to develop [broader categories of thought] for aspects of the world that are important to them and to which they are exposed with some frequency. (Holland et al., 1986, p. 38)

We look for problems which we have the *personal* craft to solve. Usually, problems which we cannot solve are not interesting to us. This personal craft knowledge includes strategies which we are able to employ and clues about how to recognize the situations in which to employ them. The kinds of strategies we use are constrained by personal knowledge and experience and grow with it. Polya does not address how general strategies are acquired. I will make this point from a developmental perspective, drawing from an experiment of Piaget's in which he explores a child's act of invention.

In this experiment Piaget asks a child to put a watch chain into a little box. The child begins by putting one end of the chain into the box (see Figure 1). Drawn by its own weight, the chain slips out. The child tries this procedure several times. After a few unsuccessful attempts, she gets a new idea: She places the chain on a flat surface, rolls it up into a ball, and puts the whole thing into the box. Still later, the child tries the experiment again by beginning with the unsuccessful method, but only for a short time. She quickly returns to the successful method and accomplishes the task (Gruber & Voneche, 1977, pp. 238–239).

Piaget argues that the first time the child uses the successful method, she has to invent new means. Piaget offers this as an example of an *accommodative* process, which, by Piaget's definition, is about constructing new mental schemes for unfamiliar situations. The second time she uses the successful method, after retreating for a short time to the unsuccessful one, the girl is controlling her

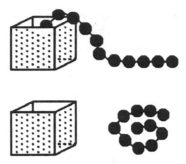

Figure 1. A Piagetian experiment where a child tries to place a watch chain in a little box.

behavior mentally. Piaget offers this as an example of an *assimilative* process, which, again by Piaget's definition, is about refining mental schemes so that they are able to adapt to variations of familiar situations.

Piaget continues to argue that there is no such thing as pure accommodation. For a constructivist like Piaget, new knowledge does not appear spontaneously but must be formed out of old knowledge and new pieces of knowledge acquired from one's interactions with the world.

Piaget argues that invention requires both inductive and deductive processes. Unlike many theorists, he views them as being components of a continuous process. For him, induction is an accommodative process which uses *anticipation* or "hypotheses of subjective origins" (Gruber & Voneche, 1977, p. 270). Anticipation relies on familiar mental schemes, which may or may not be reliable depending on how they, themselves, were formed. For example, the initial schemes were unreliable for the girl in the experiment. She anticipated different results from her actions than those which actually occurred. Anticipation is accommodative, because it reaches beyond observed events. It is a guess about the effects of one's actions based upon one's model of the world.

One only begins to examine one's model of the world when an anticipation fails. *Reciprocal assimilation* is Piaget's term for the experiments which are performed in order to examine failing anticipations. Recall that the girl tried the unsuccessful method several times before switching to a different method, and even though she switched to a successful method, she returned briefly to the unsuccessful one. Piaget argues that this "empirical groping" gave the girl opportunities to acquire more objective data surrounding the unexpected events. However, even experimentation may not protect subjective qualities from being attached to physical characteristics. The mental schemes produced through reciprocal assimilation may contain a mixture of salient and subjectively interpreted data.

Only a synthesis of these schemes can provide the means for dissociating the subjective from the objective. This synthesis is the *deductive* process and involves the coordination of invariant features among schemes, the decoupling of the salient from the subjectively interpreted data (Gruber & Voneche, 1977, p. 270). One imagines that, with each new successful trial, the girl had more "experimental evidence" from which to construct the appropriate mental scheme.

It is difficult to imagine how this girl could develop a general method of inquiry from one learning experience alone. The bridge between situated knowledge and general principles must, itself, be constructed. On this issue Polya is mostly silent.

In *Mindstorms* Papert argues that Turtle Geometry can serve as a means for building bridges between things like Polya's heuristics and a learner's personal knowledge. Papert's comments show how leaps of reasoning—typical of inductive thought—can be mediated by Logo.

The Logo Turtle is a creature which lives on the computer screen. In its simplest form it has a position and a heading. The child writes programs in the Logo language to navigate the turtle (forward, backward, left, or right) around the screen. The trace of the Turtle's path is used to make designs or explore aspects of Turtle Geometry. One theorem in Turtle Geometry is "The Total Turtle Trip Theorem" (TTT theorem):

> If a Turtle takes a trip around the boundary of any area and ends up in the state in which it started, then the sum of all turns will be 360 degrees. (Papert, 1980, p. 76)

The theorem is powerful, because children can actually use it to inform their design process. It is intelligible because the theorem is tied to the turtle's behavior and, thus, easy to grasp. It is also general because it applies to a variety of geometric objects: Squares have four sides each of 90 degrees, triangles have three sides each of 120 degrees (outer angles), and "circles" have as many sides as one finds visually sufficient (Papert, 1980, p. 76). Using Turtles and Turtle Geometry supports what Papert calls *syntonic* learning; that is, from Freud, "ideas which are acceptable to the ego" (Papert, 1980, p. 221). Turtle Geometry is *body* syntonic, because walking the turtle around on the screen is much like one's own walking (Papert, 1980, p. 63). It is *culturally* syntonic, because the idea of "angle" in Turtle Geometry (e.g., right and left turns) connects with activities children do outside of school, like riding a bicycle (Papert, 1980, p. 68).

> [Turtle Geometry] adds a new element to Polya's advice: "To solve a problem look for something like it that you already understand. The advice is abstract; Turtle geometry turns it into a concrete, procedural principle: *Play Turtle. Do it*

yourself. In Turtle work an almost inexhaustible source of "similar situations" is available because we draw on our own behavior, our own bodies. (Papert, 1980, p. 64)

Papert's approach is *constructive* in Piaget's developmental sense, because current experiences benefit from previous experiences. It's *constructionist* in Papert's sense, because Logo provides opportunities for new kinds of experiences which are constructive in nature. Turtle Geometry situates ideas like Polya's heuristics in a constructionist context.

I believe Polya really wanted to talk about problem setting—or what I call *design problems*. Design problems are constructionist: They are about creating situations which are problematic in ways the "problem solver" can handle. Design problems take into account the learner as well as the body of knowledge "out there" which it is valuable for the learner to acquire. Design also captures the creative aspects of engineering and the engineered aspects of composing.

In order to place ideas about design within a musical context, we will need to emphasize those formulations of musical thought which are process oriented and deemphasize formulations of musical thought which are structure oriented. This is what the next few sections attempt to do.

FORM CONSTRUCTION

For the music theorist A. B. Marx (1795–1866), there are as many musical forms as there are works of art (even though previous works of art are often used as models for subsequent works of art). Music's form "is the way in which the content of the work—the composer's conception, feeling, idea—outwardly acquires shape" (Bent, 1987, pp. 28–30). The notion of the form "acquiring shape" captures the idea that form is a constructed process, what another theorist, Rudolph Reti, has called *form building* and what I call *form construction*. The point is that a composition is not entirely planned beforehand. The plan stays a little ahead of the music of which it is a plan. A composer works from the current state of the plan to the musical details, and from these details to the construction of new components of the plan (Reti, 1961).

The idea of form construction sounds peculiar. Within the Western classical tradition, we could probably list the number of musical forms on a sheet of paper, yet there are thousands of compositions, and, we might argue, there are as many "forms" as there are compositions. The reason form construction sounds peculiar is that the word *form* is used to mean two radically different things. Marx and Reti are using *form* as an inductive process. They are talking about *form in the making* rather than *ready-made* form.[1]

---

[1] This way of contrasting process and product comes from the anthropologist of science Bruno Latour, who distinguishes "science in the making" from "ready-made science" (Latour, 1987).

Traditionally, *form* is used to describe the over-all structure of a composition, what the musicologist Willi Apel describes as "the structural outline—comparable to an architect's ground plan" (Apel, 1972, p. 327). Often times, we want to be able to say something about large numbers of pieces. Under these conditions, having general classifications of pieces is useful. Even A. B. Marx, the same theorist who argued that musical forms are unlimited, found this practice so useful that he invented the term *sonata form*. Not only analysts, but composers, have found it useful to think of musical forms as structural models. Charles Rosen argues that one of the principle agents of stylistic development is the mixing of form elements into new forms. In order to construct hybrids of them, form classifications must already exist (Rosen, 1988, p. 57).

How we use the word *form* depends on what we want to use it for. The traditional notion of *form* provides an economical way to remember and access general musical knowledge. However, this use of *form* assumes that the knowledge being organized is already present. A more operational notion of *form*—as form construction—describes how problems are constrained by elements of form and how problems contribute to new elements of form.

Situating Form Construction

> *While the objective of the Trukese navigator is clear from the outset, his actual course is contingent on unique circumstances that he cannot anticipate in advance. The plan of the European, in contrast, is derived from universal principles of navigation, and is essentially independent of the exigencies of his particular situation.* (Suchman, 1987, p. viii)

Form construction is about making plans as well as using them during the compositional process. Giving plans this double service leaves room for what Suchman calls *situated actions,* by which she means "actions taken in the context of particular, concrete circumstances" (Suchman, 1987, p. viii). The notion of a *plan* as traditionally conceived is similar to the notion of *form* as traditionally conceived. They are both about the structure of the product rather than inductive processes which give rise to it.

The traditional planning model is more goal oriented than either Suchman or I find realistic. Suchman argues that, even in relatively conventional problems, "structure is an emergent product of situated action, rather than its foundation" (Suchman, 1987, p. 67). I have found this to be the case in a recent problem-solving study of my own. There, I found that problem solvers used a wide range of strategies on the same problem. The main purpose of these strategies was to find out more information about the problem. Sometimes their strategies were conventional, while, at other times, they were highly idiosyncratic, drawing from personal knowledge no one could have anticipated (Gargarian, 1990a). A synthetic notion of planning leaves room for the personal craft knowledge of the designer and how his or her previous successes shape future quests.

COMPOSITIONAL STRATEGIES

This section explores form construction and compositional thinking, by using the procedural perspective of the Logo programming language.

Compositional Problems[2]

A good composer makes a composition sound as if it were an inseparable whole. In fact, a composition is made up of many composition parts. Knowing that you can make a part, and then add it to another part to make a bigger one, and so on, makes composing a less complex process than it may appear to an outside listener. For example, the following musical phrases are represented as Logo lists. I give the names *part1* through *part4* to four phrase-lists using the Logo primitive MAKE. These four phrases are the parts of a simple song.

```
MAKE "part1 [[cl 2] [dl 2] [el 4]]
MAKE "part2 [[el 2] [dl 2] [cl4]]
MAKE "part3 [[cl 2] [el 2] [dl 2] [el 2] [cl 2] [gl 2] [gl 4]]
MAKE "part4 [[gl 2] [gl 2] [cl 2] [el 2] [dl 2] [el 2] [cl 4]]
```

The song is defined by the Logo procedure TUNE (below), which uses the Logo procedure PLAYPHRASE to play each of the phrases defined above.

```
TO TUNE
PLAYPHRASE:part1
PLAYPHRASE:part2
PLAYPHRASE:part3
PLAYPHRASE:part1
PLAYPHRASE:part2
PLAYPHRASE:part4
END
```

Composing the four part of TUNE, one by one, is a simpler problem than composing TUNE all at once. This well-known problem-solving strategy of subdividing problems into simpler subproblems is called *decomposition*.

Design and Exploratory Strategies

Problem-solving strategies work best when we know what our problem is. Oftentimes we use exploratory strategies to search for interesting problems. For example, *part2* is actually *part1* with the notes reversed. This can be demon-

---

[2] The Appendix provides a glossary of Logo primitives and procedures used in this chapter.

strated by typing, PLAYPHRASE :part1, and then typing, PLAYPHRASE MAPNOTES (REVERSE :part1) :part1.

The procedure REVERSE reverses the phrase with the name *part1*. The procedure MAPNOTES maps just the notes of the reversed phrase onto the phrase with the same name while leaving the rhythms unchanged. Similarly, *part4* is actually *part3* with the notes reversed. This can be demonstrated by typing the following:

```
playphrase :part3
playphrase mapnotes (reverse :part3) :part3
```

MAPNOTES and REVERSE are operations which can be used to explore new phrase possibilities using old phrases as points of reference.

Self-Referencing

The above demonstrates than an old phrase can be used as a means to a new phrase. I may have written part 1 of TUNE, then *got the idea* to reverse its notes to produce part 2. From this view, solving part 2 is actually a result of resetting part 1. The same could be said for parts 3 and 4. The use of previous musical results (e.g., part 1) as a resource for new solutions (e.g., part 2) is a very powerful exploratory strategy. I call this strategy *self-referencing*. Trying to be inventive without a point of reference is usually disastrous. Composers need to construct the boundaries of problems. Self-referencing does it automatically. Self-referencing also helps during the listening process, since the product of self-referencing is a pattern which shares properties with its predecessor and, thus, allow listeners the ability to benefit from previous listening.

Problem Space and Search

At the beginning of my discussion of TUNE, I asked how parts could become a seamless whole. This is partially addressed by self-referencing, which causes each subsequent part to become a response to some previous one. I also said that I *got the idea* of reversing the notes of part 1 to get part 2, and reversing the notes in part 3 to get part 4. However, it's not enough to have the idea of "reverse." There are many little ideas like "reverse" that are part of the craft of composition. How does a composer know which one to use when? Part of "getting ideas" is recognizing situations in which some idea seems fruitful. Self-referencing is one strategy which produces a framework in which to think about what to do next (or to *not* think about what *not* to do next). Given a previous solution, some chunk of music, there are operations a composer is likely to think of applying to it (e.g., like REVERSE) and others which he or she would find inappropriate to even consider.

Ideas are drawn from a pool of ideas which seem relevant to the task at hand. In a problem-solving terminology, this pool of ideas is called the *problem space*. When the problem space is large, we need strategies for making it small (or smaller). When it is small, we can use relatively crude strategies like trial and error to search through the problem space. Self-referencing can be thought of as one of many strategies for keeping the problem space small enough so that trial and error will work.[3]

Building Abstractions

Self-referencing is one design strategy. Another is *building abstractions*. The Logo procedure MAPNOTES was an example of an abstraction: MAPNOTES looks at notes and is blind to everything else. Having an infinite number of compositional choices from moment to moment is not freedom; it's paralysis. A composer has the compositional freedom he or she wants only after the space of possible problems has been reduced to a manageable few.

In order to demonstrate the abstraction building process, I first need some musical scales and Logo procedures. As in TUNE, I will use Logo's list structure to produce a pattern of note-duration pairs, this time to make musical scales rather than melodies. I will not argue that list structure is the most natural way to represent musical data; rather, my emphasis will be on illustrating the power of abstractions.

The two scales shown below are the C major and C minor scales both in ascending order. The Logo primitive MAKE assigns the names *cmajor* and *cminor* to the following scale lists.[4]

```
MAKE "cmajor
[[c1 4][d1 4][e1 4][f1 4][g1 4][a1 4][b1 4][c2 4]]
MAKE "cminor
[[c1 4][d1 4][d#1 4][f1 4][g1 4][g#1 4][b1 4][c2 4]]
```

I also want to make an abstraction which allows me to distinguish between the shape of a melody, its *contour,* and the particular notes of which it is comprised. A *contour* is a pattern of positions along a scale, not some particular scale but a *generic* scale. The contour of a melody plus its associated scale results in the melody. Figure 2 illustrates this.

In Figure 2 one finds a horizontal line of boxes numbered from 1 through 8. Each box is a contour position. Above and below the box are the C major and C minor scales (respectively). Notice that there is one note for each box. Above

---

[3] "In spite of the primitive character of trial and error processes, they bulk very large in highly creative problem solving" (Simon, Newell, & Shaw, 1979, p. 148).

[4] [c1 4] is to be read "the note *c,* in the first octave, with a duration of 4 Logo WAIT units."

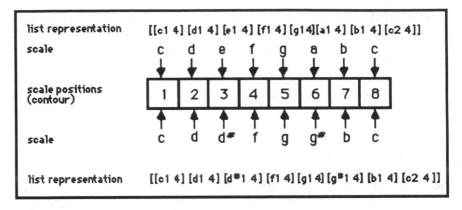

Figure 2. The numbers 1 through 8 define contour positions whose note values change depending on whether they refer to the major or minor scale (above and below, respectively). The Logo list representations for each scale assume a constant duration of 4 (in Logo WAIT units) for each note.

and below the scales are the way I represent these scales in Logo, as lists of note-duration pairs.

Typing, PLAYPHRASE :cmajor or PLAYPHRASE :cminor plays the scales. Typing,

```
PLAYPHRASE CONTOUR [1 3 5 3 1] :cmajor
PLAYPHRASE CONTOUR [1 3 5 3 1] :cminor
```

uses the same pattern of contour positions, [1 3 5 3 1], to select notes from different scales. The same contour can express many different patterns of notes, depending on what scale it is applied to. Of course a different contour applied to the same scale will produce a different note pattern as well.

Given these new abstractions, I will proceed to rewrite TUNE. The melodic phrases in TUNE (parts 1 through 4) are expressed below as contours without rhythm. (Recall that *part2* was the reverse of *part1*, and *part4* was the reverse of *part3*.) Let's name the contours *shape1*, *shape2*, *shape3*, and *shape4* (parts 1–4, respectively).

```
MAKE "shape1 [1 2 3]
MAKE "shape2 REVERSE :shape1
MAKE "shape3 [1 3 2 3 1 5 5]
MAKE "shape4 REVERSE :shape3
```

We can now apply these contours to the C major scale to get the original phrases minus the rhythms.

```
PLAYPHRASE CONTOUR :shape1 :cmajor
PLAYPHRASE CONTOUR :shape2 :cmajor
PLAYPHRASE CONTOUR :shape3 :cmajor
PLAYPHRASE CONTOUR :shape4 :cmajor
```

We can do the same thing for rhythmic data by giving the extracted durations of parts 1–4 the names *duration1*, *duration2*, *duration3*, and *duration4* (respectively). Typing,

```
MAKE "duration1 EXTRACTDURATIONS :part1
```

uses the procedure EXTRACTDURATIONS to extract durations from *part1*. MAKE assigns the name *duration1* to this new duration list. Recall, that the duration pattern of *part2* was not reversed in *part1*, just the notes were. Therefore, typing:

```
MAKE "duration2 :duration1
```

causes *duration2* to inherit the rhythm of *duration1*. Similarly, typing:

```
MAKE "duration3 EXTRACTDURATIONS :part 3
MAKE "duration4 :duration3
```

causes *duration3* to be defined and *duration4* to inherit it. With contour, scale, and rhythm defined, I can reconstruct the phrases found in the procedure TUNE from duration, contour, and scale parts.

```
PLAYPHRASE MAPDURATIONS :duration1 CONTOUR :shape1 :cmajor⁵
PLAYPHRASE MAPDURATIONS :duration2 CONTOUR :shape2 :cmajor
PLAYPHRASE MAPDURATIONS :duration3 CONTOUR :shape3 :cmajor
PLAYPHRASE MAPDURATIONS :duration4 CONTOUR :shape4 :cmajor
```

I could also abstract out the scale part of the expression by writing a revised version of TUNE (shown below). Notice that the C major scale is replaced by the abstraction (i.e., variable) ''scale.''

---

⁵ It might be easier to read these expressions if parentheses are included; for example, PLAY-PHRASE (MAPDURATIONS :duration1 (CONTOUR :contour1 :cmajor)).

```
TO REVISED-TUNE :scale⁶
PLAYPHRASE MAPDURATIONS :duration1 CONTOUR :shape1 :scale
PLAYPHRASE MAPDURATIONS :duration2 CONTOUR :shape2 :scale
PLAYPHRASE MAPDURATIONS :duration3 CONTOUR :shape3 :scale
PLAYPHRASE MAPDURATIONS :duration1 CONTOUR :shape1 :scale
PLAYPHRASE MAPDURATIONS :duration2 CONTOUR :shape2 :scale
PLAYPHRASE MAPDURATIONS :duration4 CONTOUR :shape4 :scale
END
```

Now, typing REVISED-TUNE :cmajor plays the original tune. On the other hand, typing REVISED-TUNE :cminor plays a new version of TUNE with the C minor scale.

This suggests a powerful idea, namely, that abstractions become concrete pattern elements at higher levels of abstraction. In music, higher levels of abstraction embrace longer spans of time. Within one span of time certain details will vanish, and within another, certain abstractions become concrete details. As a composer, I want to look at different kinds of data, depending on the span of time I am "viewing." Abstractions help me to navigate across different spans of time.

Compositional Complexity

We might also say that the abstractions for different spans of time help me to sculpt the characteristics of the current problem space. Being able to abstract out particular kinds of data is a useful way to manage the complexity of a problem. One way to think about design strategies is that they help designers to manage *compositional complexity*. For example, the procedure TUNE-VARIATIONS[7] (shown below) accepts a list of scales (any number of them) and applies the scales, one at a time, to the subprocedure REVISED-TUNE.

```
TUNE-VARIATIONS :scale-list
IF EMPTY? :scale-list [STOP]
REVISED-TUNE THING FIRST :scale-list
TUNE-VARIATIONS BUTFIRST :scale-list
END
```

---

⁶ *Scale* is a variable name. When evoking REVISED-TUNE, the real scale will replace *scale* throughout the procedure.

⁷ TUNE-VARIATIONS is the name of the procedure. But it is also a command within the procedure. This self referencing is called *recursion*. Each time TUNE-VARIATIONS calls itself it removes whatever is in the first position of the list with the variable name :scale-list. Then it behaves as if it was called for the first time. However, it again calls itself, and so on. Eventually, list :scale- will be empty of list elements and stop. That's what the expression: IF EMPTY? :scale-list [STOP] is for.

Typing TUNE-VARIATIONS [cmajor cminor] plays REVISED-TUNE first with the C major scale and then with the C minor scale. Typing TUNE-VARIATIONS [cmajor cminor cmajor] plays REVISED-TUNE three times, using the major and minor scales, and then the major scale again. Previously, we thought of *scale* as an abstraction. At this higher level of abstraction *scale* becomes a concrete entity out of which new scale patterns are made! What happened to the notes, rhythms, contours, melodies, and so on? They're still there, though outside the boundaries of this new design setting.

Relations Between Composing and Listening Strategy

In the above Logo demonstrations you may have noticed that previous Logo programs were incorporated in subsequent ones. While the results became increasingly complex, the degree of complexity during the design process remained relatively constant. Decomposition, self-referencing, and abstraction building were the three strategies used to keep design complexity from getting out of control.

The compositional process seldom gets more complicated than this. One might argue that this is a trick, that problem complexity has really shifted from the problem-solving phase to the design phase of the process. However, I argue that this is not true, since selecting and using one of the mentioned strategies is not, itself, a particularly complex problem, nor is the new problem produced by the result of the strategy.

I will briefly make comments about the reconstructive process (i.e., about listening) which complement those made about the constructive process (i.e., about composing). Most musics in the world have a notion of scale (i.e., of notes which divide the octave into discrete steps), even though the number and size of the steps will vary. The notion of scale makes it easier for a listener to compare notes and to judge melodic motion. Therefore, scale is not only useful in the design process; it is a useful encoding device for apprehending and remembering melodies.

The current state of developmental theory in music is relatively primitive. Nevertheless, it appears that children can recognize contour (as I have described it) before the age of 2 and simple phrases a little later. Only by the age of 5 can children begin to distinguish musical keys (i.e., relations between scales). More subtle (e.g., *chromatic*) alterations of melody are not detectable until a few years later. However, given a constant scale, a listener can recognize that two melodies are different by recognizing differences in their contours alone (Dowling & Harwood, 1986, pp. 90–152). Therefore, contour apprehension, which occurs early in development, remains useful after scale pattern apprehension has been acquired.

The idea that there are natural links between the constructive and reconstructive process will be a background theme in section 4 of this chapter.

NATURALISTIC EXAMPLES

In the summer of 1990 I was at the University of Campinas in Brazil, where I gave some lectures on the compositional process. In one lecture I explained that I had been writing some music for children's stories, and proceeded to play and explain excerpts from one of the stories. An unexpected response to that lecture gave rise to some new thinking which I report here. Retelling the experience provides me an opportunity to illustrate three themes: composing, interpretation, and the sociology of negotiating musical meaning.

Composition and Design

The story described in the Brazilian lecture is called *The City of Storms.*[8] In the story, the children are caught in a city where it always rains. The children are frightened, but no one understands why, since, because it always rains in the city of storms, no one who lives there notices. The story is about how the children find a way out of the city and how they eventually return home safely.

The first musical excerpt I used in the Brazilian lecture was the "storm music," which I will call *rainstorm.* In the early phase of writing *rainstorm,* I wrote parts A and B without the piano or horn parts. (See Figure 3. Time goes from left to right.) Parts A and B have been written in such a way that the end of part B allows a return to part A (notated by the looping arrow in Figure 3).

Two design strategies are illustrated by these actions.

1. *Decomposition* (or modularization): represent a problem as a collection of simpler subproblems. By making a part A and another part B, I had two simpler problems than if I had worked on the problem of the two parts seamlessly joined.
2. *Recombination* (or synthesis): combine solutions into a bigger solution. By making B so that it would return to A I was able to produce a larger musical segment from two smaller ones.

I will not describe how parts A and B were made except that they were composed of yet smaller and simpler parts before they were combined into larger and more complex ones.[9] At every step in the compositional process I want to limit the number of things I have to think about. This is what decomposition provides. At the same time, I want the steps to accumulate into musical gestures that are bigger than the sum of the parts, i.e., more expressive than any of the parts are by themselves. This is what recombination provides.

---

[8] This story was written by Chris Cleary.
[9] One can imagine how this might be true by reflecting on section 3 of this chapter.

(repeat)

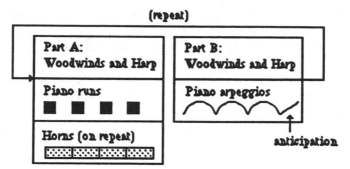

Figure 3. Parts A and B of the children's story *The City of Storms*. Time moves from left to right. The different "layers" of part A include the woodwind and harp, the piano runs, and sustained chords in the horn. The different "layers" of part B include the woodwinds and harp, and the piano arpeggios.

Interpretation and Expectation Theory

In order to make *rainstorm* more frightening, I added fleeting piano runs to part A (the dark boxes in Figure 3). These runs are a metaphor for thunder. I then added the piano arpeggios in part B to make the return to part A more dramatic. Three of the piano arpeggios have an arching contour (i.e., they go up and down), while the last one only ascends. My assumption was that this provokes a sense of *anticipation,* because it is different from the other arpeggios and, thus, tells the listener that something new is going to happen.

This, at least, is how I imagine a listener will respond to it. As the composer, I am in a privileged position, since I know what will come next; I wrote it. In fact, something new does happen. The return to part A includes the use of sustained horns (the four rectangular boxes filled with dots in Figure 3). The additional question I have to ask myself is whether the listener, lacking my privileged knowledge, will make the expectation I expect him to make.

Anticipation is a term used by musicians to refer to musical expectations. It is similar in many ways to Piaget's notion of anticipation. In both cases the observer makes "predictions" based on intuitive knowledge. When "predictions" fail, more active inspection is required.

Expectation theory explores these processes within a cognitive framework. The best example of expectation theory applied to music is Leonard Meyer's *implication-realization* model. The *implication* stands for what the listener thinks is possible, and the *realization* stands for what actually happens.[10] My theory of

---

[10] "Our understanding of a past event often includes not only our knowledge of what actually occurred but also our awareness of what might have happened" (Meyer, 1973, p. 112).

the listener in the above example is that he or she will hear the first three arpeggios as similar, and the fourth as different from them. The recognition of difference should evoke in the listener the expectation that something will change even though the particular change will be difficult for the listener to predict.

This explanation is consistent with current theories of expectation that say that a new expectation will begin to form when some regularity has been interrupted. Interruptions can occur either because an expected event does not occur or because an unexpected event occurs (Mandler, 1984, pp. 171–188). In my music example, the listener might expect a fourth arpeggio similar to the first three. Because a similar arpeggio does not occur, a new expectation begins to form in the mind of the listener.

Expressivity

Of course, if the listener does not catch the arpeggio cue, he or she will not be surprised. However, in retrospect, he or she can recover from surprise if he or she is able to reconstruct events using the arpeggio cues as data. This is the natural course of interpretive experience, from anticipations and failures to reevaluations and recovery. However, if in retrospect, the listener is unable to reconstruct events using anticipatory cues (e.g., the arpeggios) as data, he or she will be confused rather than surprised. My conjecture is that music that is unfamiliar to a listener will often create such confusion and will be less expressive because of it. For me, *expressivity* is tied to a listener's ability to successfully anticipate events or recover from surprise.

ReDesign

I still found that *rainstorm* was lacking in dramatic effect and got the idea of adding a new preliminary music module to set the mood of *rainstorm* (rather than changing anything within *rainstorm* itself). Figure 4 shows the revised music for *rainstorm*, including a new music module, *set mood*, and the horn part which serves as a bridge between *set mood* and *rainstorm*. (Again, time moves from left to right in Figure 4.)

Set mood performs its mood-setting function by being "playful." The contrast between *set mood*'s playfulness and the more "serious" mood of *rainstorm* makes *rainstorm* more serious, more frightening.[11]

Including *set mood* illustrates a third design strategy which is difficult to name. I will call it *context-object alternatives*.

---

[11] Roughly speaking, by *playful* I mean "structurally obvious and upbeat," and by *serious* I mean "relatively less structurally obvious and slower."

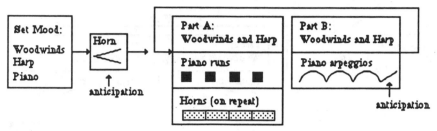

Figure 4.   The revised music for *rainstorm*. Time moves from left to right. This figure adds to figure 3 a new music module, *set mood*, and a connecting horn part.

3. *Context-object alternatives.* In any musical situation where I notice difficulties, I have two general choices. I can either change the musical object
   that is problematic, or I can change the context in which it is heard.

A design strategy like *context-object alternatives* illustrates two important
characteristics of design which I inherit from Brown and Chandrasekaran. The
first is that *strategies operate at the generic level.* One hopes that working at the
generic level creates the possibility for quick navigation across a number of
problem-solving spaces. The second characteristic is about the problem-solving
space itself. *The problem-solving space is huge in design problems* as compared
with traditional problems, because it is comprised of a number of candidate
problem spaces. Design problems look for plausible problems rather than seek
solutions to particular problems (Brown & Chandrasekaran, 1989, pp. 2–9). My
strategy of deciding whether to change the musical object or change the context
in which it is heard has both of these design problem characteristics.

My use of these design ideas retains the constructionist's perspective, because
notions like *generic* and *problem space* are defined in terms of the learner's
personal knowledge. Both the object and context to which this strategy was
applied were a result of my previous efforts.

Corrective Methods

The crescendo in the bridging horn part (between *set mood* and parts A and B in
Figure 4) creates anticipation because a crescendo can only get so loud before
something else has to happen. Once again, this was my reasoning for how the
listener might respond, not necessarily how he or she actually would respond.

Most of the Brazilians listening to my lecture found my arguments persuasive
except for one of the students in the University's composition department. I will
call him José. José felt that I could still make improvements and recommended
the following three (shown in the edit boxes, in Figure 5).

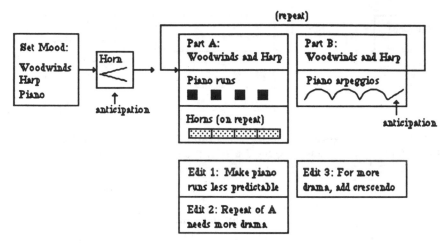

Figure 5. Included are José's three ideas for editing the music, two edits for part A and one for part B.

  Edit 1: If the piano runs are suppose to suggest thunder, they should be less predictable (like thunder). Try a more irregular distribution of them, perhaps during the repeat of A (i.e., after the thunder-pattern has been firmly established).

Edit 1 says that my thunder metaphor could have been more convincing. Notice that José suggests how to achieve an unpredictable pattern of runs by first supplying a more predictable pattern. In this way, the expected does not occur. This is a good example of using anticipation.

  Edit 2: The repeat of A needs more drama, because it doesn't have *set mood* and the crescendo in the horn to prepare it, like the first appearance of A had.

Edit 2 says that the second appearance of A doesn't work as well as its first appearance. This criticism also tells me that its first appearance worked all right, at least from José perspective.

  Edit 3: The anticipation of part B returning to part A could be heightened by giving a crescendo to the woodwinds and harp during the last piano arpeggio.

Finally, edit 3 says that my anticipation hypothesis for the return to A from B could also be made more convincing. José suggests that I use a crescendo, much as I did in the horn part after *set mood*.

  José's criticisms went beyond an expression of his likes and dislikes. In them one finds specific *corrective methods* (Papert's *debugging strategies*) for making the music ''better.'' In general, the fact that there are corrective methods gives me the courage to make provisional musical statements. The design process frequently uses previous solutions to define the context for new problems, including the refinement of old problems. Said simply, corrective methods depend on self-referencing.

The Sociology of Negotiated Musical Meaning

All three of José's comments attempted to improve the dramatic effect of the music by adding new elements of anticipation. What these anticipations do is draw from the variety of ways a listener might reason about the music. A composer's first listener is himself or herself. However, the *objectification of experience* (to use Piaget's term) requires that the composer incorporate ways of reasoning exhibited by other listeners into his or her own, more "subjective" experience of music. This may seem like a harsh, even cold, way to characterize one's growing musical experience. It's less harsh if we understand *objective* to mean *shared cultural experience,* and *objectification* to mean *increasing the experiences one shares with others in one's culture.* The goal is not to make experience impersonal; rather, the goal is to make shared experience more personal.

A composer's first efforts are often unexpressive. They become more expressive each time he or she introduces new anticipatory elements. Giving purpose to pattern has its difficulties. Even so, these difficulties are substantially diminished if we are aware that a music's expressivity is, itself, designed. With the awareness of a new type of problem we can begin to explore methods for dealing with it. It's no wonder that most beginning composers become discouraged, and only the most stubborn persist.

If I am wise and incorporate José's corrections into subsequent versions of the music, is "my" music mine, José's, or ours? I think the answer is "yes" to *all* of these questions. My conversation with José is similar to the kinds of conversations (or reflections) I frequently have with myself during the compositional process. It is through such conversations that I am able to calibrate my meanings in terms of other people's meanings. One could say that I have many *critics* like José in my head. I can speak to them by saying, "What would X do if he were in my shoes?" Each critic responds in a particular way.

The point is that meaning is socially constructed. In order for culture to regulate my behavior, I have to have pieces of shared culture in my head. This view of the social construction of meaning is quite similar to Vygotsky's when he discusses children at play. He points out that, while play involves imaginary situations, it is still based on rules which become explicit when there are conflicts among players about what some action means. Even if the rules change frequently, the way they change is negotiated in the course of play so that, at each instance, there is some guiding set of rules which is shaping the character of play. For Vygotsky, how the rules change captures the socialization process.

Why do the rules change? Why shouldn't the child prefer a statement of the rules which benefits him or her alone? Or in my case: Why shouldn't I ignore José's suggestions, since my meanings are *my* meanings? For Vygotsky, play serves a mediating function between the child's spontaneous acts and those allowed by the game. The (selfish) motives of each individual are modified by the (social) goals of the group when the two come in conflict. Every child is interested in keeping the play from falling apart because, without the game, there is neither winning nor losing. This is a basic agreement on which increasingly more refined agreements are negotiated.

The conflict with which each child is faced can be characterized as a tension between his or her short-term and long-term interests, a tension which is neither purely emotional nor purely cognitive. The child is forced to notice whether everyone else is having fun, not because his or her immediate interests demand it, but because his or her prolonged interests do.

The conditions of listening or play do not require epistemic feats. In my conversation with José, I didn't need to know everything about José in order to hear his complaints. Similarly, Vygotsky's child needs to know very little about his or her playmates. The only rules which each child must attend to are those that result in conflicts. Resolving these conflicts preserves the game; ignoring them jeopardizes the continuation of the game (Vygotsky, 1978, pp. 92–104). Therefore, the child's long-term interests demand that he or she negotiate meaning.

In a sense, José was challenging my "rules of listening," much as a Vygotskyian child might challenge his or her teammates' rules of play. If I can (and want to) satisfy José's expressive requirements, I satisfy all the other people who share his expressive requirements. One will notice that the kinds of advice José gave me was quite specific. If I take his advice seriously, there is a particular course of action to follow in each case. Each action makes my music a little more social, a little more responsive to what others experience as meaningful.

Media for a Constructionist Musicology

Section 4 has extended section 3's process-oriented approach to musical thinking into a discussion of listening and the construction of shared experience. My hope is that, in exploring the constructive nature of musical thinking, I am preparing the way for a new musicology that uses computers to explore topics in music, much as Turtle Geometry is used to explore topics in mathematics. What do I mean by this analogy?

The main tension in the design of media for a constructionist musicology is between making music as it currently exists more teachable, and making a more learnable music. The two approaches have similarities and can even overlap, though the latter approach expresses the constructionist's stance (Papert, 1980, p. 221). Papert's Turtle Geometry is illustrative. On the surface, there is little about Turtle Geometry which resembles traditional mathematics, yet important ideas in mathematical thinking (e.g., variables, functions, recursion, etc.) are to be found there. Instead of asking himself, "How can I make a computer-based Euclidean geometry?", Papert asked himself questions like "How can I make important mathematical ideas, like those found in Euclidean geometry, more learnable?" For me, it is clear that the idea of making a more learnable music has the greater chance of breaking through the obstacles that separate music lovers, not only from new musical knowledge, but from the musical knowledge they already have and find difficult to understand or express using current media.

ACKNOWLEDGMENTS

This research was supported by grants from the IBM Corporation (Grant #OSP95952), the National Science Foundation (Grant #851031-0195), the McArthur Foundation (Grant #874304), The LEGO Group, and the Apple Computer Inc. The preparation of this chapter was supported by the National Science Foundation (Grant #MDR 8751190 and #TPE 8850449), Fukatake, and Nintendo Inc., Japan. The ideas expressed here do not reflect those of the supporting agencies.

REFERENCES

Apel, W. (1972). *Harvard dictionary of music* (2nd ed.). Cambridge, MA: Belknap Press of Harvard University Press.

Bent, I. (1987). *Analysis* (Glossary by William Drabkin). New York: W. W. Norton and Company.

Brown, D. C., & Chandrasekaran, B. (1989). *Design problem solving: Knowledge structures and control strategies.* London: Pitman Publishing.

Dowling, W. J., & Harwood, D. L. (1986). *Music cognition.* New York: Academic Press.

Gargarian, G. (1990a). *The four stone problem.* Unpublished paper, MIT Media Laboratory, Cambridge, MA.

Gargarian, G. (1990b). *Towards a Theory of Music Anticipation.* Unpublished paper, MIT Media Laboratory, Cambridge, MA.

Gruber, H. E., & Voneche, J. J. (1977). *The essential Piaget: An interpretive reference and guide.* New York: Basic Books.

Holland J. H., Holyoak, K. J., Nisbett, R. E., & Thagard, P. R. (1986). *Induction: Processes of inference learning, and discovery.* Cambridge, MA: MIT Press.

Latour, B. (1987). *Science in action.* Cambridge, MA: Harvard University Press.

Mandler, G. (1984). *Mind and body: Psychology of emotion and stress.* New York: W. W. Norton and Company.

Meyer, L. (1973). *Explaining music: Essays and explorations.* Chicago: The University of Chicago Press.

Papert, S. (1980). *Mindstorms: Children, computers and powerful ideas.* New York: Basic Books.

Polya, G. (1973). *How to solve it: A new aspect of mathematical method.* Princeton, NJ: Princeton University Press.

Reti, R. (1961). *The thematic process in music.* London: Faber and Faber.

Rosen, C. (1988). *Sonata forms* (rev. ed.). New York: W. W. Norton and Company.

Simon, H. A. (1985). The science of design. In H. Simon (Ed.), *The sciences of the artificial* (pp. 129–159). Cambridge, MA: MIT Press.

Simon, H. A., Newell, A., & Shaw, J. C. (1979). The processes of creative thinking. In H. Simon (Ed.), *Models of thought* (pp. 144–174). New Haven, CT: Yale University Press.

Sloboda, J. A. (1985). *The musical mind: The cognitive psychology of music.* Oxford: Clarendon Press.

Suchman, L. (1987). *Plans and situated actions: The problem of human machine communication.* New York: Cambridge University Press.

Vygotsky, L. S. (1978). *Mind in society: The development of higher psychological processes.* Cambridge, MA: Harvard University Press.

APPENDIX: GLOSSARY OF LOGO PRIMITIVES AND PROCEDURES

BUTFIRST *list*
The primitive BUTFIRST outputs everything but the first element of a list.

CONTOUR contour-list scale
Contour numbers are used by this procedure to extract notes from an ascending scale
    exp: SHOW CONTOURS [1 2 3 2 3 4] :cmajor = =>
        [[cl 4] [dl 4] [el 4] [dl 4] [el 4] [stfl 4]]

EXTRACTDURATIONS phrase
The procedure EXTRACTDURATIONS makes a list of durations from a list of note-duration pairs
    exp: SHOW EXTRACTDURATIONS :cmajor = => [4 4 4 4 4 4 4]

EXTRACTNOTES phrase
The procedure EXTRACTNOTES makes a list of notes from a list of note-duration pairs
    exp: SHOW EXTRACTNOTES :cmajor = => [cl dl el fl gl al bl c2]

FIRST *list*
The primitive FIRST outputs the first element of a list.

MAKE "name [*list being named*]
The primitive MAKE names a list

MAPDURATIONS duration-list phrase
The procedure MAPDURATIONS maps a pattern of durations onto the notes of a phrase

exp: SHOW MAPDURATIONS [3 1] :cmajor= =>
       [[c1 3] [d1 1] [e1 3] [f1 1] [g1 3] [a1 1] [b1 3] c2 1]]

MAPNOTES <note-pattern><phrase>
The procedure MAPNOTES maps a pattern of notes onto the durations of a phrase
exp: SHOW MAPNOTES [c1 d1 e1] :cmajor= =>
       [[c1 4] [d1 4] [e1 4] [c1 4] [d1 4] [e1 4] [c1 4] [d1 4]]

PLAYNOTE [note duration]
The procedure PLAYNOTE plays a note-duration pair
exp: PLAYNOTE [a1 20]= =>

PLAYPHRASE [[note duration] [note duration][etc...]]
The procedure PLAYPHRASE plays a list of note-duration pairs
exp: PLAYPHRASE [[a1 20] [e1 20] [a1 20]]= =>

REVERSE list
The procedure REVERSE returns the reverse of a list
exp: SHOW REVERSE [[c1 4] [d1 4] [e1 4] [f1 4]] = => [[f1 4] [e1 4]
       [d1 4] [c1 4]]
       SHOW REVERSE [1 2 3 4] = => [4 3 2 1]

THING *name*
The primitive THING outputs not the *name*, but what the name stands for.

WAIT duration-units
I assume 20 wait units equals 1 second.

Gregory Gargarian develops media for exploring Constructionist Musicology; relating ideas from design, music composing and listening, psychology, and computing.

Espistemology & Learning Group members from left to right: Mitchel Resnick, Hillel Weintraub, Gregory Gargarian, and Idit Harel.

Epistemology & Learning Group members from left to right: Edith Ackermann, Isaac Jackson, Kevin McGee, Aaron Brandes, Uri Wilensky, and Alan Shaw.

17

Different Styles of Exploration and Construction of 3-D Spatial Knowledge in a 3-D Computer Graphics Microworld

Judy E. Sachter

INTRODUCTION

This chapter discusses some aspects of children's cognitive styles and their construction of reference frames while exploring 3-D computer graphics. The study focused on the children's use of different representations and strategies when constructing, transforming, and displacing objects in a 3-D microworld called J3D (Sachter, 1990). It also aimed to find quantitative and qualitative changes in children's spatial learning and development. The study's conceptual framework drew upon spatial cognition, child development, mental imagery, gender differences and cognitive styles related to spatial cognition, and the representations and manipulation of objects and their viewing in 3-D computer graphics.

When I first learned 3-D computer graphics, I wanted to rotate the "eye" in one of my animations, in order to slowly move around and view a scene from the other side. In many computer systems, it is not possible to rotate the "eye." I remember telling my teacher that I wanted to rotate the "eye," "over there." He looked at me with great surprise and said "just rotate the whole scene. It's the same thing." This had never occurred to me! I had thought of the scene as a stable world. I knew that *I* could move to another place to view the scene, but I didn't think of moving *the scene*. All of a sudden, I realized that both result in the same effect—in 3-D computer graphics, both were equally possible!

Part of my initial misunderstanding of this possibility was probably based on previous experiences in the real physical world, not the virtual world of 3-D computer graphics. Often, the strategy chosen to imagine the other side of something depends on the size and nature of what we are imagining. If it is an object, we often think of rotating the object. However, if it is a large building, we think of viewing it from another vantage point. From this experience with my teacher, I realized that the *same visual effect could be achieved through different means*—logically, it is the same to rotate the scene and to change the viewpoint. This "grouping" made me think about space differently. These kinds of *grouping of transformations* becomes very powerful in spatial problem solving and, I believe, is also an indication of spatial ability in general.

In the simulated world of 3-D computer graphics, as in the mind, there are many occurrences where groupings of transformations are possible. J3D provides a "microworld' (Papert, 1980) for exploring and discovering grouping such as rotation vs. changing the "eye," scaling vs. moving the "eye" or the object, and translation vs. moving the "eye" and/or the "coi" (center of interest). I had hoped to see this type of coordination—the optimum understanding of transformations—in the children who worked with J3D.

In 3-D computer graphics several aspects of spatial cognition come together to form a coherent spatial learning environment. In J3D, for example, users are given a fixed 3-D Cartesian coordinate system and a set of operations which allow them to locate, modify, and displace objects relative to this fixed reference frame. The children could modify their own point of view relative to these objects. J3D was designed to provide children with a microworld for learning to manipulate transformations of objects, and the views of these objects, through the use of positive and negative numbers and decimal fractions solidly bound to the Cartesian coordinate system.

The study's participants were fifth-grade children with varying spatial abilities. How these children learned about spatial and metric concepts was investigated while they constructed images and animated them with J3D. The children participated in both structured exercises (to learn about J3D) and in unstructured play with J3D on their own. In general, the larger study demonstrated that the children who used J3D improved in their spatial understanding and their ability to solve spatial problems both on and off the computer, as measured by a battery of spatial tests and tasks (see Sachter, 1990). All these children also improved in their organization of spatial concepts as seen in the language they used to describe space, in their drawings representing 3-D space, in their understanding and use of the Cartesian coordinate system, and in their ability to coordinate objects and view transformations.

Prior to looking at various strategies used to construct the reference frame by individual children, it is important to review some of the issues related to the choice of strategies and, subsequently, how these choices reveal individual styles.

Spatial Cognition and Reference Frames

Piaget and Inhelder (1967) characterize three major types of relations or properties of space: topological, projective, and Euclidean space. *Topological proper-*

ties are the qualitative relations among objects. *Projective space* is the coordination of viewpoints (actual and virtual), and the figures considered in relation to
these viewpoints, such as straight lines or parallel lines, that remain invariant
under projective or perspective transformations. *Euclidean, or metric, properties*
require the concepts of straight lines, distances, measurements, parallels, and
angles to be fused into a single operational whole. These relations, completed by
the construction of the reference frame, are established between objects and
determine the location of objects within an organized whole.

The *reference frame* is a construct which underlies projective and Euclidean
space and is an important factor in the performance of various spatial and
developmental tasks. A reference frame is a systematic representation of spatial
relations among object which provides a set of coordinates for expressing
transformations of such relations (Pufall & Shaw, 1973). The development of the
reference frame progresses from merely subjective to a more objective presentation of spatial relations. Piaget viewed it as a homogeneous progression, from
using local, toward global, frames of reference. For Piaget, the coordinate
system, as described by mathematicians, was nothing but an elaborate version of
the most stable and reliable reference system for describing objects and movements in space. The construction of the coordinate system indicates the culmination of Euclidean thinking.

Physical objects are perceived and coded with respect to a cognitive coordinate system (Marr & Nishihara, 1978; Rock, 1973), which has an effect on
recognition, information retrieval, and spatial transformations (Just & Carpenter,
1985). In the mental representation of objects, along with the implicit origin and
axes of the objects, there is also implicit information about the point from which
this object is viewed. The occurrence of a viewing point also implies projective
space, with all the distortions and occlusions that occur in perception. Projective
space is also addressed by Piaget's three mountain experiment, which requires
the ability to take someone else's point of view. This coordination of perspectives occurs around 9 or 10 years of age and is said to demonstrate the movement
away from egocentrism and to indicate greater differentiation between self and
other.

The reference frame is not necessarily a stable global construct. Olson and
Bialystok (1983) declared four general classes of referents: ego, observer,
object, and environment. What becomes an important issue is how, why, and
when a particular reference frame is chosen. Consequently, choosing the appropriate reference frame becomes one of the more difficult problems in both spatial
and cognitive style tasks. This choice can become complicated by the fact that
the reference frame used depends on the context, the materials, and the complexity of the problem posed. These variables can affect the strategy and the
reference frame used, and consequently can affect the performance on spatial
tasks. DeLisi and DeLisi (1981) found that the manner in which children
imagined geometric transformations corresponded to their understanding of reference axes, distance relations, relations of equality, and measurement (DeLisi et

al., 1981). As with the coordination of perspectives (projective system), age 9 marks the completion of the framework appropriate for the comprehension of the Euclidean systems. At this age, mental imagery, in cooperation with these operations, also becomes dynamic and anticipatory. For these reasons, fifth grade (age 10) is a pertinent age to look at the child's construction of the reference frame.

There is a great body of literature that studies children's abilities in mental imagery and spatial cognition through rotation and perspective problems. (See Sachter, 1990, for a review.) The most important aspect in terms of the construction of spatial concepts is that rotation and perspective problems are logically and algebraically similar, but are not psychologically similar. Some of the differences in rotations and perspective changes are thought to be due to differences in strategies (Just & Carpenter, 1985); in the ability to code, isolate, and activate the critical spatial predicates needed to solve the task (Olson & Bialystok, 1983); or in the ability to use language to explicate spatial thought (Olson & Bialystok 1983; Huttenlocher & Presson, 1973). *Based on this, I believe that children constructing images within the J3D microworld are obliged to deal with these spatial concepts explicitly through using the object and view transformations, by specifying these changes with both language and mathematics, and by subsequently seeing the constructed computer image.*

Gender Differences, Cognitive Styles, and Spatial Cognition

Gender differences and cognitive styles are important elements to consider when studying spatial cognition. The issue of gender differences in spatial ability has been one of the most persistent differences found in all abilities research (McGee, 1979). The difference between females and males in spatial ability has been well documented and persistent in the past; usually, if there were sex differences favoring males, it is an indication that there was a "spatial content" in the test (Eliot & MacFarlane, 1983). The sources of gender differences in spatial cognition are still under debate, because it is very difficult to separate the genetic, hormonal, biological, and sex-related brain differences, and psychosocial influences (Halpern, 1986). Of these possible sources of difference, the most relevant to this chapter is the *gender differences in strategy use.*

Cognitive style refers to individual differences in modes of perceiving, remembering, and thinking (Halpern, 1986). Many assessment tests for cognitive style are based on how an individual uses, organizes, and processes information. Several of these tests also have an underlying spatial element. Some researchers believe that differences in cognitive style as well as in gender may also reflect strategy differences (Linn & Peterson, 1985, 1986; Globerson, 1985). Ackermann (chapter 14, this volume) believes that there can be inconsistencies among children and within each child's performances due to the child's style, modality of task description, and/or the context within which the task is given. Strategy difference may pertain to acquiring a strategy, choosing the correct strategy for the task, and/or efficiently using a particular strategy (Linn & Peterson 1986; Globerson, 1985, Halpern, 1986). A well-known cognitive dimension is field articulation: field-dependent and field-independent styles. The assessments for field-dependent and field-independent cognitive styles have revealed gender differences, with a larger proportion of males exhibiting a field-independent style. However, as Halpern (1986) points out, on nonspatial tests for field articulation there are no gender differences.

Many researcher have addressed the question of the extent to which spatial ability can be affected by training. As other researchers (Halpern, 1986; Linn & Peterson, 1985; Globerson, 1985; Witkin, 1978, 1981, Liben & Goldbeck, 1980, 1984) have shown, intervention can minimize gender differences on certain spatial tasks, change cognitive styles and strategies, and improve performance on many spatial tasks. I have also shown that spatial abilities can improve from instruction, experience, and practice at explicating the essential spatial information. The children's experiences in my study affected their deeper constructs— the reference frame (Sachter, 1990).

Although I did not expect significant quantitative changes through my intervention, they did appear. Many of the tasks on measurement and the coordinate system are analyzed in a more qualitative way to try to access the children's understanding of the operations, of strategies, of their use of natural language to talk about space, and of their understanding and use of the graphics system. The main focus was on the reference frame, and on how well it was constructed and applied through various Euclidean and computer tasks.

My goal was to introduce children to multiple strategies for organizing space, for choosing transformations, and to encourage their use of the operations that the graphics system made available. I looked at their strategies for specific tasks prior to, and after, the intervention. I also checked for differences between boys and girls in their strategies in this particular environment. The results of this larger study are discussed in Sachter (1990).

The J3D Computer Graphics Microworld

J3D provided a viewing and transforming microworld. Children could manipulate one or more basic geometric polyhedral objects by changing their size, proportions, position, and/or orientation in space. These objects could be thought of as malleable building blocks to be used in the construction of images. A more complex object or scene can be constructed out of geometric primitives (e.g., a cone, cube, sphere, and cylinder). Scaling is used to create the desired size and proportions. Translation is used to position the parts in the desired relationship to other parts. To correctly position the part, it is necessary to take into consideration the original object, its current size, and the displacement of its boundaries. The rotation can be figured by knowing the orientation of the original object and the desired orientation, and by specifying the axes and degree of rotation from the original.

The capability of J3D to display 2-D views of 3-D objects offered the children *concrete visual feedback* of their synthetic 3-D world. They also had control of spatial transformations through the Cartesian coordinate system. Thus, the system set the Cartesian coordinate system within a concrete graphical framework. The numerical values of coordinate space became less abstract, since they were used as a language for dealing with space in order to create images.

In J3D, children interacted with the computer through a keyboard-entered command language that requires the specification of transformation commands in terms of Cartersian coordinates. The syntax of the command obliged the children to both name the spatial transformation desired and consciously and explicitly to use the coordinate system as the frame of reference (see Figure 1,

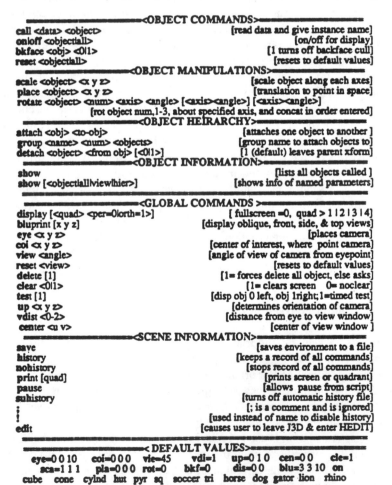

Figure 1. J3D - Command Guide.

the short version of the J3D Command Guide; for a longer version of the J3D Manual, see Appendix A in Sachter, 1990).

The concepts and syntax of J3D were introduced to the children as a means of building a conceptual domain. The vocabulary of the system allowed us to discuss what they could do with J3D. It also allowed us to point out alternate strategies for constructing images. Due to the complexity of J3D, I designed several learning sessions progressing from very uniform and structured tasks to open-ended projects. The first few exercises dealt with one specific operation only, while the later projects were left up to the children.

My interventions were also structured for a progression from more to less assistance. In the beginning, I worked very closely with the children, in a think aloud, step-by-step process. Later, I was assisting children at their request, or when they seemed stuck or confused. I was an available "expert system"—an integral part of this microworld.

Each child went through the same sequence of exercises and projects, but at his or her own pace. Each child had 15 sessions of 45 minutes each (roughly 11.5 hours total) with J3D. The level of complexity reached in the five projects depended on the individual, and the children were supplied with (various kinds of) support in designing, planning, and executing their projects.

The children were also asked to do several exercises as a posttest. In addition, a final interview was done to investigate: (a) how they understood the system, (b) how they would teach it to others, (c) what they found important, (d) what language they used, (e) what explanations they had created for themselves, and (f) what explanations they had appropriated from the experimenter. The final interview was also intended as a way for the children to (g) present their work and talk about their plans, problems, and feelings regarding J3D.

ASSESSING THE DEVELOPMENT OF CHILDREN'S SPATIAL FRAMEWORK THROUGH EUCLIDEAN AND PROJECTIVE TASKS

The analysis of the many spatial tests and tasks administered to the children allowed me to construct a pyramid representation, or "building block," of spatial components of Euclidean and projective concepts (Sachter, 1990). These building blocks allowed me to grasp each child's spatial framework, and to understand *what type of spatial problems* he or she could or could not solve. This information allowed me to document *what children brought to the learning experience and what knowledge they constructed as a result of their experience.* It also provided a method for predicting where children might have more difficulties with J3D.

Among all participants, only one child, David, coordinated the "view and rotation" problem prior to the intervention. However, the pretasks indicated that his "spatial framework" was almost fully developed; he had already constructed the necessary framework for the Euclidean and projective tasks prior to the study. After working with J3D, 8 out of the 10 children could solve this task either through change of view or rotation. Six of these children understood completely how to do these two transformations in J3D. Moreover, it is important to mention that all children were able to use J3D and, with varying degrees of prompting, to solve all J3D tasks. It was possible to use J3D—and the coordinate system embedded in it—without being able to coordinate measurement in 2-D. One of the reasons for this might be that children can extract correct coordinate points without necessarily being able to plot them. In order to place a point it is important to coordinate the two axes, whereas to extract a point, it is sufficient to think about one axis at a time. This same principle holds true for J3D. Since the children could think about one parameter in one axis at a time, they were able to use the system. Some children changed one parameter at a time, while others often changed more than one parameter at a time.

To demonstrate, let's review a portion of a "history file" of the command Jenni used to solve a given task with two cubes offset by their width in X and depth in Z (with their edges just touching). She had to place one cube offset from the other in two dimensions. Jenni started by changing one axis at a time: she first changed the X axis, then the Z axis, then she went on to change the Y axis.

```
call cube cc          [Bring in two objects]
cal cube c
dis
pla c 3 0 0           [Changes X axis]
dis
pla c -1.5 0 0        [Satisfied with X value]
dis
pla c -1.5 0 2        [Starts on the Z value]
dis
pla c -1.5 0 4
dis
pla c -1.5 0 3
dis
pla c -1.5 0 3.5      [Satisfied with Z value]
dis
pla c -1.5 -1 3.5     [Starts on the Y value]
dis
pla c -1.5 .25 3.5    [Satisfied with Y value]
dis
```

In contrast, David immediately changed two parameters at a time. He also kept the dimensions of the cube in mind when dealing with the offset.

```
call cube c           [Bring in two objects]
call cube cl
place cl -1 0 1        [Moved cube in X and Z simultaneously]
dis 4
place cl -2 0 2        [Adjusted cube in X and Z simultaneously]
dis 4
```

Some children tried one axis at a time to determine the correct axis, while others changed more than one at a time. Jenni was lowest spatially among all the participants in the study. She "adjusted by axis" in order to achieve the picture. Although she had not yet coordinated measurement in 2-D, she could use J3D by just keeping in mind only one axis at a time.

One interesting thing which I examined (since it relates to the projective tasks), was how the children think about the objects that they are viewing on the computer screen. I expected they would gain understanding of 2-D representation of 3-D objects by working in J3D. I also expected that, from working with J3D, the children could more easily imagine that these 2-D images were just a "window" into a virtual 3-D world.

At the beginning of the study children tended to think more about representing 3-D objects in 2-D than about the object itself in 3-D. This seemed to change through the study. In the pretests, the children seemed to think of these 3-D representations (on paper or on the computer) in terms of their position in 2-D space or in terms of how they would draw (represent) them in 2-D. They did not think of them as virtual 3-D objects. For example, one child's strategy report for the Rotations test was related to the shape being able to come off the page. This was a way of talking about a 2-D representation being expanded into 3-D with full movement in space. Psychologically, it was no longer attached to the 2-D page.

I also found that children improved in thinking about these 2-D images. There was a subtle change in their own reports about the strategies they used in the standard spatial tests, and in their ability to draw 3-D objects and to draw different views of an object. This ability to think about a 3-D object (and imagine it moving, rotating, and stretching in space) goes together with the underlying ability to think of these objects in three dimensions.

Thinking about these virtual objects as actually 3-D objects was one of the problems for the lower spatial children. These children didn't consistently think of the virtual objects as 3-D. Often, when looking at the screen and seeing the object represented in 2-D, these children would start trying to adjust the image by choosing the 2-D *screen* or *picture* as their reference, not the *object* it was representing in 3-D.

Two interesting incidents illustrate this point. In the example of Jenni's and David's commands above, we can see how they differ in their thinking about space. For example, when David changed his command from (-1 0 1) to (-2 0 2), he was thinking about the cube as a 3-D object. His adjustment showed that he *considered the object in 3-D* and changed both the X and Z (or width and depth) of the object at one time. Jenni, on the other hand, was making her adjustments and fine-tuning the picture so that it *looked* like it was correct. She *thought of the object as 2-D*.

The difference in what it represented (3-D) and how it looked (2-D) was something Jenni often confused when working at the computer. Jenni thought about it in this way even though the changes she made were in three axes. She was able to understand and imagine all the possible transformation for creating a particular image, but when she started working with J3D her focus shifted to the 2-D screen, not the virtual 3-D world that the screen represented. This facility in *understanding the representation of 3-D objects* goes along with the increase facility in *imagining what they look like from different views and in being able to transform them.* After the children explored and used the system by transforming objects and changing the view, they gained a deeper understanding of all the possible changes in the object and in the view. They were better able to make sense of building invariants of both representations and reciprocal transformations.

A LOOK AT THREE CHILDREN THROUGH TWO SPATIAL TASKS

This section describes three children's construction of the coordinate system, and the coordination of transformations, through two different tasks. Two particular exercises are presented below in order to explore some of the children's microgenetic changes.

*   *TASK-1. Constructing Referents and Plot Points in 2-D.* This task required that the children plot two points (-1 2 0, 3 -.5 0) on a grid, and more importantly, that they explicate, or label, the axis and numerical referents. This task was only administered as a posttask with the help of the researcher. The children worked by themselves, and the researcher aided the children through asking questions or providing reminders of previously introduced concepts or strategies. The children had to decide what was important as a referent and then to plot the two points. As mentioned previously, this type of task relates to the coordinate system, and thus is very important in J3D. It essentially allowed the children to demonstrate what they knew about the coordinate system by having to generate it.
*   *TASK-2. Changing the View of a Given Scene.* This task was an indicator of coordination of rotation and change of perspective. It indicated which children were able to understand and/or coordinate these transformations. The task used a grid divided into four squares on which several objects were placed to create a scene. A hut, a cylinder, and a cone were each placed on different squares. This task can satisfactorily be achieved through either changing the eye or a global rotation. It can also be accomplished through place or translation; however, this was only a partial solution because one of the objects, the hut, would also have to be rotated. The easiest way to attain this is through changing the eye, because it is the most global change and it requires the fewest commands in J3D. To achieve this through rotation, all objects would have to be grouped and this would require many more com-

mands to J3D. To use rotation, the children had to understand what rotates, what is the referent for rotation, and the nature of local and global rotations, since just turning the hut does not produce the desired effect. When the children were asked to predict how they would implement their solution on the computer, this sometimes may have caused them to realize they had not thought through a possible solution far enough, or had incorrectly anticipated an outcome. Sometimes, through thinking about how to implement their solution in J3D, they would switch their solution or strategy.

These two tasks were the most difficult. They marked the *coordinations of concepts in Euclidean, projective, and J3D tasks.* The Euclidean Task-1 required that children label referents and plot two points on a grid. Solving the transformational Task-2 required both a coordination of projective concepts as well as a coordination of transformational concepts. Analyzing these two tasks helps us understand how individual children solved these spatial problems.

Three children, who represent "extreme" model cases in spatial ability, will be discussed here. *David* was the child with the highest spatial pretest scores; *Tiffa* and *Jenni* had the lowest spatial pretest scores. Jenni and Tiffa are different in that Tiffa's posttest scores went down and Jenni's posttest scores significantly improved.

David was a stocky white boy who was fairly serious, especially about school and learning. He was often involved in his own thoughts and projects. Jenni was a very petite, vivacious, and outgoing Hispanic girl who was always interested in and distracted by what was going on around her. Tiffa was a very tall, quiet, and mature black girl who was very soft spoken. She was known for being a hard worker and for sticking with problems that were very difficult for her.

Analysis of TASK-1: Constructing and Coordinating the Coordinate System

Only 3 of the 10 children were able to complete this task correctly; 4 other children were able to do parts of the task (i.e., label the axes, or label the numbers, or plot the points). This task was difficult for the children. Even those who could complete all parts had to be prompted. David, Jenni, and Tiffa's answers are shown in Figure 2. David, the highest spatial participant, demonstrated a level of spontaneous response not seen in the other children. The children were asked to plot two points; (-1 2 0) and (3 -.5 0).

David's case. This task was not very difficult for David. He had coordinated measurement in 2-D prior to the study. In the pretask, when asked how he had measured in 2-D, he wrote: *"I measured how far from the side and top in the first box, and put the dot in the same place in the second box."*

Of the three children, David was the one who was able to plot a point in the pretest. During this task, David immediately marked the X and Y axis and

PLEASE PUT THE REFERENCE NUMBERS IN THE GRID
AND PLOT THE FOLLOWING TWO POINTS:
(-1 2 0) AND (3 -.5 0)

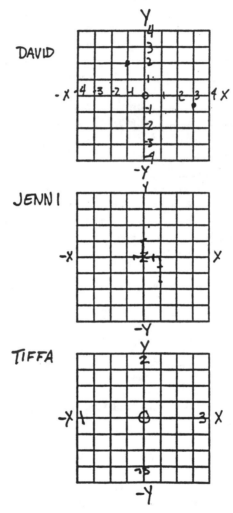

Figure 2.   David's, Tiffa's and Jenni's Construction of Coordinates in Task-1.

plotted the two points. When asked if there was any other information he thought would be helpful, he added the positive numbers to the graph. When asked again if he thought this was enough information for someone to understand, he added the negative numbers and said, *"It is now."*

Jenni's case. This was a more difficult task for Jenni. She had not coordinated measurement in 2-D prior to the study, nor was she able to do so after the study. In the pretask, she placed two points, one next to the correct number in each axis. The two axes were not coordinated into one single point. She was able to label each axis—both positive and negative—correctly in the posttask. Jenni even indicated the Z axis by putting a Z at the origin. During the interview, I asked her three times if she could "think of any other information that would be needed on the graph in order to plot the two points." This question was asked several times, to see if she could think of any other information needed on the graph (such as numbers along the axes), and to determine how confident she was in her answer. Below is a portion of the transcript of this session, when Jenni was placing a point (-1 2 0) on her graph.

Judy: What does the first number mean?
Jenni: Minus, it's minus right here, this one I got is minus one, then right here? [She drew a line from zero to the left halfway along the line to the first intersecting line and marked it with a short line]
Judy: All right.
Jenni: -1 and two. 2 and zero. Over here. [She drew another line from zero to one full unit up in Y]

Jenni drew lines from the origin and placed a point in -X, and then drew another line from the origin to a point in Y (see Figure 2). If each square of the graph was equivalent to two units, then the end points were placed at the correct distances from the origin. She labeled the axes but did not label the reference numbers along the axes. The axes helped to orient her, but the absence of reference numbers prevented her from using the grid as a consistent global reference frame. As a result, the first point (a set of two lines) seemed to be in one scale, and the second point (two lines from the origin to two points) in another scale. While Jenni was able to measure in 1-D and extract the coordinates for a point by the end of the study, she was unable to generate and plot a single point in 2-D. We can see that it is possible to use the Cartesian coordinate system and J3D without being able to coordinate measurement in 2-D. My assumption is that, if she could have spent more time with J3D, she could have coordinated measurement in 2-D.

Tiffa's case. Like Jenni, Tiffa could not coordinate the measurement in 2-D either before or after the study. She was able to find her way about the coordinate system, one axis at a time. In the pretask, Tiffa put a point above 7 on the X axis and a point to the left of 10 in Y axis, instead of placing a single point at (-7 10). As we can see in Figure 2, she used the numbers to *label a point* rather than as a *reference from which to mark a point.* She wrote "1" for the point (-1 2 0) placed almost at the left edge of the grid (-X axis), "2" almost at the top edge of the grid (Y axis), "3" almost at the right edge (X axis), and "-.5" at only 1 square less than the lower edge (-Y axis). The numbers 1,2,3, and -.5 are all very close to being the same distance from the origin she marked. She did not put in reference numbers, but she labeled the axes; she did not deal with these numbers as measurement, but rather she used them as labels.

Below is a portion of the session, which reveals Tiffa's understanding of the axes and directions along the axes. Her difficulty was making what she knew explicit, and making use of what she knew to solve the task at hand. Tiffa needed scaffolding to even get started on this task.

Judy: What information would you need to be able to read this grid? Remember when you made your data? What information did we have to put on the graph paper?
Tiffa: The points, the picture, and, and that's about it.
Judy: Would we need anything else? If we wanted to plot a point, would there be any other information we would need to know about those three numbers?
Tiffa: [silence]
Judy: What do those three numbers mean?
Tiffa: [unsure] X,Y and Z?
Judy: OK, so what would we need on this [grid] to let us know what those number really are?
Tiffa: X,Y and Z.
Judy: Great. Could you do that for me?
Tiffa: Uh, just put this here?
Judy: What do you think?
Tiffa: [She writes the axes on her paper]
Judy: Good, OK, now if you could plot those two points for me.
Tiffa: [silence]
Judy: Do you think you have enough information to figure out where to put those two points?
Tiffa: [She labels the X and Y axes on the grid]
Judy: OK, then add whatever information you need so that you can plot those two points.
Tiffa: I don't need anything else. Let's see, let's see. Is that what you want?
[Here we can see that Tiffa became unsure of what she was doing when I asked if she needed other information. She often looked at me for the cues, answers, or even for approval of her answer when we worked together. This tendency of looking at me for confirmation of her work became more pronounced near the end of the study as she dealt with more complexity.]
Judy: What have you just done? Explain to me what you just did.
Tiffa: Set the -1 on the negative side of this X.
Judy: Uh huh.
Tiffa: This side is over at 3. Yeh, and two in Y, it's not negative so I put it at the top.
Judy: Do you think that's enough for someone else to understand what those numbers mean if they looked at it?
Tiffa: [She nodded yes]

Tiffa could not yet perform all of the 1-D measurement tasks, extract a coordinate point or coordinate measurement in 2-D in the posttasks. She solved this problem by using the numbers themselves as indicators of the points, rather than by putting the numbers on the grid to be used as referents.

Summary of TASK-1. Among these three children we see different styles of understanding 3-D space and the Cartesian coordinate system. All three children were able to use the coordinate system within J3D, even though their ability to coordinate the system varied. David *knew the system* quite clearly and could make his understanding explicit for himself and for others. Tiffa and Jenni could *use* the system and *understood* the axes, but they were *not yet able to coordinate the axes into a whole system of references.* Jenni was able to start systematically by defining her own references (the numbers along the axes) and use these implicit referents (the numbers were not written on the graph). Tiffa was *not yet able to define these referents systematically.* She used the numbers themselves (local referents) next to the points as a label. My assumption is that more time for Jenni and Tiffa was needed to attain a coordinated system of references. According to Jenni's starting level, she made a great deal of progress from using J3D. I think that Tiffa was a child who was juggling the multiple concepts and was just beginning to sort them out when the study ended. Some children need more time than others.

Analysis of TASK-2. Coordinating the Eye and Rotation Transformations

In this task, the children were asked to write ''what could have caused the difference between one picture and three others'' (see Figure 3). The data from TASK-2 show the same overall pattern for David, Jenni, and Tiffa that we saw on TASK-1. Jenni and Tiffa were able to solve this task, but in a way that was not as coordinated a solution as David's.

The children's solutions to this task seems related to De Lisi, Locker, and Youniss's (1976) hierarchy of three types of movements in space—transposition, intermediate, and transformation. *Transposition* reflects an understanding of movements as displacement, and *transformation* reflects a coordination of change of position and change in the object's character. De Lisi's hierarchy of transformation is similar to what I found in the children's solution to this task. Most of the lower-spatial children in the study thought that translation (transposition) was the solution in the pretask, and all but one of the children, Tiffa, progressed to see the solution as either a rotation and/or as a change of view in the posttask (transformation). The rotation and change of view take into consideration, not just the displacement in space (as does transposition), but also the transformation of the objects and the relations between those objects. David was able to do this task prior to the study. Jenni and Tiffa were not. Jenni and Tiffa saw the changes as a translation or change of position prior to the study; in fact neither of them reported the possibility of a rotation or change of view in the pretask. After the study, Jenni was able to see the solution as either a rotation or change of view, but Tiffa still saw it only as a change of position. Let us examine each child's thinking about this task more closely.

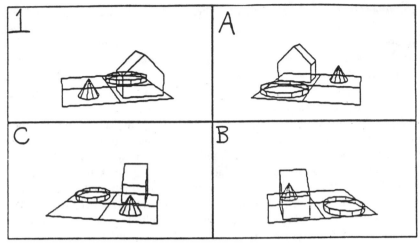

Figure 3. In Task-2 the children were asked to indicate what could have caused the difference between picture 1 and the other pictures A, B, and C.

David's case. In the pretask, David did not yet understand the reciprocal relations between rotation and a change of view in the pretask. From his answers (below) we can see that he saw each picture as a separate problem with possibly a different solution. He reported only one type of transformation for each picture without having coordinated the concepts involved. David very quickly understood what J3D offered, and he tried to incorporate what he had learned from the introduction to J3D. In his pretasks, he used the language proposed in the lecture and guessed the axis of rotation. He wrote,

David Pre:
A: Rotated on X? axis.
B: Changed point of view
C: Rotated on X? axis

David Post:
Eyepoints; rotation of bottom with other things grouped.

Below is a portion of the posttask transcript where the rotation solution was discussed. David's answers to the posttask revealed that he understood that all of the pictures could be achieved through *either* eye point or rotation. Notice that he spontaneously qualified how it would be possible to succeed through a rotation. For David, the transformations of rotation and change of view became reciprocal by the end of the study.

Judy: Now, you wrote down rotation. Rotate what?
David: Rotation in Y.

Judy: Anything else I would need to know to rotate that?
David: Are all the things attached? ["Attach" is a command in J3D that is used to attach one object to another object]
Judy: So, would they have to be attached?
David: Or group. ["Group" is another command in J3D that allows several objects to be called by one name and transformed the same through one set of commands]

David knew the axis of rotation for the scene. He saw that the relations between the objects was fixed and had to be maintained. He understood how to do this with J3D. In order to use a rotation strategy, the relations between objects had to remain fixed. The two methods for fixing the relations between objects in J3D was the "attach" or the "group" commands.

When discussing the change of view strategy, I asked David if he could tell me where the eye points were for the different pictures. He immediately began figuring out the coordinate point of the eye for each view. I stopped him and asked him to describe it in more general terms. He said "backwards" for the view that was the opposite of the anchor view (front). After he generated this type of answer, I set up an anchor for him by stating that the reference picture #1 was seen from the front.

Judy: So, here in #1, I'm seeing it from the front. Where am I seeing it from in A?
David: In back.
Judy: And in B?
David: The side.
Judy: And in C?
David: The other side.

All the children who wrote down a change of view strategy were able to respond and immediately give the correct direction from which the scene was viewed once the reference of a given view was set up for them. However, it was difficult for them to specify their own anchor. Jenni was able to set up her own anchor.

Jenni's case. In the pretask, Jenni saw the difference in these pictures only as a change of position. She wrote:

Jenni Pre:
A: The hut moved dyagelly at number 1.
B: You moved it to the side.
C: The hut moved to the side.

Notice that the relations between the hut and the other objects were not even mentioned. She refers only to the hut for A, B, and C. This object was more salient because it was taller than the other objects, and it was a recognizable canonical object. Those children who said that the difference in the pictures was a change of position often mentioned only the hut. I believe that they chose the change-of-position solution because, like Jenni, they were only looking at the hut in relation to the base or to the viewer. Their focus was localized on the objects rather than on the more global relations between objects.

In the pretask Jenni saw the solution as a translation or change of position of the objects. However, on the posttask, she only thought that the pictures could be made through rotation and change of the view. She wrote, *"You rotated them A-B-C; rotation, eye points."* Jenni also wrote that the change was the result of a rotation. When asked if she could think of any other way to explain the changes, she asked back "Eye point?" When asked again if she could think of any other explanation, she went back to a rotation strategy. However, whenever pressed, she returned to the eye point as the strategy to explain the pictures. Jenni thought that I had created the pictures by changing the eye. She was the only child who provided herself with an explicit anchor. Under the four pictures Jenni wrote: *"1.base,A.back,B.side, and C.back side."* Even though she had written *"rotation"* as her first solution, the eye strategy seemed dominant for her. Below is a portion of this posttask session, discussing what she had written.

Judy: OK. How would we have to do it if we were going to rotate it?
Jenni: [she shrugs her shoulders]
Judy: What happens if I just rotate the house? Will I get the right picture?
Jenni: No.
Judy: So tell me what is rotating.
Jenni: You're rotating the house and the whole picture.
Judy: So how could I do this on the computer, then? [Trying to see if she remembered the attach or group commands]
Jenni: Eye points, with the eye points. [When she thought about it, she probably thought that it was either too complicated or impossible to rotate all these objects together.]
Judy: With the eye points. But if I was going to do it with rotation, how would I do it?
Jenni: I don't know. [She may not have remembered that the attach or group commands or she was unable to apply their operations to this problem]
Judy: Well, would I want to just rotate each object, or all of them?
Jenni: All of them. So, eye point. [Jenni understood that if you were going to rotate everything, then the obvious transformation in J3D would be a view change]
Judy: Do you think I rotated them, or I changed the eye point?
Jenni: Changed the eye point.

It is difficult to say whether Jenni switched back and forth between the eye and the rotation strategies because she understood the difference of complexity in J3D, or because she understood that the two operations were equally possible. Another possibility is that, if she *looked* at the objects, they appeared rotated. However, if she *thought* about how to achieve the image in J3D, she thought about it as a change of view. What is not clear here is whether Jenni was able to disentangle the two transformations. It seems that focusing on one strategy would almost cause her to shift to the other strategy, just as focusing on the image on the screen would cause her to shift from what she knew to what she saw.

Tiffa's case. As mentioned above, Tiffa was the only child who saw the answer to this problem in the pre- and posttasks as a change of position. Several other children mentioned that this was a possible solution, but they understood that it had to be used along with rotation (for the hut). However, Tiffa, whose spatial ability scores actually dropped from the study, maintained that change of position or transposition was the only possible solution throughout the interview in the posttask. Let's take a closer look at how she thought about this and what actually changed in her thinking between the pre- and posttask. In the pretask, Tiffa describes the hut's movements in 2-D simultaneously.

Tiffa Pre:
A: The hut moved diagonally from 1.;
B: The hut moved diagonally again from A.
C: The hut moved diagonally again from B.

Notice that she did not explicitly mention the other objects or the base, although the base can be inferred because of the use of the word diagonally. This word refers to movement in 2-D in relation to the base.

Tiffa's thinking never changed from translation. She had changed the eye and used rotation a great deal in her animations. She was able to talk about rotations and came up with eye points. It is not that she was not familiar with these transformations. I believe that she simply did not see them as part of the solution for this particular problem. She looked at this problem more locally, focusing on the position of the objects. In the posttest she started to consider the relations of several objects when she talked about moving more than just the hut. She was aware that changing the position of the hut was not enough to achieve the picture. She mentions a rotation for the hut, which indicates that, for her to understand it, the hut needed to be in both the right position and in the right orientation. In the interview, I tried to prompt Tiffa to see other possibilities, but her thinking did not shift from translation. She started to think about rotation for just the hut, but she settled back to a change of position as a way to solve the problem. From then on, she stayed with this strategy, as we can see in the transcript below.

Tiffa: The picture in A, yeh, the picture A, the house has jumped over to this side and you could have turned it around. [Silence for a moment while she thought about it then she restated what she thought the answer should be] The home has jumped diagonally to the other side.
Judy: What's the difference in one and B? What's changed?
Tiffa: The cone jumped to the opposite side of it.
Judy: OK.
Tiffa: And what is this?
Judy: It's just a fence or cylinder. Just call it a cylinder, that's fine.

Tiffa:	So, it's moved to the other side.
Judy:	OK. C?
Tiffa:	Well, the hut jumped diagonally to the other side, the cone has jumped diagonally to the other side a little bit, and cylinder jumped to the other side.
Judy:	Ok. That's a lot of changes. So, basically, to do that on the computer, we'd have to place everything, because everything has moved?
Tiffa:	[Nods her head yes]
Judy:	Now, can you think of any other way to explain the changes?
Tiffa:	No.
Judy:	OK. Look at one and look at A.
Tiffa:	Yeh.
Judy:	OK. So there's no other way to change that, to get A from one, except for moving the objects around.
Tiffa:	Right.

Tiffa could see no other solution to this problem. However, she had begun to consider more than one object's position, as indicated by the position changes.

Summary of TASK-2. David, Jenni, and Tiffa were each able to solve this task in varying degrees of coordination. Only David was able to coordinate these transformations and understand their interactions after the study. Jenni and Tiffa saw this task as a change of position rather than a rotation or change of view in the pretasks. In the posttask Tiffa maintained this solution, but Jenni saw it as a change of view or rotation transformation.

DIFFERENT PATTERNS OF INTERACTION AND STYLES OF MASTERING THE J3D MICROWORLD

Issues of style are very central to spatial cognition. This is why I previously reviewed the theoretical background concerning style issues relating to gender and space. In this section, I will discuss the children's style of interaction (with the system and with me) that I observed.

As stated previously, from the children's point of view, I was an integral part of the J3D microworld. Therefore, my style of interaction with the children should be analyzed as well. From analyzing the transcripts, and from my observations and interactions with the children, I came to realize that I had a *relational style* of working with the children. I was in fact using different techniques, hints, questions, and methods in helping the children toward their own proximal development. As we saw above, my interactions with David, Jenni, and Tiffa were different. I was able to work with them in different ways, sensitive to their styles of work and their spatial abilities. The pretests and pretasks helped me acquire knowledge about the children, which was later implemented in the ways I helped each of them move toward their zone of proximal development. I used a different language and different methods with each child, and I was reflective about their personal development and knowledge in my questioning and hints. I did not do the thinking for the children, but I found ways to interact with them so that they could do the thinking.

Much in the style of Lampert (1988) on mathematical discourse, I also tried to establish an intellectual discourse with the children—a spatial-mathematical discourse—that enabled them to develop their concepts and skills. By examining the *patterns of speech,* the duration and amount of what was said to each child, and how each child responded in the learning sessions, I was able to gain insight into the dynamic of our spatial discourse.

For example, the pattern of discourse between David and me shows that David often cut me off and that he responded with very brief answers. David was a very independent learner. He was an "explorer" of the system and did not want any maps or other hints. On the other hand, the pattern of speech between Jenni and me is more like a symmetrical alternation between the two of us: The duration of each part is often close to equivalent. It was more of a negotiated "dialogue." The pattern between Tiffa and me shows long explanations by me and single-word responses on Tiffa's part. From this we can already see different patterns of styles and cognitive processes in the interaction. I also found that this pattern revealed both the quality and style of our interactions. By looking more closely at the content, it was possible to see the quality of the scaffolding that each child required. *Children required different types of scaffolding*—psychological, emotional, social, and cognitive. Thus I proceeded differently for each child.

For example, Jenni learned in a relational way and needed a great deal of scaffolding in the *mathematics* involved in J3D. What is interesting about this is that I thought of Jenni as a very independent child, and yet her notebook is filled with statements such as *"I need more help from Judy."* Tiffa also needed scaffolding, but in a way that is different from Jenni. Tiffa created what I believe to be one of the most complex and difficult animation projects. She could and did work on her own; however, she did so only after we had planned both the strategies and commands *together.* She needed a great deal of scaffolding in planning and strategy, but once she understood what she needed to do, she could work very hard on her own. Tiffa was usually an independent learner, but because of the complexity of the system, she gradually shifted to be a more dependent learner.

In addition, I asked the children in my study how they would *teach J3D to other children* (following Harel, 1988). What children actually learned and appropriated—and what learning styles they used—clearly appeared in their explanation for how they would teach J3D to another child. For example, David told us that he would teach others in the exact way he had worked and solved problems on the system. He was able to describe what was essential in *using and knowing* the actual computer system.

Judy: How would you explain the system to other children in your class?

David: Well, I'd tell them that it's a system where you can have, you know, different shapes and put them together and turn them and see different places with the computer. And then I'd show them how to place, rotate, and how to scale. Then I'd show them how to group and attach.

Judy: Anything else you think you would need to add to help them understand how the system works?

David: Yeh. Tell them about x,y and z axises, the axes. And, you know, tell them that objects are like one in 3 directions. [The extent of the objects]

Judy: That's right. So what would you teach them? Let's say you were going to give them a class, what would you teach them in your first class?

David: Um, about the axes, x, y and z, and how to rotate, place, and scale. And how to call in objects.

Judy: What would you teach them in the second class?

David: Um, how to group things. I'd tell them how to group things, how to attach things, and how to get them to put them, to know how, to show how to get it so, like in the right place so that it's right next to them so you can group them.

David appropriated the *language and the concepts* of the transformations available in J3D, and his straightforward answer showed that he would teach these concepts in the order he learned them.

On the other hand, Jenni appropriated the language and concepts of J3D, but she also *integrated my explanations and my language* as an integral part of her knowledge of the system. She was more interested in communicating *how* she would teach to another, rather than *what* she would teach.

Judy: OK, if you were going to teach a class to others in your class. What would you teach in the very first class so that they could use this system?

Jenni: In the very first class I will teach them all the commands that Kimba use and that stuff. And how to get them and the history of it and how to go to the files, and all that stuff. [Kimba was the name of the hard disk for the computer]

Jenni: In the second class I will teach them how to use the keyboard and if they had a big problem I could help them and do some like projects they have to do and all that stuff. And, and two I'll teach them the data they have. And if like they need help, I will teach them how, to help them and how to go to the files, and how to go to J3D. And what to do when you get into J3D, that you have to type your name.

And then the second question they ask you if you need any help.[This was a message to the user on the system]

Jenni: I think, if I was a teacher, I would have to explain a lot and how to use the rotations, place, and scale because they haven't used it. They have only used Logowriter and they go like LT 90, that means LT left and RT right. And to place it goes FORWARD and BACKward. But in Kimba, with the program that we are using right now, is rotate or scale, place, but I think I would teach, I would really have to explain that a whole bunch, a whole bunch of times.

Judy: How would you explain it?

Jenni: I'd explain that what they have to do is R O T for rotation and they have to put the X rotation, or the Z or whatever, or the Y. If they want to put it, to place, it will be difficult for them because they have not used that, that command. And so I will have to put like place and I'll have to teach them how to place it. Then what they will have to do is look at the paper and like it has a 1, 2, 3 minus and a Z and X and in Y. And they're gonna have to look at things that they will have to do to put it where, to want to place it. And for scale what they use—in Logowriter to scale it, and like it is difficult to scale in Logowriter.

Jenni's detailed explanations of the system did for "her students" what I had tried to do for Jenni. I used concepts from Logo, which she knew and was familiar with, to explain something new to her. I also helped her learn her way around the computer, and I was there to provide explanations for her when she requested help. We see these same kinds of concerns in Jenni's proposal of how she would teach others about the system. We also see that Jenni did understand J3D in a way that was different from David's more formal and explicit understanding.

Jenni and David represent two different ways of interacting with J3D and with me. Each child wanted something different from me and each child required different kinds of assistance. Jenni wanted *a connection, a dialogue, a relationship,* while David used me as a *source of information.* These two children typify a number of style issue which I see as coalescing There is the soft/hard mastery of Turkle (1984) and Turkle and Papert (Chapter 9, this volume), the field dependent/independent of Witkin (1978, 1981), and the analytic/relational learner of Hale-Benson (1986).

David demonstrated his hard mastery in his planning and his scientific approach. In his first project, David came with a drawing on graph paper of a person, with each part labeled for the geometric primitive that he would use. Once he understood the system better, he did not even bother writing these kinds of things down. He could tell me all the commands that he would need and reconstruct whatever else was necessary. The focus of David's animation was on the details of the commands for the movement for his sword. This was evident in his animation, which was not that interesting to watch but was interesting for the complexity of the transformations he was trying to control. In the post interview, David's entire focus for his discussion of his animation was on the *complexity of rotating his sword in two different axes and moving the eye simultaneously.*

David could also be described as a field-independent child. He related to space formally and often chose the most invariant and global referent for solving spatial tasks. In his description of a spatial layout he was the only child who used a formal description of the setting: *"First get a grid 3 × 3."* David was able to restructure and organize his space to solve the spatial tests and tasks with a high degree of consistency. His explanations to other children were tied clearly and articulately to the formal representation of the Cartesian coordinate system. This is consistent with David's independence as a learner and with his resistance to my interventions and my strategies. In other words, David could also be considered an analytic learner.

David is field independent and has an analytic learning style, but this does not preclude his intense engagement in what he was doing with J3D. His notebook revealed that most of his entries were related to how much he liked doing his projects and/or a status report of his current project. He focused both his intellect and his aesthetics on the more technical aspects of the system.

On the other hand, Jenni is a child who approached J3D as a soft master. Much like David, she was very engaged in her work and in her learning process. However, her engagement was in her *relation to things, people, ideas, as well as in the aesthetic and emotional content of her work and environment.* When asked to "plan" a project, she would draw lots of pictures. However, the drawings often did not have anything to do with her projects. This finding is similar to Ackermann's (Chapter 14, this volume) finding about differences between children's drawings and their actions or verbal descriptions. In one task, when the children were to describe a spatial layout to a friend, Jenni not only described it but also gave detailed instructions on how and where to glue the pieces. This gluing indicates that she is a builder and a concrete thinker. This type of thinking was also revealed when she created her projects. She had an initial idea, and then she would start in a *bricoleur* fashion to add parts or new objects, look at them, think about them, then make more changes and adjustments. While David entered several commands with changes in more than one axis at a time, Jenni seldom did. She understood that the J3D allowed this, yet she wanted to see the resulting picture after almost every change she made. All of these incidents point to a negotiating way of interacting with J3D. We have seen another aspect of her soft, relational style in her naming of objects. Everything was named after something or someone connected to her personally. She was also the only child who even noticed that the name of the hard disk on the system was called "Kimba." Most of the time when she referred to the computer she called it Kimba. Jenni not only anthropomorphized the computer but even made jokes about the *"little mouse that's attached to Kimba."*

Jenni is also a child who could be described as more field dependent. We saw her tendency to be swayed by the visual image on the screen. Previously I discussed how she seemed to switch back and forth between a rotation and change of view strategy. Each time she would focus on a different part of the display she would switch strategies. She was also swayed if I questioned her on her choice. This behavior is both related to her field dependence and her relational learning style. In addition, in almost every entry in her notebook, she mentioned me either as a helper or as someone she liked. For example, on April 25, 1988, she wrote: *"I was confused at the first time. But then Judy helped me a lot. I think I am finished with my animation. I like Judy a-lot. Judy is a good helper. She is nice and sweet. I thank her a-lot."* If we compare this to David's comments in his notebook, we can really see the difference between them. When he finished his animation, he said, *"I finished my sword animation."*

To summarize, Jenni and David provided fairly clear examples of an emerging "clustering of styles" (e.g., Weir, 1986). The tendency for this emerging clustering was found in many of the other children. This clustering that I am referring to can be captured in relation to Jenni and David as a continuum, with a hard mastery, field-independent, analytic learner on one end, and a soft mastery, field-dependent, relational learner on the other. Their particular style was evident across the board.

What becomes especially interesting in the analysis of these children's styles, is that this "clustering" also corresponds with *how they related to space* (especially the coordinate system). David understood and related to space in a very formal and logical way. He related to J3D, the computer, and to me in a very similar manner. Jenni on the other hand, was relational in her understanding and use of space and in her interactions with J3D, with the computer, and with me. Witkin (1978, 1981) found that the ways in which people solve spatial tasks is related to field dependence–independence. He also claims that the differentiation of articulated or global (reference frame) and degree of autonomous functioning (self-object differentiation) could be determined from his spatial tests. David and Jenni are good examples for a strong correspondence in how they relate to the reference frame, to J3D, to their knowledge, and to me as a coherent clustering.

Allowing for Epistemological and Relational Pluralism in the Construction of Spatial Knowledge

Usually, the coordination of perspectives task has been treated *formally and abstractly*. With J3D this changes: Children were able to *play with rotation and perspective-change concepts, and were even able to choose which they prefer to use*. For coordinating the two, they had to understand the isomorphism between them as well as build invariants. After playing with J3D, the children were able to imagine more transformations (both object and view) than before. All the children were able to solve all of the J3D tasks, and many of them were able to clearly understand the multiple solutions and coordinate them.

A clear difference in how different children thought about space emerged through their description of the spatial relations. From various tasks it was apparent that some children thought about the image as a 2-D drawing, while others thought about a 2-D representation of a scene in 3-D space. Many of the children shifted in the posttasks from the 2-D drawing strategy to the 3-D strategy. In other words, through exploring space in J3D, their thinking about space and their representation of space changed. This ability to think about a 3-D object (and imagine it moving, rotating, and stretching in space) coincides with the underlying ability to think of these objects in 3-D. This increased facility in representing objects coincides with the increasing facility to imagine object transformations and how objects appear from different views. J3D provided children with the opportunity to play with the coordination of these transformations in different ways, and therefore they were more able to build invariants of both representations and reciprocal transformations.

One last aspect of this 2-D to 3-D shift can also be thought of as a shift in the "field:" from a field-dependent and perceptual strategy to a field-independent one or focus on what is known (representation of a 3-D scene). This shift occurred most often among the field-dependent children. For example, when Jenni, a field-dependent child, was looking at the screen, she thought about the image as 2-D; however, if she though about how she would create the scene, she shifted to a 3-D strategy. This subtle difference can reveal the style of a child as well as influence the performance on spatial tasks.

By analyzing the dynamics of the interaction within the learning environment, I was able to identify learning styles and to propose different kinds of support. My style of coaching also allowed for multiple styles to emerge and function in this environment, so children could act with their own emotional, cognitive, social, and spatial functioning. And I tried to provide each of them with an adequate kind of scaffolding (e.g., emotional for Melvi, social for Paul, informational for David, and mathematical/cognitive for Tiffa and Jenni—see Sachter, 1990). Each child constructed his or her own knowledge about space and appropriated the language and concepts from J3D and from me in his or her own way. Only the finer grain analysis reveals the individual differences in what children appropriate and how they provide supports for themselves in the construction of their own knowledge. Both *how* and *what* children appropriate also reflects their style.

Style, Gender, and Spatial Cognition

I found differences in performance between boys and girls on the standard spatial tests and on the Euclidean and projective tasks in the pretests and pretask. These findings correspond to previous research in the literature. However, in the posttests and tasks there was no significant differences between boys and girls.

I do not believe that the gender issue is as crucial as previously thought. In their recent article, even Linn and Hyde (1989) mentioned that gender differences in spatial ability are declining. One reason for this decline might be that education is moving more towards accommodating more styles of learners. I did not see a particular pattern of strategies, or style, that was particular to just boys or just girls. Rather, I saw individual differences that were fairly coherent within each child. And at the end, both boys and girls improved in their spatial abilities. The ANOVA showed no gender interactions, the only main effect was improvement for each individual in spatial performance (see Sachter, 1990). This demonstrates that different kinds of improvement or strategies do not relate to gender but to preferential strategies in choosing the reference frame.

DIRECT AND INDIRECT SPATIAL LEARNING

A deeper understanding of the representation of 3-D objects was also exhibited in children's drawings (indirect learning). Their drawings changed to show a greater understanding of perspective, hidden surfaces, foreshortening, and so on. I was not teaching these children now to draw, yet their drawings improved. I saw as much improvement in the representation as I used to see when I taught drawing in high school.

J3D is an integrated learning environment which offers multiple accesses to spatial understanding. A combination of visual, verbal, formal, and informal modes encouraged children to reflect upon and integrate different spatial representations. J3D was accessible for children of all styles, and provided children with the opportunity to investigate, learn, and coordinate projective and Euclidean space while they create images and animation. Children *actively used* these concepts, making them explicit through perceptual and cognitive explorations in spatial problem solving.

Children were not just learning about spatial concepts; they were *actively and explicitly using them* to construct images with J3D. Transformations of objects and views are specified through the command language, which ties the name of the transformation, the metrics of the Cartesian coordinate system, and the object to be transformed with the "concrete" perspective image. All of the operations and their anchoring to the Cartesian coordinate system helped in the construction of the reference frame.

The J3D environment was found to help children explore and use the Cartesian coordinate system even if they had not yet attained coordinated measurement in 2-D. Therefore, it is a viable environment to explore these concept prior to acquiring them.

The children improved their spatial skills quantitatively and qualitatively regardless of their styles and spatial ability. By integrating different ways of dealing with space, J3D enhanced children's understanding of space, as well as their ability to solve spatial problems both on and off the computer. Children corrected their own behavior through feedback from J3D and explored space in ways that are not available in any other media. Changes in the children's representations became evident in many ways. They were more clear and explicit in communicating spatial information: The language they used to describe space and transformations of objects in space improved, as did their drawings representing 3-D space, and their understanding and use of the Cartesian coordinate system. There was some progress in the mathematics necessary to work in this system, and in the naming of geometric forms. In short, J3D, from a learning perspective, allows children to work with transformations, measurement, visual representations of perspective, and to manipulate these with tools that children do not normally have access to.

Many children in the study gained a mastery of spatial concepts by coordinating both rotation and perspective. J3D offers both a choice and dynamic control over these operations. Thus, most of the children began to understand the relationship between mental rotation and perspective change through exploring the differences and similarities in object and view transformation.

EDUCATIONAL IMPLICATIONS

J3D may be viewed as a narrow setting, with children isolated one-to-one in a room, working a computer. However, the conclusion we can draw from the examples of the children's learning and developmental changes is important. It is essential to bring spatial concepts into the life of children, not only because many of these are related to mathematics and various fields of science, but because spatial ability is also related to a number of professionals that actually require this particular knowledge. For instance, admittance to dental or architecture school is dependent on spatial ability. In fact, many of the spatial tests I used were developed for vocational and guidance "screening."

However, we should not always be concerned with what children will do in the future, but provide them with meaningful experiences here and now, helping them develop general thinking skills, flexibility, grouping, coordination and planning skills, as well as the skills needed for solving complex problems. Complex systems and virtual environments, such as J3D, provide an opportunity for exploration which stretches the children's thinking *here and now* in ways that are meaningful to them. In school mathematics, children have to memorize a definition for a point and a polygon, but it means nothing to them. When they were creating data in J3D, they needed these concepts to create real images. They needed the mathematical knowledge in order to manipulate the images they themselves created. In the virtual world of J3D, the children were not learning *about these concepts but were actively using* them for manipulating objects in space through doing art, animation, Euclidean mathematics, geometry, and decimal fractions; they were doing space, doing mental imagery, and doing 3-D computer graphics.

ACKNOWLEDGMENTS

I want to thank the children who participated in my study for all the time, energy, concentration, and creativity that they put into this project. I want to thank the teachers, Joanne Rhonkin, Marquita Jackson-Minot, and Maria Teresa Rodriguez, for their patience and cooperation. I especially want to thank Seymour Papert for allowing me the freedom to develop my ideas and research, and Edith Ackermann for her rich understanding of how children think, for her patience and gift in dealing with the minute "nitty gritty" of designing and analyzing tasks for children, and for all the interesting and exciting conversations about spatial thought, styles, and gender issues we have had, I gratefully thank Idit Harel for her excellent support and her help in putting this chapter together.

REFERENCES

De Lisi, A.M., & Delisi, R. (1981). Children's strategies in imaging spatio-geometrical transformations. *International Journal of Behavioral Development*, *4*, 201–222.

De Lisi, R., Locker, R., & Youniss, J. (1976). Anticipatory imagery and spatial operations. *Developmental Psychology, 12*(4) 298–310.

Eliot, J., Smith, I., & Macfarlane, M. (1983). *An international directory of spatial tests.* Windsor: NFER-NELSON.

Globerson, T. (1985). *What is the relationship between cognitive style and cognitive development?* Paper presented at Third Tel-Aviv Annual Workshop on Human Development, Tel-Aviv, Israel.

Hale-Benson, J. (1986). *Black children: Their roots, culture, and learning styles* (rev. ed.). Baltimore, MD: Johns Hopkins.

Halpern, D. (1986). *Sex differences in cognitive abilities.* Hillsdale, NJ: Erlbaum.

Harel, I. (1988). *Software design for learning: Children's construction of meaning for fractions and logo programming.* Unpublished doctoral dissertation. MIT Media Laboratory, Cambridge, MA.

Harel, I., & Papert, S. (1990). Software design as a learning environment. *Interactive Learning Environments, 1*(1), 1–32.

Huttenlocher, J., & Presson, C. (1973). Mental rotation and the perspective problem. *Cognitive Psychology, 4*, 277–299.

Just, M. A., & Carpenter, P. (1985). Cognitive coordinate systems: Accounts of mental rotation and individual differences in spatial ability. *Psychological Review, 92*(2), 137–172.

Lampert, M. (1988). *The teacher's role in reinventing the meaning of mathematical knowing in the classroom.* Unpublished paper, Michigan State University, East Lansing, MI.

Liben, L., & Golbeck, S. (1980). Sex differences in performance on Piagetian spatial tasks: Differences in competence or performance? *Child Development, 51*, 594–597.

Liben, L., & Golbeck, S. (1984). Performance on Piagetian horizontality and verticality tasks: Sex-related differences in knowledge of relevant physical phenomena. *Developmental Psychology, 20*(4), 595–606.

Linn, M., & Petersen, A. (1985). Emergence and characterization of sex differences in spatial ability: A meta-analysis. *Child Development, 56*, 1479–1498.

Linn, M., & Petersen, A. (1986). A meta-analysis of gender differences in spatial ability: Implications for mathematics and science achievement. In M. Linn (Ed.), *The psychology of gender: Advances through meta-analysis.* Baltimore, MD: The Johns Hopkins University Press.

Linn, M., & Hyde, J. (1989). Gender, mathematics, and science. *Educational Researcher, 18*(8), 17–19, 22–27.

Marr, D., & Nishihara, H. K. (1978). Representation and recognition of the spatial organization of three-dimensional shapes. *Proceeding of the Royal Society* (pp. 269–294).

McGee, M. (1979). Human spatial abilities: Psychometric studies and environmental, genetic, hormonal, and neurological influences. *Psychological Bulletin, 86*(5), 889–918.

Olson, D. R., & Bialystok, E. (1983). *Spatial cognition: The structure and development of mental representations of spatial relations.* Hillsdale, NJ: Erlbaum.

Papert, S. (1980). *Mindstorms: Children, computers, and powerful ideas.* Basic Books.

Piaget, J., & Inhelder, B. (1967). *The child's conception of space.* New York: Norton & Co.

Pufall, P., & Shaw, R. (1973). Analysis of the development of children's spatial reference systems. *Cognitive Psychology, 5,* 151–175.

Rock, I. (1973). *Orientation and form.* Orlando, FL: Academic Press.

Sachter, J. E. (1990). *Kids n' space: Exploration into spatial cognition of children.* Unpublished doctoral dissertation, MIT Media Laboratory, Cambridge, MA.

Turkle, S. (1984), *The second self.* New York: Simon and Schuster.

Weir, S. (1986), *Cultivating minds: A Logo case book.* New York: Harper & Row.

Witkin, H. A. (1978). *Cognitive styles in personal and cultural adaptation.* Clark University Press.

Witkin, H. A. (1981). *Cognitive styles: Essence & origins.* New York: International University Press.

PART IV

CYBERNETICS AND CONSTRUCTIONISM

Children playing engineers. . .

HIPPO RAY FOR COMPUTER

Children playing psychologists. . .

The Agency Model of Transactions:
Toward an Understanding of Children's Theory of Control

Edith Ackermann*

INTRODUCTION

Cybernetics was defined by Norbert Wiener as the study of "control and communication in animals and machines" (Wiener, 1952). *First-order cybernetics* provides a description of regulatory processes in terms of circularities, feedback, and retroactions. *Second-order cybernetics* describes the evolution of complex systems in terms of self-organizing principles, emerging behavior, and equilibration processes. Researchers in cybernetics explore these phenomena by building working artifacts.

In exploring cybernetic ideas with children, our overall purpose is to develop and explore languages for describing the functioning of "simple-minded intelligent artifacts." We want to compare languages used by children with languages developed by scientists during the early days of cybernetics. We want to contrast descriptions produced while children observe an artifact's behavior ("playing psychologist") with descriptions useful to their building and programming ("playing engineer"). Finally, we want to compare languages used to describe *intelligent artifacts* (objects that act in a personlike way) with languages used to describe living creatures and inanimate objects, or things. Such a project is no doubt ambitious and requires a group effort in its realization.

Many reasons have led us to choose this topic, not the least of which is technological. At M.I.T., the time has come when we can offer children a

---

* This chapter is based on an Address given at the 11th Annual Meeting of the Archives Jean Piaget on Genetic Psychology and Cognitive Sciences, University of Geneva, Switzerland, September 1990. It represents work in progress. An extended version of this chapter will appear in the Proceedings of the Conference.

laboratory for building self-regulating devices. By a "self-regulating device," I mean a mechanism able to read or *sense* certain features in its environment (such as light, sound, or obstacles), to measure or *evaluate* their values in relation to internally fixed referents, and to *adjust its behavior* accordingly.

Our group has developed the building blocks out of which many kinds of "artificial creatures" can be built. The "creatures" are usually made out of LEGO bricks, gears, motors, and sensors, and controlled by a special version of the Logo programming language. Students in the Epistemology and Learning Group have created a variety of simple-minded sensorimotor artifacts capable of all sorts of goal-seeking and regulatory behaviors, such as sensing light, avoiding obstacles, and responding to sound. More recently, Fred Martin and others have designed a set of "electronic bricks" that can be wired directly onto the creatures, allowing for their "autonomy" from the desktop computer. While the work of Nira Farber (this volume) and Fred Martin (this volume) focuses on the functioning of a single "creature" in interaction with its environment, Mitchel Resnick (this volume) is currently building a computer-based microworld for exploring the behavior of very large populations of such simple-minded creatures.

The children we work with (most upper elementary and high-school students) are generally fluent enough in programming to design their own creatures (sometimes with the assistance of an adult). Under such circumstances, both experimenters and children find themselves in unusually rich terrain for exploring the functioning of artificial creatures. Not only can children *observe* the creatures' behaviors as they are moving around in a natural or "social" environment (usually a box with obstacles, lights, and sounds, as well as with other creatures), but they can *influence* their behaviors by acting upon their sensory input. Even more important, children can *modify* the creatures' behaviors *from within,* by reprogramming or rewiring them. In other words, children can switch roles from "playing engineer" to "playing psychologist"—from being the creatures' designer to being their external observer.

In this chapter, I focus on a specific issue that attracted my attention as a developmental psychologist. I analyze how children gradually come to disentangle purpose and causation, or psychological and physical explanations, when describing the behaviors of artificial creatures, as well as the behaviors of people and of things. Of particular interest are questions such as: Under which circumstances are children likely to favor psychological or physical explanations? When and how do children distinguish between the behaviors of animate and inanimate creatures? How do children gradually integrate causality and purpose when describing the behavior of artificial creatures that have the peculiarity of being objects yet act in person-like ways.

A survey of other researchers' work, together with my own preliminary results, indicates that, very early on, children actually construct a synthesis of these two kinds of explanations to make sense of the functioning of—and transactions among—people, things, and artifacts. The main characteristic of this synthesis is the description of a transaction in terms of "who" impacts "whom" (and how), and "who" is impacted by "whom" (and how). Causal chains are, in other words, understood in terms of how elements control one another's behavior, either through direct or mediated action (A *does* something to B, versus A *tells or signals* something to B).

Such a search for agency requires that children animate the actors in a transaction. The agency model, I claim, forms the core of what will become a cybernetic view of the world. And, like cybernetics, it provides a conceptual framework for explaining behavior across the range of the living and the inanimate. The ability to animate objects is a crucial step toward the construction of cybernetic theories. It is by no means a sign of cognitive immaturity.

CAUSALITY AND PURPOSE AMONG CYBERNETICIANS

We know from the history of cybernetics (and later, of AI and cognitive science) that as soon as the first intelligent artifacts were built, many fundamental concepts such as "self," "purpose," "intentionality," and "free will" needed to be reconsidered. The reason for this questioning is the profoundly ambiguous nature of these early artifacts. They were physical objects, yet they behaved in a somewhat human-like fashion. Their dual nature led both their builders (engineers) and their observers (psychologists) to engage in heated debates about the nature of their "intelligence." Could they be called intelligent in the first place? And if so, how could one best describe their intelligence?

The Macy Conferences provide the richest existing trace of the spirit in which these early discussions evolved (Von Foerster, Mead & Teuber, 1953). In studying the Macy Conferences, we notice time and again that engineers and psychologists quite consistently picked different sets of concepts for describing the functioning of self-regulating devices. More recent debates within the fields of AI and cognitive science seem to confirm the polarities already observed during the Macy Conferences (e.g., Boden, 1978; Dennett, 1987; Minsky, 1986). The story goes as follows:

Through actually building intelligent systems out of unintelligent parts, engineers make it clear that goal-orientedness (or knowing how to reach a goal) by no means requires the system's awareness (its knowing that it knows how to . . .), or intentionality (its deciding to . . .), or free will (if willing, it could . . .). Engineers usually insist that no vital principle needs to transcend, or live independently, from a material substrate. To them, if mind might well emerge from matter, the building of a mind—out of matter—does not require the use of higher-order concepts such as purpose and intentionality. For engineers, such concepts are not operational or useful in their work.

In contrast, most psychologists (as well as educators) study behavior *as it becomes meaningful to—and controllable by—a subject*. This is not surprising, since it is their job to help people use whatever reflecting capabilities they have (self-awareness) as a means of monitoring their own behavior. To the psychologist, the concept of "subject" is a useful construct, and so are the concepts of "purpose" and "intentionality." Their role is to capture at a glance what seems so specific to human cognition: namely, the ability to act upon its own activity as if it were a subject of inquiry, to evoke objects that are not physically present, to act (mentally or physically) upon objects (real or symbolic), and to choose the most appropriate among a set of possibilities to achieve a goal. Even Piaget, whose interest as a structuralist was in studying "what people *know how to do*" as opposed to "what they *think they know how to do*" (Piaget's own words), spent many years of his life trying to understand how babies gradually outgrow early reflex activity and become able to initiate, adjust, and inhibit action at their own will (Ackermann, 1990). In the enormous progress achieved during the first 2 years of their lives (the sensorimotor period), babies no doubt move from being entirely driven by many uncontrollable needs to partially monitoring their drives through self-correcting activities (circular reactions) and, later, through reflection (reflective abstraction). This transition from *reflex* to *reflective* activities, or from response to command, needs somehow to be captured by the cognitive psychologist.

CAUSALITY AND PURPOSE IN LAYPEOPLE: ADULTS AND CHILDREN

Developmental psychologist generally assume that cognitive growth starts with an initial state of indifferentiation between a subject and his or her environment (or of a dualism between the self and the outside world), and that it moves progressively toward a state of greater differentiation. The subject is thus enabled to perceive and describe the world (thing and others) as being separate from himself or herself. Even if such a view is generally accepted, the following two questions nevertheless remain:

1. Is this process of differentiation different when dealing with things and with people (or with inanimate and animate objects)?
2. Is this process as smoothly incremental and as universal as developmental psychologists generally assume?

People's ability to progressively disentangle purpose and causality gains to be situated within this broader developmental framework. Research in this domain leads to a somewhat contradictory picture.

On one hand, psychologists like Michotte (1963), Leslie (1979, 1984), Heider and Simmel (1944), and Steward (1982) suggest that one of the primary distinctions people make in understanding and dealing with the world is between things they react to as social objects (personlike), and things that they react to as nonsocial (thinglike). Very roughly speaking, social objects—or personlike things—are assumed to be active agents, capable of initiating behavior from within, and of directing, inhibiting, and modifying their behavior after an analysis of its effect or consequences. In other words, social objects are perceived as having some *controlling intelligence* that helps them monitor their activity. In constrast, nonsocial objects—or things—are assumed to be passive receivers, or recipients of others' actions. The action of a thing is nonintentional and not initiated from within. Instead, it is determined by external forces that act upon it. *Actions happen to them, rather than their causing actions to happen.*

This group of researchers claims that people recognize quickly, and at a young age, the difference between the functioning of social and nonsocial objects, and that people then regulate their behavior accordingly. These researchers consider that people usually describe social objects in psychological terms, and nonsocial objects in mechanical-causal terms.

On the other hand, we know from research by Piaget (1975), Carey (1985), diSessa (1982, 1988), Inagaki and Hatano (1987), and Turkle (1984) that young children do not, most of the time, distinguish mind from matter, or psychological from physical reality. Consequently, many things, such as moving objects, appear to them as endowed both with material properties and with will. To use Piaget's words:

> In early stages of their development, children do not draw limits between themselves and the external world. This leads us to expect that children will regard as living and conscious a large number of objects which are, for us, inanimate. (Piaget, 1975, p. 77)

Actions such as movements of an inanimate object are often seen as a result of a conscious effort. And if an agent *knows how* to do something, young children assume that it also *knows that it knows how* to do something.

CAUSALITY AND ANIMACY: A CLOSER LOOK

In the face of such apparently contradictory results, it is useful to look more closely into the existing body of research, in an attempt to develop an explanation for the apparent disparities. Such a preliminary survey is a necessary prerequisite to analyzing our own data. It has actually provided me with a model, or rather with a lens, through which I can make sense of children's attempts to disentangle the concepts of animacy and causality.

> There is a celebrated monograph, little known outside academic psychology, written a generation ago by the Belgian student of perception Baron Michotte. By cinematic means (shapes moving on a screen) he demonstrated that when objects move with respect to one another, within highly limited constraints, we see causality. (Bruner, 1986, p. 17)

Let me briefly describe Michotte's experiment on the perception of causality:

- In a first situation (1), a shape A moves toward a shape B, makes contact with B (hits it), stops, and then B moves away. All subjects immediately describe shape A as launching shape B.
- In a second situation (2), the action begins in the same way. Yet after A contacts B, both shapes continue in the same direction. In this case, shape A is described as dragging shape B.
- If, as in the third situation (3), the time span increases between the moment when A hits B and the departure of B, people tend to split the episode into two parts: B is no longer seen as responding to the action of A but is described as initiating its own movement.

Michotte's experiment was initially designed for adults. It has since been replicated with young children (Piaget & Lambercier, 1958) and with infants (Leslie, 1979, 1984). Leslie was interested in the origins of such perception of causality in very early childhood. His experimental procedure consisted of measuring signs of surprise in 6-month-old infants. Leslie showed infants a sequence of cinematic episodes that we, as adults, see as "being caused." He then interspersed one noncausal episode (sequences showing action at distance), and the infants, he claims, showed startled surprise.

Yet another variation of Michotte's experiments was undertaken by Fritz Heider and Marianne Simmel (1944), who used a bare animated film to demonstrate the immediacy of "perceived intention." They presented adults with a scenario made out of a small moving triangle, a large moving circle, and a boxlike empty rectangle. All the shapes moved in and around the empty box. Observers unanimously described the movements as a series of animate moves with clear social intent, like chase, fight, protection, attack, and so on. According to Bruner, the scene was usually perceived by adults as two friends being pursued by a large, bully-type creature who, upon being thwarted, broke up the house in which he had tried to find them. All the scenarios produced instances of social causation.

Finally, Judith Steward brought Michotte's experiment a step further, by showing that very specific properties of movement systematically trigger intentional rather than causal interpretations. In an experiment called "Object motion and perception of animacy," Steward presented adults with 35 displays programmed on an Apple II computer. The displays showed moving dots in a variety of situations.

Either the source of a dot's movement is unknown (as dot just starts), or it is triggered by something else. In some cases, the dots move together in a straight line. In other cases, they don't. One dot might overtake another through sudden acceleration, or it might decelerate and stop. Dots might change the course of their trajectory, and make detours around obstacles. Steward has varied the spatiotemporal constraints of dots' movements in such a way as to produce apparent "animacy" or "causality." Her question to the subject was very simple: "I have done a series of simulations of movement of objects and creatures. I will show them to you one by one, and you tell me if you think they are objects, creatures, or whether you cannot tell."

Steward shows that subjects plainly see goal-seeking persistence, or purpose, when dots initiate behavior, when they overcome obstacles, and when they accelerate and change the course of their trajectories. Inanimate objects, in contrast, are supposed to conserve their heading, their direction, and their speed. If they do not conserve their speed, inanimate objects can only decelerate (or die out).

Note that, with the exception of Leslie, this first group of researchers essentially studied adults. Their findings are nonetheless widely used to show that people recognize quickly, and at a young age, the difference between the functioning of social and nonsocial objects, and that people then regulate their behavior accordingly (Bruner, 1986).

Research by Carey, DiSessa, Piaget, and Inagaki and Hatano, on the other hand, shows that purpose and causation are not always as clearly distinguished as suggested by the first group of researchers. Young children, as well as adults, tend to personify objects and, at times, to objectify persons. In Piaget's study on animism, young children quite generally express the idea that objects, such as a stone or a piece of wood, cannot be hit or broken without feeling the impact. In a similar way, a watch cannot give the time without knowing that it does so, and a boat cannot carry people without making an effort and, of course, it feels that it is making an effort.

A more careful reading of children's protocols, however, shows that their analysis of the circumstances under which an object is likely to feel an impact is extremely subtle. My favorite example comes from Ali, age 8½. The experimenter asks Ali whether he thinks that a cloud could feel things—like, for example, a sting. The child answers that, of course, a cloud cannot feel a sting. How could it, since it is only air? Later in the interview, however, Ali comes back and mentions that clouds actually do feel wind and warmth, since it is both wind and warmth that drives them. Another child, around the same age, thinks that a wall cannot feel anything ("because it is strong!"). It is only when someone hits it really hard and knocks it down that it feels something ("because *that* would break it"). The point here is that if children may well be animistic, they are so in an extremely selective fashion. The interaction between elements needs to make sense, and moreover, the personification of an element needs to respect and possibly explain physical laws or psychological principles (Hatano & Inagaki, in preparation)

What does this apparently conflicting body of research tell us about children's ability to disentangle purpose and causation?

First, it reminds us that intentions do indeed constitute a fundamental and quite primitive category with which personal experience and transactions between objects (alive or not) are organized. Young children tend to view physically caused events as being psychologically intended. This does not imply that children simply project humanlike properties to all physical or biological agents indifferently. By *agent* I mean an element (alive or not) that is currently acting upon another element during a transaction. Children introduce increasingly subtle distinctions between specific situations. They attribute more or less control (will) depending on whether they see an agent as being omnipotent—and omniscient—and also, on whether they perceive the limits of their own ability to impose their will over people and things (Inagaki & Hatano, 1987).

The examined body of research, moreover, helps us identify specific properties of an agent's behavior which trigger purposive rather than causal explanations (Michotte, 1963; Steward, 1982). If a blob initiates a movement by itself, if it "knows" how to change direction or speed along its way, and/or if it "insists" on a goal-seeking motion, both children and adults tend to *animate* it, or to describe it in psychological terms. They give it a soul (anima), or a brain, to account for the self-regulatory aspect of its behavior. On the other hand, if a blob starts moving and changes direction or speed under the impact of another blob, both children and adults tend to *objectify* it. One could say that such a blob has no inner locus of control, and thus no *anima*.

However, our own explorations—as well as a closer look into children's responses to Michotte's and Heider and Simmel's experiments—indicate that causality and animacy are not always as clearly differentiated (as suggested by Michotte and others). In a recent doctoral thesis, Thommen (1990) studied children's perception of "intentional causality" (her words) when presented with Heider and Simmel's animated film. Her analysis shows that children between age 3 to 12 only progressively construct clear distinctions between purpose and causation when describing the scenario (see also Gilliéron & Thommen, 1987).

Moreover, in analyzing the exact terms used by young subjects in Michotte's experiment (Piaget & Lambercier, 1958), and in asking them to be explicit about the prerequisites and consequences of each blob's activity, we see that children certainly mingle intentions and causes, yet in a very consistent way. They animate or disanimate agents as they focus on particular aspects of their activity.

THE AGENCY MODEL OF TRANSACTIONS: A STEP TOWARD A THEORY OF CONTROL

Children's explanations of mechanical-casual realities, as well as of biological and psychological realities, are remarkably consistent across domains. They are best captured by what I call an "agency model of transactions." Such a model becomes progressively refined during ontogeny. It varies across situations and evolves as a transaction occurs. The story goes as follows: Imagine an agent A (alive or not alive) acting upon a recipient B, either by directly *doing* something to B (impacting it) or by *telling* it something (giving it a command). If the child does not know—or pay attention to—what has triggered A's behavior in the first place, then A tends to be seen as an active agent initiating behavior "at its own will." And usually, as A becomes animated, B gets objectified. Now, as soon as you ask children to think about the consequences of A's behavior, they turn their attention to the recipient B and begin to envisage its ability to respond. My claim is that, as soon as this shift of attention takes place, young children actually animate B. Instead of being a simple recipient, B thus turns into an agent. The child focuses on *its* feelings and *its* ability to act, or react, and by doing so, dismisses B's initial objectlike passivity. Once focused, B gains life and autonomy. It can now feel an impact, bounce off, hit other elements, and hit back.

Note that it is only insofar as B is able to react to A that A's action can be described as a signal. In effect, how could a signal *flow* from A to B, if A's action (physical impact or command) did not affect B's behavior somehow? If B *acts forward* (impacting a third element C), we—researchers—usually describe the event as a linear "casual" chain. If instead, B *acts back* on A, modifying its behavior, we think of the event as circular causality, or feedback. In both cases, the actors at play (alive or not alive, agents or recipients) can be said to *control one another's behavior*. They do so either via a physical impact (A *does* something to B) or via instructions (A *tells* something to B). In the first case, we—researchers—tend to describe the transaction as a case of physical or mechanical causality. In the second case, we talk about information or signal processing. Unlike adult researchers, young children do not seem to distinguish between mechanical causality and signal processing. Instead, they consistently animate agents under scrutiny. And since recipients (who were previously objectified) can themselves become "alive," children are able to view a transaction from different perspectives. They learn to describe how different elements (actors) affect or *control* one another's behavior. Whether these actors are alive or not alive, or whether they act—and affect a recipient's behavior—by actually "pushing" it (physical impact) or by sending it a "message" (information), seem less relevant. The agency model, on the other hand, facilitates the distinction between linear and circular causality. Such a distinction becomes possible as soon as the child understands that a given agent (B) could both *act forward* by impacting a third element (C), and *act backward* by reacting to a first element (A).

Many questions can be asked based upon this agency model of transactions. Here are a few: What triggered an agent's behavior? Does an agent recognize the consequence(s) of its own activity? If it does, can it modify its behavior accordingly? Can a recipient be sensitive to an agent's impact? How and why will it respond? In answering these questions, children refine their descriptions of a transaction, while at the same time, they reveal how they articulate purpose and causation. Note that, very often, children pose these questions for themselves without an adult's intervention.

The objective of my current research on children's development of cybernetics explanations is to probe the explanatory power of the agency model in a variety of settings. I use "agencies" as a framework for designing experiments, for generating questions, and, above all, as a lens for interpreting children's spontaneous descriptions. My long detour into children's theories of human and nonhuman transactions was a prerequisite to studying their developing theories of minds (their own and other creatures' minds). When describing the functioning of simple-minded artificial creatures (interacting with their environments, or among themselves), children do, indeed, think in terms of agencies (of "who" is controlling "whom" or "what"). And agencies, I suggest, are an essential step toward a cybernetic view of the world.

SUMMARY

In this chapter, I discussed how children come to disentangle *purpose* and *causation*—or psychological and physical descriptions—when explaining the behaviors of "simple-minded intelligent artifacts," as well as the behaviors of people and of things. I argued that, very early on, children attempt to build a synthesis between these two kinds of explanations, and that they do so in a similar way when explaining the functioning of people, of objects, and of living and artificial creatures. The most striking characteristic of this synthesis is children's focus on "who" is impacting "whom" (and how), and "who" is impacted by "whom" (and how) in a given transaction. Both people and things are understood in terms of how they *control* each other's behavior, either through direct or mediated action (A *does* something to B, or *tells or signals* something to B, and B *acts or signals* back accordingly). Such an agency model of transactions requires that the actors at play be animated. It forms the core of what will become a cybernetic view of the world. And, like cybernetics, it provides a conceptual framework for explaining control and communication across the range of the living and the inanimate. Young children's tendency to *animate* objects constitutes a crucial step toward the construction of cybernetic theories. It is by no means a sign of cognitive immaturity.

ACKNOWLEDGMENT

I wish to thank Aaron Falbel, Idit Harel, Mitchel Resnick, and Carol Strohecker for their support and help in writing this article. Their suggestions, criticisms, and encouragements were precious to me. I also wish to thank whose whose ideas informed my writing. I am deeply grateful to Bärbel Inhelder, Guy Cellérier, Andy DiSessa, Heinz von Foerster, Christiane Gillièron, Ernst von Glaserfeld, Seymour Papert, Jean Piaget, Marvin Minsky, Evelyne Thommen, and Mike Travers. Above all, I wish to thank all the members of the Epistemology and Learning Group, my current and former students, and my colleagues from the F.P.S.E., in Geneva. They are all living in my mind and heart. I especially wish to thank the children whose creative and generous minds are a main motivator in all my work.

REFERENCES

Ackermann, E. (1990). Circular reactions and sensori-motor intelligence: Why Piaget's theory meets cognitive models. *Archives de Psychologie, 58,* 65–78.

Boden, M. (1978). *Purposive explanation in psychology.* London, UK: The Harvester Press.

Bruner, J. (1986). *Actual minds, possible worlds.* Cambridge, MA: Harvard University Press.

Carey, S. (1985). *Conceptual change in childhood.* Cambridge, MA: MIT Press.

Dennett, D. C. (1987). *The intentional stance.* Cambridge, MA: MIT Press.

DiSessa, A. (1982). Unlearning Aristotelian physics: A study of knowledge-based learning. *Cognitive Science, 6,* 37–75.

DiSessa, A. (1988). Knowledge in pieces. In G. Forman & P. Pufall (Eds.), *Constructivism in the computer age.* Hillsdale, NJ. Erlbaum.

Epistemology and Learning Group. (1990). *Constructionist learning* (ed. by I. Harel). A Media Laboratory Publication. Cambridge, MA: MIT.

Gillièron, C., & Thommen, E. (1987). La perception de la causalité sociale chez l'enfant de 3 à 9 ans. *Psychologie et education, 3/4,* 158–161.

Hatano, G., & Inagaki, K. (in preparation). Everyday biology and school biology: How do they interact?. In S. Paris & W. Stevenson (Eds.), *Cultural perspectives on literacy, cognition and schooling.*

Heider, F., & Simmel, M. (1944). An experimental study of apparent behavior. *American Journal of Psychology, 57,* 243–259.

Inagaki, K., & Hatano, G. (1987). Young children's spontaneous personification as analogy. *Child development, 58,* 13–26.

Leslie, A. M. (1979). *The representation of perceived causal connection.* Unpublished doctoral thesis, Department of Experimental Psychology, University of Oxford.

Leslie, A. M. (1984). Spatiotemporal contiguity and the perception of causality in infants. *Perception, 13,* 287–305.

Michotte, A. (1963). *The perception of causality.* New York: Basic Books.

Minsky, M. (1986). *Society of mind.* New York: Simon & Schuster.

Papert, S. (1980). *Mindstorms: Children, computers and powerful ideas.* New York: Basic Books.

Piaget, J. (1975). *The child's conception of the world.* Totowa, NJ: Littlefield, Adams. (Note: The discussion on animism is found in pp. 194–206)

Piaget, J., & Lambercier, M. (1958). La causalité visuelle perceptive chez l'enfant et chez l'adulte. *Archives de Psychologie, 36,* 77–201.

Steward, J. (1982). *Perception of animacy.* Unpublished doctoral thesis, University of Pennsylvania.

Thommen, E. (1990). *La perception de la causalité intentionnelle chez l'enfant de trois a douze ans.* Unpublished doctoral thesis, University of Geneva.

Turkle, S. (1984). *The second self.* New York: Simon & Schuster.

Von Foerster, H., Mead, M., & Teuber, L. (Eds.). (1949–53). *Cybernetics: Circular, causal, and feedback mechanisms in biological and social systems* (Transcripts of the 6th, 7th, 8th and 9th Josiah Macy Conference). Caldwell, NJ: Progress Associates.

Wiener, N., (1952). *Cybernetics, or control and communication in the animal and the machine*. New York: John Wiley & Sons.

Stephen Ocko Photography

Damal and Shawn, Project Headlight students, explore the workings of a LEGO/Logo car they built.

19
Children and Artificial Life

Mitchel Resnick and Fred Martin

INTRODUCTION

Scientific ideas have their greatest force when they begin to seep out of the scientific community and into the general culture. This has happened with computer-science ideas during the past decade. As computers have proliferated throughout society, so have computational ideas and computational metaphors. Mental mistakes that were once seen as "Freudian slips" are now viewed as "information-processing errors" (Turkle, 1984). Indeed, computational metaphors are influencing the way people think about things in nearly all disciplines, in nearly all parts of society.

Ideas from the emerging field of Artificial Life could have a similar influence in the next decade. Like biology, Artificial Life aims to explain how animals behave and how they evolve. But Artificial Life (or ALife, as it is sometimes called) tries to achieve this goal through a radically different approach. Rather than observing real animals, ALife researchers try to create artificial animals, typically in the form of robots and computer simulations. Some ALife researchers (Deneubourg, Goss, Franks, & Pasteels, 1989; Travers, 1989) are creating "artificial ants" on the computer screen, hoping to gain a better understanding of how real ants build nests and find food. Other ALife researchers (Reynolds, 1987) are creating "artificial birds," hoping to gain a better understanding of how real birds move together in flocks. In short, ALife researchers think that the best way to understand life is to build it. (For an overview of ALife research, see Langton, 1989.)

Artificial Life is not merely a field of research, but a set of powerful intellectual ideas—in particular, ideas about how complex systems (like living creatures) develop, interact, and behave. As ideas from Artificial Life infiltrate the culture, it is important to develop ways to share these ideas with children. Giving children access to ideas from the forefront of scientific research is, in general, a powerful pedagogic approach. When children sense that they are sharing in a new and dynamic enterprise, they are more likely to invest them-

379

selves in the process of learning. Thus, children can both benefit from and contribute to the dissemination of new scientific ideas.

In certain fields, such as high-energy physics, it is difficult to make cutting-edge ideas accessible and relevant to children. But that is certainly not the case with Artificial Life. There is something compelling and exciting about the idea of "Artificial Life." The study of Artificial Life is full of objects that are, in Sherry Turkle's phrase, "betwixt and between"—objects that straddle the fuzzy boundary between the living and the inert (Turkle, 1984). Such objects are the source of both tension and fascination. And that makes them rich terrain for learning.

Through ALife projects, students can explore a set of important scientific ideas that are generally ignored in precollege classrooms. In particular, students can explore ideas about *systems*. For example: How does the complex behavior of an ant colony emerge from the simple actions of individual ants? In working on ALife projects, students focus particularly on biological and ecological systems. But many of the ideas they learn (ideas like *feedback* and *levels of organization* and *emergence*) apply equally well to physical systems and social systems. Thus, ALife projects hold the promise of providing students with a new framework for thinking about a wide range of phenomena in the world.

In this chapter, we discuss how (and why) to make Artificial Life ideas and activities accessible to children. We draw on several years of experiences in both classrooms and informal-education settings (see, for example, Martin, 1988, and Resnick, Ocko, & Papert, 1988). Some of the examples involve computer-based systems that are already available commercially (like Logo and LEGO/Logo). Others involve systems that are in the research stage at our laboratory at MIT. With these tools, children can explore how (artificial) creatures behave in different environments, and how they interact with other (artificial) creatures. In the course of such projects, children explore some of the central themes of Artificial Life research.

LOGO AND LEGO/LOGO

One could argue that Artificial Life came to the classroom a long time ago, in the form of the Logo turtle (Papert, 1980). After all, isn't the Logo turtle a type of artificial creature? Well, yes and no. For the most part, students (and teachers) have tended to focus on the Logo turtle as a "drawing turtle": they use the turtle to draw geometric shapes, patterns, and pictures. But for the purposes of Artificial Life, it is more useful to think of the turtle in a different way—not as a drawing turtle, but as a "behavioral turtle."

Imagine, for example, a Logo program in which the turtle continually moves forward, but turns 160 degrees whenever it "sees" a red pixel under it. The turtle starts to have a "personality"; one could say that the turtle is "scared" of the color red. In this program, the Logo primitive COLORUNDER acts as a crude "sensor" for the turtle, providing the turtle with information about the "world" in which it lives.

In versions of Logo with multiple turtles, more complex examples are possible. Imagine a Logo program in which one turtle runs around randomly, while a second turtle "chases" the first (always setting its heading toward the first). The first turtle can be viewed as the "prey," the second turtle as the "predator." This simple microworld suggests many interesting experiments. If the prey is faster than the predator, will the predator ever catch the prey? If so, how long will it take?

This type of project begins to capture the spirit of Artificial Life. ALife projects typically involve a cycle of activities: build a new simulation, analyze what happens, develop a new theory, then modify the simulation to test the new theory. Every simulation leads to new questions and new simulations. In this way, ALife projects blur the traditional distinction between "theoretical" and "experimental" science. ALife projects blend theory and experiment, analysis and synthesis.

The integration of LEGO bricks with Logo programming (known as LEGO/ Logo) opens new possibilities for Artificial Life activities in the classroom. With LEGO/Logo, children can write Logo programs to control machines that they construct out of LEGO building pieces (including not only the traditional LEGO bricks, but also LEGO gears and motors and sensors). Students have used LEGO/Logo to build (and program) all sorts of things: merry-go-rounds, conveyer belts, automatic doors, moving sculptures (see, for example, Resnick, Ocko, & Papert, 1988). Most LEGO/Logo projects in schools today seem to focus more on "machines" than "creatures." Students often build machines that they have seen in the world—or fantasy machines that they would like to see in the world. But there is great potential for using LEGO/Logo as a construction set for artificial creatures.

In building LEGO/Logo creatures, *sensors* are particularly important. Using sensors, a LEGO/Logo creature can sense the world around itself—then change its behavior depending on what it senses. For example, a LEGO/Logo creature with a touch sensor can be programmed to change direction whenever it bumps into an obstacle. The motion of the creature is not fixed: It depends on what obstacles are in the room. With sensors, LEGO/Logo creatures don't just *act in* the world, they *interact with* the world.

ELECTRONIC BRICKS

Although LEGO/Logo is a rich construction environment, it does have some limitations. One problem is that LEGO/Logo machines must be connected with wires to a desktop computer. Wires are a practical nuisance, particularly when children use LEGO/Logo to create mobile "creatures." Wires get tangled with other objects in the environment, they get twisted in knots as the creature rotates, and they restrict the overall range of the creature. More important, wires are a conceptual nuisance. It is difficult to think of a LEGO/Logo machine as an autonomous creature as long as it is attached by umbilical cord to a computer.

The wiring problem could be eliminated by using an infrared link, as in television remote control. But we decided to make a more serious modification: We began to build the electronics *inside* the LEGO bricks (Martin, 1988). With these *Electronic Bricks*, students no longer need to connect their LEGO creatures into a personal computer. Rather, they can build computational power directly into their LEGO machines and creatures. No more umbilical cord.

We have created about a dozen types of Electronic Bricks, falling into four categories. There are *Action Bricks* (motors, lights), *Sensor Bricks* (light sensors, sound sensors), *Logic Bricks* (and-gates, flip-flops, timers), and a *Programmable Brick*. The Programmable Brick is a fully programmable computer with the power of an Apple IIe, built inside a LEGO brick the size of a deck of cards. Students can create different behaviors for their creatures by wiring Electronic Bricks together in different ways, much in the spirit of Valentino Braitenberg's *Vehicles* (Braitenberg, 1984).

Consider, for example, a simple creature with a Light-Sensor Brick (pointing upward) and a Motor Brick. The output from the Light-Sensor Brick is connected to the speed input of the Motor Brick. When the Light-Sensor Brick detects light above a certain threshold, it sends a signal to the Motor Brick, and the creature moves. When creature is in the dark, it stops. We dubbed this creature *Wary* (Figure 1). If you then replace the light-sensor with a sound-sensor and a Flip-Flop Brick, the creature might be called *Obedient* (Figure 2). Every sharp sound "flips" the state of the Flip-Flop Brick. So the creature stops moving when you clap your hands, then starts again when you clap again.

Students have worked with Electronic Bricks in several ways. Some have observed pre-built creatures, trying to figure out how the creatures work—much as ethologists observe animals (Granott Farber, 1990). Others have built creatures of their own, trying to create new behaviors from simple behavioral building blocks (Martin, 1988; Bourgoin, 1990).

THINKING ABOUT SYSTEMS

Viewing the world in terms of *systems* is a fundamental, organizing idea throughout the natural sciences, social sciences, and engineering. Yet precollege education rarely addresses systems-oriented concepts. Part of the problem is that students (and teachers) have not had appropriate tools to "mess about" with systems. New tools like LEGO/Logo and Electronic Bricks can change that. Through our observations of children building artificial creatures with LEGO/Logo and Electronic Bricks, we have found that they explore a wide range of systems ideas—including interaction, feedback, levels, and emergence.

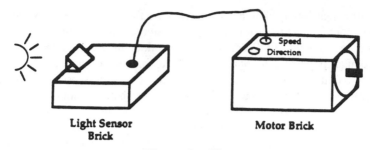

Light Sensor
Brick

Motor Brick

Figure 1.   Wary.

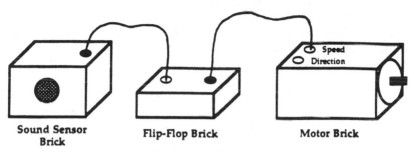

Sound Sensor
Brick

Flip-Flop Brick

Motor Brick

Figure 2.   Obedient.

Interaction. Systems are defined not only by their components or elements, but by the ways in which those component interact with one another. In LEGO/ Logo and Electronic Brick projects, interaction occurs at several levels: interactions among the components that make up a creature, interactions between the creature and the environment, and interactions between the creature and other creatures.[1]

In even the simplest activities, children begin to gain a sense of the interaction between creatures and the environment. Imagine a LEGO creature with a built-in motor to power its motion. When a child connects an Electronic Brick light sensor to the motor, the creature immediately begins reacting to changes in light. Moreover, children quickly discover that a creature's behavior can be changed not only by modifying the creature itself, but by changing the environment in which the creature lives. For example, children can add more lights to the environment, or make the lights flash. In many cases, the creature, placed in a new environment, reacts in unexpected ways, revealing new aspects of the creature's behavior—and driving home the importance of thinking about creatures in the context of their environments.

Feedback. Real creatures are not preprogrammed with an exact set of actions. Rather, they constantly modify their behaviors based on interactions with

---

[1] Of course, interactions between the creature and other creatures can be viewed as a special case of interactions between the creature and the environment.

the environment. Many engineered systems use the same strategy. A rocket, for instance, continually makes mid-course adjustments to stay on its desired course.

Children can build LEGO creatures that work on the same *feedback* principle. One popular project is to build a creature that moves toward the light. A feedback-based approach works as follows: If the creature senses that the light is brighter to the left, turn a bit to the left; if it senses that the light is brighter to the right, turn a bit to the right. With this simple strategy, the creature will (with a bit of weaving) move toward a bright light.

Of course, there are limitations to this strategy. For example, the creature will not necessarily move towards the brightest light in the environment. Imagine that there are two light bulbs near the creature: one bright bulb and one dim bulb. If the creature happens to "see" the dim bulb first, it might move toward that bulb, ignoring the brighter bulb. This problem is often referred to as the "local maximum" problem. Such problems are typically not discussed until college engineering courses. But LEGO creatures provide a meaningful context for children to start exploring such problems as early as elementary school.

Levels. As students play with artificial creatures, we are particularly interested in how the students think about the creatures. Do they think of the LEGO creatures as machines, or as animals? In fact, we have found that students (and adults) regard the creatures in many different ways. Sometimes students view their creatures on a *mechanistic* level, examining how one LEGO piece makes another move. At other times, they might shift to the *information* level, exploring how information flows from one Electronic Brick to another. At still other times, students view the creatures on a *psychological* level, attributing intentionality or personality to the creatures. One creature "wants" to get to the light. Another creature "likes" the dark. A third is "scared" of loud noises.

Sometimes, students will shift rapidly between levels of description. Consider, for example, the comments of Sara, a fifth grader (Martin, 1988). Sara was considering whether her creature would sound a signal when its touch sensor was pushed:

> *It depends on whether the machines wants to tell . . . if* we *want the machine to tell us . . . if we* tell *the machine to tell us.*

Within a span of 10 seconds, Sara described the situation in three different ways. First she viewed the machine on a psychological level, focusing on what the machine "wants." Then she shifted intentionality to the programmer and viewed the programmer on a psychological level. Finally, she shifted to a mechanistic explanation, in which the programmer explicitly told the machine what to do.

Which is the correct level? That is a natural, but misleading, question. Complex systems can be meaningfully described at many different levels. Which level is "best" depends on the context: on what you already understand, and on what you hope to learn. In certain situations, for certain questions, the mechanistic level is the best. In other situations, for other questions, the psychological level is best. By playing with artificial creatures, students can learn to shift between levels, learning which levels are best for which situations.

Emergence. In many systems, certain behaviors or patterns *emerge* from interactions among system components. For example, the patterns in a bird flock emerge from the interactions among individual birds. Similarly, the behavior of a market economy emerges from the interactions among millions of economic actors. These behaviors or patterns are not explicitly programmed or represented in the system components. Rather, these emergent behaviors represent a higher "level" in the system. This higher level must be described with different parameters than those used to describe the lower level components.

In many animals systems, there are two types of emergence. First, the behavior of each individual creature emerges from interactions among the "agents" that make up the creature's mind (Minsky, 1988). At the same time, the behavior of the entire animal colony or society emerges from the interactions among the individual creatures. In short, the colony level emerges from the creature level, which in turn emerges from the agent level.

With LEGO/Logo and Electronic Brick creatures, children can begin to observe and experiment with emergent behaviors. Consider a simple LEGO creature with a light sensor pointing upward. Imagine that the creature is programmed with two rules: (a) move forward when you detect light; (b) move backward when you are in the dark. When this creature is released in the environment, it exhibits a type of emergent behavior: It seeks out the edge of a shadow, then happily oscillates around the shadow edge. The creature can be viewed as an "Edge-Finding Creature." This edge-finding capability is not explicitly represented in the creature's two rules. Rather, it emerges from those rules.

Here is another example. When we started to develop LEGO/Logo, one of our first projects was to program a LEGO "turtle" to follow a line on the floor. The basic strategy was to make the turtle weave back and forth across the line, making a little forward progress on each swing. First, the turtle veered ahead and to the right, until it lost sight of the line. Then it veered ahead and to the left, until it again lost sight of the line. Then it started back to the right, and so on. This behavior can be represented by two simple rules: (a) if you are veering to the left and you lose sight of the line, begin to veer right; (b) if you are veering to the right and you lose sight of the line, begin to veer left.

We tried the program, and the turtle followed the line perfectly. But as the turtle approached the end of the line, we realized that we hadn't "programmed in" any rules for what to do at the end of the line. We didn't know what the turtle would do. We were pleased with the behavior that emerged: The turtle turned all the way around and started heading back down the line in the other direction. This "end-of-line" behavior was not explicitly programmed into the turtle. Rather it emerged from the interactions between the turtle's rules and the unfamiliar environment at the end of the line.

Of course, these examples represent rather simple cases of emergence. But emergence is an ill-defined and poorly understood concept. Simple cases are probably the best place to start—perhaps not just for children and novices, but for scientists as well.

THINKING ABOUT THEMSELVES

Playing with Artificial Life systems can influence the way children think about systems of all kinds: physical systems, political systems, economic systems. But perhaps most important is how it influences the way children think about *themselves* as systems.

While building and programming artificial creatures, children naturally ask questions abut themselves. In some cases, Artificial Life activities encourage children to reexamine things that once seemed obvious. As children try to make their creatures move, they reexamine how they themselves walk. And they reflect on the advantages and disadvantages of walking versus rolling, of legs versus wheels. (These activities exemplify what Papert, 1980, calls "body syntonic" learning.)

As children add light sensors to their creatures, they wonder: What would it be like to have only one eye? Or three? As children work with sensors, they also gain a deeper understand of how their own senses work. At first, many children think that LEGO sensors will work "by themselves." They put a touch sensor on the front of a creature, for example, and they expect the creature to automatically change direction when it bumps into something. They don't realize that they must *program* that behavior into the creature (by writing a Logo program, or making the appropriate connections among Electronic Bricks).

This mistake is not all that surprising. Johnson and Wellman (1982) showed that fifth-grade children generally view the brain as the organ of mental life. Thus, children see the brain as essential for thinking, dreaming, and remembering, but they deem it irrelevant to walking, sneezing, or sensing. After building and programming artificial creatures, children generally have a much different view. They recognize the important role that the brain plays in processing sensory inputs and orchestrating actions by the body.

Through our work with Artificial Life and children, we hope to gain a sharper sense of how children think about their own minds. As children build and program artificial creatures, how will their images of the mind change? Karen Thimmesch, a teacher at Galtier Magnet School in St. Paul, Minnesota, has begun to investigate this question. She asked her fourth-grade students to draw pictures showing how information is transmitted and processed inside their own heads.

The children's pictures indicate a wide range of metaphors—in some ways mirroring the metaphors of mind that scientific researchers have used through history. Some students used transportation metaphors, showing cars and bicycles carrying information around the brain (Figure 3). Other used communications metaphors, showing telephone wires (Figure 4) or walkie-talkies throughout the brain (Figure 5). Some children relied on computational metaphors, showing a little person at a computer terminal inside the head (Figure 6). Of course, scientists these days prefer distributed (not centralized) computational metaphors of the mind, with "societies" of agents interacting with one another (Minsky, 1988). Some children had similar ideas (Figure 7). The most unusual picture, perhaps, was an ant colony in the brain (Figure 8). This might seem strange at first, but many ALife researchers and cognitive scientists view ant colonies as one of the best metaphors for the brain/mind (e.g., Hofstadter, 1979). In this view, each individual (ant or neuron) is capable of very little, but collectively they are far more than the sum of the parts.

How will children's images of their minds evolve as they spend more time with artificial creatures? So far, we do not know; we are just starting to study this question. But we expect that Artificial Life activities will influence children's ideas in a fundamental way. No one expects children to come up with answers to ages-old questions about the mind, but it is important for them to think about these questions, to play with new ideas and try them out. At the least, LEGO/Logo and Electronic Bricks will give children a better set of tools for thinking about an important set of questions.

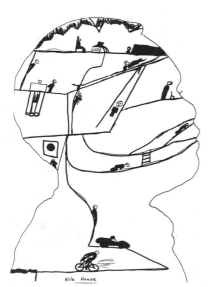

Figure 3. Transportation metaphors.

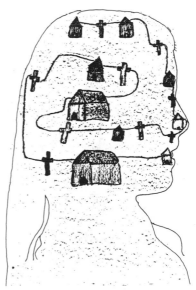

Figure 4. Communication metaphors.

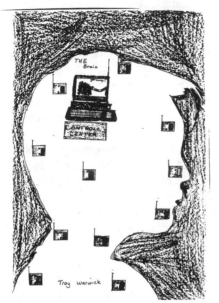

Figure 5.   Wireless communication.

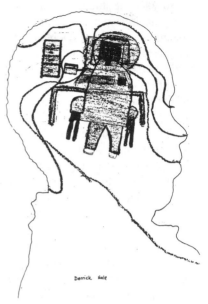

Figure 6.   Hacker in the head.

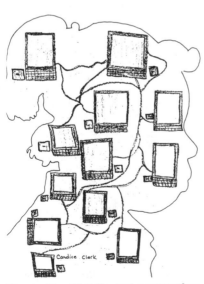

Figure 7.   Distributed computing.

Figure 8.   Brain as ant colony.

IS IT TOO SOON?

Some people might wonder whether it is appropriate (or feasible) to introduce ideas from Artificial Life at a precollege level. After all, scientists themselves do not have a very good understanding of the mechanisms (or even the meaning) of Artificial Life. Shouldn't we wait until scientists figure it out before introducing it in schools?

Our answer is an emphatic *no*. Although ideas like emergence are still poorly understood, certain core ideas of Artificial Life are clear. And new computational tools (like LEGO/Logo and Electronic Bricks) make it possible for precollege students to explore these ideas, at least qualitatively, if not formally. By building and programming artificial creatures, and by discussing and thinking about the results, children begin to view the world through a systems-oriented lens. The fact that scientists are still struggling to construct the intellectual framework of Artificial Life can, in fact, be turned to advantage. Too often, school science insulates students from the excitement that drives real scientific research. By exploring Artificial Life, students can share in the excitement.

Scientists, too can learn a great deal from the introduction of Artificial Life into the classroom. In many cases, the best way to clarify a new (and still-fuzzy) idea is to try to make it accessible to children. In developing explanations and tools for children, researchers are forced to confront the core issues in a domain. They must strip away levels of detail and formalism, and focus on the central concepts of the domain. As a result of this process, not only do students get a better sense of the domain, but so do the researchers.

ACKNOWLEDGMENTS

Many of the ideas in this chapter are based on collaboration with Seymour Papert, Stephen Ocko, Edith Ackermann, and Brian Silverman. In addition, Mike Eisenberg and Franklyn Turbak provided helpful comments on a draft of the chapter. We are particularly grateful to Karen Thimmesch of Galtier Magnet School of the St. Paul Public Schools for sharing her experiences and students' drawings with us. Our research on LEGO/Logo is supported by grants from the LEGO Group and the National Science Foundation (Grants 85101-0195, MDR-8751190, and TPE-8850449). Some of the ideas in this chapter were previously presented in a paper titled "LEGO, Logo, and Life" (Resnick, 1989).

REFERENCES

Bourgoin, M. (1990). Children using LEGO robots to explore dynamics. In I. Harel (Ed.), *Constructionist learning*. Cambridge, MA: MIT Media Laboratory.

Braitenberg, V. (1984). *Vehicles*. Cambridge, MA: MIT Press.

Deneubourg, J. L., Goss, S., Franks, N., & Pasteels, J. M. (1989). The blind leading the blind: Modeling chemically mediated army ant raid patterns. *Journal of Insect Behavior, 2*(5), 719–725.

Granott Farber, N. (1990). Puzzled minds and weird creatures: Spontaneous inquiry and phases in knowledge construction. In I. Harel (Ed.), *Constructionist learning.* Cambridge, MA: MIT Media Laboratory. (See also this volume, Chapter 15)

Hofstadter, D. (1979). *Godel, Escher, Bach: An eternal golden braid.* New York: Basic Books.

Johnson, C. N., & Wellman, H. M. (1982). Children's developing conceptions of the mind and the brain. *Child Development, 53,* 222–234.

Langton, C. (Ed.). (1989). *Artificial life.* Redwood City, CA: Addison-Wesley.

Martin, F. (1988). *Children, cybernetics, and programmable turtles.* Unpublished master's thesis, MIT Media Laboratory, Cambridge, MA.

Minsky, M. (1988). *The society of mind.* New York: Simon & Schuster.

Papert, S. (1980). *Mindstorms: Children, computers and powerful ideas.* New York: Basic Books.

Resnick, M. (1989). LEGO, Logo, and life. In C. Langton (Ed.), *Artificial life.* Redwood City, CA: Addison-Wesley.

Resnick, M., Ocko, S., & Papert, S. (1988). LEGO, Logo, and design. *Children's Environments Quarterly, 5*(4), 14–18.

Reynolds, C. (1987). Flocks, herds, and schools: A distributed behavioral model. *Computer Graphics, 21*(4), 25–34.

Travers, M. (1989). Animal construction kits. In C. Langton (Ed.), *Artificial life.* Redwood City, CA: Addison-Wesley.

Turkle, S. (1984). *The second self: Computers and the human spirit.* New York: Simon and Schuster.

Stephen Ocko Photography

Rachel and Mimi, Project Headlight students, build an amusement park with LEGO/Logo.

20

Treasureworld:
A Computer Environment for the Study and Exploration of Feedback

Aaron Brandes and Uri Wilensky*

FEEDBACK AS A POWERFUL CONCEPT

Cybernetics, the study of self-regulating mechanisms, was a strong scientific movement during the period from the 1940s to 1950s (e.g., Von Foerster, 1953; Wiener, 1954). The concepts of positive and negative feedback were used to study subjects ranging from goal-driven mechanisms, to family systems, to the human brain and body. The word *feedback*, like many scientific terms, has passed into popular parlance. People say things like "The teacher gave me feedback about my paper." In this case, they may mean "criticism," "praise," "a grade," "comments on." However, the teacher–student system will only form a feedback loop if the student takes the teacher's response as a measure of the ways in which the paper deviates from some kind of "goal state," and then revises it in that direction.

Feedback is one of the mechanisms we use in daily life, yet we may be unaware of it. We are constantly using feedback to act and navigate in the world. The thermostat, for example, operates on a feedback principle. A desired temperature is set. The actual temperature is then measured. If this temperature is lower than the desired temperature, the heating system is turned on. If the temperature is higher, the heating system is turned (or left) off. If there is a cooling system, the corresponding appropriate actions are taken. Yet many people believe that the thermostat is like a valve, and they will therefore turn it up higher than the desired temperature to get the room to heat up more quickly (e.g., Kempton, 1986). Thus we may miss opportunities to learn about feedback from mechanisms around us through misapprehension of how they work.

---

* This work is a collaboration. There is no primary author.

It is also possible that the sheer effectiveness of these devices suppresses any need to understand them. We may think, for example, "the thermostat keeps the room at the right temperature." No explanation is needed. In a similar way, it is easy to steer a car without conscious thought about the feedback process involved.[1] The hands turn the steering wheel, the wheels of the car turn, and our eyes detect any difference between where we are heading and where we want to go. The difference between the desired state and the actual state is usually detected without our conscious attention. Just as subconsciously, our hands respond to the difference, adjusting the position of the steering wheel. Conscious thought enters only when a problem arises.

Our focus here is on "negative feedback loops," in which the response to the feedback decreases the difference between the current state and the desired state. In contrast, in a "positive feedback loop" this difference is increased. Consider, for example, a sink or shower with its hot and cold faucets reversed. Sensing that the water is too cold, a person will turn the "hot" faucet. Since this is really the cold faucet, the water will get colder, and the person may continue turning that faucet on more, or turning the other faucet off. The expectation of a negative feedback loop is so strong and unconscious that it interferes with understanding the situation. Interesting system behavior can also result when two negative feedback mechanisms with differing goals interact. It has been observed, for example, that on average Italians prefer to be physically closer to people they are talking to than do the English. An Italian and an Englishman in conversation may therefore perform quite a "dance." As the Italian moves closer, the Englishman will back away, provoking the Italian to continue the pursuit.

The approach of our research is to put children in a negative feedback loop. Making explicit part of the feedback loop provides the student in the loop an opportunity to learn about feedback, while simultaneously allowing us to observe and study the development of this learning process. The game, *Treasure*, is the tool we developed to accomplish these goals. In our research we were interested in whether there would be stages in learning to play the game, and what differences in style could be observed. Although learning and understanding feedback was our initial research focus, during our research other concepts—of strategy, information, and model building—became important to our assessments as well.

Before discussing our methods and results in detail, here is a brief summary. We found that the group of children (primarily fourth graders) we studied were able to use sensory feedback to find a hidden treasure. Nevertheless, this was a nontrivial task. Most children went through a common set of stages in mastering the search for the treasure. Differences in style in mature play were also observed.

---

[1] The authors remember wondering, as children, how they would learn to steer. Watching someone else drive (especially in a movie or on television), it was not at all apparent what the connection was between the movement of the steering wheel, and the amount the car turned.

WHAT IS TREASUREWORLD?

Treasureworld is a LOGO based learning environment for exploring strategy and feedback. We intend to create a number of games for *Treasureworld*. Our current research uses just one game, *Treasure*, which is based on the children's game of "hot and cold."[2] Each time a child plays, the location of the treasure is randomly selected. The object of the game is to find the treasure by moving a LOGO Turtle around the screen. After each move the Turtle gives sensory feedback. It sets its *color* and emits *sounds* to indicate how far it is from the treasure.

Treasure begins by asking the player for his or her name. The player's name is used to give the game a number of personal touches. The player is given an option to get directions for the game. There are four commands available to move the turtle: "cfd," "cbk," "crt," and "clt." These are analogous to the LOGO commands "fd," "bk," "rt," and "lt," which move the turtle forward or back, and turn the turtle right and left. For each command, the distance to be moved or the angle to be turned must be specified. To help the player interpret the color feedback, a line of turtles showing the colors from hottest (red, pink, . . .) to coldest (. . . , gray, dark gray) appears at the top of the screen. In the current implementation there are 14 different colors. The turtle begins at the home location (Figure 1). The game proceeds with the player issuing commands to move the turtle. The turtle then gives color and sound feedback based on its distance from the treasure. When the turtle comes to within five units of the selected location, the treasure has been found. The player is then congratulated by name and treated to a display of graphics (including a treasure chest opening and coins coming out) and music (the theme music from "Looney Toons" cartoons). The player then has an opportunity to have his or her moves replayed (see Figure 2a). This is possible because we created software which stores a log of all of the player's moves (see Figure 2b). As researchers, we found the logs to be a valuable tool for capturing and examining data.

The player also has an option to display a map of the colors corresponding to the regions of the screen[3] (as seen in Figure 3).

These options give the players a chance to review what they have done, and to learn from the experience. This option can be thought of as second-order feedback, because it is feedback on the strategy as a whole, not the individual move.

In designing *Treasureworld*, our goal was to create an environment for the study of feedback in which students with a variety of styles could be successful.

---

[2] To play this children's game, one child leaves the room and an object is hidden. When the child returns the other children give the child verbal feedback as to how far the child is from the treasure. This feedback can range from the simple "hot," "hotter," to the more metaphoric "You're ice cold" or "you're burning up."

[3] Because we measure distance as the sum of the horizontal and vertical distance, the map is collection of nested diamond-shaped regions.

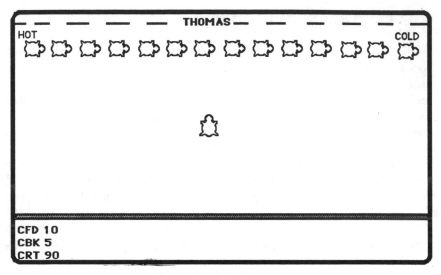

Figure 1. Initial Screen.

Each of the turtles in the "strip of turtles" at the top of the computer screen is a different color, ranging from red (hottest) to dark gray (coldest). The "action turtle" is white, and positioned at the Logo "Home" position ($x=0$; $y=0$). The bottom of the screen is the LogoWriter "Command-Center," where the user types commands to move the turtle in search of the treasure. As the user starts the game, he or she is asked to enter his or her name, which appears at the top-center of the screen throughout the game.

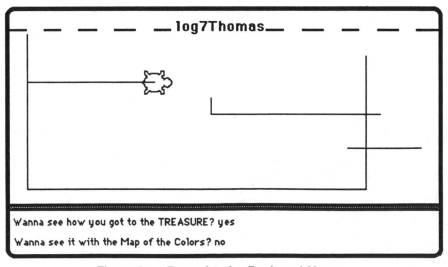

Figure 2a. Example of a Replay of Moves.

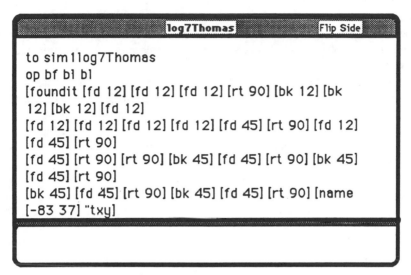

```
to sim1log7Thomas
op bf bl bl
[foundit [fd 12] [fd 12] [fd 12] [rt 90] [bk 12] [bk
12] [bk 12] [fd 12]
[fd 12] [fd 12] [fd 12] [fd 12] [fd 45] [rt 90] [fd 12]
[fd 45] [rt 90]
[fd 45] [rt 90] [rt 90] [bk 45] [fd 45] [rt 90] [bk 45]
[fd 45] [rt 90]
[bk 45] [fd 45] [rt 90] [bk 45] [fd 45] [rt 90] [name
[-83 37] "txy]
```

Figure 2b.   Example of a Log.

We learned from other microworlds that the principles of *low threshold* and *syntonicity* would be valuable for engaging the children (Papert, 1973, 1980). Since we wanted children to reflect on their actions, we would provide them with opportunities to view things from different perspectives.

Feedback requires response to "differences which make a difference" (Bateson, 1972). In a rich and complex world, selecting which differences to

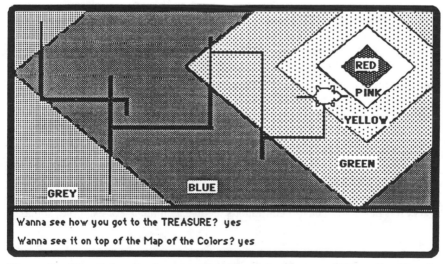

Figure 3.   The Color Regions on the Computer Screen (With a Replay of Moves).

attend to and interpret is a complicated (and often subconscious) task. In our microworld, the significant differences (change in sensory feedback) are made explicit. The player can then concentrate on interpreting the difference and responding to it.

We chose sensory feedback (sound and color) over words or numbers to encourage syntonicity. *Syntonic learning*, in contrast to *dissociated learning*, is learning that engages a person's sense and knowledge of something familiar. Sensory feedback is directly engaging; the turtle can be experienced as trying to communicate with the child. Using both color and sound increases access for children of different cognitive strengths.

Low threshold means that it should be easy to begin playing. We achieved this by using a small number of commands. These commands are very similar to LOGO Turtle commands. Since the children were familiar with the LOGO environment, the directions could be focused on the goals of the game. The meaning of the feedback is constant from game to game. Although location of the treasure is chosen randomly at the beginning of the game, it remains in the same place throughout the game. These regularities support an incremental learning process.

During the game, children respond to the feedback, possibly drawing on previous experiences during that game. Reflection from a more global point of view is encouraged at the end of the game by optionally replaying all of the moves and feedback responses. Children can see where they repeated an action or took a circuitous route. Looking at a map of the different color feedback zones offers another shift in perspective. Children can see the relative size of the zones, their shape, and how far each zone is from the treasure.

Our basic goals led to the design decisions and criteria just described. These criteria influenced further decisions. For example, we considered having motion commands for big, medium, and little steps. The child would then not have to make number selections. The resulting world would be simpler (in terms of choices) but less rich. We did not want to encourage unnecessary limitations. By encouraging exploration, we hoped a fuller learning experience would result.

Another important decision involved whether the feedback should be continuous (any change in the distance to the treasure changes the feedback, with small changes corresponding to small feedback differences) or discrete (all positions within a certain range of distances from the treasure result in the same feedback response.)[4] Having a small, discrete set of feedback responses also makes the problem of feedback interpretation much simpler, because different responses are easily distinguished. This puts more emphasis on the response to the feedback. It is possible to have a continuous feedback channel (for example, sound or

---

[4] Of course, even floating-point numbers are literally discrete on a digital computer.

number) in addition to a discrete one (for example, color).[5] However, we wanted these modes to complement each other. Furthermore, we did not want to make things unnecessarily complicated. Because the feedback responses are not continuous, some information theoretic aspects (such as how frequently to sample) enter more strongly into the game.

RESEARCH PHASES

Our research with *Treasureworld* involved two main phases. In the first phase we worked with children individually. In the second phase we worked with a classroom of children, with the collaboration of their teacher. The data we gathered included our written observations, videotape footage, logs of *Treasureworld* play, notes kept by the children, and observations made by the classroom teacher. The purpose and procedure will be presented for each phase. Observations of the children's play of the game, and further analysis, will follow.

Individual Interviews Phase

Goals. Initially we worked with individual children. In this phase we had a dual purpose. First, we wanted to see if the game "worked." Would children like it? Would it be too hard or too easy? Another goal was to explore the thought processes of the children as they played in the feedback environment. We could thus begin to formulate an understanding of the process and to make adjustments for the classroom phase and for subsequent research.

Methodology. We worked with the children one at a time, outside the classroom. Some of the students had seen the game and were eager to try it. Other children were selected by the classroom teacher. We aimed for a mix in gender and ability.[6] We introduced ourselves and the game to the children. During and after the game, we asked questions to evoke their thoughts and feelings. Why did you do that? Where do you think the treasure is? Could you find it again, no matter where the computer hides it? Did you like playing the game?

---

[5] On our target platform, the IBM PC jr, there is a limit of 16 colors; however, a virtually continuous range of sounds and numbers is available. The choice of the PC jr was dictated by our desire to support the growth of a *Treasure* "culture" by having the whole class play at once. We worked with children who were part of Project Headlight, an MIT assisted program in the Hennigan Elementary School. Hennigan is an inner-city public-school in Boston. Children have daily access to a network of IBM PC jrs.

[6] Some children who became "stars" in playing the game had difficulty in academic work.

Results. These initial observations were very encouraging. The children were very enthusiastic about playing the game. They showed great persistence in searching for the treasure, often taking well over a hundred moves to find the treasure. Typical patterns in the process of learning to play the game were observed. Differences in style also became apparent.[7]

Classroom Phase

Goals. We next used *Treasureworld* with a class of 19 fourth graders (a Spanish/English bilingual-class in Project Headlight). In this phase, children would have many opportunities to play the game. There would be a greater chance to explore the concepts of feedback and strategy. By working with a whole class, we hoped that a *Treasure* "culture" would emerge. Children could share their experiences in playing the game. Through classroom discussions, we explored the concepts of feedback and strategy together. We also intended to make more observations of children's play, and to increase our data base of game logs. This would help us build a better model of the children's learning experience, and to observe a wider range of playing abilities and styles.

Methodology. Children in the class already knew us from work we had done with them earlier.[8] We initiated our new phase of work with the class with a series of "pretest" interviews. The purpose of the interviews was to give us a baseline sense of each of the children in the class. At this point we also selected five children for closer observation according to their gender, ability, and personality.

We then met with the whole class to explain what we would be doing for the next few weeks. *Treasure* had developed a good reputation by word of mouth, so the children were looking forward to playing. The game was explained as being a computer game similar to the game of "hot and cold."[9] The goal was to find a hidden treasure. We stressed that the process of how they looked for the treasure was interesting to us. To encourage self-reflection, we gave them notebooks we had designed for them to record their experience.[10] During the first few sessions with the game, much of our effort was spent helping the children resolve their

---

[7] We observed that some of the children had difficulty getting the turtle to do what they wanted, particularly if the turtle was not moving horizontally. As a result we created some software using the turtle to explore the use of angle and distance.

[8] Before beginning this phase of the project we worked with the class using software we designed to help them exercise their ability to control the turtle, and to use angles and estimate distance. (See footnote 7). The children were asked to make notes on what they had learned. The use of the software helped prepare for using *Treasureworld* as a class activity.

[9] We asked the children if they were familiar with the "hot and cold" game, and they said they were; and we did observe them later playing the "hot and cold" game proficiently.

[10] The notebooks were modeled on the process-notebooks used by Idit Harel in her research (e.g., Harel, 1988).

technical problems in using the software, and making sure they understood how to play. From then on, the children played the game twice a week for 4 weeks. We gathered information on the children's process through three sources: direct observation, the logs created when the children played the game, and their notebooks.[11]

During a typical day, a cacophony of computer beeps rang out as the children played *Treasure*, in the Headlight computer pod. The computers were arranged in a large circle and also linked in a local area network. Some children talked to each other, and others bragged about how many times they found the treasure. We helped the children with technical difficulties and observed their play of the game. No attempt was made to "instruct" them in finding the treasure. After playing, the children were usually given time to write in their notebooks. We also worked directly with the class in a discussion format to explore the concept of strategy. More will be said about this in the results section.

We concluded our class sessions with a competition, in which the children formed five teams of three or four children. The teams were instructed to work together to find the treasure in as few moves as possible.[12] The children were enthusiastic about the team competition. All the teams did well by some measure (e.g., one team found it the greatest number of times, one had the best single game, one had the best average, etc.).

We conducted postinterviews with five of the children we had followed closely and held a competition among them to see who could teach *Treasure* the best. The competition involved teaching *Treasure* to other children.[13] The other children were introduced to the game, and allowed to play for half an hour, in order to get a baseline for their ability. Only one of them was able to find the treasure. Next, each was paired with one of the experienced children. These sessions took place one at a time, enabling us to observe and videotape the process. The children who were teachers were told they could use whatever method they wanted to teach the other children. This competition had a clear winner.

Results. Observations of stages and styles in the play of the game will be presented in separate sections. A few notes on our classroom discussions of strategy follow.

---

[11] The notebooks were intended to give us a window into the feelings, difficulties, and insights the children experienced during the process of mastering *Treasure*. Some class time was spent discussing and working on the note-writing process. Nevertheless, we found that the children did not tend to write much, and that much of what they wrote did not give us additional insight into their process.

[12] Choosing the fewest number of moves as a measure of proficiency biased our competition towards a more abstract style of play, one which we were accustomed to. Had we chosen to minimize time, however, rather than number of moves, the concrete players would have fared much better.

[13] Inspiration for this teaching activity came from the work of Idit Harel (see the "learning by teaching" principle in Harel, 1988, and Harel & Paper, 1990).

In our classroom discussions we found that the concept of strategy seemed difficult for the children, especially in the context of games.[14] We had more success when we asked them for strategies they might use to get a sibling to do a chore for them. Among the ideas they came up with: offer them something they wanted, threaten to tell the parent on them, take something away from them until they did what you wanted. They seemed to particularly enjoy being able to express the ''sneaky'' plans.

The classroom teacher was away at a conference during our class discussions of strategy. After her return, she was surprised when one of the girls in the class asked her, ''Do you think about us after school?'' This provoked a discussion in which the children raised such questions as ''Do you have strategies to make us learn?'' and ''Do you do use tricks to get us to react in a certain way?'' This was a novel way for the children to look at things and provides a concrete example of how they brought experiences from the game into other areas in their life.

DEVELOPMENTAL SEQUENCE OF STAGES

At first *Treasure* players *did not respond to the feedback by taking corrective action*. This stage was characterized by *moving randomly* around the screen. Even when they constrained themselves to staying on a single horizontal or vertical line, their step sizes often vary wildly, ranging from very small steps to steps that wrapped around the screen many times. Typically, after a child had ignored feedback, we asked: ''Did you just get colder or hotter?'' When the child responded ''colder,'' we then asked: ''so, are you closer or farther from the treasure?'' Often, the child would respond ''farther,'' and then, on the next move, continue in the same direction. Most children responded correctly to questions about both the warmth of the turtle color (or sound) and the interpretation of the color as distance, yet they were just as likely to move in the direction opposite to that indicated by this knowledge as they were to move treasureward.[15]

Sometimes we asked the children to guess where the treasure might be. Not only did they not have a guess, but the question appeared strange and sometimes amusing to them. It appeared that the concept of a fixed but invisible location for the treasure was foreign and hard to grasp.

---

[14] In one class we had the children list games they were familiar with. The first and largest category of games they listed were video games. In addition they came up with outdoor games, board games, and card games. But when asked to name strategies in these games they were at a complete loss. They were unable to abstract any rules from the remembered contexts. In Monopoly, for instance, they came up with strategies such as ''buy properties'' or ''get money.'' In general, in the context of games, they confused strategies with goals.

[15] In one case, Juan, on playing his first game, moved the turtle all over the screen for a protracted period of time. When we asked him what he was doing, he said that he wanted to see all the colors. Alas, we were blind researchers at the time and encouraged him to seek the treasure rather than enjoy the colors. After all, mad pursuit of coins is much preferable to stopping and smelling the flowers.

In the next stage, children *moved the turtle in a straight, usually horizontal line*. Some children did this the very first time they played *Treasure*, skipping over the first stage. Typically, the children moved the turtle to the right, and when encountering the end of the screen, "wrapped" to the leftmost edge and then continued in the same direction. They were content to watch the turtle move and retrace its steps over and over. Initially, while the turtle may have passed over the same trail, it may not have landed on precisely the same spots it had before, so the feedback pattern may have been different for each pass across the screen. However, the children often used the same numeric arguments to the movement commands, so the turtle did land in exactly the same places as before, resulting in the same feedback pattern. Assuming a stable world, a world in which treasures stay put and distance means what we expect it to, no new information can be gained by going back to the same locations. Yet, this *perseveration* persisted. Indeed, perseveration was not limited to this stage alone: it occurred at virtually every stage of *Treasure* proficiency.

In the next stage, we observed a very marked change. The children *began to respond to the feedback with corrective action*. If the result of the previous move is to make the turtle "colder," the child immediately moved the turtle back to where it was before. Often, we observed expressions of excitement when this discovery was made. They had gained a measure of control over the environment. They could undo the undesirable. They had discovered the *reversal rule*.[16] As this stage progressed, the colder regions were experienced as extremely unpleasant. One child demonstrated her discomfort particularly dramatically. When she moved away from the treasure (in her words, "I got colder"), she would exclaim, "Oh, no," and bury her face in her hands. After a few moans, she would peek back up at the screen and, when seeing the colder color again, would repeat the performance. Sometimes it would take a few minutes for her to get the gumption up to move again. The discouraging feedback was experienced as pain. (*Getting colder "is bad."*)

In the transition period between the reversal stage and the next stage, the children seemed literally stuck. They typically moved in only one dimension, and since moving away from the warmer sections was experienced as painful, they therefore *found the warmest sections of the line* and just stayed there basking. After a few moments of contentment, a child might attempt a small move out of the warmth, but when this was inevitably followed by a colder turtle, she hastily returned to her spot.

In the next stage, we again noticed a crucial moment. Frustrated by her immobility, the idea suddenly dawns that she can move out of her comfortable line into a new dimension, to start *exploring the plane*. In all observed cases, this

---

[16] Not all children adhere to the strict form of the reversal rule. Some children at this stage, reverse their heading but use a slightly different magnitude, and so don't end up at the exact same location as they were at before. For more on this, see the Styles section.

meant that the child turned 90 degrees and searched *perpendicularly to the line* she had been traversing. Acclimation to the new line proved rapid, and soon she would find the warmest region on this new line. This procedure was then iterated as the child spiraled in to the treasure region.

At this juncture there was an observed divergence in the class. Some of the children continued to play as they had before responding to the local feedback. However, some children began to look at things from a more global perspective. They paid greater attention to the map of the colors displayed at the end of a game (which by now they had seen a few times from "lucky" strolls into the treasure area) and began to construct mental maps of the domain. Before making their next move, they would *visualize* the color map and hypothesize *a specific location for the treasure*. Often they would point to a specific spot on the screen and say: "I think the treasure is here." This is in marked contrast to their earlier puzzlement if asked where the treasure might be.

The next obstacle that the children encountered was passing the treasure by. By using the spiraling strategy, the children entered a zone of proximity to the treasure. However, because they had gotten accustomed to moving the turtle in large steps, they often leaped right over it and landed on the other side. In large part, this is due to the progressive reduction in color region size, the closer one gets to the treasure. Initially this was very confusing to them. They had gotten used to the idea that they could find the best color on a line by moving in a hotter direction. Once they got colder, they would reverse their heading and thus converge on the best color. This, however, only works if the step you are taking is smaller than the size of the region. When you are close to the treasure, the regions are not very wide, so if your step size is too large, you will miss it. It was while struggling with the frustrations of this stage that some children first asked us: "How big is the treasure?"

The solution to this dilemma led to the next stage, which we call *step-size refinement*. The children learned to reduce their step size as they got close to the treasure. In many cases, the trigger for this response seemed to be arriving in the pink region, the second hottest area. In the teaching competition, for example, one child explicitly invoked this rule, saying: "When you get to the pink, you gotta use a lower number" (of turtle steps).

The situation is further complicated by the following fact about *Treasure-world*. The radius of the innermost feedback region, the red color zone (which sounds the note high c) is 10 units, but the zone of the treasure, the region which triggers the animation and announces you have won, has a radius of 5 units. This means that, while you are in the red region, you can no longer use feedback to find the treasure; you must either search the whole space or develop a more sophisticated strategy for deducing the treasure location. One such strategy is to take very small steps[17] while in the red zone, and notice at which point you

---

[17] Some children referred to these as "baby steps"—a reference to the popular children's game "May I."

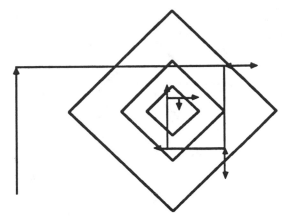

Figure 4.   Example of an Edging Path.

entered it and at which point you exited. Then you can *go back half the distance* you traversed and you will be in the middle of the red zone, on top of the treasure. This strategy can be generalized.

Recall the stage at which the children made the breakthrough and learned that they could move off of a line by turning 90 degrees. Typically, a child had been moving along a line in a warmer direction, when suddenly he encountered a colder color. Knowing now that he had just gone past the best color on his line, he applied the reversal strategy, returning to where he was, and then turned either right or left. This dynamic had the effect of making the turns happen at the edges of color regions. Figure 4 illustrates the path of a child proceeding in this manner.

As we can observe, the child has taken a circuitous path due to this "edging" effect. In some cases this pattern can lead the child to loop[18] around the treasure, always very close, but ever just out of grasp. One child solved this problem by discovering the generalization alluded to above. Whenever you have found the best color on a line, note where you entered that region and where you exited it, and go half way between. Only then make your turn. Following this "centering" strategy results in a much cleaner and shorter path to the treasure, as shown below in Figure 5.

By the time children have attained the latter stages of this developmental sequence, they have achieved a level of mastery of *Treasure*. In the process, they have moved from the stance of "getting colder is bad," indicative of the reversal stage, to the new stance of "*getting colder is information*." Now, when they are moving towards the treasure and encounter a colder region, they no longer hang

---

[18] For a more detailed example of looping behavior see the Styles section.

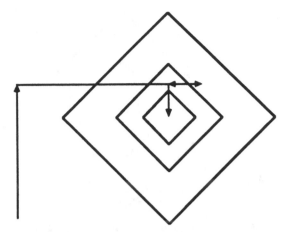

Figure 5. Example of a Centering Path.

their heads and moan. Instead they say "Oh, okay, it's the other way," and head in a new direction.

DISCUSSION OF CHILDREN'S LEARNING

In general, the children's enthusiasm for the game was striking. This enthusiasm cannot merely be attributed to the special attention of the researchers (i.e., Hawthorne Effect), and the opportunity to spend class time playing a game (i.e., not regular school work). The children wanted to play even when we were not there. Furthermore, the estimation game we developed for working with distance and angle did not elicit the same kind of enthusiasm. The pleasure most children experienced when first finding the treasure was palpable. This would seem to be partly due to the challenging nature of the task. The children experienced finding the treasure as an accomplishment. Some children were competitive about how many times they had found the treasure.

Another component of the children's enjoyment arises because it is reassuring and satisfying to find a hidden object. There may be an analogy with children's delight in playing a peekaboo and hide-and-seek. These games tap into fears and desires that lie beneath the surface of our consciousness. The game also possesses an element of "moderate novelty" (Piaget, 1952). There is novelty in that the treasure is hidden in a new location each time the game is played. At the same time, strategies and insights from previous games can be applied. This recognition of something familiar in something new is also pleasurable. The treasure location is random; hence, there is a small chance that it will be the same from one game to the next. As one child observed in her notebook, "Today I learned that the treasure can be in the same place."

Learning about Feedback, Strategy, and Information

How did we gauge what the children learned? We used direct observation of the children's play as a starting point. Changes in their play of the game became evident over time. By replaying the logs of the games and viewing videotapes, we noticed regularities and differences in how the children played. We were guided by comments made by children in their notebooks and during interviews, class discussion, and the competitions to refine our ideas and questions. For further information, we interviewed the classroom teacher.

What did the children learn about feedback? A key question is, What is going on in the early play of the game when children do not respond to the feedback by retreating if the feedback indicates that they are getting "colder" (further away from the treasure)? One hypothesis is that they are exploring the situation, "smelling the flowers." While that may be an aspect of their behavior, our hypothesis is that the main reason for their behavior is that they do not initially understand feedback, nor do they realize its value in the process of playing the game. Evidence for this is that, although adults may experience some difficulties in finding the treasure, they generally respond to the feedback by attempting to move in a direction which will decrease their distance from the treasure. However, the children needed to first learn that it is important to interpret the change in feedback. When asked, the children were able to correctly interpret whether the change in color and sound feedback meant they were getting "hotter" or "colder." They did not, however, necessarily make this interpretation spontaneously. Furthermore they had to learn to act in response to the feedback. The child who was most successful in the teaching competition made this an explicit rule. Once children realized that the feedback required interpretation and appropriate response, they attempted to use the feedback to get closer to the treasure. As we mentioned earlier, this was not always an easy task: when children were near the treasure, but stepping over it, frustration was frequently the result.

The experience that using feedback can get them to a goal was new and powerful for the children. During their initial play of the game, children often expressed discouragement, seeming to believe that they would never find the treasure. However once they found the treasure, most were confident that they could find it again. Even if they encountered difficulties in their subsequent searches, they did not abandon the strategy of responding to the feedback as a way of finding the treasure. As they refined their understanding of the game, they came to see that they could have a general method of play, which would work no matter where the treasure was hidden.

The children learned to use information. The sensory feedback is information, if one knows how to interpret it. Knowing that one has moved away from the treasure helps one learn more about where the treasure is. Initially, however, many children react to the moving away as a negative thing. One of the girls, for example, was so afraid of making a mistake that she was initially almost unable to choose a move. Later, the children realized that they could use this information to take corrective action. This is an example of learning from "mistakes." Children were able to experience mistakes as a natural part of the learning process.

Models can be useful in interpreting and assimilating information. As mentioned in the observations section, the question "Where do you think the treasure is?" seemed initially to take children by surprise. They were looking for the treasure precisely because they didn't know where it was. If the feedback indicated that they were far from the treasure, they looked elsewhere. However, as indicated in the discussion of perserveration, they often returned to cold regions. Their earlier understanding of where the treasure was diminished with time. As some players developed, they began to build up more of a sense of where the treasure might be. A "sense" can include an association of an area of the screen as being near the treasure, a mental image of the map of colors, and other possibilities.[19] In the team and teaching competitions, children were frequently seen pointing to where on the screen they thought the treasure was.[20]

Along with building up a model, some children began to make and test hypotheses. In the early stages of a game, this means going to an area where the player thinks the treasure might be, and exploring there. The idea might be disproven, in which case the child tries somewhere else. If the child thinks he or she is getting very close, an exhaustive search of the area might be started. Children varied in their ability to search an area systematically. The frustration of children who had unsuccessfully searched an area where they believed the treasure to be was very evident.

Making and testing their own hypotheses in the school environment was a new thing for many of the children. The children tended to rely heavily on adults for validation of their progress. In this reliance, the classroom teacher conjectured a cultural factor. Most of these children come from Hispanic families, in which the adults make all of the decisions. Many parents choose what their children eat and wear. These children face fewer decisions than many other children their age. This game offered these children an opportunity to make decisions on their own. Initially, however, many children took the approach of trying to get hints about the treasurer's location from us. Telling them that the computer had hidden the treasure, and that we didn't know where, helped to shift the task to one of their engagement with the computer.

---

[19] Much of the language we commonly use are visually based (for example, the words *picture* and *image*). Even the more abstract-seeming word *idea* comes from the Greek word *idein*, meaning to see.

[20] During the teaching competition Thomas was observing Larry (who he had just taught how to play) search for the treasure. Thomas insisted that Larry was near the treasure. "No way, man," was Larry's response. Thomas remained confident, even though he initially had trouble in pinpointing the location of the treasure.

What do we mean when we talk about the children's learning? We do not claim that they have assimilated a series of abstract principles. We do believe, however, that they have contacted these principles in a meaningful way. This is manifested in the increasing stability of their understanding of the game. Lack of such stability is linked to the recurrence of perseveration. The most striking perseveration was noticed during the phase of one-dimensional play. The child finds the point on the line closest to the treasure. Failing to reach the treasure, the child continues to move along the line. Consider another situation. The child reaches the "pink" region and is quite near the treasure. By taking steps that are too large, the child steps over the treasure. The inexperienced child may explore the area and then suddenly go off looking in another area. This pattern may repeat. A child with a stronger sense that the treasure must be nearby may become rather frustrated but is not likely to wander off to a cold area.

There is some structure of understanding that develops in the child's mind. One of the goals of our future research is to explore this process more fully. We believe that the understanding developed in playing the game supports the development of a set of "mental muscles." The experience of playing the game promotes an ability to take advantage of a number of regularities in the *Treasure* microworld that reflect regularities in the world. The complexity of events in the world may hide such regularities. Feedback is in operation all around us, yet we may not be aware of it. Information given to children in school is often so balkanized that it would be difficult to build up a coherent model of it.[21] *Treasure* is simple enough to allow construction of a model of where the treasure is, and how distant from the treasure the different color/sound feedback zones are. Furthermore, the use of this model is rewarded by greater ease in finding the treasure. *Treasureworld* thus provides a positive, concrete experience of model building with which other similar experiences can begin to resonate. We believe that the kind of learning discussed in this section is a valuable contribution to the development of the children's metacognitive skills. The convergence of experiences of success based on internalizing or operationalizing the abstract principles discussed here will foster a sense that there is another way of looking at things. This process is analogous to the childrens' insight that "teachers have strategies." Discussions with the classroom teacher support our view that growth of this sort occurred.

STYLES IN TREASUREWORLD

Any discussion of style, in order to be centered, must place itself with respect to the two extreme positions vis á vis individual differences in problem domains.

---

[21] Papert (1980, p. 39) describes the resulting image of human knowledge as "a patchwork of territories separated by impassible iron curtains."

The first of these, which we shall call the *flat position*, essentially says: Any individual differences detected in approaches to problem domains are reflections of the person's unique gifts and perspective. All approaches are equally good. Any approach can lead to success in any domain. The educational mission of a teacher holding this position is to work with and encourage the development of the student's individual style, to provide an environment in which it can flower (e.g., Turkle & Papert, 1989).

The second of these, which we shall call the *hierarchical position*, says: For each problem domain there is one right approach, one right way to solve the problem. Any problem-solving effort that does not use this approach is inferior. The educational mission of a teacher holding this position is to impart the correct approach to the student, to ferret out the student's bad problem-solving approaches and to replace them with better ones (e.g., Brown, Bransford, Ferrara, & Campione, 1983).

We came to this study with a prejudice to steer a middle course between the Scylla of indiscriminate acceptance (flat) and the Charybdis of judgmental rigidity (hierarchical). In *Treasureworld* we were convinced that a number of very different styles would be successful. However, we believed that the nature of the domain would lend itself to a style that favored abstraction over concrete representation, focusing on higher level goals (black-boxing) over absorption in detail, and an ability to shift perspectives over a less differentiated view of situations.

Another confusion that often arises in discussion of style relates to the level of description to which the word *style* is applied (Falbel, 1985). In one such level, a style is synonymous with a strategy. In this sense an individual can choose from his or her grab-bag of styles the one most appropriate to the particular situation. At a different level, a style is almost synonymous with a personality. It is fixed and immutable, coloring the individual's actions through all situations.

In order to elucidate the manifestation (or emergence) of styles in children playing the game, it will be useful to contrast the play of two children.

Thomas and Jose: Two Styles in Treasure Play

Beginning play. Thomas is able to find the treasure the first time he plays. However, it takes quite a bit of exploring: 134 moves. While it appears that he has discovered the strategy of "if you are getting much colder go back" fairly soon in his development, he does not exhibit confidence that he can find the treasure again. When asked at the start of his second game if he has a guess as to where the treasure is, he shakes his head and shrugs his shoulders. During the course of his second game, the researchers repeatedly ask him if he has a guess as to where the treasure is, and he invariably answers that he does not. Through his first 4 days of playing, he still ignores feedback at times. He often makes unnecessary turns (for example, the feedback continues to indicate that he is getting closer, but he turns to the side).

Jose notices us playing the game in a prototype version and, attracted by the music and the colors, asks if he can play. He understands what to do immediately and, with great confidence, he grabs the keyboard. At first he moves only in horizontal or vertical lines, but then he begins to make turns and thereafter speedily attains the treasure. When asked if he can do it again, he says, "Of course." At the beginning of the second game, when asked where he thinks the treasure is, he points to the location where he had just found the treasure. After one move in that direction gave him disconfirming evidence, he immediately turned around and spontaneously told us that the treasure was on the opposite side of the screen this time. Jose played three times his first day and found the treasure in less than 60 moves each time.

Development (over next 3 weeks). Both Thomas and Jose learn to vary their step size. Thomas, however, soon settles on selecting from a palette of three step sizes: 10, 3, and 1. Jose varies his step size considerably, sometimes choosing steps as large as 100 and often choosing step sizes between 1 and 60. Thomas soon formulates explicit rules to govern his motion of the turtle. He says: "If you are going forward and the sound gets lower, turn back. If it gets higher, keep going until it gets lower again, then go back one move and turn." Of all the children, Thomas notices the sound feedback most consistently, and responds to it rather than the color. Indeed, during phase 3 of the project, when he is teaching another child to play the game, he admonishes him: "Don't look at the colors, listen to the sound."

In contrast, Jose cannot articulate how he moves the turtle. When asked to explain his strategy, he responds with a list of the places he has recently visited before arriving at the treasure. Jose is perceived by the class to be an expert at *Treasure*. Class members often direct questions about the game to him, and he is happy to help them. His help usually consists of wandering over to their terminal, seizing the keyboard, and solving the problem on his own. The he cocks his head and says, "See, it's easy, that's how you do it." Thomas, on the other hand, is not highly regarded. He is a peripheral class member and not often questioned about *Treasureworld*.

Teaching Others. During phase three of the project, five students were selected to teach five novice *Treasureworld* players how to play the game. Thomas and Jose were among these five. Jose was paired with Ahmed, the only novice child who was able to find the treasure in the pretest encounter with the game. Thomas was paired with Brad, a child who seemed to flounder during the pretest.

Just before Brad came into the room, Thomas asked us, "How do you want me to teach?" When we replied that "he was the teacher and he could teach any way he wanted," he said with a determined expression on his face: "I'm not going to be a normal teacher."

Thomas began by telling Brad, "I'm going to play a game first, and you watch me, then you'll play." As Thomas played, he stopped to point out whenever he was applying a rule. After he had won, he asked Brad to play. He watched carefully as Brad played. Whenever Brad made a move that violated Thomas's rules, Thomas immediately corrected him, pointing out which rule he was violating. In some cases, however, he actually gave Brad "bad advice," that is, advice which led him down a longer path to the treasure.

Jose, on the other hand, did not offer Ahmed a chance to play by himself. Jose took charge of the keyboard and found the treasure rather speedily, stopping at various points to "explain" why he turned in a particular situation. An example of Jose's explanations: "It's easy, you see. Do you get what I'm doing?" Ahmed invariably replied that he did.

Even though we were convinced that Thomas's teaching had been much better than Jose's, we were nonetheless expecting Ahmed to win. We did not believe that Thomas's superior teaching would overcome the large handicap that Brad had begun with. To our surprise, Brad won first place and Ahmed tied for second. While Ahmed showed some improvement in his game, Brad's improvement was dramatic.

Dichotomies. We would like to make two distinctions of style implicit in the discussion of Thomas and Jose. The first of these uses the word *style* in the "strategy" sense, the latter more in the "personality" sense.

The first distinction is between those who use many different step sizes in moving the turtle (the variable-step-sizers), and those who use only one or a few step sizes (the fixed-step-sizers). From the above cases, it is evident that Jose is a variable-step-sizer and Thomas a fixed-step-sizer.

A typical first "rule" learned by the *Treasureworld* player is what we call the *reversal rule*. It says: If you are going in a certain direction and you get "colder," go back to where you were. Fixed-step-size players apply this rule rigidly and go back to exactly where they were. Variable-step-size players reverse their heading but, because they may step back a different quantity than they went forward, usually do not return to the exact same place from which they came. In some cases they may vary their step size a great deal in this situation and jump a whole range of colors.

Different styles lead to different difficulties in finding the treasure. A child, for example, who has a fixed step size (a step size of 5 is a common one) may endlessly repeat the traverse of a rectangle surrounding the treasure. In Figure 6 we can see how Sula is stuck in such a loop.

Sula starts off at point A. The first step gets her to point B, which turns the turtle pink. Feeling she's getting closer, she takes another step in the same direction, to point C. Now she has crossed over the red zone without knowing it, since the turtle does not change color. Another step in the same direction now gets her to point D, where she hits the yellow. Seeing that matters have gotten worse, she turns and continues around the rectangle, never getting to the red.

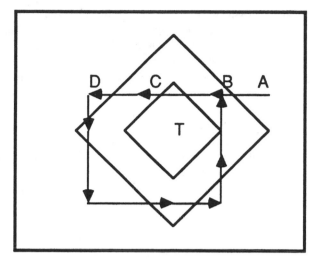

Figure 6.   The Traverse of a Rectangle Surrounding the Treasure.

Notice that, even if she applied the reversal strategy, going back to the pink (point C in Figure 6) before turning, she would still be stuck in such a rectangle, albeit a tighter one. The combination of the "bad luck" of point of entry into the pink region and a fixed step size has doomed her to this Sisyphian circumnavigation. Children with a variable step size strategy do not as often get into this particular bind. Once they are in such a rectangle for a while, they will vary their step size and break the pattern, thus increasing the likelihood that they will wander into the red.

One factor that influences the choice of style in this case is comfort with moving the turtle. Most children begin as variable-step-sizers. However, after encountering difficulties with controlling the turtle (for example, getting it back to exactly where it was before in order to verify an hypothesis) they narrowed their selection of steps and became fixed-step-sizers. Many were therefore able to solve the problem of controlling the turtle by making use of a restricted set of options with which they felt comfortable.

A second distinction of style that emerges from the previous discussion is between the "rule-based" style, and the "situational" style. We would say that Thomas's style in playing *Treasureworld* is "rule-based," while Jose's style is "situational." Jose's confidence in his ability to get out of any bad situation that he might encounter in *Treasureworld* did not foster a need to reflect on his strategy and explicitly formulate a set of rules. While it might be said that he was still following rules, just a large number of very specific situational rules, Jose was never able (despite great efforts on the part of himself and the researchers) to express what those rules were. Thomas, on the other hand, did not initially feel confident in his ability to win at *Treasureworld*. It may be surmised that this lack of confidence and consequent desire to protect himself from failure led him to step away from the game a little, to stop the ceaseless activity of playing, and to reflect on what he could do to ensure that he did not get into trouble. This led to the formulation of explicit rules. We found that "rule-based" treasure players tend to be fixed-step-sizers, and "situational" players tend to be variable-step-sizers. The initial lack of confidence that characterizes the rule-based players leads them to adopt the more controlled fixed-step-size. In this way, a style in the sense of personality shapes the "lower-level-style" (strategy) of the players.

In addition, much of the difference that we observed in the play of rule-based players vs. situational players is captured in the recent literature on situated action (e.g., Agre, 1989; Suchman, 1987). Agre, for example, contrasts the traditional AI view of planning with the notion of "situated activity" in the following way.

> In the *planning* view of everyday activity: "If an agent's activity has a certain organization, that is solely because the agent constructs and deploys a symbolic representation of that activity, namely a plan. Everyday activity is fundamentally planned; contingency is a marginal phenomenon. An agent conducts is everyday activity entirely by constructing and deploying plans. The world is fundamentally hostile. Life is a series of problems to be solved."
>
> In contrast in the *situated* activity view: "Everyday life has an orderliness, coherence, and laws of change that are not the product of any representation of them. Everyday activity is almost entirely routine, even when something novel is happening. Everyday activity is fundamentally improvised; contingency is the central phenomenon. An agent conducts its everyday activity by continually re-deciding what to do. The world is fundamentally benign. Life is a fabric of familiar activities." (Agre, 1989, p. 11)

The parallel between the style of Jose and the situated action model is striking, similarly that of Thomas and the planning model. Agre goes on to argue the superiority of the situated view over traditional planning models. This, however, is not our contention here. Of greater relevance is his observation of the marginality of the situated view in traditional AI and cognitive psychology. Similarly, we discovered that Jose had been marginalized by the traditional academic school system. Indeed he had been classified as learning disabled and had stayed back two grades.

FURTHER RESEARCH DIRECTIONS

Treasureworld is work in progress. There are many directions to go in pursuing further research. As we have said earlier, our main research goal is to gain a deeper understanding of the process by which the child assimilates the concept of feedback. It is our hope that by doing so, we will provide a foundation for the construction of new feedback learning environments and so bring the study of feedback to a more prominent position in the educational life of the child.[22] A "feedback curriculum" would cut across many of the usual divisions of discipline currently fashionable in the school. It is central to the study of biological systems (e.g., Bateson, 1972; Dawkins, 1976), physical systems (e.g., Gleick, 1987), computers, the study of mathematics as process (e.g., Vitale, 1989), and to newer cybernetic models of psychology (e.g., Minsky, 1987).

Our work with *Treasure*, however, has also left us curious about many questions that arose out of the details of the game. We plan to experiment with a number of variations. The next paragraph is a quick summary of some of these ideas.

What would happen if the turtle left a trail when it moved? The children would no longer have to remember what the feedback told them last time; they would be able to see it on the screen. Would this alter in any way their perseveration behavior? What differences might we observe if we chose to separate the feedback channels, one game with sound feedback, another with color feedback? Will some kids learn to auditorize their environment instead of visualizing it?[23] Treasure provides 14 gradations of feedback. What if we provided continuous feedback? Would this change eliminate looping behavior? Would the traversal paths be less ragged?

We would also like to work with a broader range of children. With older children we would like to work on writing programs for the turtle to find the treasure (Abelson & diSessa, 1980). What additional power would be gained from this concretization, the reifying of strategy? Would situational style players be interested in writing such programs? Would they be able to write such programs without abandoning their style? Another research question is, At what age do children begin to respond to feedback in *Treasure* the way adults do?

The children we worked with were primarily Hispanic. The Hispanic culture has been characterized as a "soft" culture (Turkle, 1984), which may be associated with a more situational style. Would the same style dichotomies be observed in a different cultural milieu?

Lastly, we plan to develop the other games in *Treasureworld*. Among these are one-dimensional and three-dimensional analogues of *Treasure*, variations in which various obstacles (both linear and planar) are placed on the terrain, and worlds in which the treasure moves. One interesting variation involves changing the meaning of the feedback from a measure of distance to the treasure to a measure of height above sea level. The treasure would be "buried" on the highest mountain, Everest. In this variation, following the feedback would be

---

[22] Ackermann (1989) has pointed out, "The empowering effect of feedback for a human subject intelligent enough to take advantage of it" (p. 14).

[23] See Nagel's "What's It Like to Be a Bat" (1979) for an illuminating discussion of the difficulties of switching sensory modalities.

much more complex. One might climb up a very tall hill, the Matterhorn, only to find that one can't get any higher and have to descend in order to find another slope.

Another variation moves closer to the original "hot and cold" game by providing relative feedback. Only two feedback signals, "closer" and "farther," would be given, so no absolute measure of distance could be calibrated. Still another game involves putting two children in the feedback loop, one to interpret the feedback and one to give it. They could play on two computers across a network, and the feedback giver would be constrained to give nonlinguistic cues. Through their interactions, they would develop a feedback language in which to have a conversation about feedback. A final variation is one in which the goal of the game is changed. Instead of finding the treasure, the child is asked to draw a color picture of the "world" as he or she has understood it from the feedback obtained. This variation could be very interesting for exploring some of the epistemological issues involved in the construction of worlds.

We all navigate through the world usually receiving feedback only from the narrow range of our senses. Yet somehow we construct a more or less coherent picture of the whole, though we may not know where the treasure is located.

ACKNOWLEDGMENTS

We would like to thank Seymour Papert for the inspiration to begin this research and the incisive comments which kept it on track. There is not space enough here to enumerate the many ways in which we received encouragement and support from Idit Harel. She was a constant support, starting from the beginning design of the research through the final drafts of this chapter. We would like to acknowledge Edith Ackermann, Mitchel Resnick, and Hillel Weintraub for their extensive comments on drafts of this chapter. In addition we would like to thank Mario Bourgoin for his technical advice, and Judy Sachter for her artistic graphics in the treasure chest animation. To Gilda Keefe we give our special thanks for sharing her classroom, her enthusiasm, and her insights with us. To the children themselves, our gratitude for their openness to explore something new and for the fun we shared. Finally, we would like to thank the students, researchers, and staff of the Epistemology and Learning Group at MIT for the atmosphere of support and constructive criticism that provided an essential backdrop to our research. Without all this multicolored feedback we would not have been able to take the corrective action that resulted in this writing.

This research was supported by grants from the IBM Corporation (Grant # OSP95952), the National Science Foundation (Grant # 851031-0195), the McArthur Foundation (Grant # 874304), the LEGO Group, and the Apple Computer Inc. The preparation of this chapter was supported by the National Science Foundation (Grant # MDR 8751190 and # TPE 8850449) and Nintendo Japan. The ideas expressed here do not reflect those of the supporting agencies.

REFERENCES

Abelson, H., & diSessa, A. (1980). *Turtle geometry: The computer as a medium for exploring mathematics*. Cambridge, MA: MIT Press.

Ackermann, E. (1990). Circular reactions and sensori-motor intelligence: Piaget's theory of early cognitive growth. *Archives de psychologie, 58*, 65–78.

Agre, P. (1989). *The dynamic structure of everyday life*. Unpublished doctoral dissertation & Tech. Rep. No. 1085, MIT, Cambridge, MA.

Bateson, G. (1972). *Steps to an ecology of mind*. New York: Chandler Publishing Co.

Bateson, G. (1979). *Mind and nature: A necessary unity*. New York: Dutton.

Brown, A. L., Bransford, J. D., Ferrara, R. A., & Campione, J. C. (1983). Learning, remembering, and understanding. In J. H. Flavell & E. M. Markham (Eds.), *Handbook of child psychology: Cognitive development* (Vol. 3). New York: Wiley.

Dawkins, R. (1976). *The selfish gene*. New York: Oxford University Press.

Falbel, A. (1985). *Sorting out the issue of style*. Unpublished paper, MIT Media Laboratory, Cambridge, MA.

Gleick, (1987). *Chaos: Making a new science*. New York: Viking Penguin.

Harel, I. (1988). *Software design for learning: Children's construction of meaning for fractions and Logo programming*. Unpublished doctoral dissertation, MIT Media Laboratory, Cambridge, MA.

Harel, I. & Papert, S. (1990). Software design as a learning environment. *Interactive Learning Environments Journal, 1* (1), 1–32.

Kempton, W. (1986). Two theories of home heat control. In D. Holland & N. Quinn (Eds.), *Cultural models in language and thought*. Cambridge, UK: Cambridge University Press.

Nagel, E. (1979). What is it like to be a bat? *Mortal Questions*. New York: Cambridge University Press.

Minsky, M. (1987). *The society of mind*. New York: Simon & Schuster.

Papert, S. (1973). *Uses of technology to enhance education* (AI Lab. Logo Memo No. 8, AI Memo No. 298) Cambridge, MA: MIT.

Papert, S. (1980). *Mindstorms: Children, computers, and powerful ideas*. New York: Basic Books.

Piaget, J. (1952). *The origins of intelligence in children*. New York: International University Press.

Suchman, L. (1987). *Plans and situated actions: The problem of human machine communication*. Cambridge, England: Cambridge University Press.

Turkle, S. (1984). *The second self: Computers and the human spirit*. New York: Simon and Schuster.

Vitale, B. (1990). Structures in relations vs. processes. In C. Hoyles & R. Noss (Eds.), *LOGO and mathematics: Research and curriculum issues*. London:

Von Foerster, H. (Ed.). (1953). *Cybernetics: Circular, casual, and feedback mechanisms in biological and social systems*. Caldwell, NJ: Progress Associates Inc.

Wiener, N. (1954). *The human use of human beings: Cybernetics and society*. Boston: Houghton Mifflin.

Aaron Brandes and Uri Wilensky discussing their Treasureworld.

21

MultiLogo:
A Study of Children and Concurrent Programming

Mitchel Resnick*

INTRODUCTION

In many computer applications, people need to control several objects at the same time. For instance, someone might want to program a group of graphical objects to move across a computer screen in a coordinated dance. Someone else might want to program several robotic machines to walk across the floor at the same time—perhaps in synchrony with a video image on the computer screen.

These coordinated activities, simple though they might seem, are very difficult (if not impossible) to program using traditional programming languages like Pascal or Logo. The problem is that traditional languages are based on a single process that executes instructions one at a time. This *sequential paradigm* does not match the way the real world works: people and animals act in parallel; objects interact in parallel. As a result, many real-world activities can not be modelled in a natural way with sequential programming.

The ideal solution is to use a *concurrent* or *parallel* programming language—that is, a language that allows programmers to control multiple, interacting processes.[1] During the past decade, computer-science researchers have developed dozens of concurrent languages (for an overview, see Gelertner, 1986). But there has been little empirical research on how people learn, use, and understand concurrent-programming languages. Such research is critical for improving the design and teaching of concurrent languages. There is a long list of unanswered research questions. For example: In what ways do these new languages simplify the task of programming? In what ways do they make the task more difficult?

---

* A version of this chapter appeared in *Interactive Learning Environments*, *1*(3).

[1] Some researchers make distinctions among the terms *concurrent*, *parallel*, and *multiprocessing*, but there are no standardized definitions or distinctions. In this chapter, I use these terms interchangeably to refer to languages that allow programmers to control multiple processes.

What factors influence the learning of concurrent programming? What existing mental models influence people's understanding of concurrent programming?

Some researchers expect that people will have difficulty learning to program with concurrent languages. Empirical studies have shown that novice programmers, using traditional *sequential* languages, have significant difficulties. In learning concurrent languages, novices must cope with many of these same difficulties plus a host of new ones, most notably issues related to synchronization of multiple processes. Indeed, some researchers worry that "the complexity of (concurrent) programming—all those processes active at once, all those bits zinging around in every direction—is simply too great for the average programmer to bear" (Gelertner, 1986).

On the other hand, some previous research seems to suggest that concurrent languages could facilitate the task of programming (at least in some situations). Several researchers (Pea, Soloway, & Spohrer, 1987; Bonar & Soloway, 1985) note that novice programmers (using traditional sequential languages) often assume parallelism where none exists. Would these novices find parallel programming more natural and intuitive?

To explore these issues, I developed a concurrent extension to Logo called *MultiLogo*. MultiLogo provides new metaphors and constructs for controlling multiple processes at once. Its primary goal is to give people (particularly nonexpert programmers) a simple yet powerful model for thinking about and programming concurrent processes.

I conducted an experimental study with a small group of elementary-school students. The students used MultiLogo to control the concurrent actions of robotic machines. In this chapter, I analyze the students' work with MultiLogo, with special emphasis on the "bugs" in students' programs. Some of these bugs, no doubt, reflect weaknesses in the design of MultiLogo. Others, however, are likely to arise in all types of concurrent programming. I divide these general bugs into three primary categories, which I call *problem-decomposition* bugs, *synchronization* bugs, and *object-oriented* bugs. For each category, I discuss examples and possible causes of the bugs. This analysis provides a framework for understanding ways to improve the teaching and design of concurrent-programming languages.

MOTIVATION

My work on MultiLogo was motivated, in large part, by my involvement in the development of a computer-based construction system called LEGO/Logo (Resnick, Ocko, & Papert, 1988). As students work on LEGO/Logo projects, they often want to control several robotic machines at the same time. After building a LEGO amusement park, for example, a child might want all of the rides to run simultaneously. To do that, some form of concurrent programming is needed.

As its programming language, LEGO/Logo uses an expanded version of Logo. Students can use any of the traditional Logo primitives and control structures (IF, REPEAT, etc.), plus any of 20 new primitives added specially for the LEGO environment (such as ON, OFF, and SENSOR?). To turn on a LEGO motor, the programmer first tells the computer which port on the LEGO interface box it should "talk to." Then the programmer simply types ON, and the motor turns on. A typical LEGO/Logo program is shown below. The program is designed for a LEGO car with touch sensors on the front and rear bumpers. The program turns on the car motor, then keeps checking each sensor. Whenever the car bumps into something, the program changes the direction of the motor (and thus the direction of the car).

```
to bumper-car
talkto :motor-port
on
check-sensors
end

to check-sensors
listento :front-sensor
if sensor? [rd]        ;; rd is for "reverse direction"
listento :back-sensor
if sensor? [rd]
check-sensors
end
```

The LEGO/Logo programming language is adequate for a wide variety of applications—and, indeed, children have used it to program many different types of projects. But certain applications expose the limitations of the LEGO/Logo language. Consider, for instance, the CHECK-SENSORS procedure shown above. Although this procedure works as desired, it presents certain conceptual difficulties for novice programmers. To understand the procedure, a programmer must think of the computer alternating between the two sensors—first checking the front sensor, then the back sensor, then the front sensor, and so on. A model in which each sensor is checked continuously and concurrently would probably be much more intuitive for novices, since it would more closely model the way "real" sensors (like eyes and ears) work. Indeed, in working with LEGO/Logo, many novices attribute some sort of intentionality to sensors. They seem to believe that each sensor plays an active role in checking itself and in informing the computer (or the motor) when it has been pressed.

In other cases, the need for concurrency is even more compelling. Imagine that we want to modify the CHECK-SENSORS procedure so that the computer flashes a light for five seconds every time the car reverses direction. We could write a subprocedure FLASH-LIGHT, then make the obvious modification:

```
to check-sensors
listento :front-sensor
if sensor? [rd flash-light]
listento :back-sensor
if sensor? [rd flash-light]
check-sensors
end
```

This procedure has a bug: What if the car bumps into something *while* the computer is flashing the light? The car will not reverse direction until *after* the computer has finished flashing the light. In short, the computer cannot flash a light and check the sensors at the same time. We could modify FLASH-LIGHT so that it "time-slices" between the two activities, alternating between checking the sensor and flashing the light. But this "solution" has several drawbacks. When implemented in a high-level language, time-slicing is usually quite slow, so the light might flash irregularly, with a noticeable pause each time the computer checked a sensor. Equally important, this "fix" represents another step away from modularity; thus, it makes the programming task more conceptually complex.

This example reveals the need for what we might call *check-and-act* concurrency: a program needs to check for a condition and execute an action at the same time. Similar issues arise if we try to control two (or more) devices at the same time. For example, we might want a LEGO robot to walk around the room while a light on its head flashes continuously. This example calls for *act-and-act* concurrency: a program needs to execute two actions at the same time. As with check-and-act concurrency, there are sometimes ways to simulate act-and-act concurrency within the sequential paradigm, but at a cost of decreased modularity and increased conceptual complexity.

Some versions of Logo (and other languages) have offered programmers limited forms of concurrency in the form of *sprites* and *demons* (see Resnick, 1988, for more details). These limited approaches are often useful, but they do not go far enough. They help in only certain specialized situations, and they do not provide a conceptually clean model of concurrency.

DESIGN OF MULTILOGO

MultiLogo aims to provide a more general solution to the concurrency problem. It provides new constructs to help people think about and program all types of concurrent activity. This section describes the primary constructs of MultiLogo.

Agents. MultiLogo introduces a new object known as an *agent*. Each agent is like a separate version of Logo. To create concurrent activity, a MultiLogo programmer creates several agents, then asks each agent to execute Logo instructions *at the same time*.[2] Besides executing traditional Logo (and LEGO/Logo) instructions, each agent can also communicate with other agents.

MultiLogo agents differ from "processes" in other concurrent-programming languages in that MultiLogo agents have stronger "identities." Users can create agents with distinctive "personalities," each with its own name, procedures, variables, and turtle. Agents were designed in this way so that programmers can more easily coordinate and keep track of the (concurrent) activities of various agents.

Communication. MultiLogo agents need to communicate with one another to share data and to synchronize their activities. They communicate primarily by sending messages to one another.[3] MultiLogo messages are in the form of expressions for the recipient agent to evaluate. For example, the message FD 40 tells the recipient agent to move its turtle forward by 40 units. The message PRINT :NAME tells the recipient agent to print the object associated with its variable NAME. And the message START tells the recipient agent to run its START procedure.

Agents can send messages in several different ways. For example, an agent can DEMAND another agent to evaluate an expression immediately, interrupting its current activity if necessary. Or the sender could ASK the other agent to evaluate the expression "whenever it gets a chance."

To understand the differences between various types of communication, it is useful to imagine each agent maintaining a queue of expressions that it needs to evaluate. At any moment, the agent is evaluating the first expression in the queue. When an agent finishes evaluating an expression, it pops the expression off the queue and begins evaluating the next expression in the queue. If the queue becomes empty, the agent remains "dormant" until it receives another message.

Consider what happens when one agent DEMANDS another agent to do something. For example, an agent named MANAGER might evaluate the following expression:

manager ⟶ demand :flasher [onfor 20]

In this case, the message (ONFOR 20) gets pushed onto the *front* of FLASHER's queue (Figure 1). If FLASHER was in the process of evaluating an expression, the

---

[2] The current version of MultiLogo is implemented on a single-processor computer. So the agents do not actually perform actions at the same time. Instead, MultiLogo time-slices between the agents, doing a little of one action, then a little of another. But this time-slicing is implemented at a "low level," so it runs very quickly, making the actions seem concurrent. Most importantly, this low-level time slicing is completely invisible to the user. As far as the user is concerned, the agents perform actions concurrently.

[3] MultiLogo's use of agents and message passing was motivated, at least indirectly, by previous work on object-oriented languages like Smalltalk (Goldberg & Robson, 1983) and Actor languages (Hewitt, 1977).

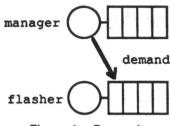

Figure 1.   Demand.

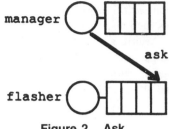

Figure 2.   Ask.

remainder of the evaluation is pushed down to the second position on the queue. After FLASHER finishes executing the message (presumably turning on a light for 20 time units), FLASHER resumes execution of the interrupted expression.

Consider, on the other hand, what happens if the MANAGER agent ASKS (instead of DEMANDing) that FLASHER turn on the light:

manager ⟶   ask :flasher [onfor 20]

In this case, the message is placed at the *back* of FLASHER's queue (figure 2). FLASHER executes the message whenever it completes executing all of the earlier expressions in the queue. So DEMAND places messages at the *front* of FLASHER's queue, and ASK places messages at the *back* of the queue. In either case, MANAGER behaves the same: it simply sends a message to FLASHER, then continues with whatever else it is supposed to do. MANAGER does *not* wait until FLASHER finishes executing the message; thus, ASK and DEMAND initiate parallel activity (assuming MANAGER has more instructions to execute).

When an ASK or DEMAND message is evaluated by the recipient agent, the resulting value is of no use. In particular, the agent which sent the message has no access to the value of the message. Thus, messages sent with ASK or DEMAND can be considered ''send-and-forget'' messages. MultiLogo has two other communications primitives (DEMAND-AND-WAIT and ASK-AND-WAIT) which behave differently. After sending a message with one of these primitives, the sending agent waits until the recipient agent finishes evaluating the message. At that time, the recipient ''sends back'' the value of the message. Since the sending agent waits for a response, these types of messages are *not* used for initiating parallel actions. But they have important uses. For example, DEMAND-AND-WAIT can be used to inspect the current state of another agent, and ASK-AND-WAIT can be used to synchronize the actions of several agents (see Resnick, 1988, for more details). The programming projects in this study focused on the ASK form of communication.

Meta-level commands. Agents are always in one of three states: *active*, *dormant*, or *paused*. An agent is *active* if it is in the process of running a program. An agent is *dormant* if it currently has no program to run. An agent can influence the state of another agent by executing a *meta-level command*. For example, the command HALT causes an active agent to become dormant.

Interface. This study used an early version of MultiLogo with a very modest user interface. The screen was divided into three windows. In one window, the user typed messages to the agents. Consider, for example, the following command:

manager ⟶ forward 50

The prompt indicates the name of the agent (MANAGER). This command asks the agent named MANAGER to move its turtle forward by 50 "turtle steps."

A second window displayed printed output from the agents. The third window was for turtle graphics. As mentioned previously, each agent has its own turtle.

Example. Let's return to the example of the LEGO car with two touch sensors. We can create a MultiLogo agent for each sensor, and one for the car motor.[4] To make the car reverse direction whenever one of the sensors is pressed, we can write:

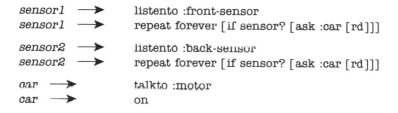

```
sensor1  ⟶    listento :front-sensor
sensor1  ⟶    repeat forever [if sensor? [ask :car [rd]]]

sensor2  ⟶    listento :back-sensor
sensor2  ⟶    repeat forever [if sensor? [ask :car [rd]]]

car  ⟶        talkto :motor
car  ⟶        on
```

Suppose (as in the earlier example) we also want a light to flash for a few seconds whenever a sensor is pressed. We can create a new agent named LIGHT to be in charge of flashing the light. Then we can change the instructions for SENSOR1 and SENSOR2 so that they send two ASK messages: one to the CAR agent (asking it to reverse direction), and one to the LIGHT agent (asking it to flash for a few seconds).

EMPIRICAL STUDY: METHODOLOGY

I tested MultiLogo with students at the Hennigan Elementary School in Boston. Eight Hennigan students used the MultiLogo system during May and June 1987. In this chapter, I focus on four of the students. This group included two fourth-grade students (one girl and one boy) and two fifth-grade students (one girl and

---

[4] In my examples, I use suggestive names for the agents. Students typically did not name their agents: they used the default agents, which were identified by numbers 1 to 10.

one boy). Each of the students worked with MultiLogo for at least four sessions, with each session lasting between 45 and 90 minutes. I will refer to the students by their initials: FB, NL, DB, and SM. With one exception, I always worked with students on a one-to-one basis. (During FB's final session, she was joined by her classmate BW.)

All students had at least one school-year of experience programming in Logo, using a version of Logo called LogoWriter. (In fact, the students were part of a special computer-intensive environment, in which students worked at the computer for roughly an hour each day.) Two of the students (the two fifth graders) had some previous experience with LEGO/Logo; during the previous school year, they had each spent about a dozen one-hour sessions working on LEGO/Logo projects.

The MultiLogo sessions were in the form of semistructured interviews. In a typical session, I suggested a particular project for the student to work on, and I explained any new programming concepts or primitives needed in the project. As the student worked on the project, I asked questions to probe the student's thinking. If the student ran into difficulties, I provided hints and suggestions. All sessions were tape recorded, and all computer interactions were saved in computer files.

During the study, I guided students through a sequence of projects. Each project involved writing a MultiLogo program to control a particular LEGO model. (The students did not build any LEGO models during the study; they were given fully constructed models.) The sequence of projects served as only a rough framework; I did not follow the sequence blindly. If a student suggested a new idea for a project, I typically helped the student follow through on the idea (as long as the project seemed to touch on "interesting" concepts). Also, if a student had difficulty with a particular concept, I typically introduced an additional project to reinforce (and probe) the student's understanding of the concept.

The following sections describe the basic sequence of projects, with sample MultiLogo programs for each project.

Walker/flasher projects. The first group of projects involved a LEGO walking machine with a light on its "nose." These projects were designed to introduce students to MultiLogo's central metaphors (agents and communications). Through these projects, I hoped to analyze students' difficulties in learning and using these basic metaphors.

First, I asked students to make the machine walk back and forth. This task does not use any MultiLogo features; students could imagine that they were typing at a traditional LEGO/Logo interpreter. Then I asked the students to make the light flash while the walker was moving back and forth. This is a very difficult task using a traditional sequential approach. As students worked on this problem, I introduced the idea of MultiLogo agents.

After the students had worked with agents for a while, I asked them to make the walker and flasher start at the same time. The solution to this task requires communication among agents, so I introduced the MultiLogo primitive ASK.

There are two primary approaches to this problem. In the "hierarchical" approach, a MANAGER agent sends messages to a WALKER agent and a FLASHER agent:

walker ⟶
```
to walk
talkto :motor-port
repeat 6 [onfor 30 rd]
end
```

flasher ⟶
```
to flash
talkto :light-port
repeat 20 [onfor 4 wait 2]
end
```

manager ⟶
```
to walk-and-flash
ask :walker [walk]
ask :flasher [flash]
end
```

manager ⟶   walk-and-flash

An alternate approach uses just two agents. In this case, the FLASHER agent sends a message to the WALKER agent, then starts its own FLASH procedure.

walker ⟶
```
to walk
talkto :motor-port
repeat 6 [onfor 30 rd]
end
```

flasher ⟶
```
to flash
talkto :light-port
repeat 20 [onfor 4 wait 2]
end
```

flasher ⟶
```
to walk-and-flash
ask :walker [walk]
flash
end
```

flasher ⟶   walk-and-flash

Touch-sensor projects. The next set of projects involved the use of LEGO touch sensors to control the walker/flasher. These projects were more difficult than the initial walker/flasher projects in several ways. First, the touch-sensor projects generally required the coordination of a larger number of agents. Second, problem decomposition tended to be more difficult in these projects: It was generally less obvious how many agents were needed and what each agent should do. Third, the projects required an understanding of the agents' queuing method for incoming messages.

To start, I reviewed the LEGO/Logo primitives SENSOR? and WAITUNTIL, and I gave several short examples of how to use touch sensors. Then I posed a task involving the LEGO walker plus two touch sensors. The goal was to write a program with the following behavior: if I pushed one of the touch sensors, the walker should walk back and forth several times; if I pushed the other touch sensor, the light should flash for a while. A solution to this task (making use of some procedures written in the previous section) might look like this:

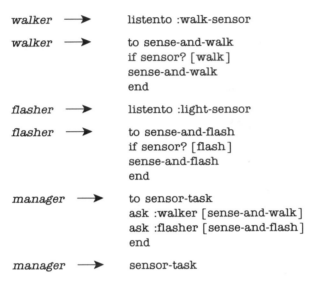

walker   ⟶   listento :walk-sensor

walker   ⟶   to sense-and-walk
               if sensor? [walk]
               sense-and-walk
               end

flasher   ⟶   listento :light-sensor

flasher   ⟶   to sense-and-flash
               if sensor? [flash]
               sense-and-flash
               end

manager   ⟶   to sensor-task
               ask :walker [sense-and-walk]
               ask :flasher [sense-and-flash]
               end

manager   ⟶   sensor-task

After students completed that task, I added an extra requirement: If I pushed the walker's touch sensor *while* the walker was walking, the walker should do another walking cycle when it finished its current cycle. That is, the walker should "remember" that its touch sensor had been pushed while it was walking. The LEGO light and its corresponding sensor should behave similarly.

To solve this task, students needed a more detailed model of agent communications. Most important, they needed to understand: what should an agent do if it receives a message while it is already active? I explained that each agent has its own queue and that new ASK messages are placed at the end of the queue. (In some cases, I also introduced the primitives DEMAND and DEMAND-AND-WAIT.) The new sensor task can be solved by dividing responsibilities among more agents. In the solution to the previous task, the walker agent was responsible both for checking a sensor and for making the walker move. These two jobs should be divided between two agents. That way, one agent can continue to check the senor even while the walker is moving.

LEGO turtle projects. The final set of projects involved a LEGO "turtle." Whereas the LEGO walker has only one motor (allowing it to move forward or backward), the turtle has two motors (allowing it to turn right or left, as well as moving forward and backward). I introduced the turtle projects, in part, to observe how students coped with problem decomposition and synchronization in projects with two motors. In addition, the turtle projects were a natural setting for introducing meta-level commands like HALT.

To start, students controlled the LEGO turtle using direct commands. Then I asked the students to write standard "turtle" procedures to make the turtle go forward, backward, left, and right. For example, the procedure to make the turtle go forward might look like this:

left-wheel $\longrightarrow$ talkto :left-motor-port

right-wheel $\longrightarrow$ talkto :right-motor-port

lego-turtle $\longrightarrow$ to lego-fd :time
ask :left-wheel [clockwise onfor :time]
ask :right-wheel [clockwise onfor :time]
end

As a final task, I asked the students to write procedures to coordinate the motions of the graphics turtle and the LEGO turtle.

EMPIRICAL STUDY: ANALYSIS OF RESULTS

In general, students appropriated the idea of agents sending messages to one another quite easily. By the end of four sessions, all of the students had successfully programmed the walker/flasher projects and the touch-sensor projects. Moreover, they seemed to grasp the power and usefulness of concurrent programming. One student (FB) described MultiLogo to a classmate in this way:

Remember how we were trying to do that program with the people walking and music and snow falling? Well, here there are different agents, and each agent can do something on the screen at the same time. You get it?

At times, however, students were confused by the new programming paradigm. As NL explained at the end of her first session:

It's sometimes confusing. You're asking two different agents to talk to two different things to do two different things. And so everybody's doing something else. And it's confusing to figure out what you are doing and why you are doing it and who told you to do it.

In my analysis of the results, I will steer away from the "success stories" and focus instead on students' mistakes and misconceptions, or "bugs." These mistakes can serve as clues to the thinking processes and mental models that students use during MultiLogo programming. My central purpose in analyzing students' bugs is to gain insights into the way students think about concurrent programming. (My analysis focuses exclusively on bugs related to concurrent programming. In writing MultiLogo programs, students made some mistakes unrelated to concurrent programming. I ignore such "traditional" bugs.) I divide the students' programming bugs into three primary categories:

- *Problem-decomposition bugs*. These bugs arise out of students' difficulties decomposing problems into actions to be performed concurrently by multiple agents.
- *Synchronization bugs*. These bugs arise out of students' difficulties coordinating and orchestrating the activities of multiple agents.
- *Object-oriented bugs*. These bugs arise out of students' confusion among different types of "objects" (e.g., agents, procedures, motors, ports) in the MultiLogo system.

These "bug categories" are not neatly disjoint. Bugs in one category interact with and influence bugs in other categories. For example, a programmer cannot think about synchronization issues independently from problem-decomposition issues. Nevertheless, a rough division of bugs into categories is a useful first step towards understanding how novices think about MultiLogo. For each category, I will present examples from the students' work and speculate as to the causes and origins of the bugs. (In presenting students' programs, I sometimes "clean up" the code in order to illustrate a point more clearly. In doing so, I make every effort not to distort the spirit of the original code.)

Problem-Decomposition Bugs

Problem decomposition plays an important role in computer programming. To solve a complex problem, programmers typically divide the problem into simpler subproblems and write procedures to solve each of the subproblems. Each of these subproblems might be decomposed into yet simpler sub-subproblems, and so on recursively. This type of decomposition, which might be called *functional decomposition*, is useful not only in programming, but in all types of problem solving.

In concurrent programming, an additional form of problem decomposition is needed. While dividing a task into functional pieces, programmers must also decide how to divide the pieces among agents for concurrent execution. This aspect of decomposition, which might be called *agency decomposition*, does not replace functional decomposition. Rather, the two approaches are complementary; they represent two different dimensions in problem decomposition. Functional decomposition focuses on *what* needs to be done; agency decomposition focuses on *who* should do it.

Examples of problem-decomposition bugs. Two of the students (FB and NL) ran into problem-decomposition difficulties right away, in the initial walker/ flasher task. FB used a standard functional decomposition approach: she began by writing two procedures called LIGHT and MOTOR:

```
Agent 1  ⟶    to light
               talkto "a   ;; light plugged into port a
               onfor 20 wait 20
               end
Agent 1  ⟶    to motor
               talkto "b   ;; motor plugged into port b
               onfor 40 rd
               end
```

Notice that FB used only a single agent. Before writing the procedures, FB explained her approach:

> I'll write one (procedure) for the light and one for the motor and put them together in one program so you can call the program by itself. Cause you can't repeat two programs and do them at the same time. You can repeat one program with two little programs in it.

But after writing the procedure, FB realized that she didn't know how to "combine" the two procedures so that they would execute at the same time:

> You could do REPEAT 200 [MOTOR LIGHT], but then it will do MOTOR and then it will do LIGHT. You have to combine them. So how do you combine them? I want to leave these (subprocedures) alone, but I want to put them together. Without writing a procedure, putting them together . . . You said one agent does one thing, but if we combine them, then we could (do more than one thing at a time). But how do you combine two programs without writing one program for them all?

Eventually, all students in the study succeeded in decomposing the walker/ flasher task into two loosely coupled processes. But their grasp of agency decomposition was still quite fragile. This fragility was evident when they worked on the tasks involving the LEGO touch sensors. On the most advanced touch-sensor task (in which the walker and flasher must queue up incoming messages), all of the students (at least initially) had difficulty decomposing the task into "parallel" subtasks.

Consider, for example, the case of DB, probably the most proficient Logo programmer in the group. DB had little trouble with the walker/flasher activities, and he started with an agent-based approach for the touch-sensor tasks. He made one agent responsible for all flasher-related activities:

```
Agent 1  ──►   to walk
               talkto "b       ;; motor plugged into port b
               repeat 5 [onfor 30 rd]
               end

Agent 1  ──►   to onwalk
               listento :walker-sensor
               ifelse sensor? [walk onwalk] [onwalk]
               end

Agent 2  ──►   to light
               talkto "a       ;; light plugged into port a
               repeat 10 [onfor 20 wait 20]
               end

Agent 2  ──►   to onlight
               listento :light-sensor
               ifelse sensor? [light onlight] [onlight]
               end

Agent 1  ──►   to sense
               ask 2 [onlight]
               onwalk
               end
```

This program worked well. The decomposition into two agents played an important role: The walker could be started even while the light was flashing, and vice versa. This feature would be difficult to implement with traditional Logo. But then I pushed the walker's touch sensor *while* the walker was moving. It had no effect. I suggested that DB change the program so that the walker could "remember" if its touch sensor had been pushed while it was walking; if it had, the walker should do another walking cycle.

DB understood the problem immediately: "Ah. That's tricky. So it has to keep looking for that (the sensor) even when it's doing the walk." To solve this problem, however, DB resorted to his sequential time-slicing instincts. He explained his plan for the flasher:

> It's going to flash the light on and off, check the sensor, then flash the light on and off . . . So before it turns the light on every time, it's going to check the sensor, whether it's been pushed again.

He changed his light procedure:

```
Agent 2  ──►   to light
               talkto "a
               repeat 10 [if sensor? [light2] onfor20 wait 20]
               end
```

DB explained that LIGHT2 would "do the same thing" as LIGHT itself. That is, it would make the light flash 10 times (on for 2 seconds, off for 2 seconds), checking the sensor between each 4-second flash cycle. (In fact, DB could have simply used LIGHT in place of LIGHT2.) Thus, DB's LIGHT procedure time slices between flashing and checking. This approach, while clever, has a flaw: What if I press and release the sensor *during* one of the flash cycles? Then the procedure will never "know" that the sensor was pushed. When I posed this problem to DB during the next session, he quickly came up with a solution: "We can do it [the flash] for only 1 second," that is, use finer time slicing.

That is a clever patch. Indeed, it adopts the same approach that I used in writing the underlying software to simulate multiple processes. But the patch has problems. It is not possible to write fast time-slicing routines in Logo itself (since Logo, like other "high-level" languages, is quite slow). So DB's procedure might still "miss" the push of the sensor. Moreover, DB's solution is much more complicated than it need be, and it would be very difficult to modify or extend. Using concurrent-programming constructs, it is possible to write a much simpler, more modular solution. (Eventually, DB developed an excellent solution to the touch-sensor task. His solution used seven different agents: two to check the sensors, one to run the walker, one to run the flasher, and three to start the whole thing going.)

Causes of problem-decomposition bugs. In thinking about problem decomposition, some students seemed stuck in the sequential paradigm. They continued to think in terms of "a little for this agent, a little for that agent." This sequential, time-slicing approach was particularly evident (and deeply entrenched) in NL's and FB's thinking. I asked NL and FB to explain how they would coordinate a "real-life" situation in which two people must execute tasks simultaneously, and (at least initially) they both stuck with their time-slicing approaches. Consider this excerpt from my conversation with NL:

M: Let's forget about the computer. Let's say you were going to wash some dishes and I was going to brush my teeth. How would you set it up? So I'm standing at a sink.
N: And I'm standing at a sink.
M: What are you going to do?
N: I'm going to wash a dish. Wash, wash, wash. (To me:) Brush your teeth. And you're going to brush your teeth. And I'm going to wash another dish, and I'm going to tell you to brush your teeth again.

My conversation with FB was very similar. I asked her to "program" a situation in which she had to sweep the floor and her brother had to set the table for dinner:

F: I'm going to tell him to start setting the table, which he won't do. Anyway, he starts on the table, then I go back and start sweeping.
M: So you're going to ask him to set the table, and then you're going to start sweeping.

F: But when I tell him to do it, he only does one plate. But there are five people that he
has to set places for and he only sets one plate. Because he has to repeat this thing.
And I have to repeat. I only make one stroke with my broom. But we have to repeat
it forever. But there is no way both of us . . .

When pressed, NL and FB quickly recognized and admitted the nonsensical
nature of their "programs." Indeed, pressing students to think about "real-life"
models proved to be a good way to nudge them towards a "parallel" programming style. But NL's and FB's initial "solutions" to the real-life problems are an
indication of just how strong their sequential-thinking models are.

It is possible that some students had trouble decomposing problems into
concurrent subtasks precisely *because* of their expertise in traditional programming. The students in the study were among the best Logo programmers in the
school; they could quickly appeal to standard "cliches" of traditional programming (such as time-slicing and functional decomposition). Unfortunately, these
cliches sometimes got in the way as the students tried to master the new
programming paradigm.

BW, who worked together with FB during FB's final session, provides an
interesting contrast. BW, though a good student, had limited Logo programming
skills and had never seen MultiLogo. Nevertheless (or perhaps as a result), her
instincts on agency decomposition were quite good. At the start of the session,
FB (a veteran of three MultiLogo sessions) gave BW a short MultiLogo tutorial.
Then I posed the touch-sensor task. BW suggested creating new agents for each
of the sensor-checking procedures, an excellent suggestion that FB ignored. It is
possible that BW's lack of Logo skills made it easier for her to embrace the new
paradigm. BW would have had great difficulty writing the program to implement
her idea, but she grasped the overall concept of concurrent programming very
quickly.

Synchronization Bugs

Perhaps the most pervasive MultiLogo bugs involved the synchronization of
multiple agents. These bugs differ from the problem-decomposition bugs discussed in the previous section: in a prototypical synchronization bug, a student
successfully decomposes a problem into subtasks for different agents, but then
has difficulty coordinating the activities of those agents.

Examples of synchronization bugs. Students' synchronization bugs tended
to fit into two broad categories: *unintended sequentiality* and *unintended concurrency*. In an unintended-sequentiality bug, the programmer attempts to make two
(or more) agents act concurrently, but gets sequential behavior instead. The
simplest (and most common) example involved the initial walker/flasher activity.
Three of the four students in the study initially wrote procedures similar to these:

```
Agent 1  ──▶     to walk
                 repeat 100 [onfor 80 rd]
                 end

Agent 2  ──▶     to flash
                 repeat 200 [onfor 10 wait 10]
                 end

Agent 2  ──▶     to walk-and-flash
                 flash
                 ask 1 [walk]
                 end

Agent 2  ──▶     walk-and-flash
```

As written, agent 2 will make the light flash 200 times; *then* it will ASK agent 1 to make the walker move forward and back 100 times. The program is still functioning sequentially; the WALK-AND-FLASH procedure does not exploit the potential for concurrency. To make the two activities (walking and flashing) occur concurrently, the two lines in the WALK-AND-FLASH procedure should be reversed: agent 2 should ASK agent 1 to make the walker move; then (while agent 1 is doing that) agent 2 should make the light flash. (It is somewhat ironic that proper concurrency, at least in this case, requires proper *sequencing*.)

Similar difficulties arose in more advanced activities. NL stumbled into a three-agent version of this bug when she tried to coordinate the actions of the screen turtle and the LEGO turtle. At first, NL wrote:

```
Agent 1  ──▶     to both-fd :num
                 ask 2 [talkto "b onfor :num]   ;; one motor in port b
                 talkto "a onfor :num    ;; other motor in port a
                 fd :num
                 end
```

This procedure works quite well, but the screen turtle doesn't move until *after* the LEGO turtle is finished (since agent 1 controls one of the LEGO turtle wheels *and* the screen turtle). To fix this bug, NL realized (correctly) that she needed a third agent. But she added the third agent like this:

```
Agent 1  ──▶     to both-fd :num
                 ask 2 [talkto "b onfor :num]
                 talkto "a onfor :num
                 ask 3 [fd :num]
                 end
```

The program now uses the screen turtle of a different agent, but the screen turtle still does not move until the LEGO turtle finishes. NL ultimately solved the problem by placing the screen-turtle command (ASK 3 [FD :NUM]) *before* the LEGO-turtle commands.

In *unintended-concurrency* bugs, the problem is the reverse: the programmer wants two actions to be sequential, but they end up concurrent instead. DB encountered a subtle unintended-concurrency bug while programming the LEGO turtle. He began by writing these turtle procedures:

```
Agent 1  ——▶   to trt
               talkto "a  ;; left motor in port a
               onfor 30
               end

Agent 2  ——▶   to tlt
               talkto "b  ;; right motor in port b
               onfor 30
               end

Agent 3  ——▶   to tfd
               ask 1 [trt]
               ask 2 [tlt]
               end
```

The TRT (for turtle-right) procedure turns one of the turtle's wheels for 3 seconds—making the turtle turn in an arc. TLT (for turtle-left) turns the other wheel for 3 seconds—making the turtle turn in the opposite direction. TFD (for turtle-forward) runs the TRT and the TLT procedures concurrently—making both wheels turn so that the turtle moves forward. These procedures, when used individually, all worked fine. Problems arose when DB wrote a SQUARE procedure:

```
Agent 3  ——▶   to square
               repeat 4 [tfd ask 1 [trt]]
               end
```

This procedure looks analogous to a traditional turtle-graphics SQUARE procedure. But the procedure does not work: instead of tracing out a square, the turtle goes forward for 12 seconds, then turns right for 12 seconds. To understand the problem, consider what happens when agent 3 executes the SQUARE procedure. Agent 3 executes the following sequence of commands:

TFD
ASK 1 [TRT]
TFD
ASK 1 [TRT]
TFD
ASK 1 [TRT]
TFD
ASK 1 [TRT]

But in executing TFD, agent 3 simply sends two messages: a TRT message to agent 1, and a TLT message to agent 2. So in executing SQUARE, agent 3 does nothing other than send messages. Agent 3 sends 12 messages in all—eight messages from the four TFD commands, and four messages from the four ASK 1 [TRT] commands. Importantly, agent 3 does *not* pause between sending these messages. After sending the two messages as part of its execution of TFD, agent 3 immediately sends a TRT message to agent 1. And after sending the TRT message to agent 1, it immediately executes the next TFD and sends two more messages. And so on.

All of these messages get queued up by agents 1 and 2. Agent 1 gets eight TRT messages in all; agent 2 gets four TLT messages. Agents 1 and 2 gradually work through their queues. For a while, both agents have messages to execute; agent 1 executes TRT while agent 2 executes TLT, so the LEGO turtle goes forward. After 12 seconds (four TLT commands of 3 seconds each), agent 2 runs out of messages in its queue. Agent 1 continues to execute TRT messages by itself, and the turtle turns to the right. DB ultimately solved this synchronization problem by changing the TFD procedure so that it *waits* until one of its "subagents" is finished:

Agent 3 ⟶
```
to tfd
ask 1 [trt]
demand-and-wait 2 [tlt]
ond
```

Causes of synchronization bugs. There seem to be two major causes of synchronization bugs: failure of the conversational metaphor and assumption of "excessive parallelism."

Failure of the conversational metaphor. Novice programmers often make use of what Pea (1986) calls the "conversational metaphor"—that is, they imagine themselves having a conversation with the computer (or, in the case of turtle graphics, with the turtle). This metaphor is deeply rooted, Pea notes, since the programmer "has communicated throughout an entire lifetime in a conversational manner." The conversational metaphor can be very helpful in thinking about programming, but it also leads to some misconceptions. Indeed, Pea argues that many novice programming bugs are caused by programmers' attempts to generalize from natural-language conversations to programming conversations. For example, some novice programmers expect the computer to have human-like interpretive capacities, going beyond the information given in the code. In effect, they expect the computer to "read between the lines," just as a good human listener does.

In MultiLogo programming, the conversational metaphor is even more problematic. MultiLogo "conversations" are different not only from natural-language conversations, but also from Logo "conversations." In a typical Logo conversation, the roles are clear: the programmer is the initiator, and the computer/turtle is a relatively passive recipient. The programmer gives commands, and the computer/turtle executes them (and, perhaps, sends back a response). In a MultiLogo interaction, the situation is much different. After the programmer gives a command to an agent, the agent might send a message to another agent, which, in turn, might send a message to yet another agent (or back to the first agent), and so on. An agent, unlike the computer/turtle of sequential Logo, is not solely a recipient. Each agent can play a dual role, both initiating and receiving commands.

As a result of these differences, programming in MultiLogo requires new metaphors. Writing a MultiLogo program is more like *orchestrating a conversation among others* as opposed to *having a dialogue with another person*. Unfortunately, children typically have little experience orchestrating conversations (or other actions) among groups of people. They have few metaphors or models to draw upon. So they tend to apply more traditional conversational models—often with buggy results.

The failure of the traditional conversational metaphor is manifested in several different ways. Consider, for example, the standard synchronization bug in the walker/flasher procedure:

Agent 2   ⟶
```
to walk-and-flash
walk
ask 1 [flash]
end
```

For at least two students (FB and NL), this bug seemed to arise (at least in part) from an inappropriate extension of the conversational metaphor. FB, for example, explained the procedure like this: "Well, you start one, then you ask the other one to start." Rather than orchestrating the interaction between agent 1 and agent 2, FB apparently imagined herself having conversations with each of the two agents. In this way, FB could view each agent as a passive (that is, noninitiating) recipient, much like the turtle/computer in traditional Logo programming. Since a different agent received each of the two commands, FB expected that the commands should run concurrently.

Interestingly, both FB and NL found the walker/flasher task much easier when I suggested that they add a third agent to coordinate the activities of the other two. NL, for example, quickly typed a procedure of the form:

Agent 3   ⟶
```
to walk-and-flash
ask 1 [walk]
ask 2 [flash]
end
```

This approach fits much more naturally with the traditional Logo conversational metaphor. Each agent has *one* clearly defined role. Agents 1 and 2 act like traditional turtles, carrying out instructions; agent 3 is an initiator, like a Logo programmer. Moreover, the hierarchical structure of the agents in the WALK-

AND-FLASH procedure seems to be a much more familiar organizational structure for the students; even in elementary school, children have already dealt with many hierarchies. NL, for example, quickly labelled the third agent as "the teacher." FB used a similar metaphor. She imagined herself and her brother as agents 1 and 2. Then she added: "My mom would be agent 3."

The conversational metaphor also falls short along another dimension: it does not provide a strong model for situations in which one agent wants to communicate with another, but the recipient is already "busy." In real-life conversations, this situation is unlikely, since we get sensory feedback. We know if another person is already talking or otherwise occupied. In Logo "conversations," we never need to worry: if the turtle/computer is busy executing instructions, we can't even type any new instructions. Thus, many programmers are totally unprepared for MultiLogo-style interactions among agents. They are unaccustomed to thinking about whether the recipient of a message might be busy. Consider, for example, DB's attempts to program the LEGO turtle to walk in a square (described early in this section). In orchestrating messages among agents, DB never seemed to think about whether a message's recipient might already be executing a message.

Assumption of "excessive parallelism." In writing programs in traditional sequential languages, novices sometimes exhibit what Pea (1986) calls "parallelism bugs." That is, they assume that several lines of a program can be "active" or executing at the same time. Soloway, Bonar, Barth, Rubin, and Wolf (1981), for example, found that 34% of the students in an introductory Pascal course assumed a type of parallelism in the execution of a WHILE loop: They thought that the program *continuously* monitored the WHILE test condition as it executed the body of the loop, exiting from the loop as soon as the test condition became true. Similarly, Pea (1986) found that more than half of the students in one high-school BASIC course expected IF-THEN conditional statements to act as demons, executing *whenever* the conditional predicate became true.

Students programming in MultiLogo exhibited a related bug: they sometimes assumed that a single agent could do more than one thing at a time. In some cases, the bug manifested itself in familiar ways. For example, some students assumed that an agent could continue to check an IF statement while performing other actions. But the bug also had new manifestations in MultiLogo, making it even more prevalent than in traditional Logo programming. It was very common, for example, for students to think that an agent could send messages *and* perform other actions at the same time.

In at least some cases, this assumption of *parallelism within an agent* seemed to be an underlying cause for the walker/flasher synchronization bug:

```
Agent 1    ──→    to walk-and-flash
                  walk
                  ask 2 [flash]
                  end
```

After NL wrote a procedure similar to this, I asked her to explain the meaning of the line ASK 2 [FLASH]. She replied: "Can you please do this for me? I'm busy walking." Clearly, she imagined that agent 1 sent the message *while* it was walking.

FB had a similar misconception about an agent *receiving* a message: she thought that the agent (if busy) could continue with its current activity *and* execute the message at the same time. In one particular case, an agent was making a LEGO light flash, when another agent DEMANDed that the agent execute the message ONFOR 100. FB predicted that the light would go on for 10 seconds, then resume flashing. This prediction was correct, but her reasoning was flawed. Her explanation:

> This is how I thought about it. The procedure was running. Then that little guy who goes around and picks people found out that you wanted something else to happen. This is the light, going on every other minute. But then over here it has another whole procedure, and it wants the light on. And it does it. And it meets with this (the flashing procedure) but it also fills in the times when it's off. So it will run continuously together.

Clearly, FB imagined that the agent was executing *both* procedures (the flashing and the ONFOR 100) at the same time. In her mind, the ONFOR 100 command "fills in" and turns on the light for the periods during which the flashing command would have otherwise turned the light off.

The excessive-parallelism bug seemed relatively robust, persisting even in the face of my repeated warnings that agents can do only one thing at a time. What factors could cause such a robust bug? Most analyses of parallelism bugs have focused on novices' use of natural-language interpretations for programming commands. Bonar and Soloway (1985), for example, explain the Pascal "WHILE demon" bug like this:

> In natural language, *while* is typically used as a continuously active test . . . This kind of control structure is unusual in a programming language. More typical is a construct in which the loop condition gets tested once per loop iteration (e.g., the WHILE loop in Pascal). The surface link between the two kinds of "while" allows a novice to infer similar semantics.

This analysis provides a reasonable explanation for parallelism bugs in sequential languages. But it does not adequately explain students' excessive use of parallelism in MultiLogo. In MultiLogo, students' parallelism bugs do not appear to be linked to misinterpretation of particular words (like WHILE or IF). Other factors seems to be at work.

In some cases, the bug was probably caused by the students' overgeneralization of a new concept. When a new concept is introduced, students are likely to use it (at least initially) in some inappropriate contexts. In this case, students tended to overuse the new idea of concurrency, applying it (inappropriately) to individual agents.

The use of LEGO devices might also have contributed to the strength of the bug. Consider a situation in which an agent turns on a LEGO motor (or light), then performs some other action. Some students seemed to think that the agent needed to perform some *continuing action* in order to keep the motor (or light) on. This model gave students the false impression that the agent was doing two things at the same time.

Probably the most important factor, though, was the way students identified agents with people. I encouraged this identification in my explanations, and students quickly adopted the metaphor. But this personification of agents had an unintended side effect. Some students seemed to reason that agents, like people, should be able to do several things at the same time. Indeed, students were most likely to attribute multiple simultaneous actions to a single agent precisely when the agent was performing actions that a person *could* do simultaneously. The misconception that an agent should be able to simultaneously perform an action and send a message (i.e., talk to someone else) is a case in point; people can certainly walk and talk at the same time.

This factor was highlighted when I asked NL to think about a "real-life" situation in which she had to wash some dishes and I had to brush my teeth. How would she "program" these actions? She replied: "I'm going to do the dishes, and *while* I'm doing a dish, I'll tell you to brush your teeth" (emphasis added). If people can do it that way, why not agents?

Object-Oriented Bugs

MultiLogo includes many different types of objects: agents, turtles, ports (on the LEGO interface box), motors, sensors. This multitude of objects sometimes caused confusion for the students in the study. The students did not seem to have a clear model of which commands influenced which types of objects, or how each type of object interacted with the others.

These confusions led to a collection of bugs that I call *object-oriented bugs*. Although some of these bugs might arise in traditional Logo programming (particularly in LEGO/Logo), they seem far more common in MultiLogo programming, due to the greater variety of object types.

Examples of object-oriented bugs. The most common object-oriented bugs involved confusions between agents and other objects. In particular, students often mixed up which commands affected agents, and which commands affected other objects (such as motors). This confusion was most evident when students wanted to *stop* objects. In almost all cases, students had difficulty understanding the difference between stopping an agent, stopping a procedure, stopping a motor, and stopping a turtle. In FB's first session, for example, she programmed agent 1 to make the LEGO walker move forward and back several times:

Agent 1 ⟶   repeat 100 [onfor 50 rd]

When FB wanted to stop the walker, she typed:

Agent 2 ⟶   halt 1

This command halts agent 1—but it does not turn off the motor that agent 1 was controlling. So the walker keeps moving (although it no longer reverses direction). This result surprised FB, but she quickly came up with an explanation: she must have told the agent to HALT while it was executing the RD command. In her mind, the HALT command stopped only the RD; the ONFOR command was still working, so the walker continued to move.

SM also had problems when he tried to stop the walker. He started the walker with a REPEAT instruction similar to the one that FB used. When he wanted to stop the walker, he typed OFF. The motor turned off, and SM thought he was done. But a few seconds later, the motor turned back on, much to SM's amazement. The reason: the OFF command simply turned off the motor, it did not halt the agent. The agent was still running its REPEAT instruction. So the next time the agent executed an ONFOR command (within the execution of the REPEAT instruction), the motor turned back on.

I explained the problem to SM, and he came up with an alternative solution: He told the agent to HALT. But that led to the same problem that FB had: the agent stopped, but the motor kept going. In fact, to stop both the agent and the walker, you must give a sequence of two commands, and the commands must be in the proper order. First you must HALT the agent, then tell the agent to turn OFF the motor.

NL had similar problems with a turtle project. Her problems resulted from a confusion between agents and turtles. She wanted to use two LEGO touch sensors to control a screen turtle (with each sensor making the turtle turn in a different direction). But NL had difficulties, largely because she continually confused agents and turtles. She wanted to use two agents (one for each touch sensor) to control one turtle. But the concepts of agents and turtles were so closely associated in NL's mind that she had trouble thinking about them separately. Both in her comments and her code, she kept referring to turtles when she meant agents, and vice versa.

Causes of object-oriented bugs. It is not surprising that the students had some difficulty distinguishing between different types of objects. In their previous Logo experience, the students never needed to make such distinctions. They could, for instance, think of "Logo" and the "turtle" as the same thing. To stop a graphics procedure, it didn't matter if they thought about "stopping the procedure" or "stopping Logo" or "stopping the turtle." The results were the same.

This type of thinking, however, leads to problems in MultiLogo programming. NL, for instance, had a particularly strong association between "Logo" and "the turtle." In the first session, when I said something about typing commands "to Logo," she interrupted: "I like to think of it as talking to the turtle." In fact, she had even given a name (Harry) to the turtle, and she referred to the turtle by its name. This close association between Logo and the turtle can be very useful in traditional Logo programming. But the close association probably made it difficult for NL to separate the concepts of agent and turtle in MultiLogo.

These problems were probably exacerbated by my decision to allow students to refer to agents by number rather than giving the agents names. With agents identified only by number, it was easy for students to confuse agents with turtles (which are identified by number in LogoWriter), or with ports on the interface box (which are identified by letters and numbers). If the students had given agents names, they might have been more likely to view the agents as distinct entities.

The distinction between agents and interface-box ports was further confused by the fact that both objects seem to be involved in some type of communication. Agents send messages to one another (using ASK and DEMAND), but agents also send messages (like ON and OFF) to interface-box ports. Thus, the roles of agents and ports can easily be confused.

LESSONS

The empirical study revealed certain common problems for novice MultiLogo programmers—overgeneralization of parallelism, misuse of the conversational metaphor, continued reliance of sequentialist techniques, overpersonification of agents, confusion among various types of objects. These same problems (or closely related variants) will likely arise as novices begin to use other concurrent-programming languages. Some of these difficulties could be eased by *changes in the design* of concurrent-programming languages. But the learnability of a programming language is not a property of the language alone; the way in which the language is taught is equally important. So *changes in pedagogy* might be needed. Below, I discuss possible changes in design and pedagogy, based on the three categories of concurrent-programming bugs.

Problem-decomposition bugs. When students had difficulty decomposing problems into subtasks for separate agents, I often asked them to write informal "programs" to solve "real-life" problems, such as household chores. This tactic seemed to work well. Some students initially gave solutions heavily influenced by "sequentialist" thinking, in effect time slicing between different people rather than having the people work in parallel. But the students quickly recognized the nonsensical nature of the time-slicing approach, and they developed new solutions based on concurrent actions by different people. Moreover, the students were able to transfer this idea to the programming domain, solving programming tasks that had earlier presented difficulties.

In future use of MultiLogo, it would be a good idea to make even greater use of such "real-world" examples. These examples should be supported with discussions about different approaches to problem decomposition. It is important for students to gain an understanding of the differences between *functional* decomposition and *agency* decomposition, and a better sense of how and when to use each type of decomposition.

Synchronization bugs. To work through synchronization bugs, it is a good idea for students to "play agent"—that is, act out what each agent is supposed to do. This activity requires a group of students, each playing the role of a different agent. Messages can be represented by pieces of paper that agents deliver to one another. Each agent/student should carry some sort of box or folder to hold a queue of messages. By acting out MultiLogo programs in this way, students can see how MultiLogo programs are much more like *orchestrating a conversation among others* rather than *having a dialogue with another person*. Thus, they can begin to develop a broader version of the conversational metaphor. Students can also confront their "excessive-parallelism" tendencies by carefully acting out their scripts, making sure to do only one thing at a time. After acting out a program, students should trade roles and act it out again, so that each student can see what the process looks like from different perspectives. This tactic could help students develop an ability to "decenter"—that is, put themselves in the place of different agents.

Object-oriented bugs. Perhaps the most important antidote to object-oriented bugs is a more explicit introduction to the various types of objects in MultiLogo (agents, turtles, motors, etc.). In introducing MultiLogo, it is important to discuss which commands affect which objects, and how various objects relate to one another.

Changes in the design of MultiLogo's *agent* construct could also be helpful. MultiLogo agents are designed to be as general as possible. Each agent starts out identical; it is up to the user to give each agent particular features. For example, if a user wants one agent to control the motor of a car, the user can customize the agent as follows: name the agent something like CAR-MOTOR, plug the car motor into port A on the interface box, and type the command TALKTO "A to the CAR-MOTOR agent. Then any command typed to the CAR-MOTOR agent will control the car motor.

This approach provides the programmer with a great deal of flexibility. But it can also lead to confusion. Some students (understandably) got confused between the TALKTO command for choosing a port on the interface box, and the ASK and DEMAND commands for sending messages to agents. The problem is that the message-passing metaphor is being used in two different ways: in one case to refer to messages sent from one agent to the interface box, in the other case to refer to messages sent from one agent to another.

One way to avoid this confusion is to create *specialized agents*—in this case, agents designed to talk to specific ports on the LEGO interface box. For example, one particular agent would be responsible for all instructions sent to port A of the interface box. Perhaps the agent would be named PORT-A. So to control a LEGO device plugged into port A, you would simply send the appropriate message to the PORT-A agent. This approach unifies the two forms of communication; the TALKTO command could be eliminated.

Similarly, it is not clear that all agents should have personal turtles. It would be worth experimenting with a version in which certain specialized agents controlled the screen turtles. Those specialized agents could be seen *as* turtles, not as *having* turtles. With this approach, the confusion between agents and turtles might be reduced.

FUTURE DIRECTIONS

My work with MultiLogo raises as many questions as it answers. Among the possible directions for future research:

Empirical studies. My initial empirical study suggests many possible follow-ups. For one thing, it would be interesting to observe nonexperts as they gain more experience and work on more complex MultiLogo programs. What programming difficulties would be most persistent? What new difficulties would arise? In addition, it would be worth investigating how previous programming experience (with traditional sequential languages) affects a person's ability to learn concurrent programming. My initial study gave mixed indications on this question. Finally, it would be interesting to study how children apply concurrent programming concepts and metaphors to other domains. Does experience with MultiLogo affect the way they approach other complex (but noncomputer) design tasks? Does it affect the way they think about multi-object physical systems (like the solar system)? Does it affect the way they think about their own minds?

Other models of concurrency. MultiLogo represents just one approach for introducing concurrency into programming. MultiLogo is well suited for certain concurrent programming tasks (such as robotic control), but it is ill suited for others. For example, it would be difficult to use MultiLogo to model behaviors involving hundreds or thousands of concurrent processes—such as the flocking behavior of birds or the foraging behavior of an ant colony. I am currently developing a new concurrent language for these types of applications (Resnick, 1991). This new language, tentatively called *Logo, is being implemented on the Connection Machine, a massively parallel computer with thousands of processors. With this new language, I hope to explore how people (particularly children) learn new ideas about *emergent* and *self-organizing* behaviors.

These types of projects can lead to new insights into how people learn, use, and understand concurrent programming. Such insights are critical in a new field like concurrent programming. If concurrent languages are difficult to learn and use, they will never have a widespread impact. Indeed, the growth of concurrent programming could ultimately be paced by the ease with which programmers are able to learn and use the new ideas of concurrency.

ACKNOWLEDGMENTS

Hal Abelson and Seymour Papert provided intellectual guidance in the design, development, and testing of MultiLogo. Chris Hanson, Bill Rozas, and Andy Berlin (of the MIT AI Lab), and Allan Toft (of the LEGO Group), generously shared their time and expertise in helping me implement MultiLogo. Edith Ackermann, Mike Eisenberg, Andee Rubin, Brian Silverman, and Franklyn Turbak provided helpful comments throughout the course of the project.

The LEGO Group, the National Science Foundation (Grants 851031-0195, MDR-8751190, and TPE-8850449), and the General Electric Foundation have provided financial support for my work with MultiLogo.

REFERENCES

Bonar, J., & Soloway, E. (1985). Preprogramming knowledge: A major source of misconceptions in novice programmers. *Human-Computer Interaction*, *1*, 133–161.

du Boulay, B., O'Shea, T, & Monk, J. (1981). The black box inside the glass box: Presenting computing concepts to novices. *International Journal of Man-Machine Studies*, *14*, 237–249.

Gelertner, D. (1986). Domesticating parallelism. *Computer*, *19* (8), 12–16.

Goldberg, A., & Robson, D. (1983). *Smalltalk-80: The language and its implementation*. Reading, MA: Addison-Wesley.

Hewitt, C. (1977). Viewing control structures as patterns of passing messages. *Journal of Artificial Intelligence*, *8* (3), 323–364.

Mayer, R. (1981). The psychology of how novices learn computer programming. *ACM Computing Surveys*, *13* (1).

Papert, S. (1980). *Mindstorms: Children, computers, and powerful ideas*. New York: Basic Books.

Pea, R. D. (1986). Language-independent conceptual 'bugs' in novice programming. *Journal of Educational Computer Research*, *2* (1), 25–36.

Pea, R. D., Soloway, E., & Spohrer, J. C. (1987, Winter). The buggy path to the development of programming expertise. *Focus on Learning Problems in Mathematics*, *9* (1).

Resnick, M. (1988). *MultiLogo: A study of children and concurrent programming*. Unpublished master's thesis, MIT Dept. of Electrical Engineering and Computer Science.

Resnick, M., Ocko, S., & Papert, S. (1988). LEGO, Logo, and design. *Children's Environments Quarterly*, *5* (4), 14–18.

Resnick, M. (1991). Animal simulations with *Logo: Massive parallelism for the masses. In J. A. Meyer & S. Wilson (Eds.), *From animals to animats*. Cambridge, MA: MIT Press.

Soloway, E., Bonar, J., Barth, J., Rubin, E., & Woolf, B. (1981). Programming and cognition: Why your students write those crazy programs. In *Proceedings of the National Educational Computing Conference*, pp. 206–219.

Stephen Sherman Photography

Mitchel Resnik (center) discusses his work at the Epistemology & Learning Group Research Seminar. To his right, David Chen and Alan Shaw; to his left, Hillel Weintraub and Gregory Gargarian.

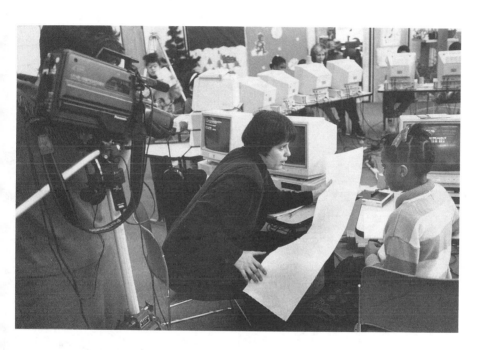

PART V

VIDEO AS A
RESEARCH TOOL
FOR EXPLORING
AND DOCUMENTING
CONSTRUCTIONIST LEARNING

22

The Silent Observer
and Holistic Note Taker:
Using Video for Documenting a Research Project

Idit Harel

THE ROLE OF VIDEO IN ISDP RESEARCH[1]

The quantitative and qualitative research techniques that were used for the Instructional Software Design Project (ISDP) involved the extensive use of videotaping. Four different approaches for using video were used for documenting ISDP. In what I named VideoMode 1, I utilized video as a *holistic interview-recorder*. In VideoMode 2, I utilized video as a *silent observer*. In VideoMode 3 the medium was used as a *video-based note taker*. VideoModes 1, 2, and 3 contributed greatly, but differently, to the data collection process, and especially to the quantitative, qualitative, and comparative analysis of the study's results. VideoMode 4 was a process of conducting research and observation of phenomena through *chunking and editing* and through *preparing video presentations*.

The videotaping was done for several purposes: first, for an assessment of children's learning of mathematics, programming, and software design during ISDP; second, for a documentation of the development of the project's culture in the whole class, among particular students, and in relation to the teacher; and third, for a comparison of the experimental class's knowledge with that of two control classes.

I must admit that video making was not one of my primary research goals, and I do not value my video data as being "beautiful" or "good" in the conventional artistic senses of film and video production.[2] I only wish to describe here how

---

[1] ISDP was a 6-month-long inquiry of children's Logo-based learning project, and was conducted at Project Headlight, in a Boston inner-city public-school. In ISDP, a fourth-grade class was engaged during one semester in the design and production of educational software to teach fractions. See Harel, 1988, 1991; and Harel and Papert, this volume.

[2] It is important to mention that video making was not a central goal of the research itself. The techniques I used would probably be considered quite inappropriate among most film- and video-

video was used for my specific research. I do not claim that certain uses of video as a researcher's tool are better than others. Also, I am not concerned with creating a hierarchical ranking of various uses of video. Rather, I wish to describe how the implementation of various video techniques in ISDP contributed to the data collection and research analysis. I did find that each of these different uses of a videocamera captured certain aspects of the research better than other research tools could have done. Video assisted me in systematically capturing conceptual, learning-related, and developmental phenomena. I claim that certain data on such complex phenomena could only be captured, and later analyzed in detail, through video.

VIDEOMODE 1: USING VIDEO FOR A HOLISTIC DOCUMENTATION OF INTERVIEWS WITH RESEARCH PARTICIPANTS

The holistic characteristics of video documentation[3] were utilized in several contexts during the ISDP research. For establishing a base line about children's knowledge of fractions and Logo programming before ISDP began, 51 children from three classes (one experimental and two control classes) were given written and computer-based tests and were also interviewed at length on video, using the Piagetian clinical method. The camera was placed on a tripod during these interviews, focusing sometimes on both the researcher and the child, and at other times only on the child.

Today, the most common piece of technology researchers use in interviewing is the audiotape. It is usually used for recording interviews when a word-by-word transcript is crucial for the research. The audiotape is preferred over handwritten notes because it records the data in a more "objective" way and frees the researcher from taking careful notes during the interview. This approach enables him or her to focus on the person being interviewed—which makes the process of

---

making communities. I used video as an observer and note taker (these techniques will be described in detail later in this chapter). I point out that there is a difference between taking handwritten notes for oneself and taking notes for others. The videocamera could be used for both; however, I used it mostly for 'taking notes' without considering an audience other than myself. I therefore did not give special attention to the quality of the shots (images, background, sound), nor to the message these shots might convey to people other than me. In any case, it turned out that the video methods I had tested were very informative and important to the research enterprise, despite the low quality of the audio and the visuals.

[3] See Nira Granott Farber (1990) for a discussion of this issue of the "holistic" aspects of video-recording.

interviewing much more "friendly and comfortable" for all participants. In addition, audiotape allows for postinterview replay and reanalysis of any given moment in the interview—an advantage it has in common with the videocamera. A disadvantage of the videocamera, in comparison with the audiotape, is the effect it can have on the ambiance of the interview. Most people feel more comfortable and less intimidated in front of an audiorecorder than in front of a camera. However, this was not a problem for most children in my study, who had become accustomed to the several videocameras used by various researchers at Project Headlight.

Any advantages in terms of comfort would in this case have been offset by the importance of being able to view the students' facial expressions and body language, which, for the purpose of answering certain research questions, were as important as what was actually said (or not said) during the interview sessions. Since most of these interviews focused on the idea of constructing and talking about representations of fractions, children often used movement and facial expressions for expressing their ideas. They were also asked to work with some manipulative materials (blocks, clay, drawings, pegs)—activities that could only be captured in detail on video. I therefore opted for what I considered a superior method of recording children's conceptual understanding and their multiways of expressing their knowledge and ideas to me.

After the preinterviews and tests were done, ISDP started. All three classes (experimental and controls) followed the regular mathematics curriculum, including a 2-month unit on fractions. However, the control classes differed from the experimental class, and from each other, in their computer learning experience. When the Project ended, posttests and interviews were conducted with the experimental and control groups to document the differences in their performances and knowledge. All these interviews were again recorded in VideoMode 1. These pre- and postvideodata allowed me to view segments back to back, and to capture, for example, any growth or change that occurred in children's understanding of fractions and their representations, or in their attitudes towards mathematics in general. I could measure response time when needed, look for regulations, and code the information systematically according to categories of interest. As I watched the videos over again, new categories for analyses emerged. Some aspects of the qualitative and quantitative analysis of each child and the cross-analysis of several groups of children could not have been done through the use of notes or audiorecorded interviews.

Finally, VideoMode 1 was often used *during* the period of ISDP as well. For example, if I had certain questions I wanted to ask the teacher or the children about their projects and learning, I videotaped the person in the process of answering and reacting to my questions. The camera was placed on a tripod for these interviews. In summary, close to 80 hours of video data in the form of VideoMode 1 were collected for the ISDP research.

VIDEOMODE 2: USING VIDEO AS A "SILENT OBSERVER" FOR DOCUMENTING PARTICIPANTS' DEVELOPMENT DURING A PROJECT

In VideoMode 2, the videocamera was placed on a tripod in one position for an entire session and simply allowed to run (often for an entire hour). VideoMode 2 was used to capture classroom discussions, brainstorming sessions, one or two children working on their software projects at their computer, and the teacher's or the researcher's interactions with her students. VideoMode 2 was my *major* way of using video in ISDP. Since ISDP lasted close to 4 months, VideoMode 2 captured a great quantity of developmental phenomena. It was used much like *another observer* who takes extensive notes about children in action.[4] However, it was different from a human observer, since it captured data more "objectively" and more comprehensively than even the most experienced human researcher could do by hand.

VideoMode 2 not only captured data in an objective and holistic way, but also "freed" me as a researcher. I needed to be an active participant in this environment. With the use of VideoMode 2, I did not have to be concerned about the camera, and I was able to devote my full attention to my work with the children. Therefore, from the children's and teacher's point of view, I became more of a helper in the culture than an observer.

I collected close to 60 hours in video in VideoMode 2, which allowed me to later observe children and teacher learning, designing, and interacting—often in situations when I was not directly present.

I found that VideoMode 2 was the most objective way of documenting children at work. Whatever happened in front of the camera was taped, without preplanning or any fixed agenda. The only "agenda" I had was, for example, to "capture Tim and Monica once a week in VideoMode 2." But I did not ask them questions, nor did I tell them what to do, or how to act, at the times when the camera was there to record them. I therefore believe that using the camera in VideoMode 2 was the least intimidating for the research participants. Since no person carried the camera, the participants felt quite free to act the way they usually do. In certain situations, however, the participants did react to the camera. They approached the camera and spoke to it, demonstrated things to it, or joked with it. These situations, in fact, revealed very important ideas that were present in children's minds on a given day, revealed information about their projects, and captured moments related to social play. I believe that such

---

[4] At the end of each session I took many handwritten notes, but usually on issues I was involved with directly and personally at that day. The camera, however, was usually placed next to children I did not plan to work with on a particular day. Therefore, it collected data for me—data that I could easily miss (in quantity as well as quality) if the camera was not collecting it for me.

moments could not have been so beautifully captured if a person, not a tripod, had been holding the camera. Here is an example.

The Importance of VideoMode 2 in Investigating Tim's Case. Tim, one of the most successful children in what we describe as "school mathematics," usually scored high on school tests and was a very proper, self-disciplined, and organized student. Not surprisingly, Tim developed much greater knowledge of fractions and Logo after ISDP. Although he scored high in the posttesting, it turned out that the most important revelation, captured by video, was not the effect of ISDP on "how he got better in solving school-like problems," but closely related to what I discovered about other aspects of his experience. In the video, I saw new facets of Tim's personality, and observed how they affected his style of involvement in ISDP and, hence, his learning. VideoMode 2 recorded the many occasions when Tim spoke spontaneously to the camera about what he was doing at that time. Tim was never asked to speak to the camera, but he liked very much to do so. He would often turn around, look straight into the camera's lens, and say things such as: "This is the six o'clock news. And we focus today on Tim's Fractions Software ,. . ." He would then demonstrate his piece of software, step-by-step, to his imaginary "six o'clock news audience," explaining his fractions representations, and his Logo-related discoveries. At other times, he would say to the camera, "Wait. I will return shortly after I help Cassina with her programming, and will tell you more about my very, very cool project."

At times, Tim also introduced his partner Micky to his imaginary "news audience": "This is my friend Micky. We work together every once in a while. His project is cool, too. Let's look at what he has accomplished so far." Tim and Micky presented each other's progress to the camera, told jokes to it, and socialized in front of, and with, it. They "collected" a great deal of data for me about their own processes and progress in the project.

First, I believe they would not have done all that if I had been carrying the camera. Second, with 17 children around me, I was not able, even if I wanted, to invest a great deal of time with any one child. I could not play and joke with children in the same way they did with my camera. I could never have recorded such detailed reports of their projects as they voluntarily presented to the camera.

To summarize, VideoMode 2 captured two important aspects of Tim's personality. It revealed a "playful Tim," very different from the "successful, proper, shy, quiet" Tim familiar to his teachers and me. The camera on a tripod did not intimidate him. The opposite: He was captured as a free, spontaneous, uncensored, and much more joyful child who blossomed in the absence of adults. Tim expressed himself very differently when he was left alone, or with a couple of friends with whom he could fool around and exchange ideas. In this playful mode, Tim did extremely creative, yet disciplined, work on a project that was meaningful for him.

Another aspect of Tim's work that was captured in VideoMode 2 was his relationship with Micky. They sat next to each other during the 4 months of the project. Much like professional adults, they worked together, had fun together, and helped each other on fractions and Logo programming. Individually and collaboratively they were trying to accomplish the same job. The camera recorded their unusually relaxed and non-competitive relationship. Yet it also recorded how each of them was very concerned about his own processes and product, which later resulted in two different pieces of instructional software.

VIDEOMODE 3: USING VIDEO AS A "NOTE-TAKING"TOOL

In VideoMode 3, the videocamera was carried by me and directed at taping interesting events. Certain aspects of VideoMode 3 are the closest to conventional video-making techniques. When certain events occurred that seemed to me to be significant for answering my research questions, I videotaped them instead of taking notes by hand. VideoMode 3 was used mostly for capturing something that was interesting *conceptually*. Although the quality of the image and sound were not necessarily my first priority, I did sometimes use it for capturing a "good shot" of a child at work; "a close-up" of someone's laugh, joy of accomplishment, frustration; or an interesting interaction among children or between a teacher and a child. However, much like VideoMode 1, these shots were more purposeful and subjective, and were directed at recording certain things that were important for me personally, as the researcher—for later observation and analysis.

VIDEOMODES 1, 2, AND 3: THEIR IMPORTANCE TO THE ANALYSIS OF BOTH THE QUANTITATIVE, QUALITATIVE, AND COMPARATIVE RESULTS

By the time I had completed my study, I had accumulated close to 100 hours of video in the form of VideoMode 1. This data included about 80 hours of pre- and postinterviews with 51 fourth-graders, 5 hours of interviews with the teacher during the project, and 2 hours of interviews with her a year after the project ended. In addition, my colleague Carol Stein (a professional editor who collaborated with me on the editing project) interviewed me about the project, and together we interviewed Seymour Papert as well. I also had close to 60 hours of video in the form of VideoMode 2, which showed children working at their computers, giving classroom presentations, and brainstorming (Goldman

Segall's footage was available to me as well[5]). And finally, I had images of the Headlight computer pods, including close-up shots of the children's computer screens, as well as close-ups of their designer's notebooks showing explanations of their story boards, designs, and plans and how these related to the final pieces of software.

These video data were used in the analysis of the study's results to supplement my personal hand-written observations, the children's daily Logo files, the contents of their designer's notebooks, and their written fractions and Logo tests. Video made significant contribution to the analyses of individual children's work in ISDP, as well as to the comparative analysis of the three classes of children. Although the other data (nonvideo) I collected was as important, I cannot imagine conducting and analyzing a constructionist research project of this kind without the video data I had collected. Here are two examples.

The Contribution of VideoModes 1, 2, and 3 to the Investigation of Debbie's Case. As I analyzed Debbie's case, I often had to consider the video data. My data in the form of VideoMode 2, for example, enabled me to observe Debbie often sitting by herself at the back of the classroom. She looked self-conscious and insecure. The video captured how rarely she participated in classroom discussions and how seldomly she interacted with the other children outside of the classroom.

I had not expected ISDP to transform Debbie's personality and social life. However, I discovered in my video segments that her particular style of involvement and her thinking and learning did change in ways that I had not anticipated. On camera during ISDP, she appears deeply engaged in her designs and programming work, which convinced me that something in the ISDP approach had "clicked" for her. My earlier video segments demonstrated that she didn't connect with the regular classroom activities. However, later video data showed that she connected powerfully to this particular project. For example, as I observed her independence and her stubbornness on video from the ISDP period, I realized that these characteristics were probably a strength for her in a project of this kind. She was able to work on her own, in a private manner—but she could also share her ideas via the computer screens without being concerned about direct communication with others. The video I had in VideoMode 3 showed that Debbie developed ideas about teaching and explaining which she applied in a direct, sometimes stern, manner that contrasted with her usual intimidated and isolated stance.

Another change that was captured on video in VideoMode 1 was the way in which Debbie's initial lack of excitement about fractions in the preinterviews

---

[5] Ricki Goldman Segall's video data (Chapter 23, this volume) was also available to me at that time. Although she did not have any particular data on ISDP, she did have many images of the children I had worked with, of their teacher, and of the school. She also provided me with several excellent video segments about Debbie. I thank her for letting me use some of her beautiful video clips in my edited tapes.

gave way to a growing interest and comprehension. The extent of this appropriation is evidenced in the general knowledge of fractions Debbie displayed in the videotaped interviews conducted before and after the project. As stated previously, like most children in the preinterviews, her fractions knowledge was limited and she was insecure and vague. After the project ended, the video helped me compare her language, performance, and definitions with those of 50 other children. It showed that Debbie felt much more comfortable when talking about fractions than other children did, and that she overcame many of the rigid notions she demonstrated in the preinterview.

The video also captured for me how Debbie came to be known for her good ideas and how she enjoyed feeling creative and successful. Other children wanted to see or play with her software, and gave her positive comments: "I love it!" or "This is fresh!" Then, they would ask her to teach them how to do things: "How did you ever make these colors change?" In VideoMode 3, I also taped how Debbie's representation of the house became part of the general classroom culture. A few weeks after Debbie completed her representation of the house and the wagons, Tim's house appeared on video, and then, Paul's. Of course, all these video data complemented the school-test scores, and the results from Debbie's written tests.

In retrospect, Debbie's case was extremely rich. Yet, she did not have the "ideal" personality for participating in the type of experimental investigation that required a great deal of collaboration with the researcher and a continual sharing of personal ideas, thoughts, knowledge of various kinds, designs, and programming problems. Interacting with Debbie was sometimes difficult, and I often felt I had to play games with her to elicit a meaningful response. Video-Mode 2—that is, the "silent observer"—was crucial for collecting data on a child like Debbie. Such children are often ignored by researchers in favor of children whose personalities and attitudes make them easier or more enjoyable to work with. (In fact, I did not plan to focus on Debbie at first, and I had much more data about other children in her class.) With the assistance of my video as the "silent observer and note taker," I was able to develop a sense of who Debbie was. It was the reviewing of all my data (video and nonvideo) in integration that made me decide that I should choose to investigate—and, more importantly, to present—her case to teachers and researchers, not only because of its intrinsic interest, but also because of the general importance of gathering and presenting data on children who are socially and academically at risk.

The Contribution of VideoModes 1, 2, and 3 to the Investigation of Sherry's Case. Another demonstration of the high value of video data is the case of Sherry. Sherry was a slow worker, easily distracted, and quite disorganized in her thinking and writing. Her concentration was intermittent, and she was rarely fully engaged in her regular school work, as was captured in the earlier video segments. However, the camera later captured Sherry's ways of enjoying ISDP. In VideoMode 2, I was able to record her *processes* of designing one of the more interesting pieces of software in this class. Given her personality and style of work, organizing a project of this kind was in itself an important learning experience. Her Logo program was not as large or complex as some of the other children's but the video data made me realize that it was quite an accomplishment for her. My video data emphasized, for example, that, for Sherry, the *length* of the project was a crucial factor in enabling her to become engaged in it and see it through to a finished produced. The video shows that she did not accomplish much during any individual session. Still, it was rare to see her as involved with her other school work as she was in ISDP. Moreover, the videocamera, the videocamera captured Sherry's unique body language, which made me realize that Sherry's style was to move and dance as she thinks and solve problems—behaviors which are certainly not encouraged in other classroom settings, but which enabled her to function effectively.

Sherry did not write much in her Designer's Notebook (unlike Debbie). But even the little that was videotaped about her notes and designs provided a window into her progress. She started with what she described as "fractionizing shapes." And later, she created in her Notebook a "generic design" for all the screens that show "fractionized shapes." The camera also recorded how the month of April (i.e., the second month of the project) was a transitional period for her. Sherry then stopped working on shapes and started to think about a very different kind of representation: *The Clock*. The video data allowed me to capture this process of transition, and to explore "with her" the discoveries she made as she was moving her fingers on the computer screen, calculating angles, taking notes, and programming her animation of the Clock.

Sherry did well on most items in the videotaped postinterview, but the most interesting moment in the postinterview occurred when she looked around the room and chose to talk about the clock as a representation of a fraction. Only the camera could capture how she "struggled" at this part of the interview. Although Sherry had spent an entire month programming a clock in Logo, during the interview it seemed she was still at a transitional level of understanding the different properties of this representation. A great deal of information was nonverbal in this interview: her shy smile, her animated big eyes, and her use of her hands to express and explore many of her thoughts. Videotaping was crucial for understanding and analyzing what was going on with her. Sherry was thinking of what the clock represents in relation to fractions. The clock as an object is quite confusing, since it represents both fractions as area (in its shape divided by the clock's hands), as well as fractions in time (days, hours, minutes, seconds, etc.). This segment of the interview raised many epistemological questions in my mind in the same way it did for Sherry. But I could always observe Sherry on video, again and again, and ask: What is really going on in Sherry's mind?[6]

---

[6] One thing I am planning to do in the future is to show children moments, such as the one described here of Sherry, and analyze these moments with them. This points towards another important use of video as a research tool.

VIDEOMODE 4: DOING RESEARCH THROUGH VIDEO CHUNKING AND EDITING

After I completed writing my thesis (Harel, 1988), the large amount of raw audiovisual information collected for the original research purposes in Video-Modes 1, 2, and 3 was reanalyzed, chunked, and/or edited to produce several short segments that would be useful for documenting the project. What do I mean by *useful*? Why was editing an important research project in itself?

Often teachers request curriculum materials from our group. They need materials that will guide them in implementing Constructionist projects with computers, and they seek ways of adopting the Epistemology and Learning Group's pedagogical approach in their classrooms. As stated previously, this presents a dilemma: the open-ended and Constructionist character of ISDP (as well as of other projects in the E&L Group) does not easily lend itself to conventional step-by-step guidelines, worksheets, or exercises. In addition, teachers are part of a complex and rather rigid system that often does not allow them to try new things or explore new pedagogy, even when they want to be innovative.

Therefore, one goal of VideoMode 4 was to create a series of video segments with which to document several aspects of ISDP, and—at the same time—to situate it within the theoretical framework of Constructionism.

In VideoMode 4, I wanted to explore whether video can be a flexible medium that conveys complexity to others. I attempted to create a series of videotapes that could inform and inspire teachers and researchers alike, without destroying the holistic character of the project (see Appendix). We found that we could do it most effectively by capturing on video, for example, someone who was a "real" teacher speaking about her own experiences in the project.

SUMMARY

During ISDP and afterwards, I was able to experiment with using video as a research tool in the following ways: VideoMode 1 was utilized as a *holistic interview recorder*; VideoMode 2 was used as a *silent observer*; and VideoMode 3 as a video-based *note taker*. I gave examples of how each of these three approaches contributed greatly, but differently, to the data collection and analysis. Some examples demonstrated how all VideoModes together—when combined with hand-written notes, the participants' project-portfolios, and other data—contributed to the investigation of the case studies about the children and their teacher, and to the documentation of the project.

I found that video, which is usually considered to be a qualitative data recorder, assisted me, not only in the qualitative analysis of the results, but also in the quantitative and comparative analysis. Video is a medium which has a great potential for comparing individual children's and groups of children's learning and development over time and in detail. Although good ethnographic research can also be conducted without the use of video, in my examples I attempted to show that certain *kinds* of data could only be captured through video.

In addition, I described VideoMode 4 as a process of *conducting research through video chunking and editing, and preparing video presentations.* Video is a holistic and multidimensional medium, that could play a great role in teachers' development and in the presentation of Constructionist ideas that do not readily lend themselves to a step-by-step presentation.

I must make some remarks about the "objective" and "subjective" aspects of my video recordings. I see all VideoModes as *subjective* in one sense: In VideoModes 1, 2, and 3 I placed the camera and "framed" what *I* wanted to capture, and in VideoMode 4, I edited the segments for communicating ideas that *I* wanted to convey about the project and its theoretical approach. However, I do see VideoMode 2—the silent observer—as the most objective of these four modes, for two reasons: first, because I did not have direct control over what was going on in front of the camera; second, because I think children behave differently if the "camera's eye" is operated by a person as opposed to operating by itself on a tripod. In all four cases the participants reacted to the presence of the camera. However, my data revealed that I was only able to collect certain kinds of information via VideoMode 2—information related to social play, freedom of expression, and uncensored behaviors of the participants. Therefore, the data I collected in VideoMode 2 often revealed precious insights about the participants that I could never have gathered otherwise.

Yet, to some degree, all VideoModes are also *objective*, since one can always go back to the video data, reobserve them, retrieve more information, replay segments, and look at the same data in many different ways. One can also present such data to various researchers and get their opinions about the meaning of any given recorded moment—something I often took advantage of during my data analysis.

Finally, I hope the 'video cases' I described above (of Tim, Debbie, and Sherry) will inspire the readers' thinking about the potential power of video as a researcher's tool. My explorations of video as an information-recording medium and as an information-analysis medium were quite preliminary and specific to ISDP. A great deal of exploration about video is taking place within our research group and elsewhere.[7] Further investigation of these issues is needed for developing the field in relation to the modification and refinement of the techniques described in this section, and the development of additional techniques that could be used for different types of research.

---

[7] See, for example, the papers in the October 1989 issue of the Special Interest Group on Computer & Human Interaction (SIGCHI) Bulletin, *21* (2); and Hanbardt (1986).

ACKNOWLEDGMENTS

I wish to, first of all, thank Linda Moriarty and her students for their great contribution to the ISDP research. I thank all the other teachers and students from Headlight who participated in the study. I thank Carol Stein for her collaboration on the video editing project, and for her valuable contribution to the many fruitful discussions we about video, video making, and video editing—during the year of our working together. I thank Seymour Papert for his support and ideas throughout the period of ISDP and afterwards. Seymour's contribution to my ongoing thinking about my research in general, and with video in particular, is always enormous. I also thank him for his constant and insightful input to the editing project. I thank Ricki Goldman Segall for giving me some footage from her large video archives, and Nira Granott for discussing with me many of the ideas presented in this chapter. Finally, I thank Edith Ackermann, who provided me with many insights about research with and without video, and for her useful comments on previous drafts of this chapter.

This research was supported by grants from the IBM Corporation (Grant # OSP95952), the National Science Foundation (Grant # 851031-0195), the McArthur Foundation (Grant # 874304), the LEGO Group, and Apple Computer, Inc. The preparation of this chapter was supported by the National Science Foundation (Grant # MDR 8751190 and # TPE 8850449) and Nintendo Japan. The ideas expressed here do not reflect those of the supporting agencies.

REFERENCES

Granott Farber, N. (1990). Through the camera's lens: Video as a research tool. In I. Harel (Ed.), *Constructionist learning*. Cambridge MA: MIT Media Laboratory.

Hanbardt, J. (Ed.). (1986). *Video culture: A critical investigation*. New York: Visual Studies Workshop Press.

Harel, I. (1988). *Software design for learning: Children construction of meaning for fractions and logo programming*. Unpublished doctoral dissertation. MIT Media Laboratory, Cambridge, MA.

Harel, I., & Stein, C. (1989). *Children as software designers: A video series*. Cambridge MA: MIT Media Laboratory.

Harel, I. (1990). On realistic constructionism: Children designing software for learning mathematics. *Journal of Mathematical Behavior*, 9(1).

Harel, I. (1991). *Children designers: Interdisciplinary constructions for learning and knowing mathematics in a computer rich school*. Norwood, NJ: Ablex.

Harel, I., & Papert, S. (1990). Software design as a learning environment. *Interactive Learning Environments Journal*, 1 (1), 1–32.

Papert, S. (1990). Introduction. In I. Harel (Ed.), *Constructionist learning*. Cambridge, MA: MIT Media Laboratory.

APPENDIX

The following is a short description of the content of each of the edited tapes and the rationale for its editing.

Tape 1. An Overview of the Instructional Software Design Project

Here we investigated the ways in which we could create a half-hour-long documentation of ISDP. This video is divided into five units. We edited each unit so that it could be viewed on its own if needed, and that all five units together would form a whole. For introducing and discussing concepts and ideas, we interlaced in each unit concrete images with abstract voice-over by Papert or Harel, side by side to close-ups of the teacher or the children talking about their concrete experiences, and many images of children and the teacher at interviews or in action.

Unit 1.1 Constructionism vs. Instructionism. This unit emphasizes that in ISDP children are the designers and makers of personal and real products. It shows how children were designing software, and how in this process they learned about fractions and Logo. We also wanted this unit to be an introduction to the integrative principle of ISDP. That is, the learning of fractions, Logo programming, reading and writing, designing, communicating, evaluating, and producing were integrated into one project in a constructionist way. Papert himself introduces these ideas in this tape.

Unit 1.2 What is a Faction? This unit summarizes the ways in which children think about images and experiences that remind them of fractions or situations where they use fractions. It emphasizes that children come to the ISD project with many rigid notions about what fractions are. By editing clips from preinterviews, this unit highlights the variety and plurality of ideas children have on fractions and their representations. It emphasizes the importance of allowing children to think about their own thinking. The general message is: "This was the children's knowledge base when they started the project. They then built their new knowledge from there."

Unit 1.3 Learning by Teaching and Explaining. This unit highlights the idea that people learn best when they need to explain something to others or represent complex information to people who do not yet know this information. How do children come up with ideas of what to teach, represent, and design? This unit captures several brainstorming sessions from the ISDP class, and children's discussion on what is difficult about fractions. It demonstrates how children came up with ideas for teaching about fractions to other children, and how these ideas developed from discussion in the classroom into the children's programming. This unit also highlights the role of the teacher as facilitator of the brainstorming process in the classroom. Children reflect on what was difficult for them and come up with ideas on how to design screens to make it easier for other children to understand. The teacher asks the children to draw upon their own experiences with fractions from everyday situations, and they are thinking about their own thinking and learning.

Unit 1.4 Learning through Representing. Why is children's knowledge of fractions so poor and limited? How can children develop *deep understanding* of fractions? The claim made by Papert and Harel in this unit is that schools usually emphasize the "how" (algorithms), but ISDP emphasized learning and knowing the "why" and the "when." In ISDP, children gained their understanding of the deep structure of fractions knowledge through constructing representations. As Papert says in this segment, "representations are the *deep structure* of any kind of knowledge, while algorithms are the *surface structure* of mathematical knowledge or any other knowledge." Another point that is being highlighted here by Harel, is that the *children* construct the representation—not the teacher. This is what Papert calls child-centered "Constructionism" vs. teacher-centered "Instructionism."

Unit 1.5 Learning More is Easier than Learning Less. This unit highlights the idea that integrating the learning of subjects and skills is more meaningful to children than learning each in isolation. Learning more is easier than learning less, since, for children, learning several things together (e.g., fractions, programming, designing, representing, explaining, etc.) makes much more sense than learning each one separately. In ISDP, for example, mathematics is not learned in isolation and Logo is not learned in isolation. When studying both together, children gained deeper understanding of each.

Tape 2. A Case Study of the Teacher

This tape includes the teacher's reflections about her experience in the project, and her reflections on her students' experiences. It documents her role and contribution to the project. It highlights her facilitating role. It also captures her concerns about implementing a project of this kind in her classroom. Although the teacher is raising the issue of the need for a long and intensive period of time for ideas to develop and take root in children's minds, she has many concerns about the length of ISDP. The teacher also claims, for example, that she and her students learned Logo along the way and did not need to have expertise in fractions or Logo before the project started. In addition, several video clips were edited to show the teacher's gradual process of appropriation of the project. Through the images and voice-overs of her speaking, viewers can see her changing as the project progresses, in terms of the ways she interacts with her students, the kinds of issues she picks up for discussion in the classroom, and her conversations with the children at the computers.

Tapes 3, 4, and 5. Case Studies of Three Children

These video portraits document three children's processes in ISDP. But many inferences could be drawn about learning and schooling in general. Each tape emphasizes the differences among the three children in relation to their styles of involvement during the project, their ways of learning fractions, their processes of learning and doing Logo programming, their relations with the teachers and their peers, and how their processes relate to the project's educational philosophy, pedagogy, and underlying principles.

Tape 6. Children's Ideas of What Fractions Are

This tape includes four units (each is 30 minutes long) edited on the base of my interviews with 51 children that were videotaped before and after the experiment in 1987. Here, we wanted to investigate the impact of these tapes as "eye openers" and "discussion generators" about children's fractions knowledge. We selected the segments that illustrate the best the diversity in children's styles of responses, as well as the diversity in their misconceptions and/or levels of understanding.

All these units are dealing with the same set of *epistemological questions*: What does it mean to know fractions? What does it mean to understand representations of fractions? What do different representations, models, and explanations, mean to various children who did, or did not, participate in ISDP (i.e., a comparison)? Here is a short description of each segment in this series.

Unit 6.1 What is a Fraction? Here we edited a series of definitions given by children about what is a fraction. The interview questions that elicited the video data for this unit were: What is a fraction? Do you like fractions? Are you good in fractions? Are they hard or easy? What is hard about fractions? What is easy? When did you start learning about fractions? When you close your eyes and think about fractions, what do you see? (Or, what comes to mind? What images do you see? What do you think of? What else?) Can you learn about fractions outside of school? What outside of school reminds you of a fraction? Can you give an example of a fraction outside of school? What in this room reminds you of a fraction?

Unit 6.2 Children Solving Representational Problems with Pattern Blocks. This unit is about children's ways of solving mathematical problems related to proportion and ratio.

Unit 6.3 Children Solving Representational Problems With Cuisennaire Rods. Different problems about part–whole relations and proportional reasoning were given to the children. The camera captured their reactions, problem-solving techniques, and answers.

Unit 6.4 Children Drawing Representations for Thirds and Fifths. Different drawing problems were given to the children. The camera captured their techniques of drawing and revealed their ideas about the equality of fractional parts, as well as their general concept of a fraction as area.

Jacqueline Karaaslanian Photography

Stephen Sherman Photography

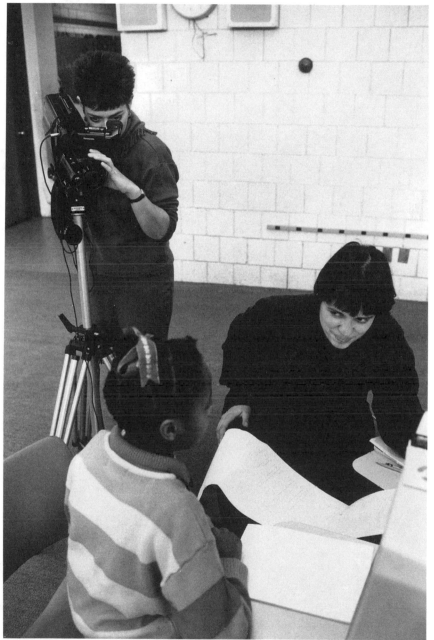

Using video as a research tool

465

23

A Multimedia Research Tool for Ethnographic Investigation

Ricki Goldman Segall

THE TOOL, *LEARNING CONSTELLATIONS*

Multimedia tools can help organize video and text data into meaningful categories and be of great assistance during the process of data analysis in building
educationally and anthropologically sound theories. In fact, it is my contention
that certain discoveries in my study about children's thinking could not have
been made without the use of a unique multimedia research environment called
Learning Constellations. *Learning Constellations* was built for investigating the
thinking of children and then for creating case-study descriptions. *Learning
Constellations* is comprised of a set of six videodiscs and a specifically designed
HyperCard application providing access to video observations, transcripts of the
video, text and video annotations, and textual analysis. The underlying premise
of *Learning Constellations* is that the anthropological approaches of Clifford
Geertz and Mary Catherine Bateson provide a powerful model for thinking about
and designing multimedia research environments. In addition, *Learning Constellations* allows users other than myself (e.g., teachers and researchers) to examine
my original documentation and add new levels of interpretation by including
their own written observations to the existing descriptions. In a sense, users
become researchers, building their own theories about the interpretations of the
selected video and text data. Consequently, as users add their text and video
annotations to the basic material, *Learning Constellations* becomes a growing
video and text document or archive.

The conceptual models used in designing *Learning Constellations* were ethnographer Clifford Geertz's notion of *thick descriptions* (Geertz, 1973; Ryle,
1971)—which bring the reader or viewer closer to understanding the intention of
the 'native' experience—and Mary Catherine Bateson's notion of *disciplined
subjectivity* (Bateson, 1984; Erikson, 1950). These two notions form the under-

lying themes of this chapter. It is my hope that this chapter and other articles addressing issues of video and videodisc as research tools (Hockings, 1975; Mead, 1975; Gerstein, 1986; Goldman Segall, 1988; Mackay, 1989; Lampert & Ball, 1990; Rochelle, Pea, & Trigg, 1990; Harel, Chapter 22, this volume; Granott, 1990) will contribute to a deepening of the discourse among researchers about the rigor of qualitative research techniques in the light of new technologies.

Multimedia Video Ethnography for Discovery and Communication

Multimedia video ethnography is what I term using video and videodisc technology in conjunction with computer-linked interfaces for studying cultural growth and change. It combines what has traditionally been referred to as *visual* or *multivocal ethnography* when it is used in conjunction with computer applications to organize and analyze the video and text data. My approach is similar to the recent study of preschools in China, Japan, and the United States conducted by Tobin, Wu, and Davidson (1989). In fact, their research method also used video as a tool for eliciting meanings, as did my study.

> Our research methods are unlike those used in most comparative research in early child education. We have not tested children . . . We have not measured the frequency of teacher-student interaction . . . Although we touch on all these issues . . . our focus instead has been on eliciting meanings. (p. 5)

My research differs most significantly from Tobin et al.'s in the fact that the extensive video data in my study was developed into a databank accessible to me and to other users in many ways. By working with my video data on videodisc, discoveries about the children's thinking were made which would not have been possible using conventional research tools. Having random access to my data enabled me to segment the pieces or chunks of video data, to organize them into meaningful categories, and then to reconstruct the chunks into fine-grained case studies of children (Goldman Segall, 1990b, and Chapter 13, this volume). The random-access videodisc environment also enabled me to communicate with my viewers and readers in a manner which gave them the opportunity to build their own meanings. Moreover, by using this medium, I established different relationships with my viewers and readers; they became part of the research effort. Consequently, my resulting case studies, to some extent, reflected the interpretation of the various users of *Learning Constellations*.

In short, it is my contention that multimedia video ethnography promotes both making discoveries within the data and communicating the discoveries with other users. Ultimately, discovery and communication in the research process become less distinct pursuits.

THE RESEARCH SITE AND GOALS

The overall goal of Project Headlight, as Seymour Papert, its originator, often proposes, was to find a way of entering into the culture of the school system in order to make incremental changes to the lives of children and adults (Papert, 1986). With this in mind, a section of the Hennigan School was selected to be the site of Project Headlight, because it was a school facing problems similar to many American inner-city schools problems such as: how to deal with children at risk, how to cope with the drug problem, how to provide opportunities for children from diverse ethnic and socioeconomic backgrounds, and how to encourage learning in the sciences. Additional reasons for selecting this school were that, first, the open-style architecture with large area "pods" seemed the perfect place to make the changes Papert wanted to make within the school system, and, second, that the Hennigan proposal was the only proposal originating from teachers and not from the school administration. As a result of selecting a traditional school, our research goals were kept within certain bounds— fundamental changes to the overall structure of the school would be constrained; changes affecting a small section of the school consisting of 12 teachers and their classes would be enhanced.

My own research within Project Headlight began in the fall of 1985. My goal was to understand how this particular constructionist culture could provide children with the physical, social, and intellectual space needed to understand their own thinking about the things they build, the things they do, and the things they imagine. In other words, what I documented on video is how children expressed their thinking within this growing culture. I studied three children in great depth. Each of these children had their own different interests and would set up situations to work out ways of understanding what was on their minds. The content areas were examined to the extent that they illustrated how each of these children delved into their own style of thinking (see Goldman Segall, 1990a, 1990b, Chapter 13, this volume). I was curious about how they linked their experiences together, integrating them into the web of their life. I wanted to know why one child was able to appropriate these experiences as her or his own and another was not. In short, my study examined the process of successful or unsuccessful appropriation of Project Headlight ideas and resulted in the finding of three dominant and preferred thinking styles (Goldman Segall, 1990b, and Chapter 13, this volume).

ISSUES IN VIDEO ETHNOGRAPHIC RESEARCH

Becoming a *Participant Recorder*

Since the goal of my video research study at this school was to gain insight into the thinking of children, I set out to use a research tool—videomaking—and implement a methodology—the ethnographic approach—to gather data by encouraging self-expression and communication.

This process included using video as an investigative tool for looking at how a culture could grow with the appropriation by children of computers to enable them to think about their thinking processes. I initiated this study by asking questions that reflected their own programming, talking, and playing. The questions I asked were influenced by Carl Rogers' reflective listening techniques (Rogers, 1961). The deeper origin of my questions stemmed from my genuine interest in how children understand their own thinking.

Due to the invasiveness of videotaping, I often waited to be invited by the children to see what they were doing. Sometimes I asked for permission to participate with the children while they were working. This does not mean that I did not regularly walk around recording many things in and around the open space—the computer pods—wherein the computers were arranged. However, when I sat down beside some children working, I asked whether or not they wanted to tell me (and the camera) what they were doing or thinking. If the answer was "no," then I did not record. Combining the recording capacity of video with my meandering approach, responses were elicited rather than forced. With the camera in my arm or on my hip, I was less a participant observer and more a *participant recorder*.

Creating a Change in the Culture with Video Technology

When thinking about using new technologies with which to do research, the tendency is either to discredit the possibilities or to exaggerate the potential. One tends to forget that the individual researcher using the technology is a more significant indicator of the potential of the research than is the power of the tool. Even a well-designed tool is only as good as its user. Often, the *bigger* or more sophisticated the technology, the less potential there is for observing what is really happening. The point is that it is not enough to use better technologies to do the same things "better." The idea is to let new technologies enter our lives in a comfortable way in many domains so that something new can happen to the lives of people. We need to think about the emergence of new technologies in the way we think about art, filmmaking, or transportation. Thinking about bigger and better carriages did not necessarily lead to exploring the planets, and as Papert says, thinking about better Impressionism did not bring about Picasso's Cubism. Papert's theory is that, when we think about new technologies, we need to think about how technologies extend our natural cultures so that new kinds of things can happen to people. If Papert is correct, as I believe he is, about cultures growing in the context of technologies, then there is a need to consider the impact upon the source culture when video is collected, viewed, and then shared so that it becomes part of the existing culture. As Papert has stated (Goldman Segall, 1989a):

Ricki Goldman Segall is working in the same Hennigan School and is exploring some exceedingly different ways of using this machine. She hangs around the school and tries to get pictures, unobtrusively, of what the children are doing and sometimes tries to use her presence as a way of evoking discussion. By interviewing the children and letting the children interview her, they talk about things in different ways, and this is part of the "picture-making" becoming part of the culture of the school: its presence there changes the way children think about what they see on television at home because they have been so intimately connected to the "television-making" in the school. And the way they talk to Ricki has a lot to do with the reactions they make to everything to do with moving images on screens everywhere in society. It's all part of a complex meshing of different processes. This is the way we have to see new technologies.

Thus, when we think about a possible effect of a particular researcher who uses video technology as a tool within a particular culture, we need to address how the children in that culture appropriate the researcher's video research (Goldman Segall, 1990c). If permitted, as it was in my case, *the child begins to "direct" the research and the researcher becomes the child's cameraperson who follows the direction of the child.*

Describing Events or Persons

To build a comprehensive video and text description of the children in this Logo culture, I used Clifford Geertz's concept of *thick descriptions*. Thick descriptions are descriptions that are layered enough to uncover the intentions of a given act, event, or process. What makes a description *thick* is the quality of the description. Gilbert Ryle, an Oxford scholar, first coined the expression *thick descriptions* as a means of differentiating between what is really happening when the same action appears to be happening (Ryle, 1971). For example, he asks: If there are five people sitting on a rock, each with his hand on his chin, how do we know which of these persons is really the thinker of thoughts, "le Penseur," as he calls him.

In a video research environment, thick descriptions are video images which retain and convey the original meaning (as the ethnographer understood them at the time of videotaping). Neither the quantity nor the resolution of the images make the descriptions thick. What creates thickness is the ability of the visual description to transmit what is really being said for purposes of "commensurability," as Geertz would say (Geertz, 1983).

The importance of thick descriptions in a video or videodisc environment is that they provide us with a way of coming to terms with the problem inherent in observational research—it "tends to resist any kind of systematic evaluation" and, like all interpretive approaches, it is "imprisoned in its own immediacy or detail" (Geertz, 1973, p. 24).

In order to address this issue of systematic evaluation in my research, I applied the notion of thick descriptions to the chunking of video data (Goldman Segall, 1989b). Each chunk of video was segmented with enough contextual information to best preserve the original meaning. When chunks required editing, they were placed together in ways which aimed at maintaining the original spirit of the event.

Reaching Conclusions from Selected Video Data

In a multimedia research environment every user accesses different video chunks, viewing the selected data through different eyes. The thickness built into the description of the act, event, or process provides a measure to ensure that conclusions, although not the same, fall in the same range (see, for example, the cases of children in Goldman Segall, Chapter 13, this volume).

To build thick descriptions into a chunk, one can begin by finding the smallest unit of meaningful content. Whether this be a contraction of the eyelids, a word, or the constructing of a program in Logo, *content granularity* is decided by examining the original purpose or intention of the person who contracted her or his eyelids, spoke, or wrote a program. Since researchers are bound, as Weber would say, in their "own webs of interpretation," (Geertz, 1973, p. 5), their conclusions are often limited by previous experience. However, in a multimedia environment, researchers share their original documentation, allowing users to more closely examine the footage of the person who experienced the event.

Maureen Hansen, a teacher from California, spent considerable time researching the children's thinking as presented in *Learning Constellation*. This is what she wrote in one of her personal annotations in this environment:

> The *Learning Constellations* package is a most liberating item for the researcher. The "stuff" of the research is the actions, words, contexts, and inferences that live through the film that hang on the line to dry, to blow in the wind, to twist around the cord and each other, to be viewed by the neighbors, and, perhaps, to fall to the ground. The data for us is the children, teachers, classrooms, [and the children's] ideas, fears, and strengths. *Learning Constellations* gives us this data to use for our purposes. (Hansen, July 1990)

Addressing *Point of View* and Interference

The search for understanding the meaning of an event often leads to problems of interference with what is going on as well as with the personal bias in reporting it. The more the researcher participates, the greater the possibility of interfering with what is happening. Similarly, the more the researcher participates, the greater the bias. What my research has shown is that participation need not cause negative interference, and that point of view can enrich our understanding and inform us of what was going on when the event was recorded.

According to Geertz (1973) and Bateson (1984), the ethnographer—no matter how strongly committed to living in the culture without changing or manipulating any events for data collection—affects the environment.

Geertz emphasizes the fact that "anthropologists don't study villages, they study in villages" (1973, p. 22). "Culture exists in the trading post, the hill fort, or the sheep run; anthropology exists in the book, the article, the museum display, or sometimes, nowadays, the film" (1973, p. 16). For Geertz, if you want to understand anthropology or any science, then you should examine what those who study it actually do. Thus, in order to understand what anthropology is, it is important to describe what anthropologists do. According to Geertz, anthropologists do enthnography. They establish rapport, select informants, take notes, keep journals, and collect any other relevant data such as maps, genealogies, or texts. Anthropologists communicate their experience of the culture.

Bateson describes the process of data collection as the phase that least requires the interference of the researcher, because the anthropologists do not manipulate or change the environment to generate data; they study it as it is. This does not mean Bateson is naive about the influence of the participating observer upon the culture being studied. Far from it. She is aware of the delicate relationship between the observer and the research subject. As Bateson says:

> Anthropologists sometimes speak of their field as their laboratory, but in general our knowledge is based on observation rather than manipulation. Where we act for change it is to achieve goals seen as valuable rather than to generate data. Usually, our experiments are those arranged by history and most of our variables are embedded in the flux of human life and cannot be isolated, having neither beginning nor end but unfolding over time . . . Each life history, and the record of each community with its own distinctive and interlocking patterns of adaptation, is valuable and to be recorded, a unique experiment. (Bateson, 1984, pp. 24–25)

Ethnographers begin their documentation by accepting the fact that what they record in their field notes is already an interpretation of an event. The recording of the event is, in some respect, "fiction," because it is a picture of what the person who is participating in the event is experiencing. Moreover, the observers and recorders, by their presence in the environment, affect the culture within which they are collecting their data. Readers of the social sciences often have a tendency to accept the results of researchers who have gone into the field to do their studies without questioning the underlying biases of this initial phase of the documentation; they do not ask the following questions: When do ethnographers put pencil to paper? When do they turn on the camera? What do they select to record, and what do they exclude? What is in the frame, and what is not? What detail is focused on, and what is placed in the background? What do ethnographers experience while they are recording, looking through the viewfinder? When do they stop experiencing the event?

The main question to ask is not whether or not the results were influenced by the presence of a video ethnographer, but rather how ethnographers provide thick descriptions in their recording of the people, processes, or events to understand the meaning. They do this *by carefully describing their involvement* with the cultures they study. In short, doing ethnography means bringing personal biases and expectations into full view as part of the whole picture.

In video ethnography, the problem of bias or point of view is greater. Each time the camera is turned on or off, point of view comes into play. Thus, two central concerns of using video as a research tool are: how does one know that what is being videotaped is research data and not merely an impressionist view of events; and how does one know that the video selected for either linear or nonlinear usage is most representative from the whole body of video data?

One way of looking at these issues is to examine the relationship between bias and interpretation. The issue is complicated because, even if a given point of view is biased, an interpretation can still be enjoyed as humorous or interesting. The documentary film *Roger and Me*, by director Michael Moore, exemplifies this seeming contradiction. The viewer has an opportunity to "journey with" Moore through Flint, Michigan while he attempts to get an interview with Roger Smith, Chairperson of General Motors. The movie was thought scandalous by those who expected this documentary to tell the "truth" about Flint. Some agreed with the interpretation and did not think it was biased. Others, who did not agree, said it was a misrepresentation of what happened in Flint when General Motors closed its factory. But still others, accepting the strong point of view *and* the fact that is was not the whole truth, felt it contributed to their understanding of Flint. The latter were interested in the fact that everyone in the movie—from the woman who sold the rabbits "for food or pets," to the visiting wealthy partygoers in a local prison, to the workers at General Motors—had an interesting story to tell.

Why is point of view so often excluded from informing us about the subject under investigation? Why have we researchers tended to adopt models, for doing research, that do not incorporate the personal, subjective, and interpretative approach? Investigation into the understanding of personal styles of cognition (e.g., Kogan, 1983; Turkle, 1984; Gilligan, 1982) and of involvement or appropriation (e.g., Fox Keller, 1983; Papert, 1990) suggests that *research could benefit by acknowledging the intimate relationship between the seer and the seen, or between the observer and the observed.*

In conclusion, video recording for research purposes cannot be without point of view. Even in the most "objective" research projects with the video camera on a tripod in the corner of the room, the researcher has chosen where to place the camera, how "tight" or wide the shot will be, at what angle the camera will record, and who will be in the camera's view. Moreover, her or his decision to use the camera as a stationary object also reflects a point of view. One tends to think that the less a researcher manipulates the camera, the more objective the point of view. However, this may be missing the central issue. Even the "hidden" camera is a result of the researcher's perspective about (a) how she or he views the culture, and (b) what her or his reaction is to it.

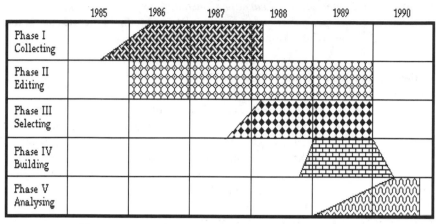

Figure 1.   Timeline of Longitudinal Video Study.

The point is that new multimedia technologies can create a space in which the context and the culture are easily felt, accessed, and communicated to others. They can give users freedom of movement within the source material while maintaining the integrity of the original event. To build this kind of environment, I specified two constraints upon my design wherein thick descriptions could be created, not only by myself, but also by other users. First, I ensured that the body of work was robust, and, second, I linked chunks of information into meaningful groupings which best adhered to (my interpretation of) the intention expressed by the informants.

THE RESEARCH PROCESS

This section consists of an abbreviated examination of the five phases of my research process (Goldman Segall, 1989c, 1990b). The central theme of this section is that many decisions and ideas occurred in the process which were not defined at the outset. Moreover, the entire project grew through my own constructionist process. The five major phases (see Figure 1), as I now define them, are:

- Collecting data by observing and videotaping my interactions with the children.
- Editing linear "movies" and nonlinear chunks from the video data.
- Identifying, selecting, classifying, and categorizing the video segments for videodiscs.

- Building the interface for *Learning Constellations*
- Using *Learning Constellations* to analyze data and to build theories about the children's styles of thinking.

Collecting the Video Data (1985–1987)

Learning to Use the Research Tool. Phase I of my video research project started when I first took the videocamera into the Hennigan School on my regular biweekly visits. By having to decide when to turn the camera on, what to videotape, how to hold the camera, and most importantly, how to respond to the children with this invasive tool in my hands, I defined the scope of the project. To put it as simply as Temaner and Quinn (1975) do, I faced three core questions: "What to shoot? How to shoot it? How to put it together?" In this phase, I constantly asked myself how much effort it would require to become proficient enough with the technology to capture the images on videotape that would hold together as a unified body of work.

Even in those early stages of videotaping, I produced results that I had not been able to produce using fieldnotes and audiotape recorders. Perhaps this was due to the excitement of using a medium which allows for instant viewing, reflection, or correction; one can critique one's own work immediately. Daily, I would view both the content and the technique of my shooting. This combination of instant self-instruction and feedback from Leacock (e.g., 1975), Davenport (e.g., 1987), and others taught me how to look at my research environment without prejudging it, how to see what was worth filming and what was not. For me, using video as an ethnographic research tool meant capturing images of the culture by using the camera as an expressive medium. With the camera, I could better respond to what the environment *told* me to record. To state this in Erik Erikson's words—as Bateson uses them—I wanted to attain *disciplined subjectivity*.

> The process is an aesthetic one, one of listening for resonance between the inner and the outer, an echo that brings the attention into focus. Poets work this way as the curve of a leaf evokes the poignancy of a past moment. Therapists work this way, moving back and forth between their own task of self-knowledge and the task of understanding a patient. Indeed, I have always thought of this effort to become aware of and draw systematically on internal processes in the terms of Erik Erikson's description of clinical method as "*disciplined subjectivity.*" (Bateson, 1984, p. 201)

Style of Responding to the Children. In my approach of collecting data with the videocamera, I asked the children fewer questions, waited longer for their responses, made fewer suggestions, and guided the discussion less than when I interviewed children with an audiotape recorder or wrote fieldnotes. If I did ask a question while using the camera, I waited longer for their response. I found that the longer I waited without filling in the gap of silence, the more comfortable we both felt being together. I also found that an intimate space was created by sitting silently beside the child while she or he worked. I was not there to guide, instruct, teach, or lecture. I was there because I wanted to share the experience with a child.

Learning how to elicit children's thinking rather than encouraging them to reflect my own thinking was a major challenge. Children want to please adults, they want our approval, and they want to tell us what we want to hear. Consequently, I accepted whatever they told me as a gift. Although I asked children questions and sometimes sat with them in a closed room with the videocamera turned on, I thought about our discussions as conversations and not as interviews. (Cole, 1989)

My "roaming" technique of videotaping included approaching a child and commenting upon the immediate situation. My remarks and/or questions followed this pattern: *Can I sit here and watch what you are doing today? Do you want to tell/show/talk about what you've been doing? That looks interesting. Would you like to tell me about it? Hi, Andrew, what are you working on today? Your game has really changed. What have you been doing to it lately? What have you been working on since the last time we talked? I really missed you this past week. Where have you been?* These questions were not scripted; they were responses to the situation. If it felt comfortable to take the next step into the conversation, I did; I did not venture further, if the child did not invite me to continue a conversation.

Constraints of Research Tools: Performing for the Camera. The videocamera is an excellent tool for eliciting responses. The camera can stay propped on the lap or on the shoulder. The researcher can choose to maintain eye contact regularly, if not most of the time, only checking the image in the viewfinder from time to time to make sure that the child is within the frame. Conversations in the presence of cameras can evolve in a way that limits, but does not discredit, the performance aspect of videotaping. Moreover, continuous exposure means that the children become less conscious of the camera. In fact, they seem to relax in its presence.

What needs to be questioned is the assumption that the performance of the participants somehow diminishes the credibility of the research. Research is no less valuable if the children's personalities are "brought out" while using the camera. In fact, one of my goals in studying the emergence of new technologies in a school culture was to examine how children appropriate a technology and make it their own. In the case of appropriating video, this means that some children become more animated than usual, more dramatic, and more *full of the stuff of life*. Videotaping children tends to provide them with expressive tools for responding to situations. When we introduce paints to children, we bring out new responses to the physical world of color and texture; children exposed to the videocamera may also develop new expressive means of communication (Goldman Segall, 1990c). From my experience over a 3-year period, I found that some children are more articulate in front of the camera, suggesting that the camera contributes to their expressiveness.

Developing an "Affectionate" Style of Shooting. A breakthrough in my work occurred one afternoon when filmmaker David Parry, who was visiting the Media Lab, came to shoot with me at the Hennigan School. Parry showed me how to move with the camera into the center of the action without disturbing the activity. Parry held the camera in both his hands in front of him. He moved the camera in and out of the center of the activity. I was shocked. However, the children behaved comfortably with Parry, because he was comfortable with what he was doing. From that day on, my camera work changed; the camera moved with me. When I participated in the activities with the children, the camera was turned on and was close to them. Eventually, I *stopped thinking about the camera* and just used it *invisibly*. By the end of Phase I, I had developed a style of shooting which was immediate, intimate, and affectionate. It consisted of the following techniques:

- holding the camera on my right hip or lap (with the viewfinder pointed up) and the microphone in my left hand or on a table to ensure direct eye-to-eye contact with those children with whom I was in conversation;
- holding the camera quite close to the center of the action to re-create a feeling of intimacy;
- pointing the camera up, giving the viewer the feeling of looking up to the child;
- following the activity with the camera to give the viewer the sense of moving his or her eyes with the activity—in other words, to re-create reality;
- videotaping one interaction for as long as the interaction lasted; and
- stepping back from the activity to *pan* the overall atmosphere to provide context.

In conclusion, my data collection phase could best be described as becoming technically proficient as well as emotionally and intellectually engaged. This attitude of caring about the children and feeling comfortable with my research tool, the videocamera, laid the foundation for the next phase, editing the video footage—a phase which overlapped with the shooting phase and continued for more than 3 years.

Editing for Linear and Nonlinear Presentation (1986–1989)

In the editing room, images can be juxtaposed to create new ways of looking at the footage. Children's anecdotal comments become alive with a certain amount of editing; they lose their truthfulness when overworked. Moreover, in the editing room, I discovered what sequences I had missed because I turned off the camera too soon, ran out of tape, or did not have charged batteries. The importance of this process of shooting, viewing, and then editing taught me how to look at the environment more carefully and to videotape with a more watchful eye on my next visit to the school. If I were to itemize the major turning points during the linear editing phase, they would be the following:

- showing and presenting the footage to filmmakers and researchers;
- building video sequences, then scenes, then stories;
- not using a narration—letting the children talk without using a voice-over describing what the video ethnographer sees or wants the viewer to pay attention to;
- experimenting with the same footage to show how different slices of the same video could bring deeper interpretations—simulating a videodisc environment;
- editing collaboratively with a colleague (for a fresh point of view); and editing alone (for intimacy with the data and closeness to one's art and intuition);
- changing from linear to nonlinear thinking for videodiscs environment; and
- becoming video proficient: buying a camera, setting up an editing suite, experimenting with many cameras and in different editing suites, and teaching other researchers of children's thinking how to use and how to think about the camera.

While editing, we also paid attention to: (a) the timing—the length of a given cut in the overall relationship to all the individual cuts; (b) the balance between the diversity and stability of various shots to ensure that the viewer could focus on what was important and be stimulated enough to maintain the focus over a period of time; and most importantly, (c) the thematic development—starting from the opening shots to the closing ones and credits.

Arranging Chunks for Linear and for Nonlinear Delivery. At this phase of the project, I was joined by Brazilian filmmaker Vivian Orni Mester, who was interested in the selection and editing of video for videodisc environments. Our first problem was to compare the process of editing for creating linear *stories* to editing for nonlinear stories. I use the term *story* in the sense that the data needed to be organized in a manner which made descriptive and narrative sense. Our guiding principle while editing was to be honest to the story we were telling, given the limitations of the footage.

To date, there are no conventions for videodisc chunking or for placement, often called videodisc *real estate*. Some designers opt for sectioning off an existing linear piece into bite-size chunks. Others organize a linear piece for easy chunking at a later date (as was done in the American Broadcasting Corporation's [ABC] videodisc called *The Holy Land*). When a piece edited for linear presentation is chunked, the beginnings and endings of the cuts can be problematic. (L-cuts are divided so that the sound under a video shot is stopped abruptly.) Another problem is that the context is usually destroyed. Furthermore, a short or long cut (which worked well in the linear story) may not stand on its own in the nonlinear story.

In deciding how to edit for videodisc environments, we designed (with the assistance of graduate student Hans Peter Broadman) a HyperCard application called *Star Notes* for making decisions about how to select relevant scenes, how to chunk video sequences, how *big* the chunk needs to be in order to communicate the message, and what chunks go well with other chunks, and for what purposes. This process is described in detail in the next section.

Selecting Video Segments for Videodiscs (1988–1989)

The following six steps describe our process of moving from thinking about the video data as scenes to thinking about the data as multimedia chunks.

The first step which we implemented was to re-view the 70 to 80 hours of relevant video data. Each viewing deepened the previous experience I had with the children; each viewing brought me closer to understanding what the children meant when they did or said certain things. Sharing these moments with a colleague on a daily basis added a fresh perspective.

The obvious question at this step was: How would we decide which segments were the most representative from the body of material? While watching another time, we dubbed large pieces of video onto about 15 1-hour ¾-inch tapes. Our chunks were long pieces to be refined alter. At a later point, we dubbed finer-grained chunks directly from the original footage of the VHS source tapes onto 10 1-hour videotapes of 1-inch video stock. This step took approximately 6 months.

The second step we implemented was to work on the design of a HyperCard tool called *Star Notes* for logging the scenes from the entire body of data. HyperCard, an Apple application for the Macintosh computer, was released in Fall 1987. Each chunk can be described on a ''card,'' a ''window,'' or a defined space on the computer monitor which resembles a filing card. Cards can be arranged in 'stacks' according to the categories from a keyword box. When calling up a stack, each card in the stack will appear and then be replaced by the next card in the stack. Searches can be carried out easily as each word in a field is an object to be found and displayed. Lampert and Ball define this process in the following way:

> Hypermedia is a new concept in educational technology. It combines elements of multimedia environments for learning and teaching with recent development in computer software called ''hypertext'' (Ambron and Hooper, 1988, Jones, 1990; Richards, Chignell, and Lacy, 1990; Wilson and Tally, 1990). Hypertext grew out of a system called ''memex'' imagined by Vannevar Bush in the 1940's. Bush (1945–1988) foresaw the possibility of building electronic linking tools, based on ideas about how people connect ideas in flexible networks, to enable scientists to cope with the ''information explosion'' occurring in many fields. Hypertext is a

representation of multiple and flexible links between discrete pieces of data which allows users to navigate among multiple paths through a network of chunks of information and to build and store their own links. When the data to be linked include video, audio, and graphic as well as textual information, the representation is called multimedia. (Lampert & Ball, 1990, p. 5)

On each card in *Star Notes* there was a space for the following information: Name (of scene), Description (of scene), Source (which tape number it came from), Date (that the video was shot), and most important, Keywords (which later became the themes). Each card (as shown in Figure 2) contained a list of categories, or Keywords—stacks of cards in the same category that were instantly accessible by clicking with the "mouse" on the name of the Keyword.

Step three consisted of entering the text data which corresponded to each chunk of video: a brief description, the name of the chunk, and the tape on which it was to be found. Although the data entry was time consuming and often tedious, it changed the nature of the research project. With *Star Notes*, we could subdivide the video data into discrete units. By describing each scene, we could manipulate the information of each card as a separate entity. (By working as a team, the categories which emerged reflected both of our interpretations of the footage.)

In step four, we assigned Keywords or Themes to each card by watching the corresponding video. While categorizing, no predetermined set of Keywords

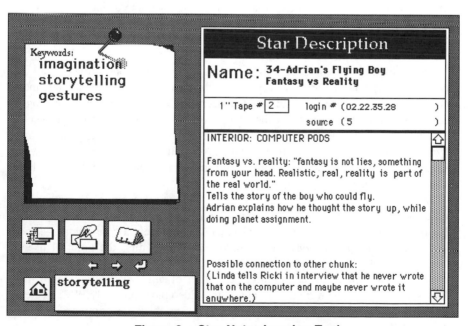

Figure 2. *Star Notes* Logging Tool.

existed. They emerged from the data. We would watch the video and then decide on the Keywords according to the content. At first the process was quite slow, but it accelerated as the content continued to point to about ten Keywords which represented the underlying themes running throughout the footage. The themes which emerged were: *Inventing, Imagination, Girl/Boy Talk, Story-telling, Lying and Punishment, Discipline, Reflecting on oneself or others, Teaching/ Learning, Gestures, Cooperative Learning, Curriculum, Independent Play, Space, and Reflections.*

In step five, these thematic Keywords were organized into stacks, or groups of cards, in order to compare and contrast the data. For example, all the cards with *Inventing* as a Keyword were grouped together online and in hard copy. In this way, we could determine which thematic categories were the most dominant and representative of the entire body of footage. (In a sense, the thematic Keyword stacks helped us understand what was often an unarticulated undercurrent in my videotaping.) These stacks became the foundation upon which *Learning Constellations* was built and, more importantly, upon which the video data were discussed by the community of Project Headlight researchers.

Not only were cards grouped into stacks, but stacks were grouped within stacks and searches were done throughout the stacks to link various subgroups. For example, the word *punishment* kept recurring in the descriptions even before punishment became a Keyword and an eventual theme. A simple search linked many punishment cards together for us to compare the context in which children thought about punishment. For Josh, punishment meant having to do anything he did not want or choose to do, such as following the school curriculum when he had a better idea for his own project. For Andrew, it meant being "grounded"— not being able to go outside the house for a long period of time. This kind of comparison aided the design and analysis.

In this linking and comparing the text data, unexpected connections began to occur. For example, Andrew's story about a boy travelling from planet to planet could be cross-referenced with his teacher, Linda Moriarty, teaching Logo commands in a class project on the planets during their constellations project. Did Andrew get his idea from her constellation project? Unfortunately, with *Star Notes* we could not view video simultaneously with the cards. *Star Notes* was similar to an indexing file, with sorting and linking capacity *about* the video but not *with* the video.

In the beginning of step six, the Keyword stacks were grouped together by arranging the stacks into what seemed like unified 30-minute videodisc *chapters*. However, only having each individual videodisc represent a core Theme—such as *Inventing* or *Imagination*, for example—seemed to miss the point of users being able to build *thick descriptions* to get close to the meanings of what the children were doing. By combining the notion of *thick descriptions* with the Keyboard Themes, we were able to chunk the video more precisely. We selected video chunks which we thought would represent thick descriptions and we recorded those chunks.

Regular discussions took place about whether or not the chunks should make sense if viewed linearly, from beginning to end. After all, why not take advantage of both linearity and nonlinearity if possible? From these discussions, an idea emerged that each videodisc could function as a chapter. However, unlike a chapter in a book, the user would have the advantage of being able to move to a related theme, find out more about each person, search for recurrences of a word or phrase, and most importantly, keep track of what we wanted to save along the way so that it can be grouped together as a cluster.

In short, by deciding about the real estate of the videodiscs, we paid closer attention to the notion of themes and thick descriptions. The end result is that the video on each videodisc seems to be woven together syntactically and semantically. Moreover, there is a storylike order of the whole body of six videodiscs:

- *Videodisc One* is the introduction and overview;
- *Videodisc Two* is an in-depth portrait of one child, Josh, at home and at school;
- *Videodisc Three* followed the *Invention* and *Imagination* themes of the children working with Logo and LEGO/Logo;
- *Videodisc Four* is a close look at Andrew's *Storytelling* and his efforts to distinguish between fantasy and reality.
- *Videodisc Five* is a description of Mindy's *girl/boy talk* and the children's views on *punishment, lying*, and the interpersonal aspects within the learning environment.
- *Videodisc Six* is the end, a closure to the videodisc set with a variety of people talking about the relationship between education, technology and humanity.

Looked at as a whole, the set of six videodiscs reflects diversity, because we discovered alternative ways of arranging the video on the videodisc—without judging which was best. The children's stories, as we understood from the original footage, guided each videodisc separately, but our Themes and *thick descriptions* established the constraints within which we negotiated the videodisc real estate. Each of the six videodiscs can be thought of as a small story, a novella; the set of six as a visual book. Our end product, *Learning Constellations*, shows that building stories with video data may still require the basic structure embedded in a good story: a beginning, character and plot development, and an end.

Building the Interface for *Learning Constellations* (1989–1990)

The purpose of building *Learning Constellations* was to connect the video data with the computer access in order to analyze the data. However, the environment was also conceived as one wherein my observations and interpretations of children would be shared. To accomplish this task and build the interface for

Learning Constellations, David Greschler, an expert HyperCard programmer
and developer, joined our team. In this section, I will describe the final product
we designed and how it works.

Overview of the Tool, Learning Constellations. Unique to *Learning Constellation* is that each (Hyper) card can be thought of as a *star* and the combining
of stars as the building of thematic constellations. I chose the title *Learning
Constellations* because stars group together differently from different perspectives in the universe. The linking of one set of stars to another is dependent upon
where one is located at a given moment. The fact that we draw conclusions from
what we are able to see and grasp from these different perspectives is not only a
good metaphor for thinking about how we think, but also a helpful model for
designing an ethnographic tool where different users will have an opportunity to
explore a range of themes.

Upon entering the system, several introductory cards appear describing the
project and explaining how to think about units or *Stars* of discrete video and text
chunks (see Figure 3).

The Galaxy Map (Figure 4) acts as the main artery through which all
navigation occurs. It has two main functions. First, it provides an easy touch-
stone to prevent getting lost amidst the groupings of data. Second, it separates
large domains of data. By clicking on any of these domains, the next level of
operation occurs. In other words, one can begin the exploration by watching the
15-minute video that I filmed, edited, and transferred to videodisc called *The
Growth of a Culture*.

Figure 3. An Introduction Page.

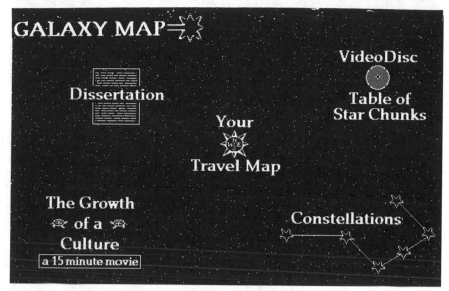

Figure 4.   The Galaxy Map.

Another option is to click on the Dissertation domain (Figure 5). Special video icons take the user to the actual video footage relating to that chunk of text. These Video Notes are represented by an icon resembling a video camera. Clicking on them immediately activates the selected video.

Another domain is the Videodisc Table of Star Chunks (see Figure 6). This domain can be thought of as a linear table of contents listing each of the video chunks on the six videodiscs. To be more precise, the video was put onto the discs in chunks which could make sense linearly if played as half-hour mini-movies on each subject. However, each chunk is independent and can be accessed nonlinearly. This table of contents provides the user with the actual breakdown of the chunks for skimming through the topics and making choices. Clicking on a selected line brings one to the Video Star card on the computer screen and to the corresponding video on the monitor (Figure 7).

Arriving at the selected video chunk (Figure 7), one can read the transcript; find the background information; search according to person, topic, or word throughout the system; go back to the last operation; go forward to the next video chunk on the videodisc; and "grab" this chunk to place it into a Constellation group with other video chunks. While viewing, one can control the speed of the video by using the Video Control Panel at the bottom of the card.

An extremely important feature of a research tool is the ability to make annotations and keep track of these annotations. Two types of annotations are possible in this system. When the *Write* button is clicked, the user has a choice of whether to make a regular Note or a Footnote. If the choice is to footnote, the cursor turns into a pencil icon (see Figure 8). When a word or phrase in the text is

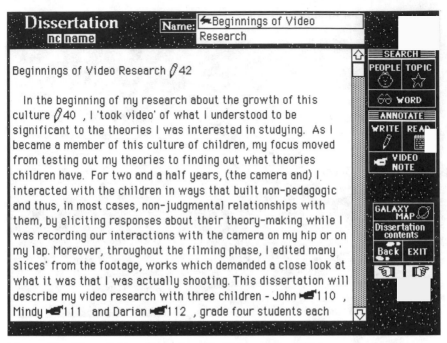

Figure 5.   Dissertation Domain with Video & Text Notes represented as icons.

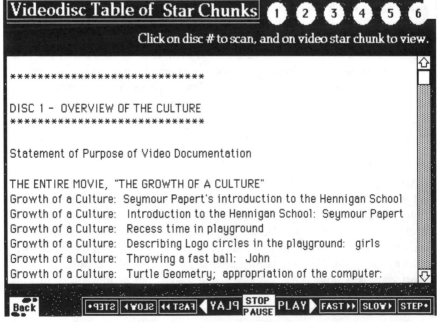

Figure 6.   Videodisc Table of Contents with easy access to all chunks on discs.

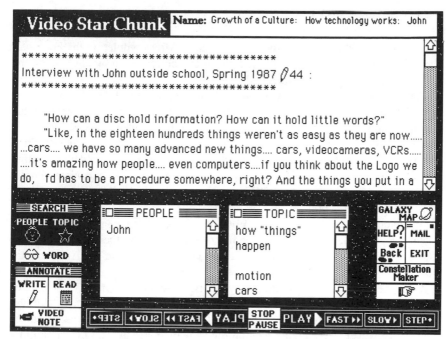

Figure 7. Video Chunk with People and Topic Search fields open.

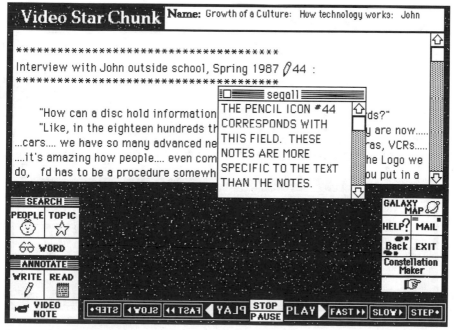

Figure 8. Text Footnotes.

clicked on, a field for writing footnotes appears. After completing the Footnote, the field is closed by clicking on the field; it can be reopened by clicking on the pencil icon, permanently embedded in the text.

Another type of annotation is called Note (see Figure 9). Notes are stored according to the person's name. (Thus they are accessible, not only in the specific chunk where they were made, but also in the public and private notebook domains.) By clicking on the Note icon, a writing field pops up where written observations about the data can be recorded. When closing the field after writing the annotation, one is asked whether this is a Private or Public Note. Public Notes only go out to other users; Private Notes only go the Personal Notebook; choosing Both does both.

When choosing either Private or Both, one is asked to categorize the note by Theme. By placing the note in a Theme, one decides why the chosen chunk of video is significant. To read, the Read button is clicked. One's private annotations are found in the Private Notebook (see Figure 10).

Once the constellation is built, it stays in the system for others to view. One of the built-in constraints of *Learning Constellations* is that the chunks are defined by the researcher. This protects the data (somewhat) from being taken out of context. However, an alternative chunking is available to users. One can build a grouping of minichunks, defining the beginning and end point of each chunk, by using the Videonote builder—a videodisc editing tool. (Researchers who are

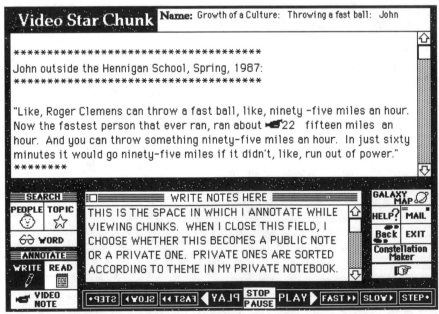

Figure 9.   Notebook Annotations: for public or private use.

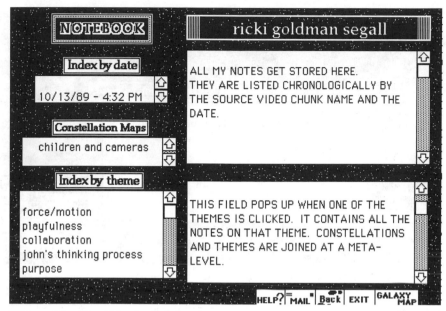

Figure 10.   The Private Notebook.

concerned about not having their research restructured by users need to consider how this affects the interpretation of their data by others.)

Building "constellations" by linking related video together to analyze similarities and differences is a useful tool for exploring ideas. For example, one of the constellations I built is called "children and the camera" (see Figure 11). I wanted to examine how Josh's behavior *in front of the camera* changed throughout the 2 years of videotaping. I selected eight video chunks ranging from my first video encounter with him to the last one, and organized them chronologically (see Figure 12). What I discovered by viewing these video chunks together was that Josh was initially quite shy in front of the camera; however, he became quickly comfortable and even, toward the end of my research, held the camera and described a movie he wanted to make about himself in the school.

Embedded in the design of *Learning Constellations* was the belief that our interpretations of video data are affected by the ways in which the interface for accessing video on videodisc is designed. As such, our goal was to present the chunks of video in ways which would preserve the integrity of the original data while enabling a synthesis of data. Our simple and accessible design features combined with the ability to link video into constellations served the purpose of keeping the interpretations as close as possible to the original event. The key to understanding the conceptual basis of *Learning Constellations* is not to look for complexity but to think about transparency, thick descriptions, and conviviality (Illich, 1973).

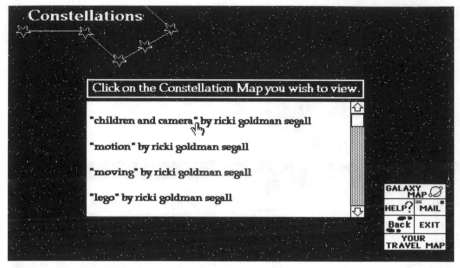

Figure 11. List of Constellation Contents.

4.5. Analyzing Data in an Videodisc Environment

In this section, I will describe the phase closest to the present time, the phase of reconstructing individual case studies of the children from the linked chunks of video data. In other words, this phase covers the period of using *Learning*

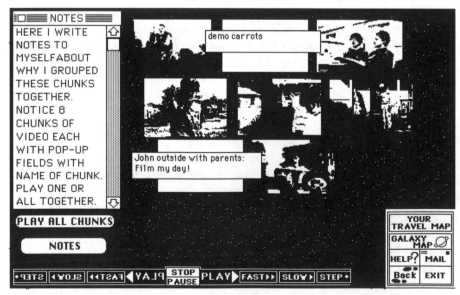

Figure 12. The Constellation: "Children and Camera" with digitized images.

Constellations as a research tool (for analyzing the video data) to the period of writing detailed case studies. This phase can be thought of as a period of deconstruction leading to reconstruction.

The Search function, the most basic multimedia tool, proved to be a simple yet powerful tool. Searching for a word, a person, or a topic through the whole body of research data led to new connections. For example, two words which kept reoccurring were *good* and *bad*. By following the path of either word, I found different meanings in what originally appeared to be a similar usage.

Not so dramatic were (and still are) the daily uses of the Topic search button. While I was transcribing the audio track of the video onto the cards in *Learning Constellations*, I entered topics—which seemed to best describe what I thought was going on in a given video chunk—into a Topic field. In a sense, one could think of the Topics as the Keywords/thematic field in *Star Notes*. The process of deciding the topic name and how to categorize each chunk was similar to how the Keyword categories developed in *Star Notes*. The central difference is that, in the Topic linking of *Learning Constellations*, the video chunk is activated and can be viewed instantly. Moreover, the contextual informatoin—the transcripts, dates, names of people in chunk, and annotations—is also available and can be copied into a writing section of the interface (in the Dissertation Galaxy).

The best example of a search through Topics which led to a discovery was when I followed the topic *How Things Happen/Work*. This topic occurred quite often (as could be expected in a Logo constructionist culture); children and adults were regularly building things, reflecting on their constructions, and coming up with new ideas. However, I had always thought that one particular chunk of video—when Josh tells me about what he would buy for everyone if he were rich—was *only* about how Josh feels about his relationship with his family members. What I discovered, however, is that this is only one interpretation, and that others are equally significant.

In the chunk of video, Josh is sitting in my car telling me about what he would buy if he were a millionaire. He would get "all the Buddy Holly records ever made" for his dad, "a big house and a maid to clean it" for his mother, and so forth. When I asked him what he would buy for himself, without hesitation, he told me:

> There's this store in the Dedham Mall and it's called, The Enchanted Forest. It's a store and everything in the store is stuffed animals. They're, like, minks, and everything; and they're stuffed animals; and there's, like, a giant one, like, as big as this car, and they have, like, they have a string hung across the thing and *it doesn't need power. It doesn't need power.* And this little guy is on his unicycle and it's a little bear. This little stuffed animal bear and it goes back and forth. *It doesn't need any power*, it just, like, put it one side and it keeps on rolling. *[It] won't stop unless you stop it. You have to get it started but it won't stop!*

Had I not had *Learning Constellations*, this chunk may have remained a cute anecdotal comment about a young boy's fantasy rather than being understood within the context of his fascination with the source of energy. Linking this chunk to other chunks of video—his constructing things that move and his reflecting upon these kinds of moving objects—built layers of richness about Josh's thinking about moving things. More importantly, it instigated my reflecting upon the pervasiveness of his thinking style. This analysis, accomplished by connecting seemingly unrelated chunks, became possible with the linking of video from simple searches throughout the video data.

Annotating and reading annotations was another step in analyzing the video data. Using *Learning Constellations* enabled me to reflect upon the video in a way I had never done when it was simply on videotape. With the multimedia environment, flashes of insight which led to ideas could stay online and be accessed later. Moreover, in *Learning Constellations*, notes are categorized by theme. As a result, building categories took place without my specifically looking for links in the data. This Theme field also provides a list of previous themes, as an aid for remembering the previous categories.

Using "Videonote" for isolating and combining related chunks helped to make more in-depth analyses. The following example illustrates the importance of this feature. A reoccurring theme in my videotaping of Josh was how he seemed to think with objects, in much the same way as does Papert. At first this comparison between Josh and Papert struck me as idiosyncratic and not related to a style of thinking. However, both these themes came together in a small Videonote that I built from two segments within two chunks. In the first video segment, Papert, in an interview, points at the camera and says: "They're pointing that camera at me . . ." Josh, in a conversation with me, points to the camera saying, "And like when they made video cameras, like you're shooting me now. When they made them, they probably thought about cameras." The two gestures are almost identical. Is this just coincidental, or are they both appropriators of physical objects—in this case the camera? The case study (as excerpted from Goldman Segall, 1990b, in Chapter 13, this volume) shows that Josh, like Papert, tends to be comfortable using objects around him *to think with*.

Another level of analysis occurred by using the slow motion feature. An example of this is when Linda Moriarty, Josh and Andrew's teacher, describes Josh in one video segment and Andrew in another. Her hands move differently when speaking of the two children. Not only do they move differently, they connote different meanings. By using the slow motion feature of *Learning Constellations*, the contrast is more evident. Another example is when Mindy tells me about Josh and Joe while I videotape her in her classroom. During this conversation, there are several interruptions. The slowed-down video shows her responses to a classmate, her teacher, another classmate, and me, the interviewer. In slow motion, we can see the way she responds to different people and how she never loses track of her conversation, no matter how many times she is interrupted. Her dramatic personal presence is highlighted in a way I might never have seen had I not slowed down the movement of the video. Particularly helpful is that the sound is cut-off while the video moves slow or fast. Without sound, the focus is on the gestural.

One could ask why slowing down the movement is important for researchers studying human behavior. One response could be that facial imaging, a topic under investigation by computer cognition researchers, relies on understanding the meaning of gestures (Ekman, 1973; Burson, Carling, & Kramlich, 1986; Landau, 1989). In terms of this study, the focus on gestures enables one to link what one says with what one means to uncover what is really being said.

The final step in this research analysis phase was to reconstruct the video portraits into written case studies. In this step, it was necessary to build portraits or case studies of the school culture and three children who experienced the introduction of Project Headlight. The case studies are the results of my research (and are excerpted in Chapter 13, this volume). In writing the cases, I was able to access my video data as I wrote. This prevented many subtle but significant errors in my reporting. However, my interpretations are still not the *final* ones. *Learning Constellations* stores my dissertation as a text document with a footnote tool for others to add their comments. In this way, it is my hope that *Learning Constellations* will continue to grow as teachers and researchers use it in the coming years.

CONCLUSIONS: CONTRIBUTIONS OF MULTIMEDIA RESEARCH

My original goal in designing *Learning Constellations* was to create a multi-media research environment which maintained the integrity of the original source material. Through my use of Geertz's notion of thick descriptions and Bateson's belief in disciplined subjectivity as thematic guidelines, I hope I have contributed to the ongoing discussion of how researchers can trust their conclusions from video-based research data. Reflecting upon Geertz's and Bateson's theories provided me with a language with which to come to terms with issues related to the bias and interference created by the participant recorder upon the culture being studied. I discovered that, if I wanted to build thick descriptions, I had to come as close as I could to the children; I had to *interfere* and use my point of view in the most disciplined manner possible. Anything less than my complete immersion in this culture would have been, for me, a thin description.

An unexpected result of this study was that, by using this intimate method of recording responses on video, the children became co-directors of the video-making—affecting the style of my videomaking. Moreover, by working with the video data intensively on *Learning Constellation*, the children's styles of thinking affected the genre of the written case studies. I believe that this occurred because of the growing relationship between the video *participant recorder* and the children I was studying in situ and on video.

Working with the video data on *Learning Constellations* brought me to make discoveries I believe I might not have made without *Learning Constellations*. One could argue that a *better* researcher would not have needed video and *Learning Constellations* in order to have found pervasiveness in Josh's thinking style. My response to this argument is that it seems fruitless to speculate on what another researcher would have found had she or he used other quantitative or non-video-based qualitative methods. I can respond by stating that I do not think that I could have found this and other findings without this method. There are several reasons for this.

First, being human, I cannot observe, participate in meaningful conversations, write notes, notice a full range of ambience in the environment, and reflect upon it—all at the same time. I am referring, not only to my personal mood that day that makes me responsive or not responsive, but, more so, to what I am capable of doing well at any given moment in time. My limitation is to think deeply about one thing at a time while having control over tools which have become familiar. Knowing that I was videotaping these conversations with children, and that I would design a multimedia tool to access my data at a later date, gave me the opportunity to respond as fully as I could to the child while I was recording.

The second reason is related to the first. When my tools were audiotape recorders and fieldnotes, my results tended to be *thin* anecdotal descriptions of what was happening. The audiotapes and fieldnotes of Shannon, the first child I studied, did not encourage me to *get to know* Shannon. With Josh, Mindy, and Andrew, I was able to "be with them" on tape over a 4-year period. I would be inspired to return to see them and find out more. Transcribing my hours of audiotape was an uninteresting ordeal, whereas transcribing the video on the videodiscs allowed me to look more closely, not only at what the children were saying, but at what they meant when they said things. Very often, their gestures—which I could see on video or videodisc—led me to the meaning.

A third reason for why I believe I was able to reach new findings in my data using *Learning Constellations* was that it enabled me to plod repetitively through the data, to check my intuitions with my colleagues and the teachers in order to rethink the meaning of what I was seeing, and to annotate my reactions while watching even tiny slices of video. I do not think I would have been able to know Josh or Andrew through their teacher's *eyes* had I not been able to slow down the motion of the video of this teacher speaking about the two boys, and watch it many times while speculating upon the meaning of her gestures. This fine-grained analysis took time and patience, but brought me closer to those I studied.

I am not suggesting that, by using multimedia video ethnography as a research tool to explore children's thinking styles, children are going to be protected from the trials and tribulations of growing up in a rough inner-city school environment. What I aimed to accomplish was to find yet another important piece in a difficult puzzle about children's thinking styles by using video and videodisc technology. It is my hope that using video technology in order to build detailed descriptions of children's thinking—about the things which concern them—will be a contribution to both the understanding of children and the development of future research technologies. It is my contention that using *Learning Constellations* for gaining access to research data, for building links, and for annotating, is an effective and reliable method for making discoveries and communicating them to others.

ACKNOWLEDGMENTS

Building *Learning Constellations* was a cooperative venture shared by Vivian Orni Mester, a filmmaker from Brazil, and David Greschler, an expert HyperCard programmer from Boston. Their dedication to this project is the stuff from which I find the energy to write about the process of creating a tool to explore the thinking of children. I thank them for believing in my dream and helping it come into fruition. I also want to thank both Mary Catherine Bateson and Clifford Geertz, whose writing helped me think through the problems of becoming a multimedia ethnographer of children's thinking. I thank my colleagues at the Media Lab, especially Seymour Papert and Glorianna Davenport for encouraging me to pursue this emerging field with such rigor and Idit Harel for editing this volume on the various constructionist approaches to learning environments. However, my deepest gratitude goes to the children and teachers of the Hennigan School who provided the substance of this work, to my husband, Avner, and my friend and mentor, Silvia McFadyen Jones.

REFERENCES

Bateson, M. C. (1984). *With a daughter's eye*. New York: Pocket Books.

Burson, N., Carling, R., & Kramlich, D. (1986). *Composites*. New York: Morrow.

Cole, R. (1989). *The call of stories, teaching and the moral imagination*. Boston: Houghton Mifflin.

Davenport, G. (1987). *Interactive multi-media on a single screen display*. Unpublished paper, MIT Media Laboratory, Cambridge, MA.

Ekman, P. (1973). *Darwin and facial expression: A century of research in review*. New York and London: Academic Press.

Erikson, E. H. (1950). *Childhood and society*. New York: Norton.

Fox Keller, E. (1983). *A feeling for the organism: The life and work of Barbara McClintock*. San Francisco: W. H. Freeman.

Fox Keller, E. (1985). *Reflections on gender and science*. New Haven, CT, and London: Yale University Press.

Geertz, C. (1973). *The interpretation of cultures*. New York: Basic Books.

Geertz, C. (1983). *Local knowledge*, New York: Basic Books.

Gerstein, R. G. (1986). *Interpreting the female voice: An application of art and media technology*. Unpublished doctoral dissertation, MIT, Department of Communications Technology and Culture, Cambridge, MA.

Gilligan, C. (1982). *In a different voice: Psychological theory and women's development.* Cambridge, MA: Harvard University Press.

Goldman Segall, R. (1988). *Thick descriptions: A language for articulating ethnographic media technology.* Unpublished paper, MIT Media Laboratory, Cambridge, MA.

Goldman Segall, R. (1989a). *Thinking about the future.* (A documentary video about the future of global issues in education). Cambridge, MA: Cambridge Center for Adult Education.

Goldman Segall, R. (1989b). Thick descriptions: A tool for designing ethnographic interaction videodiscs. *SIGCHI Bulletin* (Special Interest Group on Computer and Human Interaction), *21*, 2.

Goldman Segall, R. with V. Orni Mester & D. Greschler (1989c). *Learning constellations* [6 Videodiscs and Software package]. Cambridge, MA: MIT Media Laboratory.

Goldman Segall, R. (1990a). Learning constellations: A multimedia research environment for exploring children's theory-making. In I. Harel (Ed.), *Constructionist learning.* Cambridge, MA: MIT Media Laboratory.

Goldman Segall, R. (1990b). *Learning constellations: A multimedia ethnographic research environment using video technology to explore children's thinking.* Unpublished doctoral dissertation, MIT Media Lab, Cambridge MA.

Goldman Segall, R. (1990c). Creating video cultures in the schools [work in progress].

Grannott, Farber, N. (1990). Through the camera lens: Video as a research tool. In I. Harel (Ed.), *Constructionist learning.* Cambridge, MA: MIT Media Laboratory.

Hochings, P. (1975). Educational uses of videotape. In P. Hockings (Ed.), *Principles of visual anthropology.* The Hague, Paris: Mouton Publishers.

Illich, I. (1973). *Tools for conviviality.* London and New York: Marion Boyars.

Kogan, N. (1983). Stylistic variation in childhood and adolescence: Creativity, metaphor and cognitive styles. In P. H. Mussen, *Handbook of child psychology* (Vol. III). New York, Chichester, Brisbane, Toronto, Singapore: John Wiley and Sons.

Lampert, M., & Ball, D. L. (1990). *Using hypermedia technology to support a new pedagogy of teacher education.* East Lansing, MI: Michigan State University.

Landau, T. (1989). *About faces: The evolution of the human face.* New York, London, Toronto, Sydney, and Aukland: Anchor Books.

Lawler, R. W. (1985). *Computer experience and cognitive development: A child learning in a computer culture.* West Sussex, UK. Ellis Horwood.

Leacock, R. (1975). Ethnographic observation and the Super-8 millimeter camera. In P. Hockings (Ed.), *Principles of visual anthropology.* The Hague, Paris: Mouton Publishers.

Mackay, W. (1989). EVA: An experimental video annotator for human-centered design. *SIGCHI Bulletin* (Special Interest Group on Computer and Human Interaction), *21*, 2.

Mead, M. (1975). Visual anthropology in a discipline of words. In P. Hockings (Ed.), *Principals of visual anthropology.* The Hague, Paris: Mouton Publishers.

Papert, S. (1986). *Constructionism: A new opportunity for elementary science education* (Proposal to the National Science Foundation). Cambridge, MA: MIT Media Laboratory.

Papert, S. (1990). Introduction. In I. Harel (Ed.), *Constructionist learning*. Cambridge, MA: MIT Media Laboratory.

Rogers, C. (1961). *On becoming a person*. Boston: Houghton and Mifflin.

Roschelle, J., Pea, R., & Trigg, R. H. (1990). *Videonoter: A tool for exploratory video analysis*. Palo Alto, CA: Institute for Research on Learning.

Ryle, G. (1971). *Collected papers*. New York: Barnes and Noble.

Temaner, G., & Quinn, G., (1975). Cinematic social inquiry. In P. Hockings (Ed.), *Principals of visual anthropology*. The Hague, Paris: Mouton Publishers.

Tobin, J. J., Wu, D. Y. H., & Davidson, D. H. (1989). *Preschool in three cultures*. New Haven, CT and London: Yale University Press.

Turkle, S. (1984). *The second self: Computers and the human spirit*. New York: Simon and Schuster.

AUTHOR INDEX

V

Van Sommers, P., 230, *233*
Vitale, B., 413, *415*
Voneche, J.J., *232*, 237, *268*, 313, 314, *331*
Von Foerster, H., *378*, 391, *415*
Vygotsky, L.S., 297, *309*, 330, *332*

W

Wachsmuth, I., *81*
Watt, D., 6, *11*, 58, *83*, 163, *190*, *191*
Weir, S., 6, *11*, 58, *83*, 163, *190*, *191*, 359, *364*
Weizenbaum, 187, *191*
Wellman, H.M., 385, *390*

Werner, H., 296, *309*
Wertheimer, M., 295, *309*
Wertsch, J.V., 296, 297, *309*
Wiener, N., 16, *27*, 367, *378*, 391, *415*
Wilensky, U., 197, 200, *203*
Winnicott, D.W., 230, 231, *233*
Witkin, H., 276, *294*, 339, 357, 359, *364*
Wittgenstein, L., 168, *191*
Woolf, B., 437, *445*
Woolgar, S., 162, *191*
Wu, D.Y.H., 468, *497*

Y

Youniss, J., 349, *363*

SUBJECT INDEX

11.7.92
11.7.92

$80.75
80.75

Midwest

#52715

Scarce 4.08 $200